BEYOND THE ROBOT

BEYOND THE ROBOT

The Life and Work of
Colin Wilson

GARY LACHMAN

A TARCHERPERIGEE BOOK

tarcherperigee

An imprint of Penguin Random House LLC
375 Hudson Street
New York, New York 10014

Most TarcherPerigee books are available at special quantity discounts for bulk purchase for
sales promotions, premiums, fund-raising, and educational needs. Special
books or book excerpts also can be created to fit specific needs.
For details, write: SpecialMarkets@penguinrandomhouse.com.

ISBN 9780399173080

Printed in the United States of America
1   3   5   7   9   10   8   6   4   2

To Outsiders everywhere

Reality is *not* what happens to be most real to us at the moment. It is what we perceive in our moments of greatest intensity.

—Colin Wilson, *The Craft of the Novel*

My life's task is to light a fire with damp sticks. The drizzle falls incessantly. Yet I feel that if only I could really get the blaze started, it would become so large and fierce that nothing could stop it.

—Colin Wilson, *Phenomenological Journal*, January 31, 1965

CONTENTS

INTRODUCTION

A PILGRIMAGE TO TETHERDOWN

In the summer of 1983 I found myself traveling to Cornwall, in the far west of England. For the past several years I had been reading the work of a writer whose ideas interested me deeply and I was on my way to meet him. His name was Colin Wilson.

Wilson had achieved overnight fame in 1956 at the age of twenty-four with his first book, *The Outsider*, a study in existentialism, alienation, and "extreme mental states." No one was more astonished than Wilson himself to discover that this work dealing with the angst and spiritual crises of figures such as Nietzsche, van Gogh, Dostoyevsky, T. E. Lawrence, H. G. Wells, and others had become an instant best seller. But surprisingly it had. Reviews were glowing and critics tripped over each other to hail England's own "home-grown existentialist." After years of struggle, sacrifice and hard work, Wilson had made it. *The Outsider* was "in."

The glory, alas, was short-lived. Fame, especially in England, is fickle, and after the initial praise—A MAJOR WRITER, AND HE'S ONLY TWENTY-FOUR, the headline of one review ran—the press and serious critics soon turned on what they were now calling a "messiah of the milk bars."[1] The tag came from Wilson's association with a group of writers the press had christened the Angry Young Men—roughly equivalent to America's Beat Generation—people like John Osborne, Kingsley Amis, John Braine, and others. Although Wilson had very little in common with them, he was guilty by association, and when the critical tide turned against these angry men, he was caught up in it. In practically no time at all, Wilson went from being a boy genius to persona non grata, a status among the literary establishment that he labored against for the rest of his career and was never quite able to throw off.

It was after this critical thrashing that Wilson left London and moved to a remote village in Cornwall. Here he hunkered down and over the years developed what he called a "new existentialism," an "evolutionary," optimistic philosophy which would eventually include areas of the occult and mysticism. He hoped this would counter the bleak dead end in which he believed the existentialism of Sartre, Camus, and Heidegger had found itself, and in which most of modern culture had also become mired.

Wilson's idea of an optimistic, evolutionary existentialism excited me. I had spent the past several years tracking his books down, reading everything by him that I could find. That was why I found myself at the tail end of a two-month sojourn in Europe—much of it spent visiting "sacred sites"—making the journey down to Cornwall to meet him.

I had first come across Wilson's work some years earlier, in 1975, when I was nineteen and living on New York's Bowery, playing in the band Blondie. I had recently developed an interest in the occult.[2] Punk was on the rise but remnants of the previous hippie generation could still be found, and among the books I read at the time was Wilson's *The Occult*, which had been published in 1971 and which briefly reestablished his reputation after the critical bashing following *The Outsider*.

What was exciting about *The Occult* was that Wilson approached the mystical, magical, and paranormal from the perspective of existential philosophy. It was not a book of spells or accounts of haunted houses but an attempt to understand occult phenomena in terms of a philosophy of consciousness that Wilson had been developing for more than a decade and which I later understood was based on the work of the German philosopher Edmund Husserl, whose phenomenology became the basis for existentialism.

Explanations of phenomenology and its importance for Wilson and for human consciousness in general will be found in the pages that follow. Here I will say that the essence of Husserl's philosophy, and the aspect of it that made the most impact on Wilson, was what he called "intentionality."[3] Simply put, this is the recognition that consciousness does not passively *reflect* the world as a mirror does, which had been the standard idea of consciousness since the philosopher René Descartes established it in the seventeenth century. Instead it actively reaches out and *grabs* it—although we, for the most part, are unaware of this activity. Consciousness, then, for Husserl, is not a mirror but a kind of hand. And while a mirror reflects what is in front of it whether it wants to or not—it has no choice in the matter—our hands, we know, can have a strong grasp or a weak one or, in fact, none at all.

It was something along these lines that Wilson tried to get across to me when I finally arrived at his home, called Tetherdown, near the small fishing village of Gorran Haven, on a scorching July day. I had called him from a phone box in Penzance, where I was staying. He was friendly and immediately invited me to come and stay the night; he even offered to pick me up at the train station in St. Austell, the nearest one.

Two things stand out immediately from that first trip to Tetherdown. One is Wilson's house, set back from the Cornish cliffs, where he had lived with his wife, Joy, since 1959. It was filled floor to ceiling with more books than I had ever seen outside of a public library or a well-stocked shop. Thousands of them crammed the bookshelves that lined practically every wall; the most recent estimate of the number of volumes in Wilson's library was thirty thousand, not to mention the LPs, cassettes, and later CDs and DVDS and other items that made up his research material.

My other strong memory is of a long, wine-fueled evening during which Colin did his best to explain Husserl's ideas about consciousness to me. The essence of it escaped me later but by the time I went to sleep that evening I was sure I had it in my grasp. We continued the conversation the next morning, before I headed back to London. I can remember Colin sitting with me, outside his kitchen, in the bright morning sun, telling me that if he made a certain mental effort, he could reproduce a mild version of the effects of mescaline, the drug that had prompted Aldous Huxley's influential book *The Doors of Perception*. I believed him and was determined, at some point, to be able to do this myself.

When I returned to Los Angeles, where I lived, I began a correspondence with Wilson that lasted over the years, and I would later visit Tetherdown again on several occasions, getting to know Colin, Joy, and their children, and building up a friendship. In the late 1980s and early nineties, Colin came to Los Angeles to give talks, and each time he came, we met. On one occasion I was house-sitting for one of the owners of the Bodhi Tree Bookstore, where I worked at the time—it was the preeminent "metaphysical" bookshop west of the Rockies—and I invited Colin and Joy to stay with me. During his stay he came to the shop and spent a huge sum, filling up boxes of books to be shipped back to Cornwall.

In 1996 I moved to London. Over the years I made the journey to Cornwall or met with Colin on his trips to London; on more than one occasion I interviewed him and wrote articles about his work and reviews of his books for some London newspapers.[4] I always found him warm, generous, upbeat, and encouraging. One of our last meetings was at a conference in London in 2005, where he introduced me to the writer Graham Hancock. Afterward with Joy and their son Damon and his family—Colin enjoyed being a grandfather—Colin took us to an Italian restaurant; he liked food and the wine flowed. I saw him again briefly in 2009 when he gave a talk in London, but as my young sons were with me and hadn't the patience to sit still, I had to leave before saying good-bye.

It was sometime in 2011 that I heard that Colin had suffered a stroke following a difficult spinal operation. I knew he had had problems with blood pressure and the news of the stroke was not welcome. I had kept up our correspondence—carried out by e-mail now—and we had exchanged copies of our books; I even dedicated one to him.[5] But now it seemed clear that his health had taken a turn for the worse. At first the prognosis seemed hopeful but after a time it was apparent that damage had been done and his condition would not improve.

I was in Holland when I heard the news that Colin had died. It was the weekend of December 6–7, 2013, and I was there giving a lecture. A text message from a mutual acquaintance came late at night telling me of his passing. His death at eighty-two following a severe illness was not unexpected but it nevertheless came as a shock. Like so many of his readers, I had somehow believed that he would go on forever. Now that constant flow of books had stopped.

I could not make the funeral, but a memorial service was held for Colin on October 14, 2014, at St. James's Church in Piccadilly. Oddly enough it was the place I had last seen him, at the talk I had to leave abruptly a few years earlier. The poet William Blake—whose poetry Wilson admired and had written about, featuring it prominently in *The Outsider* and other books—had been baptized there, and it was a place where many other "alternative" thinkers had lectured. Among others who had gathered to celebrate Colin's life and lament his passing, I was asked to speak, and in the five minutes allotted me, I tried to sum up the essence of his work. An impossible task, you might say, considering that he had written more than a hundred books about a dauntingly wide range of subjects. But Colin himself came to my aid.

In *The Occult*, the book that began my journey into Colin's philosophy, he writes, "A single obsessional idea runs through all my work; the paradoxical nature of freedom."[6] In the five minutes I had, I tried to explain what Colin meant by this, attempting to condense in a few words what he had spent a lifetime investigating.

What is the "paradoxical nature of freedom"? It is the curious truth that when our freedom is threatened, we know exactly what it is and why it is important and are willing to risk our lives in order to protect or regain it. Its value is unquestioned, indubitable, and insistent. "It was," Colin writes, speaking of freedom in the context of German tanks rolling into Warsaw or Soviet ones into Budapest, "something solid and definite that was being stolen, as a burglar might steal the silver."[7] But once the threat has vanished, somehow, imperceptibly, the *meaning* of our freedom dissipates; its value dissolves and becomes unreal, and we fall into the trap of taking it for granted, as we do most of the things that matter to us in life, a human failing Colin referred as a version of original sin.

When we live comfortable, complacent existences, freedom, or any other of our deepest values, becomes just a word, and because our *grasp* on our values grows limp, we waste our lives on trivialities, getting caught up in smaller immediate concerns and losing sight of the bigger picture, what Colin called the "bird's eye view." When this happens our idea of freedom becomes "blurred and indefinite" and "seems to shimmer like a mirage."

"When I am confronted by a danger or crisis," Colin writes, "I see it as a threat to freedom, and my freedom suddenly becomes positive and self-evident—as enormous and obvious as a sunset."[8] Yet when the threat recedes, or the crisis abates, the sunset of freedom fades, and we slip back into a state of dullness and apathy, a lack of gratitude that we accept as "human nature."

Colin "always accepted the fundamental reality of freedom" and had spent his life trying to uncover the inner mechanisms that enable us to grasp it. The vision, he believed, was "not an illusion or mirage," as so much of the wisdom of the world, from Ecclesiastes to the absurdist playwright Samuel Beckett, one of Colin's bêtes noires, would have us think. But if it is not an illusion—if the vision of freedom, or meaning and purpose, is real—then what happens? What goes wrong? Why does something we are willing to die for become, for many of us, a burden, a weight, something we want to *escape* from, as the title of a once popular book has it, and which we experience whenever we are bored and feel faced with the challenge of "killing time"?[9]

"The trouble," Colin saw, "is the *narrowness of consciousness*," a shrinking of our awareness that reduces it to a mere reflection of the physical world and numbs our ability to appreciate the values and meanings that give our life purpose. This narrowness, he argued, "lulls us into a state of permanent drowsiness, like being half-anesthetized, so that we never attempt to stretch our powers to their limits." And a consequence of this is that we never discover exactly what our limits are. We accept our dim, half-awake state as normal, as reality, and unless some crisis conveniently shakes us out of it, we live this way and die, having no idea what life, ours or anyone else's, was about.

But in those moments when freedom and the values that give our life meaning are perceived as concrete, indisputable *realties*, we *know* this isn't true, that our lives here are involved in something bigger than ourselves, that something important is at risk and that we are playing for very high stakes.

What causes this narrowing of our consciousness? And why is crisis able to widen it? The culprit is an evolutionary labor-saving device that Wilson called "the robot." This is a kind of servant who *does his job too well* and has taken over control of our lives from its master—that is, ourselves. The robot, let me point out, is not a villain. It is merely a helper, a necessary one, who, seeing that we lack the courage and commitment to really live our lives, has decided to live them for us. He has not, as we may think, usurped our power. We have positively given it to him. But it is time to take it back, time to go beyond the robot and begin, in a paraphrase of T. S. Eliot, to "live the life we have lost in living."[10]

This is the central theme, the "overwhelming question"—another nod to Eliot—that will be at the heart of this introductory overview of Colin Wilson's life and work.[11] What I will try to do here is to make clear some of the basic ideas and aims of Wilson's philosophy in hopes that it will prompt readers unfamiliar with his work to seek out his books and read them for themselves.

For a dedicated reader like myself, one of the odd and frustrating things about Wilson is that many people know his name, and are familiar with some of his books on the occult, ancient mysteries, and crime, or one of his novels, such as *The Mind Parasites* or his Spider World series, but are unfamiliar with the body of ideas that make up his philosophy and inform all of his work. His friend Robert Ardrey, author of the influential book *The Territorial Imperative*, once told Wilson that he wrote too much. Wilson agreed, but admitted that he couldn't stop. "I write," he once wrote, "as a dog with fleas scratches."[12] He told me at one point, "I had so much to say, I thought I wouldn't be happy until I was seventy and had fifty books behind me." Yet he was aware of the problems with this, especially in an age of increasing specialization. "The trouble with having so much to say," he told me, "is that you write too much and cover too many subjects." In addition to this there is the sheer pressure of work: "You're also forced to write at a tremendous pace, just in order to make living."[13]

I am not sorry that Wilson wrote so much, but I can appreciate that readers wanting to get an idea of what he is about might find it difficult to see their way in. They can see this book as a kind of Rough Guide to Wilson's philosophy.

Mention of philosophy and abstruse terms such as "phenomenology" and "existentialism" may give readers unfamiliar with Wilson second thoughts and suggest that they will find him too abstract and difficult. The opposite is true; Wilson writes some of the most readable prose in modern literature—certainly in the "alternative" genre—and, as one reviewer put it, "has a narrative style that can make the pursuit of any idea seem like exciting detective work."[14]

It was this that gripped me when I first read *The Occult* forty years ago. As a good existentialist, Wilson is always concrete, not abstract. He uses examples from his own life and the lives of others in order to get his point across, and is adept at coining metaphors and analogies that give the reader a clear picture of what he means. He is also one of the great synthesizers, bringing together and linking up in new ways important insights and discoveries of other thinkers; following up the leads Wilson provides in books such as *The Outsider*, *The Occult*, *Mysteries*, and many others is like getting a liberal arts education.

Readers of Wilson will know this and need no inducement to go back and reread his work; I leave it to those less familiar with him to enjoy an enlightening and educating experience.

So let us take a look now inside this Outsider and see if we can get an idea of the life and work of Colin Wilson.

CHAPTER ONE

THE ANGRY YOUNG MAN

On May 28, 1956, an unusual book appeared on the London literary scene and quite literally took it by storm. World War II had ended more than a decade earlier, but the Britain the book appeared in was still recovering from the Blitz, rationing, and its demotion from an empire to a small and rather fragile island nation. Bomb sites and shattered buildings were still part of the London terrain, and Britain's fall in status was reflected in its cultural consciousness. In 1951 the Festival of Britain, dedicated to technology and innovation, tried hard to kick-start a sense of recovery, but the response was sluggish and the doldrums that had settled over the Sceptered Isle seeped into every aspect of its life, including its literary one.[1] The outlook there was pretty bleak.[2] The end of World War I had seen the rise of a new generation of writers. Figures such as T. S. Eliot, Virginia Woolf, Aldous Huxley, James Joyce, and D. H. Lawrence had emerged from the aftermath of the "war to end all wars," and their grim determination to "tell the truth" and depict "reality" made the previous generation of writers seem hopelessly outdated. Bernard Shaw, H. G. Wells, G. K. Chesterton, and others from the Edwardian era were still writing, but the optimism and progressive thinking that had characterized what I have called the "positive fin de siècle" now rang hollow and it was clear that the new crew was representative of an unmistakable change in sensibilities.[3]

Ten years after Victory in Europe and Hiroshima, nothing similar had happened, at least not in Britain, and the epigone of the first wave of modernism seemed to have settled into producing good but not particularly exciting work. Cyril Connolly, one of the most influential critics of the time, placed the blame on James Joyce's forbidding monster *Ulysses*, which, Connolly argued, was a very tough act to follow, something Joyce discovered for himself when he produced *Finnegans Wake*, which, for all its puns, mythology, and linguistic hijinks, was not what one could call a novel. Joyce, it seemed, had taken the novel as far as it could go, and there appeared to be little left for those who came after him to do, even himself.

This sense of anticlimax and reduced expectations most likely played a part in the vertiginous success of a book that, in one sense, should not have been successful at all. Not that it wasn't good or didn't deserve the acclaim it received. But as its author soon found out, most of the hue and cry the book prompted was for the wrong reasons.

The book was *The Outsider* and its author, a twenty-four-year-old Leicester lad named Colin Wilson, was an unlikely candidate for celebrity, more like what used to be called a "high school dropout." For the past several years Wilson had drifted from job to job, tramping across England and France, often doing cheap manual labor, and at one point he was so insolvent that he had taken to sleeping rough on London's bucolic Hampstead Heath, to escape paying rent, but also to avoid the payments he was obliged to make to his estranged wife for the maintenance of their son.[4] He was, in his own words, "a bum and a drifter," who occasionally had encounters with the police; at least one policeman had told him that it was illegal to sleep in England without a roof over one's head.[5] Wilson did not have the benefit of a university education, something most of Britain's literati had, and his tousled hair, turtleneck sweater, and general unkempt appearance were not standard issue for upcoming British writers.

And if the author was not cut from the expected literary cloth, his book certainly wasn't either. *The Outsider*, a work of literary and philosophical analysis, was concerned with the spiritual dilemmas of an eclectic and somewhat incongruous collection of characters. This angst-ridden group included the philosopher Friedrich Nietzsche, whose misappropriation by the Nazis had given him a bad reputation in English-speaking countries; the dancer and choreographer Vaslav Nijinsky, who had died insane in London just a few years earlier; the military hero T. E. Lawrence of Arabia; the painter and suicide Vincent van Gogh; the French philosopher, novelist, and playwright Jean-Paul Sartre, at the time probably the most famous writer in the world; and forgotten figures such as the playwright Harley Granville-Barker. Others included were H. G. Wells, Fyodor Dostoyevsky, and Leo Tolstoy. There were also some unfamiliar names, such as the German novelist Hermann Hesse, who was practically unknown in England at the time; and the Greek-Armenian esoteric teacher G. I. Gurdjieff, who had a bad reputation for taking A. R. Orage away from his proper work as a literary editor and for somehow being responsible for the death of the New Zealand writer Katherine Mansfield.[6] What all these individuals and others had in common is that they all exemplified a character type that Wilson identified as "the Outsider."

Who or what is the Outsider?

A more detailed answer to this question will be found in the pages that follow. But for now we can say that the Outsider is someone who sees "too deep and too much" and that most of what he sees is "chaos."[7] He or she lives in the world with a sense of "strangeness" and "unreality." The safe, stable reality that most of us perceive is for the Outsider an illusion, a facade obscuring a more dangerous and threatening possibility: that of nothingness, nihilism, and the void, the complete inconsequentiality of human life and all its achievements. For the Outsider, the values and meanings that constitute life for most people— a good job, a big home, a nice bank account—are empty and makeshift; they are, at best, "attempts to gloss over, to make look civilized and rational something that is savage, unorganized, irrational."[8] That is to say, for the Outsider, most people's lives are inauthentic, based on untruths and the avoidance of reality. But the Outsider "stands for Truth."[9] He stands for Reality. He seeks a meaning and purpose that the everyday world cannot provide and his salvation lies in understanding this and embracing it with total conviction.

Other names appear in Wilson's heterogeneous mix, but by now the reader should have an idea of what reviewers, cracking open their copy of *The Outsider*, would have confronted. Although the sun never set on the English empire—at least not until after World War II—its cultural, literary, and philosophical tastes were often parochial and insular. The English were also notoriously impervious to ideas—their forte is pragmatism—and if there was one thing *The Outsider* was full of, it was ideas.[10] That a book that declared that "the Outsider cannot live in the comfortable insulated world of the bourgeois" and that "it is as impossible to exercise freedom in an unreal world as it is to jump while you are falling" skyrocketed to the best-seller list has to be one of the great ironies of modern literature.[11] Another is that the success this irony achieved would drive its author, if not into exile, certainly into a kind of literary no-man's land which he would escape only through much hard work, determination, and sheer brute endurance. Such a fate might have crushed most beginners, but the author of *The Outsider* was, as you might expect, an Outsider himself, and the years leading up to his paradoxical success were ones of effort, challenge, and the difficult business of actualizing one's freedom.

Colin Henry Wilson—he never used his middle name in any literary work—was born into a working-class Leicester family in England's Midlands on June 26, 1931. The Depression had hit Great Britain by then and needless to say times were tough. The effects of World War I were still felt throughout the United Kingdom, and the worldwide economic slump only added to an already difficult situation. Wilson's father worked long hard hours in a boot and shoe factory earning little more than three pounds a week, roughly twelve dollars at the time. It was a barely livable wage. Although Wilson says his family— there were later brothers and a sister—was never really deprived, there were times when the money was short, and on at least one occasion the young Wilson had no food for his school lunch break.[12]

Wilson candidly admits that he was the reason his parents married; neither

really wanted to but his mother's pregnancy forced the issue.[13] He also admits
that he didn't really like his father, but acknowledges that he was a "hard worker
and good breadwinner." Yet the fact that "working a forty-eight-hour week"
must have struck his father as "a poor substitute for living" must have had something to do with the eventual Outsider's desire to escape the dreary treadmill
of everyday life, its endless routines and repetitions.[14] It was a fate that practically everyone around the young Outsider shared. "No one dreamed of escape,"
he later remarked about the people in his childhood, "because no one thought
there was any escape. Instead they contented themselves with the pub, and the
football match on Saturday afternoon, and dreamed of winning the football
pools."[15] Most everyone around him was satisfied with this, but from an early
age, Wilson had other dreams.

Wilson's father was bad-tempered and irritable—not surprising, given he
had been forced into marriage in his late teens—and he and Wilson's mother
often quarreled. On occasion this led to blows.[16] Wilson's father consoled himself, as many other fathers did, by spending evenings at the pub drinking beer.
Wilson admits everyone at home was relieved when Dad left for the pub, but
the drinking did cut into the family finances. Wilson says that the first sentence
he wrote was "Dad drinks beer," an achievement about which his father was not
happy.[17]

Wilson's mother was different; in fact the two hardly seemed suited to each
other. His father was sentimental and emotionally turbulent, his mother cool
and detached, a difficult mix that in Wilson produced a dedicated family man
who was given to sudden demonstrations of affection, yet who also needed
solitude and who could appear to those who didn't know him as aloof and
withdrawn. To compensate for her unhappy home life, Wilson's mother read
magazines such as *True Romance*, but also novels by D. H. Lawrence and A. J.
Cronin—famous in his day for *The Citadel*—which she borrowed from the local
library. She was an intelligent woman who daydreamed of a better life, and
would share her woes and dissatisfaction with Colin and his brother Barry as
she got through her chores. Wilson would later write, "I have long suspected
that imaginative working-class women are the evolutionary spearhead of society, since the narrowness of their lives imparts an intensity to their daydreams
that middle- and upper-class women, lacking the desperation, find harder to
achieve."[18]

Wilson's mother's daydreams of a more rewarding existence communicated
themselves to the young Colin and her response to unhappiness served as a
counter to his father's bitterness at an impoverished existence. The "narrowness"
of her life imparting an "intensity" to her daydreams is an example of Wilson's
belief that adverse conditions may often be of more value to a creative person
than more ostensibly nurturing environments. Two of Wilson's heroes, Bernard
Shaw and H. G. Wells, had been born into impoverished families and had to

overcome many obstacles and difficulties in their early years before achieving any kind of success. Their early struggles ensured that they would not balk at later challenges, and instilled in them an optimism and drive based on a vivid awareness of the *value* of the things they fought for. They were inoculated against the kind of pessimism and spoiled-ness that, Wilson believed, is often associated with an easy life in which everything is handed to you. The novelist Marcel Proust and the playwright Samuel Beckett, for example—two writers Wilson often refers to—both came from well-off families. Proust was a notorious hypochondriac and Beckett developed a numbingly pessimistic vision of life, depicted in painfully static plays such as *Endgame*. This belief in the power of early effort to minimize pessimism and despair plays a central role in Wilson's philosophy.

Yet Wilson also admits that "the most essential fact about my childhood is that I was spoiled."[19] By this he means he was the darling of his extended family. His mother was the first of many brothers and sisters to produce a grandchild and young Colin was doted on by his grandparents, aunts, and uncles. His maternal grandparents regarded him as "altogether remarkable," a conviction that he came to share. He was told that he was "pretty" and "clever" and that great things must be in store for him. This fuss and adulation instilled in the young Wilson "a certain basic conviction that life and fortune mean well by me," an optimism and certainty of success that both buoyed him and led to later friction with his critics, who found his frank assessment of his own powers and abilities too forthright for their tastes, especially coming from an Englishman.[20] For the English, good upbringing should root out "any element of what might appear to be self-assertion or egoism," with the result that one develops an instinct to "suppress any stirring of impatience or originality. . . . Good manners," in this case, means "to be like everyone else," a difficult assignment for an up-and-coming Outsider.[21]

The praise Wilson received led to him getting used to "being the strongest, and to exerting a certain authority over my brothers and cousins."[22] It also later led to him "thinking of myself as a prodigy."[23] And although he soon realized that he was "not half the prodigy I thought I was," it was just as well he wasn't disillusioned, as it preserved him from the "fallacy of insignificance," the prevailing idea that human beings are humble, unexceptional creatures whose potentialities are severely limited, a belief Wilson would take exception to in *The Age of Defeat*, his book about the "loss of the hero."[24] It also led to him becoming something of a performer. He learned to recite poems and sing songs and was often put up on a table to entertain the family. Looking back, Wilson is amazed at the kind of confidence he displayed then, compared to the excruciating shyness and reserve that colored his teens. But the adulation fed a self-confidence not yet undermined by the doubt and self-division he would later struggle with. It was responsible for "occasions on which I wanted to do something, and have done it with an ease that has astonished me—an ease that is somehow foreign to the subjective and introspective part of me."[25] Self-division, the quarrel between two opposing visions of ourselves, became one of the central themes of Wilson's later work. In his early years this took the form of "two opposing impulses: distrust of the world, and the sense of immunity, complete confidence."[26]

Yet at the same time that Wilson received unconditional approval from his family, he also felt the beginning of a need that would remain throughout his life. This was the desire for solitude, the urge to retreat, to withdraw from life's racket into some interior realm where the noise of the everyday world would not reach him. This hunger for contact with the inner world of ideas, dreams, and imagination, detached from the melee of life ("living," Wilson says, "is always like trying to write a letter with the radio on, the children screaming, and the house on fire"), was symbolized for the young Wilson by the tub of Diogenes, the eccentric living quarters of the ancient Greek Cynic philosopher, who ignored the requirements of social life and lived as he pleased amid the bustle of the city.[27] "When I think back on my childhood," Wilson reflected, "it seems to me that my life has been dominated by a desire to contract into a point."[28] Wilson's philosophical bathtub or contracted point would take many forms, from a sleeping bag on Hampstead Heath to a remote cottage in Cornwall.

Wilson was unsure if his childhood was happy—he suspected most childhoods are much the same—but certain early experiences must have made an impression on him. One of his favorite ways of expressing a mode of enhanced consciousness was by describing the experience of a child at Christmas. In *Beyond the Occult*, which Wilson believed was his most important nonfiction book, he spells out what he calls eight "levels of consciousness."[29] Wilson calls Level Six the "magical level," referring to what the writer J. B. Priestley called "delight," a state of unalloyed happiness and excited expectancy.[30] Level Six, Wilson writes, "is what happens to a child on Christmas Day, when everything combines to make life seem wonderful."[31] In *Poetry and Mysticism*, Wilson speaks of the "peak experiences" that provide evidence for our ability to enter such enhanced states of consciousness. "Peak experiences" are what the psychologist Abraham Maslow, an admirer of Wilson's work, called the moments of sudden joy and happiness that seem to come to most psychologically healthy people. Driving back to Cornwall from Scotland, Wilson found himself in "one of those moods of the 'glory and freshness of a dream', of feeling far more *awake* than usual. All negative elements—doubts, fears, the sense of contingency— vanished from consciousness. It was the kind of mood I had often experienced as a child, particularly at Christmas, as if the mind itself is a Christmas tree covered with coloured lights."[32] Christmas today might not be quite the same as it was in Wilson's childhood, but the point is made.

It is commonplace in biographical writing to find the roots of a mature personality in early childhood experience; amid Wilson's standard childhood adventures—fistfights, shoplifting from Woolworths, gratuitous lying—a few stand out as early signs of the later philosopher.[33] One is what Wilson called his "distinct tendencies to sadism . . . a violent intolerance toward anything that seemed to me weak or silly."[34] "Sadism" might be too strong a word; when he was a boy this took the form of teasing children he thought lacked "vitality." Later it would appear in his antipathy toward any form of self-pity, an impatience with self-indulgence, and his high regard for self-discipline, toughness, and a strong will. "If you allow the will to remain passive for long periods," he wrote in *New Pathways in Psychology*, his book about Maslow, "it has the same effect as leaving your car in the garage for the winter. The batteries go flat. When the batteries go flat, 'life fails.'"[35]

Will is a central theme in Wilson's work, from *The Outsider* to later books such as *Super Consciousness*, and it is linked to Husserl's intentionality, the insight that consciousness is active, not passive. But the will for Wilson is not simply a matter of brute assertiveness, of having one's own way at the expense of others; his critiques of willful individuals such as the Marquis de Sade and Aleister Crowley make this clear. The will for Wilson is not enough; it does not work in a vacuum and is directly related to our perception of *meaning*. The people in Wilson's childhood who were content within their limited horizons made no effort to change their lives because *they saw no reason to*. For such people, "as life drags on repetitively, they get tired; they stop making effort; it is the *will* that gets run down."[36] They experience what Wilson calls "life failure," the feeling that life has become, as it did for Shakespeare's Hamlet, "weary, stale, flat, and unprofitable."[37] As he never tires of repeating, "close-upness deprives us of meaning."[38]

When life is "in your face," as it was for the people around the young Colin, we can't see beyond it, and our expectations and desires shrink, as does our will and incentive to make efforts. Holidays excite us, Wilson says, because they remind us of the world that extends beyond our immediate environment; they remind us of "wider meanings," and this "sharpens the appetite for life—that is, the will to live."[39] As he writes, "the deeper my sense of the 'meaningfulness' of the world, the fiercer and more persistent my will."[40] It was Wilson's perception of meanings that extended beyond the pubs and football matches of his childhood that fueled his will to escape his limited origins.

Along with his sadism, another example of what Wilson called his early "sexual perverseness" was one he shared with other creative individuals, like the poet Rainer Maria Rilke.[41] As a young boy Wilson loved to dress up in his mother's clothes, including her underwear.[42] Authorities such as the pre-Freudian sexologist Havelock Ellis suggest that such behavior "indicates a tendency to homosexuality," as did, for Ellis, Wilson's attachment to his mother and dislike of his father. But Wilson never observed any trace of homosexuality in his makeup.[43] What his early cross-dressing did amount to is a "panty fetish," to which Wilson candidly admits. "At a very early age," he confesses, "before I had ever heard of sex, I used to put on my mother's knickers when I was alone in the house, and experience a curious thrill at the silky feeling of the rayon against my body."[44] From then on, Wilson writes, "the sight of knickers always caused a certain sexual arousal."[45] Wilson suggests that his predilections as a young boy were not necessarily a sign of sexual precociousness, but an effect of the biologist Rupert Sheldrake's notion of "morphic resonance," a kind of telepathic inheritance of acquired characteristics. Knickers—women's underwear—first appeared in the mid-nineteenth century and soon became a standard ingredient in pornography. Wilson suggests that a century and a half of lurid excitement over a glimpse of these "forbidden" items—the Victorians referred to them as "unmentionables"—imprinted itself in the male psyche, hence his excitement over his mother's underwear as a child well before he knew anything about sex.[46]

Sex is a central theme in practically all of Wilson's work, from his early phenomenological analysis in *Origins of the Sexual Impulse* to philosophical erotic novels such as *The God of the Labyrinth* and his study of fraudulent gurus, *The Devil's Party*. It is not too much to say that while for many drugs were a means of accessing intense states of consciousness—think of Aleister Crowley, Timothy Leary, and more sober advocates such as Aldous Huxley—for Wilson sex was the preferred method. Yet "method" is not quite right, as it suggests that sex was something Wilson went out of his way to pursue, or that he performed it ritually, as in Tantric Yoga. He was not a Tantrist, nor a Casanova, Henry Miller, or even a D. H. Lawrence, and aside from his childhood transvestitism Wilson's sex life, candidly depicted in his autobiographies *Voyage to a Beginning* and *Dreaming to Some Purpose*, was not especially frenetic or comprehensive. He even says he was somewhat puritanical about it as a child, and didn't care for the dirty stories his school friends often told. What Wilson brought to sex was a keen phenomenological insight and analysis. Writing in his journal during the 1960s, a difficult time for him, he asked, "What do I wish to do as a philosopher? If I had to express it swiftly and accurately, I would say: to be able to express the meaning-content of the sexual orgasm in words."[47] "It ought to be possible," he believed, "to get the mind into a state of intensity approaching a sexual orgasm, and keep it like that all day." A cursory reading might suggest this expressed a desire to enjoy a daylong orgasm, but pleasure is never Wilson's aim in writing about sex. He is never prurient. What interests him is its "meaning-content," the insight, often glimpsed in the orgasm, that "behind the ordinary façade of reality, there is a power like a million hurricanes, a great wind. It is like a current of a million million volts."[48]

Wilson's early sexual puritanism didn't last long. By his adolescence, like most boys, he thought about sex constantly, and his search for the "meaning-content" of the orgasm began around the age of fourteen, when a casual fantasy about his French teacher introduced him to that particularly intense state of consciousness. Fantasy would not become reality for some time, and his French teacher had nothing to do with it, but before then Wilson had experienced another kind of altered consciousness. When he was about ten an uncle gave him a book, *The Mysteries and Marvels of Science*. It marked for him the beginning of "disinterestedness," a withdrawal from the human (all-too-human, in Nietzsche's phrase) world that he inhabited until then, and an entry into the wider world of knowledge. In *A New Model of the Universe*—a book that would later feature largely in Wilson's *The Occult*—P. D. Ouspensky tells of the impact a volume of physics had on him as a boy. As he surreptitiously read it during a Latin class, "all round me walls are crumbling and horizons infinitely remote and incredibly beautiful stand revealed . . . For the first time in my life my world emerges from chaos. Everything becomes connected, forming an orderly and harmonious whole."[49] Ouspensky experienced the delight that the release from the stifling personal world and the immersion in the *impersonal*, in the *objective* meanings that surround us, can have on certain individuals. The young Wilson felt something much the same.

A tattered copy of a pulp science-fiction magazine added to Wilson's delight. Astronomy fascinated him, as did Wells's novels *The Time Machine* and *The War of the Worlds*. For his eleventh birthday his mother gave him a chemistry set. Horrible smells and sudden bangs soon disrupted the Wilson home. Not long after, filched copies of *Amazing Stories*, *Fantasy Magazine*, and *Thrilling Wonder Stories* and various chemicals needed to produce satisfactory explosions were added to the penknives, fountain pens, magnifying glasses, and other trinkets the young Wilson pocketed from Woolworths. His new love of science changed him and his world. For one thing, it revealed a great distance between himself and the adults around him. Although petted and treated as a boy wonder, Wilson felt contempt for most grown-ups. "They seemed," he felt, "to understand so little."[50] He never met an adult he could wholly admire. He was insatiably curious about the world and was constantly coming across some essential information that the adults had either forgotten to mention or didn't know themselves and didn't care to find out. A history class unveiled the secrets of the prehistoric age, Jules Verne's *Twenty Thousand Leagues Under the Sea* informed him about Atlantis, and a question to his grandmother, a spiritualist, about life after death added to his growing store of knowledge. That no one had told him about these things before amazed him.

"The craving for a 'system,' an explanation of the world, seems to date back as far as I can remember," he later wrote.[51] "Something altered in my picture of the world" when he discovered science. The distrust he had felt up until then dissolved. Knowledge, he was beginning to understand, was power. It seemed that at last he could understand "human destiny." Most people might be contemptible creatures, the eleven-year-old decided, but this was because they "were too lazy to care about anything beyond their immediate needs."[52] Wilson had never met anyone who was interested in ideas *for their own sake*, a predilection uncommon among the working class, and rarely found in general. But Wilson saw that the limitations he had been born into—and those of humanity en masse—could be transcended through a passionate devotion to knowledge. There were the essential things that truly mattered; science dealt with those. And there was everything else, what Wilson called the "trivial." Triviality was the source of everything that disgusted him about the adult world. Thinking back on "the most violent quarrels and scenes of my childhood," he recalled, their cause was always something "trivial." "An overwhelming, monstrous triviality, a parasitic triviality that ate its way into all values" characterized the world of his childhood.[53] Is it any wonder that in later years he would characterize the essence of his philosophy as an escape from what the philosopher Heidegger called "the triviality of everydayness"?

Science was a relief from this essentially petty world of overwrought emotion and inconsequential anxieties. Its coolness and detachment were intoxicating. The name Albert Einstein appeared in the sci-fi pulps young Colin read and with Wells he soon became his hero. He borrowed volumes of chemistry from school and read them cover to cover, added popular science magazines to his growing collection, and was disappointed when he discovered that the atomic bomb had already been invented. Although he had hoped to be the one to do it—adding his name to the list of great scientists that included Galileo, Newton, and Einstein—he nevertheless was excited by the news. He went from bottom of the class to a top-grade student and became the teacher's pet in his science classes. Popular science books by Sir Arthur Eddington and Sir James Jeans added to his reading. He enjoyed a certain celebrity at school by being able to correct his teachers and earned himself the nickname "the Professor."[54] His curiosity was not limited to purely scientific concerns however, and a discussion among his classmates about the riddle of where space *ended* led to what we might see as the first glimmer of the kind of existential questions that would later obsess him. He wrote a twenty-page letter to Sir Arthur Eddington about this, asking him if he could tell him what the universe was all about. But when he asked the librarian if she knew his address, she told him he had died earlier that year (1944). By this time Wilson's contempt for adults had even affected his appreciation of his heroes, and he concluded that Eddington wouldn't know the answer anyway.[55]

His discovery of science had a curious side effect. Einstein's relativity shifted into a kind of moral relativity, a misunderstanding and misapplication of his ideas that was not limited to thirteen-year-old boys. This shift was to some extent an expression of his contempt for adults. In an attempt to rationalize this, Wilson developed his ideas about what he called "superiority," the notion, based on psychiatrist Alfred Adler's concept of the "inferiority complex," that people are motivated by the need to see themselves as "extraordinary."[56] This idea was revived in 1974 by the cultural anthropologist Ernest Becker in his book *The Denial of Death*. Becker's basic argument is that all human beings have a deep-seated need to *be somebody*, to stand out from the crowd, to be an "object of primary value," to show that he or she "*counts* more than anyone else."

Years later Becker's ideas would inform Wilson's mammoth account of criminality through the ages, *A Criminal History of Mankind*. But in 1944, Becker hadn't written his book, and the thirteen-year-old Wilson had worked it out for himself. Adler's use of Nietzsche's idea of the "will to power" came as a revelation to Wilson, and seemed much more accurate than the psychologies of Freud or Jung, which he had learned about, with Adler's, from a textbook on psychology. Adler argued that we all suffer from an inferiority complex and, to compensate for this, we all struggle to achieve a sense of superiority, or at least for the approval and high esteem of our fellows that come with this. Wilson recognized that although adults seem to be reasonable and fair, this is an illusion, and that most disagreements among them are settled through sheer self-assertion ("Now, you listen to me!"). The adolescent Wilson concluded that if such is the case, then there is no objective right or wrong—this was a myth that adults used to control children. These are purely relative terms, with no final meaning. The reality behind them is pure self-assertion, that is, dominance, an idea that would come to inform Wilson's later philosophy. As he wrote, echoing his younger self's belief, "Nobody is right; nobody is wrong; but *everyone* wants to be thought right."[57] This insight into our powerful need for self-esteem and the submission of others to our demands would reemerge decades later in the mature Wilson's explorations into human psychology, just as the tension he felt between his distrust of the world and the feeling of complete confidence would reemerge in the Outsider's confrontation with "Ultimate Yes and Ultimate No."[58]

What Wilson's reading did in 1944 was inspire him to write an "Essay on Superiority," a curious blend of Einstein and Adler that produced in Wilson the fear that in "questioning too deeply," he had cut himself off "from the rest of the human race."[59] He felt that he had "destroyed in [him]self a certain necessary basis of illusion that makes life bearable for human beings." He had crossed this boundary in the name of truth, but had come to discover that truth "had no power of intensifying life; only of destroying the illusions that make life tolerable."[60] His angst was so great that he was surprised to wake up and find himself alive the next morning.

What began then was a long period in which futility seemed to be the answer to the question of the meaning of existence. "It was," he writes, "the worst and most depressing period of my life."[61] A glib and ungenerous biographer might conclude that Wilson's whole oeuvre and unremitting emphasis on optimism and life affirmation was a reaction to his long teenage depression, a manic, lifelong effort to keep his cosmic anxiety at bay. That someone might work toward an alternative to depression rather than accept it, as some do, as an ultimate truth about reality, seems a more perceptive and reasonable assessment. Wilson's futility, however, wasn't rooted solely in precocious existential agony. His ideas about superiority weren't the sole source of his unhappiness. "There was a social maladjustment," he realized, "for which the ideas provided the excuse."[62] At thirteen he had few friends, and the sexual awakening that troubled him had no outlets. "Sex"—or the lack of it—"played as important a part as my eschatological doubts in making me wretched in my early teens."[63] He spent "three years in my bedroom, reading and writing." He admired a "certain ideal of cold brutality and intellect," a penchant for the unromantic and austere that remained throughout his life; one of Wilson's favorite writers was the Austrian novelist Robert Musil, whose *The Man Without Qualities* met this taste for clarity, precision, and sheer intellectual toughness.

He wrote to stave off boredom and despair. One product was his first book, *A Manual of General Science*, an ambitious attempt to summarize all knowledge, written over his summer holidays in 1944, using popular encyclopedias and library books as his sources. What began as an exercise to fill one notebook led to cramming as much information as he could about physics, chemistry, astronomy, and everything else into six. He eventually abandoned the project but emerged from it with two insights. One was that being forced to summarize a subject in a few pages increased his ability to understand it—an educative by-product that many writers, myself included, have benefited from. It also introduced him to the "intense pleasure" of working on a book, a "feeling of inner health" after a hard day's work, a relief from the usual world of "neurotic daydreams."[64] He had discovered the "sheer immensity of the world of ideas" and it was like exploring some "marvellous unknown country" with "limitless horizons." His long days of writing were relieved by long bicycle rides, extensive excursions into the countryside, where he raced for miles as fast as he could, often cursing motorists along the way. After abandoning *Manual*, he set himself other strenuous intellectual tasks: reading all of Shakespeare, as well as his contemporaries, working through Russian literature, or absorbing the history of art.[65]

Films were also a relief; like many young boys he haunted the Saturday matinees. Westerns and later Technicolor musicals—with their blonde leading ladies—fueled his daydreams. (Wilson applauds both film and comic books as a better means of getting an education than the schools he attended.) At this stage he decided that if he was ever going to escape the "vegetable mediocrity" around him, it would be through the "effort to be great." An ordinary life was out of the question. It was "genius or nothing," a challenge many creative people set themselves. This emphasis on being great and on genius would return in unhelpful ways during the initial excitement around *The Outsider.* Now they were an absolute necessity for maintaining his inner direction.

That inner direction found itself sorely challenged. The sense that everyone around him had no idea of the abyss of nothingness before which everyday life teetered led the angst-ridden teenager to loathe everyone he came into contact with. If his disgust with mediocrity and illusion was, at bottom, a religious sensibility—*vanitas vanitatum*—it was also, he later recognized, not a particularly good recipe for a "cheerful and well-adjusted adolescence."[66] Literature became an avenue of escape. Poetry became a special discovery, and Wilson enlarged his library with "characteristic amorality," liberating books from bookshops and libraries. Through poetry he could retreat from life, avoid people, and enter a beautiful and more meaningful world.

It was not until 1946, when he was fifteen, that he realized that he was not the only person in the world who was troubled by the question of the meaning of human existence. The BBC had started a new radio network, the Third Programme, and that evening Wilson tuned in to hear the third act of Bernard Shaw's philosophical comedy *Man and Superman.* The third act, known as "Don Juan in Hell," is the philosophical heart of the play and is often performed by itself. Wilson had already seen the film of Shaw's *Caesar and Cleopatra*—starring Claude Rains and Vivien Leigh—but wasn't intrigued enough to read Shaw's other works. This was different. The central tension of "Don Juan in Hell" is a kind of Platonic dialogue between Don Juan and the Devil, in which Don Juan argues Shaw's "creative evolutionist" philosophy against the cultured nihilism of the Devil. Hell, it turns out, is not a place of torment, but a world of comfort, pleasure, and endless discussions about love. There one has nothing to do but amuse oneself, a damnation that Don Juan finds insufferable. Heaven, to which he wants to escape, is a place of effort and activity; it is the home of the "masters of reality," while hell is the home of the "unreal and of the seekers of happiness."[67] It is in heaven that the work of aiding life in its "incessant aspiration to higher organization, wider, deeper, intenser self-consciousness, and clearer self-understanding" takes place. In hell, people sit around and tell each other how wonderful they are.

The effect of hearing that broadcast remained with Wilson throughout his life. Shaw became one of his permanent heroes; in later years he would find it impossible to read "Don Juan in Hell" without a feeling of awe.[68] He would go on to write a biography of Shaw, and came to understand that what excited him about Shaw's writing was its "irresistibly *optimistic* forward movement," his "clarity" and "conviction that any problem will yield to a combination of reason, courage and determination."[69] With Musil, Shaw is another writer whose intellectual toughness and lack of sentimentality exhilarated Wilson—that he was invariably funny helped too—and Shaw's optimism, clarity, and refusal to give in to despair became central ingredients in Wilson's own writing. Shaw's status among litterateurs today is less high than it has been, but for Wilson there is no doubt that he is "the greatest figure in European literature since Dante."[70]

What resonated with Wilson was that someone else had actually thought and written about the problems that preoccupied him. He was struck by the revelation that he was not *alone*. He listened to the play again and then read it and the next forty-eight hours were like a "mental earthquake." Yet it wasn't enough to quell his doubts. He often went into churches and argued with priests about the existence of God and the meaning of life. The poetry of T. S. Eliot helped dissipate his depression in a way that Shaw could not.

Wilson left school at sixteen. His ambition then was to become a scientist, and while studying for a math exam in order to get his B.S. he took a job at a wool factory. The hours were long and the work hard, and the three months he spent there gave him a "glimpse into an abyss of boredom and repetitiveness."[71] When he passed his exam he got work at his old school as a laboratory assistant. The work was much easier than at the wool factory and entailed taking classes, and at first he enjoyed it. But by then a new problem had arisen. He had spent the past few months writing plays—one was a sequel to *Man and Superman*— and a short story he had written was accepted by a magazine put out by a factory where an uncle worked. Shaw, Eliot, and other writers had worked on Wilson's sensibilities and although a certain fundamental appreciation of science and its rigor would remain with him, he had lost all interest in it and no longer wanted to become a scientist. He wanted to become a writer, a career switch that did not go unnoticed by his employers, who nevertheless turned a blind eye to the loss of one of their star assistants. But by the end-of-term exams it was obvious. He did miserably and he was let go with two months' severance pay.

It was during his period as a lab assistant that Wilson underwent two important experiences. Although the work was easy, it was not a time of peace. Petty quarrels with one of his professors dragged him down into the trivial. The misery, boredom, and depression continued and he filled notebook after notebook with expressions of his disgust and later burned them. He read endlessly, writing analyses of Joyce, Ibsen, Pirandello, and sent off stories that failed to get accepted. He did not necessarily enjoy writing, but did it obsessively, in order to keep back the sense of total futility that he was afraid would overwhelm him. Then, during the Easter holiday of 1948, it did.

He had spent a whole day reading a book about Russian literature, a gloomy prospect in itself, when, getting up to make a cup of tea, he blacked out. An electric sensation filled his brain and as he stood in the kitchen he became aware of nothing but blackness. Something flowed through him and he realized that it was an insight into "what lay on the other side of consciousness." It was an "eternity of pain," and a recognition that "*life does not lead to anything*" but is an "*escape from something*."[72] It was an escape from some indefinite but ever-present horror, a "metaphysical horror," we might say, borrowing the term from the philosopher Leszek Kolakowski, and it would reappear as the "vastation" experienced by many of Wilson's Outsiders. "All the metaphysical doubts of years," Wilson felt, had culminated in "one realization." "What *use* is such truth?" he asked. The futility seemed complete. Even writing about it was futile.

He managed to salvage some positive sense out of the emptiness. Nihilism became a kind of active belief. Not the *absence* of beliefs, but the active belief in Nothing. After reading excerpts from the *Tao Te Ching* in *The Bible of the World* he associated his Nothing with the Tao. A dubious identification, no doubt, but it gave body to what he felt. He seemed to have reached a boundary of skepticism beyond which he could not go, a kind of gleeful solipsism in which he illogically tried to convince others that they did not really exist (illogical because if they did not exist, then whom was he trying to convince?). Then another dark insight brought everything to a head. Writing once again, he felt a revulsion at the sense of renewal it triggered, a stubborn return of the animal insistence on living. He would not be tricked again by this false reconciliation with life. The boredom, misery, pain, and emptiness would only return the next day. In order to prevent this he made a decision. "*I will not go on living like this*," he thought. He would kill himself.

The idea cheered him. The decision to end his life brought a certain distance from it, a certain freedom; he had at last mastered his destiny. Even the complaints from his professor about coming to his evening class late didn't disturb him. While the other students prepared their materials for analysis, Wilson went into the storeroom. There amid bottles of cobalt chloride, silver nitrate, potassium iodide, and other chemicals was a bottle of hydrocyanic acid. He grabbed it, removed the stopper, and inhaled the distinctive almond smell. Just as he was about to put the bottle to his lips, something happened. Suddenly, a vivid realization of what exactly would happen if he drank the stuff invaded his mind. His imagination had involuntarily stepped a few moments into the future and the burning and retching that would precede death were palpable. He seemed to become two people. "I was suddenly conscious of this teenage idiot called Colin Wilson, with his misery and frustration," a "limited fool" whose death would probably be a relief for everyone, and a "real me" who told his other self that if didn't rid himself of his self-pity "he would never amount to anything."[73]

Wilson's moment of duo-identity was much like a similar mental split he would experience decades later, during another period of intense strain. This later split inspired his notion of a "ladder of selves," which he spelled out in *Mysteries*, his sequel to *The Occult*. Here it led to the sudden undeniable revelation that what he really wanted was not less life, but more. His other self whispered in his other ear: "Think what you'd be losing if you killed yourself." In that moment the richness of the world, its sheer complexity became concrete.

The objective meanings beyond his limited personal self rushed in on him and made the idea of suicide suddenly laughable. There was, he suddenly *knew*, a whole world out there and he was about to chuck it away. It was a moment of what Wilson would later dub "Faculty X," our unrecognized power of *grasping reality*, of brushing aside the cobwebs of our petty personal selves and seeing the world *objectively*. He replaced the stopper, put the bottle back on the shelf, and returned to class.

Wilson's brush with death showed him that suicide was no answer, but it did not solve his problems. The need to work remained, as did the inevitable bouts of boredom, depression, and misanthropy. He applied for jobs and was happy when he was turned down and miserable when he was hired. He joined a drama club out of boredom; later, during his *Wanderjahr*, he would think of becoming an actor. A job as a tax collector ended ignominiously. He took an exam to become a civil servant and to his horror he passed. He was posted to Rugby, not far from Leicester, and had his first experience of the terror of landladies. He was kicked out of lodgings. When some unexpected money came to him, he left the job after a year, and used his windfall to cycle to the Lake District, in order to see something of the countryside. He misjudged the distance and had to return to Leicester after a few days' frantic pedaling, at which point he entered the RAF in order to fulfill his National Service.

At first Wilson enjoyed his National Service. The square-bashing left him feeling physically fit and happily exhausted, with little time for his existential worries. He had by this time discovered the *Bhagavad Gita*, the Hindu religious classic, and started to practice concentration. It was not meditation per se, but an attempt to focus his mind, to achieve the kind of detachment that often came to him through poetry. The notion of reincarnation and the ubiquity of Brahman gave him a sense of an existence spanning eternities. He began to feel a certain idealism, the sense that one day all men would devote their attention to the things that matter and would labor toward understanding the purpose of life.

Yet the same pettiness that plagued him in civvies now pestered him in fatigues. A kind of lethargy and corruption prevailed at his camp and eventually Wilson was faced with the kind of triviality that had fueled his adolescent misanthropy. A series of petty humiliations eventuated in a confrontation and Wilson was faced with military jail. He avoided this by pleading mental and emotional strain that gave him suicidal thoughts and capped off his tale of woe with the false admission that he was gay. The years of dressing in his mother's underwear came to good use and he admitted that his gross inefficiency was rooted in the nervous tension he felt in the proximity of so many handsome men. At the time homosexuality was tacitly acknowledged in the service but explicitly disapproved of and Wilson was treated with delicacy. His study of books on sexual perversion provided him with textbook answers to the doctor's questions and after some pressure to inform about any goings-on—Wilson had, in fact, declined an invitation to flog an officer, but he refused to tattle—he was eventually discharged as "nervously unstable." Six months after entering the RAF, he was free. His tenure had taught him that "one's salvation can lie in proceeding to extremes of indiscretion and ignoring the possible consequences."[74]

He left with a sense of clarity about his position. He began to see the answer to certain problems of existence. One was to achieve more permanently the kind of detachment that came to him now only in moments. This could be accomplished by pursuing a life of contemplation, which essentially meant freedom from life's incessant demands. Humanity, he saw, was afflicted with a kind of "original sin," the inability to *hold on to* the insight that came in such moments, as if the significance of our experience vanished like fairy gold. We were like permanent amnesiacs who forgot everything a moment after it happened. If, as seemed reasonable, we consider those moments of insight sudden flashes of mental and spiritual health, then most men suffer from a chronic illness, a kind of "reality deficiency" that prevents them from retaining the inner nourishment that experience provides in the same way that a vitamin deficiency prevents the body from retaining physical nourishment. Most of us accept this malnourished state as normal, just as many people get used to living with an illness. But some individuals refuse to accept it; they struggle against the dulling and deadening of their senses, and to their fellows they appear unusual and strange, somewhat *outside* the normal run of things.

The first thing to do was to avoid falling back into the trap of pointless, numbing work. Taking a cue from the example of itinerant eastern sages, Wilson decided to become a wanderer. He resigned from the civil service; his father thought he was throwing his future away and the act widened the rift between them. He packed a rucksack with Plato, the *Gita*, and T. S. Eliot and imagined living in a stone hut on the Aran Islands, but this daydream soon transformed into the idea that he would become an actor. This too failed to materialize and he hitchhiked almost aimlessly, spending nights in haystacks and RAF barracks; he traveled in his uniform and explained that his official discharge papers hadn't yet arrived. He practiced yoga in a youth hostel, thought of catching a boat to India, and spent a night at Stonehenge, reciting passages from the *Gita* and shivering. He came to see that, contra Hermann Hesse, being a homeless wanderer was not as romantic as it sounded. But his visions of a monastery and of a life under the stars were "symbols of intensity," much like his interest in the church. For a time then he seriously considered becoming a Catholic, but gave it up because while he could see the need for an idea of God, the "vicarious atonement" offered by Christ seemed unnecessary. But essentially the church, like his fantasy about India, was an image of the kind of transformed life he sought; it was a way of holding on to his vision of *meaning*.

Eventually he had to return home, where he knew he was considered a nuisance. He moved from job to job, mostly on building sites. Work at a fairground led to his losing his virginity at nineteen to an enterprising teenage girl. His dalliance with her cost him the job, but at least he had finally penetrated the mystery of sex, which was, however, something of a letdown. "There was a practical feeling about it," he recollected, "and an odd lack of excitement."[75] It was enjoyable enough for him to continue it for a time, until the realization that he would soon drift into normality—marriage and a family—woke him up. He wanted to devote his life entirely to the work of the mind, not slip into a frustrating conventionality. He no longer felt on the defensive; he realized that he had stopped being miserable in the old way. The sense that destiny meant well by him, fostered by his adoring family, returned. He switched from laboring jobs to being a farmhand, and after a pregnancy scare, Wilson told his amour that he had to move on.

He was still unsure what to do, but decided to head across the channel to France. He was propelled in part by his father's anger at his uselessness, but mostly by a feeling that he had started to live as he should. He stopped reading the now "morbid" Eliot and became fond of Rabelais and Blake, two life affirmers who buoyed his new sense of acceptance.

He picked apples for a week before reaching Calais. There he was struck by the remnants of the war, bought a bottle of wine and some bread, and ate by the roadside. He became involved with some fellow young travelers at a hostel, and enjoyed a brief romance with a girl who soon jilted him for someone else. The frustration was soothed by a moment of detachment, looking at the trees in the Avenue de Châtillon in Paris. And an odd book of poetry led him to the studio of the septuagenarian Raymond Duncan, a self-styled poet and arts patron and brother of the celebrated dancer Isadora Duncan. Duncan was a kind of throwback to the nineteenth century and the world of *La Bohème*. He wore a toga, sported a long beard, expounded an arts-and-crafts philosophy reminiscent of William Morris, and wrote reams of Whitmanesque poetry. Wilson found his ideas and language sentimental and turgid, but Duncan sought followers and he offered a place to sleep and meals to eat to students willing to submit to his teaching. Wilson ate and slept and used his time at Duncan's Akademia to work on the novel he had started, which would eventually become *Ritual in the Dark*, a narrative of existential suspense, far removed from Duncan's humanistic ethos. After a few weeks of submitting to Duncan's philosophy, Wilson was asked to leave when his true motives were found out.

He headed to Strasbourg to stay with a pen friend, but it soon became apparent that their sensibilities were too divergent. Since they had last met, Wilson's friend had become an ardent Marxist, who espoused Rousseau's naïve belief that men are born free but are everywhere in chains. By this time Wilson's misanthropy approached a kind of Manichaean intensity; he believed that most men are chained by their own mediocrity, and that Marxism or any political or economic system was no help here. Wilson's religious perspective argued that what was needed was not a new system, but a new kind of man, which to his friend sounded far too much like a kind of fascism. Wilson stuck it out, reading Henry James at the university library, where he met an American academic who encouraged him in his writing; he felt he had made a breakthrough, and his new acquaintance's encouragement confirmed it. He tried to find work at the university but it was too late in the semester. His continental adventure ended when his friend's family informed him with great regret that a relative was coming to stay and that sadly they would have to ask him to give up his room. Wilson knew this was untrue but it was obvious he couldn't remain in the house, and with the help of the British Consulate he found his way back to Leicester.

Three months of drifting hadn't solved his problems. They were there, back at home, when he returned. He picked up his romance where he had left it, but soon broke with the girl for good. New temporary jobs appeared. He took a position as a clerk for a metal works. He enjoyed watching the molten metal being poured into molds and then pounded by steam hammers. The sight of the red glow at dusk illuminating the bodies of the men reminded him of Blake and the "hammer of Los," which creates the visionary space that opens into eternity. He began an affair with the works' nurse, an older woman, Betty, who would become his first wife. Their unsuitability would later become clear but now he was attracted to her maturity and reserve. But inevitably the job began to bore him, the numbing automatism began to set in, and all the poetry and literature he read at night could not stave it off. The need to preserve spontaneity, to *live* rather than be lived, compelled him to fight. He tried a number of tactics: getting up earlier than he had to, sleeping on the floor, running, sitting up all night in a yoga position. Nothing worked. Whatever he tried, it seemed he couldn't escape the sense of "being what society wished to make me, merely another human being in the human anthill."[76]

He left the job and got work as a laborer digging trenches. What he needed was time to do real work, to write. He had a brainstorm and asked his boss if he could work a three-day week. It would mean less money but more time and the plan seemed brilliant. The boss refused; he quit and took another job at a chemical factory. Here he recited poetry to fend off the fog of triviality while boiling resin and moving empty crates. Then fate threw another challenge his way. Betty announced she was pregnant. A month later it was confirmed. Wilson's parents had been forced into marriage by the same complication and it seemed he was following suit. After some deliberation—Betty refused an abortion—in June 1951, at the age of twenty, Wilson married Betty, who was ten years his senior, at the Leicester registry office while she was on her lunch hour. Wilson was broke as ever, so Betty had to pay for the ring.[77] Neither wanted marriage or a child—Betty was focused on her career—but Wilson's sense of responsibility precluded running for it. Almost immediately after the wedding he hitchhiked to London. They had to live together, but it wouldn't be in Leicester. If he was going to actualize his genius and achieve greatness, it wouldn't be there.

Wilson's first marriage lasted eighteen months, all of them filled with the same battle against mediocrity he had already waged for some time. "It was an ill-fated marriage from the beginning," he reflected, when he came to write of it years later.[78] As he summed it up, "I worked in factories in London and we moved from home to home with dismal regularity."[79] Landladies didn't want children and those who would take them proved demonic. Becoming a landlady, he came to believe, was "the surest way to forfeit your immortal soul," and Wilson even wondered if the malice he felt toward these petty tyrants somehow endowed him with the evil eye.[80] On more than one occasion, following a particularly intense explosion of anger, misfortune befell his tormentor, and Wilson wondered if he was somehow responsible. Although he began to see the advantages of marriage—he was now not alone and appreciated the affection and trust Betty could give him—at bottom he wanted to write and didn't want the responsibility of providing for a wife and a child, certainly not at the same age that his father had had to.

Things, however, were not all bad. Wilson enjoyed coming home from work and finding his supper ready for him. In the evening they enjoyed the cinema, or listened to concerts on the radio. Weekends saw walks around London, often in the East End, scene of the Jack the Ripper murders, where Wilson would set much of *Ritual in the Dark*. (He would later coin the term "Ripperology" for the study of the murders.) It was at this time that Wilson began to write in the Reading Room of the British Museum, hoping to catch a wave of inspiration from its earlier habitués, such as Shaw, Wells, Marx, and Samuel Butler (author of *Erewhon* and an early philosophical critic of Darwinism). He liked the sense of order married life provided. It was much like being back in the secure world of childhood, after the tumultuous years of his teens.

But eventually the difficulties seemed insurmountable. When the baby—a boy they named Roderick—arrived, things understandably became more difficult, and life's racket was cranked up a notch. Wilson soon found that he had even less time to focus his mind on what mattered, and attempts to achieve the kind of concentration he'd had in his early days of reading the *Gita* proved impossible. An argument on Christmas Day 1952 proved the point. Wilson tried to meditate but Betty asked him to mind the baby. Later, when he tried to make up, he read to her from D. H. Lawrence. Betty thought it was boring. He left in a huff and cycled madly down King's Road. At Wandsworth Bridge, with the cold Thames below him, he looked inside himself to see what he really wanted. It wasn't marriage.

Clearly things weren't right. He thought of Nijinsky, whose poignant *Diary* he had just read. Nijinsky's wife was, like Betty, a good, sensible woman who, for all her love, had no idea of the kind of mental strain her husband was under. For all the affection and trust he received from Betty, he felt she continued to read his motivations in the most commonplace way, and did not take him on his own valuation, an unforgivable attack on his amour propre, as every man will know. She did not share his enthusiasm for ideas and felt his obsession with them was a kind of self-centeredness and insensitivity. His urge to evolve, he felt, went beyond the usual personal motivations, and when she reduced his aims and aspirations to these he reacted angrily. It is true, he admits, that "the evolutionary obsession can be interpreted as a manic egoism or will to self-assertion."[81] This was an accusation Betty had no hesitation in making and it is one not infrequently made against many would-be artists and geniuses. But his excitement about ideas was sincere and something he wanted to share with her. He was discovering new and important writers and thinkers, such as Ouspensky, whose *In Search of the Miraculous* he had found at the Wimbledon Public Library, and which introduced him to Gurdjieff, "quite obviously one of the greatest minds" he had ever encountered. Here he had also come across Richard Wilhelm's translation of the *I Ching*, with an introduction by Jung. Like all aspiring writers, he asked the oracle about his future; he received six unbroken lines, the hexagram called "The Creative." "The creative works supreme success," the oracle told him. "Furthering through perseverance." It was a prediction he had hoped to hear; "furthering through perseverance" could be seen as Wilson's philosophy in a nutshell. (He remarks that although he has thrown the I Ching coins innumerable times since then, he never again received six unbroken lines.) He would have loved it if Betty got excited about these things too. She didn't. When he got excited and tried to tell her about his ideas, she felt he was talking at her, not with her, a not uncommon complaint in unions like these.

The conclusion seemed obvious. He was either serious about his business as a writer or he wasn't. If the relationship couldn't be established on his terms, he was prepared to let it go. The marriage, he saw, was "an irrelevant interlude," a long diversion from his purpose, and it would have to end. He wasn't angry. It was a simple, clear recognition.

They separated in the new year. They had been living in a house in Kensington where Betty worked as a live-in nurse for an ill elderly woman. It was the second such setup that they had found themselves in. (The number of rooms and temporary accommodations the two had lived in would have placed enormous demands on any couple.) The first such arrangement had proved intolerable; the old man Betty cared for then demanded her full attention, resented Wilson's presence, and would often give presents one day and take them back the next. One of these gifts was a typewriter that Wilson used to type his novel; in a fit of pique, the old man took it away and Wilson fumed. The house in

Kensington was no better. The woman would fly into insane rages, accusing Betty of stealing her mail and other absurdities. Eventually it turned out that an undetected cancer of the womb was the source of her furies. Sometime into 1953, Betty gave up the position. Their furniture was put into storage, and Betty returned to Leicester with the one-year-old Roderick. The idea was that she would wait there until Wilson found them a new home. But they would never live together again.

"Implacable life," as the poet Baudelaire called it, had proved unwieldly to the young Wilson and now he had escaped its iron grip again. He wouldn't let himself be trapped. Being a failed husband and father was perhaps an ignominious fate, but going the limit had proved useful before. His reading had introduced him to an unusual canon of works, and the individuals responsible for them seemed to have been faced with problems similar to his own. No one seemed to have noticed these books or ideas and he began to see connections and parallels among them. Life hadn't been rosy for these strange characters but in some way each seemed to have contributed something that, brought together, might suggest a way out of the labyrinth and off the treadmill and into something closer to Reality. It was time to find out.

CHAPTER TWO

BEFORE *THE OUTSIDER*

The initial result of Wilson's new freedom was a plunge into anarchy—or at least into the fringe of the London anarchist movement. Some months earlier he had come across an anarchist speaker in Hyde Park Corner, an edge of London's great green space given over to free speech; among those who had honed their oratory there was Wilson's hero Shaw. A red-bearded man was preaching anarchy and Wilson was taken with his wit, if not his arguments. The speaker was Philip Sansom, an old-school anarchist who in 1945 had been imprisoned for inciting the King's soldiers to drop their rifles and ignore their duties. By the time Wilson heard him his bark was much worse than his bite, but Wilson liked him and he asked if he could join his London Anarchist Group. Formal membership in an anarchist society seems highly oxymoronic; Sansom told him there was no official membership, but if he really was an anarchist, he could come next Sunday and join him in haranguing the crowd. Wilson took the challenge. En route the next week he decided to test his anarchistic tendencies by trying to avoid the full Underground fare from Wimbledon to Marble Arch. He was caught out and handed a fine. This encounter with tyrannical authority informed his rhetoric, and for half an hour he instructed listeners on how to avoid paying transport fares. Many cheered him—he drew a large crowd—but the hard-line anarchists doubted his ideology and advised him to read Mikhail Bakunin, Prince Kropotkin, and other anarchist thinkers.

Wilson knew that anarchism, with its rejection of all forms of authority, was nonsense, or at best a kind of political and social idealism: inspiring to consider but impractical to achieve. He believed that with time and effort, society could become more intelligent and democratic, reducing the need for authority. But as we are now, we are not ready for this. He did believe in the anarchist aim of creating a society of "free spirits" who would aid each other gratuitously. The kind of "demoniacal, ruthless money-grubbing" he had seen in the workplace was a cancer that reduced men and women to laboring automatons when it did not crush them outright. Life should be about something more than that. He wanted to create an England that would nurture its talented men and women, and foster the growth of individualism. Understandably such broad sentiments weren't hard-core enough for the tough-minded politicos he rubbed elbows with, and although welcome to come to their meetings, Wilson was not allowed back on their soapbox.

He moved to another group, who was happy to get speakers. Wilson's motivation in joining these groups was much less political than personal. With his marriage collapsed he had more free time and wanted to learn how to speak to an audience, training that would come in handy a few years later, when his literary success led to many speaking engagements. (It was at this time that he worked to lose his Leicester accent, one not usually associated with intellectual pursuits.) He had once tried to speak at a Theosophical Society meeting—he was briefly a member while living in Wimbledon but found their thinking too slack—but his voice quavered and his hands trembled; he wanted to get over his stage fright. His flirtation with anarchy ended after he gave a talk about the irrational element in human nature, exemplified by a selection of Roman emperors, Jack the Ripper, and passages from Dostoyevsky. The moral was that the kind of anarchist millennium dreamt of by his comrades was impossible as long as the irrational side of human beings remained unexamined. No political, social, or economic system could alter that; only self-discipline of the kind once offered by religion. The anarchists believed that once the oppression of authority was lifted, men would love each other automatically. It was the kind of ethos that severed ties with Wilson's French friend. To the many who accepted Rousseau's dictum about being born in chains but really free, Wilson's arguments sounded like the worst kind of authoritarianism. He left anarchy after that.

The society of free spirits gratuitously helping each other had yet to appear and Wilson had to find another job. This time it was as a hospital porter in Fulham. He received patients, wheeled them around on stretchers, fetched their meals, took dead patients to the mortuary, and emptied rubbish bins. He was given a tiny cubicle to sleep in and meals. Privacy was at a minimum. For the first few weeks, Wilson was still speaking anarchically—representing the syndicalist workers—and he kept their soapbox with him at work, bicycling to Hyde Park Corner with it strapped to his back. The work wasn't hard and the pay was decent but the long, empty hours, waiting to receive a patient, were demoralizing. Cards, tea breaks, and football matches on the radio filled the void. The stagnant atmosphere bred sexual chitchat; the porters reeled off exaggerated accounts of their success or drooled over pornography. Death, too, was nearby. Once Wilson saw the body of a young woman after the postmortem. He had seen her alive a few days earlier; now her brains and intestines lying on the slab seemed to deny that humanity had any importance in the scheme of things. He asked himself what seems a naïve question, but one that would play an important part in his philosophy to come: *why* do we die? Are we so unimportant to nature? Or do we, as Shaw believed, die because we are too lazy to make life worth living?

The negation symbolized by the young woman's body was offset by a "near mystical experience."[1] Lying on his bed, he was listening to the "Liebestod" from Wagner's opera *Tristan and Isolde* on the radio. For Wilson music ranks with sex and poetry as a reliable means of inducing what he would later call "the other mode of consciousness," and he would go on to write a book about it.[2] At the time he was fascinated with the life of the dancer Nijinsky—he would feature in both *The Outsider* and *Ritual in the Dark*—and when the spirit grabbed him Wilson would improvise a dance to whatever music he was listening to. He did so then. He stood up and in his cubicle began to make slow movements with his arms. He tensed his muscles and as the music reached a climax "it seemed to penetrate the depths of my being."[3] For a brief moment he was "above time" and could look down upon life from a height. He had glimpsed some of mankind's evolutionary possibilities. Sheer concentration, an effort of will, he believed, had induced the "timeless moment," and indicated that the relentless flow of time, from life to death, could be halted.

Time may have stopped for a moment, but the relentless need to write remained. He had begun a kind of anarchist revue. It was to have been performed by the syndicalist workers but they had fractured over the poet Herbert Read's acceptance of a knighthood. Read was an anarchist and a surrealist and accepting a knighthood seemed a capitulation to the authorities, rather as if Johnny Rotten was made a peer of the realm. His ex-comrades were in a tizzy but Wilson decided to use his material for a performance of his own. He was by then an habitué of the milk bars and coffeehouses that had sprung up in postwar London. Here he found would-be artists, writers, and poets with a lot of time on their hands. Wilson convinced some of them to take part in his show. They rehearsed in a room in Hampstead and ran through several readings but the work was never properly staged.

It was, he says, a sexually stagnant time. The one time he found himself in bed with a woman—a Communist he had met after speaking at Hyde Park Corner—he experienced "*la fiasco*," as the French writer Stendhal called impotence. This was not out of lack of desire. He found his comrade's approach too forthright and banal; it made lovemaking seem "insipid." Such matter-of-fact fornication was the opposite of the mystical aura that fascinated him about sex. He dated some women at the hospital, one of whom was a vital, idealistic manic-depressive German who had been in the Hitler Youth in her early teens. In her depressive moods she spoke of the meaninglessness of life, much as Wilson had not so long before, and she would regard people as little more than lifeless puppets. Once on Westminster Bridge, she declared that if she took her clothes off or lay down in the road no one would notice. To Wilson's regret she didn't undress but began doing push-ups in the middle of traffic. No one batted an eye. She had, Wilson said, great reserves of energy, and during the war she had been able to channel them into purposeful activity. Like many Germans her age, she had little idea of what Hitler was really about, and had seen him as a kind of heroic figure. Now she had nothing to do with her energies and they collected in her until they could only be released in irrational behavior.

The woman Wilson was most interested in was an eighteen-year-old Catholic named Laura Del-Rivo. She came from a middle-class background and like him, haunted the coffeehouses and dreamt of becoming a writer. She would in fact produce two novels, one of which, *The Furnished Room*, was made into a film, *West 11*, in 1963.[4] At a coffeehouse in Charing Cross Wilson read some of Laura's work while she chain-smoked. He was impressed, both with her writing and with Laura herself. She seemed to embody what he was looking for in a woman; she was "intelligent," "completely feminine," and "devoid of resentments or self-assertion." She, however, was not interested in him, at least not in that way. She had been making the Soho scene for a while, going to parties, poetry readings, and jazz clubs, drinking and smoking grass. It was a sexually casual milieu but Wilson soon discovered that Laura was less casual about sex than he would have liked. She had her eye on another budding genius, a journalist named Bill Hopkins, who had a stronger claim on greatness than Wilson, given that he had published some poetry. Wilson decided that he had to meet this rival.

An encounter was not difficult to arrange. Hopkins held court at several cafés, and at one Wilson saw him addressing a crowd of admirers. He reminded him of F. Scott Fitzgerald and the poet Percy Shelley—romantic, good-looking, idealistic, but too rhetorical for Wilson's tastes. He was a bit disappointed; Hopkins did not match up with Wilson's image of a serious writer. But he was impressed with his personality. He seemed to be a born leader with a gift of conversation that could mesmerize his listeners. Wilson also learned that Hopkins had no interest in Laura. Once he had mentioned to her in a casual way that he would like to sleep with her. Laura explained that she couldn't do it in a casual way, as she was Catholic; she had, in fact, been educated at a convent. This seemed absurd and Hopkins said so. They eventually were lovers briefly but Laura's shyness bored Hopkins and the affair soon ended.

After a couple of meetings Wilson gave Hopkins the manuscript of what would eventually become *Ritual in the Dark*. The novel had gone through many incarnations, and had been variously influenced by Charles Dickens, James Joyce, and *The Egyptian Book of the Dead*. Wilson had originally planned for the narrative to follow the ancient Egyptian funerary texts in the way that Joyce's *Ulysses* had followed Homer. But he soon dropped his attempts at modernist prose and accepted the fact that he needed to tell a story in order to grip his readers. His walks in the East End had convinced him to recast the novel as a kind of modern-day Jack the Ripper thriller. He had been fascinated with the Ripper murders and with crime in general since his childhood, and his growing obsession with Nijinsky and other eccentric types, such as T. E. Lawrence and Vincent van Gogh, moved the work toward something like Dostoyevsky's *The Brothers Karamazov*. The central theme was the question of freedom. The hero, Gerard Sorme, a young intellectual living on a small but sufficient private income—a Wilson alter ego who would appear in later books—has a lot of it, too much for his own good. His aimless drifting is arrested when he meets a strangely fascinating but ambiguous character who may be involved in a series of murders taking place in London's notorious Whitechapel. Their conversations lead Sorme to realize that his fascination with Austin Nunne, his eccentric and mysterious friend, has shaken him out of his existential lethargy and reawakened his will to live. To say more would give the tale away; it remains a gripping story and my recent rereading brought back all the old excitement and romanticism about London in the "duffle-coated" years.[5]

Like all beginning writers, Wilson wanted immediate feedback on his opus but Hopkins took his time. A mover, shaker, and journalist, Hopkins had his fingers in many pies and kept his new friend waiting. One day Wilson walked into the A and A Café, a favorite watering hole, and found his manuscript there, waiting for him with a note from Hopkins. "Welcome to our ranks," it read. "You are a man of genius." Wilson had long known this but it was gratifying to receive corroboration. It was the beginning of a friendship that would last until Hopkins's death in 2011.[6]

Wilson, however, was not quite as taken with Hopkins's own work. It was too romantic for his disciplined tastes. It smacked of Victor Hugo, a sprawling, uncontained genius, and had more than a hint of Poe's obsession with the death of beautiful young women. Hopkins was also much more the doer and man of action than Wilson, using his media savvy to stir things up and make a splash. He lacked Wilson's determination to become great through slow, painstaking effort and had the scene maker's hunger to be "in the news"; Hopkins was in fact putting together a new journal, *Saturday Critic*, that would ruthlessly attack the substandard literature of the time. (The project would fall through because of a lack of funds.) "Although we live in an age of specialization," Wilson reflected, "where years of study are required to become a technician or mathematician, few would-be writers seem to recognize that their trade requires an equally long self-discipline."[7] This is an early expression of what Wilson would later describe as the need for "long term purposes" to motivate us and drive our will.[8] It also points to the need for an at times extreme self-belief in order to get through the sloughs of discouragement and lack of success.

The two should not have hit it off, but Wilson was captured by Hopkins's unshakable self-confidence, a certainty of his own genius that so far Wilson had found only in himself. What he had seen of Soho had disappointed him. He did not find a carefree existence à la *Bohème*, nor the kind of society of free spirits his idealistic anarchism hoped for. His disillusionment came through in his short picaresque novel *Adrift in Soho*, whose title suggests the atmosphere of aimlessness.[9] Its hero, like Wilson, is a young man from the north who is guided through Soho's bohemian life by an experienced habitué but is soon disillusioned with this underworld of poseurs and artists manqué and leaves.

Soho seemed to breed the same lack of self-confidence he had encountered in Leicester. Six months of coffeehouses and pub crawls hadn't uncovered an artist or writer who felt strongly about his work or believed it would make an impact on his contemporaries. The "fallacy of insignificance" that Wilson would critique in *The Age of Defeat* seemed par for the course amid London's art crowd. Even Laura Del-Rivo was diffident about her work. He may not have liked Hopkins's writing but at least the man had the chutzpah to believe in himself. Hopkins's problem, Wilson concluded, was that his personality was too strong; he wasted ideas and energy in brilliant talk. That his father had been a famous Welsh actor suggested that he had inherited a certain taste for histrionics. In a pre-echo of later concerns, Hopkins was too "other-directed," too focused on the immediate effect he could have on other people, and not "inner-directed" enough to put in the time and effort necessary to complete long-range work.[10]

But for the moment, two geniuses had found each other, and between them they would change the world, or at least the London literary scene. A reading of Wilson's anarchist effort, *Twentieth Century Revue*, was held in rooms above a pub in Holborn. It went over well but afterward there was a sense of anticlimax. Boredom set in among his recruits and Wilson was asked to write another play. He complied and parts of *The Metal Flower Blossom* eventually found their way into *Adrift in Soho*. But his cast found rehearsals boring as well and the effort came to nothing.

With Soho a letdown and the hospital getting too much for him, Wilson once again found himself in a familiar situation. The boredom evaded his attempts to slough it off; he felt as if his mind and spirit were rotting. Five minutes in his porter's room was like a weekend in hell. He stewed in his own apathy. Even sitting cross-legged in an empty, dusty room reciting verses from the *Gita* and making desperate attempts to focus his mind were of no help. He remembered earlier moments of delight, but could not grip their reality. An inadvertent reunion with Betty—stage-managed by his parents during a visit to Leicester—ended in another rift. It was painful but he was glad that their decision to try again—taken after spending a night together at Wilson's parents' home—was canceled soon after making it.

He began to experience strange blackouts. Low blood pressure and exhaustion probably were responsible, but this didn't explain the sense of meaninglessness that came over him. The old fear of some horror on the "other side of life" returned and along with this an increased sense of his own mechanicalness. Gurdjieff had told Ouspensky that he and everyone he knew were really just machines, and now Wilson agreed. His actions seemed to be little more than responses to the stimuli around him, as if he was a penny-in-the-slot machine. The thought of suicide returned. He couldn't accept it, so he did what he had done in the past: he moved on. He would return to France.

He gave up the hospital job, sold his books, spent a night sleeping in Hopkins's office, hitchhiked to Dover—with a night sleeping rough outside Canterbury along the way—and was soon again on the ferry crossing the channel. Some wine and a meal at a café near the Calais docks cheered him up. The Spanish music on the radio made him feel that he inhabited all of Europe. The gods were on his side. A sense of joy, expansiveness, and well-being filled him, reminding him of other peak experiences. He could "catch history like a bus." It was another moment out of time. A day or two later, history deposited him in Paris.

He went to visit a friend who lived on Rue Bayen, where he could stay. Next he needed to find work. The money from selling his books wouldn't last long. He saw an advertisement for a new American magazine called *The Paris Review* and decided to check it out. Although the days of Hemingway and Henry Miller were long over, Paris was still a magnet for aspiring artists, poets, and writers, and Americans and their dollars were still welcome there. He went to the magazine's offices and met its editor, a young well-dressed American named George Plimpton.

Plimpton later became a famous journalist, writer, and television personality; he died in 2003 and *The Paris Review* remains one of the premier English-language literary journals. In its early days it promoted the work of writers such as Jack Kerouac, Philip Larkin, Philip Roth, Adrienne Rich, and Nadine Gordimer, to name a few. Wilson got a job selling subscriptions for the fledgling *Paris Review* door-to-door to Americans in Paris. He was happy to find some sort of literary work but soon found that selling subscriptions to a literary review wasn't easy. Often all he could unload were a few individual copies and the proceeds from these barely kept him going. A couple of weeks later, a struggling and hungry Wilson heard that Bill Hopkins was en route to join him. Soon they both were knocking on Americans' doors, trying to sell copies of the magazine. They had little success and whatever profits they made were soon consumed in cigarettes—Hopkins chain-smoked; Wilson didn't—chocolate, and other essential items.

An attempt to sell copies of another review, *Merlin*, edited by the Scottish Beat writer Alexander Trocchi, met with similar triumph. Trocchi would become a friend a few years later; at the time he was subsidizing serious literary work by writing pornography for the notorious Maurice Girodias.[11] Girodias's Olympia Press and its infamous Traveller's Companion series, which was aimed at English-speaking tourists, published Henry Miller; Vladimir Nabokov's controversial *Lolita*, about a middle-aged man's obsession with a twelve-year-old girl; and the lurid *Story of O*, a 1950s precursor to *Fifty Shades of Grey*. *Merlin* published Samuel Beckett, Pablo Neruda, and Jean-Paul Sartre, among others, and Wilson would come to respect Trocchi as a writer, if not as an individual. His most famous work, *Cain's Book*, is an account of his life as a heroin addict, living on a barge on the Hudson River; it deservedly ranks as a classic of drug literature. Wilson would come to feel that like many of his contemporaries, Trocchi wasted his powers on drugs, affairs, and various "revolutionary" activities. For a time Trocchi was involved in Guy Debord's situationist movement, a kind of avant-garde street Marxism. (Debord would commit suicide in 1994.) Notoriously, in 1961, Trocchi, then on bail for a drug charge, injected himself with heroin during a live television debate on drug use. On more than one occasion, he prostituted his wife in order to finance his addiction, and he was infamous for arranging orgies, which he oversaw with a certain sadistic zeal.[12] Fleeing arrest for supplying drugs to a minor, Trocchi was smuggled across the U.S. border and into Canada by the novelist Norman Mailer, where he was helped by a young poet named Leonard Cohen, who aided his repatriation to the UK. Trocchi died of pneumonia in 1984; he was just short of sixty, his body exhausted by drugs and general abuse.

For all its literary hustle and bustle, Paris, like Soho, proved wanting. Wilson had intended to live and write there, but after two months he called it *fini* and returned to England. London held no appeal and in any case he couldn't afford it, so there was no choice but Leicester. Enduring his parents' disapproval, the twenty-three-year-old frequented the Labour Exchange. He was sent to Lewis's department store; Christmas was approaching and there was need for temporary work. If by now the reader feels dizzied by Wilson's wanderings and occupations, I don't blame him. Wilson himself was somewhat scattered. He had worked as a farm laborer, lab assistant, civil servant, hospital porter, secretary, construction worker, laundryman, clerk, in a dairy, a post office, a wool factory, among other places, all along trying to become a writer. He had been a "dissatisfied wanderer" for as long as he could remember, a "perpetual misfit" and drifter. This was not, he says, because of a bohemian temperament. All he wanted was a room, some books, a typewriter, and enough to eat. But he seemed caught in a cycle of taking jobs out of necessity and enduring them until the boredom set in and he had to leave, only to find himself in another pointless job.

One thing he found at his new job was the woman who would become his second wife. His trainer for the cash register was an attractive, intelligent, cultured young woman named Joy Stewart, to whom he took an immediate liking. She had a smile that "transformed her face as completely as sunlight passing over a lake."[13] Her slight vagueness only made her more endearing. He learned that she was engaged and was planning to join her fiancé in Canada. Just his luck. As he got to know her he saw that she was all that he wanted in a woman. In many ways, she reminded him of Laura. She was extremely well read, having absorbed Yeats, Proust (in French), Joyce, and Virginia Woolf, among others. She was attractive and literary and if he was ever going to settle down with someone, she would be ideal.

He also started a competitive friendship with a fellow new employee, a character named Flax, whose ideas about dominance and sex found their way into Wilson's third novel, *The World of Violence*, published in 1963. Flax was a military man bored with civilian life. Wilson appreciated his respect for discipline but rejected his military version and argued that the only discipline worth having was that of the mind. Flax felt that most writers and thinkers were weaklings, an assessment Wilson could understand. Flax voiced an opinion that informed some of Wilson's later ideas: that modern civilization, geared toward comfort and security, lacks challenges for highly motivated people. It is through such challenges that they develop; without them, they grow weak, their powers wasted. Flax illustrated his philosophy by challenging Wilson to races, drinking bouts, and other shows of endurance. He once fired a pistol, just missing Wilson, in order to test his nerves and boasted of being the "last man standing" at an orgy, an achievement that found its way into Wilson's phenomenological analysis of sex, *Origins of the Sexual Impulse*. Once they climbed the scaffolding around a church steeple. Wilson had to suppress a childhood fear of heights to make it to the top, but at least he showed that he wasn't a sissy.

It was through Flax that Wilson was able to get close to Joy. Flax had designs on a workmate of Joy's and the idea was to invite both girls to his apartment for a harmless weekend with Wilson as Joy's "date." Wilson had already suggested that the employees put on a Christmas show, something like his anarchist revue, and that Joy should take part. In the end the manager agreed to a performance of the first act of *Man and Superman*; it was not a success and Joy turned out to be as bad an actress as she had warned. The harmless weekend resulted in Wilson eventually convincing her to break off her engagement and join forces with him. He had to overcome much resistance, but in the end "the most marvellous girl he had ever met" admitted that she did care for him and would take her chances with this waster. It was a decision not without consequences.

After Christmas, Wilson's boss asked if he had decided to stay on. If so he would have to buy a suit—until then Wilson lacked one. "Shades of the prison house" began to close in and Wilson did not buy a suit. He was already thinking of returning to London. Joy and a workmate had decided to rent the rooms above Flax's flat and Wilson offered to redecorate them. At a New Year's Eve party, Wilson and Joy ended up sleeping together harmlessly on the floor, along with other guests. The next day, when he saw her at the flat, he announced that he had decided to return to London. She had better break off her engagement because he intended that she should come with him. She hesitated, then agreed. The next evening they slept together a little less harmlessly. The experience was "one of those moments when you feel that the gods are on your side and life is wholly good." It was like van Gogh's *Starry Night*, a sense of complete affirmation.

Wilson briefly took another job; ironically it was at a boot-and-shoe factory, the kind at which his father had worked. With Joy in his life, he felt a sense of renewed purpose and determination. He would need them for the return to London.

What he met there was a fussy landlord, more boring work, and a visit from Joy's father. Joy had broken off the engagement, left her job, and followed Wilson to London, where she quickly found work at a department store in Oxford Circus. Her parents were not happy with these developments. She was throwing away her future and being led to perdition by a penniless good-for-nothing. Her father had read enough of Wilson's letters to Joy to see that he would come to no good, and he was there to tell him so. Their conversation closed with mutual disgust. But later Joy's father convinced her to agree not to visit Wilson at his lodging; she had taken a room in another part of London, which offered her parents some relief. Wilson was understandably furious. Joy was over twenty-one—what right did her parents have to tell her what to do? Other worries soon appeared. His landlord proved impossible and Wilson had to move again. Work began to drag and he left and found another office job, this time at a garage. This was quickly followed by a stint at a wine merchant. His new landlady's daughter supplemented her income with some infrequent prostitution and often used his room for her assignations. But at least he was able to convince Joy that as he had moved, her agreement not to visit his lodgings was no longer valid. This casuistry had unexpected benefits.

Joy's parents discovered that she was visiting him again and demanded that Wilson appear before their tribunal. He didn't want to, but they would not relent until he agreed. On a hot Saturday afternoon he and Joy set out to hitchhike to her parents' home in Peterborough, not far from Leicester, a journey of about one hundred miles. Along the way Wilson had one of his most important insights, something he came to call "the St. Neots Margin," or "the indifference threshold," which he introduced in the last book of his Outsider Cycle, *Beyond the Outsider*.[14] In essence it is a way of accounting for the strange "paradoxical nature of freedom" that obsessed him throughout his life. Fundamentally it is the recognition that pain and inconvenience can stimulate our vitality far more than pleasure can.

He illustrates this insight with the story of the old woman in the vinegar bottle. A fairy sees the old woman complaining about her cramped life and transforms the vinegar bottle into a cottage. She returns to see how the woman is getting on and discovers that she is still unhappy; the cottage, she says, is damp, cold, and small. The fairy transforms the cottage into a house. When the fairy returns again, she finds that the old woman still isn't happy—she needs servants, help with cleaning, and so on. Now the fairy turns the place into a palace. But once again, the old woman isn't satisfied; the palace is too big, the servants don't listen to her, it's hard to heat. Exasperated, the fairy points her magic wand and turns the palace back into a vinegar bottle.[15] The old woman, Wilson tells us, has a high indifference threshold, meaning that she is horribly spoiled, and cannot appreciate the good things in her life. She is indifferent to them, and is just as unhappy in a palace as she is in a vinegar bottle.

What Wilson recognized is that while pleasure may not cross the indifference threshold, pain or inconvenience can. He discovered this while hitchhiking to his dutiful meeting with Joy's parents. He was not looking forward to it, but didn't particularly want to stay in London; he didn't care one way or the other. They had been walking for miles in the heat when they finally got a ride. A truck driver picked them up, but soon after, a noise developed in the engine, and the driver said he would have to stop at a garage and let them off. They started hitching again. After a while, another truck stopped. Wilson felt no joy at getting a second ride, merely a feeling of "About time . . ." Then a kind of synchronicity happened: another ominous knocking started in *this* engine. Wilson thought, "Oh no, not again," then realized this was his first *positive* response since leaving London.

The driver said he would have to leave them at a garage too. But then, he saw that if he kept his speed down, the knocking stopped. If he kept to around twenty-five miles an hour, he could keep going. By this time, Wilson was listening intently for any recurrence of the noise, and when the driver said he thought they would make it, he let out a sigh of relief, and felt a sudden surge of happiness. Then the oddness of the situation dawned on him. Here he was, crawling along in a stuffy cab on a hot day, heading to a meeting he dreaded, and yet he suddenly felt quite happy and alive and eager to get there. The fact that the truck had picked them up in the first place didn't please him; he was indifferent to it. It was only with the threat of the second truck breaking down, and the *removal of the threat*, that he felt anything positive. The indifference threshold, he came to see, "is the extent to which the vitality is asleep."[16] Pleasure and convenience—getting the lift—didn't waken his vitality, but inconvenience and its elimination did. We can also see that the attention Wilson was forced to pay to the engine—listening for the knocking—*focused* his mind, concentrated it, dismissing his earlier blasé attitude and awakening his sense of values.

The good fortune of getting a ride did not stimulate Wilson into making any kind of effort, but the threat or crisis provided by the possibility of breaking down again did. The indifference threshold, then, is the point at which we feel something is worth the effort. As Wilson came to see, bored, spoiled people have a very high indifference threshold; people with a strong sense of purpose have a much lower one. A god, we could say, would have no threshold at all: someone like this would find *everything* worth the effort and would never feel bored. As they were passing the town of St. Neots when this insight came to him, he jotted down in his notebook, "St. Neots Margin," as a trigger to help him remember it. It is one of his most important contributions to human psychology and it would do much to explain some of the bizarre activities of his Outsiders.

In fact the meeting with Joy's parents turned out successful; at least it resulted in a temporary truce. The two agreed to get engaged, which seemed to placate her mother, and they returned to London. Wilson had yet to inform Joy's mother that technically he was still married.

London provided further frustration. His landlady didn't approve of Joy's visits and said that he would have to leave; that her daughter topped up her income with prostitution—something her mother was ignorant of—struck Wilson as the height of irony. A quarrel at work (he was now at a plastics factory) led to his dismissal. He began to feel like Raskolnikov in *Crime and Punishment*, just before the murder. . . . What he needed was time to write. The fragments of *Ritual in the Dark* needed continuous, undisturbed work so he could fuse them into a real novel. But the endless jobs and perpetual moving never allowed him this. Then he had a brainstorm. A friend had told him that he was planning on spending a year in the Middle East, wandering around, and had bought a tent and a waterproof sleeping bag for the adventure. Why couldn't he do the same here in London? Most of the money he earned went to rent and the maintenance money he sent Betty for their son. He could feed himself for much less. If he started sleeping in a tent, he could do without a room, which meant that he didn't need to earn as much money, which meant that he could spend less time working and more of it writing.

He bought a cheap tent and sleeping bag, stored his books at Joy's, and immediately put his plan into action. He was already living on the edge of North London; open country was a bicycle ride away. He put down stakes near a golf course. But after a few nights he decided that he didn't need the tent; it was an effort to put up and take down and it could attract attention. The waterproof sleeping bag was enough; in the rain he merely pulled the top over his head. It was perfect. With the money from his last paycheck he could, if he was frugal—this meant no books—feed himself for a month. Eventually he worked out that he could live on two pounds a week, which was about six dollars at the time. He could, of course, no longer send Betty any money, but as she had found a new position as a live-in nurse, he reasoned that this would not inconvenience her too much. It's not clear what Betty thought of this.

Soon he moved camp to Hampstead Heath, which was closer to Joy's rooms—she was now living near Chalk Farm in North London—as well as an easy ride to the British Museum. He would wake up with the sun (most mornings; sometimes he overslept), freewheel down Haverstock Hill, and stop to have tea and bread and dripping—basically animal fat, a World War II staple for low-income families—for a few pence at a busman's café.[17] Then he would bicycle to Bloomsbury and the British Museum, deposit his rucksack—which housed all his belongings, aside from his books—in the cloakroom, and get to work.

His new regimen was better than slaving away at another job, but it was not as idyllic as it may sound. He was exhausted from the past two years and living like a tramp didn't help. Most nights he couldn't settle down until after midnight; too many necking couples were still about. Often he was woken up by a dog licking his face, a policeman shining his flashlight, or another tramp tripping over him. He greeted the bright blue early mornings through a fog of weariness. When he told Bill Hopkins about his new routine his fellow genius congratulated him on building up the "Wilson legend," but legends are not always best enjoyed by the people making them. His time at the Reading Room—he was there from nine to five—was always too short. But the evenings were even harder. Public libraries were closed; it was difficult to find somewhere to rest and read in warmth and quiet until he could head to the heath. He couldn't afford pubs or cafés. He spent some time at Joy's, but her landlady didn't care for visitors. It was, as he says, "a strange sensation, having nowhere to go, nowhere to retire to at nights, nowhere to spend the evening reading."[18] He was, in fact, living out the kind of existence that many of the characters he had read about and had written about in his notebooks had lived—the Outsiders he had been obsessed with for years—and felt the same strain as they had. But until the weather turned colder—it was, after all, summer—chez Wilson meant a patch of grass and sleeping bag somewhere on the green fields of Hampstead Heath.

His new life did come with some benefits. At the Reading Room someone had noticed him reading a book about the Danish existential philosopher Søren Kierkegaard and started up a conversation. His new acquaintance was studying Heidegger and when Wilson remarked that he had spoken on Hyde Park Corner, he suggested that Wilson should meet someone he knew. This turned out to be Alfred Reynolds, a well-read, highly educated Hungarian Jew, who had fled the Nazis in the 1930s and became involved with British intelligence. After the war, Reynolds was involved with the de-Nazification of young Germans— at which he was highly successful—and now was the leader of a movement called the Bridge. The Bridge was a peace movement that promoted tolerance, reason, and a humanistic philosophy. It was hugely popular just after the war, but by now had shrunk to only a few dozen members. These met in Reynolds's book-lined rooms on Warwick Avenue, a leafy area of northwest London.

Reynolds asked Wilson to demonstrate his talent as a speaker. After a half hour or so of preaching anarchism—or his version of it—once again on Hyde

Park Corner, Wilson had so impressed Reynolds that he asked him to become a spokesman for the Bridge. They returned to Reynolds's rooms, where he treated Wilson to a much appreciated dinner, spoke of Thomas Mann, whom Wilson had read, and Hermann Hesse, whom he hadn't, and listened to music.

Reynolds invited Wilson to attend a few meetings of the Bridge. Two dozen young men gathered in his rooms. Alfred would play music, mostly Brahms, Bruckner, and Mahler. Then there would be coffee and cake—Central European staples—before Alfred would speak. He lectured on reason, tolerance, peace, and humanism. Afterward there was discussion. It was after a few meetings that Wilson knew he could never be a Bridge spokesman. He was certainly in favor of reason and tolerance, but all the sweetness and light seemed to avoid the kinds of stresses that drove his friend Flax or the idealistic German girl he had dated, and it had nothing to say about Wilson's own existential crises. Humanistic sentiments were fine and good but they were useless to people who sought some kind of intense purpose, some aim or challenge, to devote their energies to. They could not accommodate the kind of evolutionary craving that Wilson felt for something *more* than reason, the kind of craving that drove a Nietzsche, a William Blake, a Dostoyevsky. Reynolds was antireligion; he saw it as nothing but a source of bigotry and intolerance—much as modern-day atheists such as Richard Dawkins do—and had no notion of the kind of spiritual needs that informed works like the *Gita* or drove mystics like Ramakrishna, whose teachings Wilson had read in *The Gospel of Sri Ramakrishna*.

Reynolds certainly had no use for Gurdjieff. Wilson had mentioned him and Reynolds said he would like to know more. Wilson suggested Ouspensky's *In Search of the Miraculous*, or Kenneth Walker's *Venture with Ideas*, both clear, concise, and readable accounts of Gurdjieff's philosophy. Reynolds later told Wilson that he had read Gurdjieff and had decided he was a charlatan. Wilson was surprised until Reynolds said that he had ignored Ouspensky and Walker and gone "straight to the source." This meant Gurdjieff's mammoth jawbreaker of a book, *Beelzebub's Tales to His Grandson*, a work purposely designed to scare away people like Reynolds. Its 1,200-plus pages are full of neologisms, endless parenthetical remarks, dependent clauses, and other literary booby traps, all aimed at fending off the merely casual reader. Reynolds maintained that Gurdjieff was a con man, his philosophy nonsense, and nothing Wilson could say would alter this opinion. It was not an assessment that would recommend Reynolds's insight, although Wilson thought highly of him in other ways and was grateful to him for introducing him to works by Brahms, Beethoven, and the Swedish Romantic composer Franz Berwald. The situation was a kind of rerun of Wilson's earlier encounter with Raymond Duncan, although Reynolds's beliefs were of a higher caliber than Duncan's tepid arts-and-crafts philosophy.

Wilson's dissatisfaction with Reynolds's humanist outlook led to arguments and instead of being appointed a recruiter for the Bridge, Wilson was asked to stop attending meetings, although he would still be welcome as a dinner guest. One good thing to come from Wilson's association with the Bridge was his meeting with another young aspiring writer, Stuart Holroyd. Like Wilson, Holroyd had come to London from the north—he was born in Bradford, in Yorkshire, in 1933—to find fame and fortune, and was eking out an existence writing for a small literary magazine. He was one of Reynolds's chief disciples, and his beautiful young wife, Anne—who supported them as a typist—lent a certain glow to the otherwise very sober meetings. Wilson recognized Holroyd's intelligence and knew that he had a passion for poetry. Toward the end of his welcome, Wilson suggested to Reynolds that he read some extracts from his favorite literature at one of the meetings. Reynolds agreed. It was a mistake. Wilson had decided to choose literature that expressed his point that the hunger for something *more* than reason could lead to violence if it was not recognized and allowed to express itself. Considering Reynolds's anti-Nazi past, it was a tactic guaranteed to get a response. He mentioned his plan to Holroyd, who saw his point and agreed to take part. Wilson read from T. E. Lawrence's *Seven Pillars of Wisdom*, his account of his campaign in Arabia, from the letters of Vincent van Gogh, from Nietzsche, from Dostoyevsky. Holroyd read from William Blake, and from the metaphysical poets John Donne and George Herbert. Reynolds felt that they were torturing him, twisting a knife in his bowels.[19] It was after this that Wilson was asked to stay away, but he and Holroyd became close friends. Stuart joined the crew that included Hopkins and Del-Rivo and would later play a decisive part in the writing of *The Outsider*.

Another benefit of writing at the Reading Room proved even more helpful. Wilson was looking for an article T. S. Eliot had written about *Ulysses* and when he went to the desk for help, he found himself talking to the novelist Angus Wilson, who worked there. Angus Wilson—no relation—was a short story writer whose first novel, the satirical *Hemlock and After*, had come out in 1952. Wilson was not impressed with his namesake's writing—he found the satire too bitter—but when Angus saw that Colin was furiously scribbling away he asked him what he was working on. To talk to a real-life writer, whether he liked his work or not, was thrilling, and Wilson told Wilson that he was writing a novel. The professional told the tyro that he would like to see the manuscript when it was finished, and if he liked it, he would show it to his publisher. It is the kind of thing friendly authors often say to wannabes, but Wilson felt that his luck was finally changing.

It was not changing that quickly, though. Joy had to leave her room because the landlady objected to Colin having coffee with her in the morning, before bicycling down to the British Museum. She wound up taking a new room in Stanmore, a residential district in the far northwest of London. She was working as a librarian there and it made sense, but it would be harder for Wilson to visit her. By August, he wanted to get out of London for a break. He took work at a dairy outside of London, and spent several hours a day lifting crates of milk onto a conveyor belt. He worked a twelve-hour shift, slept in a nearby field, and spent his evenings in a workman's café. To fend off boredom he started learning ancient Greek, and made friends with a woman astrologer, whose knowledge of him weakened his skepticism about astrology.

He soon had enough cash to take a holiday and to repay Joy some money he had borrowed. He took his eleven-year-old brother, Rodney, to the Lake District, hitchhiking there; the trip supplied him with a psychological insight. They had climbed Helvellyn, a hefty hike at more than three thousand feet, and walked along a ridge for hours. On the way down to Ullswater, one of the district's largest lakes, it began to rain heavily. They trudged on and got drenched, and when they finally reached their campsite, his brother threw himself down in the tent, refused hot soup, and slept in his wet clothes. Wilson concluded that such irrational and potentially harmful actions—luckily his brother didn't catch pneumonia—were a way of "getting back" at life, for forcing him to make such efforts. He wanted to spite fate, but really was only spiting himself, and Wilson later came to see that many crimes are motivated by the same irrational reasoning, as a way of getting back at a society that the criminal feels is treating him unfairly.

Another holiday, this time in Cornwall, was equally profitable and demanding. During it, they thought Joy had missed her period and were afraid that she was pregnant. Fate seemed to be treating *him* unfairly now. The complications of a possible pregnancy put a damper on the holiday and Wilson's mind filled with all the difficulties that most probably lay ahead. In Teignmouth, along the Devon coast, Joy went to the ladies' room, and when she emerged they walked along the sand. Wilson sighed, and suggested that, given the situation, they had better think about getting back to London as soon as possible. "London?" Joy asked. Then she realized. There was no need to do that, she said. Her period had come on—hence her lengthy visit to the ladies'—but in her endearing vagueness she had forgotten to mention it. Wilson's relief was palpable. As he realized the crisis had passed, he was looking out over the sea and suddenly everything was transformed and appeared to him as beautiful. It was another moment of total affirmation, like what he had felt when he first slept with Joy or when he heard the Spanish music on his second French adventure. But the relief, though important, was only secondary. What was important was that the beauty, mystery, wonder, and awe he now saw and felt as he looked toward the Exmouth peninsula were *real*; they were *objective*, and not merely a subjective response to welcome news.

The removal of the crisis had stirred his vitality—as it had in St. Neots—and his "doors of perception" were now open and he saw the world *as it really is*, as Blake and the mystics he had been reading about had seen it. The meaning radiating out of everything around him was, to speak philosophically, an "objective datum." It was, as *The X-Files* tells us, "out there," not, as the poet Keats said, "in the eye of the beholder," that is, subjective. Which meant that the world we usually see is somehow false, or at least a highly edited version of reality, as it lacks the mysterious aura of an undeniable depth and *value* he was now perceiving. But if this was what the world was really like, why don't we see it this way all the time? Or, to put it the other way around, what had actually happened when his doors of perception had opened? What had he done to open them? If he could grasp the precise mechanism involved, the mental acts that had revealed true reality to him, then he should be able to induce mystical consciousness at will. Man should be able, as Wilson writes, to learn how to "brush aside [the] veils of indifference and habit that separate him from reality."[20]

It was something he had begun to think about at the Reading Room when, inspired by his acquaintance who was studying Heidegger, he decided to study existentialism; until then, he had been unfamiliar with it. Although its roots lay in the nineteenth century with the philosophers Kierkegaard and Nietzsche, existentialism became widely known in Germany with the publication in 1927 of the philosopher Martin Heidegger's colossal fragment *Being and Time*.[21] Heidegger promised to publish the second half of his fractured magnum opus but it was never completed. Heidegger was a student of Edmund Husserl, whose philosophy would have an enormous influence on Wilson.

In brief, existentialism looks at human existence as we experience it immediately, without appeal to God, metaphysics, an ideal realm, or any of the other usual elements of traditional philosophy. It does not concern itself with epistemology, logic, or the other questions that inform traditional philosophical inquiry. It is not interested in such abstract pursuits but always has the living, suffering subject, the full human being, in mind, not merely the rational thinker. This was Kierkegaard's argument against Hegel's huge metaphysical system of the Absolute Idea: it accounted for everything in the universe admirably but was of no use to him in dealing with the demands of life. He compared it to a map of Europe on which Copenhagen, where he lived, was only a pinpoint: it would be useless in helping him get around. Existentialism asks about the meaning and purpose of human existence as it is lived, in the here and now of everyday life, not in relation to a possible afterlife or metaphysical realm of eternal values. Heidegger captured the essence of the existential view when he spoke of human existence in terms of what he called *Geworfenheit*, or "throwness," the recognition that our being in the world is arbitrary, contingent, unnecessary—pure chance. We do not *choose* to be born into our particular time and place in history, and the purpose of our existence is not apparent in the way the purpose of the things around us, our man-made world, is. We simply find ourselves here, now, a condition Heidegger characterizes as *Dasein*, "being-there." As the well-known existential formula has it, with human beings "existence precedes essence," meaning that we exist before we know *why* we do.[22] Unlike, say, a chair or a work of art, the reason for which is prior to its being made, the sheer fact of our being precedes any reason for it. We are not given a Rough Guide to reality on our entry into the world and are, more or less, on our own.

Existentialism became more widely known and popularized in the postwar years, through the work of the French philosophers and writers Jean-Paul Sartre and Albert Camus. Given the mental state of a world that had just seen its second world war, Hitler, Auschwitz, and the atom bomb, this is not surprising; a similar grassroots nihilism spread after World War I. Sartre spoke of the nausea felt at the recognition of one's arbitrariness—and that of all human institutions—in his novel *Nausea*, and Camus echoed this with his notion of the absurd, the sudden shock of meaninglessness that comes with existential insight, a theme he develops in his essay *The Myth of Sisyphus*. By the time Wilson found himself peddling subscriptions to *The Paris Review* and *Merlin*, existentialism was the height of intellectual fashion, and its sensibilities informed the Parisian literary and bohemian scenes, with berets, Gauloises, black turtlenecks, angst, and Juliette Greco, "the muse of existentialism," decorating Saint-Germain-des-Prés, the stomping ground of Sartre, Camus, and Co.

Wilson quickly realized that he had been an existentialist all along. Like Heidegger, Sartre, and Camus, he rejected "abstract philosophy" and was concerned with questions of human meaning and purpose, and like them he ruthlessly rejected all attempts to minimize our utter ignorance and susceptibility to illusion. For some time he had the idea of writing a book called *The Methods and Techniques of Self-Deception*. He shared the existential demand for authenticity, for brutal, uncompromising honesty and the courage to face reality without a blindfold, without comforting stories about God and heaven. But while Heidegger, Sartre, Camus, and most of the other existential thinkers accepted that reality was in itself meaningless—for them, it is we who give it meaning, through our choices and actions—Wilson felt this was wrong. He had felt and seen *objective* meaning, a meaning that is there, just as much as sights and sounds are. He knew that Graham Greene, a writer he disliked, had written about how, as a bored teenager, he'd played Russian roulette with his brother's revolver. Greene was in a state of complete emotional emptiness; he *knew* certain things were beautiful, but he could *feel* nothing about them, or about anything else. He was, in essence, in a state much like Wilson had been in when traveling to visit Joy's parents, but even more profoundly indifferent. Greene would load the gun with one bullet, spin the chamber, put the barrel to his head, then tighten his face into a grimace before pulling the trigger. When he heard the click of the hammer hitting an empty chamber, he would suddenly be overwhelmed with a tremendous feeling of joy; he would feel "as if a light had been turned on," and he could see that "life contained an infinite number of possibilities."[23] We could say that he had briefly obliterated his indifference threshold. The infinite possibilities were there, all the time; Greene had simply fallen into such a state of apathy that he couldn't see them.

Sartre had said that he had never felt so free as when he was in the Resistance and knew he could be arrested and shot at any time. Wilson himself knew that even sleeping on the heath, for all its inconvenience, kept him at a state of high alertness and awareness, of not taking things for granted and raising his indifference threshold. In his, Sartre's, and Greene's cases, a threat acted as a kind of trigger, intensifying concentration: Greene's grimace before pulling the trigger, Sartre's constant awareness of the possibility of arrest, and Wilson's alertness to policemen or possible attack by another vagrant. Perhaps it isn't the case that reality is meaningless, he thought, but that we are usually in a state of consciousness *too slack to grasp its meaning*, too indifferent to make the effort to grasp it. But a threat *forces* us to make it. If Graham Greene saw life's infinite possibilities after the click of an empty gun barrel turned on a light, then presumably what his illumination revealed had been there all along. The light only made it visible. He had been in the dark and now, briefly, could see. (Wilson points out that the lesson was wasted on Greene, whose vision of the world remained sour and grim.) Given Wilson's vision at Teignmouth, such an answer seemed more than possible.

After the holiday, Wilson was back in London. He took a job at a Lyons Corner House—a London café fixture since the turn of the century—working in the kitchen. He didn't last long and in any case the need to find a room was more pressing. Autumn had arrived and Wilson was getting tired of the cold and damp. The days of sleeping rough were over. From North London he crossed the Thames and found a room in Brockley in South London. He had become fascinated with western mysticism and was reading through Jacob Boehme, Saint John of the Cross, William Law, and other Christian mystics. He felt drawn to Catholicism and wondered if a monastery might be an answer to his perpetual dissatisfaction. It was at least some action he could take, something he could *do*, and the possibility of a religious answer to his existential crisis increasingly informed *Ritual in the Dark*. In the end he admitted it would not have worked. He would not have been able to embrace celibacy and, more to the point, he could not accept the need for Jesus as an intercessor nor swallow the required dogma. Although he recognized that the hunger for purpose is essentially a religious hunger, religions in the modern world could no longer satisfy it. We have grown too intelligent for them. Man must work out his own salvation. How to do that was the question.

Angus Wilson had mentioned that he would be taking a holiday near Christmas. Wilson hurried to make a fair copy of what he had of *Ritual* to give to him before he left. He bought a secondhand typewriter and managed to get the typescript to Wilson just before he took his leave. He had by then found work at a post office, sorting holiday mail. On Christmas Day 1954, he found himself alone in his room in Brockley. Joy had gone to visit her parents. Wilson didn't have the money to head to Leicester. In any case, relations with his father were still strained and he would not have been welcomed. This was unfortunate; not only could he have used the dinner, he enjoyed his family, and missed being with them. (He is, he tells us, a typical Cancer, bound to hearth and home.) It was an icy, gray day, and he sat in his cold room, enjoying a meal of egg, bacon, and canned tomatoes.[24] With *Ritual* typed and in Angus Wilson's hands, he felt at loose ends. Wrapped in blankets, he wrote in his journal. He reflected that he was in the position of many of the characters he had been reading about for years and felt a strong affinity to Raskolnikov in *Crime and Punishment*, the antihero of Rilke's *The Notebooks of Malte Laurids Brigge*, the penniless writer in Knut Hamsun's *Hunger*, not to mention Nietzsche, who, like Wilson, had drifted from room to room, a perpetual wanderer. What drove these men—and Wilson—into this self-chosen isolation? Why did they feel outside of society? He began to write about this and soon found that he had the material for a book. His reading in T. E. Lawrence, the mystics, Camus, and Sartre began to suggest some underlying pattern, and he thought of other writers and thinkers who seemed to fall into place: Hesse, Rimbaud, Ramakrishna. He jotted down "Notes for a book 'The Outsider in Literature'" at the top of a page and began to make an outline. The material seemed to offer itself; it was everything he had been reading since he was a teenager.

When the Reading Room opened in January, he bicycled the thirteen miles from Brockley to Bloomsbury and began work. Angus Wilson was not yet back from his holiday—he wouldn't return for a month—but in any case he could not wait until he heard from him to start writing. En route to the museum he remembered a strange book, *Hell*, by Henri Barbusse, the French writer whose antiwar novel, *Under Fire*, earned him worldwide acclaim and the Prix Goncourt in 1916. *Hell* is about a man who spends his days peering through a peephole at the life that goes on in the hotel room next to his. It seemed a perfect metaphor for the character of the Outsider, the man who stands apart from life and observes it, however sordid or grim.

He ordered the book at the Reading Room, read it straight through, and used a passage from it as the beginning of what would become *The Outsider*. It tells of the hero catching a glimpse up a woman's dress as it is blown back by the wind. The sudden sexual shock leads him to recognize that it is not this or that individual woman he wants, but *all* women. Not in a simple numerical sense of having an endless supply, but in the sense of the *essence* of woman, the essence of the erotic thrill his sudden glimpse has afforded him. The hero of *Hell* does pick up a prostitute, but as Wilson discovered in his fiasco with his Communist comrade, the banal act of sex cannot satisfy the strange craving for *otherness* that, as Wilson would come to argue, is at the center of the male sexual impulse, as well as that of poetry, philosophy, and mysticism. The hero of

Hell feels a craving for something that the symbols which stimulate the craving cannot satisfy, another expression of the paradoxical nature of freedom.

It was this paradoxical element of sex that Wilson was trying to capture in *Ritual in the Dark*, an element of the "un-achievable," which Wilson does not limit to sex; in fact, aside from this beginning, sex plays hardly any part in *The Outsider*. The "un-achievable," he says, is a part of "the essence of anything important."[25] C. S. Lewis felt it about the idea of autumn. In *Surprised by Joy* he talks about a kind of desire that cannot be fulfilled—"how can one *possess* Autumn?" he asks—but that filled him with an unbearable longing for something of "incalculable importance," what the German Romantics of the nineteenth century called *Sehnsucht*, "unfulfillable longing."[26] The poet Yeats had felt it about waterfalls. His longing for them was painful, as there seemed nothing he could *do* about it; drinking the water wouldn't quench it, nor would being drenched by it. He wrote, "Nothing that we love overmuch; is ponderable to our touch," meaning that the kind of longing he felt could not be satisfied in any sensual or physical way.[27] It was this kind of unappeasable hunger that led Wilson to detect a difference between human beings. Some "eat, drink, impregnate their wives and take life as it comes." But others "can never forget that they are being cheated; that life tempts them to struggle by offering the essence of sex, of beauty, of success, and that she always seems to pay in counterfeit money."[28] Something is always *missing*. Wilson's Outsiders are determined to find out what that is.

The post office job had ended and Wilson found work in another laundry, this time in Deptford, along the Thames in southeast London. He enjoyed the area, the old cobblestone streets and docks full of ships (it is unrecognizable now, since the closing of the dockyards). But when someone stole his journals one day he was furious. He offered a reward but no one returned them. Disgusted, he left.

Toward the end of January 1955, he heard about a new coffeehouse opening in the Haymarket, a broad avenue full of theaters running off Piccadilly Circus. He bicycled there and was hired. This turned out to be the most enjoyable work he had ever had. He started out in the kitchen, washing dishes, but after a few weeks was put behind the counter serving customers. He worked evenings so he could keep his days free for writing. Most of his workmates were art and drama students his age or younger, and young people made up most of the clientele. They were intelligent and the surroundings pleasant. Work there was not an insufferable burden, as all his other jobs had been, but a positive pleasure. He was allowed to help himself to food and drink and he made the most of this. He wore a white waiter's jacket and tie, kept espresso machines and percolators going, and enjoyed handling the theater crowd who swarmed the place after ten. At the end of the night, around eleven thirty, the crew would relax and Wilson experienced a feeling of comradeship; he found himself uncharacteristically liking the people he worked with. It was a change from his years of deadening, "soul destroying" work.

This cheerfulness fed his urgency to write. He filled page after page at the Reading Room, writing about people like himself, "the misfits in modern civilization, the creative men who feel out of place in the rat race." He had the conviction that "gloom and despair would be impossible if we could understand the hidden powers of the human mind."[29] He saw his Outsiders as evolutionary "throw-forwards," anticipations of more evolved types of human beings.[30] Angus Wilson had returned from his holiday and he had encouraging words about *Ritual*. Wilson was happy but knew he had to finish this new work before returning to the novel. He wrote quickly, as if everything he had read and thought in the past decade was linking up and pouring out of him in a burst of inspiration. He was happy with the way the work was progressing, and read parts of it to friends, one of whom was the biblical scholar Hugh Schonfield, later famous for *The Passover Plot*, published in 1965, which argued that Jesus had planned his crucifixion, in order to fulfill the prophecy of the Messiah.[31] They met through Stuart Holroyd, who worked as Schonfield's secretary for a time.

Working at the Coffee House led to other changes. Gabby, the manager, an easygoing Soho character, suggested he take a room at a friend's near Baker Street. Her friend turned out to be a landlady as bohemian as she was. This was a relief after years of neurotic landladies intent on persecuting him. It also led to some brief infidelities. With Joy working as a librarian in Ealing, Wilson only saw her on weekends. He thought it a pity not to enjoy some innocent flirtation with some of the drama students he served coffee to. Occasionally it was not so innocent—the details are in his autobiographies—and eventually Joy found out and was hurt. One such episode became material for one of the female characters in *Ritual in the Dark*.

One weekend he and Joy hitchhiked to Canterbury Cathedral. In a second-hand bookshop in Rochester he came upon a book called *A Year of Grace*. It was an anthology of mysticism edited and published by Victor Gollancz. Gollancz was a humanitarian of Eastern European Jewish background; he founded the Left Book Club in 1936, the first book club in Great Britain, and in 1942 he prophesized Hitler's "Final Solution," predicting six million Jewish deaths at the hands of the Nazis before anyone had heard of the Wannsee Conference. Wilson had a sudden feeling that Gollancz might be interested in his Outsiders. Gollancz understood the importance of true religious values—not the hot gospel stuff peddled by Billy Graham or Frank Buchman's Moral Re-Armament, but the kind of religious questioning that obsessed Dostoyevsky and Tolstoy and which formed the essence of the book. Back in London Wilson hurriedly typed an introduction and made a fair copy of the chapter he was working on, dealing with Nijinsky, van Gogh, and T. E. Lawrence, as well as the first three chapters, and sent them with a letter to Gollancz. A few days later he received a reply. Gollancz was interested and would like to see the rest of the book.[32]

Wilson was stunned. Angus Wilson had encouraging words, but Gollancz was an editor and publisher and his positive reply read like a vindication of all the years of hard work and sacrifice. He returned to the book with renewed energy, determined to finish it as soon as possible. His urgency was motivated by another factor too. Stuart Holroyd had published some articles on the spiritual concerns of the poetry of T. S. Eliot and Rilke in *The Poetry Review*. He had been introduced to Rilke by Wilson, who had also turned Holroyd's attention to William James's *The Varieties of Religious Experience*, existentialism, Hermann Hesse, and other writers who would soon feature in *The Outsider*. Wilson had been happy to share his excitement about these writers with Holroyd—they already had much in common—but when the articles appeared, he did feel a twinge of jealousy that Holroyd had managed to get many of the things he had been obsessed with for years into print before Wilson. And when Holroyd told him that he planned to write a critical book about poetry and religion based on the articles—what would become Holroyd's first book, *Emergence from Chaos*—Wilson was afraid that he would beat him to the punch. He was determined that *The Pain Threshold*—*The Outsider*'s original title—would be published first.

Other obstacles presented themselves. In late May, Wilson's mother took ill with a burst appendix and had to be hospitalized. Her condition was serious and Wilson was afraid she might die. He decided to go to Leicester. He had typed about half the book by then and on the way to the train station he stopped by Gollancz's office with the unfinished manuscript. The secretary assured him that Mr. Gollancz never read unfinished manuscripts, but Wilson pleaded with her and she agreed to let him leave it with a note. When he returned—the danger had passed but only after his mother endured several operations—he found a letter from Gollancz saying he had read the manuscript and very definitely would like to publish the book. Gollancz asked him to visit his office when he was back. Wilson bicycled to Covent Garden and was introduced to Gollancz, a big man with a booming voice and a bald head. During lunch—his first perk as an about-to-be-published author—Gollancz asked how he read so much at only twenty-three. Wilson told him, "Boredom." When they parted Gollancz said, "I think it possible you may be a man of genius."[33] Wilson had suspected as much all along, but now someone other than Bill Hopkins did too—and he wanted to publish his book. Wilson shared the news with Joy and then wrote to tell his mother. He doesn't mention it but one suspects he would have liked to have heard his father's reply when she told him.

An advance of twenty-five pounds—about six hundred pounds in today's money, or about a thousand dollars—allowed him to leave the Coffee House and to write full-time. It was June and Gollancz wanted the finished product by September. He tried dictating for a time but when this proved unworkable he starting typing the rest of the book straight off, not doing a first draft in longhand as he had been. Speed bumps appeared in the form of new insane landladies but by now he was used to this kind of turbulence and he had a strong intuition that there was clear sailing ahead. When he told Angus Wilson that Gollancz had accepted his book, the older writer suggested that he let his publisher, Secker & Warburg, take a look at it. He did and they liked it, but asked for significant additions to some of the chapters. Having worked on it for so long and with such intensity—he also admits he was too lazy to rewrite—Wilson decided against this and stuck with Gollancz. He received an additional advance of fifty pounds when he delivered the completed manuscript on time. But that two publishers were interested in the book confirmed his suspicion that it was an important work and would certainly make an impact.

In the spring of 1956 he was proved right.

CHAPTER THREE

BREAKTHROUGH AND BACKLASH

Having his book accepted for publication was of course a breakthrough, but it didn't change Wilson's life drastically, at least not immediately. The advance from Gollancz allowed him to take Joy on a holiday in Cornwall, but by Christmas 1955, he had to take work at the post office again. He also had to find cheaper lodgings. He found them in Notting Hill, a part of London that was then a low-rent, undesirable section of town, with a large Caribbean population and prostitutes and teddy boys—roughly equivalent to 1970s punks—making up the street life. In the late summer of 1958 it was the scene of violent race riots and clashes between the West Indies residents and the teddy boys; today it is a high-rent, very fashionable, highly desirable neighborhood, with little left of its earlier bohemian character. Wilson saw an advertisement for a room at 24 Chepstow Villas, a large, half-empty mansion that had seen better days. The rent seemed low—a pound a week—but the room itself was a disappointment. It turned out to be an empty bathroom unconnected to the water mains, really little more than a large closet. But the landlady was a painter and bohemian, and the poet Dylan Thomas, who had died a few years earlier in New York after a drinking binge, had once stayed in the basement. Part of Wilson's agreement was that he would help redecorate the place; its Edwardian splendor had deteriorated badly, and Wilson found himself plastering walls and painting windowsills. He slept on the bare wooden floor in his sleeping bag and kept warm as best he could.[1]

He returned to work on *Ritual*. In February 1956, Angus Wilson offered him the use of his cottage in Bury St. Edmunds—a market town about eighty miles northeast of London—to finish it. Wilson strapped a typewriter borrowed from Laura Del-Rivo to his haversack and bicycled there. Practically on arrival he was snowed in and by the next morning could barely get out of the place. Two weeks later he returned with the finished manuscript. He submitted it to Victor Gollancz, but the plot involving a serial killer put him off and he rejected it. Angus Wilson was less dismissive. He liked it and gave it to his publisher, who agreed to accept it on his recommendation and offered a much needed fifty-pound advance.[2] Wilson himself was not happy with the finished product. He had rewritten it several times and writing *The Outsider* had changed his perspective on it. "This was not the novel on which I had worked for so many years," he admitted, looking at the finished manuscript. In fact, he would scrap the original version and two years later start over again from scratch.

But the literary life was beginning. In March, before publication of *The Outsider*, he was invited to a book launch in Hampstead for Iris Murdoch's second novel, *The Flight from the Enchanter*.[3] He and Murdoch hit it off. She was also a philosopher and had written about Sartre and when she discovered that Wilson hadn't been to university, she offered to get him a scholarship at Oxford, where she taught. Ever the autodidact, Wilson respectfully declined. At the same party he met the poet and William Blake scholar Kathleen Raine, with whom he felt much sympathy; in 1980, Raine would found *Temenos*, a journal devoted to the "Arts of the Imagination," and in the next decade she started the Temenos Academy, devoted to the exploration of the "perennial philosophy." He also met the Bulgarian-born writer Elias Canetti, an old-school European intellectual, most known for his novel *Auto-da-Fé* and sociological study *Crowds and Power*. Wilson took a liking to Canetti—he reminded him of Alfred Reynolds—but the potential friendship quickly fizzled out. Canetti took umbrage when, prodded by Gollancz, Wilson wrote to him, asking if he could review *The Outsider*. A stern reply from Canetti's wife explained that Mr. Canetti never wrote reviews and implied that Wilson had committed an unforgivable sin by asking him to.[4] Nevertheless, it was a start.

Wilson soon moved to a ground-floor room in Chepstow Villas. It cost a bit more but was large enough to share at times with Bill Hopkins, who was then working as a night editor for the London edition of the *New York Times*. The decor was one of "fairly startling squalor and disorder."[5] According to one witness, a table crammed with books, the remains of meals, empty wine bottles, and a typewriter competed for attention with a camp bed, an inflatable mattress, a broken chair, some Einsteinian graffiti, and a picture of Nietzsche. Along with the usual suspects—Shaw, Blake, Eliot—the crowded bookshelf contained volumes on forensic medicine, complete with graphic illustrations, research material for *Ritual*. By this time Wilson was rubbing elbows with other literary people. A poet he met mentioned that he had read *The Outsider* in proof and would be reviewing it for the *Times Literary Supplement*. He introduced Wilson to editors at *Encounter*, a magazine he would later write for.[6] It was founded by the poet Stephen Spender and during the Cold War years received covert funding by the CIA, but Wilson, and most of its contributors, were ignorant of this.

These preliminaries were exciting. Wilson was rightfully happy that he had finally arrived. He had even visited his parents, allowing his father to take him to his working-men's club to show off his son, the author. He and Joy visited her parents so he could present the proof copy of *The Outsider* with his name finally in print. It did little to quell their fears for their daughter's future, but at least he could prove that he really was a writer. With publication day approaching, Gollancz asked him to get a photograph for publicity. He did, wearing his polo-neck sweater and National Health glasses. It was not, he said, a good photograph, but it appeared in all the early press and became a trademark of this soon-to-be Angry Young Man.

Publication was set for May 28. A few days before, Wilson was interviewed by a journalist from the *Evening News*. The journalist seemed rather blasé about the book, but when Wilson mentioned that he spent some months sleeping on Hampstead Heath, his interest was piqued, and he began scribbling eagerly, pressing Wilson with questions. Wilson reflected that Bill Hopkins had been right about building up the "Wilson legend." Later he would have reason to regret that such colorful "newsworthy" items would take precedent over the actual contents of the book.

On Saturday, the weekend before *The Outsider*'s release, Wilson noticed a mention in one of the evening papers that Sunday's *Observer*—a national paper—would run an article asking, "Are Men of Genius Outsiders?" Wilson bought an *Evening News* but couldn't find a review. That was disappointing. His optimism was dampened further when, returning from the cinema, he and Joy saw that his bicycle had been stolen from outside Chepstow Villas.[7] That night he had another "vastation"—the term comes from the religious thinker Emanuel Swedenborg—an attack of a sense of meaninglessness, the suspicion that the sense of having arrived he had experienced over the past few weeks was an illusion. The next morning it was clear that it wasn't.

They went to a newsagents on Westbourne Grove—now lined with expensive shops and boutiques—and bought the *Observer* and the *Sunday Times*, the two "highbrow" Sunday papers, and rushed home. The review in the *Observer* by Philip Toynbee, one of the most respected critics of the day, could not have been better. For Toynbee the book was "an exhaustive and luminously intelligent study of a representative theme of our time . . . a real contribution to our understanding of our deepest predicament," and he remarked that while such ideas as *The Outsider* presented are familiar in France, he much preferred Wilson's approach to Sartre's.[8] Cyril Connolly, the doyen of English literary criticism, shared Toynbee's view. Wilson had produced "one of the most remarkable first books" he had read, and he celebrated the "quick, dry intelligence" and "power of logical analysis" that he applied to "states of consciousness that generally defy it."[9] Like Toynbee, Connolly compared Wilson to Camus, whose *L'Étranger* had been published in England as *The Outsider* (it appeared in America as *The Stranger*), and like Toynbee he comments on his age and the enormous amount of reading he had jammed into so few years. The one criticism both make is of a certain hurriedness, the sense that the book was written at top speed, a pace that made for some small errors in quotation and a lack of grace. But Toynbee and Connolly were established men; Wilson was writing for his life and *The Outsider* was written, "as first books ought to be, out of sheer compulsion," as the literary scholar George Steiner remarked.[10]

A second scan of the *Evening News* revealed that there *was* a review, by the critic John Connell. How they had missed it is a mystery. The headline said it all: A MAJOR WRITER, AND HE'S ONLY TWENTY-FOUR. By that time the telephone in the basement flat starting ringing. Wilson didn't have one and his neighbor very generously allowed him to use his. That Sunday he may have regretted his generosity. A friend had rung to congratulate Wilson. Immediately after he hung up and walked upstairs the phone rang again. It continued ringing for the rest of that day and into the week. One phone call that most likely pleased Wilson was from his editor, who told him that he would probably make a lot of money from the book. (He did; the initial sales earned him around twenty thousand pounds—almost five hundred thousand pounds in today's money, or more than seven hundred thousand dollars. A second, third, and fourth printing appeared in short succession.) Monday's mail delivered a stack of letters of congratulation. "It seemed that every friend I ever had had decided to write and congratulate me."[11] Wilson must have felt he was back in the sorting room of the post office. Cyril Connolly had asked, "Who is Colin Wilson?" and an old headmaster of Wilson's had written to say how thrilled he was to know the answer.

The poet Edith Sitwell, of the famous literary family, called the book "astonishing" and prophesized that Wilson "will be a truly great writer." A reviewer for the *New York Times* said Wilson "walked into literature as a man walks into his own house" and that the book was "a mature study, filled with assimilated erudition." The *Sunday Times* rang to ask if he would consider reviewing for them at forty pounds a review, more money than he would make in months of "real work." The BBC and Independent Television called to ask when he could record programs. Monday's *Evening News* ran the interview with the photo of him in the polo neck and tales of Hampstead Heath. Reporters knocked on his door, and Godfrey Smith, a columnist for *The Sunday Times Magazine*, took him out for an expensive lunch. Cecil Beaton took his photograph. Kenneth Walker, whose book on Gurdjieff Wilson had admired, wrote that "*The Outsider* is the most remarkable book upon which the reviewer has ever had to pass judgement."[12] He and Walker, a Harley Street doctor, later became friends, and one can imagine their conversations about Gurdjieff and Ouspensky (Walker had known both). J. B. Priestley, another writer interested in Ouspensky, called the book "a remarkable production for a young man of twenty-four."[13] And to make things worldwide, from across the Atlantic, *Time* magazine called *The Outsider* an "intellectual thriller," and *Life* magazine asked to do a profile with pictures. They wound up doing a photo shoot with him, his polo neck and sleeping bag on Hampstead Heath, his back against the tree he had slept under, reading.

Not everything that arrived that Monday was welcome. Wilson had thought that after publication he would go to Leicester in order to bask in his glory and look at the stacks of *The Outsider* in a bookshop he more than likely had pilfered from in his youth. He had no idea of the furor that would start up and he would have been happy just to see the book in the shop window. But the excitement of the day prevented that and he remained in London. This was problematic. Betty had been in touch with him recently. She said she wanted to look for a flat in London and he generously offered her the use of his room while he was away. She was still legally his wife and had written to say that she still had hopes of a reconciliation. Wilson did not. She arrived in the middle of phone calls, reporters, and requests for interviews and felt that as his wife, she should have a share in his success. Wilson could see her point, but he was not about to leave Joy—they had been together for two and a half years by then—and so his Monday morning glory was tainted with personal and emotional complications. When the *Daily Sketch*, a tabloid, ran a paragraph about Joy, the "little woman" behind this Leicester boy wonder, Betty was scandalized. Although they had been separated now for some time, her relatives were still unaware that they were no longer together; now all Britain would know. When she left she told Wilson, "Goodbye—for always." She never agreed to a divorce and it was only in 1973, after twenty years of separation, that Wilson could initiate divorce proceedings himself and officially marry Joy. He felt protective toward Betty and in the years that followed they remained friends; he helped her when he could. He would later contribute half the cost toward a house she purchased and he gave the copyright to his book *Poetry and Mysticism* to her.

Houghton Mifflin soon brought the book out in the States and it became a best seller there too (Viking had initially shown interest but in the end declined, to their regret). By the end of 1956, it had been translated into a dozen languages. Wilson could not have asked for a more startling and lucrative debut, and whatever one may think of him or *The Outsider*, it must be admitted that his triumph is one of the greatest rags-to-riches stories of all time. Parallels with the Romantic poet Byron's success at the same age were cogent if quickly clichéd; Byron had woken up one morning in 1812 and with the publication of *Childe Harold's Pilgrimage*, all England resounded with his name. If Wilson felt such comparisons were justified, we can hardly blame him. He was sustained through many very difficult years by his belief in himself and his confidence in his powers. Now that belief and confidence were validated. He had confided in his journals that he believed he was a man of genius. Now some of the most important and respected literary critics agreed with him, and said so in the national and international press. He was being feted with a frenzy usually reserved for pop celebrities such as Elvis Presley, who had shot to stardom earlier that year with the release of "Heartbreak Hotel." Wilson would soon see, however, that such overnight success is not always an unalloyed good.

In fact, the first gray clouds had already begun to obscure this fairy tale silver lining. Earlier that May a play had opened at the Royal Court Theatre on Sloane Square, a rather different part of town from Notting Hill, and although unconnected to Wilson, it would have an impact on his career. The Royal Court had launched Bernard Shaw to fame fifty years earlier and was about to do the same with one of Wilson's contemporaries. The English Stage Company had been founded in 1955 by the actor George Devine and the poet Ronald Duncan, later a good friend of Wilson's. Their mission was to foster new dramatic talent and to revitalize a complacent British theater and they had picked the Royal Court as their base. They had already put on two plays to lukewarm response—Angus Wilson's *The Mulberry Bush* and Arthur Miller's *The Crucible*—and to keep afloat badly needed a success. Their third attempt seemed a dud too. *Look Back in Anger*, by a jobbing London actor named John Osborne, had opened on May 8, 1956, to middling to scathing reviews. Osborne had written the play in a few weeks while working in repertory theater and for some reviewers its hasty construction showed. The *Times* complained that it consisted mostly of "angry tirades" by a member of the postwar generation, and the *Daily Mail* was numbed by the "monologue of self-pity and unrighteous indignation."[14]

Others agreed that it was an unpleasant play, in which an unhappy young man expresses discontent at the modern world and takes his frustrations out on his young wife. Osborne, twenty-six, seemed to have crammed all the bitterness and disappointment of his life so far into the play's three acts and as one critic of the time remarks, sprays his "flit-gun of scorn" indiscriminately, engaging in an orgy of "truculent foot-stomping."[15] Osborne's vaguely socialist vituperation would most likely have faded out with encouraging words from the gentler critics if it hadn't been for one completely enthusiastic review that appeared in the *Observer*. Kenneth Tynan, an Oxford graduate whose first book had a preface by Orson Welles, was an enthusiastic Marxist, and in Osborne's kitchen-sink drama—the action takes place in a cramped suburban flat complete with an ironing board—he thought he saw the class war in action. Although Great Britain was then a postwar welfare state, the economic and cultural class divide was wider than ever and Tynan shared Osborne's vague recriminations against "the establishment," against the pipes, slippers, thatched cottages, and modest expectations of Little England, and against the drawing room melodramas that made up most of English theater at the time. Tynan likened Jimmy Porter's—the main character—soliloquies to Hamlet's and celebrated his vitality and honesty. He applauded the "drift toward anarchy," the "instinctive leftishness" and rejection of "official attitudes" that crowd the work.

Famously he said, "I doubt I could love anyone who did not wish to see *Look Back in Anger*. It is the best young play of its decade."[16]

Tynan would go on to be one of the most influential critics of the past century; he died in 1980. His review launched *Look Back in Anger* to success, saving the English Stage Company and making Osborne's career, not to mention giving a fillip to his own. The older critics were hushed by Tynan's praise and cowed into fearing to seem old fashioned. Soon audiences were flocking to the Royal Court to hear Jimmy Porter's complaints.[17]

Wilson saw the play and didn't like it. It reminded him of some recent novels he had read—John Wain's *Hurry on Down*, which had come out in 1953, and Kingsley Amis's *Lucky Jim*, which appeared in 1954. (Osborne was not keen on *The Outsider* either, calling it a "very good reference book.") Both Wain and Amis shared an aggressive rejection of the past, a denunciation of the establishment. Both recognized the aimlessness that had begun to predominate in the postwar world. What, they asked, was the individual supposed to *do* in a world run by big business and bureaucracy? But while Wain and Amis painted a convincing picture of the uninspiring landscape, from Wilson's perspective neither offered any positive suggestions. Amis's virulent anti-intellectualism and hatred of cultural "phonies"—encapsulated in the notorious phrase "filthy Mozart"—was especially unhelpful, and encouraged a sentimental solidarity with the "common man." Osborne's play was no better. Its "long yell of protest" was little more than a temper tantrum, and offered nothing to replace what it rejected. But the chance association suggested by their appearing at the same time forged a link in journalists' minds between *The Outsider* and *Look Back in Anger*, and suddenly the myth of the Angry Young Man was born.[18] It was to become, as one of its participants said, "the most successful post-war cultural pseudo-event."[19]

At the time Wilson tried to make clear that his own work and ideas had nothing in common with most of the writers that the critics and journalists were now lassoing into the long-awaited and much needed "new movement" that was going to save the British literary world from the doldrums—and incidentally give them something to write about. His misgivings were justified, but no one took notice. Whether he liked it or not, for the reading public he was an Angry Young Man, and so were Osborne, Wain, Amis, and other writers such as John Braine and Alan Sillitoe, whose *Room at the Top* and *The Loneliness of the Long-Distance Runner*, respectively, were literary and cinematic successes. There were some angry women too, such as Iris Murdoch (although, with all due respect, she was not so young at the time) and Doris Lessing (at the same age as Murdoch, also not so young), about whom Wilson would later say that her "preoccupation with human evolution" made her a contemporary "with whom I felt the deepest sense of sympathy and kinship."[20] He did not feel this toward many others.

Looking back at the interviews and symposia in which the Angries speak of each other, it soon becomes clear that some of the things they were angry about were their unwanted association and each other's work. There was not the loose unanimity of sensibility that linked the writers of the Beat Generation, which rose up in San Francisco and New York about a year after the Angries arrived. Indeed, the coincidence of two new English-language literary movements appearing at roughly the same time, informed with a similar rejection of convention, tradition, and the past, did not go unnoticed, and in 1958 *The Beat Generation & the Angry Young Men*, an anthology edited by Gene Feldman and Max Gartenberg, made the connection official. The Beat Generation was said to have begun with the publication in 1956 of Allen Ginsberg's *Howl* and Jack Kerouac's *On the Road* the next year, but Ginsberg had been working on the poem since 1954 and *On the Road* had been parked in Kerouac's drawer for some time before it saw print.[21] Yet although each had his own peculiar style and vision, there was more linking Jack Kerouac, Allen Ginsberg, and William S. Burroughs Jr.—the Beats' Three Musketeers—than a journalist's tag.[22] The three were longtime friends and supported each other's work. This was not the case with the Angries, who soon separated into hostile, opposing camps. But for all their attempts to clarify their own position, the writers associated with Wilson—Bill Hopkins and Stuart Holroyd—found that their disassociation from the others only added more fuel to the gossip columnists' fire.

And there was much kindling to burn. According to one eyewitness, for a time "it was difficult to pick up a publication—high or low in brow—that did not contain some story on [Wilson] or reference to his book *The Outsider*."[23] By 1957 there was even some suggestion that a biopic would emerge, *The Colin Wilson Story*, modeled on *The Tommy Steele Story*, which dramatized the sudden rise to fame of "Britain's Elvis." Wilson had become a darling of the columnists, and for all his insight into the human condition, he seemed unaware that they were quickly digging his critical grave. It was, to be sure, a premature burial, but by late 1956, there were more than a few who were happy to throw a shovelful of dirt over the self-proclaimed genius.

It was that word "genius" that began to irritate the mostly modest reading public. They were happy to see a meteoric rise, because it often promises an equally dramatic fall, and it was about time for Wilson's comeuppance. The g-word was being said a tad too often and it would fairly quickly bring Wilson down. That he himself breathed it somewhat injudiciously did not help. The Angries had helped the newspapers sell copies during the "silly season," the summer months when politics goes on holiday and journalists need content. But after a while people began to be sick of seeing an angry young man practically everywhere, denouncing everything or proclaiming his brilliance. And the serious critics who had recognized the new blood began to feel a bit less supportive. After all, these young'uns were making more money than they were, seemed to show no respect to their elders, and could soon put them out of a job. They also seemed to think of themselves as celebrities and went out of their way to get in the papers—or at least that was the appearance.

Wilson tried to maintain a serious character by giving lectures on his ideas at the Institute of Contemporary Arts, and he enjoyed meeting various literary lights: Stephen Spender, Christopher Isherwood, Edith Sitwell, Samuel Beckett (whose work he detested but was too polite to say so), Eugène Ionesco (with whom he was less polite), William Golding, T. S. Eliot, as well as art notables such as Francis Bacon and Lucian Freud. At one point he found himself in the men's room at the famous Athenaeum Club, standing at a urinal next to Aldous Huxley. "I never thought I'd be having a pee at the side of Aldous Huxley," the young Outsider said. Huxley, tall and at that point nearly blind, replied, "Yes, that's what I thought when I was standing beside George V."[24] Wilson even received fan mail from famous people. Gollancz sent him a copy of the comedian Groucho Marx's autobiography, which he was publishing. Gollancz did not give books away indiscriminately, and when Wilson asked why he had given it to him, Gollancz said that Groucho had included him along with Winston Churchill and Somerset Maugham as the three people who should receive free copies. Later, in *The Groucho Letters*, Marx reprinted his correspondence with Wilson.

But Wilson was appearing too often in the celebrity news and the publicity began to dissolve the aura of seriousness that *The Outsider* had first generated. In October, on the way home with Joy from a literary party, Wilson saw a huge crowd gathered in front of a theater off the Haymarket. Curious, the two got out of their taxi to see what the fuss was about. It turned out to be the first night of Arthur Miller's play *A View from the Bridge*, directed by a young Peter Brook. Miller was in town, as was his new wife, Marilyn Monroe; she was then filming *The Prince and the Showgirl*, with her costar Laurence Olivier. Wilson saw that the actor Anthony Quayle, whom he had recently met, was starring in the play, and dropping his name, he and Joy were allowed into the opening night party. (Oddly enough Mary Ure, who starred in *Look Back in Anger*, was also in the play; she did not think well of *The Outsider* and it's unclear if they spoke or if Osborne was there.) Olivier was there, as was his wife, the actress Vivien Leigh. And Marilyn Monroe. Wilson saw that she was having trouble hitching up her strapless dress. He introduced himself—she was, he had heard, "bookish," and after all had married a playwright—and Joy. He then spoke with Olivier. When he asked Olivier if it was true that he had asked Osborne to write a play for him—this would become Osborne's next hit, *The Entertainer*—Olivier said yes and invited Wilson to write one too. When Wilson and Joy left, he was stopped by a gossip columnist and asked why he was there. Wilson said that he had started the evening hoping to meet T. S. Eliot at another party (he failed to show, although Wilson met him later) but had met Marilyn Monroe instead. The next day it was celebrity news.

From being acclaimed as Britain's own homegrown existentialist, Wilson was quickly becoming a target for seasoned veterans, happy to take advantage of his youth, honesty, and naïveté. By this time he had been satirized in *The Spectator*, *Punch*, and the *New Statesman*. He later recognized that all the early acclaim, for all its financial reward, did him no good, except to secure a readership for his later books, which, for some time, were uniformly panned. "I was compared to D. H. Lawrence, Byron and even, God help me, Plato," he later ruefully reflected, and such a high buildup would sooner or later trigger the reverse effect.[25]

Wilson's own inexperience and lack of guile also ensured that he would put his foot in it. At a debate about the theater at the Royal Court, with Arthur Miller on the panel and Marilyn Monroe in the audience, he was baited by the humorist Wolf Mankowitz, who declared that *The Outsider* was nothing more than an anthology of quotations. Wilson's replies did not go over well. At a talk for a spiritualist society, he met a columnist for the *Daily Express*. The columnist encouraged him to say something shocking but Wilson demurred.[26] By this time Wilson was tired of being newsworthy and during his talk he expressed frustration that no one ever spoke about the *ideas* informing *The Outsider* (and we ourselves will get to them shortly). He said it was wrong to see him as a spokesman for the younger generation. His work had nothing to do with an antiestablishment attitude or Osborne's kind of anger. It was a personal statement about his own spiritual crisis and he felt like a fraud when he was touted as some kind of angry young man. The next day the *Daily Express* ran a headline: COLIN WILSON ADMITS HE IS A FRAUD. Wilson had to hastily write letters to several editors explaining what had really happened. During an interview with the journalist Dan Farson—son of the journalist and travel writer Negley Farson—Wilson spoke of "real men of genius." Farson asked, "You think of yourself as a genius?" and Wilson replied, "Oh, of course. It may prove untrue but I've got to work on that assumption." He had been working on that assumption for some time. It was indeed what pulled him out of the "vegetable mediocrity" of Leicester and a life of pointless labor. He told Farson that he was in revolt against an age in which people did not make that assumption of genius, what Maslow would call the "Jonah complex," the fear of one's destiny, one's greatness. That Wilson wanted others to make that assumption and that his own self-belief had little to do with conceit is clear from his remarks to his friends. He was only "the first one through the hedge," he told them, and insisted that the only thing stopping other people from being geniuses is their laziness, as the German Romantic poet Novalis had said.[27]

It was a theme Wilson would explore in his book about the loss of the hero, *The Age of Defeat*, how the "fallacy of insignificance" keeps many from actualizing their inborn abilities, and which led to his friendship with Maslow. But when Farson's interview appeared in a new magazine called *Books and Art* all that caught the reader's exasperated eye was that the boy wonder Wilson was declaring his genius again. He had also declared that of Bill Hopkins. Hopkins had yet to publish anything, which made his genius theoretical, but when his novel *The Divine and the Decay* appeared in 1957, sympathy for the Angries had soured and his association with Wilson ensured that it would be panned; it was. But Wilson bore Farson no grudge and later the two became friends.

Declaring your genius was nothing new in English letters. Shaw did it and so did Oscar Wilde, and the kind of provocative remarks Wilson made were not vastly different from the outrageous salvos that an earlier, similarly feisty writer, Wyndham Lewis, shot off in the 1920s and thirties. But Shaw and Wilde were Irish and funny, and Lewis had important friends, such as T. S. Eliot and Ezra Pound, who agreed with him. Wilson had only been around a short time and had produced only one book.[28] As a commentator at the time sympathetically remarked, "it has often been his genuinely innocent ignorance of the complex, dangerous forces of publicity he has blunderingly stirred up which has been mistaken for arrogance and impudence."[29]

An evening at the Royal Court toward the end of the "angry years" added another nail to Wilson's literary coffin. The occasion was Stuart Holroyd's play *The Tenth Chance*. By this time Holroyd's book, *Emergence from Chaos*, dealing with the spiritual vision of poets such as Eliot, Yeats, and Rilke, had appeared and sadly it suffered from the backlash against the Angries in general and Wilson in particular. It too was published by Gollancz, and the fact that he emphasized that Holroyd was even younger than Wilson assured that it would not receive a fair hearing. The fact that, like *The Outsider*, it presented a religious view, rather than the strident leftism of Osborne and Co. made it a target of scorn by the socially minded critics. Kenneth Tynan in particular saw Wilson as a kind of fascist, with his talk of religion, discipline, the need for a new kind of man rather than a new society, his hatred of mediocrity, lack of interest in left-wing politics, and concern about the spiritual crises of characters like Nietzsche and Dostoyevsky.

Other Angries shared Tynan's view and abhorred Wilson's antipathy toward communism. The irony is that at the time Wilson considered himself a socialist, in deference to Shaw. "I am a socialist because Shaw was," he told the journalist Kenneth Allsop, "but socialism is not very deeply ingrained in me." He never espoused any political cause, he told Allsop, and the only kind of movement he felt any sympathy with was a religious one, at least at the time. "I detest cruelty and injustice, but I feel I have more important work to do than leading crusades against them."[30] Some years later, when he came to write a book about Shaw, he saw that his hero's arguments for socialism really didn't hold water. He promptly dropped socialism after that.[31]

By the time of Holroyd's play Wilson had already had a bad experience at the Royal Court. During the early *Outsider* acclaim, George Devine, one of the English Stage Company's founders, took Wilson to lunch and asked him to write a play for him. Sometime later Wilson got around to it and produced *The Death of God*, a futuristic drama set in the twenty-second century concerning a Europe-wide war and the fate of a dictator held captive in a monastery.[32] By the time Wilson submitted the play to Devine, his star had faded and the religious character of the work would not have endeared it to the leftist playwrights associated with the theater. Wilson was prepared for possible rejection, but was miffed when the manuscript was returned months later with merely a printed rejection slip. Devine had asked him to write the play and Wilson felt he could at least have written a letter himself, explaining why he had rejected it. The curt rejection slip suggested that Devine did not want the Royal Court tarred with Wilson's now undesirable brush. Understandably Wilson wasn't happy and he wrote Devine a letter, spelling out his grievances. It was not an angry letter; it was concerned mostly with what appeared to be Devine's reneging on their agreement and the Royal Court's apparent shift to an all-leftist kind of drama.[33] But Wilson made the mistake of being persuaded by Bill Hopkins into making it an "open letter" to the Royal Court and giving it to the press. Wilson's reservations about the company's about-face were reasonable, but all the open letter produced was another round of gossip about how Wilson the boy wonder couldn't take rejection.

He couldn't take a friend's play being disrupted by his leftist contemporaries either. Holroyd's play was about Petter Moen, a member of the Norwegian resistance against the Nazis, and how while in solitary confinement and facing torture he underwent a religious conversion. Wilson admits that *The Tenth Chance* wasn't a good play—religious conversion lacks sufficient drama for the stage. Others in the audience, such as Kenneth Tynan and the poet Christopher Logue, whom Wilson had known in Paris during his *Paris Review* days, thought as much too and were not hesitant to show it. Toward the end of the play, Petter Moen prays aloud, and someone in the audience shouted, "Rubbish!" Wilson saw Logue loudly leave the theater, slamming the door behind him. Tynan soon followed, and as he passed Wilson on the aisle, Wilson grabbed his sleeve and asked if he couldn't control his noisy friends. Logue had snubbed Wilson earlier, envious, perhaps, of *The Outsider's* success, and possibly convinced by Tynan that Wilson was a budding Nazi. Tynan told Wilson to get out of his life and stormed out of the theater.

At a pub next door Wilson, Bill Hopkins, and Holroyd saw Tynan and Logue. Wilson confronted Logue on his bad manners and as he did, Anne, Holroyd's ex-wife (they had by that time separated), lunged at Logue and grabbed him by the throat. His chair was tilted on its back legs and with Anne's hands around Logue's neck, it crashed backward to the floor, landing Logue flat on his back. The pub landlord soon broke up the fracas, but at a friend's nearby Bill Hopkins quickly got on the phone and soon the *Daily Express* knew just how angry those angry young men could get. By the next morning its readers did too.

It was this kind of thing that turned the critics away from Wilson. It also made him realize that some unwanted transformation had taken place in him. He was, he saw, becoming an Insider. He was losing his own sense of purpose in the swirl of parties, publicity, and press releases. "I had become aware of what had happened. . . . I was congratulated by critics on having started a new craze, on inventing a new parlour game . . . called 'Outsider or Insider?' . . . I had become a stranger to my own book."[34] We can forgive Wilson if he felt he had fallen into Shaw's idea of hell, a place of futile amusement and entertainment. All this rush and noise and pointless squabbling had absolutely nothing to do with *The Outsider*. It was not what it was about.

And what *was* it about?

In *The Outsider* Wilson made his first attempt at analyzing a character he felt was peculiar to our age, a person with a pressing hunger for meaning and spiritual purpose in a world seemingly bent on denying him these. In the past, during the Middle Ages, such an individual could have found a home in the church, which was then the heart of life, and which provided a place, in the form of monasteries, where he could work toward his salvation—work, that is, to awaken the spiritual life within him, to grasping his purpose with an unwavering seriousness. That purpose was to become something greater than himself, to work against the laziness and complacency that keeps him second-rate and allows him to be satisfied with being "only human."[35] But today, in our modern society, which is geared toward comfort and security and motivated by purely material aims, there is no place for such a person, and his spiritual seriousness is a liability.[36] His desire to be something more than a happy, well-fed animal puts him at odds with the world around him. This type is driven by needs that the people he knows do not understand. For him the world that they complacently accept is false. He sees "too deep and too much" and his awareness of the illusions that satisfy others brings him to despair. He is not at home in the world; his permanent sense of self-dissatisfaction does not allow him to be. This dissatisfaction cannot be met by any changes to the social or economic system, as Marxists such as Tynan believed. "The question of freedom," Wilson writes, "is *not* a social problem." Only by the long, difficult, personal struggle to self-realization can the Outsider realize his goal. That realization, or actualization, as Maslow called it, requires an "intensity of will" and is fostered by anything that arouses one's "will to more life."[37]

This path is difficult. The Outsider at first feels himself a kind of misfit, a "lone nutter," and his dissonance from the Insiders, those content with the world of the second-rate, leads to neurosis. There must be something wrong with him, he believes, and he may try to fit in. Usually he fails, and winds up occupying an uncomfortable middle realm. He cannot accept the world and its triviality, but he is not strong enough to escape from it completely or to impose his own seriousness upon it. This may lead to nothing more than a life of quiet desperation, or the Outsider may smolder with resentment at the insects around him, and lash out indiscriminately—as Wilson's explorations of the "criminal" Outsider will show, this can have deadly results. But if he is lucky, there are moments of vision, when a sense of power and meaning comes to him and he sees that he is not a misfit, and that the hunger and dissatisfaction that drive him, and which drove the mystics and saints of the past, are more real than the newspapers, television, and mediocrity he abhors. It is a vision of "a higher form of reality than he has so far known," a glimpse of what Wilson calls "the secret life," that sense of affirmation he had experienced in Teignmouth.[38] But then the vision fades. The Outsider is back on earth and is left wondering what the vision was about and why he must return to the dreary treadmill. *The Outsider* examines the possibility of restoring the vision, of so strengthening one's grasp on one's sense of purpose that it is not weakened or confused by the banality of "life."

Wilson's notebooks were full of observations of such figures, of Outsiders who were not able to survive their clashes with the world and who succumbed to illness, suicide, or madness, who were not quite strong enough to impose their vision on their contemporaries. What went wrong? Why did giants such as Nietzsche, Nijinsky, van Gogh, T. E. Lawrence, and others fail? To say they failed is not, of course, to diminish their greatness. But Nietzsche and Nijinsky went insane, van Gogh shot himself, and Lawrence went into a kind of spiritual suicide, burying himself as a private in the RAF at the height of his fame. Why did so many poets and writers of the nineteenth century end in a kind of self-destruction? Shelley, Keats, Poe, Hölderlin, Schubert, Hoffman, Schiller, Kleist, Rimbaud, Verlaine, Lautréamont—this list of nineteenth-century geniuses who either died young, went mad, killed themselves, or succumbed to alcohol or drug addiction could go on.[39] Why did it happen? Could it have been prevented? All were infused with the Romantic vision that burst upon western consciousness in the late eighteenth century, the insight that informed the music of Beethoven and the poetry of Blake. This was the sense, lost in the modern age, that human beings are really gods, or at least are meant to be, if only they could overcome their laziness and timidity. *The Outsider* is an exploration of the psychological and spiritual stresses that these and other men of genius faced in the search for their true selves. "The Outsider," Wilson tells us, "is not sure who he is. He has found an 'I', but it is not his true 'I'. His main business is to find his way back to himself."[40]

In nine chapters Wilson outlines the types of Outsiders, looking at the lives and experiences of individuals who, for him, embody the characteristic challenges the Outsider faces. First there is the vision of meaninglessness, the sudden recognition that the everyday world we take for granted is not quite what it seems.

As we've seen, Barbusse's hero, peering at the world through a hole in the wall, and determined to tell the truth about it, begins the analysis. It then moves to that strange last work of H. G. Wells, *Mind at the End of Its Tether*, published in 1945, a year before his death. In it Wells argues that "the end of everything we call life is close at hand and cannot be evaded." Wells, in his last days a sick, frustrated man, has "awakened to chaos."[41] "A frightful queerness has come into life," he wrote. It was the sense that human life, hitherto seen as somehow connected to the universe beyond it, was now cut off and hurtling toward some unthinkable unknown. "Everything," it seemed to him, "was driving anyhow to anywhere at a steadily increasing velocity."[42] This is one of the most unusual Outsider documents. Wells was a man of reason, a champion of science, and an apostle of the World State, a global socialism that would create the kind of rational utopia he had written about in his many books. Once confident that through reason, science, and progressive social systems, the world, as he wrote, would be "set free," Wells was now reduced to despair at the realization that "Our loves, our hates, our wars and battles, are no more than phantasmagoria . . . insubstantial as a dream." Wells had awakened to a fundamental chaos of which the man in the street is unaware, and it devastated him.

Another who saw it was Jean-Paul Sartre. His novel *Nausea* spells out Wells's insight in meticulous detail. The hero of *Nausea* has awakened to chaos too. He sees it all around him, in a stone, a doorknob, a chair. In the midst of everyday life, Sartre's hero is suddenly struck by the *strangeness* of things we normally take for granted. The *necessity* of human life has vanished. The things we name and feel we understand begin to rebel against our superficial assumptions. A glass of beer, someone's suspenders, the root of a chestnut tree: their reality, free of the simplifying language that holds them in place, overwhelms Sartre's hero. He feels negated by their very being. "Never," he says, "had I understood the meaning of *existence*." He does now and it is threatening. He feels himself stuck in the paste of existence, unable to escape from its brute meaninglessness. The title of Sartre's major philosophical work, *Being and Nothingness*, states the dilemma in its most fundamental form.

The chaos must be faced for it to be overcome. To do that the Outsider must confront a "world without values." Wilson does this through the work of Albert Camus, Ernest Hemingway, and the forgotten playwright Harley Granville-Barker. In them he sees the beginning of an answer to the Outsider's dilemma, which in essence means finding a way to the experience of *freedom*. But as we've seen, freedom for Wilson is not a social or economic question, but an *inner experience*. It is essentially an inner expansiveness, a release from trivia and banality, a sensation of more "life"—the "life more abundant" of the Gospels, when the doors of perception are flung wide open. Meursault, the hero of Camus' novel *The Stranger* (I use the American title) sleepwalks through life. Nothing touches him. He is a victim of a high indifference threshold, and incidents and experiences that would elicit feelings in others, such as the death of his mother, leave him cold. Through a series of events he becomes arrested for a shooting. He is not responsible, but he cannot be bothered to explain and is tried, found guilty, and condemned to death. It is only at the end of the novel, when, facing execution, and disgusted at the pieties of the prison priest, he explodes into anger. The prospect of death has awakened him from his unreality, shaken him out of his indifference. He realizes too late that he "had been happy" and "was happy still." In other words he has had a moment of freedom, a moment of *reality*.

Such moments come to other Outsiders. Sartre's hero has one while listening to a blues record; the nausea disappears and suddenly *he* is more real than the world. Back in civilian life and bored by its dreary routine, Krebs, the hero of Hemingway's story "Soldier's Home," remembers the moments during the war when he did "the one thing, the only thing for a man to do," and how they made him feel "cool and clear inside."[43] These are moments when the Outsider makes contact with "the secret life," the title of Granville-Barker's post–World War I play, which depicts a bankrupt spiritual landscape, the "world without values" the Outsider must transform. One of the central characters in the play echoes Elijah's lament, "take away my life, O Lord, for I am not better than my fathers." The Outsider *wants* to be better than his fathers. That is his dissatisfaction; it is an expression of the evolutionary urge. It is what makes his life so difficult and him so miserable. The question is: how to fulfill it?

One possibility is the way of the Romantic Outsider, which Wilson sees typified in the work of Hermann Hesse. When Wilson wrote about Hesse, he was practically unknown in England or America; most of his work was either out of print or not translated into English. Hesse was still alive at the time of *The Outsider*, although it is unlikely he knew of it. If he did, he may have thanked Wilson in advance for sparking the posthumous revival of his work that began in the mid-1960s and made him a campus best seller, along with Tolkien and Kurt Vonnegut. Wilson wrote the first extended analysis of Hesse's work in English, and in *Steppenwolf* he sees "one of the most penetrating and exhaustive studies of the Outsider ever written."[44]

Hesse's Harry Haller, an old "wolf of the steppes," embodies Wilson's notion of the paradoxical nature of freedom. Haller *has* external freedom. He leads a solitary life in pleasant accommodation, with enough money to live comfortably. He is surrounded by books, music, and art, all of which he can enjoy at his leisure. He has no obligations or responsibilities and can live the life of a retired scholar. But his freedom has become a burden. He *should* be grateful for it, but there is some damper on his appreciation that prevents him: the indifference threshold again. Haller is trapped in his own personal vinegar bottle. The lukewarm, routine, unfulfilling days fill him with boredom, until they are unendurable and he thinks of suicide. But on a night when he decides to slit his throat, he stops at a café and has a glass of wine. Then the feeling of inner freedom comes. "A refreshing laughter rose in me," Hesse writes. "The golden trail was blazed and I was reminded of the eternal, and of Mozart, and the stars."[45] This an example of what Wilson would later dub "Faculty X," our strange ability to transcend the present moment and grasp the reality of "other times and places." The inner expansiveness reconciles Haller to life again. But the need to find some method of recovering it *at will* remains.

It is this question that occupies the rest of the book. The Outsider's dilemma is not merely an intellectual puzzle or a literary trope. It is something that "*must be lived.*" An answer to his despair must come through a way of life, a way of *being*; it cannot be solved with words alone but requires action. Through the lives of Nijinsky, van Gogh, and T. E. Lawrence, Wilson explores the possible answers offered by the body, the emotions, and the mind. All three, like the other Outsiders, had to answer the question: Ultimate Yes or Ultimate No? Can they affirm life, or do they reject it?

Each tries to affirm, but in the end is defeated. When Nijinsky danced, he knew that "God is fire in the head. . . . I am God in a body. . . . I am a man of motion. . . . I am feeling through flesh, not through the intellect." Lines like these run through Nijinsky's remarkable *Diary*, one of the great spiritual testaments of the twentieth century. Yet Nijinsky was unable to master the realities of everyday life, and the pressures drove him insane; as mentioned, he died in a mental institution in London in 1950. Van Gogh painted transfiguring works such as *The Starry Night*, canvases that depict a world perceived in sudden, fiery immediacy, filled with swirling energy and radiant life. They show the world as it is when the doors of perception are cleansed. They communicate directly through the emotions, without the distortions of words. Yet van Gogh was prey to depressions, to the vastations that led to his suicide from the recognition that "misery will never end." T. E. Lawrence suffered from what he called his "thought-riddled nature," from a sharp, incisive intellect and relentless self-criticism and self-discipline that would not allow him rest. Moments of perception when the world was seen—as van Gogh saw it—as "not filtered through or made typical by thought" were rare, and he became a "pipe through which life flowed." Lawrence had tremendous will, but he had little capacity for *feeling*. After a slow "mind suicide" sunken in the RAF, he died following a motorcycle accident in 1935.[46]

The limits of the body, the emotions, and the mind lead to the need for a discipline. This is necessary in order for the Outsider to overcome the challenge of "the pain threshold," an early working title for the book. If the indifference threshold is the degree to which one ignores good, beneficial, positive conditions, the pain threshold is the degree to which one is sensitive to the misery of the world. The Outsider has a low pain threshold. As we've seen, he is prone to sudden moments when reality becomes an abyss, a vast emptiness, devoid of meaning, the vastation. Wilson looks at the experiences of the philosopher William James and his father, Henry James Sr., both of whom experienced this sudden collapse of meaning and left accounts of it. William James writes of it in *The Varieties of Religious Experience*; he speaks of a "horrible fear of my own existence," symbolized by a catatonic patient, which left a "horrible dread at the pit of my stomach," and a profound sense of the insecurity of life.[47] For years afterward he suffered bouts of depression and thoughts of suicide.

Contrasted with this vision of Ultimate No is Nietzsche, who presented a philosophy of total affirmation. Nietzsche experienced the vastation, but some instinct of health prevented him from succumbing to it (James, I should say, recovered from his as well). Nietzsche is, as Wilson points out, the first philosopher of optimism; from Socrates to Nietzsche's early hero, Schopenhauer, most others believed life was a bad bargain. Nietzsche knew the other experience, the explosion of joy and yea-saying that he characterized as Dionysian, an "incredible sense of well-being and zest," of "pure will," without the "confusions of the intellect" that so burdened T. E. Lawrence. Through a life of suffering and loneliness, Nietzsche arrived at the profound vision of *Thus Spoke Zarathustra*, his call for the "superman," for those who follow the evolutionary urge and answer Elijah's lament by striving to be better than their fathers.

But to follow this call the Outsider must know who he is. And in order to do that he must confront the mystery of his own identity. He asks, "Who am I?" and discovers that he does not know. None of us do. We take ourselves for granted. We feel we know who we are and what our life is about. We haven't a clue. Tolstoy's *A Confession* shows how at the age of fifty, the great novelist began to question his own identity. This uncertainty was expressed in his short story "Memoirs of a Madman." The hero of this tale experiences Tolstoy's uncertainties as "something dreadful" which he cannot avoid because he—the personality he wishes to escape—is his own tormentor, and his efforts to "get away from himself" fail. Tolstoy finds a religious answer to his uncertainty, and at this time, Wilson felt that such an answer might serve the Outsider too, as his second book, *Religion and the Rebel*, showed. But here he cannot settle for it. Wilson continues this exploration of identity through the work of Dostoyevsky, which depicts the Outsider's slow awakening to himself and his necessary course of action. From *Notes From Underground* to *The Devils*, Wilson charts Dostoyevsky's insights into the challenges of the Outsider, from the febrile, feverish world rejection of the early work to the mystical vision of total affirmation symbolized in the ecstatic suicide of Kirilov in *The Devils*.

But Dostoyevsky's greatest contribution to understanding the Outsider and showing him a way to freedom is contained in his last work, *The Brothers Kara-*

mazov, which was published in 1880. In this book he portrays three brothers who symbolize, as did T. E. Lawrence, van Gogh, and Nijinsky, the intellect, the emotions, and the body, a tripartite arrangement that we've seen Wilson employ in *Ritual in the Dark*. Here begins the work of synthesis, of fusing together the disparate parts of the self, of harmonizing what Gurdjieff called our different "centers"—the moving, the emotional, and the intellectual parts of our being.

Here also is Dostoyevsky's statement of Ultimate Yes and Ultimate No, in his "Pro and Contra" chapter, where the brute reality of pain and suffering is contrasted with a mystical vision of affirmation. Considered by the intellect alone, Ivan Karamazov's awareness of pain and suffering justifies his wish to "give God back his entrance ticket." No cosmic plan, no great universal meaning can, Ivan believes, justify the pointless torture of a child, and yet such torture goes on daily. Yet, where the intellect says no, some deeper part of us rejects this and, as Nietzsche knew, experiences an absurd yea-saying, an affirmation of life even in the face of suffering. This is what happens to Ivan's brother, the young monk Alyosha, when he has a vision of the stars, and feels "threads from all those innumerable worlds of God, linking his soul to them."[48] With this we have entered the mystic's territory and it is here that the Outsider begins to see a way toward an answer to his dilemma.

The Outsider must become a visionary. That is his salvation. He must learn how to open his doors of perception, as Wilson did that day at Teignmouth. To explore the possibility of doing so, Wilson looks, understandably, at the work of William Blake. After examining the life of another visionary, the religious reformer George Fox, Wilson analyzes the essence of Blake's vision. Blake had the poet's intuitive understanding that our perception is intentional, that it is not a matter of passively reflecting the world outside, but of the amount of will, of attention and energy we put into it. Van Gogh did not paint sunflowers and stars as if they were bursting with vibrant life because he wanted to be original or new, as some career-minded artist who is anxious to appear different might. He painted that way because he *saw* the world that way, saw it with that kind of vitality and freshness. So did Blake. For Blake and other mystics, such a way of seeing is normal, is our birthright, but we have lost it. Yet it is possible to regain it, and Blake's way, and that of the Outsider, is through the imagination, which is another name for the intentional, willed character of perception. This was Blake's mission: "To open the eternal worlds, to open the immortal eyes / Of man Inwards, into the world of thought, into Eternity."[49]

Practical ways of achieving this change in consciousness—for this is what the Outsider's salvation amounts to—occupy Wilson's final chapter. If he is to forgo the world rejection that doomed so many of the Romantics, the Outsider must find some course of action that will lead to self-expression. We return to the need for a discipline. The Romantics were defeated by the world and by their own self-pity. The Outsider, if he is to succeed in actualizing himself, must be stronger. He must find a way to produce the vision of affirmation that will dispel his self-doubt and despair. Wilson writes of Ramakrishna's peak experience as a boy watching a flock of snow-white cranes flying against a dark storm cloud. The sudden contrast throws him into a vision of the divine mother, Kali. Years later, when the vision has faded, Ramakrishna falls into despair and decides to kill himself. When he draws a sword and, like the teenaged Wilson, is about to end his life, the vision comes again. He finds himself in the middle of a "limitless, infinite, shining ocean of light."[50] Again, the sudden threat to life awakens the dormant vital forces, and Ramakrishna is plunged into ecstasy. Is there a way to awaken this sleeping will without such threats? Can the Outsider affirm life without having to put a gun to his head? Can we, again, learn how to open our doors of perception, rather than sit passively and wait for something to happen, or worse, view the world as ultimately meaningless because *as we see it*, it presents no detectable meaning? Can we learn *how* to flick the switch that tenses the mind's muscles and pours energy into our perception?

Wilson thought an answer might be found in the strange system of "man's possible evolution" developed by the enigmatic spiritual teacher Gurdjieff. Gurdjieff was dead only a few years when *The Outsider* came out; not many people outside "the work"—the name given to his system—knew much about him. As with Hermann Hesse, Wilson's study of Gurdjieff's ideas, which he called "the complete, ideal *Existenzphilosophie*," was well ahead of the pack and introduced Gurdjieff to many thousands of readers.[51] What captured Wilson's attention was Gurdjieff's notion of "self-remembering," an awakening of consciousness to a greater intensity and vividness, precisely the state of mind that the Outsider desires. Such states are experiences of the kind of inner freedom the Outsider needs as much as other men need food and water. This freedom, this inner expansiveness, is, Wilson argues, what life itself is aiming at in its evolution. Not the Darwinian version, which sees evolution as the chance product of mindless physical forces. But a "creative evolution," pushed on by an instinctive urge to grow and actualize itself, to become, as Elijah had despaired of himself, "better than its fathers." Starting from the evolutionary ideas of the philosopher Henri Bergson, Wilson looks at the work of the little-read religious thinker T. E. Hulme, who died in 1917 during World War I. Hulme saw evolution as "the gradual insertion of more and more freedom into matter." Freedom, for Hulme, was a kind of leak of creativity in matter, and the aim of evolution was "the gradual enlargement of this leak."[52]

Hulme achieved some sense of this "leak" through religion, taking the route that T. S. Eliot had. At the time, Wilson considered this way too. He was not to continue on it, but he did see the Outsider's challenge in a religious way. What he had written here, in his first book, was only the beginning, a preliminary clarification before the real work of reconstruction began. The Outsider's problems are not his alone; they involve all of civilization. Western civilization had reached a dead end, Wilson saw, and it could only move on if the Outsiders, the men and women of vision and purpose, overcame their uncertainty, *ceased to be Outsiders*, and imposed their values on the world around them. But an answer to these questions begins with them. They must endure "the intolerable struggle to expose the sensitive areas of being to what may possibly hurt them." They must make "the attempt to see as a whole, although the instinct of self-preservation fights against the pain of the internal widening, and all the impulses of spiritual laziness build into waves with every new effort. . . . The individual begins that long effort," Wilson tells us, "as an Outsider." But "he may finish it as a saint."[53]

I have looked at *The Outsider* at length here for two reasons. One is to show that the kind of publicity that Wilson received could not really have had much to do with the actual ideas of the book. We may think Wilson exaggerated things a bit when he said that it was as difficult to understand the Outsider's dilemma as it was to grasp the theories behind quantum physics, but we get his point.[54] The ideas and problems related in the past few pages are not those that occupy most people—even today, when questions about spirituality are more common than in the 1950s. Wilson was writing about peculiarly obsessed individuals, and the kinds of problems that obsess them are not those that trouble most of us. So while we, with the benefit of more than half a century of exposure to the media, may see his response as a bit naïve, we can also see that he was right to feel that he was being successful for the wrong reasons and to be worried about this. This isn't to say that the early acclaim for *The Outsider* wasn't warranted. It was. But while Cyril Connolly, Philip Toynbee, and the other early reviewers were qualified to understand the importance of the book, the gossip columnists and paparazzi who followed them most likely had no idea what it was about. And a twenty-four-year-old writer who had struggled for years could hardly be blamed for enjoying the limelight into which he suddenly found himself thrown. What is remarkable is that Wilson survived such mistaken celebrity and went on to do serious philosophical work in the face of it. Most writers or artists subject to the kind of backlash that Wilson faced would pack up their materials and find another way to make a living.

The other reason I have outlined *The Outsider* at length is because in it in embryo is pretty much everything that Wilson would write about for the rest of his long and prolific career. The philosopher Isaiah Berlin wrote an essay called "The Hedgehog and the Fox," differentiating between two types of thinkers. In it he quotes a line from the Greek poet Archilochus: "The fox knows many things; the hedgehog knows one big thing." Wilson happily admits to being a hedgehog. One big thing informs all of his work, what he calls "the paradoxical nature of freedom," which ultimately resolves itself into a question of consciousness. If there is an answer to the Outsider's dilemma, it will be found, Wilson saw, through an understanding of consciousness, a knowledge of its workings, and a grasp of its mechanisms. Such a pursuit is generally not accompanied by much publicity. What Wilson found was that in his case, it also meant a long, uphill struggle to overcome the negative effects of an unwanted reputation.

CHAPTER FOUR

AFTER *THE OUTSIDER*

The most absurd episode of Wilson's career as an Angry Young Man took place in February 1957. It began in the waiting room of a hospital in Bedford, where Joy was having her tonsils out. By this time she had moved into Wilson's room in Notting Hill. Her parents were unaware of this; they had still not quite accepted the young genius, so she kept a small room elsewhere where she could receive mail. Wilson was visiting Joy in the hospital and had left his journal with his notes for *Ritual* out on a table. Joy's sister noticed it and decided to take a look. She opened to a page with some remarks about a homosexual friend of Wilson's and some jottings on the kinds of sexual themes running through the novel. As the novel concerned a sex murderer, we can imagine what she read. The notes in fact contained an account of Peter Kürten, the Düsseldorf serial killer, on whom Fritz Lang based his classic film *M*. Wilson would later analyze Kürten's horrifying career in his *Encyclopaedia of Murder* and other books on the psychology of crime.[1] Joy's sister was shocked but at the time said nothing. Soon, however, she reported her discovery to her parents.

The fireworks started a week or so later. Wilson and Joy were back in Notting Hill, entertaining Gerald Hamilton, the individual on whom Christopher Isherwood had based his character Mr. Norris in *The Berlin Stories*, and who had been a roommate of the dark magician Aleister Crowley in Germany in the 1920s.[2] While they were having supper, the door burst open, and Joy's father, mother, sister, and brother stormed in. "The game is up, Wilson!" Mr. Stewart shouted. To which Wilson replied, "What game?" "We've read your filthy diary," Joy's father answered, and turning to Joy he asked, "Do you know he's a homosexual and has six mistresses?"

The illogic of the remark escaped Joy's father, but Wilson realized what must have happened. Joy's sister had read his journal and mistook his notes for the novel for his own confessions. Bemused, Wilson handed Joy's father another of his journals and told him to read it. He declined, but took the journal and stashed it in his pocket. He then opened his briefcase and took out a horse whip. He was about to lash Wilson with it when, in self-defense, the now quite angry young man pushed his attacker away. Joy's father fell and her mother started battering Wilson with an umbrella, shouting abuse. The absurdity of it became too much and Wilson fell to the floor laughing. Someone among the Stewarts kicked him as he did.

A tug-of-war began between Wilson and Joy's family, with Joy in the middle. Some of Wilson's neighbors appeared, intrigued by the commotion. Seeing that Wilson was outnumbered, they joined in and started to pull on his side "until it looked as if Joy was going to come apart down the middle."[3] Wilson eventually got to a telephone and called the police. When they arrived, Joy's father explained that Wilson was a sexual pervert and that they had come to rescue their daughter from him. But when it became clear that Joy was over twenty-one, the officer explained that her family would have to leave, as she was an adult.

Frustrated, Joy's liberators could do nothing but go. But the excitement was hardly over. Wilson noticed that Gerald Hamilton had vanished; immediately the doorbell rang. It was two reporters. Wilson realized that Hamilton knew a good story when he saw one and had run off to ring the newspapers. Wilson let the reporters in, told them the story, and let them take a photograph, thinking the publicity might keep Joy's parents at bay; they were, after all, a respectable family. A few minutes later the doorbell rang again. Wilson looked out the window and saw a crowd of journalists and cameramen on his doorstep. He quickly rang an editor friend, Tom Maschler, and asked if they could stay at his flat nearby. Maschler agreed, and the two sneaked out the back way.

Afraid that Joy's parents might try to save her again, the couple decided to leave London. They headed to Devon, where they could stay with Negley Farson, the travel writer. By this time the story had hit the papers—the horse whip was irresistible—and one of them, the *Daily Express*, had printed brief extracts from the journal Joy's father had taken. Wilson had heard from Bill Hopkins that the *Daily Mail* had offered fifty pounds to print some extracts too. Wilson declined to sell his private life but allowed Hopkins to arrange a deal: the *Mail* could print extracts for free, provided that Hopkins could choose and edit them.

Soon the *Mail* ran a double-page spread, with the headline THE DIARY OF COLIN WILSON. It included a cartoon of a turtlenecked Wilson being chased by Joy's father, horse whip in hand. Wilson had hoped that the extracts might clear up the matter and show that his diary wasn't a collection of obsessive jottings about sex and murder, as the extracts in the *Express* had suggested. But while an open-minded reader could recognize Wilson's intent, in whatever context, it would have been impossible at that time for remarks such as "Death to the half-livers. The evolutionary appetite in me demands a seriousness that is far from this stupid civilization" and "I *am* the major literary genius of our century," not to have been misunderstood. The papers had also published a photograph of Betty and Wilson's son, Roderick, casting them as the forsaken wife and child, left behind as Wilson ran off with his illicit love. Wilson had to issue a statement saying, "I am not neglecting my wife. I receive £100 a month from my publisher and of that I give my wife £25."[4]

Now that the press had a "runaway lovers" story on their hands, they were loath to let it go. Journalists and cameramen turned up at Farson's house, and the telephone rang nonstop. Farson, an old newsman, soon cut a deal with the *Express*. In exchange for a photograph of the couple, the *Express* reporters would sneak them away to anywhere in England, and let them go. They decided that it was best to get out of England, and had decided on Ireland. But when they told the reporters this, they replied that their editors now demanded that they stay with them. Exhausted, the two had the newsmen take them to Ilfracombe, where they could get a ferry to Swansea, in Wales. There they were put up by the novelist Kingsley Amis. Amis was no fan of *The Outsider*; a review of it he wrote for the *Spectator* spoke of "all those characters you thought were discredited, or had never read, or (if you are like me) had never heard of." But he proved friendly and after an evening drinking whiskey with him and his wife, the two "runaway lovers" headed across the Irish Sea to Dublin, with the reporters in tow.[5] After a few days of meeting and drinking with some of the literary locals, the couple decided to visit the west country. But even there the scandal overtook them. A woman they met in a hotel in Tralee handed them a copy of *Time* magazine; in it they found a photograph of themselves and a story about the horsewhipping. Back in Dublin, in a pub a stranger asked Wilson why he didn't sue *Time*.[6]

By this time the *Daily Express* reporters had let them go. But back in Notting Hill the *Daily Mail* caught up with them and asked for an interview. Soon photographs of Chepstow Villas reached their readers, one of whom was Wilson's father. He was embarrassed that his friends would see the kind of slum his famous son was living in. Not long after their return, Victor Gollancz asked Wilson to see him. He explained that if he didn't get out of London soon, whatever reputation he had left as a serious writer would be in tatters. He should be prepared for his next book to be treated harshly. All this publicity would work against him and he needed to stop it as soon as possible.

Wilson agreed. He had been thinking along the same lines. While in Ireland, they had almost bought a house in the west country; the price was cheap but the extensive repairs would have been too costly. Wilson considered the Hebrides, but they were too far away and too wet. Then a poet friend suggested something. He rented a farm cottage in Cornwall but his work for a publisher demanded he stay in London. If Wilson wanted to, he could sublet the cottage for the next two years; the poet saw no prospect of returning there until then.

In March 1957 Wilson and Joy headed to the fishing village of Mevagissey, the closest town to the cottage, where they stayed at a guesthouse. The next day a taxi took them within walking distance of the place. A long dirt road potted with cow dung led to Old Walls, an Elizabethan cottage whose walls, some two feet thick, were made of cob, hence the name. At the end of a valley they could see the English Channel, and a stream ran near their front door. The plumbing was primitive—they had to flush the toilet with buckets of water—and there was no electricity, only oil lamps. Wilson had to install a generator which powered a dozen car batteries. The electricity was needed for lighting, but also for Wilson's phonograph; he had by this time become obsessed with music and had spent much of his earnings from *The Outsider* on rare classical recordings. Hot water was at a premium, the stove ran on Calor gas, and drinking water had to be retrieved from a well. But there was no question that they would take it. There wasn't another house nearby for nearly a mile. No neighbors, no telephone, and, most wonderful, no reporters. It was time for the Outsider to get back outside.

Yet moving to Cornwall didn't end all the bad publicity. The fracas at the Royal Court and his contretemps with George Devine and the English Stage Company (discussed in the previous chapter) took place during Wilson's time at Old Walls. But Wilson's excursions to London were infrequent. He kept a pied-à-terre in Notting Hill which he shared with the novelist John Braine; Stuart Holroyd and Bill Hopkins lived in the building too. It was a short distance from his old lodgings, but 25 Chepstow Road was an even grittier environment. (By this time 24 Chepstow Villas had been sold.) The rent was low because the owner, Peter Rachman, a notorious slumlord, needed a few "respectable" tenants in order to keep the police from closing the place down as a brothel. The women on the ground floor ran a brisk business and noisy clients kept the other tenants up at night. Wilson remarks that the prostitutes hung their laundry outside the one bathroom in the place, a colorful array of panties, a suggestive spectrum of red, purple, green, and bright yellow.[7]

Wilson wistfully remarks that the one drawback to being with Joy was that he had to forgo all the sexual opportunities that presented themselves, practically for the asking.[8] Tom Greenwell, a journalist who also lived at Chepstow Road, recalled late-night carousing and endless party invitations, and remarked that Wilson "never seemed to approve of the women his closest friends became attached to" because he believed such attachments would keep them from their typewriters.[9] Much like rock stars, the Angry Young Writers had their own kind of groupie: young, enthusiastic, eager to bed a budding genius. His love for Joy and an instinct for work kept Wilson in line.

It was just as well. Along with the distractions and distortions of success, Wilson soon recognized that for all its temptations, the kind of sexual free-for-all he found himself in was more times than not a sure path to creative dissipation. In later years, in his analysis of the life and work of creative individuals, Wilson found that the kind of skirt chasing that Holroyd, Hopkins, and other friends engaged in often led to a drying up of their talent. After the crushing reviews of his first novel, Hopkins gave up writing. Holroyd produced a few more books, but eventually stopped too; he returned to writing in the late 1970s, producing work in the paranormal-spiritual field. For all his appreciation of sex—and a reader of his work is in no doubt about this—Wilson came to the conclusion that the "sexual illusion" can be as dangerous a habit to the creative worker as drug addiction. Being away from London and all its delights allowed Wilson to focus his mind on important things. What he wanted to do was to "spend my life thinking about the question that really interested me: how to transform my consciousness at will."[10] All the hoopla about his genius and scandalous sex life could only take him away from this.

All during the Angry Young Man debacle Wilson had been working on his second book, *Religion and the Rebel*. It was essentially an extension of the ideas he had presented in *The Outsider*. But where *The Outsider* had presented its themes in the "objective" dress of a literary and philosophical study—hence Wilson's injudicious remarks about it being a "fraud"—his new book was much more personal. It included an "Autobiographical Introduction," in which Wilson told of his life up till the publication of *The Outsider*. It was also a much more passionate work than any other he would produce. This is understandable. He was writing in the face of a by now almost universal rejection of himself as a writer and the Outsider as a theme with serious philosophical implications. If there was some justification for criticism that "the Outsider" was too loose and vague a term to offer any real critical purchase—something Wilson himself soon considered, when he was deluged with correspondence from innumerable social misfits and eccentrics claiming to be Outsiders—Wilson was nevertheless determined to clarify what he meant by it.[11]

Religion and the Rebel—the title was chosen by Gollancz—presents the Outsider as "the heroic figure of our time." "My vision of civilization," Wilson wrote, "was a vision of cheapness and futility, the degrading of all intellectual standards." The Outsider was "the man who, for any reason at all, felt himself lonely in the crowd of the second-rate." He could be "a maniac carrying a knife in a black bag, taking pride in appearing harmless and normal to other people," much as the character of Austin Nunne in *Ritual in the Dark* does. Or he "could be a saint or a visionary, caring for nothing but one moment in which he seemed to understand the world, and see into the heart of nature and of God."[12]

The Outsider is a symptom of our age, and for Wilson, this was in steep decline. He or she is in rebellion against the "*lack of spiritual tension* in a materially prosperous civilization."[13] As he would write some years later, "The comfortable life causes spiritual decay just as soft sweet food causes tooth decay."[14] Outsiders, Wilson argues, are an indication that a civilization has lost its sense of purpose. He believed that our own civilization, given over to scientific humanism, abstract philosophy, and material comfort, was rapidly losing whatever sense of purpose it may have had, an assessment shared by the Outsider figures he cites. In an earlier time, when spiritual necessities were recognized as much as material ones—even more so—Outsiders could find a place within society. Now they are simply oddballs, who "appear like pimples on a dying civilization."[15] Wilson would later reflect that this attack on the "sick civilization" was "a little too violent," and that in general the mood of "world-rejection" in *The Outsider* and *Religion and the Rebel* is too great. But this is the assessment of an older man on his younger self.[16] At the time he may have had a "more narrow and intense view of the problem" than he would later profess, but this is not surprising. At this point Wilson was writing his angst out of his system. In the books that follow, he would begin to approach the Outsider's aim of how to "extend his range of consciousness," logically, step by step.[17]

As in *The Outsider*, Wilson explores some representative examples of his theme. But where his first book focused on stating the Outsider's dilemma, *Religion and the Rebel* is concerned with investigating a possible answer. If the Outsider is "haunted by the sense of the futility of life," here Wilson explores some possible ways of escaping the futility. The Outsider, he says, can be compared to a man who has been hypnotized and led to believe he is no more than an ape, condemned to live out his existence in a cage with other apes. What he needs is some means of dispelling the hypnosis.[18]

As Wilson saw in his own life, the Outsider's salvation lies in extremes. He ceases to be an Outsider—ceases, that is, to be hamstrung by his own self-doubt—by becoming possessed, by becoming "fanatically obsessed by the need to escape."[19] But "escape" here does not mean a retreat into a monastery or ashram, although, as we've seen, Wilson did consider these possibilities. "Escape" here means an escape from one's own mediocrity, from one's own lukewarm existence, and this, as we've seen, can only come about through an experience of "inner freedom," which is the result of an *"increased intensity of mind."*[20] It was a way to this intensity that Wilson hoped to find. When the Outsider recognizes this, he will also see that his sense of being out of step with society is not a sign that he is a misfit who needs to get with the program, as therapies aimed at making him well adjusted would suggest. His misery is really the teething pain of a new form of consciousness, trying to emerge through him and others like him. When he recognizes this and commits himself to the difficult effort of bringing this new consciousness into being, he will take his rightful place as the "antennae of the race," in Ezra Pound's phrase, and no longer cripple himself in a fruitless effort to fit in.

The main part of the book focuses on a religious approach to the Outsider's dilemma and is informed by Wilson's reading in western mysticism. He arrives there through an examination of the imagination and its expression in three writers: Rainer Maria Rilke, Arthur Rimbaud, and, perhaps surprisingly, F. Scott Fitzgerald, whose "crack up," following a meteoric success, must have seemed something of a cautionary tale for the paparazzi-hounded Wilson. All three faced aspects of the Outsider's dilemma, yet Wilson concludes that each fell short of the goal through a lack of discipline. This analysis is part of Wilson's examination of the meaning of existentialism, which he wants to extend to cover a broader field than that of Heidegger, Sartre, or Camus. Wilson's existentialism is closer to Goethe's notion of *Bildung*. This means the "cultivation" or "formation" of the individual—there is no clear English equivalent—his maturity or, in Maslow's term, his self-actualization. Through an examination of the lives of these individuals, we can gain some insight into the problems that face the Outsider in his attempt to know himself.

But Wilson was determined to show that the concerns that obsess his Outsiders are something more than the neuroses of oversensitive individuals. They are, he explains, evidence of the spiritual bankruptcy of the age. In "The Outsider and History" he looks at the work of the historians Oswald Spengler and Arnold Toynbee, two metaphysical historians whose work is out of favor in our more pedestrian times. Each in his own way preferred the intuitive approach over the logical. Their work proceeds through vivid insights and visions; each could be said to look at history "existentially," in Wilson's use of the term, meaning they seek some deeper, more profound grasp of it than that afforded by mere logic and reason. Each has a sense of destiny, of a direction in history, unlike their more scientific colleagues, who are satisfied with more materialist explanations and think in terms of cause and effect. Wilson wanted his readers to feel history as something living, as a process they were a part of, and not merely observing from some objective standpoint. This is what Wilson calls "the living vision of history," a "deliberate discipline of the imagination to develop a sense of personal participation in history."[21]

Spengler's major work, *The Decline of the West*, was a best seller in post–World War I Europe. Its thesis is that civilizations are like living organisms: they are born, they reach a level of maturity, and they die. As his title suggests, Spengler believed that western civilization was on its way out, and Wilson is inclined to agree. One of the symptoms of this decline is "abstract philosophy," the kind of purely intellectual thinking that early existential thinkers such as Kierkegaard and Nietzsche attacked relentlessly and which Wilson criticized in *The Outsider*. Abstract philosophy, epitomized in Wilson's time in philosophers such as Bertrand Russell and A. J. Ayer, sees questions of human purpose and destiny as meaningless, sentimental leftovers from the age of religion, which should be abandoned in favor of scientific rigor; they adhered to what was known as "logical positivism." For them meaning, purpose, destiny, and other living concerns are outside philosophy's purview, which should stick to considering only the facts. This is in complete opposition to Wilson's view of philosophy; for him it is "nothing if it is not an attempt to take one's own experience apart under a microscope."[22] The failure of abstract philosophy to do this, and its preference for mere intellectualizing, is a sign of our civilization's decline, and a spur to its heading further downhill.

Spengler was a romantic; he speaks of western culture as "Faustian," and sees Goethe's hero as emblematic of it, his insatiable quest for knowledge leading to a desiccation of the vital forces of irrational life. But where Spengler believed there was no way to avoid this decline or to stop it, Wilson is more optimistic. He looks to Toynbee for a more positive vision. Toynbee, too, sees the history of civilizations as a cycle of rise and fall. But his conclusions offer more hope than Spengler's. Toynbee rejects Spengler's fatalistic biological view and sees the rise and fall of civilizations as powered by what he calls "challenge and response." We might call it the "Goldilocks" vision of history.

For Toynbee a civilization flourishes until it reaches what he calls its "time of troubles." A challenge presents itself, which it must overcome in order to keep growing. But as with Goldilocks, the challenge must be just right. If it is too great, the civilization cannot meet it and it collapses. If it is not great enough, then the civilization overcomes it too easily. It becomes overconfident and complacent, and slides into decadence. Toynbee's point is that, unlike the Darwinian picture, which sees life flourishing best under favorable conditions, for him, civilizations—and, by extension, individuals—develop when they are faced with difficulties, with challenges that bring the best out of them. They flourish when they must focus their *will* upon some need and struggle to meet it. Without such challenges, they degenerate.

To meet the challenge successfully, the civilization produces what Toynbee calls a "creative minority," a term he borrowed from the philosopher Henri Bergson.[23] These are individuals sensitive to the needs of the time, and understandably, Wilson associates them with his Outsiders. Unlike Marxist or other scientific, materialist accounts of history—or, indeed, Spengler's—Toynbee believes that "civilizations progress because of individuals." The members of the "creative minority" go through a process of "withdrawal and return," in which they "go into the wilderness," escape from the harangue of social life, in order to contact the vital forces within them. They then return with their message, which, more times than not, the majority—Wilson's Insiders—misunderstand, but which is crucial to the civilization's survival.[24]

Toynbee interested Wilson greatly because, along with being a brilliant historian, he was also a visionary. Toynbee recounts several experiences in which he seemed to be transported back to an earlier time in history, when his imaginative evocation of the period led to a kind of time travel. Wilson cites examples of this, which he would return to in later books. In 1912, while in

Greece, overlooking the remnants of the citadel of Mistra, near Sparta, Toynbee reflected on the invasion in 1821 which had left the place a ruin. As he did, he suddenly felt as if he had been sent back nearly a century and was witnessing the slaughter as it took place. It was in fact this sudden vivid experience of "historical imagination" that inspired Toynbee to write *A Study of History* and set him the task of understanding what was behind the rise and fall of civilizations.

We will return to Toynbee's "visions" further on, when we discuss Wilson's ideas about Faculty X, but we should note here that such a *widening* of our grasp of reality so that it extends beyond the present moment was a concern of Wilson's from the start. As early as *The Outsider* he uses the phrase "the sense of other times and places," which characterizes what he means by "Faculty X."[25] In *Religion and the Rebel* Wilson asks, "How can man extend his range of consciousness?" and he looks at the mental states of most humans as being "as narrow as the middle three notes of a piano keyboard." The Outsider's business is "to extend his range from the usual three or four notes to the whole keyboard." What unites Wilson's disparate Outsiders is their "instinctive knowledge that their range *could* be extended, and a nagging dissatisfaction with the range of their everyday experience."[26] I emphasize this to show that critics who claimed that Wilson abandoned existentialism and boarded the "occult bandwagon" in the 1970s—for purely commercial reasons—are incorrect. Wilson coined the term "Faculty X" in *The Occult*, published in 1971, but the concerns that led him to an examination of the occult were with him from the start.

Toynbee was alive when Wilson discussed his work; he died in 1975 (Spengler had died in 1936). He believed western civilization had entered its own "time of troubles," and that the study of history is a preparation for the "Beatific vision"; like Teilhard de Chardin, Toynbee had a vision of some "Omega point," history's culmination in an experience of universal reconciliation. But his misgivings about the immediate future were many. All we can do, he said, is to "cling and wait," to hold on and hope that we can meet the challenge of our time of troubles successfully. Ultimately he agreed with Bernard Shaw, who said that a civilization cannot exist without a religion—without, that is, some sense of transcendental purpose, some meaning that goes beyond material prosperity. In the preface to his "creative evolutionist" play *Back to Methuselah*, Shaw suggested that since all of the world's religions are fundamentally different ways to the same truth, they should be brought together, into a kind of living embodiment of the "perennial philosophy."[27]

Toynbee agreed with some version of this. The idea has a long history in the west; a version of it was popular in Alexandrian times, it appeared in the Renaissance, and it made a powerful reappearance in the late nineteenth century through the efforts of Madame Blavatsky and the Theosophical Society.[28] Not long before *Religion and the Rebel*, Aldous Huxley popularized it in his anthology of mysticism, *The Perennial Philosophy*, which appeared in 1945. While it is no doubt a noble idea and appeals to many today because of the resurgence of intolerance and religious fundamentalism, there is something oddly dissatisfying about it. It suffers from the same drawbacks as, say, the idea that we could get rid of racial intolerance by fusing all the races together into some kind of "superrace," or that we can defeat religious prejudice by celebrating every religious holiday, whatever the religion. The kind of respect and tolerance we may feel toward different religions, while desirable and necessary, isn't the same as the kind of passionate allegiance one feels toward the religion in which one truly *believes*. Such a belief *grips* one in a way that a liberal assent of tolerance cannot. If you truly believe that Jesus is your savior, you can't have quite the same appreciation of Krishna, the Buddha, or Muhammad, however much you respect them and their believers. And the same is true if Krishna, the Buddha, or Muhammed is the focus of our belief. And while that belief can often lead to unwanted results, as the waves of violence in the name of religion common today show, the positive side of it is that it can raise one out of the usual "middle three notes" of the keyboard of consciousness, into more intense states. This is something we saw in the preceding chapter, when we looked at Ramakrishna's ecstasy at the vision of the divine mother, Kali.

The obverse of this is that not everyone is a Ramakrishna. Not everyone has the same capacity for spiritual ecstasy. But if, as Toynbee and Shaw suggest, some kind of "universal religion" is needed, we face the question of how this religion can meet the needs of the average person, of the Insiders. Wilson writes, "If it is to be as acceptable to the average navvy [a manual laborer] as to the saint and philosopher, religion must be more than the philosopher's perception of 'eternal truth'—it must be myth, dogma and ritual."[29] This was the problem Dostoyevsky addressed in "The Grand Inquisitor" section of *The Brothers Karamazov* and which Wilson analyzed in *The Outsider*. Religion *should* be a discipline toward experiencing "inner freedom," toward reaching out to the other notes on our keyboard of consciousness. Yet, as the Grand Inquisitor laments, most men do not want inner freedom. It is difficult to achieve and a burden to maintain. Most men want a simple, happy life, *panem et circenses*, "bread and circuses," and to place the responsibility of their freedom on them will only make them unhappy. This is the Outsider's dilemma too, when he realizes his true place in society as its spiritual leader.[30] If civilization can only be saved by a spiritual resurgence, *how* can the Outsiders get the Insiders to understand this and to act accordingly? Can the Insiders be saved in spite of themselves?

Wilson had already recognized this hurdle at the close of *The Outsider* when he said that "the problem for the 'civilization' is the adoption of a religious attitude that can be assimilated as *objectively* as the headlines of last Sunday's newspapers."[31] Yet "myth, dogma and ritual" are the very things that intelligent people no longer wish to accept. Eventually Wilson came to see that while the *seriousness* about life that is the essence of religion is needed, a new religion itself is not the answer. "Seriousness about life" is another way of saying "a sense of purpose," and the immediate purpose facing the Outsider is "how to become a visionary."

Yet men and women who recognize this purpose find no place in modern society; more often than not they are considered abnormal and given medication. "The ideal social discipline is the one that takes fullest account of the men of genius," Wilson writes, but this is not the case today, and the Outsider is evidence of this. Wilson suggests that the church of the Middle Ages was such a social discipline, as were the Hindu, Buddhist, Taoist, and other great churches at their height. Outsiders, people driven by a strong sense of purpose, could find a place within them. But in our secular, humanist society this is no longer so. And this is why our society is in decline. It is "dying from the head downward," meaning that it has lost is aim and purpose, something that the Outsiders could provide.

Wilson asks if a revived Christianity could stop the decline and looks at the development of Christianity in answer. Christ, he said, was a "demagogue-artist" and had "more in common with Hitler than with Ramakrishna."[32] What this ostensibly outrageous statement means is that Christ was more of a man of action than a mystic. There is no evidence in the Gospels for the sentimental view of Jesus, "meek and mild." He did not come to bring peace, but a sword. Jesus's teaching is that "most men are only half-men," and he demanded that they spend all their time trying to become whole. He wanted to make men "more alive, more conscious" and to get "more life and more will out of a great sea of half-dead matter."[33] But as we've seen, the "great sea of half-dead matter"—in other words, the majority of people—cannot accept the burden of becoming more conscious, and Christ's command that men make themselves perfect as their father is perfect (as Matthew 5:48 tells us) is generally lost in favor of the image of a Christ as a sacrifice given up to God to atone for men's sins.

This is the Christ that emerged with Saint Paul; it presents, as Shaw coined it, much more of a "Crosstianity." Instead of urging men to be great, it accepts them as weaklings. (Wilson would maintain a dislike of Saint Paul throughout his career.) When Christ said, "I am the way, the truth, and the life," he meant that in order to be "saved" from a pointless existence one had to live as he lived, struggling to become more alive and conscious, giving up concern for petty, trivial things and devoting one's life to more important matters. Paul changed the meaning of this from "*be like* me" to "*believe in* me" and let everyone off the hook. Such a religion embraces human mediocrity and rejects the evolutionary urge to "be better than our fathers" in favor of the Vicarious Atonement; it is no answer to the Outsider's dilemma. (In different but similar ways, it was against such a lukewarm faith that the Christian Kierkegaard and the anti-

Christian Nietzsche both railed.) Yet the scientific humanism that developed in the seventeenth century and that "freed" man from the dogmas of a church grown more and more worldly and authoritarian (the church of Dostoyevsky's Grand Inquisitor) could offer nothing to satisfy the Outsider either.[34] For Outsiders, the worldview of the scientists is just as inadequate as the worldview of the church. Wilson asks: can the Outsiders create their *own* tradition, and can a civilization be built on it?

Wilson looks at some "rebels" against the church, men filled with Christ's true message and with the will to follow it, but who ran into a wall with the religious authorities. The life and work of Jacob Boehme, Swedenborg, William Law, Blaise Pascal, Kierkegaard, and others are analyzed in light of the Outsider's problem. Boehme, the seventeenth-century Hermetic philosopher about whom I have written elsewhere, had the kind of vision that the Outsider seeks.[35] Looking at sunlight reflected on a pewter dish, Boehme was suddenly made privy to what he called "the signature of things," the "inmost ground or center of the recondite or hidden nature," a vision that he shared with Blake, Ramakrishna, and many other mystics.[36] The experience overwhelmed Boehme and through it he "saw and knew more in one quarter of an hour than if I had spent many years at a university."[37] Boehme then labored to express his vision in words, writing generally impenetrable books couched in an obscure alchemical language. But the gist of his message gets through in his depiction of our world as the battlefield between opposing spiritual forces, and the need to struggle against complacency and laziness. Boehme's emphasis on the will is in line with the Outsider ethos. The human soul is at the center of the battle and Boehme warned away those who did not take this seriously. At the beginning of his first book, *Aurora*, he wrote: "If thou are not a spiritual self-surmounter, then let my book alone. Don't meddle with it, but stick to your usual affairs," advice any Outsider would give to his less driven neighbors.

Analyzing the essence of "the visionary experience," Wilson concludes, "It would seem to be a sense of the multitudinousness of life, a release of energy into the brain." One effect of this is that it "revitalizes all the areas of one's memory. . . . All sorts of other places and other times are revived," another pre-echo of Faculty X. The opposite of this state is boredom and exhaustion, which narrows the brain and produces a sense of being "imprisoned in time."[38] The similarity to Toynbee's experience is clear.

Among his religious examples Wilson includes Bernard Shaw, who he sees as an existentialist in the same way that he does Plato and Goethe. For all three "thought and life" are inseparable. Their works, as Nietzsche said of his own, were "written in blood," meaning that they were not merely works of art or philosophy or literature, but were born out of their struggle to surmount themselves.[39] That Wilson considered himself cut of this cloth is clear in his remark, "I am not necessarily a writer. The moment writing ceases to be a convenient discipline for subduing my stupidity and laziness, I shall give it up and turn to some more practical form."[40] (Clearly it did not cease to be so.) Plato, Goethe, and Shaw were preeminent examples of what Wilson calls the "artist-philosopher," the creative individual who possesses great sensitivity and receptiveness, *and* an incisive power of analysis. Usually an individual has one or the other: there are many great writers who do not think, and many great thinkers who cannot write. "The ideally great existentialist," Wilson writes, "would have the ability to use his will power in analysis, and yet at a moment's notice to become completely negative, transparent and receptive." This implies "complete self-control." Such self-control is part of the "transformation of consciousness" which is at the heart of the religious ideal.

Wilson's chapter on Shaw is one of the longest in the book and for the sake of space cannot be adequately summarized here. In many ways it is a dry run for his complete study, *Bernard Shaw: A Reassessment*, which appeared in 1969. We've already mentioned that Shaw believed that a civilization cannot exist without a religion, without belief in some purpose greater than security and material gain. Along with making the "perennial philosophy" suggestion, Shaw struggled to express his own conception of a religion, or a sense of purpose beyond material comfort, in his creative evolutionist plays *Man and Superman* and *Back to Methuselah*.[41]

Creative Evolution is the title of Henri Bergson's most famous work. It was published in 1907 but the idea that life evolved not through blind, chance mutations and the "survival of the fittest," as strict Darwinians claimed, but through an inherent creative urge or drive to transcend itself had been in the air for some time. Nietzsche expressed a version of it and so did Goethe before him. Contrary to the popular misconception, Darwin did not "discover" evolution, much as Freud did not discover the unconscious: both ideas were around for a long time before Darwin and Freud offered easily grasped "explanations" for them. About Darwin Shaw agreed with his predecessor Samuel Butler that he had "banished mind from the universe." Shaw was determined to bring it back. In *Man and Superman* Shaw's Don Juan says that "as long as I can conceive of something better than myself I cannot be easy unless I am striving to bring it into existence"—the Outsider's urge to be better than his fathers. This was part of Life's "incessant aspiration to higher organisation, wider, deeper, intenser self-consciousness, and clearer self-understanding."

Wilson agrees with Shaw that man is on the threshold of a higher form of life. He adds to this the insight, inspired by Toynbee, that this threshold becomes more apparent and urgent whenever a civilization hits its decline. This is the challenge civilization must face: it must raise its level of consciousness or collapse.

This theme, of a more intense, more serious kind of life, runs through practically all of Shaw's plays, but it reaches a peculiar power in *Back to Methuselah*, in which Shaw's "Ancients" have developed such a power of mental concentration that they have mastered their bodies and can extend their life by centuries. Like Bergson and other creative evolutionists, Shaw believed that spirit and matter were engaged in a long struggle and that eventually the vortex of matter with which the universe began would be transformed into a vortex of pure mind, pure consciousness. The "leak of freedom," mentioned at the end of *The Outsider*, would become a flood. Life will have won its battle to "spiritualize" matter and will have colonized the universe.

This notion of a universe of life was shared by Alfred North Whitehead, an important philosopher who is sadly little read today. Wilson closes the book with an analysis of his work. Whitehead shares the last chapter with another philosopher, Ludwig Wittgenstein, and the differences between the two could not be greater. Whitehead believed that philosophy can omit nothing; in *Modes of Thought* he gives a litany of the states of mind the philosopher must experience: drunk, sober, sleeping, waking, drowsy, wide awake, self-conscious, self-forgetful.[42] Whitehead's aim is philosophy's traditional one of understanding the universe, but his abstract prose obscures the living, immediate quality of his thinking. His is a "philosophy of organism." The universe for him is shot through with life, and the most living thing in it is human consciousness. This places him within Wilson's broader conception of existentialism.

Wittgenstein's approach was much more selective. Rather than widening philosophy so that it leaves nothing out, he wanted to narrow its role, even to eliminate it altogether, as a disease of which one needed to be cured. Wittgenstein's most well-known remark, "What we cannot speak about we must pass over in silence," gave birth to logical positivism and linguistic analysis, two Insider philosophies Wilson rejects.[43] The irony is that Wittgenstein was an Outsider, and his attempts to end philosophy—first in the *Tractatus Logico-Philosophicus* and then, in another way, in the *Philosophical Investigations*—were motivated by the same kind of mental tensions and stress that afflicted T. E. Lawrence. Wittgenstein was as tormented a soul as Lawrence. He was said to have read *The Brothers Karamazov* dozens of times. He gave away his fortune and lived in a hut in Norway. Like other Outsiders Wittgenstein went out of his way to create difficult conditions for himself because, like the others, he knew instinctively that comfortable surroundings are a trap. What he objected to in philosophy was the glib way in which academic philosophers spoke of matters such as truth, religion, and freedom, an exasperation he shared with Kierkegaard. Wittgenstein was a kind of mystic, in the manner of Meister Eckhart; the sheer *is-ness* of things, the mere fact that they exist, was enough to stop him in his tracks. "It is not *how* things are in the world that is mystical," he wrote, "but *that* it exists."[44] That learned Cambridge dons could chatter away about such miracles infuriated him. Wilson's objection is that in turning philosophy into a "language game," Wittgenstein abandoned using the mind to try to understand the problem of how to become a visionary—how, that is, to transform consciousness. In doing so he gave the enemy an effective tool for dismissing the question altogether.[45]

Whitehead's trajectory was in the opposite direction, from Insider to Outsider. He began as an "abstract philosopher" but his philosophical integrity led him to reject this status and to create something like an "existential metaphysics." One of his definitions of philosophy is that it should be a "critique of abstractions," an attempt to return to the felt experience of reality, in all its complexity. What has happened in the modern world, Whitehead argued, is that abstractions have replaced realities. He makes this argument in his important work *Science and the Modern World*, which was published in 1925.

Whitehead says that with the rise of science in the seventeenth century, reality became "bifurcated," which means "split." This split took place when Galileo made his distinction between "primary and secondary characteristics."[46] Primary characteristics are everything that can be scientifically measured, such as solidity, number, extension, shape, and so on. These characteristics are considered "objective"; they exist in reality itself. Secondary characteristics depend on an observer. Color, smell, taste, sound: these are *added* to reality by our minds. They are "subjective," and have no independent reality. They cannot be measured and, for scientific purposes, are unreliable.

Whitehead pointed out that what this amounts to is that for the scientific view, *everything* that is of value to us as human beings experiencing the world *is unreal*. The beauty and awe we experience gazing at a sunset are not real; they are only our *subjective* response to wavelengths of electromagnetic radiation refracted through the earth's atmosphere, which are the true reality. Beauty, awe, and other *qualitative* experiences exist solely in our heads and have no relation to reality, at least to the scientific kind, which is best grasped *quantitatively*. We can measure wavelengths but not awe. Whitehead realized that this is an absurd conclusion, although most scientists hold on to it firmly. With Edmund Husserl, Whitehead saw that such a conclusion actually undermines the pursuit of truth which led to it.

Whitehead's response was to point out that the kinds of facts that science relies on are not the fundamental, "really real" things of existence, as it supposes. Rather they are sophisticated abstractions, highly selective bits and pieces that scientific analysis temporarily *wrenches* out of the whole. Reality, for Whitehead, is one; everything is part of a single organism and our fundamental experience of it is more along the lines of feeling than of thought. But because of the remarkable success of its abstractions we in the modern world have adopted scientific criteria as the only ones that can afford knowledge or truth. Yet our true relationship to reality is much more along the lines of the poets' or mystics'. The world, Whitehead argues, is in reality much more like how Wordsworth or Shelley tell us it is than how Galileo or Descartes do. Poetry is closer to the truth of things than physics. Science's vision leads ultimately to a meaningless universe. For it, "nature is a dull affair, soundless, scentless, colorless; merely the hurrying of material, endlessly, meaninglessly."[47] It is because we have accepted this as the truth that our civilization is, as Toynbee pointed out, heading for collapse.

I have written at length about *Religion and the Rebel* for two reasons. One is to show that *The Outsider* was only the beginning of Wilson's attempt at posing the problems confronting "the heroic figure of our time." The other is to show that it is an important book and deserves to be better known. Unfortunately, when it appeared in October 1957, Victor Gollancz's worst fears were made concrete. Reviews were universally bad. The anti–Angry Young Man and, more specifically, anti–Colin Wilson sentiment had settled in and the critics went out of their way to show that they were well and truly tired of the boy genius. The gist of the reviews can be grasped from *Time* magazine's headline: SCRAMBLED EGG-HEAD. Reviewers such as Philip Toynbee, who had praised *The Outsider*, had an opportunity to make amends for their misjudgment and to show they weren't taken in by this self-promoting upstart. In his review for the *Observer* Toynbee called *Religion and the Rebel* "a deplorable piece of work." It was a "vulgarising rubbish-bin," "inferior," and "deeply depressing." That Toynbee's assessment and virtual recantation was fueled by a desire to show that he would not be "taken for a ride by a kind of mad-dog philosopher" was not lost on some readers.[48] Nevertheless it set the tone, and others followed suit. For the esteemed literary critic Raymond Mortimer, writing in the *Sunday Times*, Wilson was "at his silliest when he dishes out half-baked Nietzsche." A. J. Ayer, whose tepid philosophy was, for Wilson, a sign of the declining times, wrote that Wilson's "signs of megalomania" were "distressingly apparent." Wilson's sparring partner Wolf Mankowitz wrote of "the midget Leicestershire Zarathustra."[49] It was as complete a turnaround from that magnificent May morning eighteen months earlier as one could get.

To some extent Wilson may have been partly responsible for the hatchet jobs. Remarks such as "I find that being regarded as a 'promising young writer,' or attacked as a charlatan or woolly-minded freak, tends to destroy my certainty of purpose" and "The prospect of spending my life trying to make myself worthy of a few pages in *The Cambridge History of English Literature* seems to me a particularly dreary kind of treadmill" were not going to make him many friends among the critics.[50] He was, of course, responding to the negative publicity he had endured for months, and we can forgive him the outburst. His reviewers were less understanding. With few exceptions, this round of scathing reviews set the tone for how the mainstream literary and philosophical world would respond in the next decade and a half to the books that followed. Almost uniformly the books were attacked and the prevailing sense was that Wilson should give up writing, the sooner the better.

Wilson didn't give up writing, although both Gollancz and T. S. Eliot suggested that he put his typewriter aside for a time, find a congenial job, and sit the bad reputation out. Considering that prospect brought on another vastation, and in any case, Wilson was too full of ideas to stop now. Yet he himself felt that for the present he had taken his initial impulse as far as it could go. *Religion and the Rebel* was "not a final solution of the problems" that preoccupied him; in fact it had only increased them. He was confident that he had refuted claims that the Outsider was just a fad, even if doing so meant arguing that Western civilization was on its way out. The conclusion was pessimistic, but Wilson himself had an optimistic outlook. He even felt that the prospects were promising; he detected the hint of an "intellectual revolt" in the air. Yet the responsibility remained with the individual Outsider. The collapse of civilization was not a final end; civilizations had collapsed before. If such was the case, the Outsider can only observe it with "scientific curiosity" and focus his mind on "less immediate problems." Such detachment is the sign of a great optimism. He quotes Yeats's poem "Lapis Lazuli": "All things fall and are built again / And those that build them are gay." This was an expression of the irrational appetite for life, the vitality beyond logic and reason that came to Wilson and to other Outsiders in their moments of vision. For the moment he had gone as far as discursive thought could take him. The aim now was to bring his sense of urgency back into his personal life. The timing was right for that. He would need it for the way that followed.

CHAPTER FIVE

A NEW EXISTENTIALISM

Wilson took the critical bludgeoning of *Religion and the Rebel* remarkably well. He told a reporter that he felt the criticisms were on the whole fair, and that some were even very good.[1] He did write a letter to the *Times Literary Supplement* explaining what he meant by "existentialism"; evidently their reviewer was confused by this. One point he made was that it was clear that "the term 'Outsider' has outworn its usefulness," and he would abandon it. To some degree he had already done this. A week before *Religion and the Rebel* appeared there was a launch party for *Declaration*, an anthology edited by Tom Maschler, in which the Angry Young Men—and one woman—spelled out their credos, what they believed in. Wilson was part of the group, as were Hopkins and Holroyd, as well as Osborne, Wain, Tynan, Doris Lessing, and the filmmaker Lindsay Anderson, later known for the films *If...* and *O Lucky Man!*. *Declaration* sold surprisingly well, twenty-five thousand copies in the first few weeks of publication.

What its readers soon saw was that there was a clear divide between the contributors. Tynan, Osborne, Anderson, and Lessing were all very much on the left of the political spectrum, and their credos all had something to do with focusing on social problems, with changing the system. Wilson, Hopkins, and Holroyd occupied a space much more on the right, although in truth, of the three only Hopkins thought in political terms. But Wilson's and Holroyd's concentration on religious and spiritual issues—changing people rather than the system—distanced them from the more activist contributors. Predictably they were called "reactionaries" by their more socially conscious contemporaries.

Wilson didn't go to the party. He was too busy writing away in Cornwall and was sticking to his aim of steering clear of publicity. His contribution was titled "Beyond the Outsider," a title he would return to a few years later. It was a sign that he recognized that the scope of his analysis was reaching beyond the simple Outsider-or-Insider range of his first book. He pointed out that the vision informing *The Outsider* and *Religion and the Rebel* was personal, a product of his spiritual obsessions. "I happen to be obsessed by certain ideas and I think and care about nothing else," he told the reader.[2] In essence "Beyond the Outsider" summarizes the position Wilson had arrived at with his first two books. Civilization is in decline. The Outsider is a product of this. He celebrates freedom, will, and the imagination over the intellect, logic, and reason. The Outsider is evolution's attempt to create "a higher type of man" and "new unity of purpose"; if this fails, then civilization will slide into the gulf, just as all the previous civilizations that failed the test did.[3]

One new ingredient Wilson brought into the mix was a passage from H. G. Wells's *Experiment in Autobiography*, which he would return to many times over the years. Wells, too, felt that a new kind of man or person was emerging in the twentieth century. As an apostle of science, rationality, and socialism, he could hardly have been accused of being a religious fascist, as Wilson had been. Wells pointed out that "most individual creatures, since life began, have been 'up against it' all the time." Their life was a "continual adjustment to happenings . . . They hungered and ate, and they desired and loved . . . and they died." But with the rise of progress "there has been a progressive emancipation of the attention from everyday urgencies." What used to take up the whole of life has become for many people only its background. "People can ask now what would have been an extraordinary question five hundred years ago. They can say 'Yes, you earn a living, you support a family, you love and hate, but—*what do you do?*'"[4]

For many the immediacies of life no longer command full attention, and a new kind of person, driven by new needs and appetites—for knowledge, for thought, for creative expression, for more vital experience, for self-actualization, as Maslow would call it—is coming to the fore. Wells himself was one of these people, and he complained about the time and effort that dealing with trivialities and mundanities took away from his business as an "originative intellectual worker." Such a person, Wells said, is "not a normal human being and does not lead nor desire to lead a normal human life. He wants to lead a supernormal life."[5]

Wells captures the essence of this development in an evolutionary simile. "We are like early amphibians," he says, "struggling out of the waters that have hitherto covered our kind, into the air, seeking to breathe in a new fashion and emancipate ourselves from long accepted and long unquestioned necessities." But, so far, "the new land has not definitively emerged from the waters and we swim distressfully in an element we wish to abandon." Wells himself says that he does not "in the least desire to live longer unless I can go on with what I consider to be my proper business."[6] This is the Outsider's desire as well; he, too, swims "distressfully in an element" he wishes to abandon. Although Wells and Shaw were often philosophical combatants, with Shaw favoring intuition and religion over Wells's championing of science, in this desire to be free to do their "proper business" they each shared the fundamental urge of all creative individuals to evolve.

Wilson soon got a chance to do his proper business. Before the pummeling he received for *Religion and the Rebel* he had been asked by the British Council to lecture in Oslo. In late November 1957, he and Joy flew to Norway; it was their first flight. At the hotel Wilson was met by a reporter for the *Dagbladet*, one of Norway's leading newspapers. He was surprised when she asked him questions about Sartre and Camus rather than his sex life. He soon realized he had been born in the wrong country. "The British," he concluded, "are incurably trivial-minded," a product, he felt, of their insularity as an island nation.[7] It was not in their nature to produce a Dostoyevsky, a Goethe, a Sartre, or even, perhaps, a Colin Wilson. These men were interested in questions about human destiny but in Britain such concerns were considered the occupation of cranks. The Norwegian journalists, who questioned Wilson about existentialism and literature, more than made up for the malicious titbits about his personal life that he had grown used to.

Wilson lectured in a vast hall at the university. He never used notes, training from his old anarchist days, and he began to spell out the exact difference between his ideas about existentialism and the more well-known brand coming from France. His existentialism was focused on his experiences of meaning. He appreciated Sartre's, Camus', and Heidegger's analyses of human existence but rejected their gloomy conclusions. He did so because on many occasions—a spring morning, while listening to music, or when making love—he became aware of a "sense of *meaning*," which seemed to be inherent in the universe itself. It isn't "put there," in the way Galileo believed that our qualitative experience of the world is somehow inserted into it by our own minds. The meaning is there but for some reason our consciousness is usually too dull to notice it. This meaning gets through in these moments because during them our consciousness somehow *widens*. This suggests that there is something wrong with our consciousness, some inner damper that keeps it at a low level for most of the time, and allows a wider, more intense experience of it only very briefly and infrequently. Although there were plenty of reasons to feel pessimistic—the cold war, the H-bomb, overpopulation—and Wilson's audience brought them up, *this* was why Wilson nevertheless felt an "absurd optimism." It was on this "absurd optimism," what G. K. Chesterton called "absurd good news," that Wilson would begin to build what he called a "new existentialism."

Wilson enjoyed lecturing and having an opportunity to discuss ideas without a word about angry young men. After Oslo he and Joy spent a few weeks in Hamburg, Germany, with Bill Hopkins; Wilson enjoyed that very much too. While there Hopkins read the devastating reviews of his novel *The Divine and the Decay*, which promoted an antidemocratic political agenda. Given the animus against the Angries it isn't surprising that Hopkins received a pummeling equal to Wilson's. While in Hamburg Wilson worked on the new version of *Ritual* and Hopkins worked on his second novel, *Time of Totality*, which, sadly, never saw print. In cafés they often got into discussions with students and Wilson was impressed by the seriousness with which they took ideas.

He had a chance to experience this even more the next year. In 1958 the British Council asked him to do a lecture tour of German universities. Wilson decided to combine business with pleasure and in July he and Joy set out on a camping holiday in Germany. They decided to drive, in order to see some of Europe. His first lecture was in Heidelberg, then Neustadt, then Heidelberg again. Having lunch with a professor of literature—"one of those charming and cultivated Germans that I love"—at a restaurant atop the Königstuhl, a hill overlooking the old university city, Wilson reflected that *this* was the sort of thing he had hoped for from the success of *The Outsider*, not to be hounded by journalists and paparazzi.[8] Other lectures followed, in Tübingen and Freiburg, where Wilson had hoped to meet Heidegger. He was disappointed. Heidegger had taught there but recently had retired and now spent most of his time in his chalet in Todtnauberg, in the Black Forest.

At the end of the trip Wilson did meet with one of the "big three" of existentialism. In August in Paris he spent an afternoon with Albert Camus. Gallimard, the French publisher, had put out an edition of *The Outsider*. Camus supplemented his literary income by working for Gallimard—T. S. Eliot did the same with Faber and Faber—and he had mentioned that he intended to write an introduction to *Religion and the Rebel*, which Gallimard was publishing as well. Wilson had written to Camus, saying that he would be in Paris, and Camus invited him to come to his office. Wilson was surprised when he saw the Nobel Prize–winning author. Although forty-four, Camus looked about thirty and his eyes "danced with liveliness and good humour." Wilson felt he had something of the urchin about him, "as if he was capable of knocking on doors and running away."[9]

Camus spoke to Wilson about a novel he was writing; it was called *The First Man*. Camus said he appreciated Wilson's analysis of his work in *The Outsider*, and their conversation—carried on in simple French; Camus spoke no English—focused on this. Wilson tried to express some reservations about Camus' conclusions, in as polite terms as possible, linking his thoughts to his own ideas about a "new existentialism." Although he did not say so openly, he felt that, like Sartre and Heidegger, Camus had reached a dead end. His ultimate vision seemed to be of a kind of stoicism: man must make the best of living in a meaningless universe. As Camus says in *The Myth of Sisyphus*, we must imagine Sisyphus happy.[10] But Wilson's own experiences of meaning seem to contradict this. Wilson suggested that Camus himself spoke of such experiences in different places in his work. One occurs at the end of *The Stranger*, when Meursault, facing execution, realizes he "had been happy, and was happy still" and opens his heart to "the benign indifference of the universe." A similar peak experience comes at the end of his story "The Woman Taken in Adultery," when the heroine experiences a kind of mystical unity with the African night.

Camus acknowledged Wilson's point, but when Wilson suggested that such experiences might show the way out of despair and "absurdity," Camus demurred. Anything smacking of religion or mysticism was suspect to him. He looked out the window and pointed to a Parisian equivalent of the teddy boys who loitered in Notting Hill. "What is good for him must be good for me also," he told Wilson.

To Wilson, this solidarity with the man in the street was as absurd as anything Camus ever wrote. It made no sense to reject the evidence of mystical experience, he told Camus, simply because such experiences were outside the range of the ordinary man. Wilson compared the situation to Einstein's theory of relativity: should it not have been created because the man in the street would never understand it? Camus disagreed and given his lack of English and Wilson's basic French the discussion could go no further.

Even without the language barrier it is difficult to see where they could have agreed. He and Wilson corresponded for a time but they never met again. On January 4, 1960, Camus was killed when the car he was driving in with Michel Gallimard skidded off the road and crashed into a tree. Camus wasn't wearing a seat belt and was thrown through the rear window and died instantaneously; Michel Gallimard survived the crash but died of a brain hemorrhage five days later. *The First Man* was never finished—it did not appear in print until 1994—and Camus had not got around to writing an introduction to the French edition of *Religion and the Rebel*. Camus' death, though tragic, was, Wilson thought, strangely absurd. In an essay on Camus written many years later, Wilson wondered what effect Camus' womanizing—he was a notorious skirt chaser—had had on his creativity. Was the sense of futility, of reaching a dead end, that Wilson detected in Camus' work related to his rootless existence, living in hotel rooms, ignoring his wife, and pursuing practically every attractive woman he met?[11]

In early 1959 their tenure at Old Walls was up and Colin and Joy had to find another place to live. While Wilson worked on the new version of *Ritual*, Joy went house hunting. In February she found a place in Gorran Haven, a nearby village. The price was high, around five thousand pounds, and Joy felt the house was far too big for their needs. Wilson disagreed. On hearing that the place was big he said, "Good—lots of room for books and records." His collection was expanding at an alarming rate. More than once Victor Gollancz expressed concern that he was spending far too much money; along with books and records, Wilson's taste in food and wine had also been inspired by his success. The house, named Tetherdown, was a bungalow made of green concrete blocks and was not much to look at. But a long lane led up to it, and it included a large greenhouse and chalet. Plenty of undeveloped land surrounded it and from the front windows one could see the English Channel. If they could raise the money, Wilson said they would get it.

In mid-May they moved into their new home. Wilson would live there for the rest of his life and Joy continues to live there today. For a time Wilson's parents lived there as well. They had enjoyed their holidays at Old Walls, and the idea of escaping Leicester altogether was appealing. But his father found it difficult to adjust to the change in pace and wound up spending far too much time in the local pubs. Wilson joined him on some evenings, but quickly felt doing so was a waste of time; he much preferred being home listening to music and reading. Eventually, after six months, his parents decided to return to Leicester.

Wilson's father had worked all his life and the sudden free time that living in Cornwall provided was too much for him. Without the purpose provided by work, he had no idea of what to do with himself, and could not generate an inner purpose to give him some direction. In this Wilson's father was not exceptional. Wilson often quotes Sartre's line from *Nausea* about a café owner: "When his café empties, his head empties too." Most human beings are little more than a reflection of their surroundings and need input from the outside world to motivate them. Without such input, we tend to break down, as experiments in sensory deprivation have shown. Gurdjieff said that human beings could not exist for more than few seconds without "impressions," without being "fed" by stimulus from the outer world.[12] A human being who could motivate himself without the need of being stimulated by something outside would have taken an important step toward the next stage in human evolution—would, in fact, be acting out of true free will. This was a theme Wilson would turn to some years later in his espionage novel *The Black Room* (1971).

With mortgage payments and other bills, not to mention Wilson's insatiable appetite for books and records, their financial situation settled into a state that might be called "permanent overdraft," a status, according to Wilson's calculations, that he maintained throughout his career. As is the case with most writers, money arrived in spurts, and was usually just enough, just in time. The panning *Religion and the Rebel* received affected its sales; they were nothing like those for *The Outsider*. Gollancz had finally accepted *Ritual* in its new version and had advanced Wilson a much needed five hundred pounds. Wilson told his American agent that he should ask Houghton Mifflin for a five-thousand-dollar advance on their edition, a much larger sum than for his previous books. It was welcome news when he heard they had agreed.

Although Wilson was eager to leave the Angry Young Men behind, the year before he had agreed to contribute to a joint effort with Hopkins and Holroyd. This would be a book about the loss of the hero in contemporary culture. They had decided to do this because they were unhappy with *Declaration*. The book sold well, but it only provided the critics with another opportunity to bash the

Angries; on top of that, many of the "left" contributors turned it into a chance to attack their "right-wing" adversaries. Wilson, Hopkins, and Holroyd decided that they would make a statement of what they really stood for. Holroyd would approach the problem through religion, Hopkins through politics, and Wilson through literature.

By mid-1958, Wilson had written his section of the book, but Hopkins and Holroyd hadn't even started theirs. Wilson had been writing nonstop since his teens and the seclusion of Cornwall, away from all the angry young groupies, allowed him to focus on a project exclusively. This meant that he had developed a fluency that allowed him to write a book in a few months. He sent his section off to Gollancz, who said he would be happy to publish it on its own. Hopkins and Holroyd didn't mind. Hopkins was always a better talker than writer, much more a man of action. Reflecting on the time many years later, Holroyd wrote that he was "less resilient to criticism than [Wilson], and had less conviction of my own genius and less single-mindedness in pursuing its development."[13] Holroyd's second book, *Flight & Pursuit*, a kind of spiritual autobiography, was published by Gollancz in 1959, to little acclaim and much abuse. Another autobiography, *Contraries*, appeared in 1977.

In 1959 Wilson's contribution to the "hero book" appeared as *The Age of Defeat*; the title of the American edition was changed to *The Stature of Man* by Houghton Mifflin, who wanted something more "upbeat." Reviews were critical and sales minimal but by now Wilson was getting used to this response. The theme of the book is "the fallacy of insignificance," the notion, spread by modern science, literature, philosophy, psychology, and politics, that the individual has very little control over his life and destiny, and that, in the end, he can't win.

Not surprisingly, Wilson rejected this view. He expresses his own perspective with a quotation from Louis-Claude de Saint-Martin, the nineteenth-century Hermetic thinker who wrote under the pseudonym "the Unknown Philosopher." Saint-Martin argued that men "have believed themselves to be obeying the dictates of humility when they have denied that the earth and all that the universe contains exists only on man's account, on the ground that the admission of such an idea would be only conceit. *But they have not been afraid of the laziness and cowardice which are the inevitable results of this affected modesty.*" Saint-Martin, who wrote during the Romantic revolution, believed that man is really a kind of sleeping god, and Wilson felt much the same. Laziness and cowardice are the result of the fallacy of insignificance common to the age. And although the Outsider is "the heroic figure of our time," Wilson was determined to steer clear of using the term, and he makes no appearance in the book.

Oddly enough, Wilson begins *The Age of Defeat* with a look at developments in American society. A central theme of the book is the contrast between "inner direction" and "other direction" that the Harvard sociologist David Riesman examined in *The Lonely Crowd* (cowritten with Nathan Glazer and Reuel Denney and published in 1950). With William H. Whyte's *The Organization Man* (1956) and Vance Packard's *The Hidden Persuaders* (1957), Riesman's work is an analysis of the trend in American society away from the individual and toward the group, either the business organization or society in general. The trend, which began after World War II, is toward an obsession with keeping up with the Joneses, with being overly aware and overly concerned about what the neighbors think, what they buy, what they do, and how they live, and the loss of self-confidence and belief in one's own choices that comes with this.

Consumerism, "hot" religion in the form of the evangelist Billy Graham, an obsession with film stars and other celebrities, and a general trend toward conformity, fitting in, and being a "good team player": these and other modes of "other direction" were characteristic of 1950s America, and Wilson believed that its influence was quickly spreading to Britain. One aspect of his analysis that warrants closer examination is the link between other direction and violence. An increasing emphasis on our individual "insignificance" is often accompanied by a growing resentment toward the anonymous powers that control our lives. In some, this resentment can reach dangerous levels, and the need for release, to assert one's being, becomes urgent. As Wilson writes, "It would seem that there is something about a life lived on a general level of 'insignificance' that makes for outbreaks of violence."

This aimless revolt "will tend to express itself as a defiance of taboos, a deliberate contravention of laws, in a crime of violence or a sexual offence."[14] The less we are able to be our full selves in creative, productive ways, the more the inherent need for self-expression will find release through sudden acts of transgression. As Blake said long ago, "When thought is closed in caves, then love will show its roots in deepest Hell." A society that denies individuality and emphasizes conformity will produce dangerous elements on either side of the mean: criminals and Outsiders (my use).

Wilson recognized that there have been revolts against conformity. The Angry Young Men were one, as was the Beat Generation. But the Angries kept their sights relatively low; their "rebellion," as exemplified in John Osborne's *Look Back in Anger*, amounted to little more than a temper tantrum. The Beats went further but, for Wilson, still fall short of what is needed. They achieved "vigour at the expense of content."[15] Like the Angries, the Beats knew what they didn't like and said so energetically, but had little to put in its place. Yet even their name suggests defeat. They were "beat," beaten by the system. That certain aspects of what we might call "Beat philosophy" skirt very close to criminality—and often cross the line—is an example of what Wilson means by "defiance of taboos and deliberate contravention of laws." That such transgressive behavior still attracts people to the Beats—and to other transgressive characters such as Aleister Crowley—suggests that the problem of a positive alternative to conformity still remains.[16]

Wilson expands Riesman's other direction beyond the limits of sociology. He sees it in metaphysical, existential terms as a philosophical conviction that human existence is pointless and that man is ultimately defeated. It is this assumption, rife in the twentieth century, that informs the fallacy of insignificance and is responsible for the decline of the hero in modern culture. Compared to the literature and philosophy of the nineteenth century, modern thinking has decidedly lowered its expectations. We lack the kind of metaphysical hero that Goethe's Faust or Melville's Ahab embodied, and we are content with "the cult of the ordinary chap" and a literature that depicts life realistically, rather than attacking it in order to uncover its meaning.

Wilson's analysis of the "vanishing hero" is part of what he calls "existential criticism," an attempt to apply the methods of existential analysis to literature, a methodology he used in other works of literary criticism such as *The Strength to Dream* (1962), *Eagle and Earwig* (1965, a collection of essays), and *The Craft of the Novel* (1975). It forms a part of his "new existentialism." Fundamentally he was concerned with uncovering the philosophical assumptions that inform the work of various writers. This form of criticism focuses less on what the writers in question explicitly *say*, their beliefs, and their technical ability than on how they *see* the world and how they present it to their readers. As Wilson writes, "The existential critic challenges the author's overall sense of life."[17]

In writers such as Graham Greene, for example, who presents himself as an honest, serious author, telling his readers what life is really like, without romance or illusion, Wilson detects an undercurrent of pessimism that distorts the facts in favor of Greene's rather sour assessment of things. The "reality" a reader discovers in Greene's books is one seen through a rather jaundiced lens, but unless she were aware of this, the reader would accept Greene's vision of a rather grim and sordid world as objective, and would view Greene's response— a highly sin-conscious Catholicism—as understandable, even acceptable. A similar literary sleight of hand is at work in other writers. In Aldous Huxley, Wilson recognizes a voice "for sanity and human dignity in a world that has increasingly become like a nightmare."[18] Yet in Huxley's fiction Wilson nevertheless detects assumptions about human defeat that for him abet the fallacy of insignificance. Wilson argues that in novels such as *Point Counter Point* (1928) and *Eyeless in Gaza* (1936) Huxley presents a dichotomy that runs throughout his fiction, between intelligent characters who are weak and ineffectual and strong men who are brainless, a split shared by other writers, such as Thomas Mann.[19] Wilson asks: are no intelligent *and* effective human beings possible? Must intelligence and sensitivity produce the chinless Huxleyan hero, or can a new kind of hero, intelligent and sensitive but not defeated by the world, be imagined?

The main target of Wilson's criticism is the "old" existentialism of Sartre, Camus, and Heidegger, with its assumptions about the meaninglessness of existence. More than the social pressures of conformity, this has led to the prevalence of the fallacy of insignificance in our age. Wilson's criticism is existential in that it is aimed at a writer's take on existence. Sartre's uncovering of human self-deception is laudable and his ferreting out of the many ways in which we embrace "bad faith" warrants praise, but his conclusion that "man is a useless passion" is at least debatable.[20] As with Camus, Wilson believes Sartre leaves out the evidence of mystical experience, the "affirmative and irrational mysticism" that he finds in writers such as Blake, Whitman, Yeats, Shaw, even James Joyce.[21] This is the "absurd good news" that Chesterton speaks of, the sudden yea-saying and conviction that all is good that can be found in Nietzsche and Dostoyevsky, both of whom were profoundly aware of the pain and suffering of life. The meaning of "existential" is "relating to existence," "grounded in existence or experience," as more than one dictionary tells me. As such "affirmative mysticism" exists, it certainly falls under the heading of "existential" and should be taken into consideration when any overall assessments of life, reality, or existence are being made.

As with Camus, Sartre himself speaks of such moments, although to be sure they are rarer with him than with Camus. Because of his love of the physical world, Camus is closer to the poet than Sartre, for whom the physical world was repugnant. Yet in *Nausea*, a novel that depicts the fallacy of insignificance with brutal effect, Sartre does speak of moments when the nausea vanishes and his antihero feels it "unbearable to become so hard, so brilliant," when his body feels like "a precision machine." (It happens when he is listening to a recording of the song "Some of These Days.") Yet in his overall assessment of reality and of human life within it, Sartre excludes these moments and after *Nausea* they no longer appear in his work.

After his own mystical experience, William James, an existential thinker who knew about insignificance as much as Sartre did, concluded that "our normal waking consciousness, rational consciousness as we call it, is but one special type of consciousness." James saw that all around our everyday consciousness there were other "potential forms of consciousness entirely different. . . . No account of the universe in its totality," he argued, "can be final which leaves these other forms of consciousness quite disregarded."[22] James's remarks were aimed at the "tough-minded" reductionist scientists of his day, but they can easily be applied to Sartre and Camus.[23] In their "account of the universe in its totality" they do leave these "other forms of consciousness quite disregarded."

Exactly why they do would be the focus of Wilson's analysis. For the moment, with James, Wilson was determined not to leave them out. In fact he made them the center of his philosophy, his new existentialism. They form the "positive content" that the old existentialism lacks.

In February 1960 *Ritual in the Dark* finally appeared. Wilson had worked on it for eleven years and he was pleased with the finished product, which was very different from the more modernist style in which it had been first conceived. Edith Sitwell, who had praise for *The Outsider*, gave it an excellent review in the *Sunday Times* and the book critic for the *Sunday Express* said, "Not since Dickens had anyone dealt with murder in a novel of this size and seriousness." But Wilson was not yet back in from the cold. The review in the *Observer* was scathing and went out of its way to mention "the odious *Outsider*." But the American edition, which was released at the same time, sold remarkably well and Wilson's career as a novelist had begun.

The success was welcome, as were the sales. In January Joy had announced that she was pregnant. Wilson had some misgivings; his first attempt at being a father hadn't fared that well. But in August, when Sally, his second child, was born, all apprehension vanished. He "adored her from the moment she appeared," as he did the two sons Joy would later have. Fatherhood was "a marvellous experience." Wilson was fond of saying he was a "typical Cancer," who loved his home and his family. "I was undoubtedly made for family life." The media thought so too. The paparazzi had not yet given up on the self-proclaimed genius and when Joy arrived home from the hospital she found that a photographer from the *Daily Mail* had asked to take a picture of the new arrival. She declined to be snapped but Wilson proudly held his new daughter up for the camera. The headline read, ANGRY YOUNG MAN HOLDS PLACID YOUNG GIRL.[24]

The interest with murder that informed *Ritual in the Dark* did not end with that novel. At a party thrown by the journalist Dan Farson, by then a television personality, Wilson got the idea of writing an "encyclopaedia of murder," something that hadn't been done before. Earlier he had been introduced to Robert Pitman, a journalist for the *Sunday Express*, by the novelist John Braine, with whom he shared his pied-à-terre in Notting Hill.[25] Pitman's wife, Pat, shared Wilson's interest in crime and at Farson's party Wilson was trying to remember the address of Dr. Crippen, the center of a famous British murder case. He asked Pat and she had it exactly. Wilson decided on the spot she would be an excellent collaborator. For the next year they worked together on their *Encyclopaedia of Murder*.

Wilson's interest in crime was as existential as his interest in literature. His central concern was what light a study of murder can throw upon our sense of values. "Murder," he writes in his introduction, "is the meaninglessness of life become dynamic, a dramatization of the hidden futility of life. It is the human act, with all its inherent values, placed upon the microscope slide where it cannot dissolve into the featureless landscape of all other human acts."[26] In *The Age of Defeat* Wilson had written that "man is free all the time, but he confronts his freedom only at long intervals."[27] Meaning that our indifference threshold prevents us from recognizing our freedom as a reality, and it is only in moments of crisis that we become aware of it. The criminal or murderer is only someone in whom the indifference threshold has risen higher than in the rest of us; he is even less aware of freedom as a reality than his law-abiding fellows. The essential triviality of the murderer's values highlights our own trivial values. A murderer throws away human life—his victim's and his own—often for the sake of a few pounds or dollars. Yet our own sense of the value of life is usually not much greater.

In *Crime and Punishment*, another crime thriller shot through with existentialism, Dostoyevsky's Raskolnikov reflects that for someone condemned to death, the idea of standing on a narrow ledge on a high cliff, in utter darkness and solitude, with the ocean below and amid terrible storms, is infinitely preferable to irreversible annihilation. When we are confronted with the prospect of sudden nothingness, life under any conditions seems self-evidently better. Dostoyevsky himself experienced such an indubitable awareness of the *absolute value* of life when, at the last minute, he was reprieved from execution in the Semyonovsky Square in Saint Petersburg, Russia, and this experience informed all his work. The English man of letters Dr. Johnson once quipped that "when a man knows he is to be hanged in a fortnight, it concentrates the mind wonderfully."

Such a man, like Dostoyevsky, has faced a crisis that has removed his indifference threshold entirely, and he is suddenly aware of the real value of life, something that usually escapes us. Wilson's idea of the hero is precisely of someone with this enormous "appetite for freedom, a desire to live more intensely."[28] Yet who among us can muster this appreciation of the absolute value of life at will? Who among us has not felt like throwing it all away because of some trouble or problem that we later recognized as essentially trivial? Who among us would not choose annihilation over eternal storm, darkness, and solitude?

"It is precisely this knowledge of the value of life," Wilson writes, "that the murderer lacks. But we all lack it to some extent. . . . The murderer is different from other human beings in degree, not kind." All our values are relative; the murderer "simply goes further than most people in substituting his own convenience for absolute values."[29] Wilson even detects that in the twentieth century, a new kind of murder has arisen, one aimed precisely at breaking through the indifference threshold, a dark result of the lack of inner direction and the fallacy of insignificance, as well as an example of the kind of defiance of taboos mentioned earlier. Such individuals have so dim a sense of their own reality that it is only by striking out at society in some sudden violent act that they can briefly experience some sense of their own being.

It was through Bob and Pat Pitman that in the summer of 1960, Wilson and a very pregnant Joy went on a cruise to Leningrad, a curious vacation spot during the Cold War. The other tourists included John Braine, about whom Wilson tells quite a few anecdotes, chiefly surrounding his problems with drink.[30] The fare was very low—perhaps the Russians were hoping to increase their tourism—and the ship, the *Bore II*, was brand-spanking-new and smelled of fresh paint. Wilson, however, was not keen on travel; he thought that people who go in for it are empty-headed; and at every port, including Copenhagen and Stockholm, he made for the nearest bookshop, which usually stocked some American paperbacks. At Gdansk, in Poland, while everyone went out to explore the city, he stayed on board and read science fiction.

When he did deign to put down his book and see the sights, Wilson was interviewed as a representative of the Angries, as was John Braine. But not in Leningrad. Here he was studiously ignored. Braine's novel *Room at the Top* was mistakenly seen as an attack on capitalism, a misconception Braine did nothing to clarify. It sold many copies and earned him many rubles and he was feted by the press. Wilson thought the lack of interest in him was because no one had heard of *The Outsider*. It was only later that he learned that the day before they arrived *Pravda* had run an article attacking Wilson and Camus as decadent western writers. The article was supposedly written under Khrushchev's guidance. Given this, no writer or critic in Russia would dare to give Wilson more than a polite nod. He also discovered that Dostoyevsky, who featured prominently in *The Outsider*, was considered persona non grata in the Soviet Union. He and Joy had, with some difficulty, managed to find the palace of Prince Felix Yusupov, where the "holy devil" Rasputin had been murdered in 1916. Wilson would write a book about him, *Rasputin and the Fall of the Romanovs* (1964), presenting Rasputin as an Outsider and accepting the reality of his "healing powers." But when Wilson asked their guide how they could find where Dostoyevsky had lived, he was surprised at the reaction. The guide said he didn't know, and he tried to dissuade them from looking for it. Their interest in such people from prerevolutionary Russia was odd. In the glorious Soviet republic, Dostoyevsky was no longer read.

The early sixties saw much travel for Wilson. Not long after his return from Russia he headed to the United States. The reason for his trip was financial. For Wilson "the 1960s was a decade of unremitting work to stay out of debt."[31] His concentration was so fixed on his typewriter during that decade that years later, when he was asked to write an article about the sixties, he had to confess that they had passed him by. "I had to admit that I had not noticed them—I had been too busy working to keep my bank manager happy."[32] Even with the American sales of *Ritual in the Dark*, it was a struggle to keep solvent. So when, in the spring of 1961, an American poet friend who had arranged Dylan Thomas's American tours advised Wilson on how he could tour there himself, Wilson jumped at the chance. His friend suggested contacting the Institute of Contemporary Arts, in Washington, D.C. Wilson did, and in September 1961, he was off on his first trip to the United States.

It would turn out to be a grueling ten-week endurance test, punctuated with meetings with some notable individuals, and attempts at clarifying his ideas about a new existentialism. Even at the start, Wilson had an interesting encounter. In New York, he stayed at the Algonquin Hotel—famous for habitués such as Dorothy Parker and Alexander Woollcott—and saw that Graham Greene was staying there too. Wilson was critical of Greene's work, but it seemed a waste not to meet him, so he left a note for him at the desk. Later that evening his telephone rang. It was Greene, inviting him to his room for a drink. On the way, Wilson realized that he had applied some astringent existential criticism to Greene in *The Strength to Dream*, which would be published the next year, and felt a bit sheepish about this. On entering Greene's room, he confessed and said he would send Greene a proof copy of the book, so he could read it and make any replies. Greene told him not to worry and to send him a copy when it was published. Wilson's misgivings about Greene's work weren't allayed by their meeting, but he did have an interesting time. Greene struck him as a typical product of British public schools—rather different from American ones—but Wilson was fascinated by his account of New York curio shops, where one could purchase "ghastly relics," like the mummified hand of a dead airman.

Another meeting at the Algonquin was with the actor Robert Shaw, who was then appearing in an off-Broadway production of Harold Pinter's *The Caretaker*. He would later play the assassin in the second James Bond film, *From Russia with Love*, and come to fame as the hard-bitten—literally—shark fisherman in *Jaws*.

Wilson's notoriety preceded him and he was still a familiar face. He was surprised when in a public men's room in Greenwich Village someone asked if he was Colin Wilson. But the pleasures of fame were soon obscured by the hard work of doing a lecture tour. In Washington he spoke at colleges and universities, where he was introduced as a "high school dropout" who had beaten the odds and achieved success. *The Outsider* had been a best seller in the States and although the critical turnaround had reached here too, Wilson found himself surrounded by young Outsiders of all kinds, enthusiastic about his work. He enjoyed the positive response, much as he had in Norway and Germany, but an instinct in him stopped him from taking it for granted. The admiration was delightful, especially that of the young female students, but Wilson knew that his real work was in Cornwall, at his typewriter. It would be some time, though, before he got back to it.

One of the problems of being popular on campus was that he rarely had time to himself. If he went for a meal after a long lecture and Q and A session, troops of students would follow him, and he wound up giving another lecture in the restaurant. In order to get a bit of free time, at Georgetown University, Wilson sat in on a lecture by the existential theologian Paul Tillich. Tillich was very popular in the 1960s—books such as *The Courage to Be* were widely discussed—and he was a familiar face at Esalen, California's "alternative think tank," where Wilson himself would soon lecture. Wilson was grateful for the free time but couldn't understand why the lecture room was packed. Tillich, he felt, was a poor speaker, who addressed his audience in very abstract language.

In Lexington, Virginia, Wilson had a taste of what would become a recurring theme of the tour: the after-lecture party. Standing around with a drink in his hand, being introduced to Professor So-and-So's wife and repeatedly being asked how he liked America became a kind of torture, and he could see why Dylan Thomas had succumbed. Midway through the tour, these faculty parties had melded into one, with the result that Wilson found himself switching on his automatic pilot—what he would later call "the robot"—in order to get through them. The problem with this, he would come to see, is that it tends to allow our energies to "leak," which in turn produces a distinct feeling of "life failure," the boredom and apathy that erode our sense of values. Drink or sex can stimulate us temporarily, but after their first effects, we are back where we started—even worse, because we can soon become dependent on them to bring us back to life. The key, Wilson soon learned, was to somehow stop the leaking.

One exceptional meeting happened in California, where Wilson lectured at Long Beach College. Soon after *The Outsider* had appeared, Wilson met the novelist Christopher Isherwood at a party given by the poet Stephen Spender. Wilson liked Isherwood and he kept in touch with him.[33] Isherwood had moved to America at the start of World War II—he was back in London at the time of the party—and was then living in Santa Monica, just outside Los Angeles. Wilson had written to him, saying he would be in the area, and one day at the college, he got a message that Isherwood had called. Wilson called back and arranged a visit. Almost immediately afterward he got another call. This time it was Henry Miller, whose rollicking sexual exploits in books such as *Tropic of Cancer* had only recently become available in America, after being banned for decades. The books sold well and at age seventy Miller experienced financial security for the first time in his life. He said he would like to meet Wilson and was willing to come to Long Beach. But when Wilson realized that Miller lived in Pacific Palisades, next door to Santa Monica, he suggested that Miller meet him at Isherwood's.

When Wilson arrived at Isherwood's—a lecturer at the college had offered to drive him there—Isherwood announced that he had got a call from "that dreadful bore Henry Miller" and that Miller was coming over.[34] Isherwood hadn't met Miller, but he didn't like his books. Wilson wasn't thrilled with them either, although they shared an interest in Hermann Hesse and Gurdjieff.[35] And as Isherwood had arranged to take Wilson to visit Aldous Huxley, who lived in the Hollywood Hills, and then to see the actor Charles Laughton, Wilson realized that it might have been a mistake to invite Miller along. When the doorbell rang and Miller appeared with his fourteen-year-old son, Tony, it was too late to change plans.

There was some initial awkwardness, prompted by some mild existential criticism when Wilson asked Miller if he had put the "dirty bits" into his books in order to please foreign tourists. Miller had first been published by the Olympia Press, in Paris, who also published the pornography written by the *Merlin* crowd. Miller objected to Wilson's "head knowledge" and pointed to his solar plexus as his source of inspiration. Yet Miller proved to be disarmingly charming and on the way to Huxley's in Isherwood's car, they talked shop, as most writers do.

It turned out that Huxley and Miller had met years ago and were happy to renew their acquaintance. Wilson writes, "Miller was then seventy, Huxley was three years younger, but it was Huxley who seemed the older man." Huxley was almost blind and spoke like a professor; Miller bounced "with a kind of happy vitality, like a friendly puppy."[36] Wilson tried to talk to Huxley about his existential criticism—they had been corresponding about it for some time and sadly Wilson says their letters were somehow lost. Wilson may have tired the saintly Huxley, and we can imagine that his conversation was something of a lecture— after weeks of honing his ideas down so that students could absorb them, he likely ran them off at a clip. Huxley was then focused on overpopulation, something he had written about in *Brave New World Revisited*, one of his last books, and most likely wasn't that interested in hearing about what was wrong with his chinless heroes. Miller, though, seemed impressed, and told Wilson that he had never heard anyone talk like that before.

Huxley died on November 22, 1963, on the same day as C. S. Lewis and, more famously, President Kennedy. Charles Laughton, whom Wilson met that evening, with his wife, Elsa Lanchester (of *Bride of Frankenstein* fame), died in 1962. Laughton turned out to be well read and highly intelligent—a rarity, Wilson remarks, in actors—and he told stories about Bertolt Brecht, Thomas Mann, and H. G. Wells. Elsa Lanchester told a story of how Wells, as great a womanizer as Camus, had once made a pass at her. Most likely Wells didn't know she was lesbian, a fact that came to light only after Laughton's death. He was homosexual and the two had a marriage of convenience.

Wilson's California adventure was the highlight of the tour. In spite of his best efforts, it tired him. And when he discovered that he would have to pay several hundred dollars in American taxes, it all seemed something of a joke. He came back to England with little more than what he had left with. But not quite. The need to focus his ideas so that he could communicate them clearly and effectively to different audiences had led to a sharper grasp of exactly what he was doing. He was, he saw, really talking about a leap forward in human evolution. This was something he had already hinted at in *The Strength to Dream*, a study of the imagination in literature, and part of his existential criticism.

The Strength to Dream is most remembered today for Wilson's treatment of the American pulp horror fiction writer H. P. Lovecraft. As he did with Hermann Hesse and Gurdjieff, Wilson took Lovecraft seriously well ahead of his later popularity. Wilson first came across Lovecraft in 1959, when he found a collection of Lovecraft's stories, *The Outsider and Others*, while staying at a friend's farm in Dorset. Understandably, the title intrigued him. Lovecraft died in poverty in 1937 at the age of forty-six. Most of his writing appeared in the 1920s and '30s in the magazine *Weird Tales*, and were it not for the efforts of August Derleth, he would have remained in obscurity after his death. Derleth, a prolific writer himself, established the Arkham House press in order to give Lovecraft's work the dignity of hardcovers; the name came from the fictional New England town in Lovecraft's stories peculiarly prone to "eldritch" evils, "eldritch" being one of Lovecraft's favorite adjectives (it means "weird" or "ghostly"). By the late 1960s and early '70s, Lovecraft had gone from being a half-forgotten pulp hack to having practically everything he had written in print, and he was being compared to Jorge Luis Borges and Franz Kafka, a development for which Wilson can take some credit.

Fans (I'm one myself) of Lovecraft's "Cthulhu Mythos" stories about an ancient race of extraterrestrial creatures that once ruled the earth recognize his eccentric genius, but for others he is an atrocious writer, given to hyperbole and overstatement. Wilson recognized these faults, but he also saw Lovecraft as one of his Outsiders, and in his weird fiction he saw an "assault on rationality" and an expression of Romantic "world rejection." Lovecraft's aim to terrify his readers was, Wilson believed, really an attack on modern civilization. He would later soften his criticisms of Lovecraft, but here he sees him as a literary equivalent of Peter Kürten, the Düsseldorf murderer who spent "days in solitary confinement . . . conjuring up sexual-sadistic fantasies."[37]

Derleth read the book, and remarks like these led him to challenge Wilson to write a Lovecraft story himself. Wilson accepted and produced *The Mind Parasites*, one of his most well-known novels, which Derleth published in 1967.[38] Here Wilson used Lovecraftian themes to present ideas about human consciousness that he had by this time developed in what he called his "Outsider Cycle." We have already looked at the first three books in the cycle, *The Outsider, Religion and the Rebel*, and *The Age of Defeat*. *The Strength to Dream* was the next.

Jumping ahead a bit, we can say that in the form of a gripping science-fiction horror story about psychic vampires living in the mind, *The Mind Parasites* presents the vastations and life failure that defeated the Outsiders of the nineteenth century and which Wilson recognized needed to be overcome in order for human consciousness to evolve. The heroes of the novel free themselves of the psychic parasites that have been feeding on human vitality for centuries and in the process become aware of mental powers that transform them into something more than human. Or rather they become "fully human," since for Wilson what we take to be the human standard is really something far below our true capabilities. Wilson followed up with another Lovecraftian work, *The Philosopher's Stone* (1969), which many see as his best novel, about the visionary potential of the brain, written in advance of the "split-brain" fascination of the 1980s. *The Space Vampires* (1976), about extraterrestrials who live by sucking the "life force" from others, is in the same Lovecraftian vein.

The Strength to Dream argues that the way to this kind of evolution is through the imagination. Wilson applies existential criticism to a host of writers—W. B. Yeats, J. R. R. Tolkien, Oscar Wilde, and Samuel Beckett among them—and examines how their use of the imagination embodies their values. He criticizes writers who retreat from the world and try to create an alternative one in its place: Yeats with his early poetry about an escape to "fairy land" because "the world's more full of weeping than you can understand," Lovecraft with his ancient extraterrestrial monsters. Yet he is also critical of writers who feel their job is solely to depict the world realistically, which for Wilson means to relate to it as a "static observer."[39] For Wilson, "No matter how detached and uncommitted an artist pretends to be, he is involved in a world whose direction is as positive as the current of a river. . . . It is impossible to exercise the imagination," he writes, "and not to be involved in this current." This current, he argues, is the "need for a supra-personal purpose . . . the evolutionary drive."[40]

"Every work of fiction that has ever been written," Wilson believes, "is somehow obscurely concerned with the problem of how men should live."[41] Wilson himself had already answered that question: men should live in such a way that it furthers the widening of consciousness, the lowering of their indifference threshold, and the perception of the absolute value of life. The artist who, in the service of realism, simply portrays life as it is fails to do this. This was Wilson's argument against Camus. "The artist," he insists, "has to recognize himself not merely as being able to see the world, but as also being able to *alter his perception* of it." Man, he says, "has a *will to perceive* as well as perceptions." And as Wilson discovered during his own "mystical" experiences, "perceptions can be adjusted like the range on a telescope."[42] When the artist recognizes this, then "the value of life ceases to be . . . limited by the consciousness and physical aims of the individual." Instead it becomes "a function of the limitless realm of the intellect and imagination, of the creative will."[43] "Artistic development," Wilson concludes, "is associated with certain 'evolutionary preoccupations'" with the "meaning of human life and the destiny of man."[44] That destiny, Wilson believes, lies in the evolution of consciousness.

Wilson was discovering that furthering that destiny would not be easy. On his return from America he immediately began work on the last two books in the Outsider Cycle, *Origins of the Sexual Impulse* (1963) and *Beyond the Outsider* (1965); he completed both within the first few months of 1962. Wilson worked fast "because my brain was seething with ideas." He had got used to his books being ignored by the critics, and a book that appeared that year, *The World of Colin Wilson*, by a Leicester celebrity, Sidney Campion, whom Wilson had regarded as a kind of hero in his youth, did not help. In fact, it was a positive deterrent.

Campion was a self-made man, who had risen from poverty to become a barrister and top civil servant. Like Wilson's, but on a lesser scale, his life was a rags-to-riches story and he told it in his autobiography *Towards the Mountains*. Wilson's father had given Wilson a copy of this when he was twelve and it thrilled him so much that he went on to read Campion's other volumes of autobiography. Wilson was gratified that a hero of his early days wanted to write a book about him—as was his mother when he told her—but the finished product was less gratifying. Campion had got in touch with Wilson when *The Outsider* appeared. He was then retired and living in Wimbledon, passing his days sculpting. He asked Wilson to sit for him and when Wilson did, he admitted that he wanted to write one last book: a biography of him.

Wilson thought the idea was absurd; after all he was only twenty-five. But Campion insisted. Wilson was a "great writer" and Campion was determined to write the first book about him. Wilson couldn't say no to "the *great* Sidney Campion"—as people in Leicester called him—and agreed. He arranged for Campion to visit his parents and gave him his journals from his teens and early twenties. But Campion's style was decidedly purple and it was clear that he had envisioned Wilson's story as a kind of romanticized extension of his own. When he received the manuscript, Wilson was appalled: with numbing consistency, Campion had included every romantic cliché imaginable. Wilson rewrote a great deal of the manuscript, reining in Campion's over-the-top prose, but Campion later reinserted much of what Wilson had blue-penciled. The result was embarrassing. When the book finally appeared—it was turned down by several publishers—Wilson's critics had a field day with it.

One of the problems with Campion's book was that he had no capacity for ideas. Existentialism was way beyond him. But this was precisely what Wilson was at pains to pin down in order to see what was wrong with it. He had seen the need for a new existentialism as early as *The Outsider*, the need for an existential philosophy that included the kinds of experiences he had had at Teignmouth. The old existentialism ignored these experiences and because it did, it was incomplete. Now the burden was on him to show how these experiences could be analyzed in the same way that existentialism analyzed our everyday experiences. To have the experiences was not enough. He needed to understand them, to see how they worked, and, if possible, to reproduce them.

For a long time Wilson believed that an answer to these questions could be found through sex. Sex was a central theme in *Ritual in the Dark* and, as we've seen, it is there at the start of *The Outsider*. It also played an important role in his writings about crime. In the 1880s Jack the Ripper had introduced a disturbing new type of crime that was unlike anything the Victorians had ever encountered: murder for sexual pleasure, what the Germans call *Lustmord*. The idea was so foreign to them that for a long time the Victorians believed that the Ripper was a fanatical puritan, murdering prostitutes out of a moral fundamentalism, or someone out for revenge, because his or her son had died of venereal disease caught from a prostitute. That someone could receive sexual satisfaction from the slaughter was beyond them.

Wilson had put off writing a book about sex because he assumed Gollancz wouldn't accept it; he had, after all, rejected the *Encyclopaedia of Murder* and was appalled at the sex murders in *Ritual*. But Arthur Barker had accepted the *Encyclopaedia* and he would publish Wilson's work on "sexistentialism"—to coin an obvious term—too. If Wilson's aim as a philosopher was to "be able to express the meaning-content of the sexual orgasm in words," then *Origins of the Sexual Impulse* was his chance.

Origins of the Sexual Impulse tries to answer a central question: what part does sex play in man's total being? Wilson recognizes that when it comes to sex, "the gap between man's purposes and nature's seems unusually wide."[45] For nature, sex is a means of reproduction; it ensures that the species carries on. Human beings obviously reproduce through sex, but we are interested in it for other reasons too. In fact, we go out of our way to inhibit the reproductive capacity of sex so we can enjoy it without the burden of parenthood. In this sense we can see any means of avoiding conception as being against nature. We tend to think of sex as natural in order to minimize any shame, guilt, or embarrassment we might feel about it. But in fact, sex in humans is anything but natural.

Likewise, sex in the animal kingdom is not like human sex. For animals, it is for reproduction, and the instincts involved in it are triggered at certain times of the year and by a precise organic trigger: the smell of estrus in the female, signaling to the male that she is receptive. Without this trigger, there is no sex. We think of someone with a voracious sexual appetite as an "animal," and we speak of going "wild" with sexual frenzy. Both notions are misnomers. As the playwright and anthropologist Robert Ardrey, author of *African Genesis* (1961) and *The Territorial Imperative* (1966), told Wilson, "sex is a sideshow in the world of the animals."[46] Fear, dominance, and food play much greater roles. Compared to the part sex plays in human life, for our animal cousins, it is an afterthought.

This leads to difficulties when we try to determine what exactly a "sexual perversion" is. Given our definition of "natural" sex, any sex that doesn't lead to reproduction would, it seem, fit that category. This would mean, then, that most of the sex that we engage in is perverse. Again, we don't have eating or drinking perversions in the same way that we have sexual ones. (We do have eating "disorders," but they are not the same thing.[47]) A person who tried to eat stones or plastic would soon find that he could not do it for long. His body would quickly rebel. We would certainly call this behavior perverted. But a fetishist can indulge in his or her peculiar delight at length with no ill effects: no one, as far as I know, has ever got sick or died from being turned on by panties or black leather. Nature does not interfere with our sexual perversions in the way that it would with any eating or drinking ones. Again, for most human beings, love and affection are important parts of sex, but they are unnecessary as far as nature is concerned. A woman can become pregnant through rape, by someone she hates, even by someone with complete anonymity (sex with a stranger).

The Russian religious existential philosopher Nikolai Berdyaev remarked, "It is quite possible to say that man is a sexual being, but we cannot say that man is a food-digesting being."[48] It is obvious that sex involves physical organs, just as digestion does. But it is not limited to them; it reaches beyond them to permeate our entire life, in a way that digestion and other organic functions do not. Wilson's question is: how exactly does sex do this?

Wilson's basic insight is that in humans sex is fundamentally a much more mental, imaginative process than a physical one, and that its central function is to trigger an intensification of consciousness and to promote our evolution. Wilson sees us as "co-partners" in this process and argues that "whatever the ultimate purposes of the evolutionary force that drives man, heightened consciousness surely plays some important part in them."[49] "The need for a more intense consciousness," he says, "dominates all human activity." We can say that for Wilson, sex is an important part of this drive. It aims to lower our indifference threshold and give us a glimpse of reality, to temporarily open our doors of perception.

In man, Wilson writes, "the stimulus that unites his [sexual] instincts is purely mental."[50] "The sexual orgasm," he says, "is a response to an act of will and imagination, rather than to a physical reality."[51] Wilson finds evidence for this in masturbation, which, paradoxically, he says can be seen as one of our greatest achievements. Unlike other instinctual drives, for food or drink, sex is the only one that can be satisfied through a purely mental act. We can satisfy sexual hunger with an imaginative act, a fantasy, and reach climax, but we can't satisfy hunger or thirst in the same way. No matter how hard I try, I can't imagine a steak and fill my stomach with it. I can whet my appetite in this way, but not satisfy it, yet I can imagine a sexual partner and gratify that hunger. In fact, more than one male has reported that "imaginative sex"—masturbation—can often be more satisfying than the real thing, because of its capacity to focus intently on its object, and cut out all irrelevant matters. (Hence the popularity of pornography, which achieves its effect by limiting the woman's reality to only those characteristics that make her a sexual object.) We also know that unless our imagination is gripped in some way, sexual intercourse can be as banal an operation as other physical functions, and that the loss of this imaginative grip can be disastrous.

By "imagination" Wilson doesn't mean indulging in fantasies during intercourse. He means the kind of mental intensity that can be produced by crisis, when the value of our experience is no longer obscured by boredom and indifference. It is precisely because we *lose* our mental grip on the sexual act that we need to resort to fantasies to stimulate our imagination. If sex were simply a physical affair, we would not need fantasies to turn us on, just as we don't require fantasies about eating in order to enjoy lunch; we merely need an appetite.

We are so used to taking this for granted that we don't see how remarkable it is. By pointing out the part imagination plays in sex, Wilson isn't promoting masturbation; he's merely showing that the mental, imaginative component of sex in humans is much more powerful than in our other drives. In this context, imagination has a real power and it shows, again paradoxically, that as H. G. Wells said, we are "creatures of the mind."

Another example points to the same thing. In *Ritual in the Dark* Gerard Sorme, Wilson's hero, spends a morning in bed making love. After all of his sexual desire has been drained, Sorme goes out of his basement flat to bring in the milk. As he does he catches a glimpse up a woman's skirt as she walks past. Immediately he is hit with a powerful sexual curiosity, even though seconds before he was convinced he was "spent." For eating the equivalent would be stuffing ourselves at a smorgasbord and then immediately feeling ravenous again at the chance sight of a sandwich.

If Wilson's hero is sexually galvanized by a glimpse up a passing skirt, why isn't he equally excited at the sight of the woman with whom he has spent the morning making love? Surely he could satisfy his appetite here? But the passing skirt is forbidden, strange, new, unknown, and the woman in his bed is now familiar; she has passed within the indifference threshold and is taken for granted. Her reality is *diminished* in a way that is the exact opposite of pornography. [52] If pornography limits a woman's reality to only those aspects related to sex, we can say that postcoital satisfaction dampens these and lets the rest of her nonsexual reality in.

It is forbiddenness that is the real turn-on, and that is a function of the imagination.[53] That is, forbiddenness is an *idea* we must grasp with our *minds*, although we may not explicitly articulate it in this way to ourselves. It's not sex per se that excites Wilson's hero. It is the strangeness, the newness that the passing skirt seems to promise, that jolts his erotic nerve. This is an example of what Wilson calls "the theory of symbolic response."[54] This states that where in animals the sexual instinct is triggered by the smell of estrus, in humans it is triggered by symbols, that is, by elements that appeal to the imagination. This, of course, is the essence of fetishism. But for the theory of symbolic response, even a real woman is a fetish.

The passing skirt is a symbol for the strangeness Wilson's hero perceives in the woman walking by. It is this strangeness that womanizers such as Don Juan, Casanova, and others really pursue, although they are not intelligent or analytical enough to grasp this. This is why their promiscuity, for all their success, leaves them feeling oddly unfulfilled. Each new woman promises a conquest, yet once she's conquered, the urge for another immediately asserts itself, rather as if after eating a meal one was immediately hungry. If this were the case, we would go to our doctor to see what was wrong with our digestion. Yet as we consider the imagination merely a means of creating fantasies—and not, as Wilson does, as a faculty for *grasping reality*—we do not see anything wrong with its feebleness and inability to *hold on to our experience*.

What Don Juan and Casanova really crave is the *sense of reality* that the pursuit and conquest momentarily stimulate. And they stimulate this because they cause our consciousness, our will, to focus and concentrate, just as Dr. Johnson believed the thought of one's impending hanging does. If Don Juan, Casanova, and their modern counterparts had the brains to understand this, they would recognize that *this* is what they were really pursuing, and not sex. For them, sexual conquest serves the same purpose as the revolver he played Russian roulette with did for Graham Greene. It focuses their minds briefly, and they enjoy a momentary taste of real consciousness. If they could focus their minds *at will*, the need for repeated sexual conquests and for playing Russian roulette would disappear.

The sudden, unexpected excitement that surges up when the imagination is stimulated by a sexual trigger suggests that the energy of sexual arousal comes from somewhere deeper than the conscious mind. As Wilson writes, the sexual impulse "works on a deeper level than any other human impulse"; it "overrides" our conscious checks and refuses to be "assimilated" into consciousness.[55] It is an energy, a "powerhouse," that is not immediately available to the conscious mind, but that can be triggered by the promise of newness. This vision of newness Wilson believes is at the heart of the sexual impulse, as it is at the heart of mystical and poetic states of consciousness.[56] It is a function of our minds when they are properly concentrated, when they are in focus, rather than the blurred, diffuse state they are usually in.

Wilson arrives at his insights, only some of which I've touched on here, through a wide-ranging analysis and synthesis of a variety of sources: studies of promiscuity, sexual aberrations, and perversions; developments in existential and Gestalt psychology; the ideas of Gurdjieff and the writings of D. H. Lawrence, Henry Miller, Frank Harris, Vladimir Nabokov, and other sexual prophets. Here too he begins to incorporate the ideas of the twentieth-century German philosopher Edmund Husserl into his work.

Husserl began the philosophical school known as phenomenology, out of which existentialism arose, and his ideas inform the work of Sartre, Camus, and Heidegger. As mentioned, Husserl's central insight is that perception is *intentional*. Our consciousness does not passively reflect the world; it actively reaches out and *grabs* it. As Wilson would point out, it is this insight that Sartre, Camus, and Heidegger either rejected or misunderstood. For Husserl, our perceptions are like an arrow shot at the object we are perceiving. When our minds are tightly focused and concentrated—as Don Juan's is as he attempts another seduction, or as mine is trying to be as I write this book—then the object of perception, with all its reality, is held firmly in our sights and we hit the bull's-eye squarely.

Most of time, though, we are not so focused. We take our perceptions for granted and our grasp of reality is weak. Hence the need for fantasies of forbiddenness to tighten our grip on the sexual act. Students of Husserl will know his philosophy is dense and difficult, but this central insight about the intentionality of consciousness will inform everything Wilson writes from now on. As I quoted Wilson saying earlier, we have a "will to perceive as well as perceptions." Intentionality is our will to perceive. How we can become aware of this will and learn how to consciously direct it will be one aim of Wilson's new existentialism.

One insight to come from Wilson's phenomenological approach to studying sex is that we seem to have an in-built unconscious tendency to devalue our experience, to familiarize it and bring it within our indifference threshold. As he writes, "The mind's basic mechanism is to perceive similarity between one set of impressions and another."[57] It is as if we wore blinders, rather like those worn by cab horses, limiting the amount of reality we can perceive.[58] The horse wears these blinders because his efficiency would be lessened if he didn't. The movement around him, the other traffic, would distract his attention. In a busy city, this would lead to a nervous breakdown, so in order for the horse to keep to the road, its perceptions must be limited.

Wilson suggests that something similar is the case with human consciousness. In order to be effective, consciousness needs to be limited. This is why we do not enjoy a broader, more mystical or poetic consciousness more of the time. If we did, we would not make the efforts necessary for our evolution. The sort of "challenge and response" scenario that Arnold Toynbee saw at work in history is also at work in our individual lives. The best is got out of us when we're facing challenges. Such challenges "keep the will taut."[59] Experienced continuously, the kind of euphoria that comes with sexual ecstasy, or even with a spring morning, would reduce our efficiency and make us lazy. Overindulging in meditation and other relaxation techniques can have the same effect. After taking the drug mescaline and experiencing "mystical consciousness," Aldous Huxley said that if everyone did the same there would be no war, but there would be no civilization either. No one would bother to create it, as they would be too blissed out to want to. Huxley himself said that while under the influence of the drug, he looked at a sink full of dirty dishes and felt they were too beautiful to wash.[60] Alfred North Whitehead, whose notion of "prehension," the process of *absorbing* our experience and making it our own—a key element in *Bildung*—plays an important part in *Origins of the Sexual Impulse*, said that the notion of life implies a "certain absoluteness of self-enjoyment."[61] Such absoluteness of self-enjoyment—a delight in mere being—came to Huxley when he was on mescaline. But in order to carry out evolution's directives and get things done, we have to severely inhibit our appreciation of this.

While mescaline and other drugs can give us a wonderful sense of oneness and reveal the beauty of the world—even a glass of wine can do it—they also inhibit the will. In order to prevent us from sinking into a pleasant lethargy, the force behind evolution has purposely installed internal blinders, which limit the amount of reality we perceive. It is precisely because we find ourselves stuck in a rather drab and dull world that we are driven to evolve, to improve our lot. As Wilson writes, "this seems to be the method of the 'life force' for keeping us from relaxing too much, for getting the maximum work out of each human will."[62] As I've written elsewhere, an extended stay in the Garden of Eden would have been the worst thing possible for human evolution.[63]

Yet the unconscious filter that edits the amount of reality we perceive and keeps us on our toes has one major drawback. The single-mindedness it promotes is a marvelous tool for survival and an effective spur to make efforts to overcome the difficulties in life. But the picture it presents of the world is severely limited. In effect, it cuts out all the color and shows only black and white. We need such a limited view in order to respond quickly, especially in our increasingly complex world. But it minimizes our awareness of beauty and meaning. These are irrelevant as far as survival and meeting challenges are concerned, but they are very relevant when it comes to *why* we meet them. They are what make life worth living. Because of this unconscious filter philosophers such as Sartre tell us that "man is useless passion." The filter in our consciousness that prevents us from becoming lazy has also led to our believing that the world is meaningless. This defeats its purpose, because if too much meaning makes us lazy, as Aldous Huxley discovered, not enough leads us to feel that "there's nothing to be done," as Wilson's bête noire, Samuel Beckett, a Nobel Prize winner, believed.

Husserl suggests a way out of this predicament. Though stingy, the life force is not an absolute miser, and occasionally it allows us to experience a fuller, broader, deeper consciousness. These are our poetic and mystical experiences, the "all is good" feeling that brings a sense of "absurd affirmation." For some reason, during them, our blinders are temporarily removed and reality is let in. Our doors of perception are opened, but only for a moment. Then they shut again. Yet these moments tell us that reality *is not* meaningless. In fact it is dripping with meaning, so much meaning that if we experienced it in full, we would most likely blow a psychic fuse; any number of accounts of mystical experiences suggest this. This tells us two things. One is that the world we perceive most of the time is not the world as it really is, but a highly edited version of it. The second is that our doors of perception are not permanently locked. They can open. The question then becomes, how can we open them just enough to allow more reality into consciousness, so we are not taken in by gloomy pronouncements about its meaninglessness, but not so much that we are overwhelmed by it and our will inhibited? Wilson writes, "If you examine the mechanisms of the form-imposing faculty"—that is, Husserl's intentionality—"then you can adjust them to let in 'otherness,'" the richness of reality we otherwise edit out.[64]

How to do this is precisely the focus of his new existentialism. And it led to some very interesting developments.

CHAPTER SIX

PEAK EXPERIENCES, INTENTIONALITY, AND EVOLUTION

S ex must have been in the air in 1962, or at least in the atmosphere around Wilson. As he was writing *Origins of the Sexual Impulse* a letter arrived from Maurice Girodias, master of the Olympia Press. Many of the writers Wilson moved among in Paris in 1953 had made ends meet by writing pornography for Girodias. Now he had written to Wilson asking if he would like to write a "dirty book" too. The idea appealed to Wilson. Censorship was still strict in England. Writing for Girodias would avoid this and give him a chance to talk frankly about sex. There were incidents in his sexual life that he wanted to analyze and turning them into fiction would give him the opportunity to do this. So he decided to join the Olympians.

The result was a sequel to *Ritual in the Dark*, which Wilson titled *Man Without a Shadow*.[1] He wrote it in the form of a journal that Gerard Sorme, Wilson's existential hero, keeps to chronicle his sexual experiences, much like the journal Wilson himself kept. As one might suspect, Sorme has many experiences. When Wilson mentioned to his editor at Arthur Barker that he was writing a "sex novel," the editor asked to see it. Wilson sent it to him and was surprised when he said he would like to publish it. Either the sex was less frank than he thought or the British public was more open to discussing it than he had believed. Either way Wilson was happy. Girodias was notoriously mean when it came to advances, and collecting royalties from him was apparently impossible.[2] Arthur Barker was much more generous. Wilson did receive flak from some critics about inserting "episodes that would have led to prosecution in less liberal times" in order to boost sales, something, we remember, Wilson chided Henry Miller for doing. But by staying off the Olympia Press list, he at least avoided the technical label of "pornographer."[3]

Man Without a Shadow—or, as its American edition was called, much to Wilson's annoyance, *The Sex Diary of Gerard Sorme*—is not a book one reads "with one hand," as the French literary critic Sainte-Beuve said of pornography.

The writing is crisp, clean, and convincing, but Wilson's aim is to analyze the sexual experience, not sell it. There is as much new existentialism in the book as there is sex, perhaps even more. One interesting ingredient is that one of the main characters, Carradoc Cunningham, an occultist and master of "sex magic," is based on the dark magician Aleister Crowley. In 1962 Crowley had been dead for fifteen years and was all but forgotten. Some interest in him had been aroused in 1951 by the publication of John Symonds's *The Great Beast*, an often hilarious biography of the "wickedest man in the world," as the British tabloids of the 1920s called Crowley. But he was certainly not the cult figure he is today. So once again, Wilson was ahead of the trends.

In *Man Without a Shadow* and its sequel, *The God of the Labyrinth* (1970), the last of the Sorme novels, Wilson puts into action, as it were, the phenomeno-logical insights spelled out in *Origins of the Sexual Impulse*.[4] This is an example of a working routine Wilson would maintain during the 1960s and 1970s, with philosophical books being fleshed out with fiction. It was an expression of his belief that "no philosopher is qualified to do his job unless he is also a novelist."[5] This would, of course, disqualify quite a few philosophers. His point is that an existential philosophy—a philosophy which is based on experience—should be able to embody its insights in actions, in events and circumstances that reflect reality as lived. "Philosophy may be only a shadow of the reality it tries to grasp," he writes, "but the novel is altogether more satisfactory."[6]

Man Without a Shadow also initiates Wilson's tactic of appropriating literary genres and putting them to his philosophical uses. In *Man Without a Shadow* and *The God of the Labyrinth* he adopts the erotic novel (with elements of the occult informing both). As we've seen, *The Mind Parasites*, *The Philosopher's Stone*, and *The Space Vampires* use science fiction and horror. *Necessary Doubt* (1964) and *The Glass Cage* (1966) are crime novels; the first has a protagonist based on the existential theologian Paul Tillich, and the other features a serial killer who quotes William Blake. I've mentioned his espionage novel, *The Black Room*, devoted to the effects of sensory deprivation. Wilson even adopted the nonfiction novel technique developed by Truman Capote in *In Cold Blood* for his book about a serial murderer, *The Killer* (1970), published in America as *Lingard*. Space does not allow more than a checklist of these books and I have only mentioned some of Wilson's fiction.[7] These and his other novels are all very much worth reading; they all put into gripping form many of the ideas that Wilson was developing in his new existentialism. Wilson's use of popular literary genres for philosophical purposes was seen by the highbrow critics at the time as subliterature; today Wilson's approach is a recognized strategy of postmodern fiction. So, once again, he was ahead of his time.

Girodias was not the only one writing Wilson letters. Sometime in early 1963 Wilson received a letter from America that would mark a new stage in the development of the new existentialism. It came from a professor of psychology at Brandeis University, in Massachusetts. His name was Abraham Maslow.[8] Maslow had by this time become a familiar figure at Esalen, the West Coast alternative think tank, and his humanistic psychology informed much of the burgeoning human potential movement and transpersonal psychology of the 1960s and '70s. Maslow had read *The Stature of Man* (the American title of *The Age of Defeat*) and had been impressed with it. According to Maslow's biographer, Wilson's "lively philosophical writings, offering an optimistic, even exhilarating view of humanity's unrealized greatness, inspired Maslow."[9]

Maslow considered *The Stature of Man* an "important book" and he had already started referencing Wilson's work in his own writings and would do so for the rest of his career.[10] In Wilson's fallacy of insignificance Maslow found a version of what he called the "Jonah complex."[11] This was based on the biblical story of Jonah, who tries to avoid his destiny to become a prophet. In many of his students Maslow saw something similar—a diffidence, a lack of confidence, and a tacit admission that they would not achieve greatness in their chosen fields. In fact they positively avoided the idea. They seemed to retreat from the belief that they could do any better than the average, and they were happy to embrace mediocrity, even if their own potential for greatness was obvious to Maslow. They suffered from the fallacy of insignificance and Maslow wanted to get to the psychological roots of their timidity. He was the first important thinker to truly grasp what Wilson was writing about. The two began to correspond and what Maslow had to tell Wilson about his work excited him. If Wilson inspired Maslow, the influence was mutual.[12]

Maslow had started out as a Freudian but grew tired of this approach because it focused on sick people. He then had the brilliant idea of studying healthy people instead. He discovered that his subjects—"the best specimens of mankind I could find"—were "very different, in some ways startlingly different from the average."[13] One striking difference was that these healthy people all reported having "something like mystical experiences, moments of great awe, moments of the most intense happiness, or even rapture, or bliss."[14]

Maslow called these moments of "pure, positive happiness" "peak experiences." They provided his subjects with the "ultimate satisfaction of vague, unsatisfied yearnings," in which "all separateness and distance from the world disappeared." Maslow's scientific training led him to regard mystical experiences as dubious; such things were considered nonsensical, if not pathological, hallucinations produced by hysteria. But the people reporting these experiences were *not* pathological. They were the "best specimens" of humanity available to him. So these peak experiences could not be dismissed as some aberration, or as an expression of the urge to return to the womb, the "oceanic feeling" that Freud believed was the real source of mysticism. These people were vital, active, and highly motivated. They were not recluses or introverts, withdrawn from the world or seeking escape from it. They did not want to return to the womb and retreat from life, but were eager to meet its challenges.

Most accounts of mystical experience, Maslow knew, had a religious context. But these peak experiences were not necessarily religious or supernatural. They seemed to be moments of sheer delight, a kind of overflow of happiness—we could say they were a sudden awareness of what Whitehead called an "absoluteness of self-enjoyment." They were not produced by pathological states but seemed to be a by-product of a purposeful, highly motivated life. This seemed to suggest that these peak experiences were associated with psychological health.

But as Maslow recognized, not everyone has peaks. They are part of psychological health, yet the majority of people don't have them; Maslow's subjects, we've seen, were "startlingly different from the average." This suggested to Maslow that most people (or at least the average person) are *not* psychologically healthy. Not only are neurotics, psychotics, hysterics, paranoiacs, and depressives unhealthy—practically everyone else is too. This means that the standard idea of psychological health, that of the "well-adjusted personality," is actually a standard of subnormality, as it limits itself to a level *below* optimum health. To be "well-adjusted" means to be adjusted to the average, which, Maslow saw, means accepting a level less than healthy.

It struck Wilson that Maslow's peaks were much like the experience he had at Teignmouth, or the "absurd affirmation" he found in Blake, Nietzsche, Yeats, and others. They were the moments of "absurd good news," the yea-saying his Outsiders had desperately sought and sometimes achieved. One aspect of peaks that excited Wilson was that they seemed to lower the indifference threshold. In them "the person becomes suddenly *aware* of something that he had known about previously, but been inclined to take for granted, to discount."[15] Maslow told the story of a marine who hadn't seen a woman for two years. There were none where he had been stationed, and when he returned to his base camp and first saw a nurse, the *difference* between men and women suddenly hit him, and he was amazed. In another example, a young mother was getting breakfast ready for her husband and children, when the sun suddenly streamed into the kitchen. The mother looked at the children and her husband and was suddenly overwhelmed with her love for them and her happiness.

In both cases nothing mystical or supernatural happened. They were really everyday incidents. But for some reason, the young mother and the marine suddenly grasped the *reality* of something they already knew.[16]

A few things struck Wilson about all this. One was that peaks are a natural occurrence; they are not some supernatural grace bestowed from above or a product of pathology, but are as much a part of human psychology as other psychological facts. Indeed, Maslow said that peaks are part of our biology; we are, in effect, *made* to have them in the same way that we are made to feel hungry, thirsty, or cold. Then there is the fact that they are associated with high motivation, with the kind of *purposeful* living that Wilson and his Outsiders crave. Maslow's "peakers" were driven. They had aims, goals they wanted to achieve. They used their *will*. They did not, as Samuel Beckett did, feel "there's nothing to be done," nor were they subject to the kind of ontological trapdoors that Sartre's "nausea" opened. Peaks happened to highly purposeful people, who invested will into what they did. Bored, depressive characters such as Graham Greene would not be familiar with them. The peaks people like him would experience would be those artificially induced through dubious methods such as Russian roulette. Greene's "affirmation experience" was brought about by his *clenching* his mind into a tight fist of concentration as he pulled the trigger on his revolver and prepared to have his brains blown out. But this kind of concentration—at a less intense level—is common to purposive people, focusing on the goals they are motivated to achieve.

But there was one part of Maslow's findings that Wilson questioned. Maslow believed that peaks could not be induced at will. They were a by-product of an optimistic, purposeful way of life. But you couldn't make one happen, he thought, just as you can't make yourself be happy. Yet Maslow had written about how, when he spoke to his students about peak experiences and asked them to think about any they had had, they suddenly started having them, simply by remembering earlier ones and focusing their attention on them. It seemed that Maslow had missed this point. It would play a central part in the philosophy of consciousness Wilson was developing. It seemed that the human mind had the ability to alter itself, through thought and imagination alone.

Around the same time as Wilson was absorbing Maslow's ideas, the work of another thinker came to his attention. I've already mentioned Robert Ardrey. Wilson had bought a copy of Ardrey's *African Genesis* for Joy, thinking she would like it. When Wilson read it too he was struck by Ardrey's thesis. Ardrey argued that human beings emerged from their simian ancestors on the African savannahs some two million years ago, and that the transition came about because by learning to walk upright they left their hands free to use weapons—a theme Stanley Kubrick employed in the film *2001: A Space Odyssey*.

This suggested that humanity came into existence through an "evolutionary leap," a sudden advance rather than a slow, cumulative process. The idea of such a leap had been on Wilson's mind for some time, ever since he contemplated the nineteenth-century Romantics who made up many of his Outsiders. Sometime in the late eighteenth century, a kind of "imagination explosion" took place in the West, which Wilson later attributed to the rise of the modern novel. Writers, poets, musicians, and artists found themselves experiencing strange states of a godlike ecstasy, unlike anything that had come before.[17] In Maslow's terms the Romantics experienced profound peak experiences and it was precisely their fall "back to earth" that led many to alcoholism, drug addiction, or suicide. The

Romantics, Wilson felt, were too weak and undisciplined to bridge the gap; they couldn't maintain the forward drive that created the conditions for peaks. They succumbed to self-pity and despair, believing they were stranded in a drab, dreary world.[18] The contrast between their visionary states and the "triviality of everydayness" defeated them. But perhaps they were the first sign of a change in human consciousness, of a growing hunger for the kind of inner freedom that H. G. Wells had demanded. Perhaps, like Ardrey's early humans, humanity for the past century or so was undergoing an evolutionary shift.

Wilson wrote to Ardrey and the two began a correspondence. Ardrey lived in Rome and during a trip to England he visited Wilson in Cornwall. Along with ideas about human evolution Ardrey gave Wilson some professional advice. "Brother, you write too much," he told Wilson, something Wilson had heard before.

Yet it was Ardrey's ideas about dominance that really excited Wilson. Ardrey told him that precisely 5 percent of all animal groups, including humans, was dominant. This fact had been uncovered during the Korean War, when it was revealed that surprisingly few Americans escaped from North Korean prison camps. This happened because their Chinese captors first observed the prisoners to determine which were dominant, that is, which were motivated, showed initiative, and displayed other leadership qualities. They isolated these under heavy guard and left the rest relatively unguarded. Without the "troublemakers" the others were easily controlled; they were passive and quickly accepted their situation. The number of "dangerous" prisoners was always the same: 5 percent.

Wilson points out that Shaw had known about this. He once asked the explorer H. M. Stanley (of Stanley and Livingstone fame) how many of his men could take over for him in case of an emergency. Stanley told Shaw, "One in twenty." Maslow had come to similar conclusions through a study of dominance in women. He discovered that women could be divided into three dominance groups: high, medium, and low. The level of dominance influenced their sexuality. High-dominance women enjoyed sex and were promiscuous and experimental, medium-dominance women were romantics looking for "Mr. Right," and low-dominance women were shy and afraid of sex. High-dominance women always numbered 5 percent.

This insight into dominance seemed to offer Wilson a clue about his Outsiders. He had pointed out that the Outsider is not necessarily a frustrated man of genius (although he later modified this view). But he now recognized that he or she was certainly a frustrated member of the dominant 5 percent. Wilson suggested that in early times, with a smaller population, a dominant character could more easily rise to his natural level in society. Today it is less easy. There are many more people, which means many more dominant individuals, and the competition is greater. Many dominant individuals do not get the chance to express their dominance naturally. This results in an accumulation of frustrated energies and a resentment toward the society that frustrates them. Shaw said, "All men are in a false position in society until they have realized their possibilities and imposed them on their neighbours." But Shaw also realized that this is not always easy. "The finding of one's place," he admitted, "may be made very puzzling by the fact that there is no place in ordinary society for the extraordinary individual."

This is something the Outsider knows firsthand. And if a dominant individual is frustrated for too long, he may rebel, and act out his dominance criminally. Wilson points out that in tests done with rats this is exactly what happened. In overcrowded conditions, a highly dominant or "king" rat took over a cage for himself and his harem. All the other rats were jammed into another cage. Among these were other, slightly less dominant rats, and they took to expressing their dominance in "criminal" ways. They raped other rats, ate babies, and attacked their less dominant fellows. Dominant humans in similar conditions—slums—with no positive venue for their dominance, often react in much the same way.

Yet not every member of the dominant 5 percent is an Outsider. Most do find their natural place in society. Wilson points out that every store manager, drill sergeant, pop star, or sports figure is a member of the dominant 5 percent. (Having worked in the rock and roll business for many years, I came across quite a few of them.) Yet there is a further level of dominance that exceeds even these. Members of the dominant 5 percent need *other people* to express their dominance. An actor needs his audience, a pop star his fans, a CEO his vice chairmen, a dictator his masses. Without other people, their dominance has no means of expression. They are dependent on other people. If they found themselves stranded on a desert island, their dominance would have nothing to do.

This is not true of a small number of the population. Wilson suggests that .005 percent of the population displays a very different kind of dominance, one that does not need other people. If these people found themselves on a desert island, they would be amazed at their good fortune. For them, creative work is an end in itself. They are what Maslow calls "self-actualizers." They are more interested in exploring and actualizing their own creative potential than in dominating others. A philosopher, a scientist, a poet, a mystic, or a composer can express his or her dominance through the work itself.

Members of the dominant .005 percent can, of course, express their dominance in more ordinary ways. As Wilson points out, many have been incorrigible seducers. Wilson recognizes that among creative individuals a certain promiscuity is to be expected, as part of their general appetite for newness. But unlike Casanova or Don Juan, seduction is not their main means of expressing dominance. A member of the dominant .005 percent is driven by an *impersonal* urge to evolve or actualize his abilities. In practice, self-actualization results in a kind of self-forgetting, in the sense of becoming absorbed in the impersonal pursuit of an idea or creative work. Essentially this is an *escape* from personality, a release from its stuffy constraints. As T. E. Lawrence said, "Happiness is absorption." People who express their dominance through others *never* forget themselves and often seem trapped in their personality. Members of the .005 percent do not face this problem. They have matured beyond needing the approval of others or the desire to get some immediate return from their work. These are the "originative intellectual workers" Wells spoke of. With his Outsiders, for Wilson they form "the evolutionary spearhead of the human race."[19]

Yet, Wilson asks, why have so many of them cracked up? Finding the answer to this question would constitute a step in the direction of our evolution. That is what Wilson set out to do in the sixth book of the Outsider Cycle, *Beyond the Outsider* (1965).

Wilson had used this title before, for his contribution to *Declaration*. There he wanted to show the limited use of the term "Outsider," and to express his exasperation with the problems the success of *The Outsider* had created. Here it has a more positive connotation. Wilson realized that the problems presented in *The Outsider* could be addressed only through a "careful analysis of the cultural trends of the past three hundred years, a 're-checking' of the previous calculations."[20] "A point has arrived in twentieth century thought," he writes, "when a completely new impulse and direction is needed."[21] Wilson aimed to provide this new direction by bringing together ideas of a creative—rather than a Darwinian—evolution, with Husserl's insights into intentionality. Evolution is not a mechanical process, driven by chance mutations and the struggle for survival. It is purposive and aims at increased consciousness. Through Husserl's phenomenological methods, Wilson argues, we can uncover our now unconscious inner evolutionary drive and make it conscious.

Wilson conceives this challenge of increasing consciousness as an attempt to get beyond what he calls "the sound barrier," using the analogy of early attempts to create a jet that could go faster than sound. At the speed of sound, air cannot escape from in front of the jet quickly enough, and builds up into a kind of wall. The jet must smash through this wall—when it does it makes the sonic boom— or it will itself be smashed. All the early experiments failed and the jets smashed.

Wilson sees something similar taking place in our attempts to get past what we might call the "freedom barrier." This is the point at which our capacity for freedom collapses. It is what Wilson, borrowing from the poet W. H. Auden, calls "life failure," the collapse of the will into boredom and passivity, when life becomes stale. This is another version of the indifference threshold, which is precisely our inability to *appreciate* our freedom, the "strange human incapacity to lay hold of experience."[22] Man, Wilson writes, "is like a slave who has clamoured all his life for freedom, and then discovers that freedom leaves him motiveless and listless."[23] In a phrase that Wilson will often return to, we are "like grandfather clocks driven by watch springs."[24] We have the equipment to appreciate our freedom—our moments of yea-saying show us that—but we lack the energy to drive it. Or perhaps we have the energy but *do not know how* to access it voluntarily.

The Romantics made a valiant attempt to get past the freedom barrier. They were in fact the first to recognize it as a problem and the first to feel that man is really a sleeping god. Before them men accepted their place in the universe as humble creatures of an all-powerful creator. But by the early nineteenth century, men of genius such as Blake, Byron, and Beethoven were shaking their fists at the Almighty, throwing off the constraints of humility, and celebrating man's own creativity and vision. The initial results were magnificent: the works of Goethe, Beethoven's symphonies, Blake's strange mythological epics, Hegel's enormous metaphysical system. But a less robust generation followed and the early advances stalled. These later Romantics, often ill and overly sensitive men, still felt that man was potentially a god. But by the late nineteenth century they had begun to believe that the odds were against them; the fallacy of insignificance set in and they began to accept that they couldn't win. The rise of scientific materialism had much to do with this. The world was "too much with them" and they began to embrace a kind of death mysticism.[25]

Wilson uses a vivid image to convey the situation. For the late Romantics "The human spirit was like a flame burning at the bottom of a river. Like an oxy-acetylene flame, its sheer heat could keep the water at bay. But a time would come when the flame would lose its strength, and the water would close in."[26] That is, as long as the ecstasy lasted, the Romantics could feel they were gods. Once it passed, they fell back to earth, and were crushed by the "triviality of everydayness." A line from the fin de siècle poet Ernest Dowson captures the mood: "The fire is out, and spent the warmth thereof. / This is the end of every song man sings."[27] Like many figures from the fin de siècle, Dowson used drugs and alcohol to stimulate a flagging sense of life. He died of consumption, drink, and overall abuse at the age of thirty-two.

By the early twentieth century, the gentle melancholy of the fin de siècle had hardened into a general pessimism, and the fallacy of insignificance gained ground. But another attempt at breaking the freedom barrier was made by existentialism, which Wilson saw as a kind of "Romanticism II." It differed from its predecessor in important ways. One was its awareness of the problem of language. One reason why the term "romantic" has negative connotations today is that the Romantics were too prone to float off into stratospheres of rhetoric. Wilson speaks of language as a "sensitive membrane" separating man's inner being from the world. It should respond to "every shade of meaning" we wish to express.[28] The initial Romantic impulse brought a new vitality to language, but it soon fell victim to a kind of inflation. Overuse of words such as "rapture" and "ecstasy" depleted their value and they soon became meaningless.

The existentialists brought a new rigor to language. Rather than produce clouds of ecstatic self-expression, they used language like a microscope, giving precision to dimly felt intuitions. One has only to read some of the Romantic poets and then turn to a page of Sartre or Heidegger to see the difference, although Heidegger himself was prone to present his thought in often exasperatingly obscure prose. The existentialists approached the question of freedom analytically and kept their feet firmly on the ground. The result was a language of great precision and subtlety which could capture nuances of human existence in a way that Romantic rhetoric could not. The existentialists were also tougher than the late Romantics. They had more of the everyday in them. They did not, as the poet Shelley did, want to "lie down like a tired child / And weep away this life of care."[29] They faced life without a blindfold.

Yet the existentialists, too, failed to break through the freedom barrier. They did not crack up, as the Romantics did, but they avoided this by lowering their expectations. Man is free, but existence is meaningless and so his freedom is strictly limited. For Heidegger, man can experience it only in the face of death, the recognition of his "finitude," an insight he shared with Gurdjieff. For Sartre, man is "condemned to be free," and he spends much of his life trying to escape this sentence, by embracing different expressions of "bad faith"—Heidegger's "inauthentic existence"—because freedom is a kind of terror, a hole in being. Camus is slightly less pessimistic, yet his admonition that we must "imagine Sisyphus happy" is not very inspiring. We seem to be faced with a choice between Romantic ideas of freedom, which are subject to a kind of manic-depression syndrome, and existential ones, which counsel us that the best we can expect is to stoically endure a world that is oblivious to us. This ethos was summed up in Hemingway's pronouncement in *The Old Man and the Sea* that "a man can be destroyed but not defeated." Stirring, but for people such as Wilson, who want neither to be destroyed *nor* defeated, not very satisfying.

Wilson asks: is it not possible to bring the two together? Can we not fuse Romantic vision with existential rigor in order to produce something that goes beyond both? Yes, we can, but an intellectual stock taking is in order.

"The thinker or artist of today," Wilson writes, "finds himself in a room that contains the accumulated rubbish of two hundred years."[30] He must, then, accept the Herculean task of cleaning out these intellectual stables. "If our culture is 'sick'"—as Wilson himself said it was in *Religion and the Rebel*—"we should not throw all the blame on politicians or businessmen. . . . The thinkers and artists of the past two hundred years are equally to blame."[31] The pessimism they direct at our "sick" society does not make it well; it only increases its sickness. Turning your back on society, as many of the artistic and intellectual "rebels" of the past two centuries have done, is no treatment for its illness. The Outsider cannot stand apart from the world and complain about it; he must attempt some constructive work toward making the situation better.

Wilson directs his work of reconstruction at another fallacy that has informed modern thought and led to its current impasse: "the passive fallacy." This is the belief that human beings are essentially passive, the subjects of forces working upon us from outside; in a word, mechanical. It will be seen that the fallacy of insignificance and the passive fallacy are directly related. Our sense of insignificance is rooted in the feeling that we can't win, that the forces working upon us are too strong. This leads us to abnegate our will, to give up. When we do this, our sense of insignificance increases. It should be clear that this is a very dangerous vicious circle; Wilson would later argue that it is the basic cause of mental breakdown.[32] It should also be clear that it is at the root of Beckett's belief that there's nothing to be done, or of the feeling the hero of Sartre's *Nausea* has that there's no more adventure. Insignificance, then, is a factor of passivity. But the converse is also true. The moments when we do not feel insignificant are those when we use our will, when we become active agents rather than passive subjects, when, that is, we actualize and embrace our freedom. Significance, we can say, is a factor of the will and is part of a virtuous circle. The more we will, the more active we are, and the less we feel insignificant, which leads us to use our will more.[33] It is the lack of recognition of the reality of the will that Wilson finds at the root of modern pessimism.

Wilson sees the passive fallacy at work in practically all fields of modern knowledge; here he directs his critique at philosophy, biology, and psychology. In philosophy it began with René Descartes' attempt to arrive at certainty through the process of radical doubt, which left the philosopher a passive mind, sitting in his armchair, certain only of his existence and nothing else.[34] By telling the "strange story of modern philosophy," Wilson shows how through Descartes' doubt and the philosophers who followed it—Locke, Berkeley, Hume, Kant— "Reason had proved to be a kind of forest fire that ended by consuming everything."[35] Since Descartes, "There is not a single statement by any philosopher . . . that cannot be immediately contradicted by another statement from another philosopher—or sometimes from the same one."[36] In biology the passive fallacy is inherent in the strict Darwinian or neo-Darwinian view of evolution, which sees life driven by random mutations and the pressures of the environment, with no inherent purpose. And in psychology it informs Freudian psychoanalysis and behaviorism, both of which see human beings as more or less stimulus-response machines, with little or no will. To this list we can add Karl Marx, whose vision of history is of inexorable scientific laws, by which the passive individual is carried along, like a piece of flotsam in a river. In Marx's view of history, unlike in Toynbee's, the individual is nothing, merely the subject of "historical necessity."

Against this view Wilson develops what he calls a "new foundation" based on the work of Husserl and Whitehead, both of whom reject the passive fallacy and see human consciousness as a much more active affair. To their insights he joins the evolutionary vision of Shaw and Wells, which he here links to the work of the biologist Julian Huxley—brother of Aldous Huxley—and the Catholic paleontologist Teilhard de Chardin, author of *The Phenomenon of Man* (1959). Where the strict Darwinian view sees life as the chance product of a purposeless, mechanical process, Huxley and de Chardin see in it an inherent urge to what they call "complexification," a purposive drive to increase consciousness and freedom.[37] For most of human existence this drive has been unconscious, but in recent times it has begun to become conscious. As Huxley writes, "As a result of a thousand million years of evolution, the universe is becoming conscious of itself. . . . This cosmic self-awareness is being realized in one tiny fragment of the universe—in a few of us human beings." Man, for Huxley, now finds himself "managing director of the biggest business of all, the business of evolution."[38] Where for most of our existence we had been forced ahead by the pressure of events, we are now in a position not only to recognize the direction our evolution takes, but to understand why it does and to consciously pursue it.

The experience of evolution becoming conscious of itself is felt in human beings as a desire to spend more time in the territories of the mind, the inner realms of freedom and the imagination. The physical world and its necessities used to occupy practically all human attention, but it is now giving way to a need to transcend these limits and, as it were, colonize a new dimension of reality. It is this hunger for complexification that drives Wilson's Outsiders, the "dominant .005 percent," Maslow's "self-actualizers," and Wells's "originative intellectual workers." More than this, Wilson argues that it is evidence of a clear *break* between humans and animals, something denied by strict Darwinism.

Through this evolutionary urge toward complexification, human beings have access to an entirely new dimension of reality, what de Chardin calls the "noösphere," the realm of the mind, of imagination and intellect. This is something animals cannot share. An animal's purposes are determined entirely by its present needs, generally for food or shelter.[39] It is stuck in the present and when its needs are met, it is happy. The purposes of many humans, too, are limited by these necessities: we remember Sartre's café owner, whose head empties when his café does. But as we've seen, in relatively recent times, a new type of human has appeared, whose purposes transcend immediate biological needs. He is not happy when these are met, but remains dissatisfied and seeks some satisfaction outside the present, in areas of reality no animal can enter. And where Darwinian evolution sees man as essentially passive, *pushed* ahead by the pressures of his environment, the new evolutionism sees him as actively *reaching toward* a goal. "The human level," Wilson writes, "is different *in kind* from the animal level, and possesses the potentiality of a new freedom." Man is "approaching a condition when he will cease to be a creature of biological motives . . . and will regulate all his activities by a primary motive of evolutionary purpose . . . he cannot be contented with purposes that come from outside; he hungers for an *inner drive*."[40]

For such an individual, the physical world is still a source of dissatisfaction, but it is no longer capable of satisfying him; this is the lesson of the indifference threshold: discomfort and inconvenience can cross it, but not pleasure. This is because man is a purposive animal. A machine can serve a purpose—that is why we make them. But it cannot *have* purpose. A machine cannot *want* to do anything. We have wants, but for most of our existence they have been stimulated by the necessities of physical reality. Now this is changing and we are beginning to see a human being whose wants are determined not solely by physical reality, but by another dimension of reality, that of freedom, imagination, the mind, de Chardin's noösphere. For such individuals the hunger for ideas, insight, and imagination is greater than the hunger for food, sex, self-esteem, or dominance.

This sense of a creative, active character to human existence, of an inherent inner drive to evolve, also informs the schools of existential and Gestalt psychology, both of which reject the mechanical picture of man in favor of one that includes his whole being. Where Freudian psychology sees neurosis as rooted in an individual's maladjustment to society, psychologists such as Ludwig Binswanger, Medard Boss, Eugène Minkowski, and others see it as rooted in his need to "adjust" to "*the whole of existence.*" Such adjustment, if that is the right word, must take creativity and self-transcendence as its norm, not adaptation to the average, which, as Maslow pointed out, is well below the true human norm. This is because human beings are not static, fixed creatures, but are propelled by a need to go beyond themselves, to grow. If the surest way to become neurotic is to accept, with Beckett, that there is nothing to be done, then the surest way to escape neurosis is to "induce a sense of creative purpose."[41] It is a question of the passive fallacy again. Mere adjustment to society abets this and perpetuates the neurosis. Inducing a sense of creative purpose dispels the passive fallacy and initiates the virtuous circle of using the will, leading to a sense of greater life and hence greater purpose.

Key to all this is the picture of the mind and consciousness that emerges from Wilson's "new foundations" based on Husserl and Whitehead. From Whitehead, Wilson takes two central ideas. One is Whitehead's notion of "prehension," which we touched on earlier when we discussed the notion of *Bildung*, the education or cultivation of the personality through its absorption of experience. For Whitehead, prehension is a much more active process than perception. Perception in our common understanding is a passive process. I open my eyes and look out my window and see a tree. In this scenario my consciousness passively reflects the tree, as a mirror would. With prehension, consciousness "does not merely see something; it actively *grasps* and digests; the process is active, like the stomach digesting food, not passive, like receiving a slap."[42] Think of listening to music. I can have it on in the background and its melodies accompany whatever I am doing. A tune may get through to me here and there, but I am not really attending to it. My relation to it is passive. Then think of what happens when I recognize a melody from a favorite piece of music. I focus my attention. The music becomes richer; its meaning "spreads out," as it were, and stimulates memories. It enters me more deeply and I can find myself moved by it. This is prehension; I take the experience into myself and digest it. I absorb it and it becomes part of me, just as my food does. I participate with the experience, rather than passively having it.

The other idea Wilson takes from Whitehead is that we possess two modes of perception, what Whitehead calls "presentational immediacy" and "causal efficacy," and which Wilson wisely translates into "immediacy perception" and "meaning perception." Whitehead presented this idea in a short book that is sadly too little known, *Symbolism: Its Meaning and Effect*, which was published in 1927.[43] Whitehead wrote it as a refutation of the philosopher David Hume, who contended that cause and effect is not a law of nature but merely a habit of thought. This was one of the results of Descartes' doubt, an effect of the "forest fire" of reason. Hume said there is nothing linking cause and effect; each is a separate phenomenon and cannot be found in the other. I may think that the cause of a nail entering a piece of wood (effect) is the hammer hitting it, but this is merely habit. There is no necessity for the nail to do one thing or another, even if every time I have hammered a nail it has entered the wood. Whitehead argues that Hume came to this radical and frankly nonsensical conclusion because he perceives experience through only one mode of perception, immediacy perception. In meaning perception the problem would never occur because the connection between cause and effect would be self-evident.

Simply put, immediacy perception gives us the bare facts of experience, the discrete bits and pieces that enter our awareness. Meaning perception is a kind of glue that holds these pieces together and makes them a whole. Immediacy perception is involved with analysis, the breaking up of things into their constituent parts. Meaning perception is concerned with synthesis, fusing these parts together into a unity, or rather, perceiving an original unity that our powers of analysis proceed to take apart. We can get an idea of the way the two work together if we consider the act of reading. Immediacy perception shows me the individual parts of a book, the separate words. If all I had to use was this, I would never be able to read the book. I could read individual words, but they would not make sense because there would be nothing linking them together. It is meaning perception that collects the words, as it were, and holds them together. This is why Wilson says that reading is an activity that requires two hands: one to pick up individual words, the other to hold them together. We can see this at work with a difficult book. If it is too difficult, it is as if the words we are trying to collect keep slipping out of our grasp. When this happens, we fail to "get it." We are so accustomed to the habit of doing this—for it is something we *learn* to do—that for the most part we don't notice it. But if we are drunk, say, or tired, or are looking at foreign words, it is as if we are using only one hand. An illiterate person would only see squiggles on a page and not pick them up at all. It should be clear that in moments of "nausea" or "absurdity" our meaning perception has somehow turned off and we are presented with a world of only disconnected bits and pieces.

Meaning perception is our ability to step back and see something as a whole, to see the forest, and not only the trees. Immediacy perception, as its name suggests, is our ability to focus on individual details, what is immediately before us. It is like a searchlight. It has a powerful beam, yet it has one problem: "it can only focus on one thing at a time," hence Hume's failure to see the connection between cause and effect.[44] The problem with Hume, Whitehead says—and with practically all of modern philosophy, with a few exceptions, Wilson adds— is that he uses only immediacy perception. He, and most of modern philosophy—not to mention science—is like someone who goes to a picture gallery and looks at the paintings with his face pressed up against them. He can certainly grasp much detail about the brushstrokes and texture of the paint, but he misses the whole. Yet he would contend that the brushstrokes and texture *are all there is* because that is all he sees. Stepping back and seeing the whole would be unscientific because it wouldn't be analytical.

As Wilson says, "close-upness deprives us of meaning." From the scientific perspective, any meaning must be something we somehow *add* to the bits and pieces, since it can't find it among them. An attempt to analyze beautiful scenery scientifically would fail completely. The beauty cannot be broken down into details and then added up like an equation. As Wilson says, this would be like "trying to locate the beauty of a lake by swimming in it or drinking it."[45] Beauty cannot be reduced to the parts that are amenable to immediacy perception. It must be grasped as a whole by meaning perception.

Meaning perception is involved in our aesthetic, poetic, mystical, spiritual, and religious experiences, but it is persona non grata when it comes to science. Science is not interested in meanings, but in facts, in the analysis of the bits and pieces that it believes make up the "really real" things of the universe. One result of this has been to excise everything *qualitative* from experience, everything that we ourselves may add to it, in order to see what is "really" there. As mentioned earlier, this has resulted in what Whitehead calls the "bifurcation of nature," in which the world is compartmentalized into objective and subjective halves. The person responsible for this, we've seen, was Galileo, who split the world into what he called "primary" and "secondary" characteristics. While this arrangement worked well for science, what it amounted to was the inference that everything that gave life meaning was relegated to the subjective side of the divide. This meant that it did not really exist. It was not part of the world but something we added to it, like sugar to a bitter drink. Immediacy perception is an indispensable aid in our ability to analyze and control our world. It is absolutely necessary and, as Wilson points out, is our central evolutionary advance. But working alone it presents us with a world that is hardly worth living in. Reality for it, as Whitehead said, is really "a dull affair . . . merely the hurrying of material endlessly, meaninglessly." As Whitehead remarked, from this perspective, the poets should not praise nature for its beauty, but themselves for adding it to her.

Husserl, too, was aware of the "passive consciousness" problem but his approach was different. As mentioned, his central insight is that perception is intentional. We believe it is a passive process, but as Wilson pointed out, there is a will to perceive as well as perceptions. Husserl's phenomenology is a method of uncovering this will to perceive, which he called "intentionality." At present it works unconsciously. The aim of phenomenology is to bring its processes to awareness.

Wilson includes illustrations of well-known optical illusions to demonstrate how intentionality works. Its method is essentially selective; that is to say, it *chooses* or *decides* what to perceive and what to ignore. One illustration presents a figure that can be seen as either a white vase or two silhouette profiles facing each other. Another can be seen as either a black Maltese cross or a white four-leaf clover. Another is the Müller-Lyer illusion, with two lines of equal length, one of which has forked ends, the other arrowheads. We can discipline ourselves to see either the vase or the profiles, the cross or the clover, but as Wilson says, we can't see both at once. If our attention is like a hand, it can only grasp something in one way at a time. Likewise, we can train ourselves to recognize that the lines are of equal length, but only if we exclude the forks and arrowheads. If we relax, our perception immediately sees the fork-ended line as longer, because our vision follows the direction of the forks. We can see intentionality in our habit of perceiving faces in a fire or on the moon, or figures in clouds. (This is also an example of what Gestalt ["shape" in German] psychology calls our "form-imposing faculty.") Wilson also points out that the bright colored spots we see when we rub our eyes, known as "phosphenes," can be molded into different shapes by our imagination—which is another word for intentionality. When Leonardo da Vinci wrote in his *Notebooks* that an artist should "Look at walls splashed with a number of stains" because in them he could see "a number of landscapes . . . figures in action, strange faces and costumes," he was advising that one should become aware of one's intentionality (he even speaks of the "sound of bells in whose clanging you can find every name and word . . . by indistinct things the mind is stimulated to new inventions"). Intentionality is also revealed in photographs that show famous places or everyday objects at unusual angles. We are baffled by these at first because what is being shown are elements of our perception that we usually ignore. That is to say we normally select *not* to see them, and so they appear strange.[46]

In *Introduction to the New Existentialism* (1967), Wilson's attempt to condense the argument of his Outsider Cycle into a single book, he includes other optical illusions and scientific studies that show that our consciousness is highly selective and does not necessarily present us with the world as it really is. We have already seen that our consciousness is as "blindered" as a cab horse. But we are not aware of these blinders nor of the selective acts consciousness performs in presenting us with the world. We take this world for granted and are unaware of the intentions that have gone into constituting it.

Taking the world for granted is what Husserl calls "the natural standpoint." By "the natural standpoint," he did not mean getting back to nature or anything like that. He simply meant our usual, everyday, ordinary attitude toward the world. When we open our eyes in the morning we see a world out there and we assume quite naturally that all our perception does is reflect it, as a mirror would. We do not believe that our consciousness has anything to do with forming or shaping or providing that world. It is there and we simply see it. This natural standpoint is shared by all of us. Descartes, sitting in his armchair, confronting the world and wondering what he could know with certainty about it, is as much in the natural standpoint as Sartre's café owner, emptying his head as his customers leave. Descartes raises questions about elements *within* the natural standpoint—this, as we can see, is what science does—but he never questions it, nor does he question the "I" which perceives it, and on which he bases his only certainty of knowledge.[47] As Husserl and Wilson lament, neither did most other philosophers.[48]

For Husserl this is entirely wrong. The first step in phenomenology, he argues, is to "step out" of the "natural standpoint." That is, not to take the world for granted, but to see it as something strange, fresh, new—as it does appear to us when for a moment our indifference threshold is lowered and we are amazed at the sheer fact of existence. It was this aspect of Husserl's work that awakened his pupil Heidegger to the need to renew the "question of being." It is also clear that this is the source of all poetry and nature mysticism, when we see a flower for the first time. We do this, Husserl said, by performing a mental act he called "bracketing." Put simply, we do not doubt in the manner of Descartes; we simply put aside everything we think we know about the world, all explanations about it—whether scientific or religious or any other—and "bracket" them, taking them out of the equation. We don't deny them; we simply ignore them for a time. As Husserl said, this allows us to observe "phenomena" without "presuppositions." It is from this starting point that we can begin to separate what is given in consciousness from what we unconsciously add or subtract from it. That is, it's from this perspective that we can see our intentionality at work.

This immediately raises a question. If the world I see in the natural standpoint is not the world as it is, but the world as it is presented to my consciousness—hence Wilson's remark that "everyday consciousness is a liar"—*who* is presenting it to me? And from this follows another question: who is the "I" to whom this world is being presented? Descartes doubted everything except his own existence. Everything else, he believed, was uncertain, but he felt pretty sure about who *he* was. But should he have been? As we've seen, Wilson's Outsiders experience a profound uncertainty about their identity. Descartes and the philosophers who followed him did not. They took their everyday "I" for granted. But taking the everyday "I" for granted is the same as taking the world for granted, and is another form of the passive fallacy. The "natural I" is as much a part of the natural standpoint as everything else and needs to be bracketed too. This seems to leaves us with an "I" that presents the world and another who sees it. The "I" writing this book is the one who sees it. But who is the other "I"?

In order to account for this Husserl borrowed a term from the philosopher Immanuel Kant, who spoke of a "transcendental ego."[49] Again, "transcendental" here has nothing to do with Transcendental Meditation or other popular spiritual meanings. It simply means "higher" or "above." What Husserl means is that there is an "I" behind our everyday "I."[50] This "I" is the source of the intentional acts that present the world to the "I" who perceives it. We can think of their relation as that of someone in a cinema looking at a film, unaware that in some way he is also the projectionist, putting the images on the screen. What Husserl wanted to do was to "uncover the secrets of the transcendental ego": to show the person watching the film that he is also the projectionist. That is, to bring the now unconscious intentionality of the transcendental ego to the awareness of the everyday "I." In other words, Wilson wanted to reach into the mind and become aware of the unconscious mental acts that place the blinders on our consciousness. Or, as William Blake would put it, to get our hands on the keys that open our doors of perception, rather than, as it is now, picking the locks or breaking them open.

Currently we are in the position of someone trying to find a hidden treasure, who has forgotten that it was he who hid it in the first place. In *Origins of the Sexual Impulse* Wilson compares us to a detective trying to solve a mystery, who suspects everyone *but himself*. I stare at the universe and wonder what it means. I get no answer but neither the universe nor the "I" staring at it are what they seem. Yet I am not aware of this and take myself and the poker-faced world for granted. As Wilson writes, "The world seems to be wearing a mask, and my mind seems to confront it helplessly; then I discover that my consciousness is a cheat, a double agent. It carefully fixed the mask on reality, then pretended to know nothing about it."[51] Or, in a remarkable anticipation of his work on split-brain psychology to come, "the left side of my mind doesn't know what the right side is doing." Phenomenology is a way of getting the two sides to talk to each other and, in Yeats's phrase, to "complete the partial mind."

Wilson was as profoundly influenced by Husserl's insights as he was by his discovery of Shaw, and *Beyond the Outsider* is his attempt to wed the two. He kept several "phenomenological journals," in which he returned again and again to drawing out the implications of Husserl's ideas.[52] I leave discussion of some of these to the next chapter. Here I want to focus on Wilson's synthesis of Husserl–Whitehead and Huxley–de Chardin. What is important for Wilson about this is that it does away with the need, felt in the earlier books of the Outsider Cycle, for a new religion to fill the void of meaninglessness in the modern age. Religion, we've seen, is for Wilson a *seriousness* about life, a sense of purpose and direction. As Shaw said, without this, a civilization cannot continue. Wilson agreed, but he rejected Shaw and Toynbee's idea of making a new world religion through a synthesis of the existing ones. Such an idea may appeal to reason, but no religion is driven by reason. Its essential drive must come from somewhere deeper, closer to the will. It must *grip* us entirely, not merely warrant intellectual assent. Wilson argues that a determined phenomenological analysis of consciousness reveals an inherent will to evolve, to complexification, a fundamental drive to increase and intensify our consciousness. In one sense we can say that our evolutionary purpose is to uncover our hidden, unconscious intentionality, which is itself a drive to greater meaning, greater freedom.

This drive works in us unconsciously now; we are aware of its effects but not its aims or of the way in which we can pursue these consciously. But there are clues. As we've seen, Wilson finds a great many in sex. He rejects the stimulus-response machine picture of human psychology that is a result of the passive fallacy, because it fails to accommodate the true character of human consciousness. A machine is entirely dependent on someone operating it. Unless I put a coin into a vending machine, nothing will come out. The operation is purely mechanical. Animals are a little better. They respond to stimuli around them and are not dependent on a direct command by an operator. Yet, if there is no stimulus, an animal will lie passively, waiting for one to appear, or simply go to sleep. Many human beings, it is true, are like this too (some of them occupy Beckett's plays). But many also are not. Many *go out of their way to find a stimulus*, something neither animals nor machines can do. This can range from a stiff drink to the kinds of ostensibly aberrant behavior many of Wilson's Outsiders displayed. We have an inbuilt hunger for newness, otherness, for something to cause a change in our consciousness, to dispel the fog of passivity that so easily engulfs us.

One of the basic means of doing this is sex. A man may be bored to tears but if an attractive woman walks by he immediately perks up. This is because his unconscious "meaning radar"—that is, his intentionality—has caught a blip, and detected something that can raise his consciousness, that can make it, if only briefly, more intense, more *intentional*.[53] As Wilson argues in his books on crime, much criminal violence is performed by people whose consciousness has so congealed into a thick sludge that only the most radical acts can loosen it, so that it can briefly move freely, can flow. This feeling of flow is the experience of growth, of evolution. This is not to say that Wilson condones the violence some people need in order to feel this, merely that he recognizes that in some, the need for it and the difficulty of achieving it (for we are not all equal here) necessitate such radical acts. But the difference between these people and ourselves is one of degree, not kind. We are all subject to the indifference threshold, to what Wilson calls a "tax on consciousness," but most of us find less drastic ways of dealing with it.

Sex can give us that sense of forward drive, of purposiveness, but it is not the only provider. There are others: art, science, philosophy, beauty; in short, ideas can also do the trick. But at this stage in our evolution, most of us do not respond to these stimuli with the same immediate riveting of attention that a sexual stimulus triggers. But there is no reason why this should always be so. Maslow's self-actualizers, Wells's originative intellectual workers, and Wilson's .005 percent suggest that in some people, the kind of galvanizing of attention that was once the province of sex is now shared by these more spiritual pursuits. Shaw believed that eventually they would take over from sex, and Wilson agrees. And in fact sex can be seen as a kind of watershed here. The need for food and shelter also makes us more purposive, but once these are obtained, the sense of purpose fades and only returns if these are threatened. Their stimulus is purely physical, on a level with what stimulates animals. As we've seen, sex clearly has a physical aspect, but it is almost a totally mental experience, dependent upon the imagination. With sex, the imagination can perform truly remarkable deeds. I can look at a sexy picture and, subsidized by the sexual instinct, transform it from a mere two-dimensional abstract representation to something almost real, real enough for me to have a real response to it. If I am hungry I cannot do this with a picture of a steak.

Wilson suggests that the intentionality I direct to the sexy picture and which makes it real is the same as I direct to ideas or to the world at large. Newness can come from these too. Yet it is a mistake to think of newness as a kind of aura, surrounding these things. Newness is the effect of my mind focusing on these things; it is an effect of *concentrating my consciousness*, which has the result of lowering the indifference threshold. It reveals what the writer J. B. Priestley called "the unimaginable promise of things." As he writes, "even the rusty iron of the pump, a patch of blue in a puddle, an old scythe against the wall—was almost unbearable."[54] This is the absurd good news again: things we thought we already knew are revealed as infinitely mysterious.

Again, Wilson isn't saying that a pornographic picture and a painting by van Gogh are equal, merely that the power I have to make the picture come to life is the same that I can direct at a van Gogh. It is, in fact, the same that van Gogh directed at the night sky when he painted *The Starry Night*. Van Gogh's intentionality transformed the night sky into a blaze of creative fire in the same way that my intentionality transforms a sexy picture into a reality I can respond to. To say that both *The Starry Night* and the sexy picture are false or not real, because I have to direct my intentionality to them in order for them to be effective, is to misunderstand intentionality. It is the same as saying that what is real about *The Starry Night* is the paint and canvas, the close-up or "worm's-eye view." And the same intentionality that I direct to the sexy picture I must also direct to a real-life sexual stimulus in order to respond to it; we all know what it's like to not be "all there" when making love. If the sexiness of a sexy picture is not real because I must direct intentionality to it in order to respond, then the same must be true of an actual physical partner. We know this already but have come to forget it through habit: in order for some idea or insight or experience to have an effect on us, we must realize it, that is, use our imagination to grasp its reality. We can realize ideas, but we can also realize other things.

Whether we realize ideas or a sexy picture, the process is exactly the same, except in the case of sex, my intentionality is subsidized by the sexual instinct, and my "meaning radar" is unconsciously tuned to respond to it. The picture first grabs my attention—it makes a blip on my unconscious meaning radar— then I *decide* whether to focus my attention on it or not. The act of decision in some people may happen so quickly that it seems that the enlivening of the picture takes place automatically. But this is not so; the decision to enliven it still takes place, but the individual is such a creature of habit and has so little self-discipline and self-control that he is unaware of it. Many of us do recognize that we can decide to transform the picture into something we respond to or not. This is why people of little self-control don't feel shame or guilt at indulging, while those with self-discipline recognize that they are *allowing* themselves a guilty pleasure. There is the recognition that they should be using their power of realization for something more than sexual diversion. This is something that Wilson believed many of the Romantics were guilty of.[55]

This, in fact, is the essence of Wilson's theory of symbolic response. And it applies to our experience of the beauty of nature as much as that of paintings or pornography. Wilson often quotes the poem of Yeats mentioned earlier, in which he complains that the beauty of a waterfall is "untouchable," because if he reached out to grab it, he would find only "cold stone and water."[56] The intentionality that endows a fetish with the power to stimulate and satisfy my sexual appetite, which is, for Wilson, fundamentally an appetite for newness, is the same that transforms ordinary nature into a mystical revelation of meaning.[57] This power Wilson calls "evolutionary intentionality," and uncovering and understanding it is the aim and purpose of his evolutionary existentialism.

This is the philosophy that Wilson suggests as an alternative to a new religion. It is preferable to a religion because it does not demand faith—we are too intelligent now to be satisfied with that—and can be verified through observation of our own consciousness. In essence it provides the purpose and aim, the seriousness about life that religion did, but without any supernatural aid or sacrifice of intelligence. Our evolution is driven not by random mutations or environmental pressures, but by our inherent evolutionary purpose: to understand and increase intentionality. As Wilson writes, "this is precisely the aim of evolutionary phenomenology: to change man's conception of himself and of the *interior forces* he has at his command, and ultimately to establish the new evolutionary type, foreshadowed by the 'outsiders.'"[58]

CHAPTER SEVEN

AMERICA AND THE ROBOT

Included in *Beyond the Outsider* is Wilson's account of a "psychedelic experience" he had in July 1963.[1] It is curious that in all the anthologies and books about drug literature that I have ever come across—and that includes quite a few—I have never seen Wilson's account appear. This, I suspect, is because it is critical. Wilson had read *The Doors of Perception*, Aldous Huxley's essay about his experience with the drug mescaline, a derivative of the hallucinogenic peyote plant, used in some North American Indian religious rituals. Wilson was intrigued by Huxley's account of seeing "what Adam saw on the morning of his creation," but he was also aware that such delights were not guaranteed. He knew that Sartre had tried mescaline nearly two decades earlier than Huxley, in 1936, and that he had had no such beatific visions. Sartre in fact had had a "bad trip." According to Simone de Beauvoir, who wrote about it in her autobiography, *The Prime of Life*, Sartre's visions were much more hellish. Umbrellas became vultures; shoes turned into skeletons; crabs, polyps, lobsters, an orangutan, and other strange, grimacing things followed him through Paris and for some time Sartre feared for his sanity. Huxley had said that if the wrong step was taken, the mescaline experience could quickly become a grand tour of hell, with everything offering proof of some demonic conspiracy against oneself, a cosmic paranoia. It seemed that Sartre had taken that wrong step. Wilson was quick to note that de Beauvoir's remarks about Sartre's state of mind were oddly similar to the kind of experience Sartre describes in *Nausea*, of a threatening, leering Reality, staring his hero in the face. This leads one to wonder if much of the existentialism that dominated the intellectual scene in the late 1950s was a product of Sartre's bad experience with drugs.

Wilson himself did not like the mescaline experience. He did not have a bad trip—the effects were nothing like what Sartre had experienced—but he also did not experience the visual effects that had delighted Huxley. In fact he had a premonition that he would not see "the morning of creation" and on the whole, the mescaline experiment turned out to be an irrelevancy. After some unpleasant physical effects, which made Wilson think, "I'll never touch this filthy stuff again," the drug came on.[2] Wilson found himself awash in a kind of universal love, a childlike sense of innocence and trust that he associated with Marilyn Monroe and with his daughter, Sally, three years old at the time. This feeling was pleasant enough, but Wilson felt it was *too* innocent, and that it eroded his sense of self. Huxley had celebrated the release from the self that he experienced under mescaline, but Wilson did not share his appreciation. "Self-hood," he wrote, "is a precise instrument for a certain purpose," and the sense of universal love and trust he was floating in blunted this.[3]

Wilson felt that "Adult minds are intended to be the policeman of the universe," a belief he expressed at the end of *The Mind Parasites*, his phenomenological science-fiction novel. (Some of its characters experiment with psychedelics.) When he looked at Sally he saw in her the same feeling he was experiencing, and it came to him that as he was then, he was in no condition to perform his duty of protecting her. "The job of the adult is protection and care," he felt, and "the job of all responsible human beings is the same protection and care towards the universe."[4] In order to fulfill this responsibility, one needed to "insulate oneself" against this universal love; this, Wilson believed, was the first step in adulthood. What he felt happening to him then was in fact the reverse process, as if he was being sent back into childhood, and was seeing the world through "great mists of one's own feelings."[5] As he lay there in bed, he felt as if a large and overaffectionate dog had knocked him down and was licking his face. All this love was fine, but Wilson found it a bore. "Let me alone," he wanted to say. "I want to *think*."

Another aspect of the mescaline experience that Wilson didn't care for was that it felt as if all the filters or blinders installed in his consciousness were suddenly removed, and reality was coming in at him from all directions. He described it as being like a radio without the VHF attachment: instead of being able to tune in to a particular station, it was as if he was receiving all of them at once. This was confusing and, more important, it inhibited his capacity to will, a conclusion at which Huxley and William James, another early psychedelic explorer, had also arrived.[6] Wilson had over the years developed a powerful capacity to focus his attention on what interested him. Now this ability to ignore irrelevancies was weakened. It did, he believed, make him psychic to a degree; many of the feelings he was experiencing, he said, seemed to be floating loose in the atmosphere. But whatever psychic abilities were released, they did not make up for what the drug had taken away.

Huxley and other experimenters had claimed that drugs such as mescaline could trigger mystical experiences. Wilson had his doubts. His own moments of insight were associated with a sense of *control*. They were not the kind of visual experience that Huxley had enjoyed (Wilson points out that Huxley's bad eyesight may have had something to do with this) but were more like what Heidegger meant when he talked about overcoming our "forgetfulness of being."[7] That is, they were experiences that occurred when the indifference threshold was lowered and he could perceive things without the gauze of emotion in which they are usually wrapped. These moments came when for some reason his mind was tightly focused and concentrated. But it was precisely this focus that the mescaline had dissipated. Wilson was interested in how we can get our phenomenological hands on these blinders and adjust them. But he did not think we should lose them altogether.

In the end, Wilson concluded that mescaline—and by extension other drugs—seem to "inhibit evolutionary consciousness." What he meant by evolutionary consciousness is "*all* pleasure associated with the intellect or intellectual sensibility." It is "an intensity in which consciousness is aware of itself *as activity*." It includes a "sense of responsibility" rather than "passive enjoyment." In the broadest sense it means a delight in the process of education, of *Bildung*, of growth and development, of using the mind and finding a sense of power and control in that use. Mescaline could be pleasurable and beneficial if one wanted a rest from evolutionary consciousness—that is, if one wanted a holiday from using the mind. Wilson, a confirmed workaholic, did not. He also believed that the kind of visual effects that Huxley perceived under mescaline could be obtained through the use of the phenomenological method, through "bracketing" and stepping out of the "natural standpoint." But these required using the will, not turning it off. These perceptual changes, Wilson admits, are not as profound as those experienced under mescaline or other drugs, but they have the advantage of being amenable to analysis and description, something that the psychedelic experience often eludes.[8] They are also permanent, and something we can learn how to do, not passively experience through the effect of a stimulus.[9]

In any case, Wilson had no time or chance to turn off his will or mind and take a holiday, on mescaline or not. Almost a decade after it began, the critical animus toward him seemed unabated. *Ritual in the Dark*, it is true, received some good reviews and sold well. But the books of the Outsider Cycle were more or less stillborn. Between resounding silence and overtly personal attacks, it was difficult to choose which was preferable. No one seemed to notice that the books were related and that they all addressed a common theme; a repeated criticism of Wilson's work was that it displayed no "consistent viewpoint," an assessment that makes one wonder which books the critics were reviewing. Allied with a kind of willful ignorance was a rancor against Wilson having the temerity to write at all. It seemed that his publishing a book was somehow a "calculated affront."[10] Wilson was able to stand alone, but no writer is invulnerable, especially when on the receiving end of often violent attacks.

"The reviews I've been getting for a long time now," Wilson confided in his journal, "are downright insulting in tone—patronizing, like a headmaster criticising the essay of a 6th form."[11] He felt that *Beyond the Outsider* may have been a turning point in his career, but aside from himself and no doubt Joy, not many others were aware of this.[12] He knew what it was like to feel a "generalised rage against fate," the "desire to get one's own back by smashing things." But he also knew this was "one of the most dangerous states of mind." (It was precisely the state of mind of many of the criminals he wrote about.) He wouldn't let "temporary setbacks" affect him too much. What was important was to "go on working steadily to really develop the powers that I have brought into being through discipline."[13]

Yet it wasn't only a lack of intelligent critical response that troubled him. While he could always find a publisher, bad reviews did not help sales.[14] His books had their readers but the bad publicity meant he got fewer offers to review or do magazine work or lecture. He and Joy did not live extravagantly but Wilson did like his books, his music, and his wine, and he did have a growing family. On August 4, 1965, Joy had another child, a boy, whom they named John Damon, after his godfather, Foster Damon, the Blake scholar; Foster Damon turns up as Damon Reade, the Blake scholar on the trail of a poetic serial killer in *The Glass Cage*. Wilson wondered if he would feel the same affection for their son as he did for his daughter. His wonder was brief. Human beings, he reflected, "come closest to the fulfilment of their nature in being able to love," and his new child gave him much opportunity for this. Wilson himself felt that the key to his nature was "a need to give affection." He now had another person ready to receive it.[15]

But another mouth meant more financial burden and he was already carrying a substantial weight. Victor Gollancz's and T. S. Eliot's advice must have crept back into his mind on occasion: find some congenial work, stop writing at such a frantic pace, do a book a year, instead of two or three. Moments of gloom, when the thought of a future when he couldn't find a publisher or when his books would not be read, came over him. But then he would look at Joy or hear Sally laughing and the "nightmare vanished." It was through his children that he also came to accept that "the universe does not operate entirely on material laws."[16] Early on he was aware of a telepathic link with them, which convinced him that "our minds are not mere observers, stranded in a sea of matter." They can somehow "control the universe around them," an insight he would build on in coming years.

At the moment, that aspect of the universe he most needed to control was his bank balance. The "permanent overdraft" status that would run throughout most of his career had begun and Wilson had to find more paying work. He had a long list of books behind him; nevertheless he found himself complaining that he still had to "scramble . . . for a few bloody hundred pounds."[17] Once again he looked west across the Atlantic and considered heading to America for another lecture tour. It would be as demanding as his first tour, but his time there would be rewarding, in more ways than one.

In early January 1966, Wilson left Joy, Sally, and Damon and headed to London en route to New York. He was not happy about the trip. He hated leaving home, and the thought of another lecture tour depressed him. He had drunk too much the night before and was hungover. It was unseasonably warm and so of course British Rail had to have the heating on. In this thoroughly depressing state of mind, Wilson realized the train was passing through Teignmouth, where he had had his peak experience a decade earlier, when he discovered that Joy wasn't pregnant. Then he had come to the conclusion that the sea and everything else he looked at were truly beautiful, *objectively*, and that his relief at Joy's news had merely been the means of lowering his indifference threshold and realizing this. Now it came to him: *if* the sea and the Exmouth peninsula *are* beautiful for real, *why* couldn't he see this now? He felt a kind of rage at the stupidity of *knowing* that something is beautiful but not being able to *see* it. He decided to force the issue. He made a kind of grimace, concentrated his mind, and fundamentally *willed* himself to see the beauty. It was not a pretty sight. If someone had been watching him, he said, they would have thought that he was having an epileptic fit.[18]

Some moments later he felt as if doors were opening in his head. Then it happened. There was the sea, as beautiful as it had been in 1954. The process had taken about two minutes. For the rest of the journey to London, his fatigue, hangover, reservations about the trip, and general worry about the future dissolved. A determined act of intense concentration had brought the change on, rather as if, like Graham Greene, he had put a revolver to his head. But unlike Greene, he didn't need a revolver, only the knowledge that the Teignmouth peak experience had been real and that what he saw then he could see now, if only he could push open his doors of perception. Making an enormous effort of mental concentration seemed to have done the trick. He even decided to give up drinking for a few weeks so that he could maintain the clarity he felt.

Several hours later he landed in New York. His first port of call was Hastings-on-Hudson—a train from Grand Central Station took him there— where he visited the science writer Martin Gardner. They had been corresponding for some time and upon meeting, Wilson liked Gardner. Sadly they would have a falling out, and a few years later Gardner, a founding member of the Committee for the Scientific Investigation of Claims of the Paranormal (CSICOP), whom we will meet again further on, would be attacking Wilson for his credulous belief in psychic phenomena, calling his books "scribblings" and Wilson himself an "irresponsible journalist of the occult."[19] In his book *The Quest for Wilhelm Reich* (1981), a study of the radical Freudian and sex theorist's life and ideas, Wilson would later return gentle fire by questioning Gardner's scientific omniscience.[20] Gardner had first come to Wilson's attention through his book *Fads and Fallacies in the Name of Science*, in which he attacked Reich as a crank. Wilson accepted that there were some elements of the crank in Reich, but argued that he couldn't be so easily dismissed and that this ideas about "orgone energy" deserved serious study. The kind of irritated dismissal that Gardner and his fellow skeptics delivered to Reich—and any other thinkers who stepped beyond what they believed were the proper boundaries of science—was arbitrary and unproductive, Wilson thought, and he said so.

Wilson's first lecture was at Bridgewater State University, in Massachusetts, where he was received with applause—so much that he wondered if lecturing full-time in America might be a good career move. Next was New Hampshire, where a solicitous professor's wife told him he was getting fat. He had put on weight—the result of much wine and good food—but as he was six feet tall, he carried it well. His weight, however, would become a more serious concern in later years and even then he decided to cut down on food. After his lecture at New Hampton School, Wilson was invited to a literary party, where he met the writer Calder Willingham, a novelist and screenwriter; some of his later credits include the films *The Graduate* (1967) and *Little Big Man* (1970). His novel *End as a Man* (1947) had started his career and a later work, *Eternal Fire* (1962), about a determined sexual athlete who seduces his way through a series of women, had been attacked as obscene. Wilson didn't like the book—he called it nasty—but Willingham did him a good turn. He had recently had to turn down a position as writer-in-residence at Hollins College, in Virginia. The day after the party, Wilson dropped in on Willingham before heading to his plane, and mentioned that he was looking for just such a position. Willingham got on the phone to Hollins College and after a brief conversation, Wilson was hired as writer-in-residence, starting in September. The salary was good, he would have a house on the campus, and the school would pay for his family to join him. Financial worries, at least for the next year, were over.

The good news had an effect. Driving out of New Hampton on his way to the airport, Wilson had another peak. Passing a sign pointing toward Danbury, Connecticut, he recalled that Charles Ives, his favorite American composer, had been born there. Another sign, pointing to Concord, reminded him of Thoreau, whom he had loved reading in his teens. A sudden sense of their *reality* struck him, as if they were still alive. He felt that if he wanted to, he could go and meet them. Something similar would happen in Washington, D.C., two weeks later, when he was on his way to meet Dan Danziger, a friend and fellow music enthusiast he had met on his last American trip. Suddenly the idea of the *reality of the past* came to him, as if what the psychologist Pierre Janet called "the reality function"—the sense of being wide awake and in touch with the present—had expanded to encompass the entire world. He had come across this kind of experience before. Marcel Proust had had it. His novel *Remembrance of Things Past* begins when its hero tastes a kind of cake called a madeleine dipped in tea, and is suddenly cast back into his childhood holidays at Combray in the north of France. In that moment, the living reality of the past strikes him with an almost mystical clarity. "The vicissitudes of life became indifferent to me," Proust writes, "its disasters innocuous, its brevity illusory."[21] Hesse and Toynbee had had such moments too. As we've seen, Wilson himself had hit upon them in different places in his early work. But in late January, on a snowy day in Washington, it struck him vividly. It was an important insight, one of the most important he had ever had. So that he wouldn't forget it, he gave it a name: Faculty X. "The basic aim of human evolution," he concluded, "is to achieve Faculty X." The paradox, he would later say, "is that we already possess it to a large degree."[22] In the not-so-distant future he would write a book arguing exactly this point.

After Washington, Wilson headed to Brooklyn, New York, where he stayed with a flamboyant preacher, the Reverend Bill Glenesk, in his flat on Remsen Street in Brooklyn Heights. The reverend had visited Wilson in Cornwall; Wilson had put him up and the reverend was happy to return the favor. He seemed to express his love of the theater and the divine at the same time, accompanying his sermons with crashing cymbals. Wilson enjoyed the reverend's church and even preached—lectured—there himself. The congregation so liked Wilson's talk that when he said that Christianity was basically a waste of time, they didn't bat an eye. The reverend was friends with the writer Norman Mailer, who was a neighbor. When Wilson said he would like to meet him, the reverend arranged it. Mailer decorated his walls with hostile reviews of his books, and Wilson felt that with his "tough guy" image, Mailer would have enjoyed beating up his critics—a thought that may have occasionally crossed the more gentle Wilson's mind. They talked shop and compared advances; Mailer's beat Wilson's hands down. Wilson remembered that in 1960 Mailer had run for mayor of New York as a candidate for the Existential Party. When he asked Mailer what he meant by existentialism, he replied, "Playing things by ear."

Mailer mentioned that W. H. Auden was in New York. If Wilson wanted to meet him, he could arrange it. Auden lived off Washington Square in Greenwich Village. Wilson had been reading Auden's poetry since his teens and was happy to meet him, but their lunch in Auden's apartment didn't start well. At first the atmosphere was a bit cool. Auden seemed distant and Wilson wondered if this had anything to do with the fact that he wasn't homosexual; Auden was. But then Christopher Isherwood, who was also homosexual, was very friendly with him, so he decided it was just Auden's manner. The ice broke when Auden asked Wilson what he thought of *The Lord of the Rings*, which had only recently become a campus best seller, after years of modest sales.[23] When Wilson said he thought it was one of the great novels of the century and had read it twice, Auden perked up. Auden knew Tolkien and he talked about him and his work enthusiastically for the rest of the meeting. Wilson would later ask Auden to help with some trouble he was having with the Tolkien estate. He had written an essay called "Tree by Tolkien," a play on Tolkien's own story "Leaf by Niggle." When he sent a copy to Tolkien, his lawyer grabbed it and sent Wilson a letter saying that he had to change the title, as it suggested that Tolkien had written the essay. Wilson thought this was ridiculous—his own name as author was clearly on the cover. Auden said he would do what he could. He must have put in an effective word, as the booklet, published in 1973, the same year in which Tolkien died, remained available. What Tolkien thought of it is unknown.

After Brooklyn Wilson returned to Washington, where he lectured at the Library of Congress. Here he stayed with a society hostess named Marion Leiter, who he later discovered had been a close friend of President Kennedy. Marion's husband had been in the CIA and had been a friend of Ian Fleming. Fleming based the character of Felix Leiter, the CIA agent in the James Bond novels, on Marion's husband, who in turn introduced the president to the books. A positive remark by Kennedy about Bond helped make the novels best sellers in the States. At a dinner party at Marion's Wilson made an unfortunate faux pas. He had bumped into Stephen Spender at Georgetown University; he hadn't seen him for a decade and when he mentioned this to Marion, she suggested he invite him to the party. Most of the guests talked politics, so the two writers were left to themselves. Kennedy's assassination was still a tender topic and Wilson remarked to Spender that while he believed Oswald was the assassin—he had in fact written about the case—this was surprising, since Oswald's marksmanship was generally considered miserable. But then, Wilson added, Kennedy himself had seemed one of the most accident-prone people on the planet. It was a question, he said, of which was worse: Oswald's marksmanship or Kennedy's luck, and Oswald had won. There was a lull in the party and Wilson's remark sounded loud and clear. Those who heard it weren't happy. He then compounded the offense by asking if the stories about Kennedy's philandering were true. He had forgotten that Kennedy was seen by many Americans as a kind of King Arthur and realized too late that the other guests would find his question insulting. They assured him with utter confidence that such reports were untrue, and Wilson stood corrected. A decade later Judith Campbell Exner published a memoir in which she claimed to have been one of Kennedy's mistresses, and reports of other affairs also quickly came to light.[24]

But aside from this awkward moment, the lecture tour was going well. Wilson was speaking to capacity audiences and earning much-needed money. There was other good news, more or less. Someone had sent him a newspaper clipping about a court case in Boston in which *The Sex Diary of Gerard Sorme* had been described as obscene. The judge disagreed with this, but not on the grounds that the book was a work of literature. It was no worse than Henry Miller or D. H. Lawrence, the judge said. But the idea that the author of such drivel should be considered a genius baffled him—a sentiment shared by many of Wilson's critics.

In San Francisco Wilson lectured at Pacific College; afterward he managed to take a few days off to rest. He took the opportunity to visit the poet and publisher Lawrence Ferlinghetti at his famous City Lights bookshop in North Beach—where he spent much more than he should have—and to renew ties with an old acquaintance, the poet Kenneth Rexroth. Rexroth, a respected elder poet and essayist, was notorious for being the "father of the Beat Generation," at least according to *Time* magazine.[25] Wilson had met Rexroth years earlier, when the poet visited Mevagissey, Wilson's local town in Cornwall, and recorded an interview with Wilson for his KPFA radio program. Wilson had dinner at Rexroth's flat, where he enjoyed his host's talent as a salacious raconteur.[26] Rexroth also took Wilson for a tour of Haight-Ashbury, the hippie neighborhood then gearing up for the Summer of Love, which would arrive in 1967. Wilson thought it was not that different from Soho, although he found the flower children more colorful than their Swinging London comrades. He even got the impression that *The Outsider* was an important book for some of the hippies—at least it had turned them on to Hermann Hesse, whose novels were now beginning to make their comeback.[27] (By this time Timothy Leary had written about Hesse as a psychedelic precursor in his *Psychedelic Review*.)

Rexroth had become critical of the Beat Generation—Jack Kerouac in particular—and had reservations about the flower children. Wilson did too. He felt the counterculture was simply a revival of nineteenth-century Romanticism; hence the sudden popularity of Hesse, who was fundamentally a Romantic. As the Romantics did, the dropouts had a yearning for something more than what the everyday world could give them, but, like the Romantics, they had no idea what exactly that was or how to get it. (With Auguste Villiers de l'Isle-Adam's *Axël*, they could say, "As for living, our servants will do that for us.") Drugs such as LSD suggested an answer, but as Wilson had seen, they worked by relaxing the will, putting it out of commission, and for him this was a mistake.[28]

It was a mistake, however, that the entire hippie movement seemed to be making. Countercultural leaders such as Timothy Leary and Alan Watts gave this philosophy of "letting it all hang out" some philosophical credibility, and it is no wonder that in 1967, the British underground newspaper *International Times* would run a full-page story about Aleister Crowley as a "proto-hippie."[29] Crowley's philosophy of "do what thou wilt" was tailor-made for the psychedelic generation. Wilson had said that the 1960s had passed him by, but it was not only his industry that kept him on that decade's sidelines. The fundamental idea behind the new existentialism, the emphasis on will, self-discipline, and the active character of the mind, was out of step with an era determined to "turn off the mind, relax, and float downstream." Unlike Wilson, the hippies were not interested in being the "policemen of the universe," and were very happy to take holidays from "evolutionary consciousness."[30] Wilson was not surprised when, within a few years, the "whole experiment of love and self-abandonment was petering out."[31] As he would write in the early 1970s, it was from the permissive, indulgent hippie milieu that Charles Manson would emerge, a very dark bloom among the flower children.[32]

Wilson had had his own experience of the ill effects of letting it all hang out a couple of weeks earlier. He had been lecturing at the University of South Florida, in Tampa, and a professor mentioned that Jack Kerouac lived in nearby Saint Petersburg and wanted to meet him. A meeting was arranged for that evening but after the talk a friend of Kerouac's apologized to Wilson. He and Kerouac had set out for the campus, but along the way Kerouac insisted on stopping at every bar they saw. He eventually became so drunk that his friend had to take him home. Wilson said he would be lecturing in Saint Petersburg the next day—why didn't Kerouac meet him there, and they could go for a meal? But the next day the same thing happened. This reminded Wilson of a similar story that Ferlinghetti had told him. One day Kerouac had decided that he would visit Henry Miller, who was then living in Big Sur on the California coast, not far from the Esalen Institute. Kerouac hired a cab to drive the hundred or so miles, but kept it waiting for two hours while he sat in a bar across from the City Lights bookshop, drinking. Finally he got in the cab. But when they reached Big Sur, he had no idea how to find Miller's cabin. So he told the driver to go, found a field, picked a spot, and went to sleep. The next day he found the nearest bar, called a cab, and went back to San Francisco. He and Miller never met. Ferlinghetti told Wilson that Kerouac had long ago abandoned any attempt at discipline and self-control and was drifting. A look at the work Kerouac produced in his last years suggests this. Three years after his aborted attempts to meet Wilson, Kerouac was dead from cirrhosis of the liver after years of alcohol abuse. He was forty-seven. His time on the road had reached a dead end and one wonders, had their meeting taken place, if the king of the beatniks and the angry young Outsider would have had much to say to each other.[33]

Back in Cornwall in April, Wilson kept up the pace. The last weeks of the tour had been tiring and his resolve to maintain a sense of purpose and to avoid boredom suffered. But he was happy to be home. The idea of traveling again did not delight, but he had been invited to lecture at Trinity College Dublin, Joy's alma mater, and he decided that she could use a holiday, so he accepted and brought her and the children along. During his talk the electricity failed. But Wilson had so mastered his material that this didn't stop him. He knew exactly what he wanted to say and he said it in the dark. At the end, the lights came on, and the students cheered.

The experience reminded him of a book he had read about sensory deprivation; he had made a note of it in his journals.[34] Students were known to use the black room, a sensory deprivation chamber, as an aid in taking exams. In the total darkness and silence, they would sleep for fifteen hours, then wake up completely refreshed, remembering everything they had studied. The curious thing, though, was that if they remained in the black room after this point, they would begin to go to pieces. They became bored, then panic set in. They would have hallucinations. Some became severely depressed, others psychotic. It seemed Gurdjieff was right when he said that without "impressions," human beings cannot last very long.

Wilson had an idea for a novel that would have the black room at its center. He imagined a secret organization that captured spies from both sides of the Iron Curtain and subjected them to brainwashing using the black room, in order to make them double agents. He had read that the Chinese had used such techniques in the Korean War; Richard Condon's novel *The Manchurian Candidate* (1959), made into a successful film in 1962, used a similar theme; it's unclear if Wilson knew of it. Wilson's novel would be about how someone could withstand the black room, about how agents could be trained to resist the mental deterioration that inevitably set in. That Wilson could carry on lecturing in total darkness, and that his audience could also stay attentive to what he was saying, seemed to suggest that this was possible. Mental activity could help, it seemed, in resisting the black room.

This theme had occupied Wilson for some time. In his journals he had written, "'life' can make anyone great by applying the right stimulus—this is the greatness of a Napoleon. But the real greatness is to go on striving *without great challenges*."[35] As he had recognized all along, human beings are at their best when surmounting difficulties. Yet as Toynbee knew, "it is a human characteristic to deteriorate under favourable circumstances." Without challenges, we succumb to trivialities. Hence the absurd behavior of many of Wilson's Outsiders, who went out of their way to create difficult conditions for themselves out of an instinctive knowledge that more comfortable circumstances would demoralize them. Yet civilization aims at *removing* hardship, and, as Wilson had found out during his own time on the road, giving up the comforts of civilization is no answer either. (This is something that all advocates of getting back to nature eventually have to concede.) The idea then was not to get rid of civilization, as Romantics such as Rousseau had been suggesting since the late eighteenth century, and which the hippies and dropouts had recently rediscovered, but of strengthening consciousness. The question seemed to be "Can a new type of man respond to this most difficult of all challenges—the challenge of no challenge?" That is, is it possible to maintain a high level of purpose and mental focus *without* a stimulus? Can we gird our mental loins, as it were, without a threat?

It was this question that Wilson's novel *The Black Room* (1971), which he began before he left Cornwall for his stint as a writer-in-residence, aimed to answer. It would also occupy a central place in *Introduction to the New Existentialism*, his condensation of the Outsider Cycle, which appeared in 1966. Wilson

believed that if he had contributed anything to twentieth-century thought, it
was contained in this short, lucid work. One key point he was eager to make
clear was exactly why the old existentialism hit a cul-de-sac. This was, he argues, because of a misunderstanding of Husserl's philosophy.

Existentialism, at least in the form associated with Heidegger, Sartre, and
Camus, had its roots in Husserl's phenomenology. It provided a method for
answering the kinds of questions that Kierkegaard had asked, which got the
existential ball rolling. Husserl spawned a great many phenomenologists, but
according to Wilson, practically none of them grasped his most important insight, the "transcendental ego." This is the "I" behind the everyday "I," which is
responsible for "intending" the world we see from "the natural standpoint." For
Husserl consciousness is intentional, and it is the transcendental ego that in-
tends it.

Heidegger, Husserl's student, shifted his attention from consciousness to
the question of being. In philosophical terms we can say he moved from
epistemology—the study of how we know things—to ontology, the study of the
nature of being, what it means to "be," or to say that something "is." (We can
say that Heidegger wanted to get down to is-ness.) Heidegger's method remained phenomenological—that is, descriptive—and we've seen that his work
is often illuminated by sudden patches of insight, when, in Wilson's terms, the
indifference threshold is lowered and we see beyond the natural standpoint.
Wilson disagrees with Heidegger's pessimistic conclusions, but he finds much
value in his musings on language and poetry, and his determination to avoid the
"triviality of everydayness," the stifling world of personal relations and social
gossip. By secluding himself in his chalet in Todtnauberg, Heidegger took his
own step outside, and Wilson recognized that.

Wilson's real philosophical bête noire is Sartre, with whom, we've seen, he
had a relationship based on "admiration and exasperation." Wilson admired
Sartre because in his writing he was "trying to get somewhere"; he was "thinking to a purpose, with a sense of urgency."[36] Ideas were *alive* for him, as they
were for Wilson. That is, Sartre used his mind to try to understand experience
in all its complexity, instead of ignoring it, as most of us do. Wilson had the
same admiration for Wells and this is what made him an existentialist too.
What Wilson found unacceptable were Sartre's conclusions, which, he believed,
he arrived at through some fundamental errors in reasoning. Wilson's long argument with Sartre began with *The Outsider* and reached its clearest expression
in the long essay "Anti-Sartre," which began as a review of a biography of Sartre and ended as a fifty-page treatise.[37]

Sartre got it wrong, Wilson says, when he abandoned Husserl's notion of
the transcendental ego, which he did in an early book, *The Transcendence of the
Ego* (1936). Although it is not immediately apparent from his work, Husserl was
something of a mystic. He spoke of phenomenology as a way of getting to "the

keepers of the keys of being," the source of experience that Goethe, in *Faust*, called "the Mothers." Sartre rejected Husserl's transcendental ego because it smacked too much of nineteenth-century idealism, religion, and mysticism. Sartre was an atheist and a rationalist. Consciousness *is* intentional, Sartre agrees, but there is no transcendental ego "intending" it. Intentionality, for Sartre, simply means "directed." But even this is too much for Sartre; it suggests an agent behind consciousness: being directed suggests a director. For Sartre, consciousness is *drawn* to its objects as iron filings are drawn to a magnet. It has no choice in the matter, just as the metal a magnet attracts can't resist the attraction, or move with it more swiftly. It is *pulled* by objects, as the moon pulls the tides. Where Husserl has an archer (the transcendental ego) shooting his arrow (intentionality) at a target, for Sartre we must imagine a target that pulls the arrow toward it—and an arrow that somehow gets into the bow on its own. This is a result of Sartre's determination to maintain the Cartesian passive ego, contemplating a world outside itself with which it has nothing to do. It is this determination, Wilson argues, that vitiates his position.

Having abandoned intentionality—or at least an "intender" in consciousness—Sartre was then free to develop the kind of vision of the world associated with his philosophy: that of a consciousness confronting an alien, often hostile world, and desperately trying to fill itself up in order to avoid experiencing its emptiness, which is how Sartre understood freedom.[38] It is a world based on the notion of man's contingency, the realization that there is no *necessity* for his existence, that, as Heidegger said, he is "thrown into the world" with no instruction book telling him why he is there and what he should do now that he is. Wilson points out that the reason Huxley and Sartre had such different experiences on mescaline is that while Huxley spent a lifetime developing a sense of trust toward existence, Sartre had a fundamentally suspicious attitude toward it—again, a product of the Cartesian passive ego confronting an ambiguous world.

Under the influence of mescaline, the world became threatening for Sartre because he already felt threatened by it. He despised the shallow people— *salauds*, "bastards" in English—who believed that their existence was somehow necessary and who reduced the world to their own petty occupations; this was his general argument against the bourgeoisie. The kind of "intending" Sartre recognized was a falsification of the world, a distortion of it in order to avoid recognizing the fundamental fact of existence's sheer arbitrariness. What the world was really like for Sartre is in *Nausea*: meaningless, disconnected, and threatening, much as it appeared during his mescaline trip. This, Sartre argued, is the truth of the world, and those who cannot face it cover it up with falsifications (bad faith) in order to live.

But, Wilson says, here Sartre made a fundamental mistake. The kind of world *Nausea* presents is one in which consciousness has given up its task of intending. Consciousness then feels threatened because it has abandoned its responsibility of directing its attention at reality and has become completely passive before it. Sartre believed that nausea is a more true experience of the world, but this is like saying the truth of a book becomes most clear to us when we read it exceptionally badly, with our attention limp and dull, until it is, in effect, meaningless because we do not make the effort to grasp ("prehend," Whitehead would say) its meaning. Nausea does not reveal the truth about life; it is life with one of its central ingredients—our intentionality—missing. And as Sartre's hero's consciousness becomes more passive, more insignificant, the reality of things presses in on him more closely, until he is frightened by the root of a tree or a doorknob. The sheer is-ness of things overwhelms him. Huxley, whose attitude toward the world was one of trust, was delighted by the same is-ness that frightened Sartre. Wilson may not have enjoyed his mescaline experience, but his attitude toward the world is more along Huxley's lines than Sartre's.

Wilson points out that with his talk of the "absurd," Camus makes the same mistake. Camus says that our experience of the world is like seeing someone gesticulating in a phone booth. We can see his hands gesturing and his mouth moving, but we can't hear what he is saying. This, Camus says, is a good picture of life's absurdity: it is a dumb show. But again, Camus' image is one in which an important element of experience has been subtracted. The person may *look* absurd, but I *know* that he is talking to someone on the telephone, even if I can't hear him. In order to see him as absurd, I have to deliberately ignore what I know to be reality. But Camus and Sartre wanted to say that somehow, this knowledge is inadmissible. Wilson often quotes Camus' line from *The Myth of Sisyphus* in which he gives another example of the absurd: "Rising, tram, four hours in the office or factory, meal, tram, four hours of work, meal, sleep and Monday, Tuesday, Wednesday, Thursday, Friday and Saturday, according to the same rhythm. . . . But one day the 'why' arises and everything begins in that weariness tinged with amazement."[39]

The why that Camus speaks of here is the same why that Sartre's hero experiences when he wakes up and finds himself in Indochina, and has no idea why he is there. But this is no revelation of the absurdity or nausea of reality; merely the result of a passive attitude toward consciousness and life. We remember that the protagonist of Camus' *The Stranger* sleepwalks through life and only wakes up when he is confronted with the fact of his imminent execution. If the surest way to become neurotic is to accept that there is nothing to be done, then it seems that this is exactly what Sartre and Camus are suggesting. If phenomenology is an attempt to philosophize without presuppositions, which was Husserl's initial aim, then we can see that Sartre and Camus were not good phenomenologists, since they allowed their own presuppositions about reality—its absurdity—to color what they saw. What Sartre's nausea and

Camus' absurd reveal is not the truth about reality, but the limits of everyday consciousness. But since they restricted themselves to these limits, they could see no way *beyond* them.

Wilson's response to this philosophy of paralysis is to insist on the active, intentional character of consciousness. As we've seen, it is responsible for the world we perceive. We may not know why we exist or what we are supposed to do now that we are here, but it is incorrect and a kind of philosophical sleight of hand to gaze at the world blankly as if we had nothing to do with it. Our consciousness is involved with it at the deepest levels—levels, to be sure, that we are not immediately aware of, but which it is the task of phenomenology to uncover. To stare at the world and say it is meaningless ignores the fact that the world we are staring at depends on our consciousness; again, it is the crime of which the detective suspects everyone but himself. And if our consciousness changes, so does the world. If we perceive it with greater intentionality, it responds. This is the lesson of van Gogh's *The Starry Night*.

We might say it is all relative, that between the way Sartre perceived the world and the way van Gogh did—or Huxley did on mescaline—there is no way to decide which is more true. But again, this misses the point. Van Gogh's canvas vibrates with life because when he painted it he was seeing the world with more intentionality. He was reading it more intently, thereby prehending more of its meaning. Sartre's hero is afraid of a doorknob because he is barely intending; he is reading the world very badly, and inferring all sorts of threatening things about it that exist only in his mind. To say that the difference between more intentionality and less is relative is illogical. It is like saying there is no real, objective difference between reading a book poorly and reading it well. If I read a book well I understand it. If I read it poorly I do not. There is nothing relative about that. It is the same difference as between the worm's and the bird's-eye view. A worm may perceive much detail in the part of reality it can perceive, but it is a much smaller patch than what the bird takes in, just as we can gather a lot of information about brushstrokes and pigments by putting our face up against a painting, but to get the real picture, we need to step back. Since the bird's-eye view shows us more, it is more true—or at least it has a much greater chance of being true, since compared to it, the worm's-eye view is severely limited.[40]

Introduction to the New Existentialism attacks the passive fallacy. At its heart is the same question that Wilson addresses in *The Black Room*: how to meet the challenge of no challenge, how to maintain a high level of purposive consciousness without the aid of an external stimulus. One approach to this is through an understanding of mystical experiences, through states of consciousness that are not ordinary but are neither transcendental, in the sense of supernatural or religious; we have already looked at some of these in Maslow's peak experiences. One of the drawbacks of the old existentialism is that it accepted our ordinary, everyday consciousness, the natural standpoint, as a static given, as consciousness per se. Because it refused any kind of religious or supernatural reality—we must live, Camus said, "without appeal"—it argued that all our values must be rooted in this everyday consciousness. (Hence Camus' refusal to accept any answer that his teddy boy couldn't understand.)

But these values, the old existentialism argues, are relative. In jettisoning religion or any ideal world, we are left with no *objective* standard by which we can judge values as better or worse. We are free, but we have no purpose, aside from personal or social, utilitarian ones, to give our freedom meaning. There is no *direction* to our freedom; we can do as we like, it all amounts to the same thing. Sartre tried to fill in this blank with leftist politics, an expression of his hatred of the *salauds* and bourgeoisie. Camus preferred a kind of stoic morality, handicapped by his womanizing. But in a meaningless universe, such options are mere stopgaps and are ultimately arbitrary. Heidegger came closer to an answer with his insistence on living authentically. But this depended on the grim wakeup call of a constant awareness of one's finitude, an alarm clock he shared with Gurdjieff, punctuated by occasional glimpses of "being" garnered through poetry. For Wilson this is unnecessarily pessimistic.

Yet phenomenology has shown that the form of consciousness that the old existentialism bases itself on is only one of many, and that it presents us with a highly edited picture of reality for good evolutionary reasons (we remember the blindered horse). Our everyday consciousness is, as William James argued, very narrow; as Wilson says, it is a liar. It gives us a severely limited picture, then asks us to believe it is the truth, while denying it has anything to do with what it is showing us. Accepting this limited picture of reality abets the passive fallacy and leads old existentialists such as Sartre and Camus to conclude gloomily that the best we can hope for is to stoically endure life's meaninglessness, doing our best to treat each other humanely while we do. Yet peak experiences, aesthetic experiences, poetry, natural beauty, sex, and mystical experiences all suggest a reality of much greater meaning, while Husserl's and Whitehead's analyses of consciousness tell us that this meaning is *real*, not subjective. Such experiences also tell us that the limits of everyday consciousness are not fixed, and that freedom has an inherent direction, a purposiveness, in its pursuit of evolutionary intentionality, the new dimension of the mind and inner experience, Wells's "proper business," Teilhard de Chardin's "complexification." This purpose is not supernatural, but it is "outside," external to everyday consciousness, and so can be used as an objective standard by which to gauge our actions. It answers the problem of relativity. We can ask about our choices and actions: are they in accord with our evolutionary urge or not?

Put simply: the boundaries of the mind can be extended in order to encompass a permanent awareness of our evolutionary purpose. The best way to do this, Wilson suggests, is through understanding the mechanisms of consciousness itself. Through this we can understand the exact way in which our doors of perception open and close, rather than trying to break them down or pick their locks through drugs or other stimuli. Wilson suggests that a fruitful way of approaching this is through an analysis of the "great mystery of human boredom," the tendency of consciousness to lock into place or, to mix metaphors, to congeal into a thick mass; to, that is, be subject to the indifference threshold.[41] And the most boring thing available to Wilson was the black room.

The black room makes unavoidable the question that drove Tolstoy's madman insane: "Who am I?" For within its pitch-black silence there is nothing to distract you from yourself, from your consciousness. As Wilson points out, several of his Outsiders found themselves confronting this question, and most did not fare well. It sent H. G. Wells in his last days into utter despair, and caused William James to have a nervous breakdown. Usually the necessities of everyday life, the day-to-day routine that Camus describes, distract us from this question. The black room does away with these. An instinctive, subconscious vital purpose remains, but, as Wilson points out, it is precisely the more intelligent among us who are cut off from this—intelligence questions; instinct does not—and they suffer the effects of the black room sooner than more instinctive types. But as Wilson argues, there is a deeper purpose available to us; it is what we experience in moments of "affirmation consciousness," "absurd good news," what he calls evolutionary intentionality. But, as we've seen, we, or the force behind evolution—the difference between the two is more apparent than real—have declared this for the most part off-limits, at least for the time being. The answer to the black room is to gain access to this purpose, which we have purposefully denied ourselves. This deeper impulse appears when we are facing a crisis. In the black room we must find it ourselves.

The black room shows the limitations of consciousness in high relief. But these limitations, Wilson argues, are really habits we have developed because of their evolutionary benefit. They are not fixed but variable. We have seen that some are eager to vary them: Wilson's Outsiders, Maslow's self-actualizers, those who hunger for complexification. Wilson refers to Teilhard de Chardin's belief that there is an absolute *break* between man and the lower animals, just as there is a break between a living creature and a stone. If a stone's freedom can be symbolized by a line, and an animal's by a square, then man, who is most free, should be a cube.

But Wilson points out that we are not quite there yet. We are less dependent on our environment than an animal but not yet completely free of it. We *can* enter the noösphere—with any luck I, writing this book, and you, reading it, are there—but we can't stay very long. We are soon drawn back to the buoying waters of the physical world, to the triviality of everydayness. As Wells said, we are amphibians who want to leave the sea for dry land, but haven't yet transformed our flippers into legs, and so we "swim distressfully" in a medium we wish to abandon and no longer feel at home in. *If* we were fully human, a "creature of the mind," as Wells says, we could stay in the black room indefinitely because we would be able to remain in the noösphere as long as we liked. Ideas, the "challenges of the mental world," would be enough to keep our vitality high. Boredom would vanish, our consciousness would not congeal, and we would be aware of what William James perceived in a moment of "mystical consciousness": "increasing ranges of distant fact." Our Faculty X would be in good working order and we would, like Proust, Hesse, and Toynbee, be able to move freely through time. This is why Wilson says it is a mistake to think of a "superman." Man in the proper sense does not yet exist. "We are not strong enough," he writes. "The world itself is a gigantic 'dark room' that proves that we are too dependent on physical stimuli."[42]

Humans in the real sense may not yet exist, but we have glimpses of what they will be like when they do. They come when the indifference threshold is lowered, or obliterated entirely. We remember Dostoyevsky's Raskolnikov, who would "prefer to stand on a narrow ledge for all eternity, surrounded by darkness and tempest, rather than die at once."[43] Darkness and tempest here serve the same purpose as the black room. As Wilson writes, "The fear of death has raised his consciousness of freedom to a point where he becomes aware of the absolute value of his existence." Raskolnikov's "indifference threshold has been completely destroyed; consequently, the thought of sensory deprivation ceases to trouble him." As Wilson concludes: "sensory deprivation, the indifference threshold, and states of 'mystical perception,' are directly connected."[44] What we need is a method, a way of turning our flippers into legs so we can stand upright and walk out of the sea onto the land—and finding one is exactly what Kit Butler, the hero of *The Black Room*, does.

This is the message Wilson tried to get across to his students at Hollins College. In August the Wilson entourage flew to New York. After a few sweltering days there they went to Washington, D.C., to spend a weekend with the Danzigers. Then they headed to Roanoke, Virginia. Joy was impressed by the campus, with its colonial-style architecture set on rolling hills against a backdrop of the Blue Ridge Mountains. She also liked their bungalow, also on a hilltop. It had a plush carpet, a huge refrigerator and kitchen stove, and plenty of room for the children.

The last English writer-in-residence had been William Golding, whose *Lord of the Flies* had taken over from J. D. Salinger's *The Catcher in the Rye* as a campus must-read. Wilson had met Golding in the early *Outsider* days but didn't care for his work. It struck him as being as gloomy as Graham Greene's, understandably, as Golding, too, was Catholic. *Lord of the Flies* concerns a group of schoolchildren reverting to barbarism on a desert island, and seemed a parable of original sin. Wilson notes that the zoologist C. R. Carpenter had observed that when monkeys were transported from their original habitat to a remote island, they, too, reverted to barbarism while aboard the ship: males let other males attack their mates; females stopped defending their babies. Their usual "values" had vanished. Yet once able to establish territory on the new island, their values returned. If this was an example of original sin, Wilson thought, then monkeys suffer from it too. (Years later Golding became Wilson's neighbor, but he was too polite to mention these points while his guest at lunch.)

Wilson found the workload surprisingly light, two classes a week. He was allowed to teach pretty much what he wanted, which meant that most classes were about the new existentialism. He was asked to attend a creative writing seminar, but after one appearance was asked to stay away. Wilson had a "survival of the fittest" attitude toward writing: real writers survive opposition and discouragement; wannabes drop out. Teaching creative writing classes for him was like "spreading fertilizer on weeds," a philosophy the seminar instructor found unhelpful.[45] What troubled Wilson most was the presence of so many young women. Hollins is a small, private women's college, and along with Husserl, Sartre, and Camus, in each class Wilson found himself facing a row of pretty legs, extending from newly fashionable miniskirts. He was, of course, very happy with Joy and the idea of having an affair with a student was absurd. Yet he did find it hard to "restrain the normal male reflex of glancing up a skirt as the legs change position." He even says it became a kind of game with his students.[46]

While at Roanoke he hit upon another insight. Wilson's mania for music continued and he accumulated stacks of records during his semester. He disliked the paper sleeve that came with these and ordered a supply of polyethylene envelopes. When they arrived he sat on the carpet with a row of fifty records, removed the paper sleeve, wiped the dust off the record, placed it in the polyethylene envelope, and put it back in the cardboard sleeve. After a while it struck him that he was actually enjoying what most of us would consider a tedious job. Why? Wilson hated repetitive work. Why was this so pleasurable? He remembered a quote from Herman Hesse's *The Journey to the East*, in which the hero, who tends to the musical needs of a mystical League, remarks that "a long time devoted to small details exalts us and increases our strength." Why should this be so? What made an otherwise boring job a source of satisfaction for him? What happens when we become so deeply absorbed in an activity that our consciousness focuses like a laser beam? It was a step toward another breakthrough in the new existentialism.

Probably the most important event of his time at Hollins was his meeting in November with Abraham Maslow at Brandeis University, where Wilson lectured. The two had been corresponding for years and on meeting him Wilson's first impression was that Maslow was "genuinely good." We have seen how Maslow's ideas about peak experiences influenced Wilson. Another important idea that Wilson got from Maslow was the hierarchy of needs, a kind of ladder of motivation that Maslow saw ran from basic "deficiency needs" such as food, shelter, love, and self-esteem to higher, creative "meta-needs," to "self-actualization" and the need to pursue some value for its own sake, something familiar to Wilson's Outsiders and the dominant .005 percent. Maslow's hierarchy of needs would occupy an important place in the theory of criminality Wilson was developing. Wilson saw that the history of crime—specifically murder—seemed to parallel Maslow's hierarchy, with the most recent type of murder being for self-esteem, in order to get in the papers and be known. Wilson's speculation on what we might paradoxically call the "self-actualizing" murder would inform his later book *Order of Assassins*, which was published in 1972, the same year as his book on Maslow, *New Pathways in Psychology*. In 1968 Wilson was asked to write a book about Maslow by an American publisher, and Maslow cooperated by sending him tape recordings and many unpublished papers. Wilson was working on the book when he heard the news of Maslow's death from a heart attack at the age of sixty-two in June 1970.

Wilson is candid about some of Maslow's remarks about him. Although Maslow himself was critical of the kind of anti-intellectualism associated with places such as Esalen—where he was a respected figure—he was also critical of what he felt was Wilson's overintellectual approach. He felt that Wilson was not "interested in visual aesthetics . . . in emotion experienced, or in affection . . . he derogates the cosmic consciousness in favor of the laser, narrowing type . . . he sees no use at all in the peak experience as emotion . . . Very active, pragmatic, rejects altogether and even with contempt the Taoist, the receptive, the passive. Very phallic . . ." Wilson later wryly noted that at least on one point Maslow was right, that as he got older, he would get "less sexy." Maslow himself had to curb his sexual enthusiasm; he was told by his doctor it could bring on a heart attack. Maslow did, but the heart attack came anyway, while he was jogging. He was also critical of Wilson's interest in dominance, but given that some of his ideas about it came from Maslow's own studies, this was perhaps a case of the pot calling the kettle black.

Another insight that came to Wilson at Hollins concerned the strange behavior of the planarian worm. In Ardrey's *The Territorial Imperative* Wilson read about a remarkable experiment involving planaria. Planaria are very simple creatures: they have no brain, no nervous system, no sexual organs. Two scientists, Irvin Rubinstein and Jay Boyd Best, were studying them and devised a way to test their learning ability. They put the worms in a tube full of water that forked into a Y at the end. Then they drained the water, which planaria need to live. The worms went down the tube until they came to the fork. One way was lighted and led to water; the other was dark and didn't. Most of the worms soon learned to head down the lighted tube. But as the scientists repeated the experiment several times for colleagues, they noticed something strange. The planaria, who had solved the puzzle, started to take the wrong turn, or they would lie still and do nothing and eventually die. It was as if they were saying, "Oh no, not this again," and preferred death to going through the same routine. One scientist suggested that they were bored. Without a brain or nervous system, this seemed unlikely, but the scientists decided to test it. They made the choice more difficult. Now the water was down either an unlighted tube made of rough plastic (which the worms could feel), or a lighted tube made of smooth plastic. They took a fresh batch of worms and set them to work. Because it was more difficult, only a third of the worms solved the problem, but this group would perform the experiment repeatedly *without getting bored*. They never took the wrong turn or sulked, and headed down the right tube every time.

The conclusion seemed to be that the first group did indeed get bored, but the second group cleared this hurdle by putting *more effort* into the test. Twice as much, it seemed. Doubling the effort prevented boredom. This, Wilson saw, was why he got so much pleasure from the album sleeves: he was putting more effort than was necessary into the task.[47] Our *attitudes* determine whether something is boring or not, a fact Wilson would support with an episode in *Tom Sawyer*. Tom is asked to paint a fence but he gets his friends to do it—they even pay him to let them—by *pretending* to enjoy it. His friends *expect* it to be fun, and the interest they put into it makes it so. Like the planaria, they put effort into it and they don't get bored. It was another important insight for the new existentialism. And it was in fact the "planaria effect" that provides the key to solving the problem of the black room in Wilson's novel.

By the summer of 1967 the Wilsons were back in Cornwall. While at Hollins, Wilson had secured a position as a visiting professor at the University of Washington, in Seattle, for the next term—something of a misnomer, as he had no academic qualifications. He had first thought of staying on at Hollins, but then felt that the coziness there might actually erode his sense of purpose—after all, this was a point he had been making. A larger university in a bigger city might prove better. His semester started in September and in the meantime work went on. The financial situation for once looked good. He had been able to bring home some earnings from Hollins. *The Glass Cage* had sold well—ten thousand copies in Great Britain, with similar sales in the States—and had received good notices. And it seemed Hollywood was interested in it. His agent told him that the director John Schlesinger—who later received an Academy Award for *Midnight Cowboy*—wanted to option the book for ten thousand pounds, roughly twenty-five thousand dollars. There was also interest in a film version of *Ritual in the Dark*. In the long run neither project panned out but at least Wilson got the option fees. *The Mind Parasites* had also done well and received good reviews, as had *Introduction to the New Existentialism*, which was selling well on American campuses. It seemed that the resentment critics had felt toward him for a decade was easing.

The Wilsons returned to New York in late August 1967. They decided to drive to Seattle. The trip took three weeks. Crossing vast spaces in the Midwest, Wilson could understand Kerouac's mysticism about being on the road. The workload in Seattle was heavier than in Virginia, but Wilson enjoyed the students there more. Teaching existentialism to pretty teenaged girls was like "pouring water on sand," he said. They were there because their parents paid for it. The students in Seattle were older and wanted to learn; they were more alive and curious, were, in effect, self-actualizing. He was writing *Bernard Shaw: A Reassessment* and used the book for his class on Shaw. His other class was in existentialism. Both were a success and his class size soon doubled.

At Hollins he was encouraged to lecture at other universities, and the same was true in Seattle. He spent a week lecturing in San Francisco and while there caught up with Kenneth Rexroth again. This time he saw less of Haight-Ashbury but spent time with poets and occultists at a British-style watering hole called the Edinburgh Castle Pub.[48] But a meeting with Lawrence Ferling-hetti led to one of his most insightful books, *Poetry and Mysticism*.[49] Among other things it introduced a concept that would remain a staple of Wilsonian thought: the robot.

Wilson first wrote about the robot in an essay that appeared in *Challenges of Humanistic Psychology*, an anthology edited by the psychologist James Bugental, who founded the *Journal of Humanistic Psychology* with Maslow in 1961.[50] In "Existential Psychology: A Novelist's Approach," Wilson wrote, "When I learned to type, I had to do it painfully and with much wear and tear. But at a certain stage a miracle occurred, and this complicated operation was 'learned' by a useful robot that I conceal in my sub-conscious."[51] This robot, Wilson tells us, is very helpful. He drives his car, speaks passable French, and "occasionally gives lectures at American universities." The robot is very versatile; Wilson even jokes that he sometimes makes love to his wife. The robot is a labor-saving device. He takes over repetitive tasks so that we can focus our attention on other things. Alfred North Whitehead knew about the robot when he said, "Civilization advances by extending the number of important operations which we can perform without thinking about them." If I had to think about *how* to type each time I wanted to, I could never think about *what* to type. Once I've learned a skill, my robot takes care of the how, so I can focus on the what. We all know the story of the ant asking the centipede how he can move so many legs. The centipede says, "It's easy; I do it like this," and then finds himself unable to do it. His conscious mind has interfered with an unconscious or subconscious process; in psychology this is called "hyper-reflection." The same thing happens when we become self-conscious and start to bungle things we normally do easily. We then are getting in the way of the robot.

The robot is absolutely necessary. But there is a problem. "If I discover a new symphony that moves me deeply," Wilson writes, "or a poem or a painting, the robot insists on getting in on the act." After a few times, the robot takes over, and *he* is listening to the symphony or reading the poem, not *me*. We say it has become "familiar." What does this mean? Why *should* a Mozart symphony sound less beautiful or exciting after we've heard it several times? After all, it hasn't changed. We say we have "got used to it." But what does this mean, other than that we have *allowed* the robot to classify it with repetitive tasks and, as T. E. Lawrence lamented, "become typical through thought"? Making things typical is the robot's job; the problem is that he does this to things we don't want to be typical.

Animals, Wilson says, don't have this problem. They can't learn languages or how to type, having only a rudimentary robot. But when he goes for a walk, Wilson's dog experiences the sights and smells each time as if it was the first. Wilson tells us he is often oblivious to the scenery because his robot has taken over the task of cutting out irrelevant details so he can get through a day's work. Yet when his day is over and he wants to relax, he often finds that he can't. His automatic pilot—the robot—is in gear and won't let go. Wilson is not alone in this; it is a central human problem—*the* central human problem. Descartes believed that animals were really robots. Clearly he was wrong. We are the robots. Or rather, we are like people who allow their servants to do everything for them, and subsequently feel they have lost touch with life, but don't know exactly why. Wilson is fond of quoting T. S. Eliot's line from "Choruses from the Rock": "Where is the life we have lost in living?" It's with the robot.

The problem with the robot is the same as with the evolutionary devices we have developed to enable us to filter out "irrelevant" input and focus our consciousness on the task at hand. It works *too efficiently*. Children experience life with a freshness we envy and try to recapture as we get older, because their robots are undeveloped. Yet it is no advantage to the child to retain an undeveloped robot. The exigencies of life demand one; without it, we would not be able to perform the simplest tasks, from tying our shoelaces to riding a bike, or more demanding ones, like learning a musical instrument. The robot is absolutely essential and our evolutionary intentionality would not have developed it if it weren't. If we have allowed it to overstep its duties and have become too dependent on it, this is not the robot's fault. It is a result of our accepting the passive fallacy, believing that life is something that *happens* to us, rather than something *we do*.

Now when we want to turn off the robot, we often resort to crude methods, like alcohol or drugs. These can shut the robot down, but at a price. As Wilson observed, they inhibit our ability to act. Drugs and alcohol allow us to feel the richness, the deeper meanings—the "absoluteness of self-enjoyment"—that the robot dampens, but our will and ability to act effectively is dampened too. Threat, inconvenience, and crisis can also free us of the robot. Hence the Outsider's penchant for "living dangerously," in Nietzsche's phrase. The robot recognizes that the threat requires *us* to take control and he briefly exits the driver's seat; or rather we recognize the need for this and push him out. This is why Sartre paradoxically felt most free when in danger of being arrested by the Nazis, and why many older Londoners remember the Blitz as the best days of their lives. As Wilson notes, Gurdjieff's method of induced crisis is aimed precisely at the robot. Yet once the threat recedes, the robot returns to its job of economizing on energy and doing things for us.

Outsiders feel the effect of the robot more than others; hence their desire for "life more abundant." They are willing to take enormous risks in order to throw him off, to "cast the spectre into the lake," as William Blake says. But living dangerously is most often counterproductive, as many of Wilson's Outsiders discovered. The idea is neither to get rid of the robot nor to keep administering "shock treatments" so that we can be free of him for a moment. These soon cease to work and fall victim to the law of diminishing returns, with greater shocks with less effect. We need to understand how the robot works and why we developed him in the first place. We need, that is, to develop a phenomenology of the robot. And we can see that there are times when we and the robot work together. A musician in top form can allow his robot full rein, while adding the creative nuances that make him a virtuoso. This is what the philosopher Michael Polanyi calls "attending from" rather than "attending to." If a pianist attended *to* his fingers he would be in the same situation as the centipede. He lets them do their work, which allows *him* to throw in spontaneous flashes of brilliance. When Wilson felt a quiet joy at the repetitive task of cleaning his records, it was because he and his robot were cooperating. And this happened because, as we've seen, Wilson put extra effort into the task, which means that he was more there, or "present," as we like to say today.

Wilson spells this out in *Poetry and Mysticism*, in which he also introduces two other concepts that will inform his work from then on. These are duoconsciousness and relationality, a companion to Husserl's intentionality.[52] Both are fleshed out in fictional form in *The Philosopher's Stone*. We can see both as variants of Faculty X. Wilson came to write the book after talking with Ferlinghetti about the Zen craze that had captured the Beats and much of the counterculture, mostly through the popularizing work of Alan Watts.

Although Wilson had been reading the *Bhagavad Gita* and other eastern texts for some time, he did not jump on the *ex oriente lux* bandwagon, which had already acquired many passengers. As with his feeling about psychedelics, Wilson believed that the West already had methods of achieving what Zen promised, the sudden shock of perceiving the is-ness of things. Zen, he said, had "nothing to tell us that we cannot say just as precisely in western terminology," and he was critical of the current "revival of the fashion to exalt in eastern modes of thought and disparage the western," an attitude that is not entirely missing today.[53] Wilson aimed at "detailed objective knowledge of what goes on in states of 'intensity consciousness.'" Through an analysis of Wordsworth's sonnet "Composed Upon Westminster Bridge," Wilson aimed to show that poetry can trigger the same shock effect that Zen meditation induces, which he recognized as a brief flash of "non-robotic consciousness."[54]

If robotic consciousness typifies things, so that they are reduced to an uninteresting sameness, non-robotic—or poetic—consciousness does the opposite. It is characterized by a startling awareness of *difference*.[55] It achieves this awareness, Wilson argues, by highlighting contrasts and holding *two different realities* together in the same moment. He mentions Ramakrishna's ecstasy at seeing a flock of white cranes flying against a dark storm cloud: the contrast sent him into a trance of "affirmation consciousness." But examples needn't be so exotic. We feel something the same when we are in a cozy room, listening to the rain patter on the window, or are lying in a warm bed, enjoying a few minutes of comfort before we must face the cold day. In both examples we are inhabiting two realities at once.

Related to this is what Wilson calls "relationality." This is when duo-consciousness expands, and spreads out like ripples on a lake. Wilson once experienced this driving back to Cornwall from Scotland, as he passed through the Lake District—home, aptly enough, of Wordsworth. Wilson knew the area well—he had bicycled there from Leicester in his youth—and as he passed through it, he felt as if he could reach out and touch the towns and lakes and mountains that lay beyond his sight, as if his awareness stretched out into a kind of web of consciousness, connecting it to everything.[56]

It was rather like the way he felt as he left New Hampton. Consciousness not only reveals things as a searchlight does, which can be bright or dim, depending on our intentionality. It also connects them, Wilson saw, and provides an overview, as if we were raised to a great height and could see for miles. It was the bird's-eye view, showing us "other times and places." Wilson believed that over the past two centuries these flashes of "weblike consciousness have become more and more frequent" and that human beings were on the point of developing it as "a normal faculty." The Romantics were an anticipation of this "evolutionary advance."[57] This was Faculty X and Wilson was about to write a book explaining it in detail.

CHAPTER EIGHT

MYSTERIES OF THE OCCULT

At the end of his first autobiography, *Voyage to a Beginning*, written when he was thirty-eight, Wilson wrote, "it seems likely that teaching in American universities will remain my main source of future income."[1] He preferred to be "sitting quietly at home in Cornwall, far from students and term papers and grade cards." But the money he earned with these came easier than what he received from churning out book after book, on average two or three a year—one year he even had to stretch that number to six.[2] There was more of it too, with teaching salaries for a semester equaling several book advances. He had hoped that his own work would be picked up by young readers and himself turned into a "campus hero" like Hesse or Tolkien. A paperback edition of *Introduction to the New Existentialism* did sell well at universities, but it was not in the same league as *The Lord of the Rings*, and Wilson's hopes for a Tolkien-like success quickly faded.

He finished *Voyage to a Beginning* during his last days in Seattle. It is much more of an "intellectual autobiography," as its subtitle has it, than the later *Dreaming to Some Purpose*, which often focuses on the nuts and bolts of being a full-time writer and juicy gossip about fellow authors. *Voyage to a Beginning* is essentially a survey of Wilson's life up until that point and the ideas that had driven it. As he writes, "My intention in these pages is to lay bare, as honestly as I can, the basic aims and motives of my work, and to relate them, where it is relevant, to events of my life."[3] The events of his life did not interest him enough to write a "formal autobiography," he explains, and in any case, the place for autobiography, he says, is in fiction. Nevertheless *Voyage to a Beginning* is very readable and full of incident and characters. And as one might suspect, it provides a healthy and candid analysis of his sexual experiences.

In the closing chapter, "Insights," Wilson states his central contribution to philosophy: that the problems of meaning and purpose cannot be addressed by logic alone. They can be attacked "only by varying consciousness," by developing a control of it and extending this control through language.[4] This can come about only by "becoming fully conscious of our aim, instead of pursuing it instinctively and vaguely," as the Romantics and old existentialists did. This requires a "conscious analysis of the problem." No shortcuts, whether through drugs or religious disciplines, will do.[5] "Human beings are surrounded by a wall of fog—the trivialities of the present," Wilson says. Our evolution depends on our "reaching out to the wider horizons of reality that lie beyond the immediate."[6] For Wilson this is "our deepest evolutionary purpose."[7]

On a more personal note, he admits that he missed Tetherdown, and loved England. But he couldn't stand the people there, who were intellectually static and mired in class consciousness. He preferred America. The casual friendliness of the Americans he had met made him feel that "all men *are* equal" and that the human race "*is* a family," even if he didn't care for many of his extended brothers and sisters. He felt that people in America were respected for what they were, not for their "position," and only so long as they were "not conceited" about what they were. He had an "immense affection for America. . . . It is a country where I can feel comfortable and do my best work."[8]

He would return to the States again as writer-in-residence in 1973, this time at Rutgers University in Camden, New Jersey, where he was forced, alas, to teach creative writing, much to his dismay.[9] On one occasion while at Rutgers he shared a platform with Allen Ginsberg and once again felt that a quasi-academic life in America would be an easier way to make a living than churning out book after book in England. Soon after Rutgers he was invited by his Arab publisher to visit Beirut. His books had been bootlegged in the Arab world for some time, but now his publisher there wanted to make things official and offered a decent sum as an inducement. Wilson knew his books were popular in the Arab world—Mu'ammar Gaddhafi was apparently one of his readers—but he wasn't prepared for his reception on arrival. He and Joy were the first allowed off the plane and after they were greeted by the mayor of Beirut and his entourage, they walked along a red carpet to their car. In Damascus their Palestinian hosts brought them to a reception where they met General Mustafa Tlass, the new Syrian war minister. The general told Wilson that when he and other officers were in prison under the previous regime, they read an Arabic translation of *Ritual in the Dark*, tearing out pages and passing them on, so they could all read it at the same time. Wilson was surprised to learn that he was one of the most popular foreign authors in the Middle East, a status that seemed confirmed when, on returning to Cornwall, he received an invitation to do a lecture tour of Iran, then still under rule by Shah Mohammad Reza Pahlavi. Wilson considered it, but in the end was reluctant to tour when each lecture would have to be translated, and he declined.

But this was a few years down the line. For the immediate future he was back to earning his keep with his typewriter. Yet it was from America that the inspiration for his most successful book since *The Outsider* would come, if accepting a commission strictly for the money can be considered inspiration.

Wilson had always had an interest in the occult. His grandmother was a spiritualist, he had always loved ghost stories, and he says that he accepted the idea of life after death as a young boy; he would, in fact, write a book about it years later, *Afterlife* (1985), affirming the survival of bodily death. He was a fan of the books of Harry Price, the "ghost hunter," and at the local library read everything he could find about spooks and hauntings. But by the age of ten his passion for science seized him and spirits and séances soon seemed absurd, and survival of bodily death wishful thinking. Even when his interest in science faded and he decided to become a writer, the supernatural still repelled him. He was tormented by the question of the purpose of life, but the idea that we carry on in some spiritual realm after death seemed no answer and only pushed the question further on.

While in America he had noticed the growing occult revival. At airport bookshops he bought paperbacks about ghosts, flying saucers, reincarnation, and Atlantis to read on the flight. He had seen some of the effects of the new occult craze in San Francisco, in the Haight and also at the pub where he spent time with poets and occultists. In 1960 two Frenchmen, Louis Pauwels and Jacques Bergier, had published a weird, erratic, and often erroneous compendium of occult speculation, *Le Matin des Magiciens*. It became a surprise hit, and when it was translated into English in Great Britain as *The Dawn of Magic* and *The Morning of the Magicians* in America, it was a hit there too. Pauwels and Bergier had kick-started a genuine occult revival and soon publishers were seeking out authors to meet the demand for, in the historian Theodore Roszak's phrase, "all things occultly marvellous."[10]

Wilson had read *The Morning of the Magicians* and found it so full of errors and wild speculation—it more or less started the "occult Nazi" subgenre of occult literature—that he couldn't take it seriously. So when his American agent approached him with the idea of writing a book on the occult, Wilson's first reaction was that he would have to do it with his tongue fixed firmly in his cheek. He had written about the occult before; as we've seen, one of the characters in *Man Without a Shadow* was based on Aleister Crowley, and he explores the reality of psychic healing in his book on Rasputin. Other characters, such as Joseph Atholl Gardner, an eccentric mythologist who consults a Celtic form of the *I Ching* in Wilson's novel *Necessary Doubt* and whose wife is a medium, express Wilson's skeptical attitude toward occultism. We know his interest in mysticism, unusual states of consciousness, and Gurdjieff. So the occult was not unfamiliar to him, even if his existential orientation made him dismiss it.

But he could not dismiss the offer from Random House, nor the one from the English publisher Hutchinson that his British agent received. Readers of his books on existentialism and crime might wonder what had happened to their angry young man, but in the summer of 1968, Wilson found himself accepting the commission and gearing up to get his occult research done.

Around the same time he was visited by a writer named Robert DeMaria, whom he had met in Long Island, New York, at C. W. Post University, now Long Island University Post, where DeMaria taught. DeMaria told Wilson that the university was starting an extramural department called Dowling College on the island of Majorca, in the Mediterranean off Spain. Dowling would teach creative writing and DeMaria invited Wilson to accept a three-month writer-in-residence position. The idea of an extended holiday in the Mediterranean was appealing, even if it meant teaching creative writing. And how much of a holiday it was is debatable: while there Wilson worked on his "nonfiction novel" *The Killer*, about a serial murderer, and expanded *Poetry and Mysticism*. Other writers, such as the novelist Anthony Burgess, most known for *A Clockwork Orange*, and the American poet Diane Wakoski, associated with the Beats, would also be on the faculty. Wilson accepted and in September he and his family set out for Majorca.

Wilson had another reason for accepting the job—even for thinking that getting it was a kind of synchronicity, one of the "meaningful coincidences" he would soon be writing about. Dowling College was located in the village of Deya, one of whose inhabitants was the writer and poet Robert Graves. Graves is most known today for his novels about ancient Rome, *I, Claudius* and *Claudius the God*, which Wilson had read. But he was more interested in Graves's strange book *The White Goddess*, which presents a complex theory of the origins of poetry and argues that an ancient, matriarchal "moon cult," based on a kind of "lunar magic," had in the dim past been supplanted by a masculine solar intellectual cult, responsible for monotheism and later modern science. Graves had some experience of the occult and Wilson wanted to ask his advice about writing a book about it.

The Wilsons were given a house on a hill overlooking the main square, with a stone courtyard and garden, and a well that was supplied by rainwater. The first few nights were difficult: fruit rats occupied their roof, making a racket, but they got used to this, as they did to the local cuisine. Wilson first met Graves at a party at Graves's son William's house, which was used as the headquarters of the college. They spoke only briefly, and Wilson told the older writer—Graves was seventy-three—that he would drop by his house to give him a copy of his book on Shaw. When he did Graves wasn't in—he was at the beach—and Wilson left a signed copy of the book. The next morning he got a note from Graves's wife, Beryl, saying that he should come round for a drink. Wilson did that afternoon.

Graves was tall, with wild white hair and a voice like an Oxford don. He showed Wilson around his garden and then took him down to the beach. As they changed into swimming trunks, Graves asked Wilson if he would like to try the "traverse." This was a barely negotiable passage across a cliff face, over-looking jagged rocks and the sea. Wilson accepted and Graves led the way. Wilson had to put his hands and feet exactly where Graves indicated; otherwise he could get stuck or fall. The rocks below were unwelcoming and Wilson followed Graves's instructions. As he scrambled up the rock and began his climb, Wilson realized that Graves was playing the dominance game, just as Flax had done years before. Wilson managed the traverse, and at the top of a rock followed Graves's splendid dive into the sea with a rather less decorative one. But he had passed the test. As the two came onto the beach Graves slapped Wilson on the shoulder and said, "You'll do." After that Graves was a friend and dropped in on Wilson and his family often.

When Wilson asked Graves about doing the occult book, his advice was "Don't." Graves knew it had the potential to take over one's life. He also made comments that deeply interested Wilson. "Occult powers," he said, weren't rare. "One person in twenty possesses them."[11] The exact figure of 5 percent struck Wilson; he naturally wondered if this 5 percent was the same as the group he had written about. Wilson would later conclude that "all human beings possess the vestiges of 'occult powers,'" springing from the "deeper levels of vitality, what the playwright Granville-Barker called 'the secret life.'" The dominant 5 percent are most likely more able to master these powers than other people. "Magicians, witch doctors, witches and mediums," he concluded, are members of the dominant 5 percent who have gained access to occult powers.[12]

Graves made other remarks that struck Wilson, such as his idea that true poetry is written in the fifth dimension. At the time Wilson had no idea what he meant. But by the time he came to write his book, a look at the work of J. G. Bennett, an important follower of Gurdjieff, helped him to understand that the fifth dimension is freedom. Graves mentioned that many men use a kind of sorcery to seduce women. Wilson thought of his own experiences and concluded that this was true. But what impressed Wilson most was Graves's ideas about what he called "lunar knowledge," a kind of intuitive, instinctive knowledge that Graves believed was at the basis of poetry, and how it was supplanted with the rise of our more familiar "solar knowledge," the kind of rational, logical, step-by-step approach that informs science.[13]

Graves had written about this other kind of knowledge in an autobiographical story, "The Abominable Mr. Gunn," about a math teacher at his public school. One of Graves's schoolmates, a boy called Smilley, had a strange knack for seeing answers to difficult mathematical problems instantaneously. Graves writes that as the rest of the class labored at the equation, Smilley would quickly jot down his answers, which were invariably right. The teacher asked him *how* he arrived at his answers and all Smilley could say was that they "just came" to him. Smilley somehow saw the answer *directly*, all at once. He was right so often that the teacher decided he was cheating and had him caned. On one occasion when the teacher said he had finally got it wrong, Smilley said that the answer at the back of the math book was incorrect. The teacher worked out the problem and saw this was true. Graves remarks that over time, Smilley somehow lost this power.

Graves himself had a similar knack, or at least experienced it on one occasion. He writes in the same story of sitting outside the school's cricket pavilion and suddenly having the distinct certainty that he knew everything. "Though conscious of having come less than a third of the way along the path of formal education," Graves writes, "I nevertheless held the key of truth in my hand, and could use it to open the lock of any door." He explains that this wasn't a religious or philosophical theory, "but a simple method of looking sideways at disorderly facts so as to make perfect sense of them."[14] What before had been a jumble of disconnected bits and pieces was suddenly made whole. Yet when Graves tried to write down exactly *what* he had seen, he found he couldn't, and in the process, his certainty faded. It was an experience much like William James had when, for no apparent reason, in the middle of a conversation, he found himself surveying "increasing ranges of distant facts of which I could give no articulate account." James says that the ranges of distant facts were *perceptual*, not conceptual, meaning they were something he *saw*.[15] In *The Occult* and other books, Wilson recounts several other examples of this kind of seeing.[16]

Graves's "simple method of looking sideways at disorderly facts" seemed to Wilson to be rather like the kinds of experiences he had written about, those of people such as Toynbee and Proust, and his own at Teignmouth and on that snowy day in Washington. It was beginning to look like his book on the occult would be about something more than ghosts and séances.

Wilson enjoyed his time teaching in Majorca, but there were some bumps. One occurred when a professor named George Cockcroft delivered an impromptu speech about the dangers of Wilson's philosophy. Cockcroft later had great success under the pen name Luke Rhinehart with a novel called *The Dice Man* (1971), about a psychiatrist who makes decisions by throwing dice. *The Dice Man* became an underground best seller, although its depiction of aleatory rape and murder had it banned in some countries. Cockcroft seemed threatened by Wilson's concern with human evolution and consciousness and took the occasion of a group meal to explain why. With no prior notice he stood up among the twenty or so people and announced that he had invited everyone so that he could tell them why Wilson's ideas were "dangerous and unhealthy."

Wilson had heard it before but not for a while and was surprised that Cockcroft had pulled such a stunt. As Cockcroft, a "typical" liberal professor, uncovered the "fascist" agenda in Wilson's ideas—predictably linking them with Nazism—Wilson was inclined to argue or walk out. But his patience prevailed and he listened politely while Cockcroft's denunciations "degenerated into vague generalities."[17] He then replied reasonably, pointing out his accuser's false assumptions and illogic until Cockcroft had nothing left to say. Wilson says the experience taught him the value of curbing his impatience, a lesson, he admits, he is not always able to remember.

Wilson had a less stressful encounter with Anthony Burgess, whom he liked, but whose ideas about literature he found dubious, especially his Joycean concern with linguistics.[18] He came to feel that Burgess shared the kind of gloomy outlook that he disliked in other writers, and that his own optimistic perspective rankled him. It was a feeling he detected in other acquaintances, such as the radical psychiatrist R. D. Laing, whom he nevertheless liked: the assumption that anyone with a "positive" attitude must be shallow, a prejudice inculcated by the old existentialism.[19] Wilson felt that for people like Laing, who found madness an appropriate response to modern life—and who displayed a considerable amount of this in his own life—his own optimistic purposive approach must seem a kind of personal affront.[20]

Wilson did not have much time to consider this. He had agreed to do the occult book but before starting it he had to clear the decks of other work. Back in Cornwall he began to do just that, in early 1969. In between Majorca and getting down to writing what would become *The Occult*, Wilson completed *The Philosopher's Stone*, *A Casebook of Murder*, *The Black Room*, and *The God of the Labyrinth*, the third Sorme novel and one which, like *The Philosopher's Stone*, incorporates ideas that would find nonfictional expression in *The Occult*.[21] He also finished *The Killer* (*Lingard* in America), a play, *Strindberg*, about the troubled Swedish genius, and his contribution to *The Strange Genius of David Lindsay*, a book he cowrote with J. B. Pick and E. H. Visiak, about the author of one of the most remarkable books ever written, *A Voyage to Arcturus*. Lindsay's master work can best be described as a gnostic *Pilgrim's Progress* set on another planet; it has influenced writers such as C. S. Lewis and Philip Pullman. He was producing three or four thousand words a day, sometimes six thousand. Anyone who writes for a living knows what this means. He was, he saw, becoming a writing machine, and even his remarkable discipline and work ethic was beginning to pall. For a time it seemed that the BBC might be interested in a history of crime and civilization, along the lines of Kenneth Clark's successful series *Civilisation* and Jacob Bronowski's *The Ascent of Man*. Hosting a television series like this would certainly help his overdraft and give him a break from writing. But like the film options, this fell through. Again money was scarce. There was nothing for it. The writing machine had to write.

By the time it turned its attention to the occult, the mind behind the writing machine recognized a change in its perspective. From worrying that he would have to write about ghosts and haunted houses—which, of course, make their appearance—Wilson began to see that the occult was involved with much more than this and that the evidence for it was overwhelming. Scientists who dismiss the proofs of the paranormal are simply ignoring the facts, Wilson came to see.

"My own attitude to the subject has changed," he admitted, "during the course of researching and writing this book."[22] The occult had never been one of his central interests, although he had a collection of some five hundred books on the subject. (Wilson's mania for book buying was justified as "research material.") He was not entirely skeptical, but he felt that people get interested in the occult for the wrong reasons, a sadly true reflection. He had spoken with many spiritualists and while he believed in their sincerity, it was the *triviality* of their interest in life after death, as well as the kind of life that was supposed to be, that repelled him. Compared to the concerns of philosophy or science it was, in Nietzsche's phrase, "all too human," too personal and small. A look at most spiritualist literature can, I think, confirm this. Wilson knew that "our life can offer a *reality and an intensity*" in this world now, compared to which most religious or supernatural solutions to its mysteries seem irrelevant.[23] It was this belief that had led to his new existentialism. Saying that the answer to the mystery of existence is that we in some way survive bodily death seemed to miss the point.

Yet over the two years when he researched *The Occult* he came to see that the evidence for occult phenomena—life after death, out-of-the-body experiences, reincarnation, telepathy, precognition, and so on—is convincing. His preference was still for philosophy, "the pursuit of reality through intuition aided by intellect." But to him it was clear that occult skeptics were simply closing their eyes to evidence "that would convince them if it concerned the mating habits of albino rats or the behaviour of alpha particles."[24] And this is true of us all, not only "tough-minded" materialists. Many people dismiss the occult and refuse to investigate any evidence for it, because their assumptions about reality suggest that such things don't happen. If you produce evidence that they do, they ignore it because it would cost too much effort to rethink how they see the world. The same was true of the churchmen who refused to look through Galileo's telescope. Many of today's skeptics—figures such as Richard Dawkins, for example—are in the same position as Galileo's churchmen.[25] Yet if one gets past this initial rejection, the occult begins to acquire the same status as the heliocentric theory of the solar system: that is, it is seen as fact. And in Wilson's case, the facts had convinced him.

Yet what was needed was a theory linking these facts together, not another collection of oddities to entertain uncritical readers or repel critical ones. Facts, as Wilson says, never speak for themselves. They need an interpreter. There were several good encyclopedias of the occult already in print, and earlier in the century the indefatigable Charles Fort amassed an enormous amount of data about every conceivable scientific anomaly, from extraterrestrials to raining frogs. Yet Fort's books, impressive as they are, are ultimately unsatisfying because they present their readers with heaps of fascinating material but offer no way to organize it. *The Morning of the Magicians* is little better, and actually tips its beret to Fort. Many of the books feeding the growing popular occult market were of the same sort, a handicap that continues to hamper efforts to get the occult taken seriously. If scientists and other skeptics were ever going to broaden their minds about the occult, then it had to be presented to them logically, in a way that made sense, not in a sensational "believe it or not" manner. Wilson himself had an admirably open mind but even so it took two years of steady research to convince him that his attitude toward the occult was inadequate. And this came about only because of financial necessity. No busy scientist will devote time to investigating something unless he feels it is worth investigating. And that's where a good theory comes in.

Wilson's own theory, we've seen, began with his conversations with Robert Graves, and indeed, *The Occult* is dedicated to Graves. There is, Wilson argues, a kind of intuitive "lunar knowledge" that was predominant ages ago but which we in the modern world have lost touch with. We have lost touch with it for the same reason that we cut out 95 percent of the reality we find ourselves in. In the modern world, the kind of sensitivity to psychic and occult realities that Wilson was investigating would only be a nuisance. Modern life forces us to narrow our perceptions down ruthlessly, as a survival tactic. A walk through a busy modern city offers proof enough of this. If we were aware of every bit of information assailing our senses as we crossed Times Square, we would have a nervous breakdown. As Wilson found in his research, many psychics developed their abilities through an accident, and the sudden widening and opening of their awareness interfered with their everyday lives; they found themselves unable to focus, to concentrate, and they often couldn't hold down a job. The Dutch clairvoyant Peter Hurkos was a case in point. Hurkos's clairvoyance appeared in 1943 after he fell from a ladder and fractured his skull. While in the hospital he suddenly knew that a fellow patient, who was about to be discharged, was a British agent and that he would be murdered by the Gestapo. What Hurkos "saw" came true. News of his prediction came to the Dutch resistance and Hurkos was almost executed as a spy. It was only by convincing the resistance of his new abilities that he saved his life. Yet he found that he could not return to his job as a house painter and it was only when he began to perform publicly as a psychic that he could again make a living.

At an earlier time in our history, Wilson suggests, humans had a variety of "powers" which seem miraculous or supernatural now, and which Wilson relates to the equally miraculous homing instinct of pigeons or the ability of eels, turtles, deer mice, and other animals to find their way home over vast distances. Wilson mentions water divining and the "jungle sensitivity" of the hunter Jim Corbett, among other powers. We have forgotten about these powers because they are no longer necessary for our survival. As Wilson writes, "High development of the instinctive levels is incompatible with the kind of concentration upon detail needed by civilized man."[26]

Yet, as we've seen, this necessary narrowing of consciousness has side effects that, paradoxically, are ultimately *not* advantageous to our evolution. It enables us to focus tightly on immediate objectives, but it does so by ignoring the "immense world of broader significance" that stretches around us.[27] The highly edited world that our psychic blinders present us with is easily dealt with—we have edited it so ruthlessly for precisely that reason. But it has landed us in the triviality of everydayness, in which boredom and the commonplace are the ultimate truths. A sense of meaning is necessary to release our deepest energies, yet the "forgetfulness of being" that our evolutionary blinders encourage leads us to depression, ennui, and the age-old wisdom that since there is nothing new under the sun, nothing is worth very much effort. This has resulted in our becoming "thinking pygmies," masters of a vast technologically advanced world, which dwarfs us and leaves us embracing the fallacy of insignificance.

Such a conclusion cuts away at the roots of our very life. We live, Wilson says, by "eating significance"—what Whitehead calls "prehension." If our sense of wonder is strong and our curiosity wide, our vitality increases, and we are able to grip our own existence more powerfully. We feel more real. Conversely, when our sense of wonder shrinks, when we lose the sense of greater meaning radiating out from our experience, we begin to shrivel and the life force in us dies. We are starved of significance. We feel and are less real.

These greater meanings are there; they exist *objectively*, Wilson insists. We have simply blinded ourselves to them. He refers to a fascinating book, *The Intelligent Universe*, by the cybernetician David Foster.[28] Cybernetics is concerned with automated systems of communication and control; the thermostat in your home that lowers the heating when it reaches a certain temperature is an example of cybernetics. From Foster's point of view, the entire universe can be seen as having been "programmed" by some intelligence higher than it: in cybernetics, the controller is always more intelligent than the controlled. For Foster, an acorn is a program for an oak. In fact, all life is not, as official science would have it, the product of random physical forces, but the result of programming from some intelligence we can only speculate about. Foster suggests that the information with which life is programmed is brought to it by cosmic rays.

Wilson was struck by the purposive character of Foster's ideas, and how they resembled similar suggestions from a growing number of scientists and thinkers dissatisfied with the strict Darwinian explanation of life. Wilson mentions Teilhard de Chardin, Julian Huxley, the biologist C. H. Waddington, Maslow, the psychologist Viktor Frankl, the philosopher Michael Polanyi. What these thinkers share is their rejection of reductionism, the belief that the universe and man can be explained purely through mindless physical laws, or what the writer Arthur Koestler called "ratomorphic" science, the assumption that everything important about human beings can be explained by studying the behavior of laboratory rats.[29] As Wilson had argued in *Beyond the Outsider*, many scientists were increasingly taking a risk and stating that the purely random, mechanical explanations of life simply don't cover all the facts, and in *The Occult* he offers several examples of this.[30] Intelligence, *meaning*, is at work in the universe, and our old evolutionarily inhibited mode of knowledge was a way of grasping this meaning intuitively.

To compensate for the loss of our intuitive knowledge, we have developed new ways of grasping the meanings around us. We do this through art, science, philosophy, literature: in short, through the intellect and the imagination. And this new way of grasping our reality offers a glimpse of powers we are just beginning to be aware of and understand. Wilson begins his survey of the subject with a passage from P. D. Ouspensky's *A New Model of the Universe*, which Wilson admits "never fails" to move him.[31] Ouspensky writes of when he was a journalist and had to write an article about The Hague Convention of 1907. He is bored by the idea and to avoid it, he opens his desk drawer. Inside are books with "strange titles": *The Occult World, Life After Death, Atlantis and Lemuria*, and other works of the occult. Wilson initially read this passage years ago, when he was first living in London (with Betty and their son), and he could appreciate Ouspensky's reluctance to write about politics and his craving for "*another world* of deeper meaning," which his occult library symbolized. These books, and the others that Wilson himself read, confirmed Wilson's belief in "*an intenser and more powerful form of consciousness*" than the one he seemed to share with millions of other Londoners.[32] It was an ability to grasp "*meanings, far bigger than oneself, that make all personal preoccupations seem trivial.*"[33] This power of apprehending meanings beyond the personal is peculiar to humans; it is what Wilson means by Faculty X.

Faculty X is the central theme of *The Occult*. In *The Philosopher's Stone* Wilson had written, "The will feeds on enormous vistas; deprived of them, it collapses." We have deprived ourselves of these vistas, Wilson argues, by developing our consciousness so it can focus on detail like a microscope. What we need to do now is to develop our other ability, to perceive distant meanings, to start looking at reality through our telescope. Wilson introduces the reader to the examples of Faculty X we have already looked at: Proust's madeleine, Toynbee's vision of history. While these are certainly examples of a powerful form of imagination, are they in any way occult? Wilson provides examples of when our ability to reach beyond the present can actually become the power to be in two places at once.

The novelist John Cowper Powys, author of *A Glastonbury Romance*, perhaps the greatest mystical novel ever written, once "appeared" before his friend and fellow novelist Theodore Dreiser in Dreiser's Manhattan apartment while Powys was at his home in upstate New York. Similar instances of "bilocation"— the term was coined by the Victorian psychic researcher F. W. H. Myers— happened with other literary figures; Wilson speaks of Strindberg, W. B. Yeats, and Goethe, each of whom was deeply interested in the occult. When Arnold Toynbee experienced Faculty X and felt that he had been transported to the battle of Mistra, or when Proust felt he had been sent back to the Combray of his youth, was this only a trick of the imagination, or a taste of a power to pass beyond the limits of the present that we all possess but never make use of? These powers exist, Wilson insists, and can be called upon, *if* we make the requisite effort of will. Faculty X is the ability to grasp realities not immediately apparent, realities that exceed the immediate evidence of the senses. It is the power to pierce the fog of *the present* and lift us beyond its meager boundaries.

This is the central idea that runs through Wilson's history of the occult. It is a huge book, totaling nearly a quarter of a million words; Wilson in fact was asked by his English publisher Hutchinson to cut it by half, but he refused and the book was eventually published by Hodder & Stoughton, who offered a bigger advance and encouraged Wilson to expand the book. As he later remarked, the book seemed to pour out of him and almost "wrote itself." Wilson writes of the Tarot and the *I Ching* as "lunar knowledge systems," and speaks of his own experience with the *I Ching* years before, when first starting out as a writer. He explores the links between poetry and the occult, speculates on human evolution, investigates the magic of ancient man, and examines occult staples such as witchcraft, hauntings, vampirism, and lycanthropy. He writes of kabbalists, spiritualists, mesmerists, and the strong associations between Romanticism and the occult.

All the famous mages make an appearance: Apollonius of Tyana, Nostradamus, John Dee, Cagliostro, and Madame Blavatsky are only a few of them. Some of the figures whose lives Wilson recounts he would later write full-length books about, people such as Aleister Crowley, Ouspensky, Gurdjieff, and C. G. Jung, whose notion of synchronicity or "meaningful coincidence" plays an important part throughout the book. Some of the most fascinating sections deal with precognition and the "undoubted queerness of time," in the philosopher C. E. M. Joad's phrase. Time relates to Faculty X, and like Faculty X, precognition, the knowledge of an event *before it has happened*, tells us that there is something wrong with our usual understanding of time. Wilson devotes a great deal of his significant closing chapter, "Glimpses," to coming to grips with what must be the most difficult occult power for a staunchly rational person to accept.[34]

This brief overview can only give an idea of what remains an important and eminently readable investigation into our latent powers and abilities. What the reader of Wilson's earlier books sees is that he has not thrown over existentialism and boarded the occult bandwagon. As we've seen, Faculty X, the central idea of the book, has occupied Wilson throughout his career, although it was not until *The Occult* that he gave it a name. He even remarks at the beginning of *The Occult* that "as long ago as 1957" he had spoken of a "sixth sense—a sense of the purpose of life, quite direct and uninferred."[35] Wilson was only doing what he had done all along: broadening existentialism—and all philosophy—so that it was not confined by artificial limits. He has not become an occultist, merely taken the occult as a starting point for another approach to his basic aim of understanding the mechanisms of everyday consciousness. This is the essential thing; by doing so, these mechanisms can be altered so that they allow more reality into our awareness.

Wilson could not be blamed for thinking that with *The Occult* he had opened up whole new territories of consciousness to be explored. And for the first time in years, the critics agreed. Wilson had misgivings about a promotional effort Hodder, his British publishers, proposed, a pamphlet about the book and about Wilson himself. "They won't make their money back," he thought, considering the reviews and sales he had become used to, and feeling guilty that Hodder had increased his advance. But his publishers were right. When *The Occult* appeared in October 1971, it was greeted with the kind of accolades Wilson hadn't seen since 1956. The critics who had dismissed him as a flash in the pan after announcing his genius—Cyril Connolly and Philip Toynbee—were now happy to bring him back in from the critical cold.

Toynbee even almost apologized for having "battered" Wilson in the past, remembering his trouncing of *Religion and the Rebel*. Here his tune was somewhat different. In the *Observer* he praised Wilson's "staying power, his resilience, his indefatigable curiosity," and said that *The Occult* displayed "the full array of his amiable virtues." Writing in the *Sunday Times* Cyril Connolly said he was very impressed by the book and Wilson's excellent marshaling of his erudition. He praised his "good natured, unaffected charm" and reasoning, and remarked that Wilson's "mental processes are akin to Aldous Huxley." And in the *Sunday Telegraph*, Arthur Calder-Marshall, who knew at least one character from the book, Aleister Crowley, called *The Occult* "the most interesting, informative and thought-provoking book on the subject I have read."[36]

Calder-Marshall went on to predict that *The Occult* "should secure Mr. Wilson a success even greater than he won with *The Outsider*." Exact figures are hard to come by, but *The Occult* certainly sold well enough to put Wilson back on the best-seller lists. *The Occult* did well in the States too, and was immediately put out in a book club edition. As soon as Wilson's father, who took no interest in his work, heard the title he predicted that the book would be a success. Wilson was happy that on this occasion his father was proved right. The book was translated into many languages, and over the years remained a steady seller; a new edition was released as recently as 2015. After a decade and a half of being in the wilderness, Leicester's boy genius was back in the public's good books, as it were.

He later mumbled some misgivings about the UK paperback edition, which also sold phenomenally well. He didn't care for the bright green cover or the blurb about its being "a book for those who would walk with the gods," but it was precisely those who wanted to take such a walk who bought it. On a visit to Leicester, Wilson went to Lewis's, the department store where he had met Joy, and was delighted to find a whole rack of copies. The U.S. paperback did well too, with a tattered copy reaching me on the Bowery in 1975. In an introduction to the new edition, Wilson wrote that because of *The Occult* he was "no longer stigmatised as an angry young man" and had become instead a "more-or-less respectable member of the literary establishment." (Elsewhere he commented that he was no longer "lean, wolfish, and gloomy," as he was in his *Outsider* days, but at forty had become "heavily built, round-faced, and usually cheerful."[37]) This was a welcome change, as earlier that year he had become a father again; Rowan, another son, had been born on May 26, just two days short of the fifteenth anniversary of *The Outsider*. Wilson also said that writing the book made him aware that "the paranormal is as real as quantum physics (and, in fact, has a great deal in common with it), and that anyone who refuses to take it into account is simply shutting their eyes to half the universe."

Now that his own eyes had been opened, Wilson embarked on a new career, that of a paranormal theorist and investigator. He had not given up on the new existentialism, but he now saw that consciousness was even more mysterious than he had suspected. For one thing strange synchronicities seemed to happen more often.[38] References he needed seemed to appear effortlessly. For example, writing about alchemy, he needed to check a reference. He knew it was among the many books on alchemy on his shelves, but he didn't know which one and felt too tired to look through them to find out. But he forced himself to get up and make the effort. When he took down one book, another fell from the shelves and opened at the exact page he wanted. This is an instance of what the writer Rebecca West called the "angel of the library," the remarkable phenomenon, known to many writers, of needed material appearing unbidden, as if delivered by some guardian angel. Instances of the "library angel" occurred so often that Wilson remarked that "items of required information have turned up with a promptitude that sometimes made me nervous." Wilson soon got so used to being helped by his angel that he began to feel resentful if some needed reference did not appear forthwith. Because of this he concluded that one reason such miracles don't happen as often as we might like is that if they did it would only make us lazy.

As Wilson delved deeper into occult phenomena more strange things began to happen. Premonitions seemed to occur. Driving down the long lane leading from his house to the main road—something he did practically every day—Wilson had a sudden feeling that the post van might be coming at the same time. There was no reason for him to think so, but he nevertheless slowed down. Just as his car began to exit the driveway, the post van pulled in front. They narrowly missed hitting each other. In all the times he had done this, the post van had never been there. But he had somehow *known* it would be, just as, in a story he enjoyed retelling, a musician friend *knew* that as the taxi he was in rode down Bayswater Road in London, another cab would jump the light at Queensway and hit them—which is exactly what happened.[39]

With the success of *The Occult*, Wilson was no longer a pariah and new offers of work came in. Among other things he was invited to participate in a new monthly television arts program called *Format*. He had appeared on television before but now he would be a regular panelist, discussing literature and music and interviewing guests, such as the filmmaker Ken Russell, about whom he would write a short book.[40] When Wilson turned up for the first program in January 1972, he had an unpleasant surprise. The minute he stepped before the camera he was hit with a very bad case of stage fright. His heart beat rapidly and his voice was shaky, as it had been before he had trained himself to speak in public years earlier at Speakers' Corner. His performance was so bad that it took three tries before he got through it. He was so unnerved by this that to play it safe for the next program, he asked his doctor for some tranquilizers. But they seemed to have no effect, even if he took two or three on top of a few glasses of wine, which his doctor advised him never to do. No matter what he tried, whenever he was about to be on camera, Wilson froze and had to fight down a powerful urge to run away. When he saw recordings of his performance he could see that he looked terrified. "As soon as I stepped into the studio," he said, "a watery sense of panic began to invade my stomach, and I had to resist the desire to flee."[41] It was only over time and with much effort that he was able to master his panic.

He had, of course, been out of the spotlight for some time, and overworked for years. And although one might think otherwise, *The Occult*'s success didn't ease his burden. Directly following *The Occult* Wilson was back at his typewriter finishing *New Pathways in Psychology*, his book on Maslow, and *Order of Assassins*, another book on the psychology of crime. He also tried his hand at a police procedural novel, *The Schoolgirl Murder Case*, featuring a detective named Saltfleet; he had originally envisioned a series, somewhat like Georges Simenon's Maigret novels, but after a second novel, *The Janus Murder Case*, he abandoned the idea.[42] Another project was his book about wine, *A Book of Booze*, which argued that the discovery of alcohol was one of the major steps in the evolution of consciousness. He had also begun research for his book about Wilhelm Reich, mentioned earlier. He may have been back on the best-seller lists but he was working as hard as ever.

A book about psychology and one about murder might not seem to have much in common, but *New Pathways in Psychology* and *Order of Assassins* both explore an important concept in Wilson's philosophy, what he calls the "self-image." *New Pathways in Psychology* is about Maslow, but it also explores the new schools of existential and transpersonal psychology rising up in opposition to Freud and behaviorism. In it Wilson writes that "we tend to climb towards higher states of self-awareness by means of a series of self-images."[43] By this Wilson means that we "create a certain imaginary image of the sort of person we would like to be, and then try to live up to the image." This is, in fact, the same advice he gave aspiring novelists. For Wilson the novel is a "thought experiment" in human evolution, and what fledgling novelists need more than anything else is an idea of who they want to *become*. Writing a novel is a way of exploring this question. Nietzsche captured the essence of this insight in his remark that "the great man is the play-actor of his ideals." A. R. Orage, one of the earliest English interpreters of Nietzsche, and later a student of Gurdjieff, meant the same thing when he said that "evolution is altogether an imaginative process. You become what you have been led to imagine yourself to be."[44]

The self-image is not the same as having a high opinion of yourself, or deluding yourself about your "genius." It is more like having a strong sense of your own reality and potentialities and the confidence to actualize them. Wilson points out that Sartre argued correctly that most of the time our idea of ourselves comes from other people. If someone makes clear their low opinion of us, we tend to feel diminished. If someone shows they think well of us, we are delighted. We can go through these psychological ups and downs dozens of times a day. We are mirrors for each other, but more often distorting mirrors than anything else. A strong self-image is not subject to these fluctuations, or at least it recovers from them fairly quickly. Our self-image is a product of our will and of how much freedom we experience; it is a way of remembering *who we are*, and another tool with which to strengthen our grip on reality.

Maslow had spoken of the importance of maintaining a positive attitude, and Wilson found something similar in the work of the psychologist Viktor Frankl, author of the hugely successful *Man's Search for Meaning*. This is an account of Frankl's time in the Auschwitz and Dachau concentration camps, where he developed his own school of psychology, logotherapy, which places *meaning*—not sex or power—at the center of human being. Frankl observed that prisoners who maintained a purposive attitude, a sense of expectancy, *something to look forward to*—that is, the future—did better than prisoners who had given up hope. They survived because they kept their will active, rather than succumbing to the degradation around them and becoming passive. It was through observations like this that Frankl developed a psychology based on our capacity to find meaning in even the most devastating, crushing circumstances. Frankl even wrote of "peak" or "affirmation" experiences under such circumstances, as when a group of prisoners, after a long and punishing journey, were made to stand all night in the rain in Dachau, but were nevertheless happy and cracking jokes because they saw that Dachau had no chimney.[45] They would at least not die that way.

Frankl and Maslow both saw that passivity leads to neurosis because the frustrated will turns on itself. Without an appropriate target, our energies fester and sour. Wilson was fond of recounting the story Maslow told of one of his patients, an intelligent, motivated young woman, who during the Depression supported herself and extended family by working in a chewing gum factory. She was happy to have the job, but the lack of challenge led to boredom and an inability to enjoy anything; she had become so devitalized that she had even stopped menstruating. Before getting the job she had been a brilliant psychology student and had wanted to follow an academic career, but her responsibilities prevented this. Maslow saw that she was frustrated creatively, that the boredom and "life failure" were the result of her energies going to waste. He suggested that she take night classes; as soon as she did she improved.[46] Maslow saw that the need to *use* our abilities is as fundamental as any deficiency need. If it is ignored it will do us harm. "What one can be," Maslow saw, "one must be."

Frankl recognized the same problem and developed an important therapeutic technique, what he called "the law of reverse effort."[47] This calls for the patient to *actively do* the very thing he fears. Frankl hit on this when he heard the story about a boy who stuttered badly being asked to play the part of a stutterer in a school play. He did, but when it came time for him to stutter, he couldn't. Trying to do precisely what he feared stopped him from doing it. A bank clerk came to Frankl because his handwriting was deteriorating so badly that he would soon be out of a job. Frankl told him that the next time he had to write in the ledger he should try to write as badly as possible. The clerk's handwriting improved from the moment he did this. *Trying* to write badly improved his handwriting. Passivity had led to worry, which led to his interfering with his robot, as Wilson would say. By *consciously trying* to write badly, he was no longer passive but using his will, and his symptoms vanished. Approaching his problem from a Freudian or even a Jungian perspective would have only complicated the situation. As Wilson had noted, an active will is key to psychological health.

When our will becomes passive our self-image dwindles; like the hero of Sartre's *Nausea*, our self-image can become so fragile that the mere reality of things oppresses us. The opposite effect, when our self-image becomes stronger and clearer, Wilson christened "promotion." This is when we move from a lower to a higher level, when our personality achieves a more complex stage of maturity. This can happen indirectly through art or poetry, which has the effect of raising us to a more integrated state, the effect of all good art being an increase in our sense of inner freedom. But it can happen directly, through our adopting a more demanding self-image. Wilson gives an example from his RAF days, when a private was raised in rank to a corporal and was given new duties and responsibilities, part of which included giving orders to those under him. At first the private felt awkward, as if he wasn't right for the job. But after a few days, he grew into it, and felt at home in his new rank. He was promoted, in the obvious sense of rank, but also in the sense of achieving a new sense of self-confidence, a new strength, a more well-defined personality. Do clothes make the man? According to the psychology of the self-image, in some sense it seems they do.

A strong self-image and a strong sense of values go hand in hand. As Wilson points out, the black room has its deteriorating effect precisely because within it, having nothing to reflect it, our self-image dissolves. We literally go to pieces. Yet a powerful enough imaginative grasp of one's values *should* be able to withstand the black room and maintain one's sense of self. Wilson makes this point by referring to *The Roots of Heaven*, a novel by Romain Gary. In it, a prisoner of the Nazis withstands solitary confinement by imagining herds of elephants marching across African savannahs. The elephants serve as a symbol of freedom and they give the prisoner's consciousness something to focus on, something to *grip*. In this way he maintains a sense of his reality. In the same way, in order to maintain morale, the prisoners invent an imaginary woman who shares their barracks. They bow before her, excuse themselves, offer her a seat, and so on; by doing this they maintain a sense of discipline and purpose that gives them an inner freedom their captors cannot take from them.

The opposite effect of promotion, what we could call "demotion," also occurs. This is when our self-image shrinks and begins to erode, when we become demoralized and passive, and lose a grip on our values. This is precisely the effect of the black room and prison, but also, for some people, of everyday life. In very extreme cases demotion can lead someone to perform some radical act, in order to feel themselves a *reality* again. This is the central theme of *Order of Assassins*. This third entry in Wilson's "murder trilogy" is "concerned with the criminal whose motive is *frustration of the will drive.*"[48] It is about what we can call the "self-actualization murder," if that is not being too oxymoronic. This is when the act of killing is an end in itself, an attempt to assert one's reality—a tragically futile act that results not in its aim of "more life," but in less.

The self-image, Wilson says, is directly related to the robot. The more I allow the robot to take over my life—that is, the more I live passively—the less real I feel. As I become more passive, my sense of who I am begins to blur. I actually become *less* than who I am than when I feel active and alive. (In Gurdjieff's and Heidegger's terms, we can say we have lost touch with "being.") But, as Wilson says, "this is as absurd as if my physical height varied between six feet and six inches."[49] "To have a blurred self-image," he writes, "is synonymous with feeling weak and passive." Reestablishing our self-image requires a sense of power, of being alive. Most of us accomplish this through harmless ways, even beneficial ones: we may go shopping, or we may listen to a symphony, or even write one. Or like Proust, we may stumble across a madeleine.

With the kind of criminals Wilson writes about, this need for purposive action becomes acute; their self-image is so inadequate that it requires some violent act to reestablish it. The problem is that they are too lazy to work for a socially acceptable satisfaction, and prefer the "smash and grab" approach (the essence of crime, Wilson says, is the shortcut). Or they hold a resentment against the society that they believe prevents them from achieving satisfaction, and justify their actions as a blow against some vague oppression, in an act of what Sartre called "magical thinking," basically allowing emotions to overrule reason. Wilson remarks that the difference between a human being and an electronic brain—a computer—is that while the electronic brain can respond to stimuli, the human being *looks for stimuli to respond to*. We seek out meanings to absorb, challenges to overcome. The most common stimulus, Wilson suggests, is sex, and hence he argues that many rapes are committed in order to restore briefly the rapist's self-image, his sense of his own reality, not, as one would expect, for the sex itself (and we've seen that a similar scenario informs the serial seducer). The highly dominant but frustrated personality, Wilson writes, "commits a crime *because of the sense of purpose conferred by the act itself*."[50] This is akin to the excitement teenagers feel when shoplifting. It is a warped attempt at creative action. Where the poet or painter sees himself in his work, the criminal catches a brief glimpse of himself through his crime. But this method has the same drawback as drug addiction: stronger doses are necessary and in the process the self the criminal wants to actualize is quickly eroded, because the reality it has to experience is one of irredeemable cruelty and horror.

Needless to say, this analysis does not condone the action; one would have to willfully misread Wilson in order to suggest this. It is a way of understanding some forms of crime through a psychology of the will. Closely connected to this is the concept of "the Right Man," a psychological profile Wilson borrows from the science-fiction writer A. E. van Vogt.[51] The Right Man is someone who under no circumstances can admit to being wrong and who employs a form of Sartre's magical thinking in order to maintain his sense of self-esteem and express his dominance. He creates a fantasy world to support his self-image and sustains it through sheer force of will. Van Vogt also calls this type the "Violent Man," because in his obsession with rightness, he will resort to violence to get his way. Right Men come in different shapes and sizes, from bullying husbands and domineering fathers to dictators like Hitler and Stalin and cult leaders like Charles Manson. Wilson suggests that the rise of revolutionary violence in the modern world—he was writing in the era of the Angry Brigade, the Weathermen, and the Black Panthers—is a "sign of the increasing number of 'violent men' rather than of political consciousness."[52]

With these themes Wilson presents a remarkable analysis of so-called motiveless murder—murder, that is, that does not conform to earlier motives such as gain or even self-esteem, but is performed in some way as an end in itself, as a desperate and ultimately unsuccessful attempt to take control of one's life back from the robot. In what was becoming the Wilsonian style, his analysis runs through a remarkable narrative linking the medieval Persian *hashishim*, Nietzsche, Victorian pornography, Jack the Ripper, Romanticism, H. P. Lovecraft, the Manson murders, as well as Maslow's and Frankl's ideas—to name some of the main ingredients—to argue that man is a "creature whose basic need is for significances *beyond* his everyday life."[53] A need that, in some extreme cases, resorts to violence to be fulfilled.

The success of *The Occult* prompted Wilson's publishers in England and America to ask him for a sequel. Wilson agreed, although at the time he had no idea what it would be about. And in any case he had a very full plate as it was. He had managed to calm his nerves before the camera and was doing a lot of television, although it was still an effort. He had been approached by a publisher friend with the idea of writing and editing a weekly magazine series called *Crimes and Punishment.* Each issue would focus on a famous crime and the magazine would run for only a certain time; then the issues could be bound together to form an encyclopedia, much like the very successful *Man, Myth & Magic,* which appeared at the same time. Wilson was then asked to contribute to the South West Arts Council, an advisory board which decided on funding for various arts and cultural projects, like the Cheltenham Literature Festival. His other panelists included the poets Ted Hughes, Peter Redgrove, and Ronald Duncan, and the novelist Alexis Lykiard. Although not usually a team player, the original Outsider was surprised to find that he enjoyed the work.

One unwelcome complication in early 1973 was the arrival of a Colin Wilson "groupie," a mentally unbalanced American woman Wilson had met in California during his time teaching in Seattle. Wilson says that when he first met "Kathie" she made a clumsy and unsuccessful attempt to seduce him. She was such an obviously troubled soul, however, and responded so well to his optimistic philosophy, that he ignored it and humored her. The second time she seemed more determined to succeed. She turned up at Tetherdown in February for an uninvited two-week stay, which for Wilson seemed "like eternity," although one suspects that for Joy it must have felt even longer.[54] Upon arrival Kathie told Joy, "I've come now, so you can go," an announcement the mostly unflappable Joy took with her usual equanimity. To make a long and somewhat indiscreet story short—the reader can get the full details in *Dreaming to Some Purpose*—Kathie threatened suicide if Wilson did not accept her advances. His account of his involuntary submission—dry and factual—is best told by Wilson himself, but it gives a very clear idea of how patient and faithful a wife Joy had to be at times.[55] One clear result of this unwanted tryst was that after it Wilson was afflicted with severe back pains for a month—on more than one occasion he was unable to stand. Wilson felt that the paralysis was his unconscious mind's way of punishing him for wasting two weeks in pointless self-division. Wilson later discovered that in 1989 Kathie committed suicide with an overdose of sleeping pills.

In June the backers of *Crimes and Punishment* finally gave the go-ahead and Wilson was asked to produce an article a week. But then the backers wanted to speed up the pace, and Wilson was asked to contribute three or four a week. The pay was good but the workload meant he had to produce a three-thousand-word article a day—demanding stuff, even for a professional. But by July the backers of *Crimes and Punishment* were asking for seven articles, then ten. This amounted to thirty thousand words a week, about a third of the average book. This meant that Wilson was writing an article and a half, sometimes two, a day and the equivalent of a full-length book every three weeks. The money he was earning—about £750 (roughly $1,900) a week—made the effort worthwhile but it was clear that he could not keep up this pace for very long. For one thing, it had begun to affect his sex life; like the French writer Stendhal, Wilson was unfortunately experiencing *le fiasco*—impotence—more often than he, and one suspects Joy, would have liked.

The crack-up began after Wilson spent a long evening being interviewed by two young reporters from the Canadian Broadcasting Corporation. The reporters talked too much and tended to interrupt each other. He drank too much and stayed up too late, until about two a.m. By the time he got to bed his eyes were "glazed over with boredom" and he felt as if he'd been "deafened with salvos of canon fire."[56] The next day the reporters returned for another bout. After they left Wilson did some household chores, then wrote the closing pages of *Strange Powers*, a book showing him in his new role as paranormal investigator. It was one of many similar minor works that came in the wake of *The Occult*.[57] In it he interviews the dowser Robert Leftwich, a medium named Eunice Beattie, and the physician and psychologist Arthur Guirdham, author of several fascinating books about a strange case of group reincarnation involving members of the Cathars, a medieval heretical sect. It was not a hat Wilson felt very comfortable wearing. "As an 'occult investigator,'" he wrote, "I am aware that I am thoroughly unsatisfactory. When I ought to be asking penetrating questions, or devising means of testing the truth of what I am being told, I simply listen and make notes."[58] In other words, he acted like a writer and a journalist, not a member of the Society for Psychical Research (SPR).[59] Wilson was always more interested in understanding the paranormal in terms of his own philosophy of consciousness than in "proving" its reality, which he accepted. This theoretical approach sometimes left him open to criticism by more astringent researchers.

The same day he finished *Strange Powers* Wilson was asked to review a book for *The Spectator;* later the magazine *Audio* asked if he could write an article on Verdi. He tried to relax by taking Joy to see the film *Cabaret*, based on the Berlin stories of his friend Christopher Isherwood.[60] But that night he awoke at four a.m. and thought of all the work he had to do. He was unable to get back to sleep and the tension accumulated. He even thought of going to his study and starting work on one of the *Crimes and Punishment* articles but realized that

that way lay madness. Then his heart began to pound and his cheeks and ears began to burn. He tried to stop the panic with sheer willpower, but this only made things worse. He felt his "energies churning, like a car being accelerated when the engine is in neutral."[61] The anxiety he had felt before the cameras had returned and it had upped the ante. Adrenaline coursed through his veins so much that he thought he was having a heart attack. He got up and drank some orange juice, then tried to calm himself as he would a "frightened horse." He sat for a while in the bathroom, paging through a world atlas, until the waves of fear subsided. He was able to get back to bed but then the panic started again. He felt his energies leaking away, like "milk boiling over in a saucepan."[62] The anxiety produced panic, which produced more anxiety, in a particularly vicious circle. He felt as if he was under attack by the very psychic vampires he wrote about in *The Mind Parasites*. It was important, he felt, not to dwell on "our total ignorance, our lack of the smallest shred of certainty about who we are and why we are here." Doing that, he knew, would lead to a "mental Black Hole."[63] It was the kind of vastation he had written about and it was not pleasant. He was, he knew, on the brink of a mental breakdown.

Wilson was able to calm himself and carry on with his workload. But in the evenings a "fear of fear" returned and he felt himself sinking into depression. A kind of contest began, between his ability to get his work done by ignoring the fear, and getting through another bout of it in the night. He could raise himself out of his depression through mental effort, a tactic he called "gliding," but the slightest reminder of it—something on the television news, for example—would send him into a nosedive again. Some months later, on an overnight train to London, the panic was so bad that he considered getting off at the next station, wherever it was, and walking anywhere. But he managed to calm the rising fear and to sink inside himself and untie his mental knots—much as the protagonists in *The Mind Parasites* do. Yet the attacks continued. One hit him while he was staying with the writer John Michell in his old neighborhood of Notting Hill in London. He woke up in the middle of the night and, like the protagonist of Sartre's *Nausea*, had no idea what he was doing there. He fought off the panic until dawn, left a note apologizing for leaving so suddenly, then slipped out of the house and got an early train back to Cornwall.

The essence of his panic attacks, Wilson saw, was a kind of childishness. The increasing workload meant he was pushing himself beyond even his own considerable limits, and some childish element in his psyche simply refused to do it. It went on strike and said no. Purposeful activity recharges our vital batteries but in this instance his energy tanks were not refilling, and when the exhaustion came he had nothing to replenish them with. Then he had to consciously force himself to go on, compelling himself to meet his obligations and responsibilities, telling himself he had worked much harder as a day laborer and that he was getting soft. The attacks began, he writes, "with a fatigue that quickly turned into a general feeling of *mistrust* of life," which was then compounded by self-consciousness.[64] He was succumbing to the same problem that plagued Frankl's bank clerk: his consciousness of his condition acted as an amplifier, increasing it through a dangerous negative feedback. Trying to stop the panic head-on only increased it. What he needed to do was to *forget* himself in something else, to turn his mind away from its self-collapse. When he managed to do this, he was fine.

Wilson had been at a loss as to exactly what his sequel to *The Occult* would be about. He had covered so much ground already that he was worried about repeating himself. Now his panic attacks seemed to suggest a theme. He had discovered that he could free himself of them if he managed to "wake himself up" entirely. This seemed to happen by calling on some part of himself that was more adult, more mature, than the rebellious child who was refusing to go on. He found that he could call upon a "more purposive 'me,'" what he came to call "the schoolmistress effect," as if a teacher had entered a room of noisy children and clapped her hands, bringing them to order.[65]

This notion of two selves in conflict—a truculent child and a mature adult—led Wilson to formulate a theory of human personality, what he called the "ladder of selves." Gurdjieff, he knew, taught that we are not whole individuals, but that we are really made of many different "I's," like squabbling warlords each claiming to be king and seizing power temporarily. The aim of Gurdjieff's work is to try to fuse some of these different "I's" into a whole, through strenuous efforts at what he called "conscious labor" and "intentional suffering." Wilson saw that this was true, but he also saw that these different "I's" occupied different positions on a kind of inner ladder, some lower, some higher. The shift from a weak to a strong self-image could be seen as a movement from a lower rung up this ladder to a higher one. And the opposite was true: one could move down a rung or two, which, Wilson believed, is what happened to him during his panic attacks. All purposeful activity, he saw, activates a more mature, integrated self, while boredom and passivity means a drop down to lower rungs. As we move up the ladder of selves, we make contact with more of our powers; our personality expands beyond its usual limits, and we begin to experience new abilities, such as Faculty X. Presumably, at the top of the ladder of selves is an "I" more real than those below, something like Husserl's transcendental ego. But what if we move in the other direction? If we move down the ladder of selves, our personality shrinks, we become cut off from our powers, and life takes on an increasingly dull, meaningless character. We can become so contracted that we are only a fragment of ourselves, a small knot of worries and anxieties cut off from our full selves, an example of what Yeats called the "partial mind," and which the nineteenth-century French neurologist Jean-Martin Charcot had discovered in patients suffering from hysteria. And of course our habit of cutting out most of reality and relying on the robot to live for us only exacerbates this situation.

This fragmentation of self, Wilson saw, was clearly linked to the strange phenomenon of multiple personality. This happens when through some overwhelming psychological crisis, the human personality splits into one or more other selves. Famous cases are recounted in *The Three Faces of Eve*, by psychiatrists Corbett H. Thigpen and Hervey M. Cleckley, and *Sybil*, by Flora Rheta Schreiber. Unlike the ladder of selves, in which the rungs seem to blend into one another—the self that experiences promotion is not an entirely new self, unknown to the previous one—with multiple personalities, the differences between one self and another are complete; they appear to be completely separate identities, a radical embodiment of Gurdjieff's teaching about our many "I's." But even here, the existence of a "higher" kind of self, a more mature, more adult personality, seems to be the case. Wilson saw that in many cases, among the fragments of self, people suffering from multiple personality also seemed to produce a kind of guiding self, a version of who they *could be*, if allowed to evolve. The split into other personalities could be seen, Wilson believed, as a result of a failure to develop.

Wilson believed that his ladder of selves metaphor could accommodate many of the themes he had been wrestling with since *The Outsider*. It was not, he said, really a theory, but only a "convenient description of what happens when we feel 'more alive.'"[66] This sense of being more alive seemed linked to occult experiences, and it was worthwhile seeing how far the hypothesis of a ladder of selves could reach in understanding this. It could also throw light on other issues. The kind of meaninglessness associated with Sartre's nausea, for example, could be seen as an effect of the times when we occupy one of the lower rungs on the ladder of selves. On this rung we can agree with Simone de Beauvoir when in *Pyrrhus et Cinéas* she laments, "I look at myself in vain in a mirror. . . . I experience in myself the emptiness that is myself." De Beauvoir says that she can never grasp herself "as an entire object," and like Sartre she believes this is some deep insight into the human condition. Yet Wilson disagrees. Higher up on the ladder of selves, we *can* grasp ourselves as whole, and de Beauvoir's inability to do so is an indication of her low inner pressure, and not a glimpse of a fundamental truth about human existence.

But on a more occult note, the ladder of selves was suggestive as well. It seemed to Wilson that it could be useful in accounting for a variety of phenomena, from hypnosis and possession to mystical experiences and Gurdjieff's aim of "waking up" to astral travel and other dimensions. What was needed was a bridge joining the two, some connecting link between our many selves and occult phenomena. The person who supplied this missing link was Joy. It was in fact Joy's remark about a passage in Osbert Sitwell's—of the famous family—autobiography, describing a palmist's accuracy in predicting the deaths of some fellow airmen in World War I, that first weakened Wilson's skepticism about the occult. Now she proved inspirational again.

In *The Occult* Wilson had briefly mentioned the work of the maverick Cambridge archaeologist T. C. Lethbridge, a rotund studious don who took delight in investigating strange mysteries. Lethbridge wrote a number of books on various occult themes—witchcraft, UFO, ancient religions, ghosts, precognition, and the curious powers of pendulums. Wilson liked Lethbridge's casual, readable style and bought his books, but aside from *Witches: Investigating an Ancient Religion* (1962), he did not have the time to read them. But Joy did and she told Wilson about them. He then read them as well and realized that Lethbridge was an important thinker with a fresh, lively mind and much to say. Through his experiments with dowsing—the ability to detect substances buried underground—and with using a pendulum, Lethbridge had developed a remarkable theory about the paranormal, involving different rates of time, other dimensions, and levels of consciousness, which seemed to fit in well with Wilson's ladder of selves idea. When Wilson discovered that Lethbridge lived in Devon, not far from Cornwall, he wrote to him suggesting they meet, and included a copy of *The Occult*. Soon after, he received a letter from Lethbridge's widow, Mina, saying that Lethbridge had died the year before. Wilson took the opportunity of writing *Mysteries*, his sequel to *The Occult*, to explore the full range of Lethbridge's ideas and to use these as a basis for his further investigation into the occult, the paranormal, and the supernatural.

Although *Mysteries*, published in 1978, was not quite as successful as *The Occult*, it nevertheless sold very well and received several good reviews. One critic compared it favorably with Sir James George Frazer's classic *The Golden Bough*, Toynbee's *A Study of History*, and F. W. H. Myers's groundbreaking *Human Personality and Its Survival of Bodily Death*. With *Mysteries*, that reviewer wrote, Wilson showed himself to be "scientifically objective," "carefully reasoned," "logical, incredibly informative and compellingly readable."[67] A review for *New Scientist*, a respected scientific periodical, suggests that Wilson's authority on these matters was well established. *Mysteries* was a "major work . . . an extraordinary tour de force [which] will materially help to bring both sides [science and paranormal studies] together in a way which could lead to real and important advances in our view of the universe."[68]

Such acclaim from a scientific publication for a book about the paranormal is unusual today, and shows that in the 1970s, the paranormal was treated with respect by many scientists, unlike in our more narrowly skeptical times. It was firmly part of the zeitgeist. Wilson's entry into the world of telepathy, precognition, and synchronicity seemed to have triggered an interest in these matters in others too. In *The Roots of Coincidence* (1972) the respected political and scientific writer Arthur Koestler—whose own accounts of mystical experiences Wilson referred to often and whose antireductionist writing he appreciated—wrote approvingly of paranormal research.[69] Koestler followed this with an important volume, *The Challenge of Chance* (1973), about a mass experiment in telepathy, and at his death left a munificent bequest to further psychical research. The veteran novelist and playwright J. B. Priestley summed up his belief in the paranormal and other occult matters in one of his last books, *Over the Long High Wall: Some Reflections and Speculations on Life, Death and Time* (1972). The South African botanist and anthropologist Lyall Watson began a successful writing career with his best-selling *Supernature* (1973), a "natural history of the supernatural." With *Total Man* (1972), the psychologist Stan Gooch began a series of fascinating books linking psychology, the paranormal, and Gooch's own speculations about human evolution, specifically the interbreeding of Neanderthal and Cro-Magnon man, well before such ideas became accepted (sadly Gooch has still to receive the credit he is due). There was also a revival of interest in magic, with books on Aleister Crowley and the Hermetic Order of the Golden Dawn by Francis King and Kenneth Grant, and many cheap reprints of occult classics, as well as a slew of other books of varying quality on all aspects of the occult.

Of course, paranormal or psychical research had been going on since the Society for Psychical Research in the late nineteenth century and had been given a fillip by the work of J. B. Rhine at Duke University in the 1930s. C. G. Jung, too, the most famous living psychologist, had in his last years spoken out about his interest in these matters. But with the occult revival of the 1960s and early 1970s, more liberal attitudes toward the paranormal had spread across a wide spectrum of culture. It was a kind of golden age of psychical studies and the occult, and Wilson was at the heart of it.

CHAPTER NINE

OUR OTHER SELF

L ike *The Occult*, *Mysteries* was a big book—in fact, it was even bigger. It had to be in order to cover all the material Wilson had researched. He aimed to be as comprehensive and analytical as possible, and this proved challenging. With *The Occult* he introduced the subject and gave his readers an informative and entertaining history of it, along the way bringing in his philosophy of consciousness and elements of his new existentialism. Now he intended to apply his ladder of selves to occult phenomena in general, in order to understand them and to provide a perspective from which the collection of "disorderly facts," as Robert Graves might have called them, would make sense. Since he had written *The Occult* there had been an information explosion in the paranormal and occult fields. To do it right he would have to cover an enormous amount of literature on a wide field of topics, subjects ranging from "plant telepathy, psychic surgery, transcendental meditation, biofeedback, Kirlian photography, multiple personality and synchronicity" to "possession, UFO, leys and the 'ancient religion.'"[1] As the saying goes, he had his work cut out for him.

Faced with this wealth of unconnected insight, Wilson took a deep breath and spread his investigation wide and once again he ran into some flak from an editor about the length of the book.[2] She wanted to cut it by a hundred thousand words. Given the time and effort spent and the importance of the material, Wilson was loath to do this. So as he did before, he found another publisher, Putnam, who took the book as it was. It turned out to be a good decision. The book sold well in the States—I bought a hardback copy myself as soon as it came out—and the 250,000 words Wilson fought for were welcome by his many readers.

Throughout the 1970s much attention was given to the mysteries of the mind and the strange world it finds itself in. Wilson was determined to bring the latest findings together and have it all make sense. Once again, the urge toward a system, which had begun in his childhood, returned. Wilson was quickly showing himself to be an encyclopedist of the top rank. He was a non-academic popular thinker who wrote for the intelligent general reader, a type of public intellectual rarely seen in our more cloistered time. He seemed able to absorb more material for one book than most scholars do in a lifetime and he presented his findings to an intelligent public in a seemingly effortlessly readable style. *Mysteries* proved to be a remarkable sourcebook for practically everything exciting interest in the occult, the mystical, and the supernatural at a time when the general reading public had a very open mind about such things.

His readers were curious and eager to use their minds. They felt that through reading Wilson they got something like an education, the product of a didacticism Wilson had absorbed from H. G. Wells and Bernard Shaw. (As he wrote in *The Philosopher's Stone*, "I apologize for sounding didactic. It is impossible to say anything that is not commonplace without sounding didactic."[3]) As one reviewer for the *Daily Telegraph* wrote, "Colin Wilson could make a telephone directory exciting." It was this breadth of knowledge, combined with an intensity of thought and an infectious optimism, that gave Wilson's books their peculiar positive drive.

A look at the "Analytical Table of Contents" for *Mysteries* shows exactly how much Wilson had taken on. Part One deals with the work of T. C. Lethbridge, and the four chapters Wilson devotes to Lethbridge's ideas could stand as a book in themselves.[4] Through his interest in dowsing and his use of pendulums, Lethbridge had hit on the discovery that there are different levels of reality—one could just as well say different worlds—in which the notions of time, space, life, and death that hold sway here are not applicable, a belief not unfamiliar in the occult tradition.

Lethbridge's investigations covered ghosts and ghouls, UFOs, ancient pagan religions, witchcraft, dreams, precognition, and much else. One area of his study that chimed very well with particular interests of the time was his work on megaliths, the ancient stone circles and monuments that dot England and northern Europe and which had received renewed attention through John Michell's underground best seller, *The View over Atlantis* (1969). Michell's book speaks about "ley lines," supposed ancient tracks that crisscross England, aligning different "sacred" sites such as Stonehenge and Glastonbury Tor, and which Michell speculates indicate the presence of a peculiar kind of occult force. An ancient civilization that knew about ley lines and this force forms the "Atlantis" of Michell's title.[5]

Wilson, too, was very interested in this supposed "earth force," and he had come to some interesting conclusions about it and its relation to dowsing. Yet in one sense Wilson was a bit like Moses; he pointed the way to the promised land but didn't quite occupy it himself. He was, he said, "ESP thick," and often remarked that he showed little psychic ability. He had become a host on the BBC's *Leap in the Dark*, a television series about the paranormal which ran in the mid-seventies, but he himself showed little talent for it. His mind was too rational and purposive, he said, to relax enough to be able to contact the deeper levels associated with the paranormal. His temperament was "basically scientific." It was ideas and facts that excited him, and "the process of fitting them into larger and larger patterns."[6] But in one occult practice he did show some ability. While trying to dowse at the Merry Maidens, a group of standing stones near Penzance in Cornwall, he had a surprising experience. As he approached the stones, Wilson felt the dowsing rod twist violently in his hands. What amazed him was not so much that the rod had reacted—he had already seen others dowse and noted that Joy seemed better at it than he—but that as it did, he felt nothing. There was "no prickling of the hair, no tingling in the hands."[7] It was as if he had nothing to do with it. The dowsing rod was in his hands, but he hadn't made it move. Wilson concluded that some "unknown part of my brain" reacted to some strange force that came from the stones. This force had somehow made his muscles contract and this in turn had made the dowsing rod twist.

Wilson had by this time come to the conclusion that the strange phenomena associated with poltergeists—a German word meaning "noisy spirit"—are somehow powered by this unknown earth force. Poltergeists are known to throw objects across the room, lift people into the air, start fires, cause objects to disappear, make loud booming noises, and in general raise a disturbing ruckus, and Wilson believed that the energy needed for such antics come from the earth itself. He accepted the common belief that poltergeists are associated with the anxieties of puberty and that in most cases, the source of the disturbances turns out to be the unconscious mind of an adolescent or some other frustrated, unhappy character. What was curious is that in most cases, the person involved doesn't know he or she is responsible, just as Wilson felt that he wasn't responsible for the dowsing rod twisting in his hands. Wilson researched a case involving a young woman who worked in a lawyer's office; lights kept exploding and the telephone bills were staggering because someone was calling for the time dozens of times a day. The woman, who was bored with her job, had no idea she was involved and it took some work for her to be convinced of it. Wilson did a television program on the case and interviewed the psychical researcher Hans Bender. Bender said one must be careful when telling the person responsible that she is at the center of the disturbances. The knowledge could cause severe psychological shock.

Further research and a meeting with the psychic investigator Guy Lyon Playfair at a paranormal conference in the summer of 1980 would lead Wilson to change his mind about the source of poltergeist activity. He would be forced to come to the unwanted conclusion that in fact poltergeists are actual spirits; unwanted because it was frowned upon by most scientific paranormal investigators, who believed that the unconscious mind hypothesis was more scientifically acceptable. Wilson himself agreed with this but after discussions with Playfair, and a reading of Max Freedom Long's *The Secret Science Behind Miracles*, about the Huna religion of Hawaii, he could see no way around it. Long was an American teacher who came to Hawaii in 1917 and became interested in the indigenous traditions. The Huna tradition spoke of three selves: a lower, middle, and higher self. The lower self is like Freud's unconscious, the middle self is our everyday consciousness, and the higher self is a kind of "superconscious mind," an arrangement not unlike Wilson's own ladder of selves. The Huna believed that after death these different selves separate; the lower self may become a poltergeist, the middle self a ghost, with the higher self, a kind of guardian angel which controls the future, living on.[8] After investigating a poltergeist case in Pontefract, in the north of England, involving a mysterious "black monk," Wilson had to concede that the facts suggested that poltergeists really are spirits, a conclusion he argues for in *Poltergeist!* (1981).

What interested Wilson was that some part of his mind, which he was not directly aware of, could interact with the earth force and cause dowsing rods to twist and poltergeist phenomena to take place. Exactly *what* part of the mind was he talking about?

One of the many books Wilson read while researching *Mysteries* was *The Origin of Consciousness in the Breakdown of the Bicameral Mind* (1976), by the Princeton psychologist Julian Jaynes. Wilson discovered it courtesy of his friend Ira Einhorn. Einhorn, an associate of the parapsychologist Andrija Puharich—who also worked with Uri Geller—is described by Wilson as a "one-man liaison service for parapsychologists and scientists interested in various aspects of the paranormal."[9] Wilson had met Einhorn in Philadelphia during his time at Rutgers University, and, as people were wont to do, Einhorn turned up one evening at Tetherdown. With him he had a copy of Jaynes's book.[10]

Jaynes argues that before circa 1250 BC human beings did not experience an "inner world" in the way that we do; that is to say, they did not possess the kind of self-consciousness that we have. This was because their minds were still "bicameral," which means "two chambered." The two chambers in question were the right and left cerebral hemispheres, the two halves of the cerebrum, the most recent and most human part of the brain. We also possess two brains, but the difference between us and "bicameral man" is that we experience a consciousness that is informed by both; according to Jaynes our ancient ancestors had immediate access to only one, the left. Although the fact that we have two brains has been known for centuries, exactly *why* we do remains a mystery. One neuroscientist even joked that one is a spare, in case something goes wrong with the other.

According to Jaynes, bicameral man experienced his right brain as voices he heard in his head, telling him what to do. Our ancestors believed these voices came from the gods, but Jaynes argued they were really coming from the right brain. Around 1250 BC a series of calamities contributed to the breakdown of this arrangement. The separation between the hemispheres was breached and our own modern consciousness was born. We are conscious that we are conscious, and because of this we can "talk" with ourselves, carry on an inner dialogue. Jaynes argued that this was not true of early man. He did not ask himself, as we do, what he should do in some situation, but waited for the gods—or his right brain—to tell him. As Jaynes says of the characters in the *Iliad*, which recounts events that took place in the Bronze Age, "We cannot approach these heroes by inventing mind-spaces behind their fierce eyes as we do each other."[11]

Wilson would take argument with Jaynes's central theory and say that it is *we* who are bicameral, not ancient man. But what fascinated him were some of the insights that emerged from "split-brain" psychology. He had read Robert Ornstein's work *The Psychology of Consciousness* (1972), and was impressed by some of the results from an operation known as a commissurotomy. This is when the corpus callosum, or commissure, a knot of fibers that connects the two brains, is severed, often as a means of preventing epileptic fits, which are a kind of electrical storm passing from one brain to the other. What happened in these cases is that the split-brain patient literally became two people. It had been known for a long time that the left brain is verbal—it deals with words—while the right is speechless but is geared toward patterns. This is why the cliché developed that the left brain was a scientist and the right an artist. When a patient had his corpus callosum severed, he seemed to inhabit his left brain, while the right seemed to be the dwelling place of a total stranger. A variety of experiments seemed to show this.

One of the curious facts about split-brain psychology is that the right side of the brain controls the left side of the body, and vice versa. So our right visual field is controlled by the left brain, and our left visual field by the right.[12] During one experiment a split-brain patient was shown an apple with his right eye, connected to his left, verbal brain, and an orange with his left eye, connected to his speechless, right brain. When asked to say what he had just been shown, he replied, "Apple." When asked to write with his left hand—connected to the right brain—what he had been shown, he wrote "orange." Shown two different symbols—a circle and a square—with each eye, when asked what he had seen he replied, "Square." When asked to draw with his left hand what he had just seen, he drew a circle. When asked what he had just drawn, he replied, "Square."

A patient who bumped into something with his left side—controlled by the right brain—was unaware that he had. He hadn't noticed it because in truth, he, who lives in his left brain, didn't bump into anything—it was his "other half" who had. A woman who had undergone a commissurotomy viewed a sexy picture with her left eye and blushed. When asked why she was blushing, she said she didn't know. She didn't know because it was her other half who had seen the picture.

Some split-brain patients' lives became a kind of constant tussle between their two sides, with one fighting the other over groceries or what they would wear.[13] But there are also times when the mute right brain comes to the aid of its talkative neighbor. The neuropsychologist Roger Sperry flashed red and green lights randomly into the left eye of a split-brain patient. He then asked the patient to guess which color he had just seen. As the patient hadn't seen anything—he lived in the left, verbal hemisphere, and it was the right that had seen the flash—his chances of a correct guess should have been fifty-fifty. But often the patient would say red, then suddenly shake and change his mind, and say green. Sperry realized that what had happened was that the patient's right brain *knew* the correct answer, but as it can't speak, it metaphorically kicked its neighbor under the table so he would change his guess. A similar scenario may account for what the French call *presque vu*, "almost seen," the phenomenon of having a name or word "on the tip of the tongue," but not being quite able to grasp it. It may be that our right brain knows the answer, but simply can't say it or tell its neighbor what it is.

Wilson was fascinated by the evidence that we have two people living inside our heads. He had already arrived at the idea that we have an "other self," what the early twentieth-century Belgian playwright Maurice Maeterlinck called the "unknown guest." This other self, Wilson believed, was responsible for paranormal phenomena. Now it seemed that Maeterlinck's unknown guest may be living in the right brain. The idea fit well with Wilson's ladder of selves and the phenomenon of multiple personality. This does not mean, he pointed out, that Gurdjieff's different "I's," the different selves in cases of multiple personality, or the higher or lower rungs on his own ladder of selves are located in different parts of the brain.[14] What was important is that split-brain theory supports the idea that we are not the "individuals"—meaning nondivided—that we assume ourselves to be. As Wilson says, "We are very *dividual* indeed."[15] We are made up of parts, levels, polarities, and the tension between them. Often they are at odds, but occasionally there are moments of reconciliation and affirmation, when the two sides form a new whole. Wilson nods to Hesse's *Steppenwolf* as a work that embodies the idea that a more intense state of consciousness arises from a new synthesis of the old oppositions.

Wilson suspected that the unknown part of his mind that responded to the earth force and moved the dowsing rod could have been his right brain, and that it could also be responsible for other psychic phenomena, such as poltergeists. He knew that his friend and fellow paranormal theorist Stan Gooch was not in favor of the split-brain theory. Gooch anchored the paranormal in the cerebellum, the smaller, older brain that sits in the back of the skull, which the cerebrum, the new brain, has grown around.[16] Wilson concedes that Gooch might have been right (he was a great supporter of Gooch's work), but he also felt that fixing the seat of paranormal activity—or the unconscious mind, for that matter—in some specific location in the brain is really not that important. What is important is to recognize that we are really two, that along with our everyday, rational self, there is also another, unknown self. This unknown self is involved not only in paranormal phenomena but also in what Wilson calls the "other mode of consciousness," the deeper, more relational consciousness responsible for our poetic, aesthetic, and mystical experiences.[17]

The fact of our having two brains fit in well with earlier dualities in Wilson's work. It seemed to agree with his notion of duo-consciousness and with the two modes of perception that he had found in Whitehead's ideas, as well as with Yeats's apparent intuition about our two brains in his phrase "the partial mind." It also fit well with the polarity Wilson had been wrestling with ever since *The Outsider*, Ultimate Yes and Ultimate No, the moments of yea-saying and affirmation—"absurd good news"—and the narrowness and futility of everyday consciousness. The right brain seemed on the side of Ultimate Yes, with the left favoring Ultimate No. The right brain's mode of perception was richer, deeper; it provided *meaning*, allowing into consciousness all the "irrelevant" detail that our left-brain purposive consciousness filtered out. It was the kind of perception that informed Robert Graves's method of "looking sideways at disorderly facts to make perfect sense of them," and which allows us to appreciate the beauty of a symphony or painting. The right brain's preference for patterns was the source of the bird's-eye view, that feeling of being *above* the immediate moment and the freedom from the limitations of the present it gave. It provided that feeling of vague but vital significance, reaching out into the distance, the "promise of the horizon," that was the essence of Romanticism. It saw the forest, while the left brain was fixated on the individual trees.

Drugs such as mescaline and LSD, it seemed, achieved their effects by somehow inhibiting the editor in the left brain, and allowing more of the input from the right to enter consciousness. The freshness and *newness* of the senses that came in moments of "primal perception" was rooted in the right brain; it was the left brain that made things "typical," as T. E. Lawrence knew. If, as Wilson had argued, our everyday consciousness is the result of a severe editing of the reality around us, then clearly what was being edited out was the richer, deeper, more relational input coming from the right brain. Mystics believe that in their moments of expanded consciousness they experience God. What may be the case, Wilson suggested, is that they are really experiencing the right brain.

The problem with everyday consciousness, then, must be that it was slanted too much to the left. Ever since the Romantics, poets have complained that reason, logic, and intellect have taken all the mystery out of life. Mystics, too, agreed that the ego, the "I," was the source of our miseries. Some even believed that self-consciousness itself was an evil. Walt Whitman longed to "turn and live with animals," an expression of his desire to free himself of the left brain's worries and concerns. Whitman's yearning had been repeated in different ways over the past two centuries, most recently in the desire to "turn off your mind" that informed the hippies and the counterculture. So clearly what was needed was to shift the center of our consciousness from the left side of our brains over to the right.

Or was it? Wilson agreed that there was an imbalance between our brains, but the relation between them wasn't as simple as some mystics or Romantic poets might think. In order to clarify things he wrote a short book, *Franken-stein's Castle* (1980), the castle in this case being the human brain.

Wilson had already devoted much study to the brain. He had been reading material about it since the mid-1960s. *The Philosopher's Stone* is about two scien-tists who believe that the secret to higher consciousness lies in the prefrontal lobes of the cerebral cortex, and they develop an operation that can stimulate this faculty. The result is an increase in "relationality," the awareness of other times and places; at one point one of the scientists experiences a "time-slip" back to Elizabethan England. Now it seemed clear that the source of these kinds of experiences was the right brain. The question seemed to be: what was the rela-tion between it and its more sober neighbor?

Wilson first began to think of these ideas while he was working on *The Quest for Wilhelm Reich* (1981), a critical biography of that misunderstood ge-nius.[18] As a reader discovers, although a brilliant psychologist, Reich was some-thing of a Right Man, and the difficulties of his life, as well as his imprisonment in 1957 at the hands of the FDA for transporting his "orgone boxes" across state lines, can be understood as a result of Reich's unfortunate "rightness." He started out as a Freudian; we could even say that his insistence on a satisfactory orgasm as the key to mental health made him more of a Freudian than Freud, who was repelled by Reich's ideas. Wilson had always rejected Freud's insis-tence on sex as the sole cause of neurosis, and as he researched material for his book on Reich, he came to see where Freud's basic mistake lay. It was in his insistence that the unconscious is some kind of monster, hidden in the cellars of the mind.

Freud came to this conclusion while studying with the great French neurol-ogist Jean-Martin Charcot in Paris. Charcot had rehabilitated hypnotism, which had fallen out of favor in the early nineteenth century because of its as-sociation with the German scientist and healer Franz Anton Mesmer, whom the science of the time had declared a fraud. Freud was impressed by the dis-plays Charcot had put on of his hypnotized patients, who exhibited remarkable symptoms—false pregnancies, paralysis, stigmata—all while under hypnosis. (Charcot believed hypnosis was a form of hysteria.) Freud came to see that there was some unknown part of the mind that had enormous powers, much greater than our conscious part. This unconscious mind could, it seemed, perform miracles. Since it was more powerful than the conscious mind, *it* must be the true controller of consciousness. We, our conscious selves, can only be its puppets. And since, as Freud came to believe—mistakenly—our sexual drives are the most powerful forces working in the unconscious, we are all, whether we like it or not, in the service of these drives.

Wilson agreed that the unconscious mind is enormously powerful. But he did not agree that because of this, we are its slaves.

Frankenstein's Castle begins with a look at what Wilson calls the "other mode of consciousness." He explains what he means by referring to a musician friend who told him of how once, after a long hard day, he poured himself a whiskey, and listened to a suite of dances by the Renaissance composer Pretorius. As he relaxed and sipped the whiskey, some strange happiness came over him, a feeling of exhilaration, a sense that he had somehow *become* the music. A similar experience happened to a friend who worked for the BBC. Sitting in an empty control room, he put on a record of Schubert, and suddenly it was as if he had *become* Schubert. It was as if he was *participating* with the music, had somehow entered into it and was composing it himself, and could see exactly why Schubert had written it the way he had.

Wilson felt something of the same while writing his book on Shaw. Writing of Shaw's breakthrough after years of overwork as a music and theater critic, he had a "sudden feeling of intense joy," as if his "heart had turned into a balloon" and was "sailing up into the air."[19] He had become aware, he said, of the "multiplicity of life." He was back in Edwardian London, as the hero of *The Philosopher's Stone* was back in Shakespeare's day or Proust back in Combray. But he could just as easily be in "Goethe's Weimar or Mozart's Salzburg."[20] The experience, he points out, was not one of empathy; it was, as William James had said of his own mystical experience, *perceptual*. It was not merely a matter of feeling but of *seeing*, of perceiving a reality of which we are usually blind, or toward which we are usually *indifferent*. It was a moment of seeing from the bird's-eye view rather than from our usual close-up perspective. Or, in other words, it was a moment of non-robotic consciousness.

Such moments are important because they renew us. They connect us to our source of power, meaning, and purpose, and fill us with new vitality. As Wilson came to see, the right brain is in charge of our power supply. It holds the purse strings on our strength.

Wilson knew that it was precisely such moments as these that the Romantics craved: the sense that distant realities are as real as the present moment—more real, in fact—and that life is infinitely interesting. The Romantics had such moments, but the problem was that they only seemed to make life more difficult. Moments of freedom from the robot led to an intense dissatisfaction with the triviality of everydayness—that is, with robotic consciousness. This led to the tragedy of many of Wilson's Outsiders, who were increasingly unable to cope with life, which was the robot's business. As Wilson had often quoted, they wanted their servants to live it for them. This was the problem of "the near and the far," as the writer L. H. Myers called it in a novel of that name.

Myers—the son of the pioneering psychical researcher F. W. H. Myers—set his remarkable novel in medieval India, and it begins when the young Prince Jali looks out over the desert sunset from the battlements of a castle. Jali reflects that there are really two deserts, one that is "a glory to the eye" and another that is a "weariness to trudge."[21] He knows that no matter how quickly he runs, he will never reach the sunset, and that all that he will get for his efforts is sand in his shoes. This, we can see, is the same feeling that Yeats had when he expressed his unhappiness at not being able to capture the beauty of a waterfall. All he could touch was "cold stone and water," just as all Prince Jali can touch is sand. Wilson points out that Dr. Johnson expresses that same insight when in *Rasselas, Prince of Abyssinia*, he has his hero looking over a scene of pastoral beauty which should delight him and complaining, "Man has surely some latent sense for which this place affords no gratification." There are, Johnson reflects, "desires distinct from sense which must be satisfied before we are happy."[22] These "desires distinct from sense" are aimed at the "far," at realities that are not immediately present, yet are nonetheless real. Yet we habitually associate reality with the "near," with whatever is in front of us at the given moment. The "far" is the sunset we can never capture.

Yet Prince Jali believes that "one day he would be vigorous enough . . . to capture the promise of the horizon." Myers himself was a late Romantic and lost faith in this belief; in 1944 he committed suicide, convinced that between Hitler and Stalin, western civilization was at its end. The Romantics tended to agree with Myers, yet Wilson knew that Prince Jali was right, and that vigor or vitality was the answer. Maslow had convinced him that peak experiences are a product of a positive, forward-looking attitude, and the peak experience, like Faculty X, is precisely a moment when the near and the far come together. Now, as the revelations about the right brain began to inform his thinking, it was clear that it is the part of the mind responsible for this union. And again, it is important to remember that Maslow's students started having more peak experiences simply by thinking about past ones. They seemed to "fix" them by reflecting on them. It is, as Wilson writes, as if we possess a "mirror" inside us, "which has the power to turn 'things that happen' into experience," as if thought itself "has a power for which it has never been given credit."[23] If reflection could make a housewife aware of her happiness as she hurriedly got her family their breakfast—could, that is, trigger a peak experience—then it should be able to bring the far much closer to the near.

What prevents us from bringing the near and the far together is the robot. It doggedly keeps its attention on the near. More often than not I may listen to

Schubert or read Shaw and I don't feel as Wilson or his friend at the BBC did. I may enjoy them, but the experience isn't transformative, or I may find them boring and look for some other distraction. I remain trapped in my left-brain consciousness and the sunset remains at the horizon. How can I induce the right brain, the stranger next door, to perform his act of bringing the near and the far together?

Wilson begins to answer this question by looking at how our two brains interact already. We seem to have, as he calls them, an "intuitive me" and a "critical me."[24] When the two work together we can have a union approaching genius, but when they are in opposition disaster is not far. We can see this happen when we are self-conscious. When we become too aware of what we are doing and too anxious to do it well—as happens if someone looks over our shoulder—we interfere with the normal communication between our two selves and, as it were, cut off our supply line. The critical me becomes too prominent and scares away the intuitive me, who provides the power. (The left brain is pushy and forward looking, Wilson tells us, while the right is shy and easily discouraged.) I freeze up and make even more frantic but counterproductive efforts. If this continues for too long, I may end up like Frankl's bank clerk, unable to write, or even like Wilson, panicking before the television cameras.

And yet the opposite is also true. Wilson points out that the process of writing is basically a dialogue between the two me's. One has intuitions that the other has to articulate. In the beginning, communication between the two is very bad. When Wilson first began writing, he invariably crushed his intuitions flat, killing whatever he was trying to say. But with time he improved. The left brain became better at turning the intuitions of the right into words, and the right brain would get excited at this and send up more intuitions, which the left would capture perfectly, until the two "were co-operating like two tennis players."[25] Creative dialogues like this between our two minds suggested to Wilson that we are rather like split-brain patients ourselves. He remarks that Mozart often spoke of tunes just coming into his head. Where did they come from? Mozart didn't know, but we do: the right brain. If a creative genius like Mozart was not aware of his other self, we are surely less aware of it than he was. As Wilson says, Julian Jaynes was wrong: we are bicameral, not our ancient ancestors.

A similar communication takes place in moments of deep relaxation. When the tensions and anxieties of the left brain are released through poetry or music, our inner world seems to expand, and our center of gravity shifts from left to right. We then seem to blend with our other half, and become something like a full moon, whereas, as Wilson says, most of the time, trapped in left-brain consciousness, we are only at best a quarter of our true self. Very anxious and tense people are even less than this, with hysterical patients little more than the thinnest sliver. (We can think of cases of multiple personality as the moon being sliced into separate sections.) The left brain deals with the external world. It looks outside. The right is turned inward and is concerned with our inner states. The more we are stuck dealing with things, the less access we have to our other half. But we do not have to be suffering from hysteria to lose contact with our other self. As Wilson says, we are all to some extent hysterical patients because we all accept the false idea of our self that comes from being stuck in our left brain most of the time. As William James says in his important essay "The Energies of Men," "the human individual thus lives far within his limits . . . his life is contracted like the field of vision of an hysteric subject."[26] We live, James says, subject to "an inveterate habit—the habit of inferiority to our full self," an idea that James shared with Maslow and, as Wilson makes clear in his book *The War Against Sleep* (1980), with Gurdjieff too.

Wilson discovered more about the relation between the two brains through a curious book, *The Law of Psychic Phenomena*, that was published in 1893 and became something of a best seller. Its author was an American newspaper editor in his late fifties named Thomas Jay Hudson, who had become fascinated with hypnotism. Hudson seems to have anticipated some of split-brain theory. He argues that human beings appear to have two minds. One is the "objective mind," which deals with the external world and the knowledge of the senses. This is who we mean when we say "I"; it is our left brain. The other Hudson calls the "subjective mind." Its business is intuition, man's inner world; this is our right brain. The subjective mind, he argues, possesses remarkable powers. Hudson saw that while in a trance—which, in essence, is when the objective mind, or left brain, is put to sleep—a subject could speak in foreign languages he had never learned, but had somehow absorbed unconsciously in childhood, and was now "playing back" like a recording. The subjective mind had an eidetic imagination; hypnotized subjects were able to conjure images with a 3-D reality, as if they were actual concrete objects before them, as the Serbian scientist Nikola Tesla was known to do.[27] One man placed in a trance was able to hold a conversation with the philosopher Socrates; asked to repeat what Socrates said, he delivered a remarkable lecture in dialectics.

The subjective mind was the source of the ability of "lightning calculators" to answer difficult mathematical equations instantaneously or even to tell whether a twelve-digit number was prime or not. As there is no method of discovering a prime aside from laboriously dividing other numbers into it, the calculators were somehow *seeing* the answer directly, just as Robert Graves's schoolmate Smilley and Graves himself had. The subjective mind, Hudson argued, is also clairvoyant; it "sees without the use of natural organs of vision . . . and can be made to leave the body." It can also "read the content of sealed envelopes and closed books" and, as Wilson recounted in the experiences of John Cowper Powys, Goethe, Strindberg, and Yeats in *The Occult*, it can project thoughts and the "actual physical presence" of the subject to "distant places."[28] Hudson also came to believe that the subjective mind can heal and that it can do this at a distance. He himself recounts curing a distant relative of arthritis in this way.

Wilson was amazed at reports of how hypnotists were able to have their subjects do incredible things, such as lie with their head on one chair and their feet on another and remain as stiff as a plank when someone sat on them, or pick up live coals and not be burned. In one case, reported to Wilson by an American doctor named Howard Miller, a dentist hypnotized a patient before extracting her tooth. He told her that when he did she would not bleed and she didn't. This seems unbelievable. But unless we accept that the doctor who gave Wilson this account was lying, or that Wilson was naïve, as some fellow para- psychologists have suggested, then we must at least consider the possibility that it is true. Like Hudson, Miller tried his hand at healing, and as Wilson reports, he had considerable success.[29]

If a patient can do these remarkable things while under hypnosis—while, that is, his objective mind is asleep and his subjective mind is being guided by the hypnotist—why can't he do it when wide awake? The answer, Wilson saw, lay in the relationship between the two minds. The subjective mind is incredibly powerful, as Freud said the unconscious is. But, as Wilson came to see, it *takes its directions* from the objective mind. This is where Freud was wrong. We are not, as he believed, slaves to our unconscious. An elephant takes its directions from the boy riding it, although the elephant is much more powerful than the boy. The captain of a ship is not its slave, although the ship itself dwarfs him. For Wilson, we are the boy riding the elephant, and the captain running his ship. Or at least we should be.

Why doesn't our subjective mind do these remarkable things when *we* tell it to? Because it doesn't believe us; it doesn't think we are serious enough. It knows we are weak, purposeless, and vacillating. But when our objective mind is put to sleep, as in hypnosis, it is replaced by the stern commands of the hyp- notist. Because he is a much more authoritative character than our usual vacil- lating selves, it listens to him and responds accordingly.

The subjective mind will respond to the objective mind, if it thinks the re- quest is serious enough. The relation between the two, Wilson says, is rather like that between the old comedy team of Laurel and Hardy. Stan is the right brain (or subjective mind) and Ollie is the left (or objective mind). As Wilson points out, Stan takes his cues from Ollie. But Stan has a sometimes trouble- some habit: he invariably *overreacts*. Wilson spelled out this arrangement in a pamphlet, "The Laurel & Hardy Theory of Consciousness." As Wilson says, Ollie, the conscious mind, is basically the boss, with Stan looking to him for clues as to how he should react. If Ollie is cheerful, Stan becomes ecstatic. But if Ollie is unhappy, Stan goes into the deepest despair. "So," Wilson writes, "if we wake up on a rainy Monday morning, and think gloomily, 'How am I going to get through this boring day?', Stan, our unconscious mind, starts to feel depressed." Because of this he retreats and minimizes the energy he sends up. We—Ollie—then feel even more depressed and because we do, accept that it is "one of those days," and expect the worst. As a result, Stan retreats even more and gives us even less energy, which in turn confirms our suspicions. The result is that unless something breaks this vicious circle, we have a thoroughly horrible day, and feel strangely justified, or at least accept that such things "happen." (And the reader can see that this vicious circle is identical to the one that begins when Samuel Beckett says that life is meaningless, then feels bored and that there is nothing worth doing, and because of this confirms his perception of meaninglessness, which increases his boredom and apathy. . . .)

But what about when the opposite happens, as on a vacation, or on Christmas morning? We *expect* things to go well and so we face the day with pleasant anticipation. Stan gets the message and sends up energy. We respond to this with even more excitement and, as in the case of writing, we develop positive feedback, an excellent volley between the two sides of our brain. Wilson remarks that this "feedback mechanism" seems better able to account for neurosis than Freud's sexual theories, with the implication that the "power of positive thinking" may be something more than a myth. As mentioned earlier, our own *thoughts* have a power we normally overlook. "Normal Vincent Peale"—author of *The Power of Positive Thinking*—"may not have been a great intellect," Wilson writes, "but he understood something about the human mind that Freud managed to overlook."[30]

Wilson saw that we misunderstand the relationship between our conscious mind and the unconscious, our left brain and our right. It is true that the right brain is incredibly powerful. Along with the evidence that it may be responsible for paranormal phenomena, it is clear that the right brain enables our poetic, aesthetic, mystical, and spiritual experiences. "The real business of the right," Wilson says, is "to add a dimension of *meaning* to our lives."[31] This is why the left brain/objective mind has been seen as a villain. It can act as a "nagging housewife," interrupting our moments of serenity with its insistence that we get on with things. It questions our intuitions, fills us with doubt, reduces everything to logic and reason, and rejects all mystical feeling as nonsense. It is always in a hurry and doesn't let the right brain idle along as it would like. As Wilson says, it seems as if we had D. H. Lawrence, an enemy of "head consciousness" and proponent of instinct and intuition, on one side of our brain and Bertrand Russell, a notoriously skeptical and logical philosopher, on the other. The result is a constant argument.

It's no surprise that poets and mystics have argued in favor of getting rid of our interfering ego and embracing the richer consciousness of the right brain. But there is a problem. As we've seen, while meaning is absolutely essential, *too much* meaning is counterproductive, something Wilson discovered during his mescaline experience and which Aldous Huxley and William James also came to see through their own drug experiences. Being "at one" with things is an undoubted good, but if we are at one for too long, we lose all incentive. As paradoxical as it sounds, an overflow of meaning soon becomes boring. As more than one neuroscientist has observed, the right brain has a tendency to get bored and is generally more depressed than the left. Ecstasy can last only so long. As Wilson says, right brain consciousness is as pleasant and relaxing as a hot bath, but we wouldn't want to stay in the bath all day.

The right brain also seems to lack a sense of discrimination. Wilson points to an important collection of essays by Hermann Hesse, *Glimpse into Chaos* (1919). In a discussion about Dostoyevsky's *The Brothers Karamazov*, Hesse describes a character he calls "Russian Man," a kind of antiauthoritarian figure. Russian Man has abandoned all restrictions and constraints; well before the hippies he was advocating the need to "let it all hang out," to give way to all impulses. Such abandon can be liberating, but in the long run it leads to apathy and discouragement.[32] More than this, it can lead to criminality, to being "beyond good and evil." Wilson argues that much of the "liberating" radical political philosophy of the past two centuries has advocated a rejection of discipline and an embrace of impulse that is a close cousin to the "magical thinking" of many of the criminals he investigates.[33]

True freedom does not come by throwing aside all restraint, all authority and discipline, as well-meaning Romantics from Rousseau on have suggested. It is a product of purpose and the *control* we develop in pursuing it. Meaning, Wilson says, is like food. It is not an end in itself. We convert food into energy and we convert meaning into purpose. This, Wilson argues, is the nature of the evolutionary appetite. Meaning alone is not enough. In *The Philosopher's Stone* the two scientists experiment on a workman who has had a serious head injury. They are able to induce "value experiences" in him—their term for Maslow's peak experiences—states of mystical joy and beauty. But all he can say about them is that they feel nice and make things look pretty. His mind lacks the *knowledge* to make good use of his experiences. Thomas De Quincey, the English opium eater, said the same about the ability of drugs to enhance our "poetic faculty." Opium, De Quincey said, was not enough, for "a man whose talk is of oxen . . . will dream about oxen." Meaning, if there is nothing in your head for the drug to release, there will be little poetry. This knowledge is the left brain's business: it provides the disparate *facts* that in moments of Faculty X suddenly come together. (We remember James's "increasing ranges of distant fact.") Without them, a moment of Faculty X can be nothing more than a sudden feeling of "goodness." This is why Wilson says that peak experiences or moments of right-brain consciousness are not important in themselves. What is important is that they are a sudden flash of brilliance illuminating a landscape which it is our business to *map*.

Our job, Wilson says, is to *pin down* the meanings we see in these moments, to capture them in language, in order to provide a map of the evolutionary terrain we are entering. It is not enough to say, "Oh wow!" about some mystical insight, or that "all is one." What is needed is to capture the insight in words so it can be communicated to others and help make our maps of reality more accurate. And for this we need both brains: one supplying the insight, the other turning it into words. This, again, is a kind of duo-consciousness. When insight and logic work together we have a sudden moment of reality, the kind of reality that Arnold Toynbee glimpsed at the ruins of Mistra, when what you know to be real is suddenly "really real." Wilson quotes G. K. Chesterton: "You say thank you when someone passes the salt, but you don't mean it; you say the earth is round but you don't mean it." When our two brains work together, we can say something and mean it, because we see that it *really is* true.

When we speak with only one brain, we may give cognitive assent, but we don't *feel* the reality of what we are saying, we see it only in 2-D, as it were. Both brains gives us a 3-D truth. Someone else with Toynbee would have seen only ruins at Mistra. Because he brought both his knowledge and his imagination together, Toynbee was taken up above the limits of the present. For a moment he stepped out of time and was privy to a reality much greater than what we usually perceive.

If getting rid of our troublesome pushy ego is not the answer to achieving some more vivid, vital experience, what then? Wilson suggests that the answer lies not in the fact that the left brain ego is too "bossy," but that he is not bossy enough.

We have seen what marvels the right brain can accomplish when directed by a hypnotist. We have also seen that crisis can shake us awake, overthrow our indifference threshold, and give us a sense of "life more abundant." Why can a hypnotist and crisis do what we cannot? The answer is that in both cases our right brain, unconscious mind, or whatever it is that controls our power supply recognizes that the situation is serious enough to warrant more energy, more life, more consciousness.

Our problem is that we have allowed the robot to take over practically all of our life. When the hypnotists put the objective mind/left brain to sleep, the robot and the right brain respond to his commands admirably. When a crisis arises we see that *we* and not the robot must deal with it. But as we've seen, as soon as the crisis abates, we relax and allow the robot to come back on duty. And over time, even crisis can lose its effect. Graham Greene discovered this when he found that playing Russian roulette no longer galvanized him. Even the planarian worm became so bored with crisis that it preferred dying to making the effort to save itself.

What saved the second batch of planaria? They *put more effort* into solving their crisis. This got them past an inner hurdle so that they never fell below that level of energy again. The double effort got the message across to the robot. The robot is a labor-saving device. Its job is to economize on our energy, to be, as we like to say today, "cost efficient." It decides how important a situation or task is and it passes on its assessment to the right brain, which, as we've seen, holds the purse strings on our power supply. Most of the time we need the minimum to get by and our robot knows this; as a result, the right brain loses interest and goes to sleep. Hence the triviality of everydayness, the lack of meaning, the sameness that colors life. What we need to do, Wilson tells us, is in effect become our own hypnotist. We must bypass the robot and give the right brain a command it will respect. Yet because we are so vacillating and purposeless this rarely, if ever, happens. We all make resolutions we never keep, decisions we reverse, good intentions we do not fulfill. We are accustomed to letting the robot decide. What we need to do is to override its assessment and convince the right brain that it needs to send up more energy, *when we want it to*. And this is the job of the left brain, the annoying, nagging, but absolutely indispensable ego.

The ego needs to assume its position as captain of the ship. It is, as Wilson argues, the *controller* of consciousness, and not, as we have mistakenly believed ever since Freud, a mere puppet of the dark forces within us. As it is now, when we want a change in consciousness we look for some stimulus to trigger it. This is exactly the same problem that confronts the person in the black room. Without external stimulus we go limp. When the ego is doing its job properly, when it is not vacillating and fluctuating—moving from "I" to "I," as Gurdjieff has it—it achieves a sense of control, of mastery that is its proper state. This does not mean simply pushing ourselves harder—although Wilson was prone to that—but recognizing the "intentional" character of consciousness. *We* control our moods. We decide whether to give way to them or not. If I am feeling uninspired and the thought of sitting at my computer to write this chapter fills me with dread, I can decide to take a day off or I can call my bluff and make myself do it. But I can even go further and evoke a sense of optimism and expectancy, telling myself I will do a good day's work. When this happens—and it is not unusual—the result is that after a few minutes of confronting a blank screen, I actually do start working and the day does go well.

I am the controller of consciousness. The problem is that I don't know that I am. Howard Miller, who told Wilson about the dentist who hypnotized his patient so she wouldn't bleed, called this controller the "Unit of Pure Thought." Wilson believed that Miller had discovered Husserl's transcendental ego. But with this difference: this Unit of Pure Thought is confused about its responsibilities and has adopted a stance of being a mere *observer* of what takes place in consciousness. It watches the thoughts, feelings, impressions, sensations, and memories that run haphazardly, like an engine idling. This observer believes he is only a passive witness to all this and that, as Freud believed, the mind it is observing is much bigger and more powerful than it. It is as if it is in a cinema watching random images on the screen.

Miller argued that this is a false scenario, because the observer is actually *also the projectionist* and can decide what it wants to look at. Consider what happens when we *decide* to think about something, or to conjure an image of, say, where we went on our last vacation. A second before the image appears *we* have given the command that makes it happen. But we fail to grasp what this means. As Wilson writes, our observer "sits on a chair in the corner of the room, watching the confused movie on the screen and wondering why it is so nonsensical, totally failing to recognize that *he* ought to be 'in charge.'"[34] This is like someone standing in front of an orchestra wondering why they are playing so badly when the reason they are is because he has *forgotten that he is the conductor.*

We touched on the projectionist metaphor earlier, when talking about Husserl's philosophy. The difference here is that the ego in question isn't transcendental. It is our everyday ego. *It* is the absentminded conductor shaking his head and wondering why the musicians are playing out of tune. They are because he isn't doing his job of keeping them in proper order. Once he recognizes his mistake, he taps his baton and the symphony begins.

Wilson saw that this was the way forward. What had happened on that train to London when he passed Teignmouth and *forced* himself to see the beauty that he knew was there? He had taken the role of conductor—or hypnotist—and told his right brain to ignore the robot and listen to *him.* He had made *voluntarily* the kind of mental contraction that Graham Greene had induced by putting a pistol to his head. He showed his right brain or other self that he meant business, and it complied. The process seemed to be like tightening his fist and then letting go: contraction and expansion. He had induced a crisis and then felt the enormous relief when it passed. Thomas De Quincey once asked his friend William Wordsworth how he came to write poetry. Wordsworth couldn't tell him at first, but later he saw the answer. He was waiting for the mail cart from Keswick and put his ear to the ground to hear its rumble. As he got up he caught a glance of the evening star, which at that moment appeared beautiful. He knew then how he wrote poetry. He told De Quincey, "Whenever I am concentrating on something that has nothing to do with poetry, and then I suddenly relax my attention, whatever I see when I relax appears to me to be beautiful."[35]

Here was the basic mechanism: concentration, then release.[36] It was, Wilson saw, the same principle that got one over the indifference threshold, or that had Maslow's students thinking themselves into peaks, or that enabled his inner schoolmistress to bring his unruly mental classroom to order. It wasn't a question of huffing and puffing or, as he pointed out in *The War Against Sleep*, his book about Gurdjieff that followed *Frankenstein's Castle*, of more and more "super-efforts," which can easily turn counterproductive.[37] What is needed is to "summon that state of optimism, of inner purpose, that makes the super-effort easy." This is the difference between forcing yourself to do something and doing it with a sense of purpose.

This is an important point. One of our biggest hurdles, Wilson saw, is our general feeling of reluctance, our miserly thrift with our energy, our tendency to, as William James says, give in to "degrees of fatigue which we have come only from habit to obey," and which we maintain by constantly capitulating to them.[38] James knew that if we call our fatigue's bluff and push ourselves further, we suddenly discover we have much more energy than we thought. This is the essence of the "bullying treatment" that he, Jung, and Gurdjieff employed. As James writes, "First comes the very extremity of distress, then follows unexpected relief."

This, Wilson argues, is the essence of Gurdjieff's teaching. It was the point of his complicated movements, the difficult "sacred dances" that he said he learned from the mysterious Sarmoung Brotherhood but which may just as well have come from his unquestionably fertile mind.[39] Wilson speaks of Gurdjieff's ability to draw on his "vital reserves" and tells the story of how the writer Fritz Peters, wrecked by the horrors of World War II, visited Gurdjieff in Paris and how Gurdjieff was able to "recharge" him with his own vitality. Gurdjieff knew how to overcome his own reluctance and his system was aimed at teaching his students how to overcome theirs.

As mentioned, Wilson admired Gurdjieff immensely. He was "quite obviously one of the greatest minds" he had ever encountered, and in conversation with me once he mentioned that of all the people he wrote about, the only one he regretted not meeting was Gurdjieff—although one suspects he would also have enjoyed a tête-à-tête with Shaw.[40] But he did have some reservations about his teaching, or at least thought that "there were a number of small but important points" which he believed that "master of self-observation failed to take into account."[41] One was that Gurdjieff, he felt, had exaggerated the difficulties of waking up; this was why he felt that the emphasis on super-efforts could be counterproductive. Wilson felt that nonmechanical (or non-robotic; they mean the same) consciousness is not as distant from us as Gurdjieff believed. Gurdjieff's insistence that man is so completely mechanical that he cannot "do" was understandable but not as accurate as he thought. Wilson also felt it gave his ideas, like Heidegger's, a pessimistic tone.

Wilson saw that we are always having brief flashes of non-robotic consciousness. He often quotes T. E. Lawrence on this account. In *The Seven Pillars of Wisdom* Lawrence writes of starting out "On one of those clear dawns that wake up the senses with the sun, while the intellect, tired after the thinking of the night, was yet abed. For an hour or two, on such a morning, the sounds, scents and colors of the world struck man individually and directly, not filtered through or made typical by thought."[42]

This is "primal perception." Most of us have moments of it more often than we think. Peak experiences are also moments of wakefulness, just as those complimentary tastes of Faculty X are, whenever we stumble upon a madeleine. As Wilson says, what is important about these glimpses is not how pleasant they are but the *meaning* they reveal. They tell us the absurd good news that reality is not drab and dreary but infinitely interesting, and *this* is the surest way to wake us up. We all have had the experience of being tired and suddenly becoming interested in something and feeling wide awake. Think of Dr. Watson, Wilson says, feeling rather bored at Baker Street. Sherlock Holmes asks, "Did I ever tell you about the strange case of . . ." whatever it might be. Immediately Watson is riveted. We are "asleep," as Gurdjieff says, because we believe that reality is boring, and so we tell our right brain that it might as well take a nap. Wilson believed that Gurdjieff's distinction between essence and personality is more or less the same as between the right and left brain. He remarks that when asked what being conscious in essence would be like, Gurdjieff replied, "Everything more vivid," which seems to confirm this.

Gurdjieff speaks of an organ, the *kundabuffer*, implanted in man so that he perceives only a distorted picture of reality, his version of original sin. Gurdjieff called human beings "broken machines," and he did his best to fix them. Yet Wilson suggests that we may not be broken so much as not know how our machines work. There is, he says, nothing *fundamentally* wrong with us; our flashes of non-robotic consciousness tell us this. We *are* able to experience "real consciousness," and we do so more often than we think. The problem is that we experience it only haphazardly, or by using dubious methods such as drugs, revolvers, and other stimuli, and assume it is some special treat, when our everyday consciousness is really the anomaly. Yet it can be done; it is less a case of original sin, Wilson says, than "original stupidity," a stupidity we can rectify through knowledge. If we can convince ourselves that the vision of meaninglessness, of "nothing to be done," is an utter mistake, the *intellectual conviction* that the way the world appears in our moments of Faculty X is true will work as a constant alarm clock, reminding us that reality is always more than what is before our eyes. This will, Wilson says, "awaken us far more effectively than any amount of violent and exhausting effort. . . . Meaning instantly creates energy."[43] And as William Blake knew, "Energy is eternal delight."[44]

CHAPTER TEN

INNER WORLDS AND CRIMINAL HISTORIES

The relationship between our two brains seemed to offer Wilson a clue to many mysteries. He began to think of his right brain as an ally, a hidden friend who, when needed, could come to his aid. He thought of experiences in the past when, with hindsight, this seemed to be the case. Once, in the early 1960s, returning from a visit to Leicester—where he had picked up a bad case of "people poisoning"—Wilson stopped in Cheltenham, where he knew there was a good secondhand bookshop. Joy and Sally were with him and as Joy made room in the car for more books, Wilson took Sally, who was three years old, into the shop. After a few minutes Sally grew bored and asked for Joy. Wilson walked her to the entrance and pointed to Joy, who was at the car, only a few yards away. Sally headed off and Wilson went back into the shop.

Five minutes later Joy appeared and Wilson asked where Sally was. Joy said she thought she was with him. They both panicked and ran out into the street. It was rush hour and the road was full of traffic. They could see no sign of Sally. Joy went one way and Wilson went the other. They were both desperate—Sally had never been out of their sight since she was born and now she had disappeared. Wilson "had to master a rising sense of misery and disaster."[1] Giving way to fear would do no good. He simply had to muster the determination to find his daughter.

He did. When he returned to the shop again after another search, he saw that Joy had found her. Sally had wandered around the block and Joy had seen her. Wilson had "never experienced such relief." He also noticed something else: everything now seemed beautiful. Earlier he had been exhausted after spending too much time with people in Leicester and had regretted the beer he had drunk at lunch. The long drive to Cornwall was not appealing—the scenery seemed drab and boring. Now "a bus that held us up at a traffic light seemed a delightful object." Even exhaust smoke struck him as a "pleasant smell." But his relief, however great, was not the important point, he thought; what was important was the energy he had summoned to meet the crisis. He had refused to give way to despair and, seeing this, his right brain snapped to attention. Now, as he drove through traffic in a gray drizzle, he felt no impatience, as he had earlier; there was "only enormous gratitude that everything should be so *interesting.*"[2]

There were other occasions too, when his right brain came to his rescue. Once in Los Angeles, Wilson had agreed to meet Joy, Sally, and Damon at Disneyland, where they had gone while he had given a lecture. But he hadn't decided on exactly where to meet them and when he arrived at the gates he realized he had forgotten how big Disneyland was. He looked at the crowds and thought that he would never find them. But then some instinct told him not to give way to anxiety but to stay calm and to follow his intuition. He walked and let an "inner guide" steer him through the lines at food stalls and rides. The result was that after only a short while he saw them. His hidden ally had once again responded to a serious request.

The trick seemed to be to summon the kind of control and calm discipline that later helped him overcome his panic attacks. There was nothing mystical about this. It was simply a kind of maturity, a refusal to panic, a decision to remain rational and logical and optimistic and not get overwhelmed with emotion. As he came to see, such states seemed to trigger helpful synchronicities, or at least they created the mental condition these meaningful coincidences favored. The opposite states, when our emotions take control, he came to see were less conducive to them and were more prone to lead to despair and pessimism or, in some instances, criminality.

Wilson tells an amusing story of how his right brain came to his rescue when he was asked by the Italian film producer Dino De Laurentiis to help with the script of his 1980 remake of *Flash Gordon.*[3] Wilson—who asked for his name to be withheld from the credits—was given the script, which he described as a mess, "one of the most muddled pieces of rubbish I ever read."[4] De Laurentiis had him booked at the Dorchester hotel, in London—one of the city's most expensive—and paid him several thousand dollars to rewrite this "depressing nonsense." Wilson could order whatever he wanted—usually lobster and champagne—but he had to finish the script in ten days. On the evening of the penultimate day, he still had a third of the script to go, but the material was so bad that he found himself a blank. He was completely out of ideas and was feeling on the verge of a breakdown. Then he remembered what he had been writing about recently: that the right brain will never let you down. So he lay on the bed and as he fell asleep he said to himself—or his "other self," to be precise—"Come on, old right brain—for God's sake do your stuff."

As soon as he said this, Wilson writes, he "felt an odd sense of relief and fell into a peaceful sleep." He woke early the next morning and started work. An idea came to him and he developed it. Then another came and another. The inspiration continued and he began to see his way out of the mess. He made a determined effort and at five o'clock, when De Laurentiis's secretary arrived to collect his pages—to be translated and shown to De Laurentiis—he typed out his last sentence. He then called De Laurentiis and asked to be taken to Paddington Station, to catch the train back to Cornwall. As the taxi took him up Park Lane, Wilson closed his eyes and said, "Thank you, old right brain."[5] Strangely, part of his script involved Professor Zarkov, Flash Gordon's comrade, resisting being brainwashed by Ming the Merciless's secret police. Zarkov escapes being turned into a zombie because the hypnotizing machine was used on only one of his brains. The other was untouched and left Zarkov free.[6] So it seems that our other brain can come to the aid of all of us, even comic book heroes.

Around the same time Wilson had another important experience. On New Year's Day 1979, he found himself snowed in at a remote farmhouse near the Devon village of Sheepwash. He had given a lecture to extramural students the night before and now found that he could not leave. He and the others stranded with him waited a day and then decided they had to make an attempt to get out. The snow made it nearly impossible for their tires to get a grip, but Wilson succeeded and with half a dozen people pushing his car, he managed to get up to the level road. It took an hour to clear a way through to the entrance to the farm and the main road. But then the real test began. The narrow country lane was bordered by ditches; some traffic had passed, but the snow was still deep and in many places untouched. It wasn't easy to tell where the lane ended and a ditch began, and to avoid getting stuck, Wilson had to drive slowly, "with total, obsessive attention."

After twenty minutes of this Wilson noticed a peculiar feeling. It was as if his skull was getting warm. This, he believed, was the effect of his concentration. He found that he could heighten or lower the feeling through a focus of attention. When he finally reached the main road to Exeter, about two hours later, he relaxed. When he did it was exactly the same as when he had felt the sense of relief after finding Sally, or when Wordsworth looked up at his star. Everything looked "curiously real and interesting." The hours of concentration, he thought, had somehow fixed his consciousness in a heightened state—rather as the second batch of planaria had fixed a higher level of response by making twice as much effort. He felt an enormous optimism, the sense that all problems could be solved through determined effort, and this feeling of confidence lasted the rest of the drive to Cornwall. Recounting this experience, Wilson says that thinking about it renewed the sense of certainty, rather as Maslow's students were able to trigger peak experiences by remembering earlier ones.[7]

What had happened, Wilson thought, was that the need to maintain his attention, his focus, had caused him to build up his inner pressure beyond its usual level. He compared our usual consciousness to a hose that isn't fitted tightly to the water pipe. Most of our energy leaks out and our stream of attention is weak. By forcing himself to focus his concentration for an extended time, he had tightened the hose, and now his attention was like a powerful jet. The principle was the same as when he first hit upon the indifference threshold on that journey to visit Joy's parents more than twenty years earlier, or as Hermann Hesse pointed out in *The Journey to the East*, "a long time devoted to small details exalts us and increases our strength," something Wilson knew from his experience putting his record collection into plastic sleeves.[8] By maintaining focus and not giving way to the robot, we convince the right brain that we are in earnest—Shaw even said that "the brain will not fail if the will is in earnest" (*Man and Superman*). It is simply a matter of convincing it that we are.

The relationship between our two brains offered Wilson an answer to some curious material he had encountered researching an illustrated history of astronomy Hodder & Stoughton had commissioned him to write. The coffee-table-book appearance of *Starseekers* (1980) should not put a reader off. It is a serious and very readable history, and the many illustrations help the narrative along. Wilson begins his account of man's study of the stars with a story about Edgar Allan Poe. In 1848 Poe published a book that he believed would establish him as one of the greatest thinkers of all time. Its title said it all: *Eureka*—"I've found it"—the saying attributed to the ancient Greek mathematician Archimedes, who is said to have shouted this as he ran naked through the streets of Syracuse, having discovered the law of floating bodies while taking his bath. But Poe was not satisfied with discovering a single law. His *Eureka* would solve the mystery of all space and time. Its message came to Poe in a revelation and he wrote the book in a fit of inspiration. He was so confident of his genius and the book's success that he urged his publisher to print a first run of fifty thousand copies. "I have solved the secret of the universe," he told George Putnam. Poe had sold copies—his poem "The Raven" had been a success—but Putnam was less sanguine and settled for a first edition of five hundred. Even this was overly optimistic. *Eureka* was a flop and didn't even earn the fourteen dollars Poe had received as an advance. It was one of Poe's last works and its failure crushed him. He died a disappointed man the year after its publication, following a drinking binge.

Yet within Poe's at times gripping, at times exasperating account of the birth and structure of the cosmos—full of what he called "unparticled omnipresent divine substance" and echoing some of what he had written in his story "Mesmeric Revelation"—one can find some remarkable intuitions. The book contains several cosmological insights much ahead of their time. Within *Eureka's* turgid pages Poe predicts black holes, the expanding universe, curved space, galactic clusters, the discovery of a new asteroid orbiting between Mars and Jupiter, as well as many other cosmological notions, such as the anthropic principle, not thought of at the time of his writing. Wilson was not the only one to notice this. In his foreword to a recent edition of *Eureka* the English astronomer Sir Patrick Moore writes that concerning cosmology Poe "introduces concepts which are well ahead of their time." These include anticipating Einstein, the big bang, the shape of galaxies, and, as mentioned, black holes. Poe's hunches, Moore writes, were not confirmed until Edwin Hubble began his work at the Mount Wilson Observatory in 1923.[9]

Poe was not the only writer to anticipate later astronomical fact. Wilson points out that In *Gulliver's Travels*, published in 1726, Jonathan Swift tells us that the scientists of the flying island Laputa have discovered that Mars has two satellites. The distance of the innermost satellite from the center of Mars is three of its diameters; the second, outermost satellite is five of its diameters distant, an estimate fairly close to actual fact. But, as Wilson points out, Deimos and Phobos were not discovered until 1877, by the American astronomer Asaph Hall, a century and a half later. Swift's savants say that the inner satellite has a revolution of ten hours, the outer of twenty-one and a half hours. This is a remarkable guess—if it is a guess. Phobos, Mars's inner moon, does revolve in approximately ten hours; Deimos, the outer moon, in about thirty.

How could Poe and Swift have come by this knowledge? If we are not to accept that these are just coincidences then we need to explain how people who should not know of these things obviously did.[10] An even more mysterious story that Wilson recounts had occurred in very recent times. In *The Sirius Mystery* (1976), Robert Temple told the remarkable story of the Dogon, a modern African tribe in Mali, who, like Poe and Swift, seem to have obtained specific astronomical knowledge that they shouldn't possess. The Dogon seem to know that Sirius, the dog star, the brightest star in the heavens, is actually a double star. Circling Sirius A is Sirius B, an invisible white dwarf, a very small star of immense weight (a dwarf is a star that has collapsed on itself). That Sirius is a double star was discovered in 1844 by the German astronomer Friedrich Wilhelm Bessel. The Dogon seem to have had access to Bessel's notes—or at least to an account of them. They somehow know that Sirius B—which they call Digitaria—is very small and heavy, that it rotates on its axis, that its orbit is elliptical, and that it circles Sirius A every fifty years.

How a remote tribe came to have exact astronomical information about a star that cannot be seen is not easy to explain. Temple believed that the Dogon's tradition originated in ancient Egypt and that it may have been passed on to Egyptian priests by extraterrestrials sometime in the dim past. Wilson is not happy with that idea and in general he has little patience with the Erich von Däniken "ancient astronaut" school of thought—although Temple's work is of a higher caliber than that. If ancient astronauts supplied our ancestors with precise astronomical information, Wilson asks, why didn't they also tell them that the earth is round, which would have been the most obvious thing to pass on? Unless we want to accept that at some point after Bessel's discovery, an explorer interested in astronomy encountered the Dogon and told them about it, and that they then made this a part of their mythology, we need to find some way to accommodate their uncanny accuracy, as well as Poe's and Swift's.

Wilson suggests that the answer lies in the right brain, in the kind of intuitive knowledge that Robert Graves's schoolmate Smilley exhibited, the lunar knowledge coming from what Wilson calls the "dark side of the mind." It was this kind of knowledge, Wilson argues, that guided the prehistoric people who built stone circles like Stonehenge and other megalithic sites. As early as 1906 the British astronomer Sir Joseph Norman Lockyer—founder of the prestigious scientific journal *Nature*—had argued that Stonehenge and other ancient megalithic sites should be understood as astronomical calendars. This belief was given much support and wide popularity when Gerald Hawkins, a professor of astronomy at Boston University, elaborated on it in the best-selling controversial book *Stonehenge Decoded* (1965). Hawkins used computer analysis to show that Stonehenge was a remarkably precise solar *and* lunar calendar. Both Lockyer and Hawkins received much criticism from skeptical archaeologists and astronomers, but their ideas were confirmed in 1966 when the respected astronomer Fred Hoyle published a paper in *Nature* corroborating their research. Hoyle was very important support and, with his imprimatur, the idea of the Stone Age astronomical calendar gained some grudging acceptance.

What made many conservative astronomers and archaeologists doubtful of Hawkins's thesis is that they could not believe that the people who were thought to have built Stonehenge and other megalithic structures had the knowledge needed to make a calendar of any kind, let alone one of huge stone slabs. The earliest dating for the time when Stonehenge is thought to have been erected is around 3000 BC. The accepted view of the people then was that they were at best "primitive tinkers and gypsies" from whom, as Wilson writes, one would not expect much "sophistication or culture." Yet both the astronomical and engineering knowledge embodied in Stonehenge would have required a great deal of sophistication. In 1934 Alexander Thom, a Scottish engineer, studied the stone circle at Callanish in the Hebrides and realized that whoever had erected it was able to align the stones to true north, *without* the help of the pole star, which was in a different position in Neolithic times. This argued for a formidable engineering knowledge. Like Lockyer and Hawkins, Thom was convinced that such structures were fundamentally astronomical calculators. Some prehistorians, such as Alexander Marshack, pushed our ability and desire to chart the heavens back even further, to the Upper Paleolithic. In *The Roots of Civilization* (1972) Marshack argued that a thirty-five-thousand-year-old piece of bone displayed markings that charted the lunar cycle. But if the people at that time—Cro-Magnon man—were even less sophisticated then their Neolithic descendants, how could they have calculated anything?

The other troubling question is *why* Stonehenge and places like it were built. Why did Neolithic man need such a calendar? One suggestion is that a farming people would need to know of the approach of spring, in order to plant their crops. But wouldn't they be able to tell the change of season without getting massive stone obelisks weighing more than fifty tons to stand upright? Wilson suggests that whoever erected Stonehenge, "we are probably justified in assuming that their interest in the sun and the moon dated from a period before they learned about farming."[11]

Wilson believed that prehistoric man's interest in the sun and the moon had more to do with religion than farming. Primitive man *felt* the forces of the cosmos, just as a dowser feels the location of water underground. Wilson notes that Australian aborigines can detect underground water without the need of a forked twig or dowsing rod. They can simply feel its presence. We no longer can; in our complicated lives, such feelings would only confuse us, but as the evidence of dowsing suggests, some part of us—most likely our mute right brain—still responds to them. But our prehistoric ancestors could feel the forces coming from the heavens and from the earth itself. They worshipped the sun and the moon and the earth because these forces emanated from them and they affected our prehistoric ancestors and the world around them. (This was the thesis that John Michell developed about ley lines in *The View over Atlantis*.) The same principle informs astrology, although by the time astrology developed—around the second millennium BC—we no longer felt the cosmic forces so directly and began to theorize about them.

As we've seen, the German scientist and healer Franz Anton Mesmer believed that currents of vital energy surge through the universe, and that in ourselves these energies form a kind of "animal magnetism." We've also seen that Wilhelm Reich had a similar force in mind, what he called "orgone energy." Ancient China knew of a force called "chi." The ancient Hindus spoke of "prana." The Huna of Hawaii called it "mana." In 1935 two physicists, Harold Saxton Burr and F. S. C. Northrop, of Yale, published a paper, "The Electro-Dynamic Theory of Life," which argued that living creatures are held together by a kind of electromagnetic field—an idea that was later developed by the biologist Rupert Sheldrake in his theory of morphogenetic fields. This also seems to be related to the occult idea of an "etheric body," a kind of invisible energy field that gives life to the matter making up our physical body. Sensitives can see this as our aura. Saxton and Burr discovered that the "L-field" (life field) is affected by sunspots and by the lunar cycle. Wilson also points to the old wives' tale that certain people are affected strongly by the full moon—he even notes that his own family doctor confirmed this.

There is some *connection* between us and the cosmic forces around us; as I argue in *A Secret History of Consciousness*, we "participate" with the world around us much more than we realize. Primitive humans felt this connection, Wilson argues, because their consciousness was more attuned to their right brain, which, as in the case of dowsing, is able to "pick up" these vibrations. Fundamentally, structures like Stonehenge were markers, built to spot the precise location of heavenly bodies in order for Neolithic priests and priestesses to perform their worship. They may have been "sleepwalkers," as the title of Arthur Koestler's classic history of early astronomy has it, meaning that they were not aware of *how* they knew. But *that* they knew seems clear.

There is nothing contradictory, according to Wilson, in the kind of knowledge displayed in structures like Stonehenge, even though these were built long before the rise of science. The knowledge needed to erect these monuments came to our ancestors intuitively, in the same way that Graves's Smiley knew the answers to mathematical questions instantly, and idiot savants can reel off twelve-digit prime numbers at the drop of a hat, as Oliver Sacks recounts in *The Man Who Mistook His Wife for a Hat.* Much of this knowledge, Wilson suggests, is also encoded in the Great Pyramid of Giza, and he argues that there is very good reason to believe it was used as an observatory during its construction. But it is with the Egyptians, he points out, that we can detect a shift from the older, intuitive right-brain form of consciousness to something like our own more left-brain-oriented one.

We will have more to say about the pyramids and Sphinx in a later chapter, but the important point here is that astronomy proper begins as a science only after the change in consciousness that resulted in the development of the bicameral mind. Wilson in fact turns Julian Jaynes's theory around and argues that ancient man was unicameral. His consciousness was undivided and had an intuitive connection to the world. It is we who are bicameral. We have a divided consciousness, just as much as split-brain patients do. As Wilson shows in *Starseekers*, it is because of our divided consciousness that astronomy and the other sciences were able to develop.

The loss of direct access to our intuitive knowledge and to the felt connection between ourselves and the earth, moon, sun, and stars precipitated major changes in western consciousness. For one thing, it led to the demise of the ancient Great Religion of moon and goddess worship and the rise of more masculine deities.[12] But exile from the cozy cosmic nest also meant that man had to learn things for himself, and this was absolutely necessary for our evolution. The bulk of *Starseekers* is taken up with telling the fascinating story of how we came from believing the earth was flat and at the center of the universe to our current ideas about big bangs and black holes, and Wilson's excitement in telling it is evident. But in the last chapter he returns to more existential concerns.

The divided consciousness that exiled man to his left brain and forced him to chart the heavens with increasing precision and to systematize his findings has without question been a boon to our understanding of the physical universe.

As I write, the *Voyager 1* spacecraft, which left the earth in 1977, is boldly going where no probe has gone before. It left our solar system in August 2012 and is now traveling through interstellar space. According to reports, it "will not approach another star for nearly forty thousand years" and will be "in orbit around the center of our galaxy . . . for billions of years."[13] The people who built Stonehenge may have felt the cosmos in a way we don't, but they would not have been able to even conceive of what *Voyager 1* is doing. Yet we have achieved this miraculous command of the physical world at a price. Stuck in our left brain, we feel, as the novelist Walker Percy put it, "lost in the cosmos." Although we have more knowledge of the physical universe, we have less idea of *why* we are in it than our ancient ancestors did. The fundamental questions of existence, of where space ends, and why the universe exists at all remain unanswered.

Wilson points out that they will remain unanswered, as long as we believe that the left-brain approach, which focuses squarely on the world "out there," is the only one we can use. Contrary to *The X-Files*, the truth, Wilson says, is not "out there," but "in here," in our own minds. Science peers at the universe through a telescope and asks what does it all mean. Its answer: nothing. As the physicist Steven Weinberg remarked, "The more the universe seems comprehensible, the more it also seems pointless."[14] *Starseekers* closes by looking at various ideas of our cosmic future. As you might expect, none are rosy and all embrace an unquestioned belief that human beings will be long gone before the universe meets its own inevitable end. Yet Wilson points out that the scientists who make these predictions make the same mistake that Descartes did: they accept unquestioningly the "I" peering through the telescope's lens. Wilson does not. As we have seen, his investigations into this "I" lead him to reject the idea, accepted by most of us, that life is a chance guest in a universe oblivious of it. As he does in *Beyond the Outsider* and *The Occult*, Wilson rejects the strict Darwinian view of evolution and argues instead for "an unconscious but highly purposive force"—life itself—which "organized its own emergence" and made the experiment of "divided consciousness" because instinct, or intuition, "is *too* sure of itself, and therefore lazy."[15] "Because it feels lost, bewildered, unsure of itself, the conscious ego"—our left brain—"searches obsessively for meaning." In the process "it has achieved more in three thousand years of bicameral consciousness than in the previous million years of inner unity."

Wilson believes that the force that mastered the complexity of the DNA molecule and created living organisms—opening that "leak" of freedom in matter he first speaks of in *The Outsider*—will not necessarily go out with some cosmic whimper, to paraphrase T. S. Eliot. The jury is still out until all the evidence has been examined, and the part that the mind itself plays in our experience of the physical world is understood. Kant believed that time and space themselves are products of the mind; if so, no amount of peering through a telescope will give us a clue about their true end or beginning. This suggests that in this sense, we *are* the center of the universe after all. The scientist looking at the depths of space through his telescope needs to look at the depths of *inner space*, within himself, too. As Wilson tells us, "A true grasp of the mystery of the universe will involve a true grasp of the mystery of ourselves."[16]

This will also include a true grasp of the mystery of crime. But before Wilson could turn to this, he had an opportunity to meet someone who seemed to have developed a curious relationship with his right brain.

Wilson had finally managed to master his panic attacks, but his own "mind parasites" had a tendency to return when he pushed himself too hard. While he was finishing *Poltergeist!* he was asked by *Reader's Digest* to write a short novel about Rasputin. At the same time, a publisher asked him to contribute the text to a book about witchcraft, illustrated by the artist Una Woodruff.[17] Still facing an overdraft, Wilson naturally accepted. The money was good, but the work overlapped and when New English Library, the publisher of *Poltergeist!*, refused to give him more time, he was again feeling the crunch. When Wilson had his blood pressure checked, his doctor told him it was too high. He was at risk of a stroke or heart attack and needed to lose weight. He had also been checked for a problem with some internal bleeding, which seemed to bode ill (it later turned out to be a false alarm).

Wilson was now fifty, no longer a young man—angry or otherwise—and the news depressed him. But he soldiered on and started work on the witchcraft book. An account of appalling torture inflicted on some suspected witches unsettled him and when he went out to his book shed to hunt down a reference, the depression became almost unbearable. He felt he was once again on the verge of insanity. After he found the book he needed, he returned to his study; the depression continued but he refused to give way. At that point he dropped a pencil. He was inclined to leave it, but he forced himself to pick it up, and as he did, the depression suddenly vanished. He felt as if some pernicious spirit had tried to defeat him but was finally put off by his refusal to succumb. Wilson concluded that his guardian angel had decided that the best way to get the most out of him was to keep him struggling—a conclusion that many other writers may come to also. He was not allowed to relax. He had to face these obstacles rationally and get over them, and not allow his rebellious emotions to take control. By this time he was convinced that along with our physical body, we also have an emotional one; Max Freedom Long's writing on the kahunas of Hawaii helped him to see this. This emotional body was something of a spoiled child and Wilson came to see that it was the source of his depression. He pulled himself together and got his work done. He finished the witchcraft book in a month, then took care of Rasputin, and finally completed *Poltergeist!* with a day to spare.

Soon after this he headed to Finland to take part in a ten-day seminar at the Viittakivi International Center. In 1980 a Finnish correspondent asked Wilson if he would like to participate in the seminar and now, in August 1981, after once again writing several books in a few months, Wilson was looking forward to an extended working holiday. He was especially cheerful because London-Cannon Films had finally decided to go ahead with the film version of *The Space Vampires*. They had optioned the novel two years earlier and now it would go into production. The end result, *Lifeforce* (1985), directed by Tobe Hooper, of *The Texas Chainsaw Massacre* fame, was not a success, at least according to Wilson. He tells the story of how the writer John Fowles once told him that the film version of his novel *The Magus*—another sixties campus classic—was the worst movie ever made. After Wilson saw *Lifeforce* he sent Fowles a postcard saying he had done him one better. The money, however, was good and welcome. With it Wilson was able to pay off the mortgage on Tetherdown. As he considered heading to Finland he had a great sense of relief.

What Wilson encountered at Viittakivi was a surprise and the inspiration for *Access to Inner Worlds* (1983), another short book about the left and right brain. The man who met Wilson and his family at the Helsinki Airport was an American named Brad Absetz. Like Wilson, in his early years Absetz had been dissatisfied with routine life and sought out life more abundant. His search for a more meaningful life led him by a circuitous route to Finland, where he had become one of the teachers at the institute. Viittakivi was rather like a Finnish Esalen; it was an alternative learning institute and offered classes in world religions, organic farming, meditation, and various spiritual traditions. In conversation it turned out that Absetz wrote poetry, although he made the curious remark that he wasn't sure if *he* wrote it or not. Wilson was intrigued by this and when he later read some of the poetry he found it curiously "effortless and sure-footed."[18] It lacked any "literary" character, any attempt to impress, and was also thankfully unsentimental. When Wilson told Absetz how much he liked his "concentrates," as Absetz called his poetry, Absetz told him a remarkable story.

In 1961, Absetz and his wife adopted a baby whose mother was unable to care for it; they already had four children of their own, so their decision was based on a desire to give the baby love and protection. The baby had received scarce attention in its early months and because it had been left lying on its side for long periods, its head was malformed. Brad and his wife did their best, but the child was unresponsive and cried incessantly. When the child was four and a half, it was diagnosed with abdominal cancer; it died eighteen months later.

Absetz's wife fell into a deep depression because of this, lying in bed for hours, wracked with guilt. He would lie beside her, ready to help when she briefly emerged from her depression. He got little sleep over the many months that followed—it took his wife some years to recover and at some point she needed hospitalization—but he learned how to relax himself entirely. Yet this relaxation was combined with an alertness, an attention to his wife; he had to be ready to help her at a moment's notice. One day, while in this deep but alert relaxation, he felt that his right arm wanted to move. Absetz "allowed" it to. Then he felt the same impulse in the left arm. Both arms seemed to move of their own accord. As if they belonged to someone else, he watched them perform a kind of dance, like Tai Chi movements. Later he felt his legs doing the same, and he saw that even his breathing had changed. Then once, while getting lunch at a cafeteria, he saw himself reach out and choose food he normally would not have eaten. He allowed this to continue and found that by eating this unlikely food his health improved and he lost weight. He also seemed to develop a remarkable knack for beekeeping; his slow-motion movements somehow seemed to make him "at one" with the hive, something he also brought to the Japanese tea ceremony he had begun to practice. He began to do "automatic drawings"—they reminded Wilson of Paul Klee's paintings—and made fascinating sculptures out of small pieces of scrap metal. He then began to produce his "concentrates" through a kind of automatic writing. One of these struck Wilson as particularly significant. It began, "Following the afterimage of a wise old man within me, I walked a road within me, up over forested ridges, down through meadowed valleys. . . ."

What struck Wilson about this is that it seemed an example of what Jung called "active imagination," a technique Jung had developed for creating a dialogue between the conscious and unconscious minds—or, as Wilson suspected, between the left and right brains.[19] Active imagination is something like a "waking dream" or a hypnagogic vision. Jung advised that a good way to trigger it is to imagine a scene—say, walking on a country path—and then allow the mind to create a fantasy about what you would find over a hill or around a bend, or, as Absetz did, walking down a road. Wilson wrote at length about active imagination in his short biography of Jung, *C. G. Jung: Lord of the Underworld* (1984). This is a critical but respectful look at the great psychologist's life and work, and it inaugurated a series of similar short biographies that would include other important figures in occult history: Rudolf Steiner, Aleister Crowley, and P. D. Ouspensky. As more than one reader has commented, these short introductions tell us as much about Wilson's ideas as they do about the people he is writing about; they are more "Wilson on" Crowley, Gurdjieff, or whoever than "official" biographies. Devotees of Jung or Steiner might find them lacking, but Wilson readers appreciate them.

What struck Wilson after hearing Absetz's story was that it seemed that he had somehow managed to develop a way of allowing his right brain to have more say in his life. As Wilson says, he had "reconstituted the parliament of his mind, and given the Member for the Subconscious (or the right brain) wider powers of action."[20] Yet Absetz also discovered that the idea was not to hand over total control to his other self. On one occasion, when his wife began to perform spontaneous movements herself, the two began a kind of dance. During this Absetz made sexual advances that his wife resisted. His impulses continued over her protestations until their dance skirted close to an attempted rape. Then suddenly his impulses stopped and he felt confused and not a little frightened. On another occasion, while writing a "concentrate," Absetz saw that his handwriting was changing and he felt as if *someone else* was taking him over. He resisted this and made it clear that *he* was in control. A friend who studied Zen told him that he should listen to what his other self had to say, but that in the end he must make his decisions himself. In short, the other self can be an excellent helpmeet, but we should not assume it is right about everything and hand over the reins to it.

Wilson enjoyed Finland—its forests made him think of Sibelius's music—although he was not happy that Viittakivi was alcohol-free; the nearest state-run liquor store was twenty miles away and he regretted not purchasing the bottles of Beaujolais he had seen at the airport. And the activities at the seminar were not always to his taste. He did not like group activities, and listening to well-meaning but muddle-headed speeches against capitalism and western civilization was a chore. He would have collapsed into boredom if he had not learned the lesson of his lecture tours: not to allow himself to sink into reluctance. Still it was a challenge. Wilson lectured on inner freedom, Husserl, and intentionality, but most of this went over his audience's head. He then decided to try a different approach. He taught a group a concentration exercise he called the "pen trick," which involved focusing and relaxing attention on a pen or pencil—any small object would do—as a way of building up the muscles of concentration, and combined this with a breathing technique he had learned while writing his book on Wilhelm Reich.[21] Taking a deep breath, the group exhaled and allowed the relaxation to move down through their bodies. Combining this with first focusing their minds tightly and then relaxing them—the "Wordsworth technique"—had a curious effect. Soon many of the participants felt as if they were floating. Their sense of time slowed down too. Wilson was surprised when, after he thought only a few moments had passed, he saw that they had been doing this for a half hour and had almost missed lunch.

Another interesting thing happened when, after explaining to them that moods are intentional, he asked his group to think of some depressing time in their lives. When the group had induced a state of gloom, Wilson then said, "Okay, now un-depress yourself." At first they didn't know what he meant, but he explained that as they had just consciously "depressed" themselves, there should be no reason why they couldn't do the opposite. They should be able to intend it just as they had intended their depression. Wilson had come upon this idea during his panic attacks. If he could relax enough to stop the attack and return to a state of normality, there was no reason why he shouldn't be able to relax even further, into the kind of deep calm of the mystics. His students got the idea and after a few moments had worked themselves up into a state of happy expectancy.

Wilson gave half the earnings of *Access to Inner Worlds* to Absetz. Half the book is about him; the other half explores the remarkable ability we have to, as the title says, access inner worlds. Wilson explains that as it is, we spend most of our time trapped in left-brain consciousness. For most of the time this is focused on the external world: again, the café owner whose head empties when his café does. To deal with the necessities of this world we reduce it to symbols, 2-D representations that allow us to maneuver through it quickly; as we've seen, we edit out most of reality. The unappetizing character of this consciousness has led many to reject it and to seek its opposite, the warm, buoying waters of the right brain. They want to escape "head consciousness." In order to do this some take drugs; others try to go back to nature. But, as we've seen, rejecting the left brain in favor of the right isn't the answer. Wilson writes, "I do not feel that human beings have made a mistake in evolving left-brain consciousness. For all its problems and anxieties, I still prefer the condition of being human to being a cow."[22] The aim is to learn how to go *beyond* left-brain consciousness—and the robot—not retreat into the cozy world of our animal heritage. Wilson points out that when Hesse's Steppenwolf drinks a glass of wine and is reminded of Mozart and the stars, he has brought both his brains into alignment. He has not jettisoned his left brain but has relaxed his consciousness *into* the right. Both are available to him and because they are he has a sudden sense of *reality* in 3-D.

The Steppenwolf is saved from suicide because, as Wilson writes, within him "an inner trapdoor had opened, leading into an immense Aladdin's cave."[23] This cave houses our memories, our knowledge, our experience, the stores of reality we have accumulated in our life. The wine has reminded the Steppenwolf of this, and that he is much *larger* than he believes. We all have experienced this. Whenever we are deeply absorbed in a book, it is as if we have left the world of 2-D consciousness behind and entered a larger, more meaningful one, a virtual reality that exists within us. As Wilson says, this is why the appearance of the first modern novel, Samuel Richardson's *Pamela* in 1740, was a major breakthrough in the evolution of consciousness: it provided a "magic carpet that could carry the reader off into the realms of the imagination."[24] By doing so it triggered the Romantic revolution.

As Wilson points out, this can happen with works of philosophy as much as with works of fiction. When we slow down we allow the right brain to supply the other dimension; that is why the world of a novel can often feel more real than our everyday reality. Wilson points out that the critics of head consciousness are mistaken to believe that books and ideas are just words and that life or reality is about flesh, blood, bodies, and emotions. They fail to understand the nature of imagination, that it is a faculty for *grasping* realities that are not immediately present, not for offering a substitute for the real thing. (Wilson points out that even ostensibly intellectual writers such as Aldous Huxley envy more "earthy" types and have a certain contempt for the mind because it interferes with their experience of life.) Yet it is true that, as often as not, we don't always find a way to this richer consciousness; our entrance to our personal Aladdin's cave is usually blocked. How can we learn the "open sesame" that will grant us entry into our own Aladdin's cave whenever we wish to visit it?

To answer that question, in a chapter called "The Road to Visionary Consciousness," Wilson looks at a remarkable book, *Essay on the Origin of Thought* (1974), by the little-known Danish philosopher Jurij Moskvitin.[25] Moskvitin developed his own method of entering hypnagogic states—or active imagination—and in the process came to some fascinating conclusions. Lying in the sun with his eyes half-closed, Moskvitin became aware of the spectrum that appears when the eyelashes partly cover the eye. As he peered through this it seemed as if he was watching a film in the background, "a screen or mosaic with the most strange and beautiful patterns." He felt that these patterns were somehow significant. As he watched them he saw that they seemed to be made of different geometric shapes that interlocked with each other, and that these designs were reminiscent of much religious or spiritual art. They were like "art or ornamentation created by civilizations dominated by mystical initiation and experience."[26] These patterns all seemed to be surrounded by, or made up of, strange sparks of light. Brad Absetz's automatic drawings also exhibited this geometric, psychedelic character. Other inner travelers saw similar patterns and Wilson came to believe that they were a kind of "form constant" of these realms.

Moskvitin then saw that these sparks were part of larger, smokelike forms that seemed to be floating in the air. These forms seemed to produce the same effect as a still life by a Dutch master, when what we see as a goblet or wineglass on close inspection turns out to be only a daub of yellow paint. Moskvitin concluded that just as we interpret the daub of paint as a wineglass—or whatever we are looking at in the painting—we also interpret the sparks Moskvitin observed as the world around us. Even more odd, Moskvitin came to see that these smokelike forms, which he also compared to a kind of cobweb, seemed to reach out toward the outer world from his own eyes, as if the forms were *projected* from them into the world. The way they became the objects of the external world was rather like the way the spots of light we see when we rub our eyes become whatever our thoughts turn them into, or how we see faces in clouds or shapes in a fire or figures in a Rorschach blot.[27] (And we see that this is the same form-giving power that Gestalt psychology studies.) For Moskvitin, the way we perceive the world is in essence the same way we see these inner shapes and forms. We *paint* the world with our eyes, which somehow arrange the smokelike forms and sparks into the objects we see. In short, for Moskvitin it seemed that what we take as the external world originates in us—or at least that the world we *see* has its origin in our own mind, something, we know, Wilson had already learned from Husserl.

Moskvitin, Wilson points out, is *not* saying that we create reality, as some New Age and postmodern thinking would have it. I am not the creator of the "real" world—that, Wilson says, is "something different again. . . . *But of this representation which I take to be 'reality'* [meaning my consciousness of the world] *and which is actually a 'painting', I am undoubtedly the creator.*"[28] This, in essence, is exactly the same point as Husserl's intentionality. Moskvitin seems to have observed our intentionality at work, constituting the world out of some strange fundamental "mind stuff." Moskvitin appears to have hit on what the philosopher Paul Ricoeur argued was the true meaning of Husserl's phenomenology. After pointing out that the natural standpoint consists of "spontaneously believing that the world which is there is simply given," Ricoeur says that once the philosopher has rid himself of this naïveté, he comes to see that consciousness continues to observe the world, but is no longer lost in it, that is, it is no longer passive but is aware of its active character. The "very seeing itself is discovered as a doing . . . as a producing—once Husserl even says 'as a creating.' . . . Husserl would be understood," Ricoeur says, "and the one who thus understands him would be a phenomenologist—if the intentionality which culminates in seeing were recognised to be a creative vision."[29]

Our vision is creative, just as Moskvitin seems to have discovered.

One of the most important points to come from Moskvitin's observations is that in essence there is *no difference* between our vision of the outer world and that of our inner one. That is to say, there is no difference in kind. The two visions do differ because when directed at the outer world, we are constrained by its limitations. Moskvitin says that when we look at the outer world, the "selective forms"—his name for the sparks and smokelike stuff—are forced to follow the contours of its objects, what Moskvitin calls the "sequence of external impulses," the information coming to us from the senses. But these constitute a "limitation of the otherwise unlimited combinations of the selective forms released at random from within."[30]

Our picture of the world, then, is by definition constrained by the realities of the world. But our inner world has no such restrictions, so dreams, fantasies, and visions can give imagination full rein. But even our pictures of the outer world can differ greatly. A tree that is an obstacle to a farmer can be a miracle to a poet. *Physically* it is the same tree, but the farmer's picture of it is very different from the poet's. The farmer sees something in the way of his plow, but the poet sees a source of wonder. The tree is really there, but the attitude or interest we invest in it informs our picture of it. But Moskvitin seems to be saying that even this is only a small portion of the woodlands and forests of the mind. If we think of van Gogh's cypresses we can get an idea of what he means. They seem vibrant with a reality greater than any actual tree. The world that we naïvely take to be real is only one possible world.

The recognition of the visionary character of *all* perception seems to suggest a kind of gradient, leading from the outer world to our inner Aladdin's cave—the storehouse of memories and knowledge that opens up to us in moments of Faculty X—on to the strange interior world that people such as Jung discovered in their excursions into active imagination. Like Brad Absetz, Jung and other "mental travellers," in William Blake's phrase, found themselves in an inner world that was nevertheless as objective as the outer one. This was something that in different ways inner explorers such as Rudolf Steiner, Swedenborg, Aldous Huxley, and many others soon saw to be true. Huxley spoke of the mind possessing its own "darkest Africas, its unmapped Borneos and Amazonian basins," complete with their own flora and fauna.[31] The inhabitants of the inner world whom Jung spoke with told him that he was mistaken to think of it as his. He shared it, they told him, with others—just as we share our inner world with our other self. Wilson recounts other inner voyages, those taken by R. H. Ward, René Daumal, John Lilly, Thomas De Quincey. "At the moment," Wilson says, "we know as little of these inner realms as William the Conqueror knew about the world beyond Europe." But the reports given by these and other "psychonauts," as the German novelist and inner voyager Ernst Jünger calls them, leaves Wilson no doubt that our ordinary consciousness is of "an extremely inferior and limited variety" and that the inner realm "is a genuinely objective realm, not a subjective world of dreams and delusions."[32]

When Wilson returned from Finland he began to wonder how his ideas about "divided consciousness" could help in understanding the psychology of crime. The product, *A Criminal History of Mankind* (1984), was a book of equal stature and scope as *The Occult* and *Mysteries*. H. G. Wells's *The Outline of History* (1920) had impressed Wilson as a child; now it seemed he was going to write a history of his own. England was in an economic recession at the time and Wilson says he was lucky to have a publisher commission the book.

History had never appealed to Wilson—although he had written about it in *Religion and the Rebel*—but *Starseekers* seems to have shown him its virtues. It turned out that the same divided consciousness that prompted man to try to understand the universe was responsible for his apparently ineradicable criminal streak. Wilson begins his criminal history by echoing his insight from his earlier criminal trilogy, that the history of crime seems to parallel Maslow's hierarchy of needs.

Maslow saw that our needs seem to follow a distinct pattern. Our basic need is for food. When this is fulfilled we think about a home and domestic security, a place to live. Once this is secured our need for love, sex, and companionship appears. Then we have what Maslow calls "self-esteem" needs, the desire to be appreciated by our fellows, to be liked and to win their approval, to "be somebody." When these needs are met, our higher needs for self-actualization—

what Maslow calls "meta-needs"—appear. This is the need for some creative outlet, for our personal evolution. In contrast to the earlier needs, this is not a "deficiency need," a *lack*, but a need to *use* our powers. Although in theory everyone should develop to the point where these meta-needs appear—they are a concern of the dominant .005 percent—Maslow saw that many people don't get beyond the self-esteem level, and in his last years he was preoccupied with why this was so.[33]

Wilson saw that aside from crimes of passion, the earliest murders were for simple necessities such as food and that this was true throughout most of history. But by the mid-nineteenth century things began to change. He mentions Burke and Hare, the Edinburgh "body snatchers" who in 1828 killed sixteen people in order to supply bodies to a medical school. They received around seven pounds per corpse and spent that on drink. Then, by midcentury, a different sort of murder appeared. These were crimes aimed at domestic security; they seemed to be the dominant type of murder following the industrial revolution, when many murders were committed by "respectable" people in order to secure an established home and livelihood. The Jack the Ripper murders of the late 1880s ushered in the era of sex crime; as mentioned, the Victorians could not conceive of them as such and thought the Ripper was "morally insane." Then another shift occurred in the late 1950s; Wilson saw that a kind of "self-esteem" murder began to dominate then, when the killer acted in order to "be somebody," to draw attention to himself, to become famous. Robert Smith, an eighteen-year-old who shot several people in a beauty parlor in Mesa, Arizona, in 1966, told police he did it because "I wanted to get known, to get a name for myself."[34]

Many of these killers were often of high intelligence and dominance, and felt that society was somehow to blame for not granting them "dignity, justice and recognition of their individuality"; they regarded their actions as a "legitimate protest."[35] The Moors murderer Ian Brady, with whom Wilson corresponded, felt his deeds were justified because society was corrupt; he quoted the liberationist philosophy of the Marquis de Sade in court in his defense.[36] Charles Manson launched a similar defense and believed that the murder of Sharon Tate and her friends in 1969 was no different than the bombing of Vietnam. If he was guilty of killing, so was society. (As Wilson points out, this was a classic example of what Sartre called "magical thinking.") Now, in contemporary times, Wilson argues that we are seeing the appearance of a kind of murder that is a dark mirror image of self-actualization, in which the killer's actions are a twisted expression of our need to evolve and live creatively.

The so-called motiveless murders that began to appear in the second half of the past century could be seen, Wilson thought, as a warped expression of our craving for freedom. He links them to the "gratuitous acts" that the French writer André Gide wrote about. Gide describes a character who has a sudden impulse to push a stranger off a train. "Who would know?" Gide's protagonist asks, and does it.[37] The novel in which this occurs, *Lafcadio's Adventures*, published in 1912, was a black comedy.[38] By the 1950s such gratuitous acts were being performed by otherwise "normal" people who could provide no logical reason *why* they had killed. A woman who shot a man from whom she had accepted a lift—and who made no advances on her—told the police that she wanted to see if she could kill and "not worry about it afterward."[39] After watching a television program called *The Sniper*, a man similarly compelled stole out into the evening and shot a neighbor through an open window. These are only two of many cases involving a warped expression of freedom.

The criminal, then, for Wilson "is a result of man's misunderstanding of his own potential," a "distorted reflection of the human face," a "collective nightmare of mankind."[40] Crime, Wilson argues, is an unfortunate by-product of the evolution of consciousness. "When man learned to recognise his own face in a pool and to say 'I,'" Wilson writes—when, that is, his consciousness first became divided—"he became capable of greatness, but also of criminality."[41]

Yet Wilson's aim in writing his criminal history is to show that "criminal man" has no "real, independent existence. . . . He is a kind of shadow, a Spectre of the Brocken, an illusion." It is true, he says, that human history has been fundamentally a "history of crime"—echoing the belief of P. D. Ouspensky, who said as much.[42] But, as he says, it has also been the history of creativity. "To understand the nature of crime," Wilson insists, "is to understand why it will always be outweighed by creativity and intelligence."[43] In a sense we can see the evolution of mankind since it achieved divided consciousness as a race between the two. It is a race between our need to mature and our unfortunate tendency to act as children, to seek shortcuts and take the easy way out.

Wilson thought that this childish aspect of criminality seemed supported by the conclusions reached by the psychologist Ernest Becker in his book *The Denial of Death* (1973), mentioned earlier. Becker argues that one of the most powerful drives in human psychology is what he calls the urge to "heroism," his term for what he sees as a fundamental human need to stand out. According to Becker we are all "hopelessly absorbed in ourselves," in our need to be seen as an object of "primary value in the universe." We all have a deep-seated desire to show that we "count," that we are important, that we are "somebody." As Wilson points out, this self-centeredness is clearly evident in children, who make no bones about how important they are and why the world should revolve around them. As we grow older most of us realize that this is unrealistic and we learn to accommodate our needs to those of others—although it does not take much to uncover the cosmic selfishness within. We also realize that in the great scheme of things, our existence is negligible. We are nobody. But deep down the desire for primary recognition is there. As Wilson writes, "A criminal is an adult who goes on behaving like a child." All crime, Wilson says, is like a smash-and-grab raid.

Becker's book is really an elaboration on the psychology of self-esteem; death is the final blow to that and this is why we deny it. It also relates very closely to the idea of the Right Man. As mentioned, the Right Man is an idea developed by the science-fiction writer A. E. van Vogt. It describes a type of person—there are Right Women too—who under no circumstances can accept that he is wrong. His need for self-esteem is so great and his grasp of it is so tenuous that the slightest contradiction sends him into a rage. His belief in the absolute correctness of all of his actions is so unshakable—like the pope, he enjoys infallibility—that he treats any question of it as a personal betrayal. As Wilson's criminal history shows, most of history has been written by Right Men, dictators such as Hitler, Stalin, Mussolini; emperors such as Nero, Caligula, Tiberius; monarchs such as Ivan the Terrible and Louis XVI; conquerors such as Genghis Khan and Tamerlane. These are only a few of the most outstanding examples. All showed a readiness to exterminate any who stood in their way and to eliminate opposition with utter ruthlessness. All exhibited the same childish belief that their smallest wish outweighed all other concerns and they went into violent rages if someone thought otherwise. Yet the power to indulge all one's moods does not lead to happiness. Those who have been able to do so have generally been miserable. "The great tyrants of history," Wilson writes, "the men who have been able to indulge their feelings without regard to other people, have usually ended up half-insane." For, as Wilson writes, "overindulged feelings are the greatest tyrants of all."[44]

Van Vogt also called the Right Man the Violent Man. It is this tendency toward violence that Wilson wants to understand. In their need to affirm their primacy the Right Men or Women have no qualms about using violence to achieve their ends. What is the root of this oldest of all shortcuts to achieving what we want? "*Why*," Wilson asks, "is man the only creature who kills and tortures members of his own kind?"[45]

Wilson looks at various attempts to account for this, analyzing the work of Erich Fromm, Robert Ardrey, Arthur Koestler, and other contemporary writers, as well as the work of Freud and Wells. In *Beyond the Pleasure Principle* (1920) Freud posits a death wish to account for war. In *'42 to '44*, written during World War II, Wells suggests that cruelty and violence against our fellows began when humans first crowded together in the earliest cities. Koestler argues in *The Ghost in the Machine* (1967) that a too-speedy evolution jammed man's human brain, the cerebral cortex, on top of our mammalian and reptilian ones, creating a dissonance between our emotions and our reason. Wilson sees the virtue of these and other attempts at an explanation, but in the end, for him, they beg as many questions as they answer. He sees the beginning of an answer in the shift from our older, unicameral consciousness to our new, bicameral one. Of course, humans exhibited violence before then. But it is with the breakdown of the unicameral mind—to paraphrase Julian Jaynes—that the kind of *gratu-*

itous violence and cruelty that Wilson writes about seem to make their appearance. This is a violence and cruelty *for their own sake*, something, it seems, that was not seen before this shift in human consciousness. The source of this violence, like the childish demand for primacy, seems to be the impatient assertion of the left-brain ego.

According to Jaynes, in 1230 BC, around the time of the "breakdown," the Assyrian tyrant Tukulti-Ninurta I erected a stone altar that shows him kneeling before the *empty* throne of his god. The gods, or his right brain, were now mute. Tukulti no longer felt the connection to the gods that his ancestors had, and it was not a pleasant development. A cuneiform tablet from Tukulti's time has the inscription "One who has no god, as he walks along the street, headache envelops him like a garment." Such headaches did not bode well. The man who has lost contact with his intuitive self—his god—experiences stress and too often becomes impatient and loses his temper. From now on, rulers no longer ruled in the name of the god, but in the name of themselves. They were no longer servants of the deities, but were self-assertive individuals, determined to affirm their primacy.

About a century after Tukulti, the tyrant Tiglath-pileser I began one of the bloodiest campaigns in history. As Jaynes writes, "The Assyrians fell like butchers upon harmless villages, enslaved what refugees they could, and slaughtered others in thousands. Bas-reliefs show what appear to be whole cities whose populace have been stuck alive on stakes."[46] A scene from the reign of the Egyptian pharaoh Ramses III, from around 1100 BC, shows mounds of amputated hands. The laws of the time reflect this new emphasis on cruelty. Tiglath-pileser I "meted out the bloodiest penalties yet known in world history," often for minor offenses. Even the famous Code of Hammurabi, which dates from more than half a millennium earlier, seems to exhibit a new harshness, accompanied by Hammurabi's trumpeting boasts and self-congratulations. In *The Alphabet Versus the Goddess*, Leonard Shlain argues that the rise of the alphabet in about 1700 BC inaugurated a new left-brain emphasis and that this, too, was accompanied by violence. Shlain points out that the Phoenicians, who are credited with inventing the alphabet—although other Semitic people were most likely involved in it as well—were culturally backward and, like the Assyrians, displayed gratuitous cruelty. During the Roman siege of Carthage in 146 BC—much later than the Assyrians, to be sure, who were long gone by then—the Phoenicians, who founded Carthage, "threw several hundred children, drawn from the finest families, onto the stoked fires within the bronze belly of their god Moloch. . . . This cruel deity," Shlain writes, "could only be appeased by human sacrifice."[47] That the children were their own made no difference to the rulers. "The city authorities ordered their children burned alive to save their own skins."

What has happened? With the breakdown of the unicameral mind, the impatient left-brain ego has come into existence and it has begun to assert itself.

Now, when a king defeats an enemy, it is not enough to subjugate the defeated people; he must express his wrath at their defiance by slaughtering the prisoners, thousands at a time. He then erects a monument proclaiming his victory and showing the fruits of opposing his rule: amputated hands, decapitated heads, impaled men, women, and children. This is not a case of the gods demanding sacrifice, but of the king's outraged ego being appeased and his self-importance being recognized. As Wilson's bloodstained history shows, this scenario plays itself out across the ages. Yet it is not limited to the few who have hacked their way to the top. The *detachment* from the world that allowed humans to *ask questions*—which, as we've seen in *Starseekers*, inaugurated the beginnings of science and philosophy—is the same detachment that allowed us to treat our fellows as objects, to see them as *less real* than ourselves or our tribe. The loss of contact with the gods—or the right brain—led to a kind of *stress* that impelled man to develop a new ruthlessness, a willingness to take *any* measures necessary to achieve his ends. We can see this in ourselves. If we are sitting in a café and deeply enjoying a book, a noisy child or talkative adult at a nearby table can easily lead us to murderous thoughts.

Unicameral, intuitive man took his time and for the most part was at peace with the world around him. Suddenly a new type of man, one in a hurry, always having to do something, appeared. The urge to get things done prompted impatience and the willingness to take the shortest route to accomplishing one's ends, and this often meant violence. Unicameral man most likely felt more relaxed; he belonged, was at home in the world, in the way animals most likely are, and which we try to be through the use of drugs or alcohol. This precluded the kind of assertive violence that had now come into the world. But it also meant that we had no power to distance ourselves from the present, to rise above the immediate moment and to look at the world objectively. It is the ability to do this that has given us science, philosophy, history, art, literature—everything that makes up what we have called the "noösphere," and which makes us specifically human. But it is also what allowed our capacity for cruelty and violence to grow.[48] Koestler, who was obsessed with the same question and whose work Wilson admired, recognized this. He writes, "The creativity and pathology of man are two faces of the same medal, coined in the same evolutionary mint."[49] This is why Wilson could see criminality as the shadow side of creativity, a form of the "Spectre" that, as Blake has it, we will cast off when our humanity fully awakens.

The dangers of a consciousness geared too much toward the left brain can be seen, Wilson tells us, in the examples of Sparta and Rome. The Spartans, for Wilson, are an example of "the futility of sheer ruthlessness."[50] After a decades-long war with their neighbors the Messenians, the Spartans turned their city-state into "one vast army camp."[51] "They thought and ate and drank nothing but military discipline." The result was that Sparta soon became a "living fossil." At the age of seven children of both sexes entered army camps and remained soldiers for the rest of their lives. Everything centered around this; there was no private or personal life. Everything was regimented and strictly disciplined with the State the absolute ruler. Arts, thought, religion had one aim. Toynbee compared the Spartans to a nation of warriors, permanently presenting arms—much like today's North Korea, which exhibits a similar paranoia. The Spartans "fixed their mind on one thing and one thing only, and pretended that nothing else existed." They ended not as the Assyrians did, in some final battle—when, determined to end their barbarity, in 610 BC the nations of Mesopotamia rose up to destroy Ashur-uballit II's army—but through a kind of "spiritual arthritis," an inner desiccation.

If the Spartans were the "ultimate left-brainers," the Romans could not be far behind. Like the Spartans and the Phoenicians, who excelled in naval design, the Romans were a fundamentally practical-minded people. They created no philosophy or religion of their own—they borrowed both from Athens, whom Sparta had conquered—and their achievements were in engineering, law, and conquest, all very left-brain concerns. Like the Spartans, they exhibited a "curious insensitivity and literal-mindedness" and "never learned how to inhabit the world of imagination."[52] Their other achievement is, as Wilson says, in having "invented the homicidal system of election—the deliberate development of murder as a political engine."[53] Readers of Robert Graves's Claudius novels—or fans of the television series—will have an idea of what Wilson means. The bloody history of the Caesars, filled with as many perversions, excesses, and assassinations as the human mind could imagine, was a product of their stubbornly material view of life and their ruthless pursuit of personal power and gain. Because of their materialistic outlook the history of Rome "contains more crime and violence than any other city in world history," a status sadly maintained when the Eternal City passed from pagan hands to Christian: as Wilson makes clear, the history of the church is almost as bloodstained as that of the Caesars.[54] If any evidence was needed for the truth of Wilson's remark that those "who have been able to indulge their feelings without regard to other people, have usually ended up half-insane," the lives of Nero, Caligula, Tiberius, and their fellow emperors should suffice. Throughout much of its history, Rome was a "behavioral sink," a society exhibiting the worst characteristics of human depravity, and these men, who held the destiny of the West in their hands, were often the worst examples of this.

As Wilson saw, left-brain dominance can lead to crime. But paradoxically so can the attempt to escape it. The problem with this new, determined, effective form of consciousness is that it separates one from *reality*. It was successful precisely because it turned the living world into a set of symbols and focused on the quickest way to achieve its ends, reducing everything else to a kind of cardboard stage setting. But when we are "trapped in this thin and unsatisfactory left-brain awareness" for too long, we seek ways to "break open the head," to allow in some sense of newness. The boredom that often accompanies left-brain consciousness sent Alexander the Great out looking for new worlds to conquer; when he ran out of them, it sent him to the bottle and he died in 323 BC, after a drinking binge. Yet lesser violence can also achieve a brief release from our desiccated left-brain awareness and "readjust the balance" between right and left. It can rescue us from "cold reason" and restore the "feeling of instinctive purpose."[55] Yeats knew that in completing the "partial mind . . . even the wisest man grows tense / with some sort of violence." But what Yeats experienced as an inner struggle, many act out in real life. Feckless youth may take to vandalism—or, like Graham Greene, to Russian roulette. Or a character of low self-esteem, trapped in a negative self-image, suffocating on a thin left-brain consciousness and filled with an overpowering need to *feel alive*, may resort to more desperate and deadly measures: a sudden violent *act* which will, for a brief time, free him of the robot and allow a fleeting feeling of reality. Wilson's analysis of the modern period in his criminal history is filled with many sad, depressing accounts of how the human need to strengthen a too-weak "reality function" led to some of the most harrowing cases of gratuitous cruelty and violence inflicted on human beings.

For this is what is at stake: our grasp on reality and mankind's fumbling attempts, sometimes dangerous, sometimes inspired, to strengthen it.

Yet, in the end, it is precisely the left-brain ego, which we have so far seen as something of a villain, that is our best defense against violence and criminality. We are, Wilson says, free to *choose* to develop the self-control and discipline necessary to master our impatience and egotism, or to give in to them. Wilson sees the situation in terms of two forces, what he calls Force-T and Force-C, tension and control. As he writes, "Force-T makes for destabilization of our inner being. Force-C makes for stabilization and inhibition."[56] When I am tense, my energies seem to expand, to boil over; an impatience presses for their release. I begin to tap my foot or drum my fingers on the table and let out exasperated sighs. But when I become deeply interested in something, the opposite occurs. I focus my energies to a central point; I contain them. More than this: the effort of bringing them into focus seems to increase them, like ordered beams of light becoming a laser. I "*actively apply a counter-force* to the force of destabilization," and the result is a richer, deeper experience.[57] This is an experience I can guide by making my focus even more concentrated. It is the left-brain ego which *decides* to apply Force-C rather than give way to impatience. Like the Unit of Pure Thought or Wilson's "inner schoolmistress," the left-brain ego's business is to bring order to our lives.

Wilson points out that we are faced with making the choice between giving in to Force-T—that is, giving way to tension—and applying Force-C practically all of our waking hours. Modern life is incredibly complicated and I am compelled to deal with it from the moment I wake up. It induces tensions in me that I can either dispel through releasing the impatience they produce, or somehow sublimate into creative, productive effects. "Weak people" who make little effort of control "spend their lives in a permanent state of mild discomfort, like a man who wants to rush to the lavatory." Their lives are something of a misery, with minor annoyances becoming major crises. But worse is the criminal because, for Wilson, he "makes the *decision* to abandon control."[58] This is something he has in common with the Right Man, and it is no mystery than many Right Men have become criminals. The criminal feels he is *justified* in throwing away control because it is society's fault that he commits crimes; his loss of control is an act of rebellion against it. By abandoning control he is getting back at it. For the Right Man, he usually reserves a particular issue over which he feels he has the *right* to lose control. Those around him have "forced" him to do it by crossing the line. The result is the same. Instead of mastering the resentment, impatience, feelings of neglect, and other emotional reasons for their violence, the criminal and the Right Man give way to them. The result, as Wilson says, is bad for society, but even worse for the criminal, because for the "destabilized individual" it leads to "ultimate self-destruction."[59]

Those who do discipline their impulses discover that Force-C is not merely a negative power. It is the same force that allows a musician to master his instrument, or a scholar his subject. Its aim is not merely to return us to a stable condition—as Freud and proponents of other mechanistic psychologies believed—but to order our lives and consciousness, so that we can pursue them creatively. When we develop self-discipline we discover that the exercise of Force-C can produce a pleasure immensely more satisfying than the mere giving way to our impulses, which, in the long run—and often in the short—is a sure road to ruin. The reason people seek out difficulties and challenges—situations that *create* tension—is that they enjoy the feeling of power that comes by overcoming them. (As Nietzsche said in *The Antichrist*, happiness is the feeling that "power *increases*—that a resistance is overcome.") This, Wilson says, is one reason why stress, which we are ordinarily supposed to escape, can actually be a positive thing: it compels us to reach a higher level of self-control so that we can channel it into productive uses. By not developing his Force-C, the criminal becomes more and more the victim of stress and of the inner tensions it creates. His choice of the easy way of relieving tension—through violence—assures that his chances of self-development are minimal. Control, which is another name for maturity, increases our chances of achieving real happiness, the "glimpses of *objectivity*" when we "rise above the stifling, dream-like world of our subjective desires and feelings," the world that the criminal invariably inhabits. Those who have achieved this—the great artists and thinkers—instruct those who follow. The criminal dies at his own hand, a victim of his own lack of control.

CHAPTER ELEVEN

PSYCHICS, SPIRITS, AND UPSIDE-DOWNNESS

W riting *A Criminal History of Mankind* took longer than Wilson would have liked. One reason it did, he says, is because he had to rewrite it. Considering its seven-hundred-plus pages, this could not have been a welcome task. It also meant a delay in getting the rest of the advance, which meant that, once again, money was short. His efforts, however, were well received. *Time Out* called Wilson's history of crime a work of "massive energy and accessibility" and said it reestablished his place "in a European tradition of polemical thought that includes H. G. Wells, Sartre and Shaw."[1] *New Society* celebrated its "fascinating ideas about the nature of those modern unpredictable acts of violence where the older motives of greed and sexual passion will not serve."[2] Other reviews were likewise good but the sales did not match those for *The Occult* or *Mysteries*, and it wasn't long before Wilson was looking for a subject for his next book. His overdraft had gone up again but after a meeting with his endlessly patient bank manager, he was able to secure another loan using Tetherdown as collateral. This brought a brief but welcome sense of financial security. In 1983 Wilson had decided to invite his mother to come live with them in Cornwall; his father had died in 1975 and she had been living alone since then.[3] Knowing he had money in the bank was a relief.

It would not be long before Wilson found the idea for his next book. In writing *The Occult* and *Mysteries* he saw that he had left out of his investigations one paranormal ability in particular, psychometry. This is the ability to tell an object's history simply by holding it in your hands. The term itself means "soul measuring." With his interest in time slips, Faculty X, and "the reality of other times and places," it should not be surprising that Wilson was interested in a psychic power that allowed one to step out of time and relive the past. Yet it has to be said that the title of his book on the subject, *The Psychic Detectives* (1984), is somewhat misleading.

The subtitle on the Berkley paperback edition—on my desk as I write—

"Solving Crimes by ESP," suggests a combination of Wilson's fascination with crime and his interest in parapsychology. But while criminal cases involving the paranormal are scattered throughout the book, only one chapter focuses on psychics being called in to help the police in their investigations. And while dowsers and psychometrists have often been of help to the police, Wilson admits that, with one exception, "I can think of no murder case—or, for that matter, any other important criminal case—that was actually solved by a clairvoyant."[4]

The misleading title was not Wilson's choice. The book was not written with an emphasis on crime in mind, but as a general introduction to psychometry. He had originally suggested *Telescope into the Past* as a title. But Pan Books, who had commissioned the work, wanted something more "sellable." And so, as he had already done more than once, Wilson conceded and accepted the more "catchy" title.

Readers coming to *The Psychic Detectives* expecting to find accounts of psychics solving crimes may be disappointed. But the book is nonetheless an important development in Wilson's analysis of the occult. For one thing, writing it offered him another chance at coming up with a general theory of the paranormal. In the end, however, he had to admit that a paranormal "theory of everything" remained elusive; while several theories could account for different phenomena, no one theory covered them all.[5] As William James had discovered, there seemed to be an inbuilt frustration in trying to bundle the paranormal up into a neat parcel. No sooner is everything tidy and orderly than some new evidence comes to light, providing a new loose end. *The Psychic Detectives* has the virtue of presenting these loose ends in a very logical and readable manner.

In the introduction Wilson took the opportunity to strike a personal note and air some grievances he had with some fellow paranormal researchers and also with some hard-nosed scientists who regarded parapsychology as a waste of time. A newspaper story about a poltergeist haunting was the occasion. It spoke of strange things happening: a coffin floating in the air, hymn books flying from the shelf, a weird blue haze in a graveyard. Had he heard of it earlier, Wilson said, it would have been perfect for *Poltergeist!* Yet when he tried to check on it, he found that none of the "facts" it mentioned were verifiable. The journalist responsible had written other stories and it seemed the same was true of them as well. When Wilson wrote to him, expressing disappointment that he published "true" tales of the paranormal that could not be verified, the journalist accused Wilson of "attacking" him and the correspondence quickly ended.[6]

Yet the problem of verifiable sources wasn't limited to sensational journalism. Wilson suspected his friend and fellow parapsychologist Lyall Watson of blurring the same lines between fact and fiction. Watson began his best-selling book *Lifetide* (1979)—which incidentally introduced the well-known "hundredth monkey" theory—with an account of a five-year-old girl, Claudia, who he said possessed remarkable psychic powers.[7] Among other things she could turn a tennis ball inside out, without damaging it, something physically impossible, at least according to our normal understanding. Watson said that Claudia did this by gently stroking the ball, rather as Uri Geller bent his teaspoons, and somehow reversing it through another dimension. Wilson realized that if true, this was without doubt remarkable, and brought into question the known laws of physics. He wrote to Watson asking for more details—what, for instance, had happened to the everted tennis ball? Watson's reply was somewhat evasive. He said he had kept the details about Claudia vague, because he wanted to avoid having her "embroiled in that kind of controversial circus."[8] He also said that her inside-out tennis balls always reverted to their original shape after forty-eight hours. So there was no evidence that the phenomenon had occurred, and she had in any case given up doing "strange things" with tennis balls.[9]

Wilson felt that, if this was the case, then Watson should not have used the story in his book, even if he felt convinced that it was true. Doing so put him, Wilson thought, in the same league as Erich von Däniken, who regularly made claims that were easily shown to be untrue—as, for example, his claim in *The Gold of the Gods* (1973) to have visited a secret underground library in South America, which he later confessed did not exist.

The need to be as honest, accurate, and open as possible had become paramount in parapsychology. In recent times there had been a severe reaction against it by hard-nosed, "serious" scientists, enraged at public acceptance of paranormal claims. There had always been scientists who rejected anything to do with the occult or paranormal, but recently things had turned somewhat vicious. One reason for the new, violent hostility was the celebrity of Uri Geller, whose bent spoons had received worldwide acclaim. Geller's celebrity inspired a group of scientists, popular science writers, and stage magicians to band together to not only refute particular paranormal claims, but to deny that parapsychology had any scientific validity whatsoever. In 1976 the astronomer Carl Sagan, the physicist John Wheeler, the science writers Christopher Evans and Martin Gardner, the illusionist James ("the Amazing") Randi, and other liked-minded individuals formed the Committee for the Scientific Investigation of Claims of the Paranormal. They demanded nothing less than that all "serious" intellectuals should close ranks in order to stop the spread of the paranormal "rot."

We know that Wilson had considered Gardner a friend, and he had collaborated with Christopher Evans on a series of coffee table books on the supernatural.[10] He was also friendly with Marcello Truzzi, editor of the skeptical *Zetetic Scholar*, and another a founding member of CSICOP. The intolerance toward the paranormal that these critics had developed reached a new intensity in 1979. At the annual meeting of the American Association for the Advancement of Science, John Wheeler called on his fellow true believers to "Drive the pseudos out of the workshops of science." "The pseudos" here meant scientists who were not necessarily trying to *prove* the reality of the paranormal, but who felt that it was at least worthy of investigation and deserved something more than ignorant dismissal. Wheeler and his compatriots thought otherwise. The irony is that Wheeler's own bizarre ideas about the nature of reality and its relations with consciousness—widely accepted within the field of quantum physics—echo many traditional occult or parapsychological beliefs.[11]

Yet even these self-appointed guardians of science seemed to have rather flexible ideas about the truth, as becomes clear in a story Wilson tells. In 1975 *The Humanist* magazine published an attack on the work of the statistician Michel Gauquelin. Gauquelin had run a computer analysis on some of the claims of astrology and was surprised at the results; they seemed to confirm that, as astrology suggests, sports figures should be born under the sign of Mars, scientists under Saturn, actors under Jupiter, and so on. This finding was dubbed "the Mars effect" and Gauquelin later formalized it in his book *Cosmic Influences on Human Behavior: The Planetary Factors in Personality* (1985). The physicist Dennis Rawlins—a founding member of CSICOP—read *The Humanist*'s attack and felt that it was badly done. If the idea was to discredit Gauquelin, this article didn't do it. He was then asked to take on the job himself, but after subjecting Gauquelin's findings to his own analysis, Rawlins discovered that Gauquelin was correct after all, a conclusion also reached by the skeptical psychologist Hans Eysenck.[12] Rawlins urged his colleagues to make a stronger argument. They refused. When, in the spirit of true scientific inquiry, he insisted they admit they were wrong, he was either ignored or criticized by his fellows for not toeing the party line. After years of being dismissed as a "pseudo" himself, Rawlins published a pamphlet blowing the whistle on the cover-up. In it he accused CSICOP of being nothing more than a "group of would-be debunkers who bungled their major investigations, falsified their results, covered up their errors and gave the boot to a colleague who threatened to tell the truth."[13]

This polarizing, witch-hunting mentality informing CSICOP and similar paranormal critics was a danger, Wilson argued, not only to parapsychology, but to science itself. It rejected the "open-minded curiosity that has led to all great scientific discoveries." When researchers have to worry if their work will be considered loyal, the very idea of discovery dissolves. The right way to approach the paranormal—or any study, for that matter—Wilson says, is "to be open-minded, to state the facts as you see them, and to be willing to acknowledge it frankly if you are shown to be wrong."[14] Wilson had already done this when he changed his mind about poltergeists and embraced the "spirit" hypothesis. He was not happy about this, but the facts, he saw, pointed in that direction and could not be ignored.

In *The Psychic Detectives* Wilson wanted to state the facts about psychometry as clearly as possible. This is especially important, he tells us, because psychometry has received short shrift even from professed parapsychologists. The Society for Psychical Research, founded in 1882—a brief history of which makes up one chapter of the book—practically ignored it, and subsequent "scientific" investigators into the paranormal had, Wilson says, given it little better attention. Wilson explains that this is because a mistaken association with spiritualism had given it a bad name.

Wilson intended to make up for this omission. In the process this strange ability to focus a "mental telescope" on the past—or in some cases the future—became the center of a wide-ranging investigation involving the human aura, our two brains, hypnagogic hallucinations, the Akashic Records, the spirit world, telepathy, traveling clairvoyance, psychic archaeology, and much more in what had become by now the expected Wilson blend of speculation, theory, investigation, and a sometimes daunting collection of facts.

As we might suspect, the right brain plays a central part in this story. The knowledge that comes through psychometry is the same as that which enabled Edgar Allan Poe to intuit facts about astronomy years before their verification, or that made Robert Graves believe that he "knew everything," although he had only gone through a few years of education. Exactly how the right brain receives this knowledge remains unknown, but Wilson was convinced that it does and that we live in what he would later call an "information universe," a world in which everything that has ever happened has in some way been recorded. It is this record that the psychometrist can somehow read.

The term "psychometry" was coined in the 1840s by Dr. Joseph Rodes Buchanan, a follower of Mesmer and a student of phrenology, the study of bumps on the head. Bishop Leonidas Polk—later a Confederate hero in the American Civil War—told Buchanan that he had a peculiar ability: he could detect brass in the dark, simply by touching it. When he did, it produced a metallic taste in his mouth. Buchanan was intrigued and decided to test some of his students. He discovered that they, too, could detect brass in the dark, as well as other substances, such as salt, pepper, and sugar. Buchanan found that if his students held a narcotic wrapped so they could not know what it was, they nevertheless felt its effects. If a "sensitive" touched the stomach of someone suffering an illness, he experienced a "morbid feeling." One of Buchanan's sensitives told him that he could know the mental state of the person he was touching. Buchanan gave a subject some correspondence from his files, and asked if he could tell anything about the writers just from holding the letter. His sensitive was able to talk about the people, whom he had never met, as if he knew them very well.

After carrying out hundreds of tests Buchanan came to the conclusion that the human being leaves "the impression . . . of his mental being upon the scenes of his life and the subjects of his actions," thus providing us with "a new clue to the history of our race." Through it "a glimpse may be obtained of unrecorded ages." Buchanan christened this ability "psychometry," "soul measurement."

Ancient artifacts, Buchanan believed, are "still instinct with the spirit that produced them and capable of revealing to psychometric exploration the living realities with which they were once connected. . . . *The Past is entombed in the Present!*" and Buchanan had discovered the mental telescope that would enable us to recapture it.[15]

Wilson's history of psychometry begins in its early days with Buchanan and his most important follower, William Denton, whose classic book on the subject, *The Soul of Things* (1863), Wilson reintroduced to a new readership in a reissue in 1988.[16] Wilson's narrative brings in the "Odic force" of Baron Karl von Reichenbach, "dermo-optical perception," the ability to "see" with parts of the body other than the eyes, and explains how both Buchanan and Denton became persona non grata when, after their research into our mental telescope was received positively, it suffered a critical backlash because of an unwanted association with spiritualism. Even scientists open to psychic phenomena were put off by much of the spiritualist craze, with its messages from departed aunts, floating tambourines, and ectoplasmic phantoms. It was this that led the Society for Psychical Research to avoid any mention of psychometry's founders. Indeed, the possibility of being hoodwinked by a fraudulent medium—of which, Wilson admits, there was no dearth—made the SPR often more skeptical than their skeptics, and led to the sense of failure that followed its early enthusiasm.

Wilson's account introduces readers to some important but lesser known continental psychic investigators. There is, for example, the strange case of the French novelist Pascal Forthuny, who became something of an accidental psychometrist. At a meeting of the International Metaphysic Institute in Paris in 1921, the skeptical Forthuny intercepted a letter that Dr. Gustav Geley, a leading French investigator, was handing to a psychic he was testing.[17] Forthuny proceeded to invent a tale of crime and murder linked to the writer of the letter, showing how easy it was to improvise a "reading." After Forthuny had enjoyed his joke, Dr. Geley announced that the letter had been written by the famous serial killer and real-life Bluebeard, Henri Landru, then on trial for the murder of eleven women (readers can find out about the case in Wilson's *Encyclopaedia of Murder*.) Mme. Geley handed Forthuny a fan and asked him to try again. Forthuny said he heard the name Elisa and had a feeling of being suffocated. Mme. Geley told him the fan had belonged to an old woman who had suffered from congestion of the lungs and who had a companion named Elisa. Other items brought similar success and Forthuny wondered: "Do I possess a faculty I do not even suspect?"[18]

Forthuny then became a popular psychic, much in demand, and he later acquired a "spirit guide," with whom he often argued. (If his guide was his right brain, then unlike Brad Absetz, he and his ally did not always get along.) Forthuny became involved in the spiritism of Allan Kardec—a French variant of spiritualism and one of the most important religions in modern Brazil—and his exploits were recorded by Dr. Eugene Osty, whose *Supernormal Faculties in Man* (1923) is, according to Wilson, a classic on par with F. W. H. Myers's *Human Personality and Its Survival of Bodily Death.*

Another fascinating area of psychometric research is psychic archaeology, the use of psychometry to understand the past. Wilson writes that the most impressive psychometrist of all is most likely unknown to most readers. Stefan Ossowiecki was born in Moscow in 1877 and at an early age was able to see people's auras, even after taking the eyedrops an optometrist his mother took him to had prescribed. Ossowiecki also had the strange ability to move heavy objects without touching them, what is known as psychokinesis. Once, tied in a straitjacket, he lay on the floor and moved a heavy marble statue simply by thought.[19]

That Ossowiecki was both a seer and psychokinetic exemplifies Wilson's belief that in many ways it is difficult—and perhaps pointless—to try to separate one paranormal power from another. Psychometrists are often also telepaths, and traveling clairvoyants can often exhibit precognition. Knowledge of the past may come through psychometry, or via a sudden awareness of one's past life—the evidence of reincarnation. Throughout the book one of the trickiest puzzles is whether information about some object or its owner has been arrived at through psychometry or is being "picked up" from the mind of someone who knows it. And the fact that like dowsers, psychometrists can gather insight about someone not only from objects that have *not* been in contact with the person, but from *abstract representations*, such as photographs or maps, only adds to the confusion. Not to mention the possibility of spirits. As Wilson writes, "Although we are still ignorant of why different psychics should possess different powers . . . it seems fairly clear that there is no basic difference in kind between these various abilities."[20] They are all abilities possessed by Maurice Maeterlinck's "unknown guest," who, if Wilson's ideas about the ally in our right brain are correct, may not be as unknown as Maeterlinck thought.

After meeting an old Jewish mystic who told him things about himself the mystic should not have known, Ossowiecki began to study occultism. Wilson points out that the teaching the old Jew passed on to him was not very different from what Max Freedom Long had learned from the kahunas of Hawaii: that along with our unconscious mind, we also have a superconscious mind. It is from the superconscious that psychic powers come, and in order to contact it, we need to still the body and the emotions.

Ossowiecki was studied by many of the great psychic investigators, including Charles Richet and Baron von Schrenck-Notzing, but his greatest success was as a psychic archaeologist. This began in 1935, when he was able to tell the content of a sealed package that had been left by a rich Hungarian as a test for clairvoyants. Not only was Ossowiecki able to say that the parcel contained a meteorite—"There is something here that pulls me to other worlds," he said—but the sense of something sweet he detected pointed to the confectionery paper in which the meteorite was wrapped; it still contained some powdered sugar. He was also able to pick out a photograph of the rich Hungarian responsible for the parcel, whom he had never met. Ossowiecki was then asked by Polish scholars if he could tell which of the many portraits of the great Polish astronomer Copernicus was done from life, a question that had plagued historians for some time. Ossowiecki picked out one portrait and said that Copernicus had done it himself; he was also able to tell the scholars facts about Copernicus's life that only historians would know, and even some they didn't. When scholars could check Ossowiecki's "facts," they proved to be correct.

In the late 1930s, Ossowiecki worked with the Polish ethnologist Stanisław Poniatowski in giving "readings" of various prehistoric objects about which Ossowiecki knew nothing until he held them. The team of scientists, geologists, archaeologists, and other scholars Poniatowski had assembled concurred that after a series of thirty-three experiments, Ossowiecki had described eleven prehistoric cultures. Again, not everything he said could be investigated, but what could be was and was found to be accurate. Another series of experiments brought insights into the past that, Wilson says, were also subsequently corroborated.[21]

After the German invasion of Poland in 1939, Poniatowski and Ossowiecki fell afoul of the Nazis. They both lived in Warsaw and experienced the horror of the ghetto. Poniatowski vanished into a concentration camp and was never seen again, but Ossowiecki had somehow managed to secure his account of their experiments. In 1944, while trying to escape Warsaw, Ossowiecki and his wife were arrested. She was let go but he was among the ten thousand Polish men the Nazis murdered in a two-day massacre. Poniatowski's manuscript managed to escape the carnage; it remains unpublished, but Wilson gathered material on Ossowiecki and Poniatowksi from *The Secret Vaults of Time* (1978), by the psychic researcher Stephan Schwartz, who wrote a foreword to an edition of the book. The validity of psychic archaeology received significant confirmation in 1973 when at a meeting of the Canadian Archaeological Association the respected archaeologist J. Norman Emerson announced that he had "converted" to the psychometric approach, after a series of experiments with the psychometrist George McMullen had convinced him.[22] Emerson's status was so high that rather than reject his claims, many of his colleagues decided to test them, with positive results.

Wilson also gives us a look at his own participation in psychical research. He talks about a past-life regression he participated in on live television. He took part in a similar exhibition, also on television, of something called "psycho-expansion," a way of inducing a state of deep relaxation which enables participants to relive episodes in their past and also to go back before their birth. The results, Wilson said, were disappointing, but an experiment with traveling clairvoyance—"remote viewing"—was more successful.[23] He talks of meeting the celebrated Dutch psychometrist Gerard Croiset, who preferred to refer to himself as a "paragnost," while taping a segment of *Leap in the Dark*. Croiset's powers appeared at an early age; when only six he was able to tell his schoolteacher, who had been absent for a day, that he had gone to visit his girlfriend, whom Croiset hadn't met but described to a tee. By his thirties he was working with Professor W. H. C. Tenhaeff, Holland's top paranormal investigator, and had also started using his abilities to help the police.

In Croiset Wilson detected the personality traits that seemed common to many psychics: theatricality, showiness, childishness, insecurity, and a need for attention. Although Croiset had helped the police on many occasions—Wilson recounts some in the book—on one murder case he insisted that he had solved it and that the body of the victim, a young woman, had been found. Wilson corrected Croiset: the body hadn't been found and the case hadn't been solved. Croiset grew indignant and insisted it had. Wilson did not press the point and accepted that Croiset, who was well known as a healer and radiated a great warmth and generosity, most likely felt the case *should* have been solved and had convinced himself that it had.[24]

Wilson relates a case of psychic detection—or failure of it—that he was involved in himself, concerning a missing thirteen-year-old girl whom his daughter knew. The psychic involved was Robert Cracknell. Wilson brought Cracknell to the search headquarters and then to where the girl, Genette, was last seen. Cracknell had the impression that she was dead, the victim of a sexual assault. Cracknell said the body would be found within ten days, but at the time of writing—four years after her disappearance—Genette had still not been found. At one point months later a television producer approached Wilson with the idea of making a live television appeal to anyone who felt they might have any psychic impressions about the case. The program received many callers, and the resources of the police and even the military were put at their disposal. Suggestions from dowsers, telepaths, and other psychics were investigated thoroughly, but after a few weeks, Wilson, Cracknell, and their team had to admit defeat.

Yet Cracknell proved eerily accurate when he became involved a few years later in the case of Peter Sutcliffe, the "Yorkshire Ripper." Between 1975 and 1980 northern England experienced a horrific killing spree in which thirteen women were brutally murdered and mutilated. In October 1980, after being asked by the police to help in the case, Cracknell predicted that the Ripper would strike once more before being caught. In a newspaper interview he described the Ripper's house and said he lived in Bradford.

At a lunch with the publisher of Cracknell's autobiography, which Wilson had helped get commissioned, Wilson remarked that he had been asked to appear on a television program to mark the anniversary of the Ripper's last murder. Wilson refused, saying he thought it would encourage him to strike again. As he said this Cracknell announced that the Ripper *would* strike again, in the next two weeks. Six days later the body of Jacqueline Hill was found on wasteland near the University of Leeds. The killing bore all the marks of the Ripper. Then, on January 4, 1981, Cracknell was at Tetherdown when a news-flash came over the television. A man, Peter Sutcliffe, had been arrested in connection with the killings. Cracknell was gratified to hear that he lived in Bradford; when he saw photographs of Sutcliffe's home in the newspapers, it was exactly as he had pictured it. In May 1981 Sutcliffe was found guilty and given multiple life sentences.

Cracknell had not solved the case, but his predictions about it had proved true. His varying success underlines one of Wilson's central points: that psychic powers are unreliable, or at least as reliable as other human abilities, and that psychics, like other people, are often too lazy to develop them.[25] The fact that they come naturally to them inclines them toward a more passive approach. It also illustrates what has come to be known as "James's law." William James contended that things are so arranged that "no case involving the paranormal should ever be wholly convincing."[26] There always seems enough evidence to support a believer's faith, but never enough to erode a skeptic's doubt. As in other contexts, Wilson suggests this is so because if the paranormal was taken for granted, it would diminish our need to make efforts.

One ambiguous area involving psychometry relates directly to the kinds of visionary experiences, the journeys into inner worlds, that Wilson had been writing about. Some of the most astonishing accounts of psychometry can be found in William Denton's *The Soul of Things*. Denton, a geologist at Boston University, was fascinated by Buchanan's belief that the past was still available in the present, and he decided to experiment to see if he could confirm this. He asked his sister—an impressionable young woman—if she would act as his sen-sitive. He wrapped a piece of limestone he had taken from the Missouri River in paper, told her nothing about it, and handed it to her. She had an impression of water, a river, and shells (the limestone was flaked with tiny shells), and de-scribed the setting where Denton had found the stone. When Denton handed her a piece of volcanic lava, wrapped in paper, she saw an "ocean of fire pouring over a precipice." The lava had come from Kilauea, an active volcano in Hawaii. Denton took the precaution of mixing up his wrapped specimens so that even he didn't know which was which—this ruled out the chance that his sister was "reading his mind." A piece of bone taken from limestone produced an impres-sion of a prehistoric world. A piece of meteorite produced an impression of vast, dark space and a sense of hurtling through it. A fragment of Indian pottery brought an image of American Indians.

As the experiments continued, Denton's sensitives began to be able to distinguish between different periods in an object's past; they had, as it were, learned how to "time travel," by focusing on a time further away or closer to the present. Even more remarkable, they began to actually *see* the scene they were describing, rather than just getting a general impression or knowledge about it. They were really looking through a "telescope into the past." One sensitive produced a strikingly accurate description of ancient Pompeii. Another described the home of the Roman dictator Sulla. A piece of hornstone from the Mount of Olives produced a description of ancient Jerusalem.

Denton was determined to understand this phenomenon, and he studied accounts of eidetic memory, mentioned earlier, for insights into it. Yet these temporal travelogues were at times questionable. In the third volume of *The Soul of Things*, published in 1874, Denton includes his son Sherman's accounts of his visions of Mars, Jupiter, and Venus. These, Wilson admits, are much less impressive. Venus had giant trees that looked like toadstools, and was inhabited by strange half-fish, half-muskrat creatures. People on Mars had yellow hair, four fingers, blue eyes, and wide mouths. On Jupiter the people were blonde and could fly. Needless to say, modern science tells us that Venus is much too hot to support life, that Mars is cold and barren, and that Jupiter is a gigantic ball of gas; Wilson had said as much in *Starseekers*. How, Wilson asks, can we account for psychometry's impressive accuracy in some cases and what seems sheer fantasy in others?

That question led to a look at the Akashic Records and the people, such as Madame Blavatsky and Rudolf Steiner, who had claimed to be able to read it.

Much like psychometrists and their mental telescope, Blavatsky and Steiner claimed an ability to read the record of the past. The American "sleeping prophet" Edgar Cayce and others claimed to as well. This was available to them through what occultists called the "astral light," a kind of immaterial ether upon which, as Blavatsky said, "is stamped the impression of every thought we think."[27] ("Akasa" means "ether" or "space" in Sanskrit.) While psychometrists begin with a particular object, Blavatsky and Steiner had developed the ability to enter a state of consciousness in which they could *see* earlier times, much as Denton's sensitives did, as if they were watching events unfold before them; in my book on Steiner I give some idea of how he went about doing it.[28] Yet while psychometrists most often saw a time that could be verified, Blavatsky's and Steiner's visions were of remote prehistoric periods, ages in humanity's and the earth's past, about which it is impossible to verify anything. They spoke of Atlantis, Lemuria, ancient races, and lost civilizations, eras of unknown history that they were able to see vividly, as if in 3-D. Wilson suggests that in their case, and the case of Denton's son's visions of other planets, their psychometric powers blended with the uncanny visionary ability of the subjective mind or "unknown guest," that is, the right brain.

It was precisely the similarity between Blavatsky's Akashic Records and accounts of psychometry that put the SPR off Buchanan and Denton; stories of lost Lemuria and life on Jupiter were simply embarrassing to a society trying to make psychic phenomena scientifically respectable. Wilson writes that the right brain, which "speaks" in images, "has access to such a vast reservoir of imagery that it is almost impossible to control."[29] We remember what Moskvitin said about the difference between our inner and outer vision: our outer vision is constrained by the external impressions reaching us from objects "out there," but our inner vision has no such restraints. Wilson links the visions of Steiner and other readers of the Akashic Records to the strange hypnagogic hallucinations we experience on the point of sleep, which, as mentioned, are close cousins to what Jung meant by "active imagination."[30] This suggests that as with psychic phenomena, there is no easy way to distinguish between true visions and very creative fantasies. Some visions include accurate knowledge of real events. Some are outright fantasies, as Steiner's accounts of Atlantis and Sherman Denton's of Mars seem to be. And some occupy an exciting but difficult middle ground, as many dreams do, combining true knowledge with vivid but fantastic elements. A distinction *can* be made, but it requires patience and a painstaking analysis—much like a phenomenological analysis of consciousness.

Yet we've seen how Proust's madeleine was able to retrieve his childhood in brilliant detail. Wilson suggests that this could be evidence for the neuroscientist Wilder Penfield's discovery that everything that has happened to us is recorded in the brain—a neurophysiological expression of Blavatsky's astral light.[31] Given the proper trigger, our past can be replayed in striking detail. (This may be the basis of the belief that at the point of death, one sees one's life "pass before one's eyes.") Yet we've also seen that Toynbee had a vision of the past that had nothing to do with him personally, but was a product of his *knowledge* of the past and his imaginative commitment to understanding it. We can say that in a way he was a "psychometric historian," just as Stefan Ossowiecki was a "psychometric archaeologist."

After considering this "mass of bewildering facts" Wilson reaches what might seem an obvious but important conclusion. If nothing else, the study of psychometry leads to the understanding that it is pointless to try to grasp the paranormal with our normal ideas about consciousness. It is true that no one theory seems to cover all the paranormal bases. But we will certainly get no closer to one that can by accepting the "poor quality of our everyday consciousness" as our measure. We must recognize that our consciousness itself is variable and that it governs how and what we perceive. In peak experiences and other moments of "affirmation consciousness" it becomes clear that "heightened awareness could well entail heightened powers."[32]

This was an insight that Wilson would return to. In the meantime there was other work. *Afterlife*, as mentioned, dealt with the question that inspired the

SPR: the survival of bodily death. Some of its material came from earlier books, and by now Wilson was facing the problem that he had seen as early as *Mysteries*—that it was becoming difficult to avoid repeating himself. He had already felt misgivings for doing so in his book on Gurdjieff—he had told much of his story in *The Occult*—but felt it was a beneficial necessity. In repeating himself he had "discovered an entirely new set of meanings and implications."[33] And this, in general, is true of other books in which he could not avoid writing about material he had already covered. Wilson was, after all, a hedgehog, who knew "one big thing," which he continued to dig deeper and deeper into with each new book. Readers like me who read everything he wrote often found themselves in familiar territory, but it was always seen from a new angle, a different perspective, and like Wilson, this allowed us to share his new meanings and implications.

Yet even with some repetition *Afterlife* explored new territory. Wilson begins by returning to the question of multiple personality, this time looking at the remarkable work of a Canadian psychotherapist, Adam Crabtree, for whose book, *Multiple Man* (1985), Wilson wrote an introduction.[34] One of Crabtree's colleagues brought him a client named Sarah who was suffering from deep depression; she also heard "voices" in her head. When Crabtree asked Sarah to remember what the voices said, he had a shock. Sarah tensed and she began to shout, "The heat, the heat!" Crabtree asked the voice, which was unlike Sarah's, what it wanted. It said, "To help Sarah." After some sessions it turned out that the voice was Sarah's dead grandmother, who needed help as much as Sarah did. Her spirit was wracked with guilt over how she had treated Sarah's mother, which in turn led Sarah's mother to treat Sarah badly. Over several sessions, Crabtree was able to calm Sarah's grandmother, which eased Sarah's depression, but her spirit never went away. Sarah learned how to live with her in the background, as a vague, benign presence.

Crabtree went on to discover that in many cases of multiple personality, spirit possession could serve as an equally viable explanation as a fractured ego, a conclusion that the psychologist Wilson Van Dusen had also arrived at. Van Dusen, a follower of Swedenborg, taught the reality of spirits. In his practice he found that he would have equal, if not better, results if he accepted the idea that the voices his patients heard, or the different personalities they exhibited, were those of spirits. For all practical purposes, doing so made no difference; in fact it often helped the treatment.

With these beginnings Wilson launches into an analysis of the evidence for the survival of physical death. As his readers by this time expected, he covered quite a bit of ground. He looks at the world of the clairvoyant, retraces the history of spiritualism, revisits the SPR, and celebrates F. W. H. Myers's monumental *Human Personality and Its Survival of Bodily Death*, looks again at

Rudolf Steiner and his ideas about reincarnation, and explores more recent investigations, such as the work of Raymond Moody, Kenneth Ring, and accounts of Near Death Experiences.

In the end Wilson concludes that there is sufficient evidence to suggest that survival of bodily death is a reality. He was not particularly happy about this, just as he was not happy that his investigation into poltergeists led to his accepting the reality of spirits (and we can see that each conclusion supports the other). Yet the facts as he saw them led him to it and he couldn't deny it. Yet this didn't mean that Wilson had converted to spiritualism, as an experience he relates of a session with a dubious spiritualist family showed. He still felt that the messages coming from the spirit world were invariably trivial, and were of no help in dealing with the truly important questions about the meaning and purpose of *this* life, here and now. In one sense, to know there is life after death would of course be important knowledge; it would at least offer more cheerful prospects than the gloomy outlook of the old existentialism and the materialism of science. But we would still be faced with the existential mysteries that face us every day. As mentioned earlier, to say, "Don't worry—there is life after death," is no answer to this.

Wilson makes this point when, after concluding that the spiritualist family he had visited were most likely frauds, he remarked that even if the "spirit" he had questioned—and who quickly became annoyed at Wilson's queries—proved accurate, "it would have made no difference. . . . When I listen to the tape recording of that séance," he writes, "I am seized by the uncontrollable desire to yawn, and by the conviction that 'spirits' have nothing to add to the sum total of human thought: even genuine ones."[35] What the study of spiritualism, the paranormal, multiple personalities, and other psychic phenomena does do is to turn our minds back to the mystery of the personality, to the central question, "Who am I?" with which his analysis of the Outsider began. "Every mystic," Wilson writes, "has had the curious experience of realising he is not who he thinks he is. . . . In moments of visionary intensity, his identity dissolves, and he becomes aware that it is no more than a mask." Behind the mask lies an "inner universe that bears a strange resemblance to the external universe," the ancient vision of man as a microcosm.[36] There is no question that the force behind evolution would be stopped by the mere decay of the bodies housing it. But the aim is not to enter some paradise or higher realm, but to work to enlarge the "leak of freedom" it has made in this resistant world of matter. This can be done through increasing our control over Faculty X, which, as Wilson increasingly saw, was the "power of *escaping the present moment*," an ability to step out of time that makes us "citizens of eternity."[37]

Wilson was not the only one concerned with these issues, or who believed his approach threw new and revealing light on them. Howard Dossor, a senior administrator at La Trobe University in Melbourne, Australia, was a collector of Wilson's work. In 1985, he collaborated with Wilson on editing a collection of his essays, *The Bicameral Critic*. Dossor did every Wilson reader a wonderful service by making available sixteen shorter pieces of Wilson's they might never have come across. I have referred to one already, "Existential Psychology: A Novelist's Approach," in which Wilson introduces the concept of the robot. "Civilization and Individual Fulfilment" looks at the social context of Maslow's ideas. There are essays on Christopher Isherwood, Robert Graves, Baruch Spinoza, Daniel Defoe, *Wuthering Heights*, Bernard Shaw, and Alfred Reynolds and the Bridge, and an amusing piece on being a writer-in-residence. One of the most important essays is "Dual Value Response: A New Key to Nietzsche?" in which Wilson looks at Nietzsche's sudden visions of yea-saying in terms of a powerful irrational affirmation, which overrides the intellect's usual values. It describes a phenomenon in which "A situation that has aroused a neutral or negative reaction quite suddenly arouses a very positive response."[38] Wilson gives as an example Nietzsche's response to seeing his old regiment; Nietzsche had been in the cavalry during the Franco-Prussian War but had been moved to the ambulance corps. For all his talk about will and the superman, Nietzsche was a gentle soul and hated German militarism. Yet when he saw his old regiment ride past, he experienced a "tremendous exaltation." The same occurred when as a student he saw a peasant slaughtering a goat. The blood normally would have disgusted him, but at the same moment there was a terrific crash of thunder. Nietzsche felt an "indescribable sense of well-being and zest," and felt "pure will, without the confusions of intellect—how happy, how free." It was the "absurd affirmation," overriding the everyday values of the intellect.

Howard Dossor's idea might have inspired Wilson to put a collection of his own together. He had been writing now for thirty years and the idea of making a selection from the wide range of his work in order to get his message across must have been appealing. Wilson cherry-picked excerpts from his fifty or so books that he felt conveyed what he had to say with special clarity and force. The result was *The Essential Colin Wilson* (1985), an excellent "taster" of Wilson's ideas.

Selections range from *The Outsider* and *Religion and the Rebel* to *The Occult, Mysteries*, and *A Criminal History of Mankind*, with a notable pick of some of his fiction. Wilson believed that a passage, "Vision on the Eiger," from *The Black Room*, showed his fiction at its best. In it Gradwohl, a German philosopher and part of the team trying to beat the black room, tells Kit Butler, Wilson's alter ego, about the time he and his brother climbed the north face of the Eiger, one of the most difficult ascents in mountaineering. They ran into trouble and found themselves trapped on a thin ledge in the darkness and cold, overlooking the town below. Yet Gradwohl found himself inexplicably happy. "Why did I suddenly feel so happy, hanging there like a fly, and looking at the lights?" he asks. The people below, in their warm, comfortable beds, were not happy, Gradwohl knew, because they took them for granted. They suffered from "false fatigue" and the "mistaken feeling that life is not really worth living." But he and his brother had just driven their wills to the limit and were using them to quite literally hang on for dear life. They *knew*, beyond all shadow of a doubt, that life *was* worth living. They had climbed the mountain to *remind themselves* of this. Gradwohl tells Butler that their business is evolution. "We shouldn't be drifting like the rest of the fools."

One important selection is a lecture Wilson gave at the University of Bristol in 1982, in honor of the economist E. F. Schumacher, author of the classic *Small Is Beautiful* (1973). Wilson remarks that he was planning to write a book about Schumacher when he heard that he had died, in 1977. He believed that Schumacher's ideas about "economics as if people mattered" were an extension in a social context of his own ideas, and he felt that his lecture "Peak Experiences" was one of the "clearest and most compressed summaries" of his philosophy. The central point he makes is about what he calls "the underpinning of everyday consciousness," what he refers to as a kind of "underfloor lighting." This is the basic attitude we have toward the world, and for most of us it is negative. Stuck in our robotic left-brain consciousness, we see the world as flat and uninteresting or, in many cases, feel it is out to get us. This leads to reluctance, our stinginess with our energy, and eventually to "life failure." What we need to do, Wilson says, is to somehow convince our subconscious mind that this attitude is wrong and to exchange it for a more positive outlook. This is something more than positive thinking, although of course that helps. We need to sink the knowledge, the intellectual conviction that our everyday experience of the world is a kind of cheat, down into our subconscious. "Because we easily slip into boredom," Wilson writes, "our subconscious premises tend to be negative. . . . We feel the world is basically a dull place," and because we do, we *see* it as such. Yet the effect of crisis dispels this illusion; we see, as Graham Greene did, that the world is really "full of infinite potential." If we could clearly recognize this, we could "gradually reverse the negative assumption that underlies consciousness." By doing this, we can "reprogram our underfloor lighting." Doing this would make available to us our "inner storeroom," where we have collected hundreds of reasons why life is infinitely fascinating, but which we lose sight of because of our negative assumptions.[39]

Other projects kept him busy. A new novel, his first since his aborted Inspector Saltfleet series, explored the idea of the self-image. *The Personality Surgeon* tells how Dr. Charles Peruzzi, an "overworked general practitioner," came to invent a way of improving people's self-image using a video camera and a digital paint box. Perruzi and his colleague Erik Topelius find that by adjusting a person's image of him- or herself, they can release dormant energies and levels of purpose that would have otherwise remained hidden. Toward the end of the novel Wilson introduces himself as a character and tells the tale of how he came to write the book, another sign of his innovativeness in writing fiction.

Soon after *The Personality Surgeon*, Wilson expanded on his sections on Rudolf Steiner in *The Psychic Detectives* and *Afterlife* to produce his short biography, *Rudolf Steiner: The Man and His Vision*. In a way it is an accident that Wilson came to write the book. He had been approached by a publisher in the mid-1970s with the idea of writing a book on Steiner, but when he came to do it, he found he couldn't. The style of Steiner's books was "as appetizing as dry toast," but even worse was their content, which Wilson found "outlandish and bizarre." (These were Steiner's writings about Atlantis and Lemuria.) Wilson persevered but "in large doses, Steiner simply infuriated" him, so he had to back out of the commission.[40] The publisher turned to James Webb, the brilliant occult historian, and asked him to take on the job. Webb did, but soon after he began to show signs of mental instability and on May 8, 1980, he blew his brains out.[41] After writing about psychometry and the afterlife, Wilson began to have second thoughts about Steiner, especially after reading his early philosophical works on Goethe. His excitement about these led him to write too much about Steiner in *The Psychic Detectives*, and the cut material formed the basis for his biography. Again, like his books on Jung and Gurdjieff, the reader learns as much about Wilson's ideas as he does about Steiner's. Nevertheless the book is a very readable introduction to Steiner's basic ideas.

It was around this time that Wilson returned again to fiction, beginning what would become his longest effort in it yet, his Spider World series. This came about through a meeting with his neighbor, Donald Seaman, a retired newspaperman who had begun a career as a writer of espionage novels. Wilson used to meet Seaman as they walked their dogs on the cliffs around Gorran Haven, and although Seaman had had some success with his thrillers, he frequently experienced "the difficulties of most authors who try to live by writing alone."[42] In short, he was often low on funds.

The *Encyclopaedia of Modern Murder* (1983) came about because Wilson wanted to help Seaman out of some financial difficulties. He suggested they collaborate on a sequel to his *Encyclopaedia of Murder*. Like its predecessor it is an A to Z of violence, but the follow-up featured more recent examples of the "sadism that springs out of a kind of boredom," and which was linked to a "disorder that lies in the realm of the personality."[43] Wilson very graciously let Seaman use the advance to pay his debts. Seaman then suggested another collaboration, an encyclopedia of scandal. At first Wilson demurred, and most readers would think scandal wasn't a topic that would interest him, having been at the center of it often enough in his angry days. But the more Wilson thought about it, the more it seemed possible. He came to see that "great scandals afford the same opportunity to study the curious complexities of human nature as the famous criminal cases."[44] The result was a collection of highly readable gossip about an unusual group of people: the silent film comedian Fatty Arbuckle; Carlo Gesualdo, the composer and murderer; two U.S. presidents, Kennedy and Nixon; and Carlos Castaneda, among them. Wilson later collaborated with Seaman on another murder book, *The Serial Killers* (1990), bringing his analysis of motiveless murder up to date.

Seaman, who seemed perpetually in debt, was trying to think of another book when Wilson had an inspiration. He had watched a television program about insects and he suddenly had the idea of a novel about a future earth where giant telepathic spiders rule and breed human beings for food. The hero would be a young boy, a teenager, who learns how to access his own hidden powers and frees his people from captivity. Wilson suggested that he and Seaman write it together. He agreed. Wilson's publisher commissioned the book and again Wilson let Seaman have the advance, an act of largesse that annoyed Joy, given that their own debt was as much a problem as Seaman's.

Wilson was a much faster writer than Seaman and what happened was much like the aborted collaboration with Bill Hopkins and Stuart Holroyd that produced *The Age of Defeat*. Wilson began to get excited by the idea. He researched a great deal of material on arachnids, becoming something of an amateur arachnologist in the process. As he began writing he "experienced a sensation like an aeroplane taking off." He had never felt "so completely gripped" by anything he had written.[45] Whenever Seaman asked when it would be his turn to write, Wilson's reply was "Let me do a few more pages." In the end Seaman realized the book had become Wilson's. He dropped out of the collaboration; generous as ever, Wilson allowed him to keep the advance. Wilson's inspiration carried on. In the end the result would be a four-volume work, which appeared irregularly between 1987 and 2003, that in a way is Wilson's own attempt at a *Lord of the Rings* epic. The series has achieved a cult following and Richard Adams, author of the classic *Watership Down*, called it a "really fine work of imaginative fantasy." (Last I heard there was film interest as well.) As Colin Stanley writes, with Spider World Wilson "succeeds in integrating his philosophical ideas into the framework of an absorbing and gripping story." The first volume, *Spider World: The Tower* (1987) is dedicated to Sally, Damon, and Rowan. The children's author Roald Dahl once suggested to Wilson that he write a children's book. This was it.

After finishing the first part of Spider World, Wilson needed a break. It's not surprising. He had become so excited with the idea that he wrote a quarter of a million words, which meant that it had to be published in two volumes. He had also started another collaboration, this time with his son Damon, who was now a young man. *The Encyclopedia of Unsolved Mysteries* (1987) set the mold for later collaborations and for various supermarket "tabloid" books about crime or the occult, drawing on material from previous works, such as *World Famous Unsolved Crimes* (1992) or *The Mammoth Book of the Supernatural* (1991); with some of these Rowan also took a hand. These pulpy works, taken on, one assumes, strictly for financial reasons, did not do Wilson's reputation with serious critics any good and one can question his judgment in doing them. But the money, always needed, was good, and the material itself was gripping, as all good "true crime" literature should be.

The break Wilson needed came with an invitation from Japan to take part in a tour of Buddhist monasteries. Wilson was big in Japan; beginning with *The Outsider*, practically everything he had written had been translated into Japanese, even magazine articles. When his Japanese publisher decided to put out a new edition of *The Occult*, he sent Wilson a ten-thousand-pound check, roughly twelve thousand dollars, in advance. The invitation to the tour included Joy, first-class travel, and an honorarium of several thousand dollars. Not surprisingly, Wilson accepted.

His hosts were the monks of the Koyasan monastery, one of the most important centers of Japanese Buddhism. The reason for the tour was the thousandth anniversary of the founding of the Koyasan temple by a monk named Kōbō Daishi, also known as Kūkai. The sect he founded is known as Shingon or esoteric Buddhism. It originated in the Vajrayana or Tantric school of practice in India and made its way to China and then Japan in the seventh century AD. Wilson writes that while he had learned much from Buddhism, he found its doctrine of detachment too negative, and had always preferred Hinduism's aim of union with Brahman. The aim of self-discipline, he thought, was not to detach oneself from life, as the Buddha preached, but to awaken the potentialities of consciousness, the kinds of powers he had been writing about since *The Occult*. Yet Shingon Buddhism is esoteric, and like its cousin Tibetan Buddhism, it is much concerned with the occult and states of consciousness; it employs rituals, mantras, mandalas, and other means to achieve its aim of "enlightenment in this life." This was something Wilson also pursued, and after he learned this he felt that his aims and that of the monks were closer than he thought. He and his hosts, he felt, would have much in common.

Unfortunately much of the tour was something of a blur for Wilson, whose body clock failed to adjust to the time difference, or his stomach to the cuisine. Wilson was also stunned by the celebrity he apparently enjoyed in Japan. One young professor surprised him by saying that in England he must be as famous as Charles Dickens; he was baffled when Wilson said that in fact he was not well known at all, certainly not as well as Dickens. In Japan it was different. At a book signing at a large bookstore the queue went around the block. Press conferences were packed. It was a rerun of his reception in the Middle East, with Wilson being feted by important dignitaries and applauded at huge banquets. The respect was gratifying but as usual, he soon tired of the fuss; he often had to call on his inner reserves to avoid sinking down behind his indifference threshold. Wilson noted that the monks enjoyed drinking scotch—he stuck to sake—and he was understandably charmed by the Japanese custom of handing guests envelopes filled with money after interviews or television appearances.

Wilson enjoyed his visits to the temples; the rock gardens and demon guardians fascinated him, even with his tiredness. He learned from reading Kōbō Daishi's discourses how best to approach them. He would relax completely into a state of deep calm, something he had learned how to do when overcoming his panic attacks. He would listen attentively to the silence and found that he often "penetrated to the other side" of it. The temples themselves helped him. Like psychometric objects, they had recorded the centuries of prayer and meditation, and in his relaxed state, Wilson was able to "read" this, to feel the deep spirituality of the place. Then he could catch glimpses of an "underlying reality . . . not normally accessible to the senses."[46]

The actual ceremony celebrating the temple's thousandth anniversary was, however, something of an endurance test. The vast temple, open on all sides, was located on a mountain. It was October. Wilson and the other speakers, Lyall Watson and Fritjof Capra, sat in its center, before a huge mandala. The morning began with a Buddhist service. Wilson took the precaution of wearing a leather coat, but Watson and Capra were unprepared and shivered. Wilson's lecture that day—which had to be translated as he spoke—was on what he called the "pyramid of consciousness." Our consciousness, he said, is usually like billiard balls spread out on a pool table. When we concentrate we, in a sense, rack the balls up and get them in line. But if we concentrate even further, the inner pressure *squeezes* the balls until they begin to pop up to form another layer. If we can do that for long enough, Wilson believed, a pyramid would be formed that would never collapse, because the self-perpetuating intensity would keep it in place. It was an idea he would return to.

After Japan, Wilson went to Australia, where he lectured at La Trobe University in Melbourne and met Howard Dossor, then engaged in writing his study of Wilson, *Colin Wilson: The Man and his Mind* (1990), the first book about Wilson to appear for many years.[47] Wilson found Australia somewhat less enlightening than Japan. He noted in his journal that Australian students were given to littering, even when rubbish bins were well at hand, something the Japanese would never dream of doing. He remarked that the kind of irresponsibility shown in throwing beer cans in a flower bed was the beginning of criminality.

When Wilson returned to Cornwall it was time to think of another book—or actually to decide whether or not to accept a commission he had already been offered for one. But relatively minor efforts occupied him first. He coedited a collection of essays, *Marx Refuted* (1987), whose title suggests its content. Wilson's friend the poet Ronald Duncan had conceived the idea and after Duncan's death in 1982, Wilson brought the project to completion. Wilson felt that Marx was as pernicious a blight on western consciousness as Freud and Darwin, and the book was aimed at spelling out the reasons why. It was his most political statement and he shared the bill with some heavy hitters, ex-Marxists such as Arthur Koestler and the philosopher Leszek Kolakowski, and anti-Marxists such as the philosopher Karl Popper and the then–UK Prime Minister Margaret Thatcher. Wilson was for a time a Thatcher supporter, an unpopular status in Britain, although he later changed his mind.[48] (Thatcher was the UK's Ronald Reagan.) His working-class roots might suggest a leaning toward the Labour Party—equivalent to the U.S. Democrats—but Wilson's philosophy of effort and responsibility put him in the conservative camp. He felt that the "cradle to grave" welfare state initiated after World War II only made people lazy. Wilson notes that in the book he predicted the downfall of the Soviet Union two years before it happened. He felt that increasingly there was the "possibility of a world in which communism has simply vanished, overturned by the masses it was supposed to represent. . . . History," he declared, "is not only gradual." In this case, at least, he was right, and when he heard about the fall of the Berlin wall he was gratified. *The Decline and Fall of Leftism* (1990), a short essay, dots the *i*'s and crosses the *t*'s on Wilson's political stance.

His short book *Aleister Crowley: The Nature of the Beast* (1987) was another in his brief introductions to the occult greats. Wilson had written about Crowley before. He took his "magick" seriously, but his assessment of the "Great Beast" as a man of unquestioned brilliance who was unfortunately a failure as a human being—Crowley was in many ways a Right Man—did not endear Wilson's critical study to Crowley's followers. Nevertheless the book, like the others in the series, is a very readable introduction to the dark magician's turbulent life. *Jack the Ripper: Summing Up and Verdict* (1987), produced with Robin Odell and J. H. H. Gaute, concerned another unsavory character, and brought together a collection of essays to celebrate a hundred years of "Ripperology." It was also around this time that Wilson began to contribute small pieces to Colin Stanley's Paupers' Press, a cottage publishing effort that Stanley, Wilson's bibliographer, began out of his devotion to Wilson's work. Two early efforts started what would become a decades-long friendship and association. *An Essay on the 'New' Existentialism* (1986) compressed the essence of Wilson's ideas into a concise overview and introduction. *The Musician as 'Outsider'* (1987) picks up from where *Brandy of the Damned*, his first book on music, left off, and brings Romantic composers such as Berlioz, Brahms, Schuman, and Beethoven into the Outsider discussion. Wilson admired Beethoven, who said that those who understand his music "must be freed by it from all the miseries which others drag around with them." Beethoven jettisoned his miseries by overcoming his self-pity and truculent personality and reaching for the *impersonal* bird's-eye view. The composers who followed him were less robust and by the end of the nineteenth century the imaginative explosion that had fueled earlier giants had dwindled to the tragic pessimism that Wilson felt informs the music of Mahler, Schoenberg, and other late Romantics.

While in Australia Wilson had heard from an editor at HarperCollins who asked if he would be interested in doing another book on the occult. At first Wilson was put off. He felt the same as he had before starting *Mysteries*. He had said pretty much all he had to say about the subject and felt that in writing about it again he would only be repeating himself. But while in Melbourne his mind started to play with the idea and again it seemed that perhaps he hadn't said all he had to say about it just yet. In fact he could take the opportunity to summarize all he had learned about the paranormal in the past twenty years. If he had to repeat himself, so be it. In truth, when it came time to write the book, "so much new material came to light that the real problem was how to incorporate it all."[49]

Wilson felt that *Beyond the Occult* (1988) was his most important nonfiction book—quite a status, given the many books under his belt.[50] It had earned this honor because in it Wilson felt he had brought his existential and occult ideas together in their most creative synthesis. It is true that much of the material in *Beyond the Occult* Wilson had already covered; readers of *The Occult*, *Mysteries*, *The Psychic Detectives*, and *Afterlife* found themselves in some familiar territory. We again visit the spirit world, travel in time with psychometry, meet the objective and subjective minds, look at multiple personalities, and investigate a variety of paranormal and mystical experiences. But Wilson was once again determined to fuse this disparate material into some intellectually satisfying order, and as with his book on Gurdjieff, the effort of doing this and the unavoidable repetitions it entailed triggered new meanings and implications. He also introduces much new material; for example, he takes a longer look at hypnagogic experiences through the seminal work of Andreas Mavromatis and gives an overview of the teaching of Daskalos, "the magus of Strovolos." Another new angle of approach was forging a link between peak experiences and "affirmation consciousness" and the kinds of paranormal abilities under scrutiny.

Wilson always had the conviction that "all human beings possess 'hidden powers.'" He mentions his own experience of feeling Joy's birth pangs and even her toothache, and tells of a friend who had found herself floating up above her body while seriously ill.[51] Yet it was not these kinds of "powers" that really interested him, as fascinating as they are. What had obsessed him since childhood were those "strange moments of pure joy" when he experienced "an almost god-like sensation of power or freedom." These were the peaks, the moments of the "other mode of consciousness" that had become his life-long study.

Was there any connection between the two? Were mystical or peak experiences part of a gradient that included the kinds of experiences we would call paranormal? Wilson recalled a moment when, during his first trip to France, he was hitchhiking to Strasbourg, and a truck driver had given him a lift to a roadside café. He had enjoyed a meal and a glass of wine and as he looked out at the mountains in the distance he experienced a "feeling of joy that was so complete that all the problems of my life vanished into insignificance."[52] It was not merely a feeling but a *seeing*. He knew, once again, that what was wrong with human beings is that they are too *close* to life, and that such closeness deprives us of meaning. This is what leads to the fallacy of insignificance and the pessimism that undermined the old existentialism. We need to be able to step back from the constant press of things and gain perspective. And we seem to already possess the ability to do this: a piece of cake or a glass of wine can often do the trick, as Proust and Hermann Hesse discovered. If we could learn how to activate this "distancing" at will, "our lives would be transformed." As it is we waste most of our lives dealing with minor problems that we vastly exaggerate. If we could learn how to turn on the "visionary faculty" at will, the earth itself could be transfigured, since "most of the ugliness and evil of our lives is due to stress and 'close-upness.'"[53]

Again, what fascinated Wilson about these moments of vision is that they seem to suggest a completely different way of getting knowledge than our usual step-by-step approach. "When the visionary faculty is switched on," he writes, "the mind seems to be able to penetrate reality . . . and to grasp meanings that normally elude it." Wilson came to see that these meanings can have a paranormal or a mystical content. He speaks of Jacob Boehme's vision looking at sunlight on a pewter dish, mentioned earlier, when Boehme saw into "the principles and deepest foundations of things." This, he suggests, is not that different from the kinds of experience that make up the paranormal, when people suddenly seem to have a *knowledge* they shouldn't. Both types of experience also seem to happen when we are relaxed. Boehme was content staring at reflected sunlight when he suddenly felt that he learned more in a quarter of an hour than if he had spent years at a university. Psychics speak of quieting their minds, of emptying them, in order to allow any messages to come through. In both the mystical and the paranormal there seems to be a kind of *direct* knowing, not mediated by the usual routines of the intellect. In both a kind of *shift* of consciousness occurs, a kind of *turning inward* that reveals another world.

In an important book, *Toward a General Theory of the Paranormal* (1969), the psychologist Lawrence LeShan corroborated what Wilson suspected. LeShan, too, had suspected that the kind of shift that took place in paranormal experiences was not that different from a comparable shift in the mind of the mystic. LeShan had asked the famous psychic Eileen Garrett what it felt like to receive psychic information. He interviewed other psychics too, and asked the same question. They replied that when they were receiving paranormal information "the world look[ed] different than at other times."[54] Garrett said it was a "withdrawal of the conscious self into an area of the non-conscious self." It was, she said, like being "in two worlds at once." This was much like Wilson's duo-consciousness and also like his belief that poets are naturally psychic. In a later compilation of his occult writings edited by his son Damon, Wilson makes the same point speaking of the novelist John Cowper Powys, who seems to have displayed both mystical and paranormal abilities. In his novel *Wolf Solent* (1929), Powys describes his hero's joy at finding himself alone in a train compartment. This meant he was able to give himself up to "an orgy of concentrated thought" that would expand the few hours of the journey into "something beyond all human measurement." This was accomplished by a "certain trick" of "sinking into his soul," what Powys called "mythologizing."[55] He knew how to turn away from the outer world and focus his attention on his inner one. This is the same turnabout that is at work in active imagination, hypnagogic experiences, and other inner journeys. It is also what psychics and mystics do.

Wilson gives accounts of mystical experience, provided by everyday people, in order to show that the visionary faculty is not some rare gift, but a potential of consciousness shared by everyone. Yet the "most remarkable of all accounts of mystical experience" he says must be the one Ouspensky left us in the chapter "Experimental Mysticism" in *A New Model of the Universe*.[56] Following certain procedures, which most likely included inhaling nitrous oxide, Ouspensky found himself confronting a world that was unlike anything he could imagine. It was a world in which "everything is unified." There was "nothing separate . . . nothing that can be named or described *separately*." This strange new world had "no sides, so that it is impossible to describe first one side and the other." Ouspensky found it was impossible to speak to anyone about this. As he began to explain something, new thoughts entered his mind so swiftly that before he could complete a sentence he was off on another tangent. Time had altered, and at some points seemed to stop entirely. His inner and outer worlds seemed to have changed places. Everything radiated a tremendous *meaning*, so powerful that Ouspensky was overcome by the simplest object; an ashtray brought him to the brink of madness. He experienced William James's "distant ranges of increasing fact" as if a tidal wave of knowledge rushed over him. One facet of this strange new world that remained with him was that it seemed to be made of "very complicated mathematical relations."[57]

As Wilson writes about Ouspensky's and other mystical experiences, they seem to reveal a world that is shot through with *meaning*, and trigger the recognition that the universe is not, as science and the old existentialism would have it, a collection of random events. It exhibits an overall pattern and purpose. Mystical experiences show that the universe is "a gigantic pattern, like an enormous flower." Such visions invariably fill us with "courage and optimism."[58] Wilson suggests that while perhaps not so intense, the experiences of Faculty X that Hesse's Steppenwolf has after a glass of wine or that Toynbee had at the ruins of Mistra are close cousins to the type of experience Ouspensky grappled with. And these experiences themselves were not that far removed from the kinds of peaks Maslow had spoken of, when a mother had a sudden moment of joy getting her children off to school, or a Marine suddenly recognized that women are very different from men. If these "visions" were all on the same gradient then there should be a way to "build a bridge between everyday experience and the experience of the mystic."[59]

Such a bridge exists, and it reaches from one side of our brain to the other.

The real world, the world revealed during mystical illumination, is not like our everyday world, and within it our everyday ways of knowing and understanding simply don't work. Wilson points out that the philosopher Henri Bergson realized this earlier in the century. Bergson argued that while excellent for enabling us to maneuver through the world, the intellect is not very good at grasping reality. When we try to do this, it slips through our fingers. What is time? Where does space end? Our mind numbs when faced with these questions. What was needed for this, Bergson said, was intuition, which was a way of getting *inside* the world, knowing it from *within*. The intellect looks at things from outside and analyzes experience into parts. This is good for obvious uses, but it is useless if we want to grasp the *reality* of things. The intellect falsifies reality to a great extent in order to make it manageable for us. What seems to happen in mystical moments is that we see the world through intuition, not intellect, and the experience can be overwhelming.

But the intuition that enables mystical experiences is also at work in paranormal ones. Bergson served as president of the SPR and like Joseph Rodes Buchanan, he believed that the past is still alive and can be accessed in the present. Bergson believed that the brain serves as a kind of filter—much as Wilson has argued—and that in reality we are capable of knowing everything that is happening in the universe, or *has happened* in it, but our brain filters this information out because it is irrelevant to our survival. Bergson wrote that "the whole past still exists . . . is still present to consciousness in such a manner that, to have the revelation of it, consciousness has no need to go out of itself. . . . It has but to remove an obstacle, to withdraw a veil."[60] For Bergson the obstacle was the intellect, and in the difference between intellect and intuition we can clearly see the same difference as between the left and right brain, or the objective and subjective mind.[61]

In *Beyond the Occult* Wilson introduces some new concepts which we should consider here. One is his notion of "completing," which is an extension of his ideas about Husserl's intentionality. We have already seen an example of completing, in our look at the difference between someone with a well-furnished mind having a moment of Faculty X and someone less equipped. Toynbee's "time slip" back to the massacre at Mistra happened because he brought his *imagination* and *knowledge* to his experience. He was able to fill in the blanks with what he possessed himself. Someone less knowledgeable may have had a strange sense that something had happened there, and thought no more of it. Toynbee's knowledge, acquired slowly by his left brain, provided his imagination, fired by his right brain, with the "facts" that were welded together into a moment of Faculty X.

But it is not only in mystical moments that completing is at work. If we did not add our imagination to *all* of our experience, we would, in a very real sense, not have it. "Our minds," Wilson writes, "are inclined to accept the present moment as it is, without question"; this is Husserl's "natural standpoint." "We accept the present moment *as if it were complete in itself.*" But as Wilson says, "a little reflection reveals that this is a gargantuan mistake." The present moment, he argues, is always incomplete, and "the most basic activity of the mind is 'completing' it." Wilson asks us to imagine an alien finding himself on a London bus. The world that we take for granted would appear a chaos to him because he would not know the things we do. It is our *knowledge* of things that gives them their meaning; it is what we *bring* to them. Sartre's *Nausea* depicts a world in which consciousness no longer completes things, with the result that they become alien and threatening. Without our knowledge, reality is meaningless. And as we've seen Wilson finds some form of completing at work in practically everything we do—in sex, art, philosophy. The senses, he writes, "only reveal the limited reality of the immediate present, and this would be meaningless to us unless it was 'completed' by our minds."[62]

Another important concept Wilson introduces is "upside-downness." This is a state in which the place of our long-term purposes and values is taken over by our short-term ones. These lower values are invariably egocentric and emotional, much like the values that drive many criminals. It is a condition in which our underfloor lighting is very dim. Our faith in reason gives way to emotionality and our optimism to negativity. Unfortunately, upside-downness is the norm in our culture and this is doubly dangerous because it receives the ratification of the intellect. Pessimistic writers such as Sartre, Beckett, Greene, and others—we can add any of their contemporary counterparts—tell us the world is grim and meaningless, and so we feel we are justified in giving way to negative emotions. We see no reason not to.

But, as Wilson says, giving way to negative emotions turns the world upside down. We see it through the thick fog of subjectivity. Wilson says that when we are really happy it is because we are *free* of our emotions and can see things objectively. We could even say that objectivity and happiness are the same thing. When we are upside down, we accept the worm's-eye view, make mountains out of molehills, and are more likely to abandon any kind of control and release our tensions through anger and violence. We waste our lives complaining that the world does not go out of its way to make us happy. Trivialities take on enormous importance and we begin to feel what Wilson calls "the Ecclesiastes effect," the sense that there is nothing new under the sun and so there is no reason to make any effort. But when reason arises like the sun and dispels the haze of emotion, I know that "it is worth making tremendous efforts and I summon my vital energies accordingly."[63]

This is important, not only because without making efforts our will goes to sleep and we suffer life failure, although this is crucial. Wilson tells us that when we are optimistic and live purposefully, the hidden powers that we all possess become active. As mentioned, Wilson found that when he was working well, synchronicities tended to happen, and that when he was depressed, his luck was invariably bad. Examples of this run throughout the book. He writes that while working on an article about synchronicity he mentioned the story of Jacques Vallee, the UFO researcher, and the order of Melchizedek, a California cult named after the biblical prophet. Vallee was trying to research the group but could find little about them. At one point he took a taxi and when he asked for a receipt he saw that the driver's name was Melchizedek. Vallee was struck by the coincidence and decided to see how many Melchizedeks were in the telephone book. He found one, his taxi driver. Wilson said it was as if he had stuck a notice on a cosmic bulletin board—"Needed: information on Melchizedek,—and the "angel of the library" said, "How about this one?"

When Wilson finished his article he was about to leave his study when he found a book lying on his camp-bed. It was about life after death. When he picked it up it opened to a page headed "Order of Melchizedek." It was precisely the cult Vallee had been researching. Wilson writes: "I have just about thirty thousand books in this house and I doubt whether any other contains a reference to the Order of Melchizedek. But I had to stumble on this one after writing about Vallee's remarkable coincidence."[64]

Wilson concludes from this and from other similar experiences that "synchronicities produce a sense of the underlying meaningfulness of the universe, the feeling that in spite of all appearances we are not accidents of nature who have been stranded in a universe of chance."[65] As Wilson says, "We are *all* at our best when the imagination is awake, and we can sense the presence of that 'other self', the intuitive part of us. When we are tired or discouraged we feel 'stranded' in left-brain consciousness. . . . It must be irritating for 'the other self' to find its partner so dull and sluggish. . . . A synchronicity can snap us into a sudden state of alertness and awareness. And if the 'other self' can, by the use of its peculiar powers, bring about a synchronicity, then there is still time to prevent us from wasting yet another day of our brief lives."[66]

Other paranormal experiences seem to be associated with more optimistic states and none are more bizarre than precognition. While it is not too difficult to accept that in some way, the past is still with us—after all, we have a whole technology that captures it these days, on film, video, digital media—the idea that we can get knowledge of an event *that has not yet happened* seems beyond belief. Yet Wilson provides case after case in which this has been so. This leads us to question our notions of time, but even more important, it leads us to question the idea of free will. If we are somehow able to "see" an event that has not yet taken place, but which turns out to be true, this suggests that our lives are, as mechanical science has always maintained, predictable, and that the forces working on us now make inescapable the actions we will take in the future. It is the old argument of cause and effect. Yet while in many cases it does seem that our lives follow a track already laid out—after all, according to Gurdjieff we are all machines, an assessment Wilson agrees with insofar as we remain subject to the robot—there are also cases in which precognition has enabled someone to *change* a likely future.

Wilson looks at the remarkable precognitive dreams of J. W. Dunne recounted in his popular book *An Experiment with Time* (1927). By accident Dunne discovered that he had dreams of future events, and he suggested that if people recorded their dreams, they would see that they did too. One person who took up Dunne's challenge was the writer J. B. Priestley, who called himself a "time-haunted man." In his book *Man and Time* (1964) Priestley recounts the story of a woman who dreamt that her baby drowned while at a river. In the dream, the woman is with the baby by a river and, wanting to wash, goes back to her tent for the soap. It is only a short distance and she is only away for a few seconds, but when she returns the baby has fallen into the water and drowned. Not long after, the woman did find herself at a campsite. She was by a river with her baby and wanted to wash. She had forgotten the soap, and as she was about to get up to get it, she remembered the dream. Everything was in exact detail, *except* that now she decided to bring the baby with her.

Had her "hidden guest" or "other self" somehow told her *in advance* a likely event, so that she would be able to avoid it? Perhaps our other self sends us similar messages that we ignore simply because we are not aware of them. Wilson suggests that it may not be the case that "future events have already taken place." While "fairly rigidly predetermined" our lives are not "absolutely so." Most of us have some power to alter events. But only if we do not allow ourselves to let our robot do our living for us.

But how can we get beyond the robot? Wilson was about to return to a familiar subject in order to find out.

CHAPTER TWELVE

MISFITS AND ATLANTEANS

In "Below the Iceberg," an essay about the development of his ideas, Wilson talked about *Beyond the Occult*, spelling out why he felt it was his most important work. He says "below" the iceberg rather than "the tip of the iceberg" when referring to our hidden powers because it had always seemed to him that these powers extend into the very "sea" in which our consciousness rests.[1] If our conscious mind is just the "tip" of the unconscious mind, the unconscious itself—or whatever we want to call it—reaches into even greater depths. How far these depths descend is anyone's guess. Synchronicities suggest they reach into the outer world itself, prompting the idea that perhaps both our inner and outer worlds arise from some incomprehensible *other* source, distinct from either one; this is something that thinkers such as Jung, the physicist David Bohm, and the philosopher Jean Gebser have suggested. Some of these depths have been plumbed by people such as Ouspensky, Jung, Steiner, and the other visionaries and psychonauts Wilson has labored to understand. He says that he began the book reluctantly, afraid that he was "merely regurgitating" something he had already expressed.[2] But as he went on he felt that it was worth the effort and that he was creating a "new synthesis." In fact, the effort of writing about something that he felt he already knew taught him an important lesson.

"The problem with human beings," he began to see, "is that it is possible to 'know' something without really knowing it."[3] Proust "knew" about his childhood holidays in Combray, but until he tasted the madeleine, he didn't *really* know it. This "really knowing" is the central problem of human consciousness; it is, of course, the essence of Faculty X. Wilson thought he knew all about the occult and the existential dilemma of the Outsider—after all, he had been writing about these things for decades. But in writing about them again, he realized that his knowledge was in fact superficial. "In order to really *know* something," he saw, "we must meditate upon it until we have absorbed it into our being."

(Whitehead would say we must "prehend" it.) Even writing the essay, Wilson says, brought a flash of this truth to him again. Why is it so difficult for us to *really know* something? And why do we forget it so easily once we do?[4]

Wilson had seen that we *can* really know something. His study of mystical and paranormal experience had shown him this. In such states, the "powers" that appear somehow enable us to "read the 'information' encoded in the universe around us."[5] This information can be a specific item of knowledge, such as the messages that psychics receive. Or it can be a glimpse of the true nature of reality, such as the kind of insight that Ouspensky and other mystical explorers had been granted. It can be a peek at some moment in history, as Toynbee had experienced, or a sudden return to our own past, as Proust's madeleine had given him. In each case, the experience was one of going *beyond* the present, of stepping outside the four walls of our given moment in time. "The universe seen by the clairvoyant has much in common with the universe seen by the mystic," Wilson believed. "And both are *bigger* and more complete than the universe seen by the rest of us."[6]

What struck Wilson as a new insight is that the powers that enable us to gain this knowledge seem not to have evolved as, say, our powers of understanding through the left brain have. They seem to be "already in place."[7] As R. H. Ward said about his experience with nitrous oxide, "I passed, after the first few inhalations of the gas, directly into a state of consciousness already far more complete than the fullest degree of ordinary waking consciousness." Ward spoke of "rediscovering" something "which had once been mine" and said that the state was oddly familiar, while his everyday, ordinary state seemed strange.[8] And in any case, the kinds of powers Wilson was thinking of differed from other paranormal abilities. Dowsing, telepathy, the kind of "jungle sensitivity" that the hunter Jim Corbett displayed—his *Man-Eaters of Kumaon* (1944) was avidly read by a young Wilson—and other psychic powers could be explained as leftovers from an earlier time in our evolution. These abilities had a practical application, but with the rise of civilization they were no longer useful; hence our left-brain consciousness repressed them. But there was no survival advantage whatever in being able to enter mystical states or to pick out twelve-digit prime numbers instantaneously. While amazing and fascinating, there didn't seem to be anything one could *do* with these powers, in the way that the ability to find water underground or to know if a distant relative was in danger could have practical use. This led Wilson to modify the "creative evolutionary" position he had held since *The Outsider*. Shaw, Bergson, and other creative evolutionists saw life as a blind, striving will that gradually developed the means of understanding itself and its purposes. It moved in a bottom-up direction. Yet Wilson was beginning to think in terms of descent, of life or spirit leaving realms of greater freedom and *purposefully* entering into matter in order to colonize it.

"All mystical experience," he saw, "leaves us confronted by the same fundamental question: What are we doing here?"[9] Gurdjieff once told Ouspensky that the earth is in a very bad place in the universe. He compared it to outer Siberia, where everything is hard, life is grim, and mere day-to-day existence is extremely difficult. Wilson himself says that in terms of our consciousness, it is as if we lived on a planet whose gravity is so powerful that it takes an enormous effort merely to lift our limbs. Ouspensky felt something of this after his experiences with nitrous oxide. When he "returned to earth" following his mystical states, he was profoundly depressed. He felt that the world he had returned to was "extraordinarily oppressive." It was "incredibly empty, colorless, and lifeless." He compared it to an "enormous wooden machine with creaking wooden wheels, wooden thoughts, wooden moods, wooden sensations. . . . They were terrible," Ouspensky wrote, "these moments of awakening in an unreal world after a real one, in a dead world after a living, in a limited world, cut into small pieces, after an infinite and entire world."[10] He even felt that coming back to his "normal" state was "very similar to dying or to what I thought dying must be like."[11]

We see that the world Ouspensky had visited was one perceived with his right brain—it was a living, infinite, and entire world—and that the one he returned to was one seen with the left brain: unreal, dead, limited, cut. (The right brain perceives wholes, while the left analyzes experience into bits and pieces.) We also see that his reaction to returning to his normal state was much like that of the Romantics after their flights of ecstasy: depression and a feeling that they did not belong there. Indeed, in *The Strange Life of P. D. Ouspensky* (1993) Wilson calls Ouspensky a "typical romantic," while at the same time recognizing his genius.[12] Wilson began to wonder. Mystical states seem to give us a glimpse of a world of greater freedom, more meaning, and deeper insight. Paranormal experiences seem to show that the limitations we usually accept are somehow unnecessary. The evidence of spirits seems to say that our life here on earth is only one form of life, and that in some way death is not the end of us. If all this is true, then *why* do we find ourselves here, in outer Siberia, when it seems highly likely that we could be enjoying a much easier existence in some higher spiritual realm?

The answer that suggested itself is that "life" or "spirit" or whatever we'd like to call the force at work here is "attempting to establish a bridgehead in matter." The stakes, Wilson says, are higher than we think. We are, he says, on a "colonizing expedition," and our job is to secure ground for further advancement. The problem is that "after years in these difficult surroundings" the explorers—we—have become so obsessed with simple survival that "they have forgotten why they came here."[13] We have gone native, as it were, and lost sight of our objective. And some of us, the criminal types, are so defeated by the difficulties of living in this world that we resort to ruthless, brutal methods to achieve our aims.

The problem is that we have a bad memory, as Gurdjieff knew and as Wilson now saw. And the reason for this is the robot, the "fundamental source of all human problems." It is the robot that Ouspensky and other inner voyagers return to when their brief excursions into mystical realms are over. The sheer weight of the robot produces the feeling of a "wooden world," and makes a Romantic like Ouspensky regret having to "return to earth." (It was, in fact, the romantic side of Ouspensky that Gurdjieff wanted to dismantle, with debatable results.) After a trip to the higher spheres, we all have to come back to ourselves: to the "boring old habits and worries and neuroses," the "old sense of identity built up from reactions of other people," "the dreary old *heaviness*" that makes our consciousness feel like a "dead weight."[14]

We know that this state of mind is as reliable a source of insight as the headache that follows a night of heavy drinking. Every flash of non-robotic consciousness tells us this, from a spring morning breeze to the sexual orgasm. These glimpses tell us that the world is a much more fascinating and interesting place than we think. Yet we forget this knowledge almost immediately and accept the headache that accompanies our return to earth as an accurate gauge of reality. What keeps us in the thrall of the robot, Wilson saw, is our "unconscious conviction of the truth of 'upside-downness.'" We may give lip service to peak experiences, Faculty X, completing, the indifference threshold, and the rest. But at bottom, we still feel that life is something of a joke, a long, frustrating business that is best got over with as soon as possible. Even some of history's greatest minds tell us this. Socrates said that philosophy is a preparation for death. Aristotle said that it was better not to have been born. The Buddha believed that all life is misery and suffering, and Shakespeare said it was a tale "told by an idiot, signifying nothing." More recent naysayers have joined the chorus. Because our unconscious mind sees the world topsy-turvy, we rarely make an effort to throw off the robot and get back in the driver's seat. And because of this, the vicious circle of pessimism, lack of will, and boredom leading to further pessimism goes on, with the occasional accidental peak experience gratefully accepted as a crumb of undeserved happiness.

Ultimate Yes or Ultimate No? "Until we can make up our minds about this basic question," Wilson writes, "life is bound to be a series of pendulum swings between optimism and pessimism, determination and discouragement." What we need is to grasp that the "apparent 'ordinariness' of the world is a delusion created by the robot," and that moments of absurd good news and affirmation consciousness give us a glimpse of the true character of reality.[15] This is what we need to *really* know. Freedom "does not have to come from some religious or yogic disciple," although these have their virtues. "The most reliable way of achieving it," he says, "is through *intellect*, through knowledge."[16]

Thoughts like these occupied Wilson when he began to think about his next book.

While in Japan one of the strangest encounters Wilson had was with Issei Sagawa, a young man whose macabre claim to fame was that he had spent several years in mental asylums in France and Japan after murdering a young woman and cannibalizing parts of her body. He and his victim were students at the Sorbonne at the time. During his examination it became clear to the police that Sagawa was insane and he was put into a mental institution. Years later he was considered cured and released. He wrote a book about the murder, which became a best seller, and Sagawa acquired a contested celebrity, appearing on television programs and even writing restaurant reviews.

Joy was understandably not happy to meet a killer but Sagawa explained to Wilson that ever since he was a child he had been obsessed with the idea of eating someone. His obsession began at the age of three, when his father and uncle played a game with him, which ended with Sagawa and his brother being put into a pretend pot and then eaten. Sagawa was a tiny, weak child and suffered from ill health. By his late teens fantasies of being eaten, which gave him a strange sexual thrill, had turned into fantasies of eating someone else. The idea was to absorb their "life force," much as the aliens in *The Space Vampires* do. Just before he was due to return to Japan, Sagawa gave way to his fantasies and made them real. He was easily caught and immediately admitted to the crime. Wilson found that Sagawa was not a monster—he was in fact shy, nervous, quite gentle, and somewhat embarrassed about his notoriety. But he was someone who, "for reasons even he did not understand, had been hypnotised by the sexual illusion."[17]

In Australia Wilson had heard of other similar cases. A couple had recently been arrested for the abduction and murder of four women. The man was "sexually insatiable" and the murders were the result of his uncontrollable desire, which his wife helped him satisfy. Another example, Wilson saw, of the sexual illusion. After his experience in the Buddhist temples, the idea that we are all trapped in illusion hit him with new force. He had briefly glimpsed reality while sitting quietly in the temple and focusing his mind. Such glimpses, he knew, are rare these days. They show us the true value of things. But murder cases can also open our eyes, because they depict with brutal clarity the *absence* of these values. This was why Wilson found them to be an important area of study, although friends often ribbed him about the morbid delight he must take in writing about rape and other sex crimes.[18]

Now, back in Cornwall, the problem of the sexual illusion returned and it became the focus of his next book. Donald Seaman once more needed help with his finances and in conversation he casually suggested to Wilson that he should write a book about "sexual Outsiders." Like the occult, sex was something Wilson had written about extensively, and so the prospect of repeating himself did not appeal. But the problem of the sexual illusion demanded some kind of answer. And he realized he had an excellent way to approach it. The story forms the central question behind *The Misfits: A Study of Sexual Outsiders* (1988).

In autumn 1971 Wilson had received in the mail an enormous manuscript titled *Homo Mutans, Homo Luminens*, a rough translation of which is "Man the Changer, Man the Light Giver." It was by a woman named Charlotte Bach, who had been one of the few readers of Wilson's *Origins of the Sexual Impulse*. Bach was Hungarian and had fled the country after the Soviet takeover in 1948, and the style of the manuscript made Wilson wince. By the author's own admission the ideas in it were "practically unintelligible" because of their originality, but she had added to their obscurity by writing in an abstract, turgid prose, filled with a peevish sniping at practically every other thinker she referenced. Wilson's impression was that she was a "highly abrasive and aggressive lady," most likely a "paranoid nut," who esteemed herself very highly and became combative at the slightest hint of criticism.[19] We might even say she was a kind of Right Woman.

Wilson put the manuscript aside and turned to other matters. But one day while confined to bed with a nasty cold, he decided to make an attempt at reading this magnum opus. It was tough going but fairly soon into it Wilson realized that there was *something* there. The author was obviously intelligent and very well read. She referenced philosophers, biologists, zoologists, psychologists, even alchemists—her work, she said, was essentially a form of alchemy. It was obvious that through all the thick verbiage, she did have something to say—although exactly what remained unclear. A generous, encouraging sort, Wilson wrote to her thanking her for the manuscript and saying that it was clearly an important effort. Her reply was somewhat excessive: "Thank you, thank you, thank you, and thank you again," she wrote, and explained that as she had read his letter, she burst into tears.[20]

The gist of Bach's ideas was that inside every man is a woman, and inside every woman is a man, somewhat similar to Jung's conception of the anima and animus. But she goes beyond Jung. Each sex, she argued, has an urge to *become* the other. This urge destabilizes us and is the source of sexual perversion—a question, we know, that occupied Wilson. But this instability is also the source of evolution. Nietzsche had written that "one must have chaos within oneself to give birth to a dancing star." Bach was arguing that the chaos was born of our sexual instability and the dancing star a result of the creative tension this produces. Civilization was not, she claimed, solely the product of man's need for security. It was creative, a result of the dynamic tension of his inbuilt "perversion."

Many of Wilson's Outsiders were unstable and creative, so this seemed to make some sense. But was sexual deviance *really* the motive force behind human evolution, as this difficult text seemed to be saying? Wilson admired her self-confidence; she had told one professor that compared to her ideas, the hydrogen bomb was a "pop gun."[21] He was no advocate of false modesty, but his correspondent did seem to have a knack for going over the top.

When they met in London, Wilson was surprised. Bach turned out to be a "broad-shouldered mammoth of a woman." Her "deep masculine voice" carried a thick Hungarian accent. Wilson was staying with the painter Regis de Cachard—about whom he had written an essay—and after dinner the three returned to de Cachard's flat, where Bach proceeded to drink a considerable amount of wine. She then told them her life story. With the Communist takeover, she and her husband, both lecturers in psychology at Budapest University, had fled Hungary and moved to London. In 1965, a double tragedy struck: Their son was killed in a car accident and then soon after her husband died during an operation. This plunged her into a nervous breakdown. She then decided to compile a dictionary of psychological terms, hoping this would provide some income and perhaps attract the attention of a university. When she came to the term "perversion" it struck her, as it had Wilson, that it had no clear, widely accepted definition (this was in fact why she had read Wilson's book). She decided to do some research herself. The results proved interesting.

She advertised for "deviants" to take part in a study and she was surprised at the response. Among the people she interviewed was an Oxford professor, tweed jacket, pipe, and all. At the interview he asked if he could "behave normally," and proceeded to take off his trousers. Underneath he was wearing black lace panties, stockings, and a garter belt. Bach met other transvestites and came to see that while many homosexuals experienced guilt, these "cross-dressers" didn't. Most of them were not homosexual and enjoyed a good sexual life with their wives. Their only deviation was that they felt it was perfectly normal to wear women's underwear. It was then that she began to think about what this might mean for human evolution.

Wilson listened attentively but he had his doubts about her story. Compiling a book of psychological definitions is not usually a good way of making money. And her interest in deviations suggested a more personal connection. Most likely she was deviant in some way herself, a lesbian, perhaps. But when taking her leave Bach kissed Wilson's artist friend and by his account stuck her tongue halfway down his throat. So she was apparently not a lesbian.[22]

They met a few more times in London and Bach's behavior began to trouble Wilson. She seemed to be acting—overdoing her responses at times, somewhat histrionic. But she had begun to acquire a group of followers (I met some of them many years later) and *Time Out* magazine wanted to interview her and was interested in Wilson writing an article about her ideas. This meant that Wilson would have to understand them himself. He took her to lunch at the Savage Club, and with the tape recorder running, pressed her to explain her ideas, demanding she be as simple as possible.

Transvestitism was not the only thing that led her to see human beings as what we might call "closet androgynies." She had read the zoologist Desmond Morris's paper on the strange behavior of the ten-spined stickleback fish. During mating season, the male stickleback turns black and establishes a certain territory. When a female approaches, she deposits her eggs and the male does a kind of dance while releasing his sperm. At times there are more males than there is territory, and the less dominant sticklebacks are left homeless and lose their black color. If one of these approaches a male with territory, it can be mistaken for a female. The male lets the false female onto his patch; "she" acts as if she is releasing eggs, and the true male does his dance. In this way, the population is controlled; next year there will be more territory because the false females did not, of course, actually release eggs, and so fewer offspring will hatch. A similar turnaround happens with the zebra finch. Males attract females by singing and dancing. If the female fails to respond, the male will begin to act out the female's part and the female will take on his. They have changed roles. Through much study of zoology Bach came to the conclusion that such role reversal is common in nature.

What struck Bach as important was *how* individuals respond to the urge to become the other sex. She worked out eight different character types, depending on how the deviant "tension" is handled.[23] In the end, Bach concluded that types such as transvestites and "butch" lesbians release the tension by giving in to the pull literally, by dressing as the other sex. These types she considered "normal." Because of this they have lost any chance of further evolution, having lost its "mainspring." Conventionally heterosexual males and females are also "normal." The other types are all forms of homosexuals. They maintain the tension—hence the guilt felt by many of the homosexuals she interviewed—and therefore have more possibility of growth. All this came together in a kind of revelation when Bach interviewed a young man who claimed to have experienced an eight-hour orgasm. Bach suspected that he was exaggerating, but when she read Mircea Eliade's *Shamanism* she learned of the prolonged ecstatic states experienced by tribal priests and it clicked. *This*, she saw, was what the tension of deviancy was about.

Wilson once said that his aim as a philosopher was to be able to capture the "meaning content" of the sexual orgasm in words, so it is not surprising that Bach's revelation interested him. Part of the shaman's initiation is precisely the kind of transvestitism that Bach studied, but the end of his trials is to rise *above* sex, to enter ecstatic states that transcend it, much as Wilson, following Shaw, believed was possible. In the shaman, the pull of deviancy produces such a tension that it explodes into a state of mystical consciousness. The same, Wilson saw, could be true of creative geniuses such as Beethoven, who sacrificed sex for his art, or masters such as Leonardo, Michelangelo, and Tchaikovsky, whose guilt about their homosexuality spurred them to greatness.

Yet while Wilson was struck by this, there were still some snags. According to Bach's system, he was a "normal" male, and should therefore not be creative. Yet he was, his critics notwithstanding. Wilson also began to notice odd incongruities in Bach herself. She was broad shouldered and deep voiced, yet she seemed to flaunt her femininity. At a scientific debate Wilson chaired she sat in the front row wearing an enormous hat and constantly fanned herself, distracting the speakers. She seemed not to fit into any of her categories. Nevertheless he wrote the *Time Out* article and included several pages about her work in *Mysteries*, in the context of other ideas about human evolution. She was so pleased that she made many copies of this section of the book and had them bound and distributed to her followers and potential supporters.

Wilson admits to occasionally being a "rather stupid person."[24] The answer to the mystery of Charlotte Bach, he says, stared him in the face, but he was oblivious to it. All was revealed in June 1981. Milk bottles had collected in front of Bach's flat in North London and a concerned neighbor, getting no reply at the door, telephoned the police. They broke in and found Bach's body. At the morgue the medical examiner was surprised. Her breasts, it seemed, were made of foam rubber, and her underwear concealed male genitals. Bach was a man and, by her own account, one of the types that had thrown away their chances at evolution.[25]

Wilson soon learned more about Bach. It seemed the only true item in the story she had told him was that she was Hungarian. Charlotte Bach was really Carl Hajdu and had been born in Budapest in 1920. He had claimed to be the son of a top civil servant, a baron who had lost much of his estates after World War I, and whose title had passed to Carl on his death. But this, too, was untrue. Carl had come from a working-class family and any notions of nobility were pure fantasy. He was an intelligent and sexually precocious child and at fifteen had lost his virginity to a prostitute. For a time he tried to work as a male prostitute but found that when the moment came he didn't have the heart for the job, although later necessity compelled him to improve. Hungary sided with the Nazis in World War II and for a time Carl had some connection with the SS. According to a story he told in an unpublished autobiographical novel, shortly before the end of the war, when a young soldier found him AWOL and tried to bring him back to camp, Carl shot him when his back was turned. As the war was practically over and he would no doubt have been released anyway—his papers were in order—there was no need for the killing. The soldier's "attitude" upset him, that was all. As Wilson came to see, there was a strong criminal streak in Carl.

After the war Carl had trouble with the new Communist regime and so he left for London. By this time his transvestitism had begun. After making love with his girlfriend, he became excited at the sight and feel of the satin dressing gown she had thrown over him. Then, sometime later, he was expecting another girlfriend to arrive at his flat—he was something of a womanizer—when she called and canceled their meeting. He had bought some silk stockings for her and, frustrated, suddenly felt a powerful urge to put them on. He did and then masturbated, experiencing the most powerful orgasm of his life. He immediately regretted this and destroyed the stockings, but soon he was acquiring women's clothing and dressing in them. He even made use of clothing from women with whom he had affairs. He was still attracted to women, as they were to him, but it seemed that his attraction to putting on their clothes was even more powerful.

By the mid-1950s, Carl had married a woman who had a young son and he seemed to have put his transvestitism aside. But other problems arose. He was something of a confidence trickster. At the time of the Hungarian uprising he organized a "Freedom Fighters" relief fund, but pocketed the money. He became an "agony aunt," writing articles for a "lonely hearts" column. He claimed bogus academic titles and presented himself as a hypnotist; Wilson was surprised to see that he actually owned Hadju's book on the subject. He was driven by a need to be known, to "be somebody," but there was also a deep compulsion to lie, to pretend to be someone he wasn't.

Then tragedy struck. A long affair he'd had ended painfully, and then his wife and stepson died, just as Charlotte had said about her husband and son. He locked himself in his flat and went to pieces. His transvestitism returned and for weeks he wore his dead wife's clothes. He let bills pile up and spent two months in prison for debts. Then he tried to pull himself together by reinventing himself as Charlotte Bach. This was when he advertised in *New Statesman* for participants in a study of deviance. His research was for a book, *Man and/or Woman*, which was never published. But it put him in contact with other transvestites, and with this his stint as a sex guru began. In the 1970s Charlotte eventually established an institute of human ethology and lectured on her ideas at the City of London Polytechnic. At one point he considered having a sex-change operation, but at the last minute he backed out.

But there was still another side of Charlotte Bach. She was given to petty theft. She stole small items from her printer, although she had no need for them. At department stores she would shoplift something, then return it, making such a fuss that the store would refund her even without the receipt. She was a pathological liar. As Wilson saw, Bach's criminal streak "arose out of a manic egoism, an obsession with himself that made other people seem relatively unimportant."[26] It was part of her manic need for self-esteem, an attempt at making herself feel "real," as were the false academic credentials, claims to nobility, and earlier seductions.

She had even incorporated this personality trait into her theory of evolution, writing a great deal about the biological phenomenon of neoteny. This is when members of a species do not reach adulthood and instead remain immature. Some zoologists have speculated that humans are really immature apes. At a certain point, the embryo of an ape resembles a fully developed human embryo, but the ape embryo carries on to develop the brow ridges, specialized teeth, and body hair that humans lack. Humans can be seen as apes suffering from arrested development. The advantage of this is that it allows for more possibilities; we have, as it were, not yet "specialized," and can develop in new ways. Bach took this "Peter Pan" approach to evolution and applied it to her ideas. Most human beings never mature emotionally, and this inner chaos makes possible the kind of ecstatic states she was aiming at.

Yet, as Wilson knew, immaturity is at the root of criminality. As he came to see, it was also at the root of sexual deviancy.

Wilson ultimately rejected Bach's ideas. But her life seemed to encapsulate the psychology of sexual deviance and to illustrate what was wrong with it.[27] Not in a moral sense—Wilson did not censure—but in a practical one. Sexual deviance does not meet the goals it sets out to achieve, Wilson argues, because it fails to grasp the true purpose of imagination. Wilson suspected that Bach knew this herself. As he writes, Bach "must have been aware of a certain element of absurdity as he prepared to receive his adoring disciples . . . by donning foam-rubber breasts and clambering into an outsize pair of knickers."[28] Bach must have recognized the discrepancy between reality and fantasy. She never achieved the fame she wished for, yet if she had, the reality of her situation would have come to light much sooner.[29] It was this realization that most likely led to the depression that killed her. When signs of cancer appeared, Bach failed to consult the many medical friends she had made, knowing that an examination would uncover the truth. She simply shut down and committed a kind of suicide.

Wilson recognized Bach's "conceit," "muddle-headedness," and "criminality," but he nevertheless believed she had some important insights; because of this he generously regarded her as "one of the most rewarding thinkers of the late twentieth century."[30] But it is not so much Charlotte Bach's theories that inspired The Misfits as the reasons why they were wrong. Sexual deviancy is not the motor behind evolution, Wilson argues, but a by-product of it.[31] It is a side effect of evolution's real driving force: the imagination. As he argued earlier, sex is an area of human existence in which imagination plays a central role. And nothing highlights the place of imagination in sex so unmistakably as the many forms of sexual deviancy.

Following Charlotte's Bach story, in The Misfits Wilson runs through a gauntlet of practices that some readers may find surprising, if not disturbing. What may also be surprising is that the people engaging in these "perversions" are not anonymous case studies from Krafft-Ebing or Magnus Hirschfeld, although material from these and other sexologists appears. Wilson's case studies involve some of the most famous creative individuals of the past two centuries. Among his sexual Outsiders we find philosophers, novelists, composers, and poets and we are treated to analyses of the intimate lives of, among others, James Joyce, Bertrand Russell, Marcel Proust, Lord Byron, Algernon Swinburne, Yukio Mishima, Ludwig Wittgenstein, T. E. Lawrence, Paul Tillich, Percy Grainger, and, aptly enough, the pre-Freud sexologist Havelock Ellis. What these individuals have in common is an obsession with a version of the eight-hour orgasm that inspired Charlotte Bach's vision of evolution via deviancy. They are individuals caught, to a greater or lesser degree, in the sexual illusion, captivated by the idea of some ultimate sexual experience. By looking at the means they employed to achieve this—or, ultimately, their failure to do so—Wilson says we can learn something absolutely essential about human evolution.

We've seen that Wilson believes there was an "imaginative explosion" in the second half of the eighteenth century and that he credits the invention of the modern novel as the main cause of this. The middle-aged printer Samuel Richardson most likely had no idea that his novel *Pamela* (1740) and its successor, *Clarissa* (1748), would have such an effect, but as Wilson says, Richardson taught modern Europe how to daydream, and one of the first things it dreamt about was sex.[32] Richardson's work itself tells the infinitely prolonged stories of two young women pursued by lustful men. Richardson takes his time telling the tales—both works are enormously long—making sure he reminds his readers of their moral intent. He is, he insists, on the side of virtue, but it is clear that he is captivated by the intricacies of seduction and that his own imagination is fired in the act of portraying them. In *Pamela* the heroine maintains her virtue until her pursuer capitulates and marries her, but in *Clarissa* good does not win and in the end the heroine is finally drugged and ravished in a brothel.

One of the first writers to follow in Richardson's footsteps was John Cleland, whose bawdy *Fanny Hill* (1748) was so popular that the authorities gave Cleland a handsome pension provided he write no more. Yet Cleland's tale of a young wench's introduction to the pleasures of the flesh is a relatively healthy exercise of a more or less down-to-earth imagination, the product of an age when sex was seen as one of many earthly pleasures—delightful, to be sure, but only one element in a full, robust life. The same can be said for earlier erotic works, such as Giovanni Boccaccio's *The Decameron* and equivalent passages in Rabelais. Yet very quickly something happened to Europe's ideas about sex. It would not be too off the mark to say that by the late eighteenth century, it had become obsessed with it. Soon after Cleland, the Swiss-born Jean-Jacques Rousseau produced *Julie* (1761), in which sex and freedom form a union that would continue until our own permissive age. Julie, the heroine of the novel, and her tutor, Saint-Preux, fall in love. Julie is already married but they believe that since they are in love, they are already "married in God's eyes" and have the right to consummate their passion, whatever society may say. Rousseau had already argued, in his *Discourse on the Arts and Sciences* (1750), that man was born free and that civilization only corrupts his natural goodness, so Julie and Saint-Preux's adultery only follows the dictates of nature.

The theme of rejecting society's restraints and the unabashed celebration of sexual love made the book an instant success. *Julie* was so popular that libraries lent it out by the hour. One example of Rousseau's impact on western imagination can be seen in the effect the book had on the philosopher Immanuel Kant. The citizens of Königsberg, Germany, used to set their watches by the philosopher's afternoon walk, which was absolutely punctual, rain or shine. The one time Kant missed his walk was when he was engrossed in reading *Julie*.[33] In Germany Kant's younger contemporary Goethe made an even bigger impact on western sensibilities with *The Sorrows of Young Werther* (1774), a tale of obsessed unrequited love that had all of Europe in tears. Werther's suicide—prompted by his beloved Charlotte's marriage to someone else—triggered a rash of copycat suicides across the continent. Readers, Wilson writes, had by then "learned to sympathise with ecstasies of love and transports of misery." Goethe's novel was like some potent drug and it convinced its readers that they should let their feelings go.[34] They did.

With Goethe the Romantic age had well and truly arrived. What his fellow authors then began to see was that imagination could not only bring a new realism to inner experience, as Richardson and Cleland had done. Both depict the action in their tales in minute detail, which compelled their readers to *slow down*, so that what earlier may have been mentioned in passing was now subject to a meticulous analysis. As Wilson remarks, Cleland's depiction of sex takes longer to read than the act itself. What Goethe's fellow Romantics soon saw was that imagination could also *improve* greatly on reality. So writers such as the no-longer-read novelist Jean Paul produced dreamy forests and magnificent castles that never existed and E. T. A. Hoffmann's tales revolve around magic doorways and improbable meetings with wizards and golden snakes who turn into beautiful women. The most emblematic symbol of the time was the elusive blue flower from Novalis's unfinished novel *Heinrich von Ofterdingen*; Novalis's hero sees the flower in a dream and spends his life in search of it. This dreamy romanticism was shot through with depictions of sensual delight and an association of the new freedom of the imagination with the idea of the "eternal feminine," the possession of which constituted for the Romantics the idea of some ultimate sexual experience.

Yet this ideal, like Novalis's blue flower, was always out of reach, and it was this dissonance between the ecstasies of their visions and the crudities of reality that, as we've seen, eventually defeated the Romantics. When they managed to meet a woman happy to share their bed, the dream of ultimate bliss quickly dissipated; she was just a girl like any other. Yet some Romantics were determined to achieve their ultimate experience, whatever the cost. One such was the "one man textbook of criminology," the Marquis de Sade, who has the dubious distinction of introducing western man to what Wilson calls "super-heated sex."[35] This was the product of a misapplication of the imagination, resulting in a febrile, exaggerated vision that turned the simple sexual act into something like a fever dream, something the men of the previous century would have thought insane. Through a look at de Sade's works, such as *The 120 Days of Sodom* and *Juliette*, Wilson shows how his attempt to achieve the goal of an ultimate sexual experience was doomed from the start. This was because de Sade misunderstood that what he was really in search of was not some ultimate sexual experience, but the experience of inner freedom, which, ultimately, is an experience of *reality, without the limitations of the robot*. Yet, like his fellow sexual misfits, de Sade mistook sexual experience for what we can call the "reality experience," the kind of really knowing that Wilson believes was the key to moving beyond the robot.

De Sade spent much of his life in jail, unjustly, as it turns out. Although he did have a penchant for minor acts of what would later be called "sadism"—mostly whipping; the practice was named after de Sade by the nineteenth-century German sexologist Richard von Krafft-Ebing—de Sade was not in real life the monster he is often depicted as being. His twenty-eight years in prison—what Wilson calls an "outrageous injustice"—were the consequence of falling foul of his mother-in-law.[36] She understandably took argument with his many affairs and sexual misdemeanors, and exasperated with these, she used her influence to have de Sade imprisoned, where he was soon forgotten. Yet, when enjoying a brief period of freedom during the French Revolution, de Sade, then a judge on a revolutionary committee, had an opportunity to take revenge against his mother-in-law when she came to trial. Instead, he had her name and that of her husband stricken from the death lists, saving their lives. He also used his influence to improve conditions in hospitals. For someone whose name is synonymous with delight in inflicting pain, these acts suggest a surprising compassion.

Yet while Wilson recognizes that de Sade was not a villain in any clichéd sense—he does not appear in any of Wilson's encyclopedias of murder—he rejects the modern tendency to "rehabilitate" him, to see him as a misunderstood genius, a victim of society's hypocrisy. A look at de Sade's work, he explains, is all that is necessary to see that he was an "incredibly vicious and unpleasant character." For Wilson, champions, such as Simone de Beauvoir, who talk about de Sade's "martyrdom" are "self-deluded sentimentalists."[37] De Sade is important, but not in the way that modern critics celebrating transgression see him. His importance lies in the fact that his case makes clear the self-defeating character of sexual perversions.

De Sade's "viciousness" achieved self-expression during his time in prison, when he had little to do but daydream. He always had an acute interest in sex, so his daydreams, like those of many other prisoners, became a curious blend of sexual fantasy and revenge. De Sade was a product of the shift in western consciousness that came with Romanticism, the sense that man was in some way a sleeping god. He took this idea literally and decided that since God does not exist, he would now occupy his throne. He grew up in a loveless but wealthy home; he was brought up by servants and was an archetypal spoiled brat. As he writes, "As soon as I could think, I believed that nature and fortune had joined hands to fill my lap with gifts." It seemed to him that "the whole universe should humour my whims."[38]

When de Sade found himself in prison—Wilson tells us how he got there— he found both his supreme will and access to pleasure severely curtailed. So he satisfied his will and his appetites through his imagination. In 1780 he began to write what we now consider his "sadistic" works, most representative of which is *The 120 Days of Sodom* (written in 1785 but not published until 1904), which Wilson describes as the "masturbation fantasy of a man who has been deprived of sex for a long time."[39] Four libertines, their daughters, four brothel madams, and an assortment of prostitutes and other participants—some of them children—spend four months locked in a mansion systematically exploring every possible means of sexual gratification. What their sexual sabbatical amounts to is a "wide-ranging catalogue of sexual deviations, presented with manic precision and thoroughness." What the reader who persists through this litany of perversion depicted with autistic exactitude soon discovers is that, rather than excite him to a feverish pitch of erotic ecstasy, the relentless parade of unnatural acts is ultimately boring. What he also discovers is that these practices have really little to do with sex, at least in any usual idea of it. De Sade was no longer interested in sex, but in being as shocking as possible. And the person he wanted to shock most was himself.

As Wilson wants to argue, de Sade had little imagination. During the orgies, one of his libertines reflects, "One need but be mildly jaded, and all these infamies assume a richer meaning; satiety inspires them. . . . One grows tired of the commonplace, the imagination becomes vexed, and the slenderness of our means, the weakness of our faculties, the corruption of our souls, leads us to these abominations."[40] In other words, de Sade's libertines are *bored*, and their enormous efforts at sexual satisfaction are driven not by the pursuit of some final sexual accomplishment, but by the escape from a dreary ennui. An escape, that is, from the robot.

The aim of de Sade's blasphemies, Wilson argues, is to spark in him a brief sense of *reality*, to shake him out of his thralldom to the robot. We've seen that for Wilson, sex is a means of focusing the mind, of making it, as it were, erect. But because our "reality function" is weak, we lose our grip on our experience and after the sexual fever has passed, we wonder what the fuss was about. Man is "sad" after sex because the treasure he thought he had captured has vanished. But the imagination can restore it, and it does this by heightening the sense of the forbidden, which, as Wilson has argued, is the essence of the "sexual illusion" in men.[41]

De Sade reveled in the forbidden. It excited him because by pursuing it he expressed his will and felt the sense of freedom that came with this. That is, the *idea* of the forbidden thrilled him and made him feel *real*. Yet the problem with the forbidden, as with other illicit "spices," is that it is subject to the law of diminishing returns.[42] As with drug addiction, repeated indulgence lessens the effect, which can only be restored by increasing doses, which only hasten the downward spiral. Hence the absurdities that de Sade's libertines engage in, the "infamies" they pursue in order to lessen their ennui but which ultimately only increase it.

Wilson argues that sexual deviancy became widespread after the Romantic explosion, when the kind of superheated sex that obsessed de Sade filtered down to a wider audience and, along with Victorian pornography, became de rigueur.[43] (In fact, de Sade's works were first made widely available at this time.) While earlier eras did have their sexual obsessives—Wilson relates the exploits of a few in *A Criminal History of Mankind*—they were exceptions, emperors and nobility, such as Caligula and Gilles de Rais, who had the opportunity to indulge their fantasies. By the time magazines such as *The Pearl* and *The Boudoir* were being sold to Victorian gentlemen, the kind of forbidden sex that excited de Sade was commonplace.

Wilson argues that one result of the imagination explosion was the rise of an industry aimed at supplying men with the means of igniting their inner world with flares of the forbidden. Unlike the bawdy earthiness of *Fanny Hill*, tales from *The Pearl* involved schoolgirls, nuns, sisters, and other forbidden fruits in improbable situations with numbing consistency. Sex, we could say, was being used to stimulate the imagination, rather than the other way around. That the superheated sex de Sade introduced was really a clumsy means of stimulating the reality function is clear from passages Wilson quotes from *My Secret Life* (1888), an eleven-volume sexual autobiography whose author, the mysterious "Walter," pursued his erotic obsession with "a single-mindedness that was unique, even among the Romantics."[44]

If Walter ever thought of anything other than sex, Wilson writes, "there is certainly no evidence for it." Sex was his blue flower; for him it was the "most delightful and fascinating subject in the world."[45] And a reader of *My Secret Life* soon sees that sex is something of a mystical experience for Walter, and that he would certainly understand Charlotte Bach's interest in an eight-hour orgasm.

But what is really at stake with Walter and the other sexual misfits is their feeble grasp on reality and their use of sex to momentarily strengthen it. As Wilson writes, "Walter's most powerful craving is not for sexual experience, but for *consciousness* of sexual experience."[46] He wants to have his experience, but also to *know* that he is having it. In a way we could say that in Gurdjieff's terms, he is using sex to "remember himself," to overcome what Heidegger calls our "forgetfulness of being." Like modern couples he often used mirrors, to heighten his awareness of the act. He is constantly asking his partners to *tell* him what he is doing, asking them how it feels, getting them to "talk dirty"—and even talking dirty is an example of the new forbidden character of sex. Dirt, too, is forbidden, hence Walter's erotic fantasies about women on the toilet and his compulsion to peer through the bathroom keyhole, something men of the previous century would have found demented.[47]

Where de Sade tried to kick-start his imagination using a kind of sexual dynamite, Walter takes the route of Richardson and, later, Proust. He recounts in pedantic detail the fine points of every encounter, relating "in tranquillity," as Wordsworth spoke of poetry, the experience so he can savor the fact that it *actually took place*. Yet, his quest for the ultimate sexual experience leaves him, like it leaves its other devotees, strangely empty. But the promise of another conquest leads him on, and so he continues his manic and ultimately unsuccessful pursuit, conquering women of all shapes and sizes—he even experiments with homosexuality—driven by what he feels is an insatiable desire for sex, but is really a hunger for a sense of reality, a whole self-image. As Wilson writes, with Walter and the other sexual misfits, sex is trying to become "self-reflective," that is, an *imaginative* experience, like enjoying music or poetry. In their fumbling way Walter and others like him were trying to use sex as "a device for the control of consciousness."[48]

What was problematic about this is that superheated sex, like Romanticism itself, "condemned its devotees to a world of *unreality*," and widened the gap between the world of feverish daydreams and the world of commonsense actuality, the gap between Charlotte Bach and Carl Hajdu. And as there is something "inherently absurd" about superheated sex, this gap remains wide open. As Wilson writes, no matter how "tolerant" and "liberated" we may be, we still feel that someone who remains obsessed by "this kind of thing has condemned a part of himself to perpetual adolescence," as Charlotte Bach herself argued was necessary for evolution.[49] "Sex," Wilson writes, "is important, but not *that* important," and someone who devotes his life to its pursuit is lessening, not enlarging his experience. Deviant needs for the forbidden *do not* help in our evolution. They *can* create a temporary intensity of consciousness, but ultimately they are counterproductive. As Wilson says, they are a by-product of imagination, not its driving force.

While Walter is an extreme example of someone hypnotized by the sexual illusion, in one form or another the same inability to hold on to the reality of their experience is suffered by the other figures Wilson looks at. And while the erotic peculiarities of a James Joyce or a Havelock Ellis excite a certain appetite for highbrow gossip, the mechanisms involved in their fetishes are no different from those at work in our own.[50] We are all subject to the limitations of the robot. For better or worse, the misfits Wilson investigates were obsessed with the sexual illusion because they had an instinctive craving for a more vital experience, for an intensity of consciousness that comes with being free of the robot's constraints. They did not *know* this was what they sought, but we are in a better position. We can consciously try to develop our reality function, so that we no longer need the crutch of a sexual perversion—or, for that matter, Russian roulette—to do the trick for us. Wilson points out that this is what man has been trying to do throughout his history, from the moment he first sat around a campfire and told tales of great battles of yesteryear. The development of the imagination can lead to dangerous dead ends—sex crime and suicide, for example. But the dividends outweigh the disadvantages. The aim of the imagination is not to create unbelievable fantasies of "forbidden" sex, but "to enable us to grasp the reality of other times and places, instead of being the slaves of the present moment."[51] As Wilson writes, when the reality function is working properly, it brings "a sense of *mastery over time*."[52] And for all the problems and wrong turns it brought with it, the imagination explosion is evidence for Wilson that such mastery is the goal of human evolution. His look at the sexual illusion convinced him that "man is on the brink of achieving full consciousness of his evolutionary purpose." The "feedback point" in human history when this will be made apparent is, Wilson feels, very close.

But while his mind was looking toward the future, Wilson would soon have reason to turn it toward the past.

The Misfits was not well received. Around the same time as its publication, a book about the Angry Young Men appeared and its critical tone seemed to revive the old anti-Wilson animus.[53] Anthony Burgess, Wilson's colleague from his Majorca days, gave the book warm words in the *Observer* but, predictably, the main critical response was focused on Wilson's naïveté about Charlotte Bach. The satirical weekly *Private Eye* lampooned Wilson with a drawing of him in drag, and other reviewers were scathing about his tabloid-style exposé of the sexual peculiarities of literary greats.[54] He took the criticisms in stride. He was, as always, busy. He had recently lectured in the Open Center in New York, and had returned to Japan and Australia. He had lectured in Los Angeles, where I saw him speak and we had a chance to catch up. There were other lectures, in Boston, in Big Sur at the Esalen Institute, and at the C. G. Jung Institute of San Francisco.

Yet back in Cornwall, the problem of the sexual illusion still troubled him, even after *The Misfits*. With all the talk of imagination, there was, he knew, a physical element of sex that was being overlooked. A kind of "static electricity" builds up in the genitals, and sex is a means of discharging it. It is, at bottom, an exchange of vital energies, like Reich's "orgone energy," and in *The Space Vampires* he had made this the central theme, with the vampires sucking the "life force" out of their victims. The idea of a sequel to *The Space Vampires* came to him and he would use it to settle the sexual illusion once and for all. He was already commissioned to do a second part of Spider World, and he had written the first volume of this, *The Magician*. But he felt his imagination was tiring and that the book needed a break. So he decided to turn his mind to what would become *Metamorphosis of the Vampires*.

The plot involves a descendant of the man who first encountered the vampires discovering that he has become one himself. He makes contact with other vampires and is taken to their world. Wilson found himself exhilarated, creating fantastic landscapes and remarkable beings, as if he was trying to give David Lindsay's *A Voyage to Arcturus* some stiff competition. He wrote on, slightly stunned by the flow of his imagination. Yet doing the book was a risk. Harper-Collins would not commission it; understandably, they were waiting for him to finish *Spider World*. Wilson would work on *Metamorphosis* for two years, increasing his overdraft in the process. The size of the book also increased and when it was finished he was a bit daunted to see he had written a quarter of a million words. This was the problem. It was too big and the publishers he sent it to told him so. For better or for worse, Wilson wouldn't cut it. He felt he had made his most important assault on the sexual illusion in it and could not understand how editors did not see this.

As publisher after publisher turned the book down, Wilson began to feel discouraged.[55] The old feeling of impending doom returned. His overdraft did as well, getting back to amounts he had not had to worry about for some time; at one point it reached twenty-five thousand pounds, more than forty thousand dollars. One night, after considering the possibility that he might have to sell Tetherdown, or find another university post in the States, he asked himself if he really was facing catastrophe. He was no longer young; in 1991 he turned sixty. He remembered the time, decades ago, when he almost ended it all in his chemistry class, and the smell of the cyanide bottle came back with Proustian clarity. The memory of his relief when he put the stopper back in the bottle and decided he wanted more life, not less, came back too, and cheered him. No. If he just kept his spirits up, things would work out well.

It was around this time that an idea Wilson had been thinking about off and on began to take shape. In 1991 Dino De Laurentiis got in touch with him again and asked if he could write a script outline for a film about Atlantis; De Laurentiis's coproducer on the project was Stephen Schwartz. When Schwartz asked Wilson what he knew about Atlantis, Wilson replied, "Everything," and sent him a copy of an article on Atlantis he had written for *The Encyclopedia of Unsolved Mysteries*. He had been interested in the fabled lost continent for years. He thought there was good evidence that it had actually existed, and De Laurentiis's commission brought back his curiosity.

In 1979 Wilson had read John Anthony West's *Serpent in the Sky*, a study of the work of the maverick Egyptologist René Schwaller de Lubicz. In it West mentions Schwaller de Lubicz's belief that the Sphinx was much older than the official accounts, which place its construction, under the pharaoh Chefren, in 2400 BC. This was something Wilson knew that Gurdjieff believed as well, so the idea was not too unusual.[56] Schwaller de Lubicz, who had spent fifteen years studying the temple at Luxor, said that the Sphinx showed signs of erosion by water, not by sand or wind. The last time there was enough rain to erode the Sphinx's limestone was thousands of years earlier than when mainstream Egyptologists believed the Sphinx had been built, possibly as early as 7000 BC. If Schwaller de Lubicz was right, then it may have been a *previous* civilization that was responsible for it. That previous civilization, Schwaller de Lubicz suggested, was Atlantis.

Uttering the "dreaded A-word" was tantamount to parading one's membership in the lunatic fringe, Wilson knew. But as Schwaller de Lubicz had had no academic career to worry about—he died in 1961—he had no problem with that. But West had seen that if the erosion marks on the Sphinx *were* made by water, this was something that could be scientifically tested and demonstrated. This meant that rather than depend on legends, myths, or the uncertain testimony of occultists, there was a perfectly straightforward way to establish the facts about the Sphinx, one way or the other.

Wilson wrote an outline of the script before leaving for a conference in Tokyo on human communication in the twenty-first century, where he and Timothy Leary were the main speakers. He was not certain what happened to it—he never heard from De Laurentiis about it again—but some of the material from it later surfaced in a Lovecraftian pastiche, *The R'Lyeh Text* (1995), a follow-up to an earlier similar effort, *The Necronomicon* (1978).[57] Here Wilson throws quite a bit of material from recent work into a bubbling, at times frothing cauldron, which he stirs with his tongue firmly in his cheek: along with Lovecraft we find psychometry, crystals, the Akashic Records, Crowley, spirits, the Huna, and morphic resonance, to name a few items. And, of course, Atlantis. He wanted to make the script as realistic as possible, forgetting the togas and vaguely classical Greek look that most films about Atlantis have adopted. This meant that he would base it on what he had read in *Serpent in the Sky* and on accounts by Madame Blavatsky and Rudolf Steiner, taken from the Akashic Records.

West suggested that in considering Atlantis, we need not think only of Plato's lost continent, but simply of a civilization that predated those accepted by conventional historians. John Michell, we've seen, used a similar idea in his book *The View over Atlantis*, referring to an earlier civilization aware of ley lines and earth energy, and not necessarily the doomed continent at the bottom of the sea. Schwartz wanted this to be "*the* definitive Atlantis film," and Wilson was excited by the idea and wrote accordingly.[58] Ultimately, the script involved the Atlanteans' mastery of consciousness through the use of crystals able to record all of their knowledge.

Around the same time as he read *Serpent in the Sky* Wilson had received another book, whose appearance counts, I think, as one of the many synchronicities that seemed to accompany many of his projects. It was a reissue of *Maps of the Ancient Sea Kings*, by Charles Hapgood, a professor of the history of science at New England College. Hapgood's first book, *Earth's Shifting Crust* (1958), had a foreword by Albert Einstein, which seemed to give his ideas credibility. *Earth's Shifting Crust* argues that the earth's crust is like the skin that forms on boiled milk, and that this can be shifted over the surface by the weight of ice at the poles. Such shifts have happened during geological time, Hapgood argues, with the result that the poles have been located at different places on the globe; for example, there is evidence to suggest that sixty million years ago, the North Pole was as far south as 55 degrees latitude and that it was in the Pacific Ocean.[59] These pole shifts trigger global catastrophes and Hapgood's book provides some chilling evidence of their reality.[60]

Maps of the Ancient Sea Kings first appeared in 1966. In it Hapgood argues for the existence of an ancient worldwide maritime civilization, which predated all known civilizations. Like Schwaller de Lubicz and John Anthony West, Hapgood believed there was good evidence for a highly advanced civilization prior to dynastic Egypt. He had reached this conclusion through studying medieval navigational maps known as "portolans," meaning "port-to-port." The most famous of these is the Piri Re'is map, which dates to 1513. Piri Re'is was an admiral (and pirate) in the Turkish navy (he was eventually beheaded), and his map, which Hapgood consulted at the Library of Congress, is, to say the least, startling. It shows the coast of South America *and* the South Pole, centuries before the latter was discovered. James Cook first crossed the Antarctic Circle in 1773, the first landing on the continent was most likely by the whaler Captain John Davis in 1821, and the South Pole itself was not discovered until the Norwegian Roald Amundsen reached it in 1911. But the Piri Re'is map not only showed Antarctica: it showed it *without ice*. Later soundings off the Antarctic coast showed that the contours of the continent given on the map were correct; other features, invisible to the eye but detectable by sonar and other sounding devices, confirmed the accuracy of the map. This was as remarkable as Schwaller de Lubicz's claim that the Sphinx suffered water erosion. The last time Antarctica was free of ice was around 7000 BC, nearly ten thousand years ago. According to modern science, a map of Antarctica from that time should not exist. Humans were barely getting out of the last ice age. Writing had not yet been invented and it is highly unlikely that any of our Neolithic ancestors roamed the seas. The mathematical geographic skills needed to produce a map of anywhere, let alone pre-ice Antarctica, were simply not available.

But there it was, and Hapgood found other portolans displaying other geographical knowledge that they should not possess. Hapgood argued that the Piri Re'is map and others like it are based on far earlier maps, but this still does not explain how the people who made the originals acquired their knowledge. This mystery, sadly, led to some trouble for Hapgood. The Piri Re'is maps are part of the occult grab bag making up the heady blend of *The Morning of the Magicians*, the book, we've seen, that started the "occult revival" of the 1960s. This was bad enough, but in 1968 a book appeared by the Swiss Erich von Däniken titled *Memories of the Future*. Translated into English as *Chariots of the Gods*, it became a global best seller, with its claim that in ancient times, earth was visited by alien astronauts, memorials of whose visits can be found in temples and ruins scattered around the globe. One piece of evidence von Däniken presents is the Piri Re'is map. His answer to the riddle of how its maker knew of pre-ice Antarctica is that this knowledge was given to him—whoever he was—by ancient astronauts. Obviously, the only way one could have seen the coast of pre-ice Antarctica was, von Däniken declared, from the air.

Von Däniken presented other mysteries as evidence of his theory, famously the strange giant figures and geometric designs that can be found in the Nazca Desert, in Peru. But von Däniken presented his ideas with such carelessness and lack of logic that he made the authors of *The Morning of Magicians* seem like unimaginative pedants. Popular scientists such as Carl Sagan—a later member of CSICOP—were quick to point out all the mistakes, poor reasoning, and sheer muddle in von Däniken's work, so that anything remotely linked to it was soon considered guilty of the same blunders. Hapgood's work, unfortunately, was tarred with the von Däniken brush, and soon any mention of ancient sea kings was as *verboten* as the dreaded "A-word." Yet while Wilson rejected von Däniken—his work was "absurd and dishonest"—and had little better to say about *The Morning of the Magicians*, Hapgood's reasoning, he saw, was sound. For maps like Piri Re'is' to exist, there *must* have been the kind of prehistoric maritime civilization that Hapgood suggested. As far as Wilson was concerned, Hapgood had proved, "once and for all," that a maritime people existed "in the days before the South Pole was covered with ice."[61]

In fairly quick succession, two books arguing for the existence of an unknown prehistoric civilization had fallen into Wilson's lap. Yet he had to put the idea aside. Other projects pulled him away from Atlantis (we've looked at some of them in previous chapters), but when the commission for the film came, Hapgood's and Schwaller de Lubicz's ideas returned. Then other things began to fall into place. In Tokyo, at the Press Club after the conference, he mentioned the film to some friends, and told them of Schwaller de Lubicz's idea that the Sphinx may have been built by Atlanteans. One of them mentioned that he had recently seen a newspaper article in the *Mainichi*, one of Japan's top papers, about new evidence supporting the idea that the Sphinx is much older than believed. His friend couldn't find the piece, but when Wilson was in Melbourne a week later, an editor friend said he had seen the story too and promised to find it and give him a copy. It was from the *Los Angeles Times* and it told of how the

Boston geologist Robert Schoch had determined that the erosion marks on the Sphinx *are* from water—West had asked Schoch to visit the Sphinx to determine whether they are or not. When Schoch presented his findings to the Geological Society of America, they were enthusiastically supported. Egyptologists, not surprisingly, rejected his claim. They argued that there was no way it could be true, because "people who lived there earlier could not have built it." The article concluded with the thought that "if the geologists are right, much of what the Egyptologists think they know would have to be wrong."[62]

Back in Cornwall, other projects once again drew Wilson away from Atlantis. His play based on the German poet Eduard Morike's novella *Mozart's Journey to Prague* toured the UK successfully, with music provided by the Medici String Quartet; later a CD was produced of a performance. In 1992 Wilson toured Poland to promote Polish editions of *The Outsider* and *The Mind Parasites*. Compendiums of his crime writing—*Murder in the 1930's* gives an idea of what these were like—appeared, as did the third part of Spider World, *The Magician*. In 1993 he was back in Australia for the Melbourne Writers Festival, and from there he went to San Francisco, where he lectured for the Anthroposophical Society and also at the California Institute of Integral Studies, where I had a chance to attend his workshop and catch up once again. After that he was back in New York, speaking at the Open Center. It was in the midst of this travel— "travel bores me," Wilson says, "and writing about it bores me even more"—that he heard from an old editor friend, Geoffrey Chessler, who was working for a publisher that specialized in occult literature. He asked Wilson if he had any ideas for a book. Over dinner Wilson mentioned his thoughts about Atlantis and the Sphinx, and Chessler was excited. While talking about it, Wilson remarked that he believed that the people responsible for the Sphinx, and who most likely were Hapgood's prehistoric maritime civilization, would have had a different kind of *consciousness* than our own, something along the lines of the lunar knowledge he had written about in *The Occult*.

Before his meeting with Chessler, Wilson had received out of the blue a letter from John Anthony West along with a magazine that had published an article he had written about the latest developments in his investigation into the Sphinx. This involved an examination of the face of the Sphinx by Frank Domingo, a police detective who specialized in facial reconstruction; Domingo concluded that the face of the Sphinx was nothing like that of the pharaoh Chefren, who mainstream Egyptologists believed it was. Wilson hadn't been in contact with West and West had no idea he was interested in the Sphinx, so once again, synchronicity seems to have struck. Wilson replied to West, saying that he would be in New York and that they should meet. He immediately liked West, who was enthusiastic and generous and enjoyed sharing his knowledge; "information poured out of him," Wilson felt, "like water from a village pump."[63] They watched an unedited version of a documentary West had made about the

Sphinx, and later, at another dinner with the rest of the Wilsons (his family had joined him) and the writer Paul Devereux, who specialized in megalithic sites, they talked about Wilson's idea for a book about the Sphinx. During dinner West mentioned two other writers working on similar ideas, whom Wilson should know about. One was Graham Hancock; the other was Rand Flem-Ath. Soon Wilson would become familiar with both.

Back in Cornwall Wilson wrote to Hancock and Flem-Ath (whose unusual last name is a combination of his own and his wife's). Wilson had seen a television program about Hancock's search for the Ark of the Covenant, based on his book *The Sign and the Seal* (1993). Hancock sent Wilson a typescript for his new book, *Fingerprints of the Gods* (1996), a von Däniken–style work about the evidence of an ancient civilization predating any known to "official" science, although backed up with the kind of evidence and rigorous thinking von Däniken lacked. Reading it, Wilson began to feel that it preempted his own book. And when another typescript arrived from Rand Flem-Ath, his discouragement deepened. *When the Sky Fell* (1995) was based on Hapgood's work and argued that at a time in the distant past, Atlantis existed, and was located at the South Pole. When Wilson saw that Hancock knew of Flem-Ath's work, his enthusiasm for his own book dwindled even further. Nevertheless Wilson thought Flem-Ath's work was significant, and he helped get it published by offering to write an introduction to it. Later the two would work together, with less than successful results.

In early 1994, other coincidences happened. Wilson received a review copy of Robert Bauval's *The Orion Mystery*, which argues that the pyramid complex at Giza was planned as early as 10,450 BC. Hancock drew on Bauval's work as well, and the two would collaborate on another work, *The Message of the Sphinx* (1997), furthering their speculations on a highly advanced prehistoric civilization. It seemed that almost everything that had excited Wilson about the possible Atlantean origin of the Sphinx was being covered by other writers. Yet the synchronicities involved seemed too obvious too ignore. And a further study of Schwaller de Lubicz's ideas about ancient Egypt, mostly through a reading of André VandenBroeck's book about him, *Al-Kemi* (1990), suggested that there were still some puzzles about the ancient Atlanteans—or whoever built the Sphinx—that remained to be explored. For one thing, while it was exciting to consider the possibility that civilization might be much older than we believe— and the success of Hancock's and Bauval's work made clear that many people were indeed excited—it raised the question, at least in Wilson's mind, of what *difference* it could make. If all this speculation were proved true, what, in the end, would it mean? Wilson asked the existential question: how would it help *me* to know that Atlantis really existed and that the Sphinx is ten thousand years old? He found an inkling of an answer as he looked further at the world of ancient Egypt.

What struck Wilson as he made his way through VandenBroeck's book, corresponding with him as he did, and through the difficult terrain of Schwaller de Lubicz's own work, is that Schwaller de Lubicz was convinced that the ancient Egyptians had a *different kind of consciousness* than our own.[64] In his unwieldy writings, he argued that all of Egyptian life, from the simplest everyday item to their great religious temples, was centered around what he saw as a fundamental metaphysical vision of "cosmic harmony" and "the forces that bring about the becoming of things."[65] The Egyptians, Wilson saw, had a knowledge system very different from our own. He already knew what Hancock and Bauval were now telling their millions of readers: that the Sphinx, the pyramids, and other ancient sacred sites exhibited a mathematical, astronomical, engineering, and scientific knowledge that, according to the "experts," their creators should not possess. Yet the evidence for it was there, for open-minded investigators to see. As we've seen, Wilson had already touched on this in *Starseekers*. It seemed that the ancient Egyptians—and, by inference, the people from whom they inherited much of their knowledge—had systematized the kinds of intuition and hunches that allowed Edgar Allan Poe and Jonathan Swift to make accurate "guesses" about the moons of Mars, black holes, and many other things. Schwaller de Lubicz spoke of an "intelligence of the heart," which in many ways is very similar to how Henri Bergson described intuition, mentioned earlier. As I have explained elsewhere, this should not be surprising; Schwaller de Lubicz was for a time a student of the painter Henri Matisse, who was himself a student of Bergson.[66] Schwaller de Lubicz's intelligence of the heart *enters into* things in the way that Bergson's intuition does. It see things *whole* and from *within*. This, I should point out, is also how the right brain sees things; in *The Secret Teachers of the Western World*, I argue that right-brain perception, Bergson's intuition, and Schwaller de Lubicz's intelligence of the heart are practically identical.[67]

This is a radically different way than how our own knowledge system works, which is focused on the *outside* of things. As Wilson and many others have pointed out, our knowledge is fragmentary; it is geared toward breaking the whole down into bits and pieces. It is biased toward specialization, so that we arrive at the cliché that today we know more and more about less and less, and the definition of an expert as someone who knows a lot about a little. Because our knowledge system is rooted in the left brain, this is not surprising. But if there is *another* way of knowing, one that provides knowledge that is just as valid as our own but is "unthinkably different in approach," it would indeed make a difference for us to know about it and to understand it.[68]

It would also be important for us to understand *why* we no longer have access to this kind of knowledge, in the way that our prehistoric ancestors seem to have had, and what this means for our future. At present, we have no way of seeing the universe as a whole, and our greatest minds tell us that even if we could, we would only see that it is ultimately pointless, as the physicist Steven Weinberg tells us. Yet the ancient Egyptians and the people who taught them seem to have been able to see the cosmos as a unified whole, and it was certainly not pointless to them; if Schwaller de Lubicz is right, they based their entire world on it. They seem to have had at their disposal a kind of consciousness that only comes to us rarely. Wilson's aim in writing his book would be to understand this other kind of consciousness, and to try to grasp the nature of this ancient "forgotten knowledge."[69] Doing this, he believed, could help us to get through our current state of modern alienation, the sense of being lost in the cosmos to which our increasingly fragmentary left-brain consciousness seems to condemn us. Our evolution, he believed, required us to pass through this kind of "dark night of the soul." As he writes, "Deeper insight into the process of conscious evolution depends, to some extent, on having experienced the process of alienation and learned how to transform it."[70] This, he knew, was true of his Outsiders. But as he increasingly saw, it was also true for humanity as a whole.

In *From Atlantis to the Sphinx* (1996)—its original title was *Before the Sphinx*—Wilson brought together the evidence for Hapgood's prehistoric maritime civilization, Hancock and Bauval's theories about the meaning of the pyramids of Giza, musings on Atlantis and the evidence for its reality, some startling ideas about how old humanity really is, and insights into exactly how much about the universe our ancient ancestors knew—which appears to have been quite a lot. As usual, his range is wide and his reasoning compelling. Readers of Hancock's, Bauval's, and other popular works on ancient civilizations will be familiar with the basics, but in the last chapter, "The Third Force," Wilson speculates on the meaning of all this in terms of an "evolution of consciousness."

In the work of the anthropologist Edward T. Hall he found examples of our "ancient consciousness" in modern-day North American Indians, who Hall recognized to have a different sense of time than the rest of us. Studying the Hopi, Navajo, Pueblo, and other tribes, Hall found that they all experienced time in a way very different from our own. They seemed to live in a kind of "eternal present," what Hall called "polychronic time," as opposed to the ticktock "monochromic time" of western man, a clear right-left brain divide. Writing of a long journey on horseback, Hall speaks of how, once he adjusted to the slow pace, it led to *perceiving* the world differently, in a way that was more than just the result of relaxation. As Wilson writes, "The 'right-brain' state of mind permits deeper perception." What it perceives is a kind of natural rhythm and harmony, to which we, in our left-brain rush to "get things done," are oblivious.[71]

It is this rhythm and harmony that Schwaller de Lubicz's ancient Egyptians knew and which they participated with in every aspect of their lives. This harmony can be found in a variety of forms. Probably the most ancient in western culture can be found in the teachings of Pythagoras, the Greek sage who first spoke of the "music of the spheres" and believed that number is at the basis of everything. Wilson found it in the *I Ching*, too, and in the synchronicities that seem to pop up with dependable frequency when the mind is filled with optimism and purpose.

This other mode of consciousness also allows for a kind of telepathy, or group mind. Wilson finds evidence for this in the modern world; he tells the story of how a large audience of computer enthusiasts found themselves playing a game of "group mind" electronic Ping-Pong.[72] Wilson wonders if it was some form of group mind, able to somehow use the intuitive knowledge of "cosmic harmony" and "the forces that bring about the becoming of things," that enabled the Egyptians—or Atlanteans—to raise the massive blocks making up the pyramids (one of the central mysteries is exactly how a "primitive" people could manage something that is beyond the capabilities of modern engineering.)[73] Yet, while group consciousness clearly has its advantages, it also has its limitations.

While the loss of the unifying consciousness diminished us and gave rise to different versions of a "fall," Wilson believes that our emergence from it was inevitable. Group-mind consciousness, though powerful, is static. "It cannot produce Leonardos and Beethovens and Einsteins."[74] We have evolved more in the past three thousand years than our unicameral ancestors did in fifty thousand. The left-brain approach, though difficult, is a more efficient way of evolution. Its drawback is that it creates frustration that leads to criminals, a sad by-product of the new consciousness. But the advantages again outweigh the handicaps, as Wilson argues in *A Criminal History of Mankind*.

These advantages are carried on via the imagination, which, borrowing from Gurdjieff, Wilson sees as the "third force" necessary for evolution to occur. Gurdjieff said that if we think of only two forces, as we tend to do, we remain static, at loggerheads. A third force is necessary to break the deadlock; otherwise a situation will remain stuck. For human evolution, Wilson says, the third force is the imagination.

One of the remarkable things about the study of early man is that there is evidence to suggest that he had the capacity for the same level of intelligence as our own, but that he remained static and did *nothing with his intelligence* for millions of years. It is only in relatively recent times that man began to *use* the intelligence he already possessed. Wilson says he began to use it because he saw a reason to, and this vision was provided by his imagination. And that is exactly what it needs to do now. The real problem facing us, according to Wilson, is not "wickedness or male domination or scientific materialism," but boredom, our inability to feel alive unless we are faced with a challenge, the ever-present "challenge of no challenge."[75]

This is one of the drawbacks of the new consciousness. Yet the risk was necessary, because, as Wilson argues, we are now in a position where we can *regain* our lost inheritance, while not giving up our new advantages. It is precisely the left brain that looks into its past and tries to understand it; the right brain is generally happy in the moment. The left brain can contemplate itself—something, Wilson suspects, our communally conscious ancestors were most likely not able to do. By doing this, we can see what our ancestors have to offer us and we can learn how to achieve it ourselves. And, as Wilson has shown in dozens of ways by now, this other mode of consciousness is ours for the taking, more or less. It is the *knowledge* that it is at hand that is important. And if, as seems accurate, we can define a peak experience as a sudden bird's-eye view of what we *already possess*, then the third force that will push us out of the deadlock that western consciousness has been in for some time is a kind of peak experience on a global scale. This, Wilson says, is the "next step in human evolution," and, he adds, "it has been happening for the past 3,500 years."[76]

CHAPTER THIRTEEN

ALIENS AND ANCIENT SITES

rom Atlantis to the Sphinx would be another breakthrough for Wilson, a sorely needed one when it arrived. The months leading up to it were difficult. *Metamorphosis of the Vampires* had still failed to find a publisher, and with that hanging over him, Wilson started work on another book, about rogue gurus. But whatever was stopping his vampires from finding a home seemed to be afflicting his false messiahs too; the publishers to whom he sent *Slouching to Bethlehem* (the title came from Yeats) turned it down.[1] Eventually he would place the book—his book on the Sphinx would help—and with a different title, but in the meantime he had two books doing the rounds that, for some reason he couldn't understand, no one wanted. Maybe Robert Ardrey was right all those years ago. Maybe he did write too much. Maybe he had said all he had to say and was writing now only out of habit. *Was* he just repeating himself? But he was a hedgehog, after all. What else was he going to do?

His health had suffered too. It seemed that 1994 was not a happy year. His bladder was acting up, saddling him with the old gents' complaint of having to visit the toilet more often than he would like. That was inconvenient, especially at business meetings. But blood in his urine once again brought worry and the thought of some imminent disaster. Returning to Cornwall after some business in London, he checked in to his local hospital and after the anesthetic wore off woke up to find that his doctor had removed two large gallstones. Two days later he was back at Tetherdown, once again at his desk.

In New York, he lectured at the Open Center again, and while he was there his younger son, Rowan, called to say that a letter had arrived from Japan. A television company wanted him to make a program about Lawrence of Arabia. It would mean traveling to the Middle East but the offer seemed incredible. The fee mentioned was seven million yen. A quick look at the exchange rate told Wilson that his problems were solved, at least the financial ones; seven million yen was roughly fifty thousand pounds. He could pay off his overdraft and—

God forbid—relax for a while, even go on holiday, although that was always an unlikely prospect. But back in Cornwall Wilson thought to examine this gift horse. A brief correspondence and apologetic reply revealed that a zero had been added in translation and the offer was for only seven hundred thousand yen—five thousand pounds. Wilson was understandably disappointed, even when the production company offered to increase the amount slightly. It wouldn't dent the overdraft but it was something. Yet the trip to Jordan and Syria was worth it after all. It was a treat for Joy and also for Wilson, who was pleased to visit places he had read about in Lawrence's *The Seven Pillars of Wisdom* so many times.[2]

Back home again, Wilson was asked by a publishing friend if he would do a series of short paperbacks on the usual topics. He took the opportunity to get his family into the act and conscripted Damon, Sally, and Rowan as writers. They trooped on but, understandably, were not as fluent as their father and the work stalled. Wilson came to the rescue, but he found editing someone else's work about as much fun as teaching creative writing. As the deadline approached, Papa Wilson rolled up his sleeves and corrected his progeny's sentences, editing three books at once. (One can imagine the expletives emerging from his workroom.) To make things worse, when he finished the last book—Sally's volume on great love affairs—his back went out. As had happened before, the strain had been too much and he found he could barely straighten up. For a while he had to walk with a cane. Added to this, he had come down with a terrific cold, which made it impossible for him to sleep. It was a difficult time.

Nevertheless, Wilson was able to take part in a live television presentation of psychic abilities. In March, with Dr. Friedbert Karger, a physicist from the Max Planck Institute of Plasma Physics deeply interested in the paranormal, he chaired an episode of *Beyond Belief*, a program about the paranormal hosted by David Frost. On exhibit were Uri Geller, the psychic healer Matthew Manning, and the Russian telepath Boris Tulchinsky. Colin Stanley, who was in the studio's live audience, says he witnessed "spoons and keys bending before my eyes" and that Tulchinsky's performance was "incredible."[3]

Wilson was writing away at the Sphinx book when, in June 1995, Dorling Kindersley, a publisher of illustrated books, commissioned him to do a book about sacred sites. *The Atlas of Holy Places & Sacred Sites* (1996) fit in well with the work on the Sphinx but as the deadline for this approached—Sir Richard Branson's Virgin Books had commissioned it in the end—he found he had to work on two books at once, splitting up his workweek. One suspects Wilson is understating things when he remarks, "It was fortunate that the panic attacks had taught me to control anxiety when overworking."[4] By New Year's Eve 1995 both books were done.[5]

In May 1996 Wilson was on his way to Glasgow to lecture to the Scottish Society for Psychical Research. The day before the lecture he made a side trip to Edinburgh, where he met Jim Macaulay, Graham Hancock's uncle. After lunch at his golf club, Macaulay, Wilson, and Joy went to visit Rosslyn Chapel, a strangely ornamented place that features in the stories surrounding the mysterious Priory of Sion of *Holy Blood, Holy Grail* (1982) fame. The book, written by Michael Baigent, Richard Leigh, and Henry Lincoln, tells of a mysterious society that has kept a powerful secret hidden for centuries: the fact that Christ did not die on the cross, but lived to have a family with Mary Magdalene, and that this bloodline still exists today. The book was an immense best seller and the idea was later used by Dan Brown in his own megahit, *The Da Vinci Code* (2003).

Rosslyn Chapel is thought to have a connection with the Knights Templar, the medieval band of Christian warriors who rose to great prominence and influence but were eventually imprisoned by Philip the Fair of France and Pope Clement V on Friday, October 13, 1307. What is strange about Rosslyn Chapel is that it is covered with vegetal ornamentation, which suggests pagan roots—there are images of the Green Man—and that some of the carvings depict plants and vegetables native to the New World, not Europe. But when work on Rosslyn Chapel began in 1456, and the carvings were being made, Columbus had yet to cross the Atlantic. This suggests that someone other than Columbus had made the voyage to America earlier, and that whoever it was had some links to the Templars, and Freemasonry, which is also linked to the chapel. Wilson didn't know at the time, but this visit would prove useful for some future work.

When he returned to Glasgow for his lecture, Wilson was pleased to hear that his host had had difficulty in getting more copies of *From Atlantis to the Sphinx*. When he tried to, he was told they were unavailable and that it was being reprinted. It had just been released and the first run had sold out on the day of publication. This was a good sign. The book went on to do well, better than any of his others since *Mysteries* and *The Occult*. One reviewer said that "reading the book gives a sense of vast historical horizons, a birds-eye view of our place in time."[6] It didn't reach quite the sales that Hancock and Bauval had achieved, but he was on the best-seller list again. This meant a happy bank manager and a life, however brief, without an overdraft.

In September of that year Wilson spoke at a symposium on "Ancient Knowledge" at the University of Delaware, put on by the Society for Scientific Exploration, a prestigious association of innovative scientists, open to ideas outside the mainstream. His fellow speakers were Graham Hancock, Robert Bauval, Rand Flem-Ath, Robert Schoch, and Paul Devereux. It was his first meeting with Flem-Ath, and Wilson says he took to him as if he was a younger brother. Someone else he met there was Roel Oostra, a Dutch television producer who asked him if he would be interested in making a documentary about his ideas about ancient civilizations. It would mean travel to South America, Mexico, and Egypt. The t-word might have made Wilson balk but Oostra quickly offered to include Joy in the deal and with this incentive he said yes.

The first part of the program, titled *The Flood*, involved a visit to the famous

La Brea Tar Pits in Los Angeles, where many a careless saber-toothed tiger and mammoth had ended their days.[7] In late November Wilson and Joy left Heathrow Airport for Los Angeles International. It was a long flight and on arrival both were jet-lagged. Luckily, Wilson had the next morning off and wasn't needed until the afternoon. He decided to visit Phoenix Bookshop in Santa Monica, which was run by his friend John Wright. The area brought back fond memories of Christopher Isherwood and that meeting with Henry Miller and Aldous Huxley more than thirty years earlier. He had lectured at the Phoenix before—I saw him speak there in the late 1980s and early nineties—and Wilson wanted to catch up with John, but also to inspect his section on UFOs. The success of *From Atlantis to the Sphinx* had inspired Wilson's editor at Virgin to commission him to do a book about the "abduction experience," and Wilson thought he might as well get started on the reading.

He hadn't paid much attention to ufology since the early days of the 1950s and sixties, and his ignorance showed. At FortFest, a conference put on by *Fortean Times* in Washington, D.C., in 1994, Wilson had listened to a lecture by David Jacobs, an alien abduction expert, and was absolutely baffled, having no idea what he was talking about. Now, looking at rows and rows of books he had never heard of, he was taken aback. He would, it seemed, have to do some serious research. Wilson collected dozens of books from the Phoenix and arranged for them to be shipped back to Cornwall. When one of John Wright's assistants told him that a nearby New Age bookshop was closing down and having a sale, he went there to have a look and wound up buying dozens more books. Realizing that he would be late for his afternoon filming—and seeing that the credit card bill for the morning would make Joy wince—Wilson arranged for these books to be shipped as well, hopped into a cab, and headed to the tar pits.

At the George C. Page Museum, overlooking the tar pits' oily, bubbling surface, the camera rolled while Wilson spoke of the evidence for a sudden mass extinction, occurring sometime around 11,000 BC. The record suggests that in as brief a period as twenty-five years, more than a dozen species simply ceased to exist. The cause of this global cull may have been a massive meteor striking the earth. Or, as Charles Hapgood believed, a sudden shift in the earth's crust.

The next part of the documentary was filmed in the Library of Congress, where Wilson spoke about Hapgood's ideas at the place where he began his research into the Piri Re'is map. Also in this segment was Rand Flem-Ath, who had corresponded with Hapgood, and whom Wilson was happy to see again. Then the big part of the journey began. In December 1996, Wilson, now accompanied by Joy, flew from London to Mexico. One of the main themes of *From Atlantis to the Sphinx* was the idea that before Atlantis was destroyed, its inhabitants left and colonized other parts of the globe. This, Wilson and other theorists believed, could account for the strange similarities found between places as far apart as Egypt, Mexico, and South America.

Such similarities had been noticed ever since the American congressman Ignatius Donnelly published an erudite and still very readable study of the lost continent, *Atlantis: The Antediluvian World*, in 1882. Like Hapgood, Donnelly had researched in the Library of Congress. He spent twelve years on the book and when it appeared it was an instant success. He pointed out the similarities in architecture and legends, many concerning the Flood, between Egypt and Mexico, and his suggestion that the Azores could be the tops of mountains from the lost world was so convincing that the British prime minister, William Gladstone, petitioned Parliament to fund an expedition to see if he was right. Not surprisingly, Parliament declined. Wilson's brief for this part of the film was to argue that at some point in the dim past, Quetzalcoatl, also known as Viracocha, a blond, blue-eyed, white-skinned man—or god—had led a band of similar white-skinned followers from the east, and brought civilization to Mexico and South America. Viracocha and his followers, Wilson would argue, were survivors from the last days of Atlantis, who had headed west to escape her destruction, while others of the Atlantean diaspora headed in the other direction, to Egypt.

Wilson spent two days filming at the ruins of the sacred city of the Toltecs, Teotihuacán, an ancient site thirty miles northeast of Mexico City. In its heyday Teotihuacán had been as large as imperial Rome in its prime. It was first seen by Europeans in 1520, when the conquistador Hernán Cortés came upon its ruins, much of which were buried beneath the earth. Cortés wound up there when fleeing the Aztecs. They had risen up against him after he had seized their emperor, Montezuma, who had, unfortunately for him, approached the white strangers in peace. The story is that Montezuma mistook Cortés and his party for followers of Viracocha, who legend said would return one day. Cortés repaid this trust by taking Montezuma captive and eventually murdering him. He went on to defeat the Aztec army, which marked the beginning of the end of their civilization. Part of Wilson's work included filming in a tunnel beneath the great Pyramid of the Sun and in a small chamber about which, he says, practically nothing is known.

The next stop was Tollan, also known as Tula, the legendary capital of the Toltecs, located fifty miles north of Mexico City. Legend says that a titanic battle took place there between the gods Quetzalcoatl and Tezcatlipoca. Tezcatlipoca, the Lord of the Smoking Mirror—a device which, it seems, was able to create visions of faraway places—won, and Quetzalcoatl left, promising to return (hence Montezuma's fatal mistake). In 1880, while searching for Tollan, the French amateur archaeologist Désiré Charnay uncovered huge blocks of basalt, which to him resembled the feet of some enormous statute. Charnay called these statues "Atlantides," reflecting the widespread belief among early New World archaeologists that, as Ignatius Donnelly had argued, the civilizations of South America had their roots in the ancient lost world.[8] Wilson said as much as he was filmed standing near Charnay's Atlantides. What is strange about the Atlantides is that the figures hold unidentifiable instruments in their hands, one of which, Wilson believes, resembles a modern power tool. No one knows what these strange objects are; the official guidebooks call them *atl-atls*, spear throwers, although there is no evidence for this.[9] After Tollan Wilson traveled to Oaxaca, where they filmed at Monte Albán—"White Mountain"— a huge pyramid site, dating back to 500 BC, which displays carvings showing the castrated corpses of mysterious white men.

In Puebla Wilson visited Cholula, whose pyramid, now a pile of rubble, is three times the size of Giza, and is considered the largest building on earth. From there Wilson went to Villahermosa, to film at the giant Olmec heads in La Venta. The features on these heads are strangely reminiscent of the face on the Sphinx, and suggest, as the nineteenth-century archaeologist Edward Herbert Thompson believed, that there was a connection between the two. Thompson's guess was that Atlanteans were responsible, a suggestion he made in 1879 in an article, "Atlantis Not a Myth," in *Popular Science Monthly*, three years before Donnelly's book.

In January 1997, after a brief pit stop in Cornwall, the next leg of Wilson's search for lost Atlantis found him and Joy in Egypt. Like any number of tourists, Wilson found himself looking at the Great Pyramid of Giza and wondering *how* it could have been made. He knew that moving the two and half million stone blocks, some of them weighing up to eighty tons, would prove a challenge even to modern engineers. That the builders had access to some kind of power of which we are unaware struck Wilson as highly likely.[10] The huge sarcophagus in the King's Chamber was also a mystery. It was too big to fit through the narrow passageways, so it could not have been brought into the pyramid after its completion. The chamber must have been built around it. But why was the sarcophagus empty? For that matter, why was the chamber itself empty, and why was the whole of the interior of the pyramid strangely featureless and bare, unlike those of later pyramids? Why did the sarcophagus have no lid? Even more baffling was, again, *how* it could have been made. The great Egyptologist Flinders Petrie thought its red granite could only have been cut with some kind of saw studded with diamonds—not standard issue in 2400 BC.[11] Not only this, what was one to make of the strange mathematical precision involved in the cutting? Petrie's measurements showed that the sarcophagus's external volume was precisely twice its internal volume. This would require the expertise of a jeweler—but *why* such precise mathematical relations? What could they mean? And how could the granite have been hollowed out? What tools did the people of 2400 BC have that could perform precision work that would daunt modern stonemasons? Petrie also unearthed a variety of vessels, bowls and vases, made of diorite—a stone as hard as granite—whose contours and precision were, by all accounts, beyond the abilities of the pyramids' supposed makers.[12]

Pondering these questions in the sweltering interior of the pyramid, Wilson experienced a brief sense of contact with another reality, as he had in the Buddhist temples in Japan. At the Sphinx he was also able to confirm, to his own satisfaction, Robert Schoch's conclusion that the erosion marks on it and its enclosure had been made by water, not sand. But all of Wilson's time was not spent on work. Escaping for a day before their flight home, Wilson and Joy capped off their brief Egyptian adventure with a flying visit to Luxor and Karnak, where Schwaller de Lubicz had spent years in intense study.

In March 1997, the longest leg of their travels began, a fourteen-hour flight from London to Buenos Aires, Argentina. From there they had another, three-hour flight to La Paz, Bolivia; at some twelve thousand feet above sea level, it is the highest capital city in the world. For someone who hated travel, Wilson was certainly getting a lot of it. On arrival, both he and Joy felt the effects of the thin air. Their hotel provided them with mate de coca, a tea made from the leaves of the coca plant, from which cocaine is derived, which is known to help with altitude sickness. For the Wilsons it proved less effective than the margaritas they secured at the hotel bar. Even these, though, did not prevent Joy from experiencing heart palpitations that night. Wilson spoke no Spanish, so he was forced to resort to sign language when he tried to get the oxygen canister the hotel kept for such emergencies. A brief fear of having to ship Joy home in a coffin proved groundless, but she was shaken enough by the experience to decline the trip to Tiahuanaco the next day, given that it would have meant traveling another five hundred feet above sea level.

That was a shame. Wilson found Tiahuanaco "extraordinary." Of all the ancient sites he had seen in the past few months it was the most impressive, even more than the Giza complex. For one thing, it was once a port. Lake Titicaca, with which Tiahuanaco is associated, is nearby, and poses its own mysteries. One is the presence of sea creatures in it, which suggests that at some time it was connected to the sea. How it found itself more than two miles *above* the sea was one of the questions that Wilson found himself trying to answer, sifting through Hapgood's ideas about the earth's shifting crust for clues. The massive port area of Tiahuanaco—one wharf, Wilson suggests, was able to accommodate hundreds of ships—is now twelve miles south of the lake and a hundred feet above it. The huge blocks jumbled around the ruins suggest some enormous upheaval laid waste to the site, a result, perhaps, of Hapgood's shifting planetary crust. Tiahuanaco is also associated with the Viracocha legend, and a statue supposedly of this mysterious white visitor depicts someone with a mustache and beard. This would suggest it is not of a native inhabitant, as native South Americans have little facial hair.

As in Egypt, the size of the stone blocks is staggering; one tips the scales at 440 tons. How could a people who had not hit upon the wheel manage to move them, especially in the thin air of the Andes? And why did they choose such cyclopean building materials, when they could have used smaller and more wieldy ones?

The Viennese archaeologist Arthur Posnansky studied Tiahuanaco and its surrounding area for almost half a century, and believed that it was built in 15,000 BC. Posnansky reached this conclusion by studying the astronomical alignments of the many standing stones that make up much of the structure. He saw that the two observation points dedicated to the winter and summer solstice were slightly out of alignment, but his calculation soon revealed why. Because of an astronomical phenomenon known as the "obliquity of the ecliptic," which alters the position of the Tropics over thousands of years, the observation points *were* aligned to where they should have been in 15,000 BC. This suggested more evidence for Hapgood's prehistoric maritime civilization. Contemporary archaeologists dispute Posnansky's findings, calling them "a sorry example of misused archaeoastronomical evidence."[13] Yet a German astronomical commission, led by Dr. Hans Ludendorff of the Potsdam Astronomical Observatory, studied Tiahuanaco between 1927 and 1930. They reviewed Posnansky's work and decided that he was correct, although they did bring the date of the site's building somewhat closer, moving it to 9300 BC. In *The Flood*, the archaeoastronomer Neil Steede suggests a date of 12,000 BC. He also points out that whoever built Tiahuanaco was able to smelt metal; the huge stone blocks that had been toppled revealed that they were held in place by metal clamps. The metal had been poured into the stone while molten, which suggests that the builders had some kind of portable forge, able to reach a terrific heat. This again suggests a technology not known to be available at the official time of construction.

The part of Tiahuanaco that led Posnansky to his dating was the Kalasasaya, which means Place of Standing Stones. This courtyard, girdled by a ring of twelve-foot-tall shards of granite, was for Wilson the most impressive part of the site. What struck him most was a statue known as "El Fraile" (the Friar), which resembled nothing so much as the fish god Oannes who, according to the Babylonian historian Berossus, was supposed to have brought civilization to Babylon. The Friar's huge eyes and scales suggested a similarity; he looked nothing like any friar Wilson had ever heard of. And this strange Friar was also very much like descriptions of the fish gods that the Dogon tribe in Mali, Africa, said had come from the skies, and brought civilization to earth and taught them the teachings of the double star Sirius. Looking at this unlikely Friar, Wilson began to wonder if ideas about ancient astronauts were not so improbable after all. . . .

After Tiahuanaco Wilson and Joy flew to Cuzco, Peru, where he filmed at the colossal walls of Sacsayhuaman. This strange citadel, near the old city of Cuzco, twelve thousand feet above sea level in the Peruvian Andes, was as mysterious as the Giza complex. The immense stones, some twelve feet high and weighing up to one hundred tons, were cut so perfectly that they are held in place without mortar; no knife blade can slip between them. The stones are cut in irregular shapes, like pieces of some gigantic jigsaw puzzle, yet they are perfectly balanced. Again, how they were put in place remains unknown. After this Wilson and Joy took the mountain train to Machu Picchu, their last stop on this global "search for the miraculous."

Machu Picchu had lain unknown and silent for centuries. It was left to the elements after the Incas abandoned it, sometime in the sixteenth century, until it was discovered in 1911 by the American explorer Hiram Bingham. The Incas had held out here in their last days. The Spaniards had never discovered it, and when the Incas finally gave up their struggle, they abandoned it. Like the other ancient sites Wilson had visited, it was an engineering dream—or nightmare. Again, huge blocks of stone—some weighing up to two hundred tons—were laid atop each other with such precision that the space between them was merely theoretical. Again, how could the people supposedly responsible for it have managed it? The same team of German scientists who had checked Posnansky's dating of Tiahuananco checked the astronomical alignments at Machu Picchu and argued that it was built sometime between 2000 and 4000 BC, perhaps even as early as 6000 BC, somewhat earlier than the official date of 1500 AD. But if it had been built before Greece or Rome, exactly *who* had built it, and the other astonishing sites he had visited? The question continued to bother Wilson, but for the time being he had to put it on hold.

After traveling halfway around the world, in April 1997 Wilson found himself back in Cornwall, happy to be home among his books and records. What he had seen in Egypt, Mexico, Peru, and Bolivia only strengthened his belief that our ancient ancestors had access to the kind of knowledge that, since *The Occult*, he had argued could be made available to us, if we could make the necessary shift in consciousness. The question was, *how* could that shift be made? With individuals he had some idea, but how could it happen with a whole culture, a question he had first asked in *The Outsider*? Yet now it seemed that his journey around the planet was only a prelude to studying the evidence for some possible journeys *off* it. The months spent investigating ancient sites had, we've seen, altered his ideas about ancient extraterrestrial visitors. Now, looking at the boxes of books he had shipped from Santa Monica, Wilson decided it was time to investigate the mystery of UFOs.

His introduction to the strange world of aliens and abductees had actually begun two years earlier, in March 1995, when he took part in a conference on consciousness evolution given by the Marion Institute, in Marion, Massachusetts. His fellow speakers were Rhea White, founder of the Exceptional Human Experience Network; Peter Russell, whose *The Global Brain* (1982) was an underground best seller; and Stanislav Grof, a Czech psychologist and early experimenter with the therapeutic effects of psychedelics, who went on to become one of the most respected names in the "alternative" community. Wilson had met Grof before, at Esalen and also at the California Institute of Integral Studies, in San Francisco, where Grof was a professor of psychology. When Wilson went up to greet him at the conference, Grof was speaking with someone else. This turned out to be the Harvard psychiatrist and Pulitzer Prize winner John Mack, whom Wilson had met before and whose book on T. E. Lawrence he had made much use of recently, rereading it for the documentary on Lawrence that he was about to make.[14] They did not have much chance to speak—the duty of socializing with paying attendees prevented that—but soon Wilson would discover what Mack had been up to since doing his book on Lawrence.

At the conference in Marion, Grof told a story about a psychedelic therapeutic session he held with a woman with a history of drug addiction, alcoholism, and criminality. Grof told the audience how during one particularly intense session, the woman's face froze into a "mask of evil" and she began to speak with a deep, male voice which introduced itself as the Devil.[15] The Devil then began to threaten Grof. He seemed to have a peculiarly accurate knowledge of Grof's personal life, something the woman patient would not have had. Grof told the audience that he believed he experienced a "tangible presence of something alien" during the two hours the Devil "possessed" his patient. Grof finally managed to "exorcise" the unwanted guest by meditating. The strange thing was that after this experience, the woman began to improve, giving up drugs and drink and bringing order and stability to her life. It had been a frightening ordeal, but it had proved beneficial to her. Grof tried to understand the "possession" in terms of Jungian archetypes, but Wilson wondered if that really could account for what had taken place.

On the way back to England after the conference in Marion, Wilson stopped at a bookshop in Boston and stocked up on material for his "sacred sites" book. He also picked up a book that he saw was by his friend John Mack. Wilson knew Mack was a psychiatrist and a professor at the Harvard Medical School. What he didn't know was that he was the author of *Abduction: Human Encounters with Aliens* (1994), one of the most controversial books in ufology and one that almost cost Mack his career.[16] As Wilson read the book on the flight back to Heathrow, it seemed to him that many of the cases Mack recounted were not altogether different from the strange story Grof had told at the conference.

Mack's own story of how he became involved in the abduction phenomenon was rather like Wilson's introduction to it. A psychiatrist friend had asked Mack if he would like to meet Budd Hopkins. Mack had no idea who Hopkins was, least of all that he was a New York artist who helped people who believed they had been abducted by aliens.[17] Mack had never heard of alien abductions; he figured that if Hopkins believed in them, then he was as crazy as the people he supposedly helped. But a meeting with Hopkins some months later changed his mind.

Hopkins informed Mack that for decades, across the country, people of all walks of life had claimed that they had been taken aboard alien spacecraft. Most of the aliens fit the by-now well-known description of the "grays": strange beings with gray skin, huge dewdrop-shaped heads, and large black eyes. Hopkins's abductees spoke of being taken onboard spaceships where they were subjected to some kind of invasive medical examination and, occasionally, sex with one of their abductors. Most of the cases involved some kind of time loss, with abductees claiming that hours, even days of their lives had disappeared. Mack was understandably skeptical of these claims, but when he met some of Hopkins's clients, he had to admit that they seemed to be normal, everyday people. They weren't mentally unbalanced or motivated by a hunger for attention or a desire for some excitement in their lives. Most of them had no idea that there were others like them, nor were they interested in "weird" subjects, such as UFOs or the occult. Even the accounts of the experience had a repetitious sameness. One would think that if each person were inventing his or her own marvelous tale, details would differ. But Mack found that this wasn't the case; in practically all the encounters, incidentals about the interior of the craft were strikingly similar. These were, as far as Mack could tell, ordinary people who had been subjected to an extraordinary experience which affected them profoundly. Many said their lives were changed for the better because of it.

Hopkins asked Mack if he could refer abductee cases from the Boston area to him and Mack agreed. Between 1990 and 1994 Mack saw more than a hundred individuals who believed they had been taken onboard an alien ship and "examined." The ages ran from a toddler of two to septuagenarians, and the people involved included computer specialists, musicians, teachers, housewives, businessmen, and even psychologists. Mack collated his findings and in 1994 produced *Abduction*, in which he argued that, as far he could tell, the people who claimed to have had abduction experiences were not crazy. They were not mentally ill or delusional and, based on his examinations, had truly had the experiences they spoke of. Mack believed that if this was the case, it was the responsibility of psychiatrists and academics to take these people seriously and not, as had been routinely done, dismiss them as cranks. If this meant that our ideas about reality needed to be changed, then they should be changed. As he told the BBC, "I would never say, yes, there are aliens taking people. I would say there are compelling powerful phenomenon here that I can't account for in any other way."[18]

Wilson knew of early accounts of being taken onboard a flying saucer, works such as George Adamski's *Flying Saucers Have Landed* (1953) and *Inside the Space Ships* (1955), which tell of his contact with Venusians and jaunts with them across the solar system. There were other contact stories too, like that of George King, the London cabbie and founder of the Aetherius Society, who, in the mid-1950s, had heard an extraterrestrial voice telling him to prepare himself, because he was to become the spokesman on earth of the "Interplanetary

Parliament." King did, and the Aetherius Society is still going strong today.[19] UFOs had even taken an interest in earthly politics, telling Gabriel Green in 1960 that he should run for president.[20] (Needless to say, he did not do well.) All these cases involved the kind of aliens and flying saucers that Hollywood had made popular in films such as *The Day the Earth Stood Still* (1951) and *Earth vs. the Flying Saucers* (1956). But Mack's case studies were different. As Wilson read, he began to have a strange sense of déjà vu.

One case in particular made an impression on him. It concerned a young man that Mack calls Paul. Paul had come to Mack after sessions with another psychiatrist proved unhelpful; she was unable to accept Paul's claims about extraterrestrials and was actually troubled by them. In one session Paul had asked for some sign of the reality of his experiences. A sudden inexplicable *bang* sounded and the psychiatrist was frightened. That night at home the psychiatrist experienced what sounded to Wilson like typical poltergeist phenomena: her bed bounced up and down so much that she resorted to having her house exorcised. Not long after that, the therapy with Paul ended.

According to Mack, Paul recounted an abduction that happened when he was three. Then he remembered another when he was six. He heard a strange voice in his head and then found himself with a group of aliens who seemed somehow familiar. They took him aboard their ship and showed him around. Everything seemed familiar. After he had been examined one of the aliens showed him the ship's control panel, and told him that he was from their home planet. He was taken to sleeping quarters, which again seemed oddly familiar, and told that they were his, meaning that he used them whenever he was on board.

Under hypnosis Paul came to recognize that he really had a "dual identity," one as a human and another as an alien. In fact, he *really* was an alien, but had been put on this planet to integrate with earthlings. The aliens, who had a higher form of consciousness, were trying to help humans evolve, but it was tough work, because they were so resistant to change, something Wilson could understand. Paul was tired of his difficulties here and at one point let out a sigh and said, "I want to go home."

Wilson felt that Paul's case was oddly similar to the story Stanislav Grof had told at Marion, about the woman who became "possessed" by the Devil. They both, he thought, seemed to have dual identities. These *could* be explained through standard psychology. Both had had difficult upbringings and felt themselves to be misfits in some ways, so their "other selves" could be seen as a kind of compensation for their unhappy lives. But Wilson had studied enough cases of multiple personality and possession to feel there was something more at work here. We know that he was not happy with having to accept that "spirits" were a more adequate explanation for poltergeist activity than the more acceptable notion that the unconscious mind was the culprit. Yet the facts seemed to have led him to that conclusion. He had kept an open mind in that case, so experience suggested that he do so here as well. Opening the boxes of books that he had shipped from California, Wilson felt that "whether abductions are a delusion or not, they demand to be taken very seriously."[21] In *Alien Dawn: An Investigation into the Contact Experience* (1998) that was exactly what he intended to do.

In fact Wilson had contact not with aliens, but with people who apparently had been in contact with them. In the mid-1970s Wilson had written a short, illustrated book about Uri Geller. Before meeting him, Wilson was prepared to accept that Geller was, as most of his critics claimed, a charlatan. But Geller convinced Wilson of his authenticity by reading his mind, and reproducing a drawing Wilson had made, which Geller could not have seen. But Geller's genuineness only raised more questions. One of these was about the weird events recounted in Andrija Puharich's book *Uri: A Journal of the Mystery of Uri Geller* (1974). Wilson wanted to know if the events described in the book had really happened. Geller was no longer associated with Puharich; they ended their partnership on bad terms, so Wilson felt Geller would have no qualms saying if Puharich had embellished his account. Wilson, however, was surprised when Geller told him, *"Everything* happened as Andrija describes it."[22]

To understand why this statement was surprising, one needs to know the kinds of events Wilson had in mind. *Uri* relates Geller's and Puharich's experiences with a strange group of extraterrestrials known as the Nine, who, it seemed, had singled them out to spearhead mankind's next evolutionary leap. In the early 1950s, Puharich was studying a Hindu psychic named Dr. Vinod when, while in a trance, Vinod announced, in an upper-class English voice, that he was a representative of the Nine, superhuman aliens who were behind mankind's evolution. Sometime later, Puharich met an American couple who, it turned out, were emissaries of the Nine as well. When Puharich met Geller in 1971, one of the first things Uri told him while under hypnosis was that when he was three in Tel Aviv, he, too, was contacted by the Nine. They, he told Puharich, were the source of his "powers." He told Puharich that they had been "programming" him ever since, preparing him for his mission of inaugurating a new age. (As Wilson came to see, such messianic or apocalyptic anticipation is a common theme among some abductees.)

Puharich's book about Geller is one of the most baffling documents in the whole of UFO and paranormal literature. It tells a dizzying, often confusing tale filled with frankly unbelievable accounts of teleportation, psychic messages, occult histories of the world, and a collection of other fantastic events too numerous and, in the end, mind-numbing to recount. Geller and Puharich crisscross the planet and at one point are called upon to avert a war in the Middle East which could erupt into a global conflict. During a hypnotic session, while recalling Geller's early encounters with the Nine, an alien "metallic" voice announces out of nowhere that "they" have been watching Geller for decades.

Soon after, the tape recording of this voice strangely vanishes. Other things vanish too, or appear out of thin air. Calamities are predicted but do not happen, yet other predictions do come true. This is just a taste of the kind of thing that happened around Geller and Puharich at this time. As Wilson writes, the book relates "a series of events so apparently preposterous that the reader begins to suffer from a kind of astonishment fatigue."[23] Hence his question to Geller about whether the things described in Puharich's book were true.[24] In *Mysteries*, Wilson writes about the Nine, and suggests that the phenomena were associated with Puharich himself, and that in some way, he was responsible for them, a suggestion that Puharich denied.[25]

Yet if the Nine were really interested in helping mankind evolve, and if they were really intent on presenting Geller as their representative, not to mention mankind's savior, then Puharich's book about all this was a huge mistake. It simply backfired. Puharich was a respected parapsychologist; if anything, the book made scientists he had warmed to psychical research back away. The effect was not that different from how early psychical researchers had reacted to the equally strange phenomena that accompanied Madame Blavatsky: it made them draw back, afraid of being associated with Akashic Records and accounts of mysterious letters from Himalayan mystics appearing out of the blue.

What Wilson came to see as he worked through the boxes of books on UFOs and other strangeness was that the kinds of events described in Puharich's book were more or less de rigueur in the weird world of abductees. But he also saw that, as in the case of poltergeists, psychometry, and other paranormal phenomena, when the material is studied rigorously, it becomes clear that the standard "explanations"—fraud, mental illness, celebrity seeking—simply do not work. The phenomena are too strange, widespread, and consistent to be accounted for in that way. Much of the strangeness Wilson came upon found its way into his book. He begins with an examination into the crop circle phenomenon, eerie geometric shapes cut in wheat fields that, from all reports, cannot be accounted for in ordinary ways. Although many claimed to have solved the crop circle mystery by pointing out how the shapes could have been faked—I myself know people who faked one—this did not dissuade Gerald Hawkins, of *Stonehenge Decoded* fame, from taking them seriously and arguing that the phony crop circles were just that, phonies. Through a thorough investigation of the circles, Hawkins concluded that it was possible that the genuine ones—which were far more mathematically complex than the fakes—were a "form of intelligent communication."[26] The question was: from whom?

Wilson tries to answer this question and along the way touches again on ancient civilizations and the possibility of alien visitors in earth's past. He looks at the possibility of a government cover-up and the often absurd accounts of alien encounters, such as the famous "siege of Hopkinsville," in which an entire family fought off an attack by "little shining men" who "somersaulted backwards" or floated in the air when struck by a bullet.[27] Such cases, and that of Geller and Puharich—there are many others—seem examples of what Wilson calls "deliberate unbelievableness," encounters so ridiculous that they seem guaranteed to make rational minds turn away in disgust.[28]

Much of the book is an account of the ideas and careers of important anomalists, such as the French ufologist Jacques Valle; the brilliant writer on the paranormal John Keel, famous for the "Mothman" phenomenon; and Wilson's friend, the cryptozoologist Ted Holiday, for whose posthumous work, *The Goblin Universe* (1986), Wilson wrote an introduction. (Holiday devoted his life to proving the existence of the Loch Ness Monster.) What the three have in common is the belief that UFO phenomena are part of a wider paranormal, psychic, and occult experience. They have more in common with out-of-body experiences, altered states of consciousness, visions, folklore, and legends than with the kind of nuts-and-bolts Martians of the 1950s. The main insight that Wilson draws from this is that many of the "powers" exhibited by the aliens are like the kinds of paranormal abilities he had been investigating since *The Occult.* That is to say, they have more to do with consciousness than with high technology.

This was something that one of the most prestigious names associated with UFOs suggested at the height of the early "flying saucer" craze. In *Flying Saucers: A Modern Myth of Things Seen in the Sky* (1958) C. G. Jung argued that flying saucers were "projections" of the human psyche, images of the "wholeness" the planet sorely needed at a time when it was suffering a kind of global schizophrenia, triggered by the Cold War. They were a sign that mankind needed to grow beyond these puerile conflicts and, as Jung called it, "individuate," that is, evolve into a more mature level of consciousness. Jung spoke of the "flying saucer vision," a term that Wilson's friend John Michell had adopted in his book *The Flying Saucer Vision* (1968), which argued the same point. Wilson's conclusions in *Alien Dawn* echo what Jung and Michell had argued.

Wilson's idea is rather like the belief that John Mack's patient Paul had: that *he* was an alien, who had been sent to earth to complete a mission. That mission was to help mankind evolve to a higher level. Wilson notes that this was his mission too. What he came to see is that Paul may not have been too far off the mark. As he had been arguing for many years now, human beings are far more powerful than they believe. They, in fact, possess many of the powers exhibited by the "aliens." Their problem is that they *don't know* they possess them. Wilson's idea is that the aliens—or whoever is responsible for these strange encounters—are trying to let us know that we do. They are trying to move us past our fallacy of insignificance and the deadening belief that the material world is all there is. As John Mack had said, if our ideas about reality need to be changed, then they should be changed. The aliens are here to help us do that.

Wilson notes that in his late and little-known novel *Star-Begotten* (1937) H. G. Wells, another thinker deeply committed to an evolutionary point of view, had said as much. In *Star-Begotten*, Martians bombard the earth with cosmic rays and produce "fairy changelings," a new kind of human, one much more in line with the vision of a mankind free of all trivialities. At the end of the novel the hero sees that his own son is one of these changelings and that, like John Mack's patient Paul, he is one too.[29] These "strange visitors from another planet, with powers and abilities far beyond those of mortal men," as the tag from the old *Superman* television series had it, are trying to make us more like them.

But if this is so, if the "aliens" want to help us evolve, why don't they just come out and tells us, rather than go through this strange, baffling, and ultimately confusing rigmarole? Even the most well-intentioned reader of abductee accounts soon begins to wonder if the aliens are fans of Monty Python, the Marx Brothers, and the Three Stooges. The answer, as with the paranormal, is that if the truth were just handed to us, it would make us lazy. We have to work for it, like the planarian worm; otherwise we would too easily take it for granted. UFOs fall under William James's "law" that "no case involving the paranormal should ever be wholly convincing." As Wilson writes, "the mystery is essential, to open up the way to the perception of higher-order knowledge. More positive intervention would be self-defeating, since the aim is to persuade human beings to take the crucial step for themselves."[30]

The "aliens," it seems, want to "lure free will into expressing itself and recognising its own existence." Wilson had expressed as much at the end of *The Mind Parasites*, thirty years earlier. When Gilbert Austin, the book's hero, contemplates the idea that the "space police"—beings of a higher evolutionary order that he has come into contact with—should become the new teachers of the human race, he decides against it. "Nothing could be more dangerous for the human race," he tells his comrades, "than to believe that its affairs had fallen into the hands of supermen."[31] Why? Because it would make us lazy and impede our reaching the next stage in our evolution, *through our own efforts*. Austin himself, who with his colleagues has made the breakthrough—via phenomenology— decides it is even best for his fellow humans if he disappears, "in such a way that the human race could never be certain of his death."[32] He vanishes, with his equally advanced fellows, on the spaceship *Pallas*, which was last known to be moving in the direction of Pluto, where Austin suspects that the space police have established a base. This base, it seems, is the source of the strange "saucerlike spaceships" which have appeared all over the earth since the mid-twentieth century and have on occasion made contact with some of its inhabitants. . . .

With writers such as Patrick Harpur and John Keel, Wilson accepted that there is a "psychic reality which runs *parallel* to our physical reality."[33] Ghosts, poltergeist, fairies, UFOs, and other "strange visitors" are all somehow part of this parallel reality—and as Wilson makes clear in an account of some of the wilder aspects of quantum physics, the idea of parallel realities is practically commonplace for many scientists today. Wilson speculates that the inhabitants of this other reality evolve, just as we do. So over the centuries their form has shifted from spirits of the dead, to poltergeists, to the "controls" familiar to mediums, to our own spacemen. We may not know for certain if these strange neighbors have a purpose in intruding into our reality, but their effect, Wilson says, is clear: "to remind human beings that the material world is not the only reality." They "wake us from our 'dogmatic slumber', and galvanise us to evolve a higher form of consciousness."[34]

In that higher consciousness, it becomes clear, Wilson believes, that "the mind . . . has some sort of control over the material universe." This is something the "aliens" seem to display with baffling ease, and which we ourselves can begin to notice whenever strange synchronicities occur, something Wilson himself noticed while writing the book. He noted that it frequently happened that when he glanced at his digital clock, it read 1:11, 2:22, 3:33 and so on. The odds on this happening are sixty to one, and it happened too often to be "just coincidence." It even happened once when, waking early, as he usually did— Wilson usually woke at dawn and spent the early morning hours reading—he thought to himself, "I bet it's 4:44." When he looked at the clock it was.[35]

Wilson believes that such minor phenomena are a way of letting us know that we are on the right track and an encouragement to carry on. Wilson mentions that the science-fiction writer Ian Watson—whose UFO novel, *Miracle Visitors* (1978), is perhaps a better introduction to the subject than any more "factual" account—noticed the same thing. Watson told Wilson that while writing the novel UFOs seemed to "home in" on him. Synchronicities, material about UFOs, even a visit by a sinister "man in black"—the anonymous, slightly threatening individuals that John Keel found dogging his steps—all seemed drawn to Watson.[36] Like the hero of Wells's *Star-Begotten*, John Deacon, the hero of *Miracle Visitors*, a professor of psychology studying altered states of consciousness, is drawn into speculation about aliens and eventually comes to recognize that he is one himself. According to Wilson, we all are, or at least have the potential to be.

Aliens were not the only thing on Wilson's schedule for 1998. He started his correspondence with Moors murderer Ian Brady that year, which eventually led to the publication of Brady's autobiography, *The Gates of Janus* (2001), for which Wilson wrote an introduction; as we've seen, he broke off the correspondence soon after. The dreaded t-word soon raised its head again and Wilson found himself once more on the move. A trip to Canada had him speaking at the Toronto Writers Conference. Another visit to the New York Open Center led to a meeting with Frank DeMarco, a publisher from Virginia who soon found himself publishing some of Wilson's work, including the last volume of Spider World; *Shadowland* (2003) is dedicated to DeMarco. Wilson had practically given up on finishing the series, feeling his imagination had dried up; he was most likely also inhibited by the failure of *Metamorphosis of the Vampires* to find a home.[37] But after writing *From Atlantis to the Sphinx* and the books that followed, he felt the urge for fiction again, and DeMarco's enthusiasm about the series encouraged him to return to it.

DeMarco's Hampton Roads Publishing Company would also publish a congenial, casual work about Wilson's taste in reading. *The Books in My Life* (1998) was inspired by Henry Miller's book of the same name. In it Wilson takes us on an unbuttoned walk through the literature that has made an impact on him and helped to form his own tastes and ideas. We find many familiar names— Dostoyevsky, Sartre, Nietzsche, Shaw—but there are also some surprising entries. Wilson shows a warm affection for the romantic "wish fulfilment" novels of Jeffery Farnol, a British novelist whose sweeping tales of love and high adventure were huge successes in the early twentieth century. He also shows a surprising admiration for Mark Twain. *Tom Sawyer*, he tells us, made a powerful impression on him as a boy. "From the first page, where Aunt Polly catches Tom in the larder stealing jam, I was hooked."[38] Most revealing, perhaps, was Wilson's love of a character from *The Wizard*, one of the many "boys' magazines" he read religiously. Not surprisingly, he was especially keen about a series of stories titled *The Truth About Wilson*, which depicted the adventures of a remarkable character, a kind of mysterious superman, who appears out of nowhere and vanishes just as easily. Wilson breaks sports records, possesses enormous physical powers, earns many universities degrees, has conquered death, and is hundreds of years old. "It seemed to me that Wilson was perfectly correct. There is no good reason why human beings should not learn to cheat death."[39] This was a theme that a later, more sophisticated hero, Bernard Shaw, would make central to his "metabiological Pentateuch," *Back to Methuselah*. Along with being his mother's favorite and the adoration of aunts and uncles, the fact that one Wilson could read about the amazing adventures of another must have had a hand in dispelling any early fallacy of insignificance. There are other surprises, and an essay on Sherlock Holmes as a "flawed superman" is worth the price of admission alone. Yet while Wilson admits that he likes a good story—H. Rider Haggard and Edgar Rice Burroughs were childhood raves—in the end the books that had most influenced him were those that had made him think.

Wilson met DeMarco at a party given by the chemist and paranormal investigator Alexander Imich, president of the Anomalous Phenomena Research Center in New York and, at the time of his death in 2014 at the age of 111, the oldest man in the world.[40] (One wonders if he, too, read Shaw.) DeMarco, who knew Imich, had traveled from Charlottesville, Virginia, in order to meet Wilson. The two hit it off and DeMarco told Wilson that he was a student of the work of Robert Monroe, whose accounts of "out-of-body" experiences (OBE) in his book *Journeys Out of the Body* (1971) Wilson had written about in *Mysteries*. In 1958

Monroe, a radio engineer, was resting on his sofa one afternoon when he felt his hand go through the floor. He then found himself floating above his body and soon sailing around the neighborhood in some strange "astral" form. Later he entered other, very different realms. The strange realities that Monroe soon found himself exploring—he called them "locales"—seemed, Wilson thought, very similar to how T. C. Lethbridge had spoken about "other dimensions," and were also reminiscent of some of Swedenborg's accounts of his journeys in the "spirit world."

Monroe developed a method of inducing out-of-body experiences involving synchronized sounds that establish a balance between the brain's hemispheres. Monroe called the technique "hemi-sync." When DeMarco tried the process at the Monroe Institute, in Virginia, he had a remarkable experience in which he seemed to have traveled back to Concord, Massachusetts, in the 1870s and met Ralph Waldo Emerson.[41] In October 1998, Wilson and Joy flew to Charlottesville for the launch of *The Books in My Life*; while there he visited the Monroe Institute. He declined trying out the "Gateway" course, aimed at inducing OBEs; like his ambivalence about mescaline, he felt that "this wasn't for me." But he did put on the hemi-sync headphones and in a "black room" designed for their use, he experienced something of the deep calm and peace he had felt in the Shingon temples in Japan and briefly in the King's Chamber at Giza. When he returned to Cornwall, he reread Robert Monroe's books and concluded that if his experiences were not fantasy—and Wilson felt they were not—then Monroe must be regarded as "one of the greatest paranormal investigators of the twentieth century."[42]

Wilson did not have much time to rest in Cornwall. Earlier in the year he had accepted an invitation to take part in an "ancient knowledge" lecture cruise down the Nile.[43] His companions would be other writers on ancient civilizations: John Anthony West, Robert Bauval, Robert Temple, Michael Baigent, Ralph Ellis, and Yuri Stoyanov, an authority on religious dualism and author of a remarkable book, *The Hidden Tradition in Europe* (1994). Each would give lectures to the paying guests as the boat made its way from Aswân to Karnak, Luxor, Dendera, Edfu, and Abydos. In November, Wilson and Joy left London and flew to Cairo International. Their hotel, the Mena House, was within walking distance of the Sphinx. At half-past five the next morning, they were up with the others, to witness sunrise over the pyramids.[44] As Wilson looked at these great blocks of stone, the difficulties in erecting these enormous structures hit him once again. Even if the first few "steps" of the pyramid could have been constructed using sheer manpower, which was just conceivable, how were the huge, heavy blocks lifted to reach the steps much higher up? A ramp? But because of the angle, such a ramp would soon have proven to be as difficult to make as the pyramid itself. It would have extended for miles and used as much material as the pyramid. Cranes? Not even the most powerful modern cranes could do it. Again Wilson was led to the conclusion that some *other* kind of power must have been at work.

After breakfast he and Joy went to the Museum of Cairo, where they saw the statue of the pharaoh Chefren, which had been found in the Sphinx temple. They both agreed that Chefren looked nothing like the face on the Sphinx—at least, this image of him didn't. They also saw the aerial photographs of the Sphinx and pyramids that had convinced Robert Bauval that the whole Giza complex had been designed to mirror the ancient Egyptian night sky. The pyramids matched Orion's belt—Orion was an important constellation for the Egyptians—and the Nile was the Milky Way. Wilson and Joy both felt there could be no doubt about it.

The next morning they were on a flight to Aswân, where the party was joined by a military escort.[45] A year before, on November 17, 1997, Islamist terrorists massacred sixty-two tourists at the temple Hatshepsut, a female pharaoh of the eighteenth dynasty, in Deir el-Bahri, across the Nile from Luxor. Understandably, the promoters of the lecture cruise, and the Egyptian government, were taking no chances.

In ancient times Aswân was known as Syene and it played an important part in the story of early astronomy. In 240 BC the Greek astronomer Eratosthenes hit upon a way to determine the circumference of the earth. Although we are told in school that Columbus discovered that the earth was round shortly before sailing across the Atlantic in 1492, like many other facts about the earth and its place in the universe, the fact that our planet is a sphere was known to the ancients. That such knowledge was subsequently lost suggests that the quest for lost knowledge driving many books about the ancient world is motivated by something more than crank ideas. Eratosthenes knew that at noon on the summer solstice the sun was reflected in the water of a deep well in Syene. This meant that the sun was directly overhead and that the towers around the well would cast no shadow. But in Alexandria, some five hundred miles away, where Eratosthenes lived, towers did cast shadows at noon. Eratosthenes measured the length of a shadow cast by an obelisk in Alexandria at midday on the solstice. This gave him the angle of sun's rays, which turned out to be 7 degrees. He calculated that if 7 degrees was equal to 500 miles—the distance between Syene and Alexandria—then 360 degrees would equal roughly 24,000 miles. As the actual circumference of the earth is 24,901 miles, this is a remarkably accurate figure for 240 BC. Sadly, Wilson wasn't able to find the well that Eratosthenes used, which is not surprising, given that no one knows where it is. Instead he and Joy settled for a good dinner on their boat, the *Sun Queen*.

Sailing down the Nile, on their way to Edfu, one of the most sacred sites in Egypt, Wilson remarked on the lush greenery that bordered the river, and wondered how the land must have looked in 10,000 BC, when Schwaller de Lubicz believed the Sphinx was built. The Temple of Horus at Edfu is one of the best preserved and most impressive in Egypt. On its outer walls the battle between the dark god Set and Horus, son of Osiris, is depicted, and the building texts associated with this tell the story of the temple's construction.

At Edfu they were met by the historian Emil Shaker, an authority on ancient Egypt.[46] Shaker told Wilson that he believed sound played an important part in the temple's function. Authorities such as Paul Devereux have demonstrated that megaliths have remarkable acoustic properties, and Shaker pointed out how this was also true of Egyptian temples.[47] Shaker explained that certain hieroglyphics specified the number of times a ritual needed to be performed to be successful. The ritual turned out to be a kind of chant or hymn to the sun, which needed to be done three times, while making an offering. Wilson hummed and felt that the stone amplified the sound. The chant, Shaker explained, was needed to "activate" the temple.

Wilson soon discovered what activating the temple could mean. Looking at the sanctuary, a kind of cubicle of stone, Wilson began to circle it when he noticed a kneeling form blocking his way. It turned out to be Michael Baigent, author of many books about ancient religion, Rennes-le-Château, and the Priory of Sion. Baigent had his head against the stone and was clearly meditating. Wilson quietly withdrew and after a time joined John Anthony West outside the sanctuary, who spoke to him about the importance of the Building Texts. After a while the group was rounded up and taken back to the *Sun Queen* for lunch.

After lunch, Robert Bauval noticed that Michael Baigent was missing. He was due to lecture soon and Bauval—who had organized the trip—did not want a delay, so he asked Wilson if he could step in for Michael. Wilson did. Given the possibility of danger, the group was understandably worried. Concern about Baigent grew until he appeared, two hours later, having taken a taxi back to the boat, which in the meantime had moved downriver. Wilson asked what had happened. Baigent said he wasn't sure. He said he had been meditating for a few minutes and the next thing he knew everyone had left. Wilson corrected him. He had been meditating for at least twenty minutes; Wilson had seen him. Baigent was surprised. What had seemed only a few minutes for him was really a much longer time. His meditation had somehow activated the temple and he was briefly taken into eternity, the aim, one suspects, of the temples in general.[48] Wilson believed that Baigent had tuned in to the millennia of worship that had accumulated in the stones, just as he had tuned in to a similar psychometric vibration at the Buddhist temple in Japan.

The next day found the group at the tomb of Ramses VI in the Valley of Kings. When their guide Emil pointed out that a design on a wall of a long corridor seemed a depiction of human sperm, Wilson was surprised. How could ancient Egyptians, having no microscopes, know what sperm looked like? Wilson's fascination with this mystery, however, was cut short by the effects of a stomach bug he had picked up, and which proved a nuisance for the rest of the trip. Wilson did his best to appreciate the temple of Hatshepsut but a dawn visit to Karnak defeated him, and one to the temple at Dendera was less than successful. He had wanted to see the famous zodiac painted on its ceiling ever since he had written about it in *Starseekers*. According to Schwaller de Lubicz, it proves that the Egyptians knew about the precession of the equinoxes. Wilson was able to examine the zodiac long enough to agree.

By the time the group made its last important stop Wilson had thankfully recovered. At Abydos the tour headed to the Oseirion, the mysterious tomb of Osiris that lies behind the temple to Osiris built by the pharaoh Seti I sometime during his reign. The Oseirion was discovered in 1903 by Flinders Petrie and his then assistant, Margaret Murray, who later became famous for her book *The Witch-Cult in Western Europe* (1921), which argues that the witches of medieval and modern Europe were devotees of an ancient pagan religion that worshipped the horned god Pan. What makes the Oseirion unique among Egyptian temples is that its style is much rougher and cyclopean than others. Although mainstream Egyptologists date it to Seti's reign (1294–1279 BC), its similarities to the Sphinx suggest an earlier date of construction. In fact, it is closer to Stonehenge in style and construction than anything else, formed of massive, uncouth blocks, simply laid upon each other, lacking the decorations found at other temples. The archaeologist Henri Frankfort, who worked on the site after World War I, declared that Seti I had it built, although the differences between the Oseirion and Seti's temple to Osiris are glaring. The Swiss archaeologist Édouard Naville, who took over work on the Oseirion after Petrie and Murray, disagreed, and believed it was the "most ancient building in Egypt."[49]

One of the strange things about the Oseirion is that much of it is now sunken under water, which made Wilson think of a swimming pool. A deep trench around the center of the temple suggested a moat, and the cells behind this gave the place an air of a monastery. Wilson went to the edge of the water, peering into its depths. Like Michael Baigent, he somehow found himself outside of time, so much so that Joy had to shout to him that the others were leaving and that the gates would soon be shut. Passing the later carvings on Seti I's temple on his way out, Wilson had a strange feeling that, compared to the Oseirion, they seemed to be part of the "modern world." He had seen some remarkable sites in the past year, but the Oseirion struck him as "one of the most powerful places in the world."[50] He was glad it was off the usual tourist track. A flow of sightseers would only drain it of its power, as they had that of Stonehenge, Carnac, and other sacred sites that made up the standard itinerary of "esotourism."

Back in Cornwall, Wilson for once was very happy about all the traveling he had been obliged to do. He considered the Nile cruise "field work" for a new project. When *The Flood* had aired earlier that year, Wilson had e-mailed Rand Flem-Ath to ask if he had seen it. Rand hadn't, so Wilson sent him a video copy. Not long after, Rand e-mailed Wilson back, thanking him for the copy and also asking if he would consider collaborating on a project. He needed another hand because Rose, his wife, who usually worked with him, was busy writing a novel. Wilson was interested. When Rand sent him an outline of what he had in mind, Wilson quickly became excited.

Wilson knew that Rand had corresponded with Charles Hapgood and was in touch with him until his death in 1982, when he was hit by a car. (Strangely, John Mack was killed the same way in 2004.) But Rand had not told Wilson the full story. When he did, Wilson felt certain he had the making of a best seller in his hands. Just before his death, Hapgood had written to Rand, telling him that "in recent discoveries I believe I have convincing evidence of a whole cycle of civilization in America and Antarctica, suggesting advanced levels of science that may go back 100,000 years."[51] The figure took Rand's breath away. A hundred thousand years was many times more than the accepted date for the start of civilization. Even Cro-Magnon, our direct ancestor, came on the scene only forty to forty-five thousand years ago—or at least so it was believed in the 1980s.[52] *Who* was around in 100,000 BC to possess "advanced levels of science"? In his letter Hapgood had mentioned tantalizingly that he would include much of this new information in a new revised edition of *Earth's Shifting Crust*, which he was then working on and which would come out the following year.

Rand, however, could not wait that long and he immediately wrote Hapgood back asking for more details. Weeks went by and there was no word. Finally he heard. His letter had been returned stamped "Unable to deliver. Addressee Deceased." Not long after sending his letter to Rand, Hapgood had stepped off the sidewalk in front of a moving a car and had died in the hospital. Rand heard no more from him about his startling new information, and the new edition of *Earth's Shifting Crust* did not appear. How was he ever to know? Now he asked Wilson if he would join him in trying to discover exactly what Hapgood had learned that made him speak of advanced civilizations a hundred thousand years ago.

Wilson did. The idea of a civilization on earth a hundred thousand years ago was, of course, outlandish, if we think of "advanced" levels of science in terms of our own left-brain form of knowledge. But what about Robert Graves's "lunar knowledge," the kind of intuitive knowledge Wilson had been researching, exploring, and finding evidence for over the past thirty years? The kind of knowledge Schwaller de Lubicz believed the ancient Egyptians had access to? He also knew that his friend Stan Gooch had argued in a book called *Cities of Dreams* (1989) that Neanderthal man was much more intelligent than we had believed and that there was evidence that he had a "civilization," somewhat like that of the North American Indians, one based not on technology but on a kind of harmony with the earth.[53] Neanderthal was around earlier than Cro-Magnon, who wiped him out once he arrived. Was it conceivable that Hapgood had Neanderthal in mind?

Wilson was on the case and it soon became clear that Hapgood was a very interesting character.[54] He had determined, through the Piri Re'is map, that *someone* in the very ancient past had knowledge about Antarctica that they shouldn't have, and as Wilson made clear in *The Flood*, the Piri Re'is map is only one of dozens housed in the Library of Congress that contain similarly accurate but anachronistic knowledge. One, associated with the fourteenth-century French mathematician and cartographer Oronce Finé—often Latinized as Oronteus Finaeus—is even more accurate than the Piri Re'is map, and received corroboration from the Cartographic Section of the United States Air Force.[55]

But Hapgood had also had a very good idea of where the remnants of Atlantis could be found, even though his friend, the cryptozoologist Ivan T. Sanderson, had cautioned him never to mention the "dreaded A-word." Hapgood took Sanderson's advice, but on occasion he did breathe the unspeakable to some select souls, one of which, according to the writer Charles Berlitz, was President John F. Kennedy. Hapgood believed that the tiny St. Peter and St. Paul Rocks, part of an archipelago that lies in the Atlantic Ocean just north of the equator about six hundred miles off the coast of Brazil—so small they don't register on Google Maps or any other satellite imagery—were all that was left of the great lost continent. He told Sanderson that all he needed was a wealthy backer to fund an expedition. Berlitz says that because of his wartime service with the Center of Information (later the Office of Strategic Services and then the CIA), and a connection with President Roosevelt's Crafts Commission, Hapgood felt he had a good chance of getting some government support.

Rather as Prime Minister Gladstone had petitioned Parliament to fund an Atlantis expedition, Hapgood apparently spoke to Kennedy about having jets fly over the two tiny islets, searching for signs of any structures on the seabed. In October 1963, Hapgood had apparently arranged a meeting with the president, which Kennedy's assassination the next month scotched. Hapgood then tried to get Nelson Rockefeller and Walt Disney interested, but neither took the bait.

Hapgood never found a backer for his Atlantis adventure, but his belief in the lost continent's reality infected Rand Flem-Ath, who had become fascinated with Hapgood's work through his own love of ancient maps. But Rand thought he had a better location for Atlantis than his mentor, and in any case, by now, the Atlantic seabed had been extensively explored and mapped by oceanographers who in the process did not come across a lost, sunken world. A much better candidate, Rand believed, was Antarctica. And he believed he had the math, graphs, and calculations to prove it.

When he began to send these to Wilson, his new partner could only agree. It was also clear that a bigger picture was emerging. Rand had discovered that the two-mile avenue known as the Way of the Dead in Tiahuanaco was misaligned to true north by 15.5 degrees, a misalignment that it shared with fortynine other Central American sacred sites. What could this mean? Why were all of them misaligned in the same way? Rand believed it meant that these sites *had been* aligned to what was true north, *before* the huge shift in the earth's crust, moving it some two thousand miles, that Hapgood had argued took place sometime between 15,000 and 10,000 BC. This would mean, then, that Tiahuanaco and the other sites had been built then—or at least that they had been built over other, earlier sites. That successive structures were erected on the same sacred site had become clear to Wilson when writing his *Atlas of Holy Places & Sacred Sites*. Christians had done it all over the place, as had people before them.

This was remarkable enough. But Rand had also a great many graphs and charts that showed that these sites, and others around the globe, were located according to a recognizable pattern. They were not put up merely by locals for local reasons, but were all part of a vast web of connections, markers crisscrossing the planet like a grid. It seemed that the people responsible for them had encoded each sight with recognizable mathematic, geographic, and astronomic knowledge. They formed, he believed, a kind of blueprint, based on phi, "the Golden Section, a ratio that can be found throughout nature, in everything from spiral galaxies to sunflowers."[56] Added to this was Rand's theory that the original site of Atlantis was Antarctica, which flourished there before the continent had iced over, and which had been the homeland of the prehistoric "worldwide seafaring civilization" that Hapgood had argued for long ago.

Rand was even able to predict where a sacred site *should* be, according to the pattern (the reader will have to go to the book itself to get the details about this). He was on target in finding a Mayan temple at Lubaantun, in British Honduras, where the mysterious crystal skull was said to have been discovered. In science, when a theory is responsible for accurate predictions, we tend to say that it is true. Rand's seemed to be hitting the bull's-eye.

Wilson started looking for a publisher. When Graham Hancock's agent took on the job, he asked Rand to come to London so they could pitch the idea. Wilson lent Rand the airfare. The result was a very handsome commission from Little, Brown. Then, in February 1999, the two went to New York, where they were successful again. Wilson lent Rand the airfare again, and also lent him his part of the advance so he and Rose could buy a house. Other parts of the puzzle began to fall into place. During his Nile excursion, Wilson had discovered something called the "Nineveh number," a fifteen-digit number that had been found among tablets unearthed by archaeologists while digging at the ancient site of Nineveh in what is modern-day Iraq. No one could understand what ancient Assyrians would have *done* with such a large number. But an aeronautics engineer named Maurice Chatelain, who had worked on the Apollo moon missions, had an idea. Through a series of calculations involving the precession of the equinoxes and other factors, Chatelain worked out that the number was a kind of constant figure of the solar system, a multiple of every heavenly body's rotation and revolution. By working out a slight discrepancy in the earth's rotation—caused by its infinitesimal slowing each year—Chatelain was able to determine that the Nineveh number must have been used as early as sixty-five thousand years ago.[57] If correct, this added support for Hapgood's one-hundred-thousand-year-old science.

As work on the book began, Wilson recognized that the notion of a highly advanced *science* was not the same as that of a highly advanced *civilization*. As mentioned, it was possible to have knowledge *without* all of the technological development that we associate with it. As Oliver Sacks had pointed out, "idiot savants" incapable of simple, everyday tasks can nevertheless know whether a number as long as the Nineveh number is a prime or not, just by looking at it. They can even toss large primes around off the top of their heads. The same was true, Wilson knew, of "lightning calculators." If people of our time can inexplicably do this—and fail our usual standards of intelligence—why shouldn't our very ancient ancestors have been able to as well, given that our usual kind of intelligence doesn't seem involved in the process? This, he realized, seemed to undermine the idea that ancient astronauts brought us this knowledge—we had it already—although his memory of the Friar in Tiahuanaco suggested he keep an open mind on this.[58]

Wilson had spoken with many of Hapgood's friends, asking if he had said anything about his hundred-thousand-year-old science to them. He drew a blank until he called a retired professor in Massachusetts whom, to preserve confidentiality, he called Carl. What Carl told him was astounding.[59] It was he, he said, who had put Hapgood on the trail of the hundred-thousand-year-old civilization. He was convinced of the idea for two reasons. One was that ancient man knew the true size of the earth well before the Greeks. Carl told Wilson that in *Historical Metrology* (1953) the geographer A. E. Berriman argued that although the Greeks did not know the circumference of the planet until Eratosthenes, when given in terms of the Greeks' unit of measure, the polar circumference of the earth is 216,000 stade. A stade is 600 Greek feet, and the number of Greek feet in one degree of the earth's circumference is 600.[60] Ergo a stade equals one degree of the earth's circumference. Such exactness cannot be coincidental. It meant for Carl that well before Eratosthenes, a much earlier civilization knew the size of the earth, and this knowledge was inherited, unknowingly, by the Greeks in the size of their stade.

Even more surprising was Carl's insistence that Neanderthal man was much more intelligent than we believe. As this was something Wilson himself had come to accept, that Carl insisted on it too only made his own suspicions stronger. Could Neanderthal have lived in Atlantis?

When Wilson told Rand that Carl seemed to have solved the mystery of Hapgood's reasons for believing in a hundred-thousand-year-old science, he was surprised at his reaction. Rand had his doubts, then actively dismissed the idea. Later, after looking into Carl's background, he decided that he was a fraud. Wilson couldn't accept this. True, some of the things he said were frankly unbelievable—but then wasn't that true of Atlantis itself? But Wilson felt he was too intelligent and knowledgeable to be a fraud.

But this didn't budge Rand, who thought the idea that Atlantis—which he had been trying to find for decades now—had been peopled by Neanderthal was preposterous. He simply rejected the idea as ludicrous. A friend Rand had mentioned the idea to had immediately burst out laughing. That was enough to convince him that it was ridiculous.

Wilson was unmoved. More and more material about the unsuspected intelligence of Neanderthal had come to light. There were, for instance, the fifteen Neanderthal blast furnaces that had been found near Barcelona, and a report had spoken of a kind of "superglue," a pitch made of birch that Neanderthal used to affix ax blades to handles. He had also unearthed some very interesting information about Hapgood himself: he had an interest in the paranormal, hypnosis, precognition, and past-life regression, all things that Wilson had been studying for a good thirty years. Hapgood had concluded that primitive man possessed paranormal powers, a conclusion Wilson had also arrived at. It seemed that his conclusions and Hapgood's coincided, which suggested they were on the same track. He put all this into the last chapters of the book, and as far as he could tell, Rand accepted it.

The Atlantis Blueprint turned out to be a big book. When finishing it, Wilson was also editing a version of his "phony guru" book, which Virgin published in the UK as *The Devil's Party* (2000); Frank DeMarco's Hampton Roads brought it out in the United States as *Rogue Messiahs* the same year. (It had already appeared in a Japanese edition in 1996.) Wilson had also traveled quite a bit while working on both, lecturing in New York, Milan, and Rome and making unusual stops in San Marino and Sardinia, where he spoke at conferences on ancient Egypt. He was also approaching seventy. So we can perhaps excuse him when he says that when the final proof reached him, he put it aside briefly while he finished some other work. When he did get around to it he was stunned. The proof was clearly much shorter than it should have been. Precisely two chapters shorter, in fact. The material on Neanderthal and Hapgood, like Atlantis itself, had simply vanished, as had any mention of Neanderthal in the remaining text. Rand had changed these to "people like us," which gave the impression that Wilson was speaking of Cro-Magnon, which he wasn't.

Understandably, Wilson was furious with this and immediately e-mailed Rand to ask what on earth had happened. Rand replied angrily, indignant at Wilson's inference that he—Rand—had chucked out Wilson's last two chapters without even mentioning it. He had mentioned it, in detail, but apparently he—Wilson—either hadn't read the e-mail or, if he had, had forgotten. Wilson had been writing books for the past forty-five years, so it is doubtful that he didn't bother to read an e-mail about his latest work—which, he may have reminded Rand, would not be seeing print if it had not been for his efforts. And he certainly would not have forgotten an e-mail about taking out the punch line of the book. But Rand insisted it was there.

Wilson and Joy trudged through all the e-mails the two had exchanged over the past several months. Finding nothing, Wilson asked for the date of the one in question and Rand informed him. With this clue, Joy was able to find it. Depending on your perspective, either Wilson had lazily scanned the e-mail and not noticed Rand's suggestions about a "slight restructuring," or Rand had cleverly hidden his treachery in an innocuous e-mail about personal matters, appended by pages of latitudes and longitudes. I have not seen the e-mails but as a working writer myself, any kind of change, especially at the late stages of a book—the missing material had been included in the final edited typescript—are usually spelled out up front and out loud, not tucked away where there is a good chance that someone will miss them. [61] One can see Wilson as too trusting a soul, with a willingness to believe the best in people, when perhaps a little circumspection would be warranted. This was the case with Charlotte Bach. It may well have been the case with Carl. One suspects Wilson may have wondered if it was the case with Rand.

In the end, after several acrimonious e-mails, the friendship fractured and the book, with its truncated ending, appeared. As might be expected, it was not the best seller that Wilson had at first envisioned. It does not seem to have been reviewed and some readers have expressed to me a feeling that Wilson may have strayed into territory better covered by writers such as Graham Hancock, whose follow-ups to *Fingerprints of the Gods* and *The Message of the Sphinx* have been highly successful. Nevertheless, although a choppy read, with chapters by Wilson in the first person and those by Rand in the third, and more longitudes and latitudes than the present writer can absorb—Wilson himself confessed that he only has to see a map "covered with lines drawn all over it to groan and close the book"—it does contain some fascinating material. [62] Archaeological anomalies drawn from *The Flood*; reflections on the importance of the Knights Templar (in which his trip to Rosslyn Chapel came in handy); Rennes-le-Château; the Book of Enoch; the remarkable quest of Colonel Percy Fawcett to find the lost cities of the Amazon; the roots of Freemasonry, and much more. But no Neanderthals.

Their day, however, would come.

CHAPTER FOURTEEN

ON THE WAY TO SUPER CONSCIOUSNESS

Wilson felt that *The Atlantis Blueprint* was a travesty. It was like "an Agatha Christie thriller with the last chapter missing."[1] And the soured friendship with Rand was a loss. But Wilson was a professional. He promoted the book in London and in Glastonbury, one of the sacred sights he had written about in recent years, speaking there at the Glastonbury Symposium, an annual conference on a variety of alternative topics that had started up in the early 1990s. Wilson even climbed the Tor, an eerie five-hundred-foot mound ringed by a spiraling path that rises out of the Somerset plain, topped by the ruined thirteenth-century St. Michael's church. For a large man with back problems getting on in years, this was most likely a challenge. It was AD 2000 and the millennium was on its way. A sense of expectancy bubbled in the alternative community, and had been given a nudge the year before, when the solar eclipse of August 11, 1999, plunged southern England and most of Europe into a brief darkness.

Wilson had written about the eclipse for the *Daily Mail*; his article, "Feel the Force," invited his readers to open up to the mysteries of the cosmos.[2] Many of them did. He had been writing regularly for the *Mail*, one of Britain's conservative tabloids, since 1994, on a variety of topics: crime, UFOs, the afterlife, the paranormal, hypnosis, with titles such as "When the Devil has a Disciple," about the serial killers Fred and Rose West, and "Aliens in our Midst?"[3] At the summer solstice 2000, Wilson joined a Druid ceremony at Stonehenge and wrote about it in his column.[4] The *Daily Mail* serialized parts of *Alien Dawn* and *The Atlantis Blueprint* and would do the same with some of Wilson's later books. Until his last piece in March 2010, Wilson was a familiar feature to the *Daily Mail*'s millions of readers, having contributed some eighty articles to its pages.

For someone who had started his career as an Outsider, having regular column space in a conservative middle-market newspaper (a U.S. equivalent would be the *New York Daily News*) may seem incongruous, but Wilson himself never paid much attention to these distinctions. Although he wrote about philosophy and knew as much about world literature, music, and art as he did about the paranormal—which was quite a lot—Wilson was never a highbrow snob; considering he came from a working-class family, this is no surprise, nor is the fact that the more "left" newspapers, such as the *Guardian*, took potshots at him whenever possible. With the *Mail*'s reputation for sensationalism and scaremongering, this was inevitable. This didn't faze Wilson, nor did it bother him that for some, perhaps many, he was little more than a male Mystic Meg, the astrologer for the *Mail*'s competitor, the *Sun*. Like Meg's readers, many of Wilson's no doubt took in some interesting stuff about the sixth sense or ghosts over breakfast before moving on to the sports page or gossip columns. The articles were intelligent, informative, and well written, and he voiced some unpopular views in them, and not only ones about aliens or spirits of the dead. His last piece argued in favor of the death penalty in some cases, a change of heart that had begun in 2005, when he wrote about the shooting of two police officers in Bradford in the north of England. One officer, a mother with a family of five, who had only been on the force a short time, had been killed when the gun blast pierced her body armor and penetrated her chest.[5]

Wilson had argued against the death penalty in *Encyclopaedia of Murder*, saying that "most murderers do not deserve to be executed" and that by executing those who do, we "brutalise ourselves."[6] But that was at the start of his long study of crime and killers. By 2005, he had been investigating murder for more than forty years, and his article showed why he had changed his mind. In 2010, considering the killer Ian Huntley, serving two terms of life imprisonment for the murders of Holly Wells and Jessica Chapman, both aged ten, in 2002, Wilson no longer supported the total abolition of capital punishment. The death penalty, "far from being a form of state-sanctioned viciousness," he wrote, "actually demonstrates greater compassion to both murderer and victim. . . . A truly moral society," he felt, would recognize that "no purpose" was served by keeping Huntley in his cell.[7]

In June 2001, Wilson turned seventy. It was a relatively quiet year for him in terms of publications. But *Rogue Messiahs* had come out the year before. It was called *The Devil's Party* in the UK; the title was taken from William Blake's remark about his fellow poet John Milton, who was "of the Devil's party, without knowing it," something Wilson believed was true of his false messiahs. The *Mail on Sunday* gave the book a thumbs-up, and even the *Times Literary Supplement* (*TLS*) took notice, although their review, while on the whole positive, did point out some editorial problems.

One of Wilson's main themes in the book is that the downfall of many bogus spiritual leaders is sex; they tend to become obsessed with it as an expression of their dominance over their flock. The careers of Jim Jones (Jamestown massacre), David Koresh (Waco massacre), and even less-murderous characters such as Aleister Crowley make this clear. Noting this, the *TLS* reviewer pointed out that, although Wilson had written about "the occult, magic, and other esoteric themes," the "world of sex and violence . . . has clearly engaged him most closely."[8] While acknowledging that Wilson "writes entertainingly"—"his large cast of misguided aspirants to Messianic status . . . preach, plot, quarrel, rage, rape, break every law, suffer and die . . . across his colourful pages"— the reviewer assures us that this is not in "any way an academic offering. . . . Sharper editing" could have pruned some repetition, and he could have relied less heavily on anecdote. There was also the standard reflection that because Wilson's interests range "across diverse fields," allowing for a wide perspective, there is also an unfortunate tendency toward digression.[9]

This tendency toward digression does make for an at times choppy read, a handicap the book shares with *The Atlantis Blueprint*. Before publication several chapters dealing with contemporary French philosophy, which are fascinating in themselves but seem out of context with the rest of the book, found their way to the cutting room floor. They were later resurrected in *Below the Iceberg* and are engaging evidence that Wilson kept abreast of developments such as structuralism, deconstructionism, and postmodernism. As we might expect, he was critical of all three. He takes especial argument with the work of Michel Foucault, Roland Barthes, and Jacques Derrida, some of the biggest names in postexistentialism France. Sartre had died in 1980, but had been out of fashion for some time. In an obituary for the *Evening News*, Wilson remarked that while Sartre's death may seem an "out-of-date sort of catastrophe," he was nonetheless "one of the most exciting and brilliant figures in twentieth century literature."[10]

The link between Foucault and a mad messiah such as David Koresh may not be immediately clear, but in the end Wilson found that Foucault—a homosexual who had a taste for dark eroticism, S&M, and "sex with the stranger"—was as much a charlatan as Koresh; he was an "intellectual con-man" out to deceive his readers.[11] Barthes was a "depressive romantic" whose attempt to write literary criticism as if it were phenomenology displayed his "philosophical ineptitude."[12] Derrida's rejection of meaning in any text—something he shares with the other two—was "ultimately sterile."[13] Wilson's rejection of Derrida, and his warranted exasperation with the fact that he was considered one of the most important intellectuals of the age, comes through in a brief account of deconstructionism, written for his son Rowan's literature course at Oxford, also included in *Below the Iceberg*. Rowan had found Derrida's work "gobbledegook"—"understandably," Wilson sympathized—so his father explained it to him in plain English.[14] What Rowan's literature professor may have thought of this is unknown.

Yet even without the digressions into French philosophical fashions, *Rogue Messiahs* seems to suffer from a lack of a solid center. Its main argument is that false messiahs and their followers are made for each other. The messiahs are members of the dominant 5 percent on the lookout for ways to express their dominance. Their followers are individuals looking for some meaning beyond the triviality of everydayness. The bad guru needs the adoration of his flock; unlike the dominant .005 percent, he still relies on other people to feed his self-esteem, and, as Wilson's often gruesome pages show, in some cases he will go to murderous lengths to secure it. Multiple killings surrounding Shoko Asahara, leader of the Japanese cult Aum Shinrikyo (Supreme Truth), and Jeffrey Lundgren, leader of a breakaway cult from the Church of Latter Day Saints—to mention only two examples—provide gory evidence of this. The follower, on the other hand, is too lazy to work toward his own salvation, and in exchange for a life in which all problems vanish in light of the teaching, he gives up his freedom. The complete control over his followers' lives exhibited by Jim Jones and their masochistic acceptance of it are sad evidence of the level to which a powerful need for belief and belonging can reduce someone.

Yet Wilson argues that in both cases, positive drives are at work; the problem is that they can easily become warped. The false messiah is in search of an identity; the masochistic believer has a powerful "will to believe," in William James's phrase. "Human beings need to believe," Wilson writes, "because belief leads to action and human beings are born with a need to act. . . . Without purpose, human beings feel only half-alive."[15] The problem is that this hunger for purpose can lead to some very strange altars.

Not all the messiahs Wilson looks at were monsters. He writes of Rudolf Steiner's rise to European fame after World War I, and of Krishnamurti's refusal to be a theosophical world avatar and subsequent career as a nonteacher of a nonteaching. Freud, Jung, and the spiritual writer Paul Brunton make important appearances. But in our time, many charismatic but frustrated individuals adopt the mantle of guru in order to bolster a fragile self-esteem. Their need to impress others inevitably draws them into a whirlpool of indulgence and self-destruction. Very few messiahs avoid the paranoia that seems part of their bargain with the Devil.

Yet in trying to account for the often delusional psychology of many of his murderous messiahs, Wilson enters territory which, fascinating in itself—like the axed chapters on Foucault and Co.—again seems somehow out of place. In his attempt to understand the messiah's need to "transform reality," Wilson looks at some remarkable case studies of delusional psychosis. He tells the strange story of the "three Christs of Ypsilanti," in which a psychiatrist tried to free three individuals of their shared delusion that they were Christ by bringing them together. Milton Rokeach, the psychiatrist in question, believed that the collision with two competitors would shake each Christ's awareness so that they would recognize that they were, indeed, mad.

It didn't work, for two reasons. Wilson argues that people withdraw into a psychotic other reality in the first place because they find this one—our everyday reality—too difficult to cope with. To them it is threatening and frightening; it undermines their self-esteem. They are often inadequate characters, and the necessities and demands placed on them prove too much. Rather than collapse in complete breakdown and recognize themselves as a failure, their unconscious mind provides them with an alternate reality, which, while cutting them off from our shared reality, ensures that they won't fracture entirely. In a way it is a variant of the dictum of H. G. Wells's Mr. Polly: "if you don't like your life you can change it." For the three Christs of Ypsilanti it was rather, "if you don't like your reality you can change it." Too weak to change their lives, they left them for another, more amenable world. They had no reason to leave it to return to the one they had left behind.

The other reason why Rokeach's experiment failed is that the unconscious mind, responsible for the alternate reality, is incredibly powerful. We have already seen some evidence of this throughout this book. Wilson relates the strange story of "Kirk Allen and the jet-propelled couch." Kirk Allen (a pseudonym) was an actual rocket scientist who had developed the habit of taking imaginary journeys to the Mars of Edgar Rice Burroughs's John Carter novels. It was when his interplanetary hops began to affect his work that he was recognized as a borderline psychotic and sent to a psychiatrist. Allen came to believe that his real life was on Mars, where he was a ruler, and that like John Mack's Paul, he was an alien here on earth. Allen's fantasies began after a series of emotional shocks—loss of a governess mother figure, seduction at twelve by her nymphomaniac replacement, and finally the sexual advances of a too-forward workmate. As he retreated from an abrasive and invasive world, his fantasies about his life on Mars went up a notch, and after an exceptionally uncomfortable episode, suddenly he was *there*. "He found himself sitting at his desk on Mars, dressed in the robes of his high office, then making his way to the secret room and consulting the photographs in the filing cabinet."[16] After that, Allen spent more and more time on Mars and less on planet Earth.

Wilson points out that Allen's psychotic fantasy of being on Mars had the kind of reality that we sometimes find in very vivid dreams. He also argues that it is not that distant from the kind of inner journeys people such as Jung took when engaged in "active imagination" or Rudolf Steiner did when reading the Akashic Records. But where in the case of Allen and Rokeach's three Christs, the unconscious mind's ability to provide a substitute reality is detrimental, for individuals aiming to transform their lives creatively—that is, positively—it is a powerful tool. Wilson looks at the career of the poet W. B. Yeats as an example. Yeats began as a dreamy, world-rejecting romantic poet who, like Kirk Allen, found the real world much too inhospitable. Instead Yeats sang of fairies, spirits, and Celtic myths of old. His attitude can be seen in his poem "The Stolen Child," in which fairies lure a child away to their magic lands because "the world's more full of weeping than you can understand."[17] Yeats was what Wilson would call a typical romantic, withdrawing from a too difficult, demanding, ugly world and creating a more suitable substitute in its place. He complained of "all things uncomely and broken / all things worn out and old," just as Ouspensky did on his return to this "wooden world" after his experiments with nitrous oxide.[18] It was exactly this desire for fairy worlds and magic that led Yeats first to Theosophy and then to the Hermetic Order of the Golden Dawn.

But Yeats was also a hardheaded Irishman and as he developed and matured his attitude toward reality became less defensive. He was less withdrawn and his poems took on a hardness and clarity that later earned him the Nobel Prize for literature. We can say that he began to *attack* reality, rather than flinch from it, to go on the offensive, to master life. Yeats never gave up his belief in magic, but rather than use his imagination to create an alternate reality he could retreat to, he used it to transform *himself.* As Wilson writes, Yeats's *Last Poems* (1938–1939) "reveal a man who is completely adjusted to reality and who recognizes that his own sense of purpose is somehow connected to human evolution." This is the "profane perfection of mankind" Yeats speaks of in "Under Ben Bulben."[19] Yeats, Wilson says, shows that "we are not faced with a bleak choice between self-deception and a reality that frightens and depresses us," as Kirk Allen and Rokeach's three Christs were frightened and depressed. The study of false messiahs, Wilson believes, teaches us that "the unconscious mind can transform reality *without* self-deception."[20]

Where does this transformation take place? In what Wilson calls "the second stream," the current of imaginative and intellectual activity that runs parallel to the "primary stream" of ordinary, everyday life, a nod to the distinction H. G. Wells had made long ago.[21] Most of the time the two streams are mixed and life is a burdensome muddle. But there are moments when they separate and, with the everyday demands quieted, the mind can "lift off" and soar into spheres of inner freedom, the kind of freedom Wilson had pursued for practically his whole life. It is difficult to achieve and fleeting—Wilson tells of reaching it one sleepless night in a Japanese hotel. It is not, he says, a "visitation," but something that can be achieved "by direct effort." There is no reason why these powers should respond only to self-delusion, he tells us. They are in fact presages of "the more highly controlled states of consciousness of which human beings are capable."[22]

This was the real message of the book. But given its disjointed character, it's not surprising if it was lost on some readers.

Yet with 2001 an important birthday year, there was certainly cause for celebration. A new edition of *The Outsider* was published, to which Wilson contributed a new postscript, commenting on each chapter, bringing the ideas up to date with the most recent developments in his philosophy.[23] After his excursions into ancient civilizations and the strange hinterlands of the occult, his reflections on his first work remind us that throughout his long journey, Wilson remained obsessed with the riddle that started it all, the Outsider's quest for freedom, his voyage into his own consciousness. The main change in the forty-five years since the book appeared was that its author now had a "more pragmatically optimistic" outlook than his earlier, more angst-ridden self.[24] Insights he had gleaned from Maslow, Husserl, and others had made the Outsider's existential dilemma seem more of a problem that could be solved than a crisis that must be endured.

The fundamental necessity was to overcome our deep-seated habits of passivity and negativity. Human beings live as if they are driving a car from the passenger's seat, Wilson said. They must find a way to get in front of the wheel and take control. We must learn how to contact the "secret life," our deep, unconscious source of power. "Our laziness inclines us to live too close to the surface to be aware of these impulses," he acknowledged. But if we live with "enthusiasm and a sense of purpose," we can connect with the deep wells of being.[25] Most of our problems arise from our attitudes. "It is hard for human beings to grasp that their worst fears, the things they find themselves brooding on at two o'clock in the morning, are simply spectres evoked by their own negative thoughts."[26] We have a hundred reasons to be happy; we simply *don't know* that we are. Again, it was that question of really knowing, of *convincing* ourselves that peak experiences, the sensation of becoming free, of absurd good news and other expressions of affirmation are not delusions or crumbs of grace bestowed haphazardly, but actual glimpses of reality. It was our destiny to occupy those new lands of the mind, and from his first book to his most recent, Wilson had worked at understanding how this could be done. Now, after decades of effort, he saw "that it would not be so difficult after all."[27]

The Outsider was not the only early work he would look back on. In honor of Wilson's birthday, Colin Stanley's Paupers' Press issued a new edition of *The Age of Defeat*, a gesture that Wilson appreciated. The book had been unavailable for some time and Stanley did new Wilson readers a service by bringing it out in its first paperback edition.

It was odd at first, Wilson felt, to reread a book he had written more than forty years earlier, and which he claimed not to have looked at in the meantime. Getting through the proof would surely be a chore. Yet as he began to read, his feelings changed and he realized it was one of his key books. The alienation he initially felt stemmed from "looking back at a younger self over a gulf of more than forty years."[28] In the new introduction, Wilson told the story of the origin of the book and of his early days with Stuart Holroyd and Bill Hopkins. But the new edition was not only an exercise in nostalgia. Some new material included a CD of ambient music by In the Nursery, an electronic duo, with Wilson's reading of some of his favorite poetry dubbed in; it was originally recorded at Tetherdown in 1993. The tracks may not be everyone's taste, although a reviewer gave Wilson top marks for his spoken-voice performance.[29] Like his work with the Medici String Quartet in *Mozart's Journey to Prague*, it was another example of Wilson's willingness to explore other forms of expression, something he would turn to again in the near future.

More lasting, however, were Wilson's remarks about an American psychologist whose work he had become aware of only recently. In 1999 a correspondent asked Wilson if he knew the work of George Pransky, author of *The Renaissance of Psychology* (1998). Wilson didn't. His correspondent sent Wilson a copy and he says it had the same impact on him as when he first read Maslow's writings about the peak experience. Pransky and his colleague Roger Mills had developed what they call "the psychology of mind" after Pransky had attended a lecture by a fellow named Syd Banks. Banks wasn't a psychologist or a doctor, but a welder with a grammar school education. But some years earlier he had had an experience that changed his life. Banks was attending a seminar about relationships when, dissatisfied with how it was proceeding, he decided to leave. On his way out, he got into a conversation with a therapist and during it confessed that he was a mess and that his life was nothing but problems. The therapist said he was wrong. He wasn't depressed; he only *thought* he was. This seemingly vacuous cliché electrified Banks. His *life* wasn't full of problems, but his head—or mind—was. If he could change his *ideas* about his life, it would change too.

Banks saw the logic in this and agreed. It was a self-help update on the wisdom of the ancient Greek Stoic philosopher Epictetus. Epictetus, a slave who lived in Rome in the early Christian era, counseled that it is not things that disturb us, but how we think about them. It's not what happens to you, but how you react to it that matters. The one thing in our power is our attitude toward life. By changing this, Epictetus says, we can change our life. Epictetus came to these insights through the study of philosophy, but they came to Banks like a blinding light and he eventually developed a whole spiritual teaching based on them, which he communicated to thousands of people until his death from cancer in 2009.[30]

This might sound like the most vapid self-help wisdom, but it was something Wilson had been saying in a different way for some time. He reflected on his experience in Cheltenham after losing Sally and then finding her again, when he was so relieved that *everything*, even car exhaust and stalled traffic, was beautiful. It was a variant of his belief that if we could use our imagination to grasp how lucky we are that some possible disaster *hasn't* occurred—and we can think of dozens that might happen at any time—we could achieve the same kind of peak that had been granted him when he and Joy had recovered Sally. Wilson also knew the opposite, how negative thoughts can drain us of energy and lead to life failure. His panic attacks had taught him this. He realized that if, on finding Sally, he had merely sighed with relief and carried on as normal, the peak wouldn't have come. He was *amplifying* his experience with his thoughts. Unfortunately, we can think mechanically just as much as we do anything else. It takes very little self-observation to see that our thoughts tend to follow habitual grooves; as with most things, we allow our robot to do our thinking for us. And as we habitually feel that life is out to get us, our thoughts flow from one negative idea or worry to another, with the result that when some mishap takes place, we feel we are justified in our negativity. As Wilson points out, the surest way to bring on disaster is to confidently expect it to happen.

Simplistic or not, what Banks and Pransky were saying made sense. Pransky himself had come upon Banks's ideas when a friend urged him to attend one of Banks's seminars. Pransky was depressed at the time but on listening to Banks he felt transformed. He wasn't alone. At the seminar were doctors, lawyers, psychologists, and other successful professional people. Pransky observed that these people were all "emotionally stable" and exhibited the characteristics that he came to associate with "living in a high state of well-being."[31] Wilson felt that Pransky seemed to have found himself in the company of some of Maslow's peakers, which makes sense, as both Banks's and Maslow's psychologies are based on having a positive, purposeful outlook. We can see that when Maslow's students induced peak experiences simply by *remembering* earlier ones, they were using their thoughts to alter their consciousness. Banks and Pransky's positive message, then, Wilson thought, fit in well with his earlier critique of the fallacy of insignificance.

Although he was now officially a senior citizen, Wilson's workload did not let up. In February 2002 he spoke at a conference on the paranormal in Cardiff. Not long after that he traveled again to the States to speak at a conference on philosophy at Emory University, in Atlanta, Georgia. In May of that year I myself caught up with him in London. I had been living there since 1996 and had already been down to Cornwall a few times, and I had got used to the standard Wilson routine. I was on my own during the day while Colin worked. Then smoked salmon and white wine before a delicious dinner à la Joy, while Colin watched the television news, with the parrot and two dogs in tow. Then wine and conversation until Colin headed for bed around nine p.m., for his usual five a.m. wake-up call, when he would spend a few hours reading before getting back to his desk. As far as I know, aside from illness, nothing broke this pattern.

By 2002 I had been writing pretty regularly for the *Fortean Times* and they had asked if I would interview Wilson live on stage as part of their UnConvention for that year.[32] Among others on the bill were Graham Hancock, Paul Devereux, the comedian Ken Campbell, Doug Skinner (who spoke about his friendship with John Keel), the conspiracy skeptic Jon Ronson, and the "veteran Ufological heretic" Jim Moseley.[33]

On Friday, May 10, Wilson and I took the stage at the Commonwealth Institute in London's Kensington. I had prepared some questions, but the interview soon turned into a lecture about Colin's life and work up until then. According to a *Fortean Times* writer reporting on the event, Wilson gave an "illuminating account of his progress from working-class dreamer to celebrity author, via factory, chemistry lab, civil service, RAF, bohemianism and trampery."[34] Wilson tried to get across to the audience his ideas about intentionality and peak experiences, and instructed them in the concentration exercise he called the pen trick. He also talked about his mescaline experience of 1965, saying that it had given him a feeling of "total happiness and benevolence." After a suitable moment he added, "I loathed it," and explained that he could often get the same effect from radishes.

I had dinner with Wilson afterward, accompanied by several glasses of wine, and he commented on the more skeptical turn the *Fortean Times* audience had taken since its early days in the 1970s. Most of the talk about UFOs at the UnConvention was about the "death of ufology," and focused more on the sociological aspects of the phenomena and not, as Colin had done, on the more philosophical side. Although he did not say it, I thought he must have felt that he was very much old school, and likely out of step with the new breed. I had felt something like this myself. When I first came to know people in London interested in the alternative world, I was surprised to find a much more skeptical tone than I had around people in Los Angeles. When I mentioned that I was a great fan of Wilson's work, the reaction was unexpected. Most people acknowledged the importance of the early books, *The Outsider* and *The Occult*, but the general impression I got was that he had written too much about too many things and had been repeating himself for years.

Could it be true? After all, Colin himself had admitted that it would not have been a great loss if his hero Shaw hadn't written some of his last plays. The same could have been said of Wells, who, past a certain point, seemed to write the same book over and over, something Wilson had already admitted about himself to the psychologist Jeffrey Mishlove on his public television series, *Thinking Allowed*.[35] In his forays into existential criticism he had written that over time writers such as Huxley, Hemingway, and others developed mannerisms, like a kind of shell, that accreted around the original creative force and obscured it, and that in their later works there is more shell than anything else. There is no reason why this should not be true of Wilson himself; like other writers, he suffered the same occupational hazards.[36] But as André Gide once said, "Everything has been said before, but since nobody listens we have to keep going back and beginning all over again," an aphorism that could serve as a motto for all the hedgehogs among us.[37]

Yet, perhaps being a Yank, I didn't realize that for some Brits, Wilson had become something of a typical English eccentric, someone you may enjoy listening to, but whose ideas you don't take seriously—a perspective Wilson had had to labor under for years. After a few skirmishes in which I defended his work and made my allegiances clear, I decided that it was best to do this in print, and not over pints at a pub. Aside from lectures, I still keep that counsel today.

But had Wilson really become a respected but old-fashioned elder statesman, out of step with the current fashions? Not everyone felt that. One was the singer-songwriter and musician Julian Cope, famous for bands such as the 1980s postpunk the Teardrop Explodes and other projects. Cope had become fascinated with the world of ley lines and megaliths and was a devotee of T. C. Lethbridge. He had come across Lethbridge through reading *Mysteries*, and he approached Wilson with an idea he had for a project devoted to Lethbridge's work. The end result was *A Giant: The Definitive T. C. Lethbridge*, a double-CD box set for which Wilson made spoken-word contributions set against "sonically challenging backing tracks," and wrote a short essay for the booklet.[38]

Cope and producer Terry Welbourn, another Wilson and Lethbridge fan, traveled to Tetherdown on September 11, 2001, to record the first sessions. While the world rocked with the news about the World Trade Center terrorist attacks, Cope gave Wilson a crash course in rock terminology, a new experience for the Outsider, who, as far as I know, loathed rock music as much as he did mescaline.[39] They returned the following year to complete the sessions. In October 2003, Wilson was invited to take part in a three-day musical event, "Rome Wasn't Burned in a Day"—"Three Dementianal Nights of Barbarian Rock and Roll," as Cope described it—put on by Cope at London's Lyric Hammersmith theater to mark the release of the CD.[40] Wilson gave a lecture one evening and on another was in the audience when Cope stopped the performance to pay homage to his hero.[41]

More talks followed our interview for the *Fortean Times*, such as at the Occulture Festival in Brighton, an appearance he would repeat the following year, as he would his talk in Glastonbury. But 2002 was marred for Wilson by the publication of Humphrey Carpenter's *The Angry Young Men*, a book about the duffle-coated days of late-fifties London, which Carpenter described as a "Literary Comedy of the 1950s." Wilson found the book "lightweight and unobjective," but what really troubled him is that two years earlier he had invited Carpenter to Tetherdown so he could be interviewed for the book; after all, he was one of the few surviving Angries. As he told a journalist some years later, he gave Carpenter "a very nice meal" cooked by Joy, and "we drank a very old bottle of wine." But Wilson later found out that Carpenter had already written his section on him and had only accepted his invitation so that he could say he had "interviewed" him.[42] As one might expect, what Carpenter had written was not very flattering—"He drove the knife into my back as deep as he could"—and understandably, Wilson was peeved. "What an absolute shit," was his assessment of the biographer of Tolkien and the Inklings.[43]

But aside from the personal slights, what really bothered Wilson was that Carpenter treated what Wilson felt was an important literary movement as if it was a joke. Wilson had his own argument with the Angries, and we've heard much of it in this book, but they were, after all, serious writers and not just a bunch of clowns. Wilson would have to set the record straight one day.[44]

In fact he was already thinking along those lines, or at least about his early days amid the milk bars and bedsits. Paul Copperwaite, Wilson's editor at Virgin, had approached him with the idea of writing his autobiography. Wilson said he had already written one, *Voyage to a Beginning*, and he didn't see the point of doing another. But Paul disagreed, and the more Wilson thought about it, the more he could see his point. *Voyage* had come out in 1969. A lot had happened since then—his whole career as a writer on the paranormal, for one thing— and he could start all over again from the beginning. In fact, the original version of *Voyage*, written to help Father Brocard Sewell's literary magazine, *The Aylesford Review*, differed significantly from its American release, which covered much more of Wilson's sex life.[45] So he decided to do it. But when it came time to talk about an advance, Virgin had to explain that since they had not done as well with his last two books—*Alien Dawn* and *The Devil's Party*—they would have to be a bit conservative with their offer. Wilson wasn't happy with this; the books weren't best sellers, as *From Atlantis to the Sphinx* had been, but Virgin had made their money back and then some with them. So he passed on their offer but decided to write the book anyway. Somebody would publish it.

That somebody turned out to be Mark Booth, an editor at Random House and a writer on esoteric themes in his own right.[46] Booth was aboard the *Sun Queen* as it made its way down the Nile a few years back and Robert Temple, who was also on deck, suggested that Colin meet Mark. With ancient Egypt on the riverbanks, Booth and Wilson talked shop and Booth later showed interest in Colin's ideas about a follow-up to the disastrous *Atlantis Blueprint*. When he later asked Wilson what he was working on at the moment, Wilson said his autobiography, and Booth said he definitely would like to see it. When Colin finished an outline he sent it to Booth; a few days later Booth replied, saying he wanted to publish the book. The fact that he offered a bigger advance than Virgin was no doubt also an inducement. And it was Booth himself who would come up with the book's title.

A taste of what would become *Dreaming to Some Purpose* was given to some devout Wilsonians in the *Colin Wilson Festschrift*, which Colin Stanley and Paul Newman put together in 2003, and which included Wilson's outline of the book. From 1991 to 2003, Newman, a fine novelist and writer on occult and other eccentric matters, published *Abraxas*, a remarkable literary magazine, out of his home in St. Austell, Cornwall, with help from his partner and sometime Wilson secretary Pamela Smith-Rawnsley. The two were part of a local Wilson circle, and were among those he treated to a round of drinks and a tray of sandwiches at the Ship, a pub that he and friends would frequent on occasion in Pentewan. I myself attended a few sessions and can attest to Wilson's generosity.

Abraxas's unique pages provided a very eclectic offering, with poetry, essays, fiction, reviews, and interviews all connected in some way to Wilson, but not slavishly so; often Wilson's own books received a roasting by more than one incensed reader. Over the years I contributed several articles myself, and Wilson was not chary about supplying *Abraxas*—named after the Gnostic god who features in Hermann Hesse's *Demian*—with much material. The first issue featured interviews with Wilson, reviews of Howard Dossor's book on him, and Wilson himself on Bertrand Russell; Wilson appreciated his intellect but was disgusted by his relentless philandering, a point he had made in *The Misfits*.[47] *Abraxas* 7 featured an excerpt from the unpublished *Metamorphosis of the Vampires*. In *Abraxas* 8 Wilson reviewed a biography of R. D. Laing written by Laing's son Adrian, mentioning the time a drunken Laing was arrested by the Hampstead police for throwing a wine bottle through the window of a Rajneesh center. Issue 12 had him slowly getting exasperated with a Dutch fan over the relative merits of Henry Miller. In *Abraxas* 16 he wrote about his love of the English countryside, an article originally written for a Japanese magazine.[48]

This last was an ironic twist, given that the *Festschrift* included the early polemic "Against Gardening," in which Wilson gave vent to his detestation of what is an English national pastime. He has a "strong antipathy to everything connected with gardens, gardening, and gardeners." Conversations about gardens increased his blood pressure. He found the very idea of them "stagnating" and he had never been a "particular lover of nature."[49] (Tetherdown itself is surrounded by beautiful gardens, tended, of course, by Joy.) The *Festschrift* included his introductions to Chinese editions of *The Outsider* and *New Pathways in Psychology*. There is also an interesting article about a return visit to his hometown, Leicester, twenty years later, economically transformed by the influx of Asian immigrants, a pro–open door argument that would fit in well with Britain's current immigration fears. There is also a remarkable essay titled "Bias in History," originally written for the *Daily Telegraph* in 1973, in which Wilson argues that "a biased history book or a patriotic ballad can eventually kill more people than an atomic bomb."[50] Although Wilson mostly kept a low political profile in his books, in these pieces we can see that he was not oblivious to more immediate social concerns and that his approach to them is reasonable, rational, and optimistic. He also remarked perceptively about other major problems, such as pollution, overpopulation, and global warming.

Dreaming to Some Purpose, Wilson's second autobiography, was published on May 26, 2004, two days short of the forty-eighth anniversary of the publication of *The Outsider*. While writing it he had suffered two mini-strokes, which he admits "slowed me down a bit."[51] He had been having health problems for a while. He had developed a sensitivity to cold and was taking blood-thinning tablets. His doctor had told him his blood pressure was too high and that he had to lose weight and cut back on the wine. He had received these warnings before, and seemed to follow them; at least, I know that on a few occasions in the past when he and I had dinner together he stuck to water and passed on the carbs. But Wilson, a determined family man who took his responsibilities seriously and did not succumb to the temptations—mostly in the form of the "sexual illusion"—that had ruined many of his contemporaries, could be allowed one vice, and wine was it. If he did not always follow doctor's orders, can we blame him?

Wilson came up to London to do some prepublication promotion for the book, and in May 2004, we met for an interview about it for the *Fortean Times*. He was staying at the Imperial Hotel, in London's Bloomsbury, not far from the British Museum, the old stomping grounds of Virginia Woolf, E. M. Forster, and others of the Bloomsbury Group. When I knocked on his door I couldn't tell if he heard me. But when he opened it and I walked in, he seemed to be startled by my appearance. He explained that the concentration exercises he had been practicing for years now had made him oversensitive at times to "sudden stimuli," and I guess I qualified as that. He made tea with the electric kettle and after we had settled in I asked how he came to write the book. He related the turn of events mentioned earlier, about how Mark Booth came to publish it. Of the actual writing, he said it was a great advantage to have already written *Voyage to a Beginning*. "One thing you discover as you get older," he said, "is how much you forget." But the many journals he had kept and letters to Joy and his family helped fill in the blanks. When I asked how long it had taken to write, he said not long. "I always write fairly clean copy, so I was able to get it done in a few months." When I expressed surprise that it had only taken a few months to write *The Occult*, a work of some six hundred pages, he said that if you write a couple thousand words a day, it adds up pretty quickly.

After some remarks about the literary nuts-and-bolts aspect of the book, his candor about how much money he made, as well as his sex life, he launched into the central theme of his work. "When I was young," he told me, "I had to generate an extraordinary sense of self-belief and purpose, merely in order to keep myself going; otherwise I might have ended up committing suicide. . . . From the very beginning I felt that the problem of the present age is the enormous amount of gloom that everyone takes for granted." About Samuel Beckett and *Waiting for Godot*, Wilson recalled that his response to its success in Paris was straightforward. "What fucking shit! Who is this half-witted Irishman going around saying that life's not worth living? Why doesn't he just blow his brains out and shut up?" Beckett and the other pessimists, Wilson told me, were victims of what he had taken to calling the "bullfighter's cape." "Ordinary reality is permanently in front of our eyes, rather like the bullfighter who keeps a cape in front of the bull," he said. "It's only when he twists his head that he can see straight ahead"—as Robert Graves had tilted his head a certain way and suddenly "knew everything." But "someone like Beckett just accepts the cape and leaves it there." He was determined to pull the cape away. "What I always wanted was to be in a position to be able to say, 'Now wait! All this is wrong!'

and to point out the enormous problem of modern culture. It was as if some tremendous log had fallen across modern culture and had stopped everything from moving. I saw my job was to get a bulldozer and move it out of the way."

It was not an easy task. He was still troubled by the usual Wilson complaint: that he wrote too much about too many things and that this meant that only a few people had some notion of the ideas that link all his books together. But the autobiography would solve that. "It does it," he said. "It says what all my books have been trying to say, and shows that they're all about the same thing."[52] On the dangers of negativity, a central theme in the book, Wilson admitted that he was "an extremely impatient and irritable sort of person"—he confessed that Joy often felt the brunt of this—"but on the whole I tend not to go into negative emotion at all."[53]

This claim would soon be sorely tested. If Wilson was feeling a bit bruised after mini-strokes and nearly half a century of hard work, his new book, on which he had placed high hopes, was about to a get a terrible beating and in many places would be left very black and blue. The old anti-Wilson animus was strangely in evidence in most of the reviews, this time with a crew of young Turks happy to score points by sniping at an old straw man. In their hands, the story of his life received a battering. The reviewers just couldn't accept that the boy genius was still at it and still insisting on the importance of his absurd ideas. Lynn Barber, the *Observer*'s churlish interviewer, went out of her way to make Wilson look ridiculous. Invited to Tetherdown—as the treacherous Humphrey Carpenter had been—she begins her piece on *Dreaming to Some Purpose* by telling the reader that interviewing Wilson is quite a catch. "This is the first time I've interviewed a self-declared genius, also the first time I've interviewed a self-declared panty fetishist." Driving from the train station to Tetherdown she was troubled by the occasional "fucker" Wilson enunciated, mostly aimed at Humphrey Carpenter. (One suspects he aimed a few at Ms. Barber after he read her piece.) She describes him as an "amiable tweed-jacketed cove [old-fashioned man] you see in glucosamine sulphate ads"—which gives you some idea of the level of her insight—and says she is determined to avoid the topic of "non-pessimistic existentialism," something Humphrey Carpenter didn't care for either, falling asleep on Wilson's couch while he patiently explained the difference between Husserl and Heidegger. When Barber opines on Wilson's "bizarre nomenclature"—such unfathomable conundrums as Faculty X, peak experiences, and Right Men—readers familiar with Wilson's work will suspect that she could not tell the difference between nonpessimistic existentialism and the ordinary kind if her life depended on it.[54]

Once again there was no engagement with the ideas, an absence that was glaring in most of the other reviews, and which must have infuriated Wilson. It would be pointless to rake over them, except to say they are excellent examples of the peculiar British talent for using one's ignorance to appear clever.

There were, however, some notable exceptions. A reviewer for the *New York Times* deplored the treatment Wilson received, saying that the criticisms were "as virulent as those he produced in the 1950s," and praised Wilson's tenacity and optimism.[55] Wilson's old friend, John Michell, gave the book high marks in the *Spectator*.[56] I chimed in myself with a positive review in the *Independent on Sunday*.[57] Philip Pullman, of *His Dark Materials* fame, one of the most popular writers of the time, spoke well of it too. For him the book was "fresh and vivid and full of atmosphere," and he praised Wilson's account of "his discovery that intellectual curiosity is a passion as potent as sexuality."[58] Yet one reader was so enraged at the venomous response to the book that he wrote a book about it himself.[59]

Wilson was understandably disappointed with the critical response. He had expected that *this* book would change everything and that finally the reputation of being a half-baked crank would dissolve and with any luck, serious readers would begin to take his work seriously. After being at it for nearly fifty years, that was not much to ask. Alas, it was not to be.

Yet Wilson showed enviable aplomb in dealing with the bad reviews and undisguised attempts to make him look absurd. There was always work to take his mind off any disappointment and Joy to cheer him up. He was putting together his sequel to *The Atlantis Blueprint* and was already gathering material for his own book about the angry days. There were lectures too: Liverpool for one on Jack the Ripper; London for the Questing Conference, a day of "alternative history, forbidden archaeology and hidden teachings" (he would speak again at the conference the following year, and he and I met up at it). There were talks in New York, Washington, and Virginia. He also contributed another spoken-word performance, this time to a CD about the work of his old friend Stan Gooch, who was sadly languishing in a camper van in Swansea, having given up any creative effort, after years of being ignored by the intellectual elite and writing books that didn't sell.[60] Wilson had tried to get Gooch out of his depression, offering to buy him a computer so the two could keep in touch via e-mail, but Gooch seemed unable to break out of his gloom, regardless of Wilson's efforts. His contribution to *May Day! May Day! The Stan Gooch EP*, by the ARC Collective, may have helped cheer up his old friend.

But Wilson had a chance to unburden himself of some of his own frustration in the summer of 2005, when one of the few positive reviewers of *Dreaming to Some Purpose* arrived at Tetherdown for a visit.

Brad Spurgeon, a journalist for the *International Herald Tribune* stationed in Paris, had been an on-again, off-again Wilson fan for some years when he pitched his editor about doing a story that would tie in the autobiography and the coming fiftieth anniversary of the publication of *The Outsider*. In July 2005 Spurgeon arrived at Tetherdown, plopped himself into "Joy's chair," and turned on his tape recorder. He returned the following February and realized that between the two interviews he had some twenty thousand words of unbuttoned Wilson. Some of the interview saw print in the *Tribune* but most of it remained transcribed on Spurgeon's computer. With that, and a few contributions from Wilson himself, Spurgeon produced a short book, *Colin Wilson: Philosopher of Optimism*. In it we can see how Wilson, who was never an angry young man, made sure that he didn't become an angry old one either.

One of the things I was gratified to see in Spurgeon's book is that he, too, had scared Wilson out of his wits. He had "surprised" Wilson in his garage. Wilson had "leapt in fear" when he noticed him, and explained that he is often so deep in his thoughts that anything unexpected startles him. After that jumpy beginning they settled into the Wilson living room, flanked by books, dogs, and the parrot that Wilson often accused of chewing on his library. After some general talk about his life and work, and a reflection that after many years of struggle, he believed he had "achieved a little of what Gurdjieff calls 'essence,'" Wilson remarked on the response to his autobiography.[61]

"I was pretty sure the autobiography was going to be a great success. It's as good a book as I've ever written. And when it, on the contrary, got viciously attacked, I thought, well, I know *I'm* not wrong. I'm not so stupid as not to know when I've written a good book."[62] Yet the negative response to his life story wasn't the only bad news. Wilson had by then written a few chapters of his own account of the angry decade, and had been in touch with a few of his fellow survivors: Doris Lessing, Alan Sillitoe, even the poet Christopher Logue, who had been in the anti-Wilson crowd in *The Outsider* days. Wilson gave the chapters to his agent and waited to hear the offers. None came. He hit a similar dead end when he sent Bloomsbury, who was publishing J. K. Rowling's very successful Harry Potter books, his Spider World series, which had gone out of print in the UK. A fantasy novelist friend who published with Bloomsbury suggested he try them on it and he did. But after months without a word the books finally came back with a brief note saying they were "fascinating" but not for Bloomsbury, and no explanation why. Wilson wondered how they knew the books were fascinating, as it was clear to him that they never looked at them.

It was beginning to seem as if his old fear that he would one day find himself without a publisher was coming true. Spurgeon asked if he thought the autobiography's bad reviews were the reason for the rejection slips. "No, nothing to do with that," Wilson said. Then, laughing, he added that it had to do with "Saturn being in my house," blaming his misfortune on the planetary taskmaster, whose job is to make things difficult so that we have to work hard, a philosophy Wilson himself embraced. He admitted that the rejections did make him feel gloomy. But then, not long after receiving them, he found himself sitting in his easy chair, watching—invariably—the evening television news, when the thought of the rejection slips returned. He was surprised to find that there was no sign of the "sinking of the heart that you get when you remember something discouraging." He thought: "That is interesting. No sinking of the heart at all."[63]

The reason for this, Wilson believed, was the concentration exercises he had been doing over the years, the very ones that made him oversensitive to sudden stimuli. He did them while walking his dogs, getting groceries, or driving his car—an old and slightly battered Jaguar. What had happened, he believed, was that he had "changed mentally" over the years, in the past year especially so. "I've slowly taught myself to remain in a permanent state of optimism—or realism, if you like," what he called "this curious ability to focus on external reality." He had been doing this for years—we remember his revelation after being snowed in at Devon and his recapturing his vision at Teignmouth. But now he could see that "it can be done quite deliberately by a kind of effort, almost like doing a push-up."[64] It was this that prevented him from sinking into the kind of discouragement that his friend Stan Gooch had drifted into. Realizing that the rejection of his work did not send him into a depression was, he said, almost as good a piece of news as it would have been to hear that the books had been accepted. "There was that feeling of 'It's taken you a lifetime, but you're gradually getting there.'"

As for the autobiography itself, Wilson felt that it had "succeeded totally." It was just that what he was saying "hasn't been understood yet."[65] And the reason for this is that "The English are totally brainless."[66] There was plenty of time, though. He had become something of a cult figure, and this helped. He did not feel, as someone his age—seventy-four—might: "I've been working all these years and I'm still unknown."[67] He had readers who did understand him. But he would be dead for a long time, he thought, before the wider appreciation of his work would spread. Yet he never doubted that he had something important to say. "I knew this from the beginning, when I was in my teens—that I've got something terribly important to do."[68]

The interview contains interesting Wilsonian dicta on a number of topics. Unlike D. H. Lawrence, he "never gave a fuck about my background or social status," nor has he ever "worried in the least about my reputation."[69] Serial killers are "fuck-ups." "Crime writers like to write about great criminals, a Vautrin or Professor Moriarity. But that's shit."[70] He was "absolutely, totally convinced about life after death," and was "terribly lucky not to have gone to university."[71] If he was to be remembered, he would like it to be "as the first optimistic philosopher in European history."[72]

The central message, however, was that human beings are too "defeat prone." But this will change. "Human beings will, sometime during the next century, be transformed."[73] This transformation will amount to our being "in touch with reality all the time." He may not be around to see the change, something he had already told his *Daily Mail* readers, but it will happen.[74] "We've now reached a point where it is absolutely necessary for something to happen."

The important thing to remember is that "It's the way that people *see themselves* that determines what they think they can achieve." He had been working very hard for a long time to get them to see themselves as something more than meaningless worms stuck on a meaningless planet, or robots without a mind of their own. He had been working hard to get them to see themselves as what they could be if they really made the effort: truly human beings.

Another addition to that long effort appeared in the summer of 2006. Wilson finally had his chance to have his say about Atlantis, or at least to make up for the *Atlantis Blueprint* disaster. Depending on your perspective, *Atlantis and the Kingdom of the Neanderthals* can be seen as a labor of love or one of stubbornness. It is in many ways a rewrite of the earlier book without Rand Flem-Ath's contribution. Wilson nods to Flem-Ath's theories, but his main aim was to get the chapters on Neanderthal that Wilson's ex-collaborator had chucked out into print. One of the things that had led to Stan Gooch becoming an apathetic, penurious recluse, Wilson believed, was the fact that the material on Neanderthal and Gooch's insights into them had been excised from the blueprint. Gooch had expectations of some response to his ideas and now there would be none. Wilson was determined to promote Gooch's work—he was both a friend and brilliant—and had put this sequel together to do that. That was the labor of love. The labor of stubbornness was to show that *he* would determine what would go into his book, and no one else—or so it could be seen. Flem-Ath's "treachery" had hurt him deeply and some of the few sour passages in *Dreaming to Some Purpose* made this unmistakably clear.

In either case, the end result was not really a success, and is another of Wilson's books that, as the British say, "doesn't do what it says on the tin." Meaning that like *The Psychic Detectives* it was a case of somewhat false advertising. Not that Neanderthals don't make an appearance. They do, but not until the last chapter. To get to them the reader needs to retrace many steps Wilson had already taken. Many readers were not happy with this. I myself felt that much of the book covered some very well-trodden ground. A generous reader will remember that by this time, Colin's health and age were starting to slow him down. He told Brad Spurgeon that "a couple of hours' work of writing, steady creative writing, is quite enough when you're seventy-four." The book was ill-conceived and he probably shouldn't have done it, but one suspects he had to get it out of his system before he could move on.

It was not a total loss. The chapters on ancient technologies, prehistoric global catastrophes, the Flood, the roots of Christianity, the Templars, Freemasonry, and the mysteries of Rennes-le-Château have a familiar ring and readers have to decide how much they accept the work of Henry Lincoln, Christopher Knight, Robert Lomas, Hancock, Bauval, and the other writers on ancient mysteries that Wilson bases them on. My own feeling is that, taken in isolation, some of the claims made about advanced prehistoric civilizations may not be convincing—some are outright unbelievable—but as with the paranormal, when added up they do seem persuasive and I see nothing wrong in accepting the strong possibility that something along these lines is the case. And Wilson's section on Charles Hapgood, presenting the material on him that Rand did not want in their book, is fascinating, and made me wonder why Wilson didn't think of doing a book on him alone. Hapgood's deep interest in parapsychology, psychometry, precognition, and other paranormal phenomena seems right up Wilson's alley.[75]

The most rewarding chapters for me, though, were his excursions into shamanism and what he calls "primal vision." They deal with Wilson's real métier, consciousness, and the question that had started him on this quest for a hundred-thousand-year-old science: how *could* our ancient ancestors have had the kind of knowledge that is clearly exhibited in the monuments erected around the globe that he had studied for a decade now?

To answer this question Wilson looks at the anthropologist Jeremy Narby's account of his experience with the powerful mind-altering substance ayahuasca, which Narby imbibed during a trip to the Amazon. In *The Cosmic Serpent* (1999) Narby relates how, wanting to know how indigenous Amazonian people learned of the drug's properties, and those of the thousands of other plants they use, he was told the *plants themselves* told them. When Narby tried ayahuasca, he found out how. While he was under the drug's influence, two giant boa constrictors spoke to him and passed on their ancient wisdom. The upshot of their conversation was that Narby came to see how the DNA in the plants *is itself intelligent* and that, while under the effect of the drug, the natives could understand what it said to them. It was a form of the lunar knowledge that Wilson had first heard about from Robert Graves. Wilson relates this to what Goethe called "active seeing," a way of seeing nature as a living intelligence rather than, as mechanical science does, a dead machine. Goethe's active seeing was a variant of Husserl's intentionality, and is achieved by "putting attention into seeing, so that we really do see what we are seeing instead of just having a visual impression," as the philosopher and Goethean scientist Henri Bortoft explained.[76] Wilson tells us that when, one bright summer morning, he experimented with "active seeing" on his own garden—forgetting for the moment his antipathy toward it—he felt that "the grass, the trees, the shrubs suddenly seemed more real and alive."[77] They seemed to be communicating with him, as the plants communicated with the Amazonian natives and, as Wilson surmised, the universe communicated with our prehistoric ancestors.

The chapter on those ancestors, our Neanderthal cousins, is fascinating, and collects a sufficient amount of evidence to suggest that our image of them as shambling ape men, dragging their mates behind them by the hair, is a libel on their true character. Drawing on Gooch's decades-long study, Wilson argues that, as the mysterious Carl had argued, Neanderthal could very well have been the citizens of the 100,000-year-old "advanced civilization" Hapgood had so enigmatically hinted at in his last letter to Flem-Ath. Anomalies such as a 500,000-year-old polished plank of wood discovered in the Jordan valley in 1989, engraved bones from the Middle Paleolithic (200,000–40,000 years ago), and rock art tools 176,000 years old at least suggest that our ideas about how intelligent our prehistoric ancestors were need revising.[78] When we also consider that, as mentioned, Neanderthal had blast furnaces and "superglue," maintained extensive mining operations, charted the lunar calendar, were astronomers, had a religion with rituals and a belief in an afterlife, made music and sculpture, and sewed, then the need for a revision seems imperative.[79] And that is exactly what has been happening in recent times, without, as mentioned, Gooch getting any credit for being there well ahead of the trend.[80] And if we also keep an open mind about Gooch's suggestion that Neanderthal were most likely psychic and members of a group mind—like the kind of group mind Wilson wrote about at the end of *From Atlantis to the Sphinx*—we can begin to see how a kind of "civilization of dreams," as Gooch called it, rather like the civilization of the American Indian, may have existed on our planet millennia ago.

Atlantis and the Kingdom of the Neanderthals did not garner many reviews but by now Wilson had his mind on another "lost time," that of his early days with the Angry Young Men. He would rather his book about the period, *The Angry Years* (2007), had come out a few years later. (It had after all found a publisher.) He had already covered much of this ground in his autobiography, but Humphrey Carpenter's supercilious treatment of what was in his opinion an important period in England's cultural history—Carpenter's book was an "unashamed potboiler" out of sympathy with its subject—prompted him to set the record straight.[81] We can also assume that with age, health problems, and the dimming of memory, Wilson wanted to tell the definitive story while he, and most likely the reading public, could still remember it.

I've drawn on *The Angry Years* in the early part of this book and readers will be familiar with some of the stories Wilson tells. But he goes beyond the few years of the angry decade to look at the subsequent lives and careers of his fellow Angries. Carpenter called his own book a "literary comedy," but Wilson said the real story was much more of a tragedy. He really was one of the only survivors, a writer from that time who was still writing or still alive. Of his own friends, after producing good work, Laura Del-Rivo and Bill Hopkins had both stopped writing. Stuart Holroyd dropped out, then returned briefly in the 1970s, but had stopped again. The figures who went on to have major careers, such as Kingsley Amis, John Braine, and Kenneth Tynan, were all dead and had had turbulent lives full of broken marriages, alcoholism, and other addictions. An ungenerous reader might assume that, wanting to settle old scores, Wilson went out of his way to dig up as much dirt as he could about his old enemies. But one did not have to dig very deep to see that many of them had succumbed to the sexual illusion that Wilson had weaned himself off of long ago.

Kenneth Tynan, whom Wilson recognized as one of the best theater critics since Shaw, had died in 1980 of emphysema, after a fractured career, much of which was devoted to alcohol, cigarettes, and spanking. Tynan had a peculiar fondness for female bottoms and enjoyed beating them whenever possible, "preferably with the buttocks parted to disclose the anus," as he confided in his diary of 1971.[82] As Wilson remarked, "It was essential for Tynan's self-respect to see himself as the dominant one, beating the bare behind of a recumbent girl," although he himself enjoyed being spanked and would try to get his wife involved because he liked an audience.[83] Kingsley Amis's philandering was an addiction he could not break, although he had better luck with alcohol. On one occasion, while vacationing on a Yugoslavian beach, his current wife got so fed up with his womanizing that as Amis lay sunbathing she wrote on his back in lipstick, "1 FAT ENGLISHMAN I FUCK ANYTHING," and the marriage soon broke up.[84] After years of battling alcoholism, John Braine, for whom Wilson had developed a true fondness, became a talkative, assertive ultraconservative, subject to hypochondria, depression, and increasing isolation, his creative powers dwindling.[85]

There are other gossipy accounts and the reader of *The Angry Years* will find Wilson back in true form. He provides an engaging, entertaining, and very readable narrative about what for him was "the first *group* of working-class writers that had ever existed."[86] This was the point that Carpenter, the son of a bishop and decidedly not working class, had missed. Wilson pointed out that while members of the "establishment" didn't mind being criticized by one of their own, say, an Aldous Huxley or a George Orwell, they didn't take kindly to these lower-class upstarts having a go at them. The writers of the angry years had taken the job of showing up the inadequacies of the status quo out of the hands of one of its members, and the critics could not forgive them for this. Wilson himself did not share their class consciousness, and found much of their anger fruitless, but he did recognize that the "movement was based on a real political protest that hoped to get things done, to change things," and they deserved better treatment than what Carpenter provided.[87] The urge to get things done would, with the Beat Generation's similar desire, soon have an effect; the various "revolutions" of the 1960s that we still look back on with nostalgic fondness had their roots in the bleak, angry, duffle-coated days of the fifties.

Wilson is not critical of all his old contemporaries. He speaks well of the plays of Arnold Wesker, although he rejects his Marxism. He enjoyed the novels of Iris Murdoch, although her own promiscuous life showed that women, too, were subject to the sexual illusion. And, as mentioned, he had a great admiration for the work of Doris Lessing, whose "preoccupation with human evolution," evidenced in novels such as *The Four-Gated City* (1969) and those of her science-fiction series Shikasta (1979–1983), made him feel that they were sympathetic spirits.[88] This should not be surprising. Lessing, who started out as leftist, gradually became disenchanted with communism and, by the late 1960s, had turned her attention to spiritual matters; the influence of Sufism and Gurdjieff is evident in her later work. With Wilson she came to see that it is not enough to change society, no matter how much it needs changing. What truly needs to be changed is people's consciousness.[89]

Wilson had been working on that for a long time. And now he felt the moment was right to bring together the different strands of his approach into one neat package.

Critical response to *The Angry Years* was much like that to *Dreaming to Some Purpose*. Wilson fans loved it—I gave it a rave review in the *Independent on Sunday*—but on the whole, the critics of the new establishment felt that Wilson needed a beating again.[90] It didn't occur to them that he had written "a commentary that was far livelier and more gripping than most cultural studies," as Paul Newman had remarked.[91] They did not know the books Wilson wrote about. He had made a point of rereading works he already knew well, as well as later works and biographies of all the people he wrote about, but this acumen was lost on his critics. They had taken the lazy route of "writing about Wilson in a mildly derogatory fashion," which was expected of them, although in many cases they were not particularly mild.[92] Wilson shrugged it off. He may have felt momentarily gloomy but again there was no "sinking feeling," and he had by then achieved something of the Olympian distance that characterized the late Goethe, a man untouched by praise or blame. He had been working to free himself from negative emotions for half a century. He was not going to let one more bad review spoil his efforts.

The idea of putting together a kind of how-to or do-it-yourself book about consciousness had been in Wilson's mind for some time. In 1995 he had entertained some friends while Joy was away for the weekend. One of them was an editor who was interested in commissioning Wilson to do a book about his ideas. Always happy to talk about his work, Wilson spent the weekend explaining his philosophy of consciousness. "For two days," he says, "insights poured out of me in a cascade."[93] On Monday morning his friends had to catch an early train to London, and Wilson drove them to the station. Along the way he continued to expand on his conversation of the weekend, bringing up new insights and linking them to other ideas—an example of the "relationality" of consciousness he had written about in *Poetry and Mysticism*. It was a beautiful morning, and as he returned to Tetherdown he felt that "the first thing I wanted to do was to sit down at my computer and simply type for days."[94] It was the kind of excitement he had felt decades earlier, when on a cold Christmas day in 1954, he brought together everything he had been thinking about Sartre, Camus, Wells, Hesse, Gurdjieff, and all the other figures making up the motley crew of *The Outsider*. As they had then, ideas tumbled "one over the other to get out."

When Wilson got back home he turned on his computer and over the next forty-eight hours banged out a sixty-page outline of a book. It would have different names over the years; *Mind Force* and *The Search for Power Consciousness* were some. He wanted to work on it then, but other things made him put it aside—his book about the Sphinx, for one. Like many other projects, it lay untouched for some time. Then sometime in the mid-2000s, his Japanese publisher showed interest in it and he went back to it. Finally, in 2009, it found its way to an English publisher.

Watkins Books, in London's West End, was *the* occult bookshop, having catered in its early days to clients such as W. B. Yeats and Aleister Crowley. John Watkins, the shop's founder, had been a student of Madame Blavatsky in her last years and it was she who suggested that he start a shop because there was nowhere in London in the early 1890s where one could buy books on the occult.[95] In later years, the shop branched out into publishing, but financial reasons caused this venture to cease. But in the early 2000s, Watkins returned to publishing and among its titles were new editions of *The Occult* and *Mysteries*. In 2009 it put out Wilson's short summary of his life's work, *Super Consciousness: The Quest for the Peak Experience*.

It was a perfect coda to everything Wilson had been struggling to articulate for the past half century, his last word on his "one big thing." All the themes I have tried to get across in this book are there. Faculty X, absurd good news, the near and the far, lunar knowledge, the right and left brain, the Romantics, Husserl, evolution, the robot, pessimism (in the form of Samuel Beckett), the sexual illusion, Maslow, the secret life, the bird's- and worm's-eye views, the paranormal, synchronicities, and everything else are lined up nicely and given to the reader in thirteen easily digestible chapters. Wilson is again in good writing form and expresses his insights with clarity and ease; as many readers over the years have said about his style, it is as if he was there talking to them. In a way, the book serves the same function for his later, "post-paranormal" philosophy that *Introduction to the New Existentialism* did for the existential Outsider Cycle: bringing together all the different elements of an extensive phenomenology of consciousness into a concise statement.[96] If *The Outsider* started Wilson's long philosophical voyage, *Super Consciousness* lets us know exactly what he discovered along the way.

The book begins with the idea of inner freedom, and how the Romantics exhausted themselves in the pursuit of it, the question that started Wilson's long journey. The Romantics' love of nature was an expression of their hunger for this new sensation. Romantics such as Goethe—one of the few who did not succumb to despair—responded to mountains so deeply because in them he saw *"a reflection of his own inner power, his own inner mountain landscape."*[97] Nature allowed the Romantics to escape from the prison of their everyday selves. "Inner freedom" is precisely the feeling that "'you' and your personality are not at all the same thing."[98] What the Romantics were beginning to suspect is that "man is far bigger that he thinks he is." They had the insight that their 'real you' was, in some strange way, a god.

The rest of the book, like Wilson's whole career, is a patient, determined attempt to show how each of us can find our way to that "real you."

Super Consciousness is a summary of Wilson's ideas. It would be pointless for me to summarize it here. In a way, this whole book has been an attempt at that. But two important ideas of Wilson's that I have not yet touched on play a central part in *Super Consciousness*, and I have saved my discussion of them until now.

One is what he calls his "levels of consciousness." In 1987, driving back from the Esalen Institute, where he had lectured, to San Francisco, Wilson began to think about the idea of consciousness having different levels. The idea came to him when he recalled his experience at Sheepwash, when, after concentrating for hours on not driving his car into a ditch, he felt he had pushed his consciousness up a notch, and was seeing things with a greater clarity and vividness. If he had managed to do that by concentrating, how far could he go? It was the same question as when he had relaxed himself out of his panic attacks: if I can relax myself this much, how much more deeply can I do it? Wilson began to think of consciousness as a kind of gradient, and an idea something like his "ladder of selves" began to form.

There is Level 0, which is deep, dreamless sleep. Level 1, then, is that of dreams and hypnagogic experiences. Level 2 is "the most basic level of waking consciousness."[99] This is "mere awareness—the kind of consciousness a sleepy child experiences when too tired to take much interest in anything." Here consciousness is simply a mirror, reflecting the outside world, the kind of consciousness Sartre's café owner has.

Level 3 is Sartre's "nausea." In it "'you' are clearly present, but the world around you is 'merely what it is.'" Here consciousness is "stuck, like a fly on fly paper."[100] It has "congealed." Throughout his books Wilson has provided many examples of this state, from Graham Greene's boredom before playing Russian roulette to Camus' stranger, sleepwalking through his life.

Level 4 is ordinary consciousness, how our consciousness most likely is right now. It is not as stifling as Level 3, but it is still hard work and a burden. Here consciousness has "learned how to cope with existence yet it tends to think of life as a grim battle."[101] The danger here is that it is very easy to slip back a level and feel that life is meaningless and dull; we might call this the "Beckett effect." But it is at this level that something interesting begins to happen. We find that if we make the effort and don't slip down into nausea, consciousness begins to warm up. We start to feel that maybe things aren't as difficult as we thought. "An odd feeling of inner strength begins to arise, an increased determination."[102] We begin to feel that we can *do*. If we maintain this level, 4.5, long enough, we get what Gurdjieff would have called a "shock" that "completes the octave," and what Maslow called the peak experience. The peak acts as a spark that puts us into the next level.

At Level 5 we reach what Wilson calls "spring morning consciousness." It's the feeling we get on "lovely mornings, or on holiday, when the whole world is self-evidently fascinating and delightful."[103] It is here that Hesse's Steppenwolf is reminded of "Mozart and the stars" and decides not to slit his throat. Here "Everything makes us think of something else," producing a "continuous state of interest and excitement."[104] At this level we *know* that life is good, and that nausea is not, as Sartre believed, a deep insight into the human condition, but a simple misunderstanding. We also know that we must not allow ourselves to be tricked by it. As Wilson says, our best allies here are courage and determination.

Level 6 Wilson calls "magic consciousness," borrowing, as mentioned, J. B. Priestley's meaning of the term; Priestley also calls this state "delight." It is how children feel at Christmastime, or newlyweds do on their honeymoon. Here we feel "a total reconciliation with our lives"; as Nietzsche's Zarathustra does, we can say yes to life and mean it. Problems that harried us now seem trivial. We are, Wilson would say, no longer "upside down," and have adjusted our "underfloor lighting." Level 6, Wilson says, is like level 5, but fixed, so that it lasts for days on end.

At Level 7 we experience Faculty X, and the reality of other times and places seems as clear and palpable to us as the reality of the present moment. We are no longer trapped in the present and our consciousness can range over wide areas of reality, as Arnold Toynbee's did. Here we have moved beyond the peak experience into a state characterized by a "mastery of time." We see that time is "a manifestation of the heaviness of the body and the feebleness of the spirit."[105] It is here that we can act with free will and alter destiny. It is at Level 7 that we "really know" what we know, and we know it to be true.

Level 8 is the kind of consciousness Ouspensky experienced during his experiment with nitrous oxide, or that R. H. Ward or R. M. Bucke or other psychonauts experienced in their mystical states. It is "cosmic consciousness." At this level our ordinary ideas about reality are turned upside down, subjective things seem objective, past and future coincide, everything is connected. We see William James's "distant ranges of increasing fact," but as James, Ouspensky, and others discovered, these states are usually too overwhelming to do us any good. Wilson believes that the early levels are presages, or partial revelations of the truths glimpsed at Level 8. Yet he also believes that we simply are not ready yet to take them "straight" or to make much use of them. And for some, they are so powerful that the return to earth is a depressing letdown. This is why Wilson says that for the moment, we need not concern ourselves very much about Level 8. Our business now is with the first seven levels.

Wilson notes that Level 4.5 is the halfway point between Level 0 and Level 7. It is at this point that we begin to experience our consciousness as it really is. And where it is a tough slog getting out of Level 3 and into Level 4, past Level 4.5 the going gets easier. As Wilson had said about his ladder of selves, the spaces between the lower rungs are farther apart than those between the upper ones. It is as if consciousness is a kind of pyramid, and as we get closer to the top, the steps are easier to manage. "Each level is only a short and easy step away from the previous one."[106] But it is at Level 4.5 that we begin to see that we *can* change our consciousness through our own efforts. And it is at this level where the work needs to be done.

The other idea connected to our levels of consciousness is what we might call our "robot/real you ratio." At Level 4 we are 50 percent "real you" and 50 percent robot. Nausea begins when that ratio drops to 49 percent real you and 51 percent robot. At this point life begins to "fail." Further down the scale, at 48 or 47 percent real you, our mental health begins to deteriorate. We find ourselves in the state of William James's "neurasthenics," "with life grown into one tissue of impossibilities." Even further down we are the catatonic patient—a memory of which threw the young James into a deep depression—or some of the delusional psychotics Wilson wrote about in *The Devil's Party*.

But if this is so, then the opposite is also true. At 51 percent real you and 49 percent robot, we are at Level 4.5. It is here that we begin to live; the robot is no longer doing that for us. It is here that I can use the *knowledge* that my sense of being more alive is a result of a temporary dominance of me over the robot to my advantage. I can make the conscious effort to push my consciousness into an even greater "more me, less robot" state. I can achieve states in which I am 52 or 53 percent real me. This is what happens to Maslow's peakers and Syd Banks's high achievers.

We can all reach these states simply through knowing they are true and that all that is necessary from us is a certain effort and the optimistic expectancy that the effort will pay off. We have to pay a bit in advance with a certain kind of faith in what we already know. We have to have the courage to *really believe* it, and take the risk of banking on that belief in the same way that Columbus bet everything on the truth that the world is round. If we do, like him we will find new worlds. William James said that we have a better chance of achieving something if we *believe* we can than if we believe we can't, regardless of any evidence for it. Our decision to believe in our ability to succeed is a determining factor in our success. It is important, Wilson says, not to pay much attention to setbacks and roadblocks and to avoid brooding gloomily on possible future disasters—something Wilson himself knew from experience. As Madame Blavatsky sagely said, "The mind is the slayer of the real." Wilson agrees: "Ninety per cent of our problems are self-created."[107] We need to keep aware of what our thoughts are focusing on. The best thing to focus them on is, again, the knowledge that our glimpses of non-robotic consciousness are glimpses of truth, to steal a phrase from that archnemesis of all things robotic, Gurdjieff.

The essential ingredient here is concentration, or as Wilson says in *Super Consciousness*, attention. He tells the story of the Zen monk Ikkyu. A workman, recognizing the Zen master, asked Ikkyu to write something to help him in his meditations. Ikkyu wrote, "Attention." The workman, somewhat disappointed, asked Ikkyu to extrapolate on this. Ikkyu wrote, "Attention, attention!" Exasperated, the workman asked, "What does attention mean?" The Zen master replied, "Attention means attention."[108] It was a lesson Wilson learned long ago, when moving classical LPs from paper sleeves to plastic ones: "A long time devoted to small details exalts us and increases our strength." He had learned that lesson as he focused on keeping his car out of a ditch. Every one of us can learn it in a hundred different ways, from xeroxing a book, as Wilson once did, to cleaning the house.[109] Even planarian worms can learn it. It doesn't matter what you pay attention to or concentrate on. The attention and the concentration are what count. If we do it for long enough, often enough, the billiard balls of our consciousness will slowly come together, and fuse into a hard, diamond-like pyramid that can withstand the forces of time even better than the monuments the ancient Egyptians raised in the desert sands.

This would be so because "my sense of meaning would be so deep, my interest in everything so great, that I would have passed the point where 'regress' or collapse is possible. I would be sustained by sheer perception of meaning."[110] As Husserl said, perception is intentional; here we have become sheer intention. The black room would explode in dazzling colors, our flippers would turn into legs, and we would walk boldly out of the sea onto the dry land of the mind. This is a process that had started some centuries earlier with the "imagination explosion" and had come to an acute crisis with Wilson's Outsiders. But mankind as a whole was now at Level 4, the all-important midway point.

Yet many of us are past Level 4. Wilson's study of the history of crime showed that many today have reached Maslow's self-actualization level, which would be 4.5. "All we need to do now," Wilson believed, is "to grasp it." That is the essential thing: for Outsiders to stop seeing themselves as misfits and to take up their real work as evolutionary agents. To use the mind to increase the powers of the mind. To use our freedom to create more freedom. When we have done that, mankind will have taken the decisive step in its evolution and will become, as the Romantics knew we were long ago, "something closer to the gods."[111]

CODA

WITHOUT THE OUTSIDER

*S*uper Consciousness was published to little notice, aside from that of loyal Wilson fans. I saw Colin give a talk about it at St. James Piccadilly, a well-known alternative venue in London, in July 2009. There was a large crowd and although Colin was always an engaging speaker—he never used notes and always spoke off the cuff—he did seem to digress a bit, laying into Freud and even Jung as lesser psychologists than Maslow, and taking his time getting around to his subject. His tendency to digression had, perhaps, increased with age, but that is to be expected; he had no monopoly on a weakness attributable to most men of years. He was somewhat more on target in an interview he did around the time for *The Gnostic*, a journal dedicated to "Gnosticism, Western Esotericism, and Spirituality." His interviewer enjoyed the book and agreed that it was "a summation of fifty years research into existence and consciousness and peak experiences."[1]

Once again Wilson explained that the start of his long exploration was the Romantics, the contrast between the "glimpses they had in which it seemed to them that life was absolutely wonderful" and "the way they ended up, committing suicide." That initial burst of the imagination explosion didn't last long. Soon after it the darkness fell and by the turn of the century we have Yeats speaking of the "Tragic Generation." The sixteen-year-old Wilson, reading the Romantics, wanted to know if he could "find a way of achieving these states of mind when you wanted them," that is, permanently. The reason why many of the people he had written about in *The Outsider* could not hold on to them was that "they tended to be a bit inclined to self-pity." Being English and "very Anglo-Saxon," he had a "pragmatic" temperament. He never wasted time on self-pity.

How could he? Being working class, he had to "pull his cart out of the mud," and work his way up through the "vegetable mediocrity" around him, which left little time to feel sorry for himself. If he had, he would never have "got round to writing *The Outsider*."[2] As it was, after the Angry Young Man debacle, he was "able to devote [his] life entirely, living here in the back of beyond, to this interesting problem," that of mastering consciousness.[3] He had been down there in Cornwall with Joy for fifty-three years, which the interviewer agreed was a long time.

The talk moved among familiar themes. The Romantics were weaklings. Yeats weaned himself of this weakness by going on an American lecture tour, so that he could earn money to pay off his debts.[4] Wilson knew what kind of work that entailed. When he returned from his first U.S. lecture, he was "absolutely a wreck," and "must have been dreadful to live with for [his] poor wife." Dylan Thomas didn't fare as well. "A typical example of the weak outsider," Thomas had little else but a "tremendous talent in the use of words." Being a Celt was no help either, because if you are "it is terribly easy to be an alcoholic."[5] The interviewer, a Welshman living in Dublin, laughed at this, so I assume he took no offense.

Asked about the levels of consciousness, Wilson spoke of Faculty X, "this peculiar capacity to leave ordinary consciousness behind as it were and go off somewhere else, so to speak."[6] This was something "we ought to be able to do at any particular time. . . . Our problem," he said, "is simply to be aware of more than one reality." One aid in doing this is to be able to "galvanise ourselves into some sense of urgency or emergency." With a nod to the financial crisis that had hit the world in 2008, Wilson added that this should be "unfortunately easy," in view of the world recession.[7]

Asked if he saw a link between Faculty X and the kinds of visions people such as William Blake and other mystics had, Wilson tried to make clear that his work was about "getting back to reality." Our ordinary consciousness is "a liar." It is simply "not telling us the truth about reality." And western philosophy has been little help, except for people such as Husserl and Whitehead, who were among the "few that succeeded in escaping the blind alley."[8] The "moments of vision" when, with people like Blake, we *see* that our usual way of seeing the world is inadequate, "ought to be completely natural to human beings." But for that we need to be "conscious in the right way." One of the practical problems involved in this is having the leisure to work at it, something our hectic civilization allows less and less of. Another problem is the robot, who, when we do get the leisure, promptly puts us to sleep. What is needed, Wilson saw, is a "strategy against the robot," which, he reflected, would have been a good title for the book.[9]

There *should* be a way of learning how to go from "ordinary consciousness" to "the feeling of absurd good news" that would be as easy as "taking the map of a city and saying how do you get to the city center?"[10] When he was younger he thought a religious answer might have been necessary, and he warned Joy that he might one day leave her and join a monastery. Yet, in a sense, that was as romantic a tactic as Yeats wanting to run off to fairyland. What one needed to do was to achieve a "feeling of reality, of responsibilities," which are "preferable to the irresponsible attitude of the Romantics."[11]

Gurdjieff—"probably the greatest mind of the twentieth century"—came closest to solving the problem. But his austere, grim approach could backfire. "Ouspensky, you know, finished his life as an alcoholic." Yet Ouspensky was in many ways "preferable to Gurdjieff," because he was a "more precise thinker, a more scientific thinker," and that is "the first and necessary thing."[12] Although Wilson was always "to a large extent able to produce peak experiences," because he is "basically a very cheerful sort of person," he expressed a hint of frustration about his own attempts to find a solution to the central problem, a *method* of changing consciousness. "I'm aware all the time that I set out determinedly to try and find an answer to this basic problem," but it seems he hasn't quite got there yet. It demands concentration, as he made clear in *Super Consciousness*, but he admitted that at seventy-eight "you realise that you just don't have that concentration." Or you do, but "you would need some kind of tremendous crisis to cause you to exercise it."[13]

There was some chat about the science-fiction writer Philip K. Dick, and Wilson's detestation of Saint Paul for creating the "superstition" that Jesus died on the cross for our sins. "The world would have been a far better place" without him—Saint Paul, that is. The interview closed on the insight that our best moments are when the two sides of the brain are like "two tennis players playing a perfect game," and Wilson believed that it must be possible to "work out a discipline" involving the two. He suggested that a close study of the 1950s classic science-fiction film *Forbidden Planet* (1956) may help. In it a scientist discovers the remnants of an ancient alien civilization, and has his mind blown by experimenting with one of their "simpler mind control machines." "Now," Wilson said, "that's the kind of thing that we need."[14]

It was a time of reflection, of looking back. Older works were coming back into print, courtesy of Colin Stanley's Paupers' Press. Wilson's play *Strindberg*, about the neurotic Swedish genius, had come out again. He had a fondness for Strindberg, and great respect for his creative powers, although he did feel he wasted himself in his disastrous relationships and the trivial, all-too-human problems that arise with them. *The Death of God and Other Plays* appeared too, works that had never been published. *The Metal Flower Blossom* was among them, the play he had rehearsed with his bohemian friends so long ago, before anyone had ever heard of *The Outsider*. *The Death of God* was the play that had caused his ruckus with the Royal Court Theatre. *Necessary Doubt* was written for a television production company, but never produced. The BBC bought it but didn't produce it either; in the end it served as the basis for Wilson's existential thriller of the same name. *Mysteries*, a play about multiple personalities, featured his Inspector Saltfleet. Wilson wrote an introduction for the book and reminisced about the early days, and allowed himself some grumbling about not getting credit for some work. He also mentioned a dance company in Milwaukee who staged *The Mind Parasites* as a ballet; apparently it was a success. Aptly enough, he had recently lectured on Shakespeare at the Stratford-upon-Avon Literary Festival, although he did conclude that his own talent lay more in the way of novels and books of ideas than the stage. Shakespeare, however, was still on his mind.

There were other memories. Colin Stanley issued a collection of Wilson's book reviews under the title *Existential Criticism* (2009), which showed Wilson the critic in top form. The writing is crisp, clear, and sharp and reminds us once again of Wilson's formidable range, turning easily from Emily Brontë and Thomas Mann to lesser-known figures such as the Austrian novelist Heimito von Doderer and the Finn Aleksis Kivi, whose *Seven Brothers* he rates as highly as *Don Quixote*.[15] Fifty years earlier, in 1959, when his essay "Existential Criticism" was published in the *Chicago Review*, Wilson had hoped that "within the next two decades, the techniques of existential thinking will become commonplace in England and America," a desire that, if nothing else, shows his immense optimism.[16] He had hoped that his ideas about existential criticism might "lead to a revitalization of literature in the twentieth century."[17] Like much else Wilson had hoped for, this positive sea change in our stories about ourselves seems not to have taken place, at least not yet. This may be why, when he returned to fiction, he worked in fantasy and what we would now call "teen lit." It was the one area left where the fallacy of insignificance had not firmly taken root.

He had one more brief stroll through Soho, when he was interviewed about a proposed film based on his anti-bohemian novel, *Adrift in Soho*, his gentle but firm picaresque tale of moral awakening amid the layabouts and wannabes.[18] The interview was shot on location at Bar Italia, one of the few espresso haunts left from the old days.[19] Wilson sat at a table, paging through his early work, with baristas banging plates behind him and forcing another cappuccino through the coffee machine. Wilson remembered fondly the prostitutes, spivs (British slang for petty criminal), and out-of-work actors that made up the old clientele, and read a brief passage from his youthful work.[20]

He was filmed again talking about *Super Consciousness* for a new audience, on the musician and author Philip Gardiner's satellite television program *Gardiner's World*. Gardiner specialized in UFOs, aliens, secret societies, and hidden mysteries, finding them in everything from quantum physics to James Bond. He was rightly chuffed, as they say in Britain, that he had Wilson on his show, whom he called the "grandfather" of everything the program was about. Wilson showed his age, unavoidably, but was in good form, talking about Maslow, peak experiences, synchronicities, and cosmic consciousness. He ran through the basic theme of the book and at one point expressed the hope that if enough people can learn how to induce peak experiences at will, we will be able to "change civilization." He had been at it for fifty years and had made some headway. All that is needed is for others to find their way to it. It can be done.

We face problems, of course—Wilson was no Pollyanna. He was aware of the numerous crises facing the world today, which, he admitted, seems to have found itself in a terrific mess. But there is no point in giving way to despair. In fact we need to cast off our gloom now more than ever. Synchronicities show that somehow, *our minds themselves* can change things. There is a force outside ourselves that is available to help. He was convinced of that. Upbeat, optimistic, cheerful, and excited, Wilson gave the impression that even with a world seemingly unraveling at the seams, the possibility that some great change is in the wings for mankind is not as distant as it might appear.[21]

In 2011 Colin Wilson turned eighty. He had reached a stately age and could feel that he had done good work. His efforts to lift the log of pessimism that had blocked the western mind for two centuries were paying off. Slowly, perhaps, and in small groups here and there, but his ideas had reached many people and were finding their way into the collective mind. He was not a guru. He did not have followers. A healthy instinct kept him from making that mistake and in any case he did not have the time or the interest for hangers-on. They are nothing but time wasters and each of us must work out his own salvation. But he had readers and through them his ideas would spread. It was never going to happen overnight—he learned that after the false success of *The Outsider* had quickly faded out. And in any case the kind of change he hoped for would have to happen bit by bit, one consciousness at a time, winning its freedom from the robot and becoming 51 percent itself. No sudden singularity or mystical Golden Age will free us from the responsibilities we have to face. But he has shown a way and his ideas are there for all to profit by. He was even receiving some belated recognition from the academic world, which until then, like the critics, had either ignored him or considered him a crank.

In 2009 Colin Stanley had donated his huge and pristine Colin Wilson collection to the University of Nottingham, were he had worked as a librarian, in order for a Colin Wilson archive to be established. Stanley knew, as others did, that there would be future scholars eager to explore Wilson's work. For one thing, PhD candidates are always looking for virgin territory, untouched fields of research. With an oeuvre of more than one hundred books, Wilson would be a treasure trove for upcoming academics delighted to find someone no one had written about, and excited to rehabilitate a cultural pariah. But more to the point, Stanley, like many others, knew that Wilson's work deserved to be better known, to receive serious attention, and not the shallow reception given it by his critics. The archive would provide a place for enterprising young scholars, and older ones as well, to study Wilson's work as a whole, to see it for what it was: a sustained and rigorous attempt to erect a phenomenology of consciousness. Future devotees of the new existentialism would be at home there.[22]

Wilson was understandably happy about the idea, although the fact that his work would share archival space with that of D. H. Lawrence, a writer he never really cared for, may have given him pause for thought. But he must have felt that, finally, his work would receive the kind of attention it deserved.

He had planned to attend the opening of the archive but earlier in the year his back troubled him again, and in April he entered the Derriford Hospital in Plymouth to have a spinal operation. It seemed to go well, and for a time he recuperated in a cottage hospital in St. Austell. While there Joy brought him a copy of *Around the Outsider*, a Festschrift Colin Stanley had edited in honor of his birthday. The old Outsider, it seemed, was not so alone.

Wilson was pleased with the offering and seeing the scholarly articles dedicated to different aspects of his work cheered him up. It was a handsome volume and brought together insightful and original perspectives on his writing from readers around the globe, from New Zealand, Australia, and Texas to his hometown of Leicester. The idea was that each contributor would pick one of Wilson's books to write about. The literary scholar Nicolas Tredell wrote on *Ritual in the Dark*. The transpersonal psychologist Steven Taylor did *The Outsider*. Veteran parapsychologist Stanley Krippner took on *Mysteries*. Colin Stanley devoted himself to *Introduction to the New Existentialism*, while I mused on *Poetry and Mysticism*.[23] These and other essays—nineteen in all—critically engaged with Wilson's work. They were not gushing appreciations of a favorite writer's books, something that would have bored Wilson and done his reputation no good. It was a taste of what visitors to the archive would soon be producing, and it got the original Outsider's imprimatur.

The back operation prevented him from attending the archive's opening in July but Damon Wilson came in his place, and many of the contributors attended, some crossing continents at great expense. Laura Del-Rivo, Colin's old flame and a former angry young woman in her own right, was there. Short speeches were made attesting to Wilson's importance, and Damon graciously conveyed his father and sometime collaborator's thanks. The turnout surprised the staff and faculty of the university, who were impressed that even with Wilson's absence, the archive's opening attracted many of his readers. At a gathering at Stanley's home afterward I joked that if a committee of old existentialists wanted to do away with their rivals, they could wipe us out here with one blow.

Sometime later that summer, Wilson had a stroke. Full-on this time, not the "mini" kind that made his memory while writing *Dreaming to Some Purpose* shaky in some spots and the prose a little less crackling than usual. He had returned home from convalescing after his back operation and most likely would have returned to work on his latest project, *Will Shakespeare's Hand*, an investigation into the identity of the enigmatic "W. H." of Shakespeare's son-nets. The book remains unpublished and my understanding is that the infinitely good-natured Wilson had once again got himself involved with another bril-liant but irascible collaborator and that this was the reason the project was put on hold. At eighty, Wilson was understandably slowing down, but he never stopped following up on interesting ideas, and the clues that his proposed collaborator—a recognized Shakespeare scholar—presented to solving this long literary riddle were too good to pass up. But now there was another reason why this book, and any others left waiting on Wilson's desk, would not be finished. The writing machine had finally stopped.

One of his last pieces of writing to see print was an article on the work of his old friend Stan Gooch that appeared in the *Fortean Times*.[24] Gooch had died the year before and Colin was happy to say that "it seems that the safe, academic world Gooch had turned his back on is catching up with him, as re-cent findings appear to confirm some of his long-held theories about the sophis-tication of Neanderthal Man."[25] Material provided in the article supports this claim. Lyall Watson had passed away in 2008. John Michell had joined him in 2009. The old guard of the alternative world was moving on. Colin was no doubt saddest to hear that Bill Hopkins, his fellow genius of the milk bars, had died in May, while Colin was recovering from his operation.

It is a sad duty to write of the last days of a mentor and a friend. Colin was taken to a hospital near Truro, which had a specialist stroke unit. He was there for some months before being transferred to a smaller, cottage hospital nearer home. After some time there he was allowed to return to Tetherdown.

At first there was hope that his condition might improve. But soon it be-came clear that things would not get better. He was paralyzed on one side and could not read, write, or speak. For an inveterate reader and writer this must have been a difficult blow to endure. My understanding is that he did it with dignity and fortitude.

Colin Stanley visited Wilson in September 2012, about a year after the stroke. Much had been going on in the world of Wilson studies. Valancourt Books, in the United States, had reissued new editions of some of his novels. They had asked me to write a foreword to *The God of the Labyrinth*. Other Wil-sonians were asked too, and the series introduces new readers to some of Wil-son's best work. He was pleased to see Stanley and they shook hands, Wilson using his left. The stroke had affected his left cerebral hemisphere and while he could hear and understand what Stanley said, he couldn't reply. His ability to speak was gone; that rich, round voice he had jettisoned his Leicester accent to acquire and which proved itself in Hyde Park and other challenging venues was now silent. He couldn't stand or walk, and three times a day nurses came to move him and tend to his needs. Joy of course was there, as she always had been. On later visits Stanley could detect a decline in his energy and a wavering of awareness. Yet he could still grumble at the parrot that kept munching on his books and when Gail, Stanley's wife, was talking while he was watching the evening news, he growled because he wanted to hear a report on the Meredith Kercher murder.[26] Some interests never die.

Yet clearly he was failing. Music, which he loved so much, now proved too poignant to hear. Stanley recalls that on one visit, Wilson's brother Rod was at Tetherdown, fixing the stereo. He was glad that Colin could at least spend time listening to his collection. But he later heard that the music was now so piercing to him that it often brought him to tears, and he could no longer bear the emotional pain.

Stanley paid his last visit to Colin on October 21, 2013, but he wasn't there. Stanley had been journeying to Tetherdown at least once a year for decades now, collecting Wilson's manuscripts, arranging his files, and putting his literary legacy in order. It had been a year of loss. Paul Newman, who had filled the pages of *Abraxas* with Wilson gems that no fan would want to miss, had passed away earlier that year, after a long battle with cancer.[27] I had last seen him at the Wilson roundup, after the opening of the archive, and I was sorry to hear of his death. He was a fine writer and an insightful critic, and I dedicated my book on Aleister Crowley, whose work he knew well, to him. Now, when Colin Stanley arrived at Tetherdown, he found a note saying Wilson had been taken to hospital.

He waited at a local pub and when Joy returned heard the bad news. Colin had developed a chest infection which quickly turned into pneumonia; he had been rushed to the emergency ward. She was back at Tetherdown only a short while when she got a call from the hospital saying that her husband had taken a turn for the worse and that she needed to return. There was a good chance Colin would have died that night, but he rallied, and after a time he was again transferred to a cottage hospital nearer home, where he remained for a few weeks. He seemed to be recovering well and was about to be returned to Tetherdown when he developed another infection. This proved too much. On Thursday, December 5, 2013, at 10:45 in the evening, Colin Wilson died. Joy and their daughter, Sally, were at his side. He was eighty-two.

The funeral was held on December 20 in the church of St. Goran. It was attended by family and friends. A simple headstone marks his grave. On it is engraved a symbol of a three-quarter moon, on its way to being full. Wilson had borrowed it from Yeats to use in *Frankenstein's Castle* to symbolize what our consciousness would be like when we completed our partial mind.

Predictably most of the obituaries sounded the same note. Wilson started out as an interesting writer on existential themes, then turned his hand to churning out popular books for money, as if writing for a living was a disgraceful occupation. They recognized the importance of *The Outsider* but bemoaned the fact that after it he had slipped into self-chosen second-rateness, producing reams of credulous stuff on disreputable subjects such as crime, sex, the occult, UFOs, and ancient mysteries. They ignored his early philosophical work—none of the people writing the obituaries were even aware of it—and while grudgingly admitting his powers of endurance, deplored the fact that he wrote too much about too many things and was too outspoken about his genius. The fact that Wilson died on the same day as Nelson Mandela did not help, as the great South African leader's eminence understandably overshadowed Wilson's passing. It was only after a few days and numerous complaints that the BBC, until then silent, finally announced his death. I wrote a two-page obituary for the *Fortean Times*, filling in omissions and correcting inaccuracies.[28]

An ill-conceived attempt at humor at Wilson's expense was produced for the *Independent* by the journalist Terence Blacker.[29] It sparked outrage, and not only from the true believers. After an e-mail exchange I decided that the only appropriate response to Blacker's scurrilous work was to challenge him and the editor who commissioned the piece to a duel. I did, posting my challenge on the *Independent*'s website. It was picked up by the *Fortean Times*, who tweeted it and posted it to Facebook and other social media, and Mr. Blacker soon conceded that his dark joke had been a mistake. He publicly recanted his work, writing on his blog: "Not only was I not fit to tie Colin Wilson's shoes as a writer and thinker (true), but I had been unnecessarily frivolous and insensitive at a time when there were those who were still grieving for him. He had a wife and family, someone wrote."

The fact that even in death Colin had to weather such abuse is shameful. But his readers expected it and quickly came to his defense.

In *Voyage to a Beginning* Colin had written, "If this body and brain of mine could be driven on for another hundred years or so, I could probably solve all the problems of philosophy single-handed."[30]

I don't doubt that he believed he could solve philosophy's problems; he had been working on that for most of his life. But did he really think he could live for another century? I don't know. His hero Shaw had lived to ninety-four and in *Back to Methuselah* Shaw had argued that human beings need to live for at least three centuries, in order to have the time to evolve into halfway decent creatures. Colin thought something along the same lines; *The Philosopher's Stone*, about the secrets of the prefrontal lobes of the brain, takes up Shaw's challenge that "a hundred apter and more elegant parables by younger hands will soon leave mine . . . far behind."[31] It's doubtful Wilson intended to leave Shaw far behind, but where Shaw was convinced that the kind of longevity needed to truly grasp the purpose of life would simply happen—because it had to; otherwise the force behind evolution would scrap us and start again—Colin believed he had made some headway into understanding how it might be done.

When we met in 2004 he had lowered his sights a bit. At seventy-three, Wilson said that he would like to be "the oldest writer to produce a masterpiece. . . . I'd like to produce a real masterpiece at the age of ninety." He also told me, "Life after death is also an important idea for me, because apart from anything else, it offers a basis for optimism. People are pessimistic because they believe that when they die, everything just vanishes. So if we could prove the reality of life after death, it would be an enormous achievement." And he added, "What people like me have to do is to convince people not to give up."

He did that, I think. And I also believe there is little chance of his life's work vanishing. As I wrote in my obituary, "Wilson said that human beings are like grandfather clocks, driven by watch springs; reading him, I assure you, makes our inner gears a little bit stronger." He once said, "I would like my life to be a lesson in how to stand alone and to thrive on it." For the many who stood with him, it was this and much more.

It is hard to sum up a life's work that lasted more than half a century and stretched from our prehistoric beginnings to our evolutionary future, with in-depth investigations into practically everything in between. Colin Wilson left behind a huge body of writing which is there for old readers to remember and new ones to discover. In it he opened the door to a special kind of knowledge, a kind of insight with which each of us, in our own peculiar way, can discover our "secret life" and explore other times and places. There is no one path for all, as his many Outsiders, those he wrote about and those who discovered themselves through his writing, knew. He wouldn't have it any other way. I end this book with the hope that through reading it some of us can take that evolutionary leap forward that Wilson was certain was on its way and finally get beyond the robot.

ACKNOWLEDGMENTS

Many people have helped to make this book possible. My deep thanks goes to Joy, Sally, Damon, and Rowan Wilson for the hospitality and friendship they have shown me over the years. My special thanks goes to Joy Wilson, for making her late husband's personal diaries, philosophical journals, work rooms, and library available to me and for answering many questions and telling many stories. Much appreciation goes to Colin Stanley, for his tireless efforts as a bibliographer and expositor of Colin Wilson's work and ideas and for his and his wife Gail's hospitality in Nottingham. I am very thankful for the help shown by the staff of the Manuscripts and Special Collections Room at the University of Nottingham while making their Colin Wilson Collection available to me. I would also like to give posthumous thanks to Paul Newman and to his widow, Pamela Smith-Rawnsley, for their part in keeping the Wilsonian faith alive. Thanks too goes to the other Wilsonians, too many to mention individually, who through *Abraxas* and the Paupers' Press have over the years contributed invaluably to the study and dissemination of Wilson's ideas. In the many varied perspectives they have provided on Wilson's work lay the foundation for future Wilson scholarship. My thanks goes to James Hamilton for his perceptive remarks on *The Outsider* and to Mark Booth for needed information. Anja Flode Bjorlo is due much thanks for many helpful discussions and much inspiration. My sons, Joshua and Maximillian, and their mother, Ruth Jones, as always provided important help. I would like to thank my editor, Mitch Horowitz, for being open to the idea and for recognizing the importance of Wilson's work. And lastly I want to thank Colin Wilson himself, for writing some of the most thought-provoking and exciting books of the last two centuries.

NOTES

INTRODUCTION: A PILGRIMAGE TO TETHERDOWN

1 John Connell, *Evening News*, May 26, 1956.
2 I write about Crowley's impact on me in my book *Aleister Crowley: Magick, Rock and Roll, and the Wickedest Man in the World* (New York: Tarcher/Penguin, 2014).
3 Students of western philosophy will know that Husserl's ideas are difficult, complex, and demanding, and that they are expressed in an abstract prose that makes Kant seem like summer reading. Wilson is aware of the vast literature around Husserl and phenomenology and it is not his, or my, aim to present a complete summary of it. Wilson reserves the right to take what is useful to him from Husserl's large body of work and to, in effect, ignore the rest. This policy may seem scandalous to scholars but it is essential to the kind of effort Wilson and those who write about him are engaged in.
4 See, for example, "The Sage of Tetherdown: A Visit with Colin Wilson," *Gnosis*, inter 1996, pp. 6–7; "Romanticism, Optimism, and Consciousness," *Quest*, Summer 1996, pp. 19–23, 82–3; "Inside the Outsider," *Fortean Times*, January 2014, pp. 40–3; and my review of Wilson's second autobiography, *Dreaming to Some Purpose*, in the *Independent on Sunday*, June 6, 2004, http://www.independent.co.uk/arts-entertainment/books/reviews/dreaming-to-some-purpose-by-colin-wilson-6168268.html [broken link]. An early article on Wilson, "Colin Wilson and Faculty X," which originally appeared in the summer 1995 issue of *Quest*, can now be found in *Revolutionaries of the Soul: Reflections on Magicians, Philosophers, and Occultists* (Wheaton, IL: Quest Books, 2014), 9–19.
5 Gary Lachman, *The Caretakers of the Cosmos* (Edinburgh, UK: Floris Books, 2013).
6 Colin Wilson, *The Occult* (New York: Random House, 1971), 9.
7 Ibid.
8 Ibid.
9 Erich Fromm, *Escape from Freedom* (New York: Farrar and Rinehart, 1941).
10 From Eliot's "Choruses from the Rock."
11 T. S. Eliot, "Love Song of J. Alfred Prufrock."
12 Colin Wilson, *Voyage to a Beginning: An Intellectual Autobiography* (New York: Crown Publishers, 1969), 333.
13 Lachman, "Inside the Outsider."
14 Reviewer for *London Times*, back cover of *The Philosopher's Stone* (Los Angeles: Jeremy P. Tarcher, 1989).

CHAPTER ONE: THE ANGRY YOUNG MAN

1 William Shakespeare, *Richard II*, act 2.

2 Colin Wilson, *The Angry Years: The Rise and Fall of the Angry Young Men* (London: Robson Books, 2007), 1.

3 Gary Lachman, *The Secret Teachers of the Western World* (New York: Tarcher/Penguin, 2015), 375.

4 Colin Wilson, *Dreaming to Some Purpose* (London: Century, 2004), 106.

5 Ibid.

6 For Orage, Mansfield, and their relationship to Gurdjieff, see Lachman, *In Search of P. D. Ouspensky: The Genius in the Shadow of Gurdjieff* (2006).

7 Colin Wilson, *The Outsider* (Los Angeles: Jeremy P. Tarcher, 1982), 15.

8 Ibid., 13.

9 Ibid.

10 Wilson voiced this opinion on more than one occasion, and I have heard it repeated by two other English writers who deal with similar concerns, both of whom I met and interviewed: the poet and Blake scholar Kathleen Raine, and the philosopher of language and essayist Owen Barfield.

11 Wilson, *The Outsider*, 15, 39.

12 Wilson, *Voyage to a Beginning*, 15.

13 Wilson, *Dreaming to Some Purpose*, 9.

14 Ibid., 10.

15 Ibid.

16 Wilson, *Voyage to a Beginning*, 15.

17 Ibid., 14.

18 Wilson, *The Angry Years*, 5.

19 Wilson, *Voyage to a Beginning*, 11.

20 Ibid., 12.

21 Colin Wilson, "An Integrity Born of Hope: Notes on Christopher Isherwood," in *Existentially Speaking: Essays on the Philosophy of Literature* (San Bernardino, CA: Borgo Press, 1989), 34.

22 Wilson, *Voyage to a Beginning*, 11.

23 Ibid., 34.

24 Published in the UK as *The Age of Defeat* (London: Victor Gollancz, 1959).

25 Ibid., 25.

26 Ibid.

27 Ibid., 13.

28 Ibid., 27.

29 Colin Wilson, "Below the Iceberg," in *Below the Iceberg: Anti-Sartre and Other Essays* (San Bernardino, CA: Borgo Press, 1998), 126.

30 Colin Wilson, *Beyond the Occult* (London: Bantam Press, 1988), 346.

31 Ibid.

32 Colin Wilson, *Poetry & Mysticism* (San Francisco: City Lights Books, 1970), 58–9. "The glory and the freshness of a dream" is a nod to William Wordsworth's poem "Intimations of Immortality."

33 Wilson, *Voyage to a Beginning*, 17–20.

34 Ibid., 17.

35 Colin Wilson, *New Pathways in Psychology* (New York: Taplinger Publishing; 1972), 28.

36 Ibid., 31.

37 Act 1, scene 2.

38 Colin Wilson, *G.I. Gurdjieff: The War Against Sleep* (London: Aeon Books, 2005), 119.

39 Wilson, *New Pathways in Psychology*, 31.

40 Ibid.

41 J. F. Hendry, *The Sacred Threshold: A Life of Rilke* (Manchester, UK: Carcanet, 1985), 12.

42 Wilson, *Voyage to a Beginning*, 16.

43 Ibid., 17.

44 Wilson, *Dreaming to Some Purpose*, 11.

45 Ibid.

46 Ibid., 12.

47 Journal entry for May 8, 1965.

48 Journal entry for January 15, 1965.

49 Ouspensky, *A New Model of the Universe* (New York: Alfred A. Knopf, 1969), 3.

50 Wilson, *Voyage to a Beginning*, 20.

51 Ibid., 22.

52 Ibid., 32.

53 Ibid.

54 Colin Wilson, *Religion and the Rebel* (Bath, UK: Ashgrove Press, 1992), 7.

55 Ibid.

56 Ibid., 8.

57 Ibid.

58 Wilson, *The Outsider*, 106.

59 Ibid., 9.

60 Wilson, *Religion and the Rebel*, 9.

61 Ibid.

62 Ibid.

63 Ibid., 10. Although Wilson believed that late sexual development is linked to creativity and intelligence, he also recognized that in a highly sexualized environment, such as in our modern society, the stimulation of sexual desire without a socially acceptable outlet can be the cause of damaging frustration.

64 Wilson, *Voyage to a Beginning*, 38.

65 Wilson, *Dreaming to Some Purpose*, 13.

66 Wilson, *Voyage to a Beginning*, 45.

67 Bernard Shaw, *The Complete Plays of Bernard Shaw* (London: Odhams Press, 1934), 374. Shaw's idea of heaven as a place of effort and struggle and the "masters of reality" has much in common with the vision of heaven depicted by the Swedish scientist and religious thinker Emanuel Swedenborg. See Gary Lachman, *Swedenborg: An Introduction to His Life and Ideas* (New York: Tarcher/Penguin, 2012), 115–7.

68 Wilson, *Religion and the Rebel*, 11.

69 Colin Wilson, "A Personal View," in *The Genius of Shaw*, ed. Michael Holroyd (New York: Holt, Rinehart and Winston, 1979), 227.

70 Wilson, *Religion and the Rebel*, 13. Wilson's assessment of literary figures is, by mainstream standards, eccentric, not surprisingly. The American novelist Joyce Carol Oates, who appreciated Wilson's work, questioned his opinion that H. G. Wells "may be the greatest of twentieth-century novelists." (Foreword to Wilson, *The Philosopher's Stone*, viii.) A good idea of how Wilson ranks novelists can be found in his book *The Craft of the Novel* (London: Victor Gollancz, 1977).

71 Wilson, *Dreaming to Some Purpose*, 2.

72 Wilson, *Religion and the Rebel*, 16.

73 Wilson, *Dreaming to Some Purpose*, 4.

74 Wilson, *Religion and the Rebel*, 20.

75 Wilson, *Voyage to a Beginning*, 85.

76 Wilson, *Religion and the Rebel*, 27.

77 Wilson, *Voyage to a Beginning*, 118.
78 Ibid., 120.
79 Wilson, *Religion and the Rebel*, 28.
80 Wilson, *Voyage to a Beginning*, 124.
81 Wilson, *Dreaming to Some Purpose*, 61.

CHAPTER TWO: BEFORE *THE OUTSIDER*

1 Wilson, *Dreaming to Some Purpose*, 62.
2 Colin Wilson, *Frankenstein's Castle* (Sevenoaks, UK: Ashgrove Press, 1980), 13. Wilson's book on music, *Brandy of the Damned* (London: John Baker, 1964), was published in the United States as *Chords and Discords* (New York: Crown Publishers, 1966). Wilson also contributed many articles to *Gramophone* and other music magazines and music plays an important part in much of his fiction, such as the novels *Ritual in the Dark* and *The Philosopher's Stone*. Although he's a fan of early jazz, Wilson's favorite is classical music, mostly Romantic composers.
3 Wilson, *Dreaming to Some Purpose*, 63.
4 Her second novel, *Daffodil on the Pavement*, was published in 1967. Since 1964 Laura has run a stall in London's famous Portobello Road Market, not far from her early Notting Hill stomping grounds. In 2004 her novella *Speedy and Queen Kong* was published by Paufict, a branch of Paupers' Press. She continues to write and is one of the few remaining figures from the "angry years" alive today. I have met and spoken with her about Colin Wilson and her own work on several occasions.
5 An excellent introduction to Wilson's fiction can be found in Nicolas Tredell's *Novels to Some Purpose: The Fiction of Colin Wilson* (Nottingham, UK: Paupers' Press, 2015).
6 In 1995 I had the good fortune to meet Hopkins at his flat near Portobello Road, where we talked about his work and his friendship with Wilson. He had long given up writing and had made a successful career as an antiques dealer.
7 Wilson, *Voyage to a Beginning*, 145.
8 Colin Wilson, *Poetry and Mysticism* (San Francisco: City Lights, 1970), 37.
9 This was published in 1961 and is based in part on the memoirs of Charles Belchier, a familiar Soho figure. Although it is often regarded as Wilson's Beat Generation novel, doing for London what Jack Kerouac did for San Francisco and New York, it is really an anti-beat, anti-bohemian cautionary tale, depicting the demoralizing and often squalid life amid London's wannabe artists. A film of the book is due for release in the indefinite future, but from the trailers and from conversations with the director and Wilson consultant Colin Stanley, it seems that Wilson's criticisms have been watered down in order to present another paean to hipster history. (http://www.imdb.com/title/tt1765679/).
10 Colin Wilson, *The Stature of Man* (Boston, MA: Houghton Mifflin, 1959), 6–15.
11 Wilson, *The Angry Years*, 76.
12 http://louderthanwar.com/alexander-trocchi-junk-male-an-appreciation-of-the-controversial-scottish-beat-author-who-wrote-about-heroin-and-life-by-innes-reekie/.
13 Wilson, *Dreaming to Some Purpose*, 85.
14 Colin Wilson, *Beyond the Outsider* (Boston, MA: Houghton Mifflin, 1965), 29–30.
15 Ibid., 18.
16 Ibid., 30.
17 http://www.dailymail.co.uk/femail/article-2827773/The-latest-foodie-fad-Dripping-s-healthier-think.html.

18 Wilson, *Religion and the Rebel*, 30.

19 Wilson, *Dreaming to Some Purpose*, 125.

20 Wilson, *Voyage to a Beginning*, 194.

21 As Wilson himself argues, existential thinking runs throughout western philosophy and can be found in philosophers like Plato, religious thinkers like St. Augustine and Pascal, and in poets like Goethe and Blake. But existentialism, as a specific school of thought, does seem to be rooted in Kierkegaard's "leap of faith" and Nietzsche's reflections on the "death of God."

22 Jean-Paul Sartre, "Existentialism Is a Humanism," Marxists Internet Archive, https://www.marxists.org/reference/archive/sartre/works/exist/sartre.htm.

23 From Greene's essay "The Revolver in the Corner Cupboard," in *The Lost Childhood and Other Essays* (London: Eyre and Spottiswoode, 1951), quoted in Colin Wilson, *Super Consciousness* (London: Watkins Books, 2009).

24 Wilson, *The Outsider*, 1.

25 Ibid., 3.

26 C. S. Lewis, *Surprised by Joy*, in *The Essential C. S. Lewis*, ed. Lyle W. Dorsett (New York: Collier Books, 1988), 26.

27 W. B. Yeats, "Towards Break of Day," Internet Sacred Text Archive, http://www.sacred-texts.com/neu/yeats/lpy/lpy161.htm.

28 Wilson, *The Outsider*, 4.

29 Wilson, *Dreaming to Some Purpose*, 118.

30 Wilson, *The Angry Years*, 15

31 Ibid., 14.

32 In different autobiographical writings, Wilson gives slightly different accounts of what he sent to Gollancz originally. Because these details make no significant difference to the story, I have based my account here on a combination of them.

33 Wilson, *The Angry Years*, 16.

CHAPTER THREE: BREAKTHROUGH AND BACKLASH

1 As one could imagine, the house was a setting for some bohemian goings-on. Wilson records that in January 1956, the beat novelist Alex Trocchi gave a party in one room, while his girlfriend underwent a disastrous abortion in another. (Wilson, *The Angry Years*, 78–9.)

2 One assumes Wilson later had to return the advance, as Gollancz eventually published the book.

3 This was actually written before Murdoch's first published novel, *Under the Net*, which appeared in 1954.

4 Wilson, *Dreaming to Some Purpose*, 134–6.

5 Kenneth Allsop, *The Angry Decade* (New York: British Book Center, 1958), 166–7.

6 For example, http://www.unz.org/Pub/Encounter-1959nov-00008.

7 Wilson spent a remarkable amount of time bicycling in London and out into the surrounding areas, and this is reflected in *Ritual in the Dark,* whose hero, Gerard Sorme, does the same. In 2015, with Wilson's bibliographer, Colin Stanley, I visited Tetherdown in Cornwall, to help Stanley go through the enormous stacks of papers left by Wilson after his death, some of which were later housed in the Colin Wilson Collection at the University of Nottingham. While there I also spoke with Joy Wilson. At one point she produced the original manuscript of *The Outsider*, which Wilson had ferried around with him, strapped to the back of his bicycle.

8 Philip Toynbee, "Unlucky Jims," *Observer*, May 27, 1956.

9 Cyril Connolly, "Loser Take All," *Sunday Times*, May 27, 1956.

10 George Steiner, *Tolstoy or Dostoyevsky* (London: Faber and Faber, 1980), preface.

11 Wilson, *Dreaming to Some Purpose*, 137.

12 Kenneth Walker, "The Outsider," *The Listener*, June 7, 1956.

13 J. B. Priestley, "Thoughts on The Outsider," *New Statesmen*, July 7, 1956. Priestley, one of the most read writers of the time, wrote a hit play, *I Have Been Here Before*, based on Ouspensky's ideas about "eternal recurrence," and gave him full credit in the theater program. See J. B. Priestley, *Time and the Conways and Other Plays* (Harmondsworth, UK: Penguin, 1969), 86.

14 Allsop, *The Angry Decade*, 94.

15 Ibid., 123. In retrospect, Osborne's working-class rejection of everything around him smacks today of nothing so much as the equally wide-ranging and unfocused denunciation that made the Sex Pistols famous in the 1970s. This is not surprising, as what Jimmy Porter—Osborne's foul-mouthed piece—and Johnny Rotten complain about is exactly the same thing, the sense that for people like them, Britain could offer no future. (Ironically, both Osborne and Rotten would have very successful futures indeed.) Both inform and are informed by what the critic Robert Hughes would later call the "culture of complaint," and as insightful critics of both recognized, both offer little else. They know what they don't like, and want to shout about it, but suggest nothing in its place.

16 Kenneth Tynan, "The Voice of the Young," *Observer*, May 15, 1956, quoted in Wilson, *The Angry Years*, 34–6.

17 In 1958 *Look Back in Anger* was made into a film starring Richard Burton and Mary Ure; Ure had starred in the stage production and in 1957 she married Osborne. They separated in 1963 and several wives followed; Ure died in 1975 at the age of forty-two, from alcohol and barbiturates. After years of film and theater success, Osborne's star began to decline in the 1970s and his later days were filled with debt and creative failure. He died on Christmas Eve 1994, from complications arising from alcoholism and diabetes. He was sixty-five.

18 When, where, and with whom the phrase "angry young man" originated is still a question of literary historical debate. Kenneth Allsop reports that a book with that title was published in 1951 by the religious philosopher Leslie Allen Paul, a memoir of his shift from Communism to Christianity. Various journalists have been suggested as the source, as has been the press office of the Royal Court Theatre.

19 Stuart Holroyd, "Angry Young Mania and Beyond," in *Colin Wilson: A Celebration*, ed. Colin Stanley (London: Cecil Woolf, 1988), 38.

20 Wilson, *The Angry Years*, 140.

21 Both were preceded by John Clellon Holmes's roman à clef *Go*, which appeared in 1952 and features characters based on Kerouac, Ginsberg, Burroughs, and other beats.

22 Again, the origins of the name "Beat Generation" are debatable. Some sources say Kerouac gave birth to it; some say Kenneth Rexroth, an older poet who played guru to his younger contemporaries; and some say it was the product of the journalist Herb Caen.

23 Allsop, *The Angry Decade*, 148.

24 http://www.nickelinthemachine.com/2010/01/hampstead-heath-and-the-rise-and -fall-of-the-author-colin-wilson/.

25 Wilson, *Religion and the Rebel*, viii.

26 Again the similarity to the Sex Pistols and how the press egged them on to do the same, http://www.televisionpersonalities.co.uk/pistols.htm.

27 John Rety, "So Much Work to Do," in Stanley, *Colin Wilson*, 56.

28 "To believe your own thoughts, to believe that what is true for you in your private heart is true for all men—that is genius," Ralph Waldo Emerson said. That this is also Wilson's idea of genius—and not of some caricature whiz kid prodigy—is clear from his writing.

29 Allsop, *The Angry Decade*, 161.

30 Quoted in Allsop, *The Angry Decade*, 153.

31 Colin Wilson, *Bernard Shaw: A Reassessment* (London: Hutchinson, 1969). The young Wilson could show surprising political naïveté. He once had lunch with Oswald Mosley, who in the 1930s was infamous in England as the leader of the British Union of Fascists, and afterward described him as "rather a decent chap." Mosley had given *The Outsider* high praise in *The European* and according to Wilson scholar Colin Stanley he "managed to grasp the essence of that book in a way that few others writing at the time were able to do." (Stanley, *Colin Wilson*, 15.) But according to Kenneth Allsop, Wilson's knowledge of Mosley's political career was negligible. Bill Hopkins's politics were closer to Mosley's than Wilson's ever were. In an interview in 1970, Wilson says that he has "always labelled myself a socialist" but came to reject it because "as soon as you get state control, you immediately get a universal damn-you-jack attitude, rather than the enthusiasm when people are working for themselves." He remarks, though, that he's "been against the Tories all my life," the Tories being the UK's conservative party (ibid., 180). In conversation with Wilson he told me that he believes in a meritocracy, which essentially is leadership by able and talented people. With his emphasis on the creative individual and the effort and will necessary to actualize one's abilities, it is clear that Wilson is not at home with the forced egalitarianism of either populist democracy or totalitarian socialism.

32 Colin Wilson, *The Death of God and Other Plays* (Nottingham, UK: Paupers' Press, 2008). Although he's not really a playwright, some of Wilson's theater pieces carry a certain power; see his *Strindberg* (New York: Random House, 1970), in which he takes the great Swedish genius to task for wasting his powers on jealousy and paranoia. A new edition with an introduction by Wilson was published by Paupers' Press in 2007.

33 The text of the letter appears in Allsop, *The Angry Decade*, 170–1.

34 Wilson, *Religion and the Rebel*, 34.

35 Gary Lachman, *The Caretakers of the Cosmos* (Edinburgh, UK: Floris Books, 2013), 22.

36 Although in the published text women are in scant supply, Wilson's original vision of *The Outsider* included a chapter on female Outsiders which, for editorial reasons, was scrapped. He later conceived of writing a sequel, an unwritten second half of *The Outsider* which would focus on women. He did not finish this book—it was probably not commissioned—but an outline of it remains and was published sometime in the mid-1990s as "Outline of the Female Outsider" by Abraxas Publications. "Outsiders are frustrated self-actualisers. And there are undoubtedly as many female self-actualisers as male," Wilson writes in it.

37 Wilson, *The Outsider*, 30.

38 Ibid., 42.

39 I have written about some of them in *The Dedalus Book of Literary Suicides: Dead Letters* (Sawtry, UK: Dedalus Books, 2008).

40 Wilson, *The Outsider*, 147.

41 Ibid., 17.

42 Ibid.

43 Ibid., 31.

44 Ibid., 57.
45 Ibid., 59.
46 Ibid., 77.
47 Ibid., 111.
48 Ibid., 188.
49 Ibid., 237.
50 Ibid., 252–4.
51 Ibid., 264.
52 Ibid., 277.
53 Ibid., 281.
54 Wilson, *Voyage to a Beginning*, 220.

CHAPTER FOUR: AFTER *THE OUTSIDER*

1 Colin Wilson and Pat Pitman, *Encyclopaedia of Murder* (London: Arthur Baker, 1961).
2 See Lachman, *Aleister Crowley*, 277–8.
3 Wilson *Dreaming to Some Purpose*, 154.
4 Allsop, *The Angry Decade*, 168. Allsop (168–70) prints the extracts from Wilson's diary and aside from the occasional "genius," they are mostly concerned with the kind of problems the Outsider faces. Readers for whom being serious is equivalent to being pretentious could not be expected to understand the sentiment behind remarks such as "I am the most serious man of our age" or "There is a devouring evolutionary appetite in me, a growing need to take life seriously." Wilson is also quite insightful about the drawbacks of success. He remarks that while before his fame he used his journal to record "ideas that needed clarifying" and "inner states that needed examining," now "I am dogged by lots of minor problems that come as a consequence of my fame." He concludes that "the Outsider's life tends to be a struggle between real problems and mere human problems. His job is to conquer the human problems."
5 Amis may have been a friendly host but in *The Angry Years* Wilson relates that the novelist John Wain had told him that at a literary party at the time, Wain had to restrain Amis from pushing Wilson off the roof (39). And in his *Letters of Kingsley Amis* Amis tells a journalist that a bottle of whiskey Wilson had brought to him as a gift during their flight from the paparazzi was poisoned. Wilson writes, "Since the bottle was sealed when I gave it to him, it is impossible that I could have poisoned it; this was simply the kind of thing that Amis enjoyed making up to satisfy some odd streak of malice in his fairly amiable, but also oddly unhappy, personality." (Wilson, *The Angry Years*.)
6 Wilson, *Dreaming to Some Purpose*, 157.
7 Wilson, *The Angry Years*, 104.
8 Ibid., 107.
9 Tom Greenwell, "Shared Experiences," in Stanley, *Colin Wilson*, 37.
10 Wilson, *Dreaming to Some Purpose*, 163.
11 This was one of the biggest misunderstandings about *The Outsider*, that Wilson's use of the term covered every eccentric social misfit, beatnik, or "crazy mixed-up kid." Many who read *The Outsider* do not go on to read the rest of the books in Wilson's "Outsider Cycle," nor do they recognize that for him *The Outsider* is not about being antiauthoritarian but about adopting a *greater* discipline than what ordinary society requires of us. Here Wilson is in line with Gurdjieff, who dismissed such social misfits as "tramps" and "lunatics" in favor of the "good householder," what he called an *obyvatel* (Ouspensky, *In Search of the Miraculous* [New York: Harcourt, Brace, 1949], 363), and C. G. Jung, who in his paper "Adaptation, Individuation, Collec-

tivity" argues that "individuators"—those who work toward self-actualization—must achieve higher levels of inner discipline, not "let it all hang out." "Individuation," Jung writes, "remains a pose so long as no positive values are created . . . society has a right to expect realizable values." Quoted in Gary Lachman, *Jung the Mystic* (New York: Tarcher/Penguin, 2010), 133.

12 Wilson, *Religion and the Rebel*, 1.

13 Ibid.

14 Colin Wilson, *Poetry and Mysticism* (San Francisco: City Lights, 1970), 14.

15 Wilson, *Religion and the Rebel*, 1.

16 Wilson, "A Retrospective Introduction," in *Religion and the Rebel*, ix, xii.

17 Wilson, *Religion and the Rebel*, 2.

18 Ibid., 40.

19 Ibid.

20 Ibid.

21 Ibid., 104, 121.

22 Ibid., 6.

23 See Henri Bergson, *The Two Sources of Morality and Religion* (New York: Doubleday Anchor Books, 1956).

24 The idea that the Insiders or "uncreative majority," while consciously rejecting him, unknowingly profit by the Outsider's spiritual labors was shared by other "Outsider thinkers," such as Hermann Hesse and P. D. Ouspensky. In *Steppenwolf* Hesse writes, "the vital force of the bourgeoisie resides by no means in the qualities of its normal members, but in those of its extremely numerous 'outsiders' who by virtue of the extensiveness and elasticity of its ideals it can embrace" (New York: Henry Holt and Company, 1929, translation by Basil Creighton, 70–1). And in *A New Model of the Universe*, Ouspensky, analyzing the relationship between the individual and the masses, remarks, "The blind organism of the masses struggle with the man-ifestation of the evolutionary spirit, annihilate and stifle it and destroy what has been created by it. But even so they cannot entirely annihilate it. Something re-mains, and this is what we call progress or civilization" (New York: Alfred A. Knopf, 1969, 51).

25 Wilson, *The Outsider*, 102.

26 Wilson, *Religion and the Rebel*, 2.

27 See Gary Lachman, *The Secret Teachers of the Western World* (New York: Tarcher/Penguin, 2015), 27–31.

28 See particularly the Theosophical Society's input in the first World's Parliament of Religions in Gary Lachman, *Madame Blavatsky: The Mother of Modern Spirituality* (New York: Tarcher/Penguin, 2012), 157.

29 Wilson, *Religion and the Rebel*, 119.

30 By "spiritual leader" I do not mean "totalitarian mystic," but someone aware of the values needed to keep a civilization from degenerating and possessing the vitality and determination to embody them.

31 Wilson, *The Outsider*, 281.

32 Wilson, *Religion and the Rebel*, 134.

33 Ibid., 135.

34 Although Wilson focuses on Christianity, the tendency of *all* religions to begin with inspiration and revelation and to slowly ossify into dogma, ritual, and authority is implied, a problem that Bergson addressed in *The Two Sources of Morality and Religion* as the conflict between "static" and "dynamic" religions.

35 Lachman, *The Secret Teachers of the Western World*, 288–93.

36 Abraham von Franckenberg, *The Life and Death of Jacob Behmen,* Jacob Boehme On-line, http://jacobboehmeonline.com/frankenberg.

37 Jacob Boehme, *Genius of the Transcendent: Mystical Writings of Jacob Boehme, trans.* Michael L. Birkel and Jeff Bach (London: Shambhala, 2010), 37.

38 Wilson, *Religion and the Rebel,* 166.

39 Oddly enough, Wilson used this phrase for the title of his history of forensic detection, *Written in Blood* (London: Grafton Books, 1990). Here, and with his earlier books on the psychology of crime, he anticipated by decades the fascination with the "path labs" made popular by television programs like *CSI* and others.

40 Wilson, *Religion and the Rebel,* 34.

41 The essence of the creative evolutionist philosophy, self-transformation, is at the heart of practically all Shaw's work, even the popular comedy *Pygmalion,* which was turned into the successful musical and film *My Fair Lady.* Here an uneducated Cockney flower girl evolves through her efforts—and the help of Henry Higgins—into a lady. Unfortunately today's politically correct sensibilities would most likely see such transformation as the imposition of male authoritarian principles upon a helpless socially disenfranchised female, instead preferring for Eliza Doolittle (the name tells us a great deal) to remain a "draggle-tailed guttersnipe" rather than be transformed into a duchess.

42 Alfred North Whitehead, *Modes of Thought* (New York: Free Press, 1968).

43 Ludwig Wittgenstein, *Tractatus Logico-Philosophicus* (London: Routledge & Kegan Paul, 1969), 151.

44 Ibid., 149.

45 Language indeed is an important tool in this pursuit, and like Wittgenstein, Wilson is aware of what Whitehead called the "fallacy of misplaced concreteness," the tendency of philosophers to confuse words with reality. Unlike Wittgenstein, Wilson believes in language's ability to capture and analyze reality, and in his phenomenological approach, he aims at greater precision.

46 The split was carried further by the philosopher John Locke in his *An Essay Concerning Human Understanding* (1689). Locke argues that the human mind is a "blank slate" upon which experience writes; until it does, the mind is empty. "There is nothing in the mind," he says, "that didn't get there by way of the senses." Philosophers such as Plato, Husserl, and Whitehead disagree, as do psychologists such as C. G. Jung.

47 Alfred North Whitehead, *Science and the Modern World* (New York: Macmillan, 1925), 77.

48 Allsop, *The Angry Decade,* 173.

49 Ibid., 174.

50 Wilson, *Religion and the Rebel,* 35.

CHAPTER FIVE: A NEW EXISTENTIALISM

1 Allsop, *The Angry Decade,* 175. There was a small flurry of support for Wilson after the initial attack. Some writers felt that while the book may have warranted severe criticism, many of the attacks smacked more of fear than anything else. The psychologist James Hemming, writing to the *New Statesman,* deplored the critics ganging up on Wilson and summarized the "Outsider position" neatly and fairly. He suggested that the critics were "afraid of this new style of attack upon snug preconceptions" and argued that Wilson's critics should have dealt with the ideas presented in the book, rather than "fuming around like middle-aged ladies at a vicarage tea-party into which an uninvited tramp has strayed. . . . Those who admonish Mr. Wilson to start thinking haven't even bothered to think for themselves." (177.)

2 Colin Wilson, "Beyond the Outsider," in *Declaration*, ed. Tom Maschler (London: Macgibbon & Kee, 1957), 31.

3 Ibid., 37.

4 H. G. Wells, *Experiment in Autobiography* (London: Victor Gollancz and the Crescent Press, 1934), 16.

5 Ibid., 17.

6 Ibid., 18.

7 Wilson, *Dreaming to Some Purpose*, 163.

8 Ibid., 170.

9 Ibid., 171.

10 Sisyphus is a figure in Greek mythology, forever doomed to roll a boulder up to the top of a hill, only to see it roll down again.

11 Colin Wilson, "Albert Camus," in *Below the Iceberg: Anti-Sartre and Other Essays* (San Bernardino: Borgo Press, 1998), 64–80.

12 Ouspensky, *In Search of the Miraculous*, 181.

13 Stanley, *Colin Wilson*, 46.

14 Colin Wilson, *The Age of Defeat* (Nottingham, UK: Paupers' Press, 2001), 71–2.

15 Ibid., 93.

16 See Gary Lachman, *Two Essays on Colin Wilson* (Nottingham, UK: Paupers' Press, 1994), specifically "World Rejection and Criminal Romantics," 1–36.

17 Colin Wilson, *Existential Criticism: Selected Book Reviews* (Nottingham, UK: Paupers' Press, 2009), 19.

18 Colin Wilson, *The Strength to Dream* (London: Sphere Books, 1979), 197.

19 In Mann this takes the form of the artist who pays for his sensitivity with illness, and the bourgeois who pays for his health with dullness—for example in *Death in Venice* and *Doctor Faustus*. Wilson asks if it is not possible to have a "healthy artist," along the lines of Goethe.

20 Jean-Paul Sartre, *Being and Nothingness*, trans. Hazel Barnes (London: Routledge, 2003), 636.

21 Wilson, *The Age of Defeat*, 175.

22 William James, *The Varieties of Religious Experience* (New York: Collier Books, 1977), 305.

23 Heidegger was not entirely ignorant of the "other forms of consciousness" and in his writings on poetry and language skirts very close to a kind of existential mysticism, although the obscurity of his prose, and his focus on being rather than consciousness often makes it difficult to determine exactly what he is saying.

24 Wilson, *Dreaming to Some Purpose*, 194.

25 The building was sold in 1959 after the death of its landlord. Just before they had to vacate it, Bill Hopkins arranged for a sculptor friend to make a blue plaque, like the ones the London County Council affixes to the homes of famous figures from the past, such as Charles Dickens and Sir Arthur Conan Doyle. The plaque read, "John Braine, Tom Greenwell, Stuart Holroyd, Bill Hopkins, Colin Wilson lived here, 1956–59." It didn't last long and was stolen soon after being put up.

26 Wilson and Pitman, *Encyclopaedia of Murder*, 21.

27 Wilson, *The Age of Defeat*, 151.

28 Ibid., 114.

29 Wilson and Pitman, *Encyclopaedia of Murder*, 25.

30 Wilson, *Dreaming to Some Purpose*, 183–93.

31 Ibid., 195.

32 Ibid.

33 Wilson expressed his appreciation of Isherwood in his essay "An Integrity Born of Hope: Notes on Christopher Isherwood," in Wilson, *Existentially Speaking*, 33–52. Like the other essays in this collection, this was originally published in *Books and Bookmen*, a literary journal to which Wilson frequently contributed.

34 Wilson, *Dreaming to Some Purpose*, 202.

35 Wilson writes about Miller in *The Misfits: A Study of Sexual Outsiders* (London: Grafton Books, 1988), 196–200. "Henry Miller will probably be remembered as the only major writer of the twentieth century who had absolutely nothing to say." Wilson, *Existential Criticism*, 165.

36 Ibid., 204.

37 Wilson, *The Strength to Dream*, 1.

38 In 2005 Monkfish Book Publishing released a new edition of *The Mind Parasites* with an afterword by Wilson and an introduction by me.

39 Wilson, *The Strength to Dream*, 195.

40 Ibid., 191.

41 Ibid., 189.

42 Ibid., 85.

43 Ibid., 91.

44 Ibid., 181.

45 Colin Wilson, *Origins of the Sexual Impulse* (New York: G. P. Putnam's Sons, 1963), 15.

46 Ibid., 182.

47 With eating disorders we can eat too much or too little, but *what* we eat is still food. Sexual disorders are a kind of malfunction, as in frigidity or impotence. They interfere with "normal" sexual behavior. A man who, say, achieves orgasm at the sight of an umbrella—a peculiar fetish, no doubt, but on record—does not have a sexual disorder. He is not impotent, but what excite him are not the normal sexual releasers. Urophagia (drinking urine) and coprophagia (eating feces) are in this context considered sexual perversions, not eating disorders.

48 Nicolas Berdyaev, *The Meaning of the Creative Act* (New York: Collier Books, 1962), 168.

49 Wilson, *Origins of the Sexual Impulse*, 27.

50 Ibid., 18.

51 Ibid., 54.

52 This familiarity is not limited to men. Although somewhat less prone to it, women, too, become inured to sexual partners and seek out "strangeness."

53 Even ordinary, not forbidden or highly imaginative, sex has this forbidden quality. The male must "penetrate" the female; he must "take" her, "possess" her, break down her "defenses." Even with the greatest affection there is still an element of aggression.

54 Wilson, *Origins of the Sexual Impulse*, 222.

55 Ibid., 19.

56 I imagine I should point out that Wilson is writing from a male point of view—although the fact that he is a man seems to obviate the need for this. He does suggest some insights into female sexuality, but as the sexual impulse he is trying to understand is his, it is clearly coming from a male perspective.

57 Wilson, *Origins of the Sexual Impulse*, 65. Henri Bergson made the same point years earlier when he contrasted the way in which intellect works with intuition. As he wrote in *An Introduction to Metaphysics* (New York: G. P. Putnam's Sons, 1912), the intellect "reduces the object to elements already known, that is, to elements common to both it and other objects" (7). This is an insight that Iain McGilchrist, in his important book *The Master and His Emissary*, revives in a discussion about the differences between the right and left cerebral hemispheres. See my *The Caretakers of the Cosmos*, 77–89.

58 Wilson, *Origins of the Sexual Impulse*, 67.

59 Ibid.

60 See Lachman, *The Secret Teachers of the Western World*, 39–41. See also my essay "Mystical Experience and the Evolution of Consciousness," http://www.academia .edu/18910463/Mystical_Experience_and_the_Evolution_of_Consciousness.

61 Wilson, *Origins of the Sexual Impulse*, 125.

62 Ibid., 68.

63 Lachman, *The Secret Teachers of the Western World*, 55–6.

64 Ibid., 67.

CHAPTER SIX: PEAK EXPERIENCES, INTENTIONALITY, AND EVOLUTION

1 Wilson took the title from the story *Peter Schlemihl* (1814), by Adelbert von Chamisso, about a young man who sells his shadow to the devil.

2 For more on Girodias and the Olympia Press, see John de St. Jorre, *The Good Ship Venus: The Erotic Voyage of Maurice Girodias and the Olympia Press* (London: Hutchinson, 1994).

3 Colin Wilson, *The God of the Labyrinth* (London: Rupert Hart-Davis, 1970), 293. See Wilson's afterword for his rejection of the claims that he has written pornography and his rejection of pornography itself. "Pornography involves a sense of the debasement of values," he writes, and he finds it in writing that we wouldn't ordinarily call pornographic, such as the James Bond novels, or the work of Harold Robbins. That said, in the 1960s Wilson occasionally wrote for some men's magazines, such as *Penthouse*, which his friend Bill Hopkins briefly edited—Wilson contributes to a "symposium" on sex in the first issue—and *Cavalier*. A February 1965 issue of this last has him sharing column space with Paul Krassner, Nelson Algren, and Paul Gallico.

4 In 1970 an American edition of *The God of the Labyrinth* appeared as *The Hedonists*. In 2013 Valancourt Books released a new edition, with an introduction by me, as part of its rereleases of much of Wilson's fiction. *The Sex Diary of Gerard Sorme* also appeared in 1988 as *The Sex Diary of a Metaphysician* with an introduction by Timothy Leary (Berkeley, CA: Ronin Publishing). The Valancourt edition (2013) restores Wilson's original title.

5 Wilson, *Voyage to a Beginning*, 264.

6 Ibid.

7 For a brilliant in-depth analysis of Wilson's fiction, see Tredell, *Novels to Some Purpose*.

8 Wilson gives two different years for when he first heard from Maslow. In *New Pathways in Psychology* (New York: Taplinger, 1972) he says he received the letter from Maslow in 1959 (15). In *Dreaming to Some Purpose* he says, "Four years after the American publication of my book *The Age of Defeat* . . . I had received a letter from Maslow." More than thirty years separate one date from the other, and the correspondence between Wilson and Maslow is not available for research. Wilson was in his seventies writing *Dreaming* and most likely forgot, although Maslow's biographer Edward Hoffman places Maslow's contact with Wilson around the same time as in *Dreaming*. For the sake of the narrative I will stick to the later date, with the awareness that the earlier one may be correct. This will not affect the understanding of Maslow's influence on Wilson, although, to be sure, more fastidious readers may take offense.

9 Edward Hoffman, *The Right to Be Human* (Los Angeles: Jeremy P. Tarcher, 1988), 265.

10 Abraham Maslow, *Future Visions* (Thousand Oaks, CA: Sage Publications, 1996), 59.

11 Abraham Maslow, *The Farther Reaches of Human Nature* (New York: Penguin, 1976), 34–9.

12 Maslow is referred to as "Aaron Marks" in *The Mind Parasites* and *The Philosopher's Stone*.

13 Quoted in Wilson, *New Pathways in Psychology*, 16.

14 Ibid. Wilson quotes from a paper Maslow read at the Western Behavioral Sciences Institute in La Jolla, California, in 1961, "Lessons from the Peak Experience."

15 Ibid., 17.

16 For a discussion on the link between such moments and the experience of gnosis, a sudden grasp of inner knowledge common to the western esoteric tradition, see Gary Lachman, *The Quest for Hermes Trismegistus* (Edinburgh, UK: Floris Books, 2011), 31–49.

17 Samuel Richardson's *Pamela* (1740), to be exact. There had been novels before—*Don Quixote* and *Robinson Crusoe*, for example. But these were tales of "faraway places with strange sounding names." *Pamela* was the first novel in the modern sense of being about everyday life. Readers could identify with its characters and daydream about their life in a way they couldn't with these earlier works. *Pamela* was like an early soap opera and it was an immediate hit. It taught the average person how to use his imagination in order to transcend the immediacy of his own life, and to wonder what it would be like to live in another way. See Wilson, *The Craft of the Novel*, 31–40.

18 The Romantics were subject to what Wilson calls the "Bombard effect," after the French biologist Alain Bombard. Bombard wanted to prove that shipwrecked sailors could survive being lost at sea without food and water, and to prove his point, in 1952 he decided to cross the Atlantic in a small inflatable boat with practically no provisions. He lived on squashed fish, plankton, and seawater, slowly acclimatizing his body to this diet. At one point he was invited aboard a passing ship for a decent meal. He enjoyed it, but when he returned to his journey, his body would no longer accept his meager fare and rejected it violently. It took him some time to readjust. The Romantics are like Bombard in the sense that after experiencing their ecstasies (the meal aboard the ship) they could no longer accept everyday life (squashed fish and seawater.). Colin Wilson, *Mysteries: An Investigation into the Occult, the Paranormal, and the Supernatural* (New York: G. P. Putnam's Sons, 1978), 305–6.

19 Wilson, *Dreaming to Some Purpose*, 215.

20 Ibid., 15.

21 Ibid., 16.

22 Ibid., 18.

23 Ibid., 19.

24 Ibid., 31.

25 See William Wordsworth, "The World Is Too Much With Us," http://www.poetry-foundation.org/poem/174833.

26 Wilson, *Dreaming to Some Purpose*, 39.

27 Ernest Dowson "Dregs," http://poetry.elcore.net/CatholicPoets/Dowson/Dowson63.html.

28 Wilson, *Beyond the Outsider*, 40.

29 Percy Bysshe Shelley, "Stanzas Written in Dejection, Near Naples," http://www.poetryfoundation.org/poem/174407.

30 Wilson, *Beyond the Outsider*, 46.

31 Ibid.

32 Wilson, *New Pathways in Psychology*, 39–41.

33 I should point out that "significance" here is not meant in any kind of egocentric way, in the sense of drawing attention to yourself and telling everyone how important you are, but in the sense of not feeling helpless and defeated.

34 Although its roots can be traced back to the world rejection of ancient Greek philosophy; Socrates, Wilson points out, believed that philosophy was a "preparation for death."

35 Wilson, *Beyond the Outsider*, 51.

36 Ibid., 67.

37 Ibid., 124.

38 Ibid., 125. Wilson is quoting from Julian Huxley's essay "Transhumanism," in *New Bottles for New Wine* (London: Chatto and Windus, 1957). For more on Huxley's transhumanism, see also *The Caretakers of the Cosmos*, 51–2.

39 In saying this I am not, as some pro-animal individuals might think, being "down" on animals or in any way aiming to denigrate them. But it seems clear that, as far as we can tell, animals do not seem to be able to inhabit the spheres of imagination and intellect in the way that we can. That is to say they do not possess the ability to symbolize their experience, to detach themselves from immediacy and achieve a certain distance from their lives. That not all humans do this is no argument against the fact that humans can do it.

40 Wilson, *Beyond the Outsider*, 125.

41 Ibid., 137.

42 Ibid., 76.

43 A concise expression of Wilson's appreciation of Whitehead's ideas can be found in his essay "Whitehead as Existentialist," https://philosophynow.org/issues/64/White head_As_Existentialist.

44 Wilson, *Beyond the Outsider*, 76.

45 Ibid., 72.

46 Ibid., 79–81.

47 This is the famous Cartesian formula *Cogito ergo sum*: I think, therefore I am.

48 I should perhaps point out that Husserl's "natural standpoint" and "intentionality" are very similar to what Owen Barfield calls "alpha thinking," "beta thinking," "figuration," and "participation." See *The Secret History of Consciousness* (Great Barrington, MA: Lindisfarne, 2003), 153–80.

49 Kant's and Husserl's philosophies are similar in many ways. Briefly put, Kant believed that we perceive the world through a set of what he called "categories" that organize otherwise chaotic sensory data into a stable whole. These categories include time, space, shape, and, contrary to David Hume, cause and effect; there are others but this gives the general idea. We can think of Kant's categories as a pair of glasses we need to wear in order to perceive the world. But as Kant formulates it, we can only see the world in this way, and can never see what it is like when we are *not* wearing our glasses. The world we perceive is the world of phenomena, or effects; the world as it is in itself (what he calls the *ding-an-sich*), the noumenon, or world of causes, is forever barred from our view. The part of the mind that projects the categories and enables us to perceive a world, Kant called the "transcendental ego." Husserl's intentionality differs from Kant in the sense that he never doubts whether there is a world out there—which Kant's philosophy led some of his followers to do. There is a real world outside our consciousness. We do not create it, but Husserl argues that we are certainly responsible for the picture we have of it. For Husserl, we *read* the world, as we would read a book. The book is certainly outside my consciousness, but its meaning is dormant until I read it. My reading of the world is performed through inten-

tionality. I can read it with full attention or while half-distracted. This doesn't affect the book, but it does affect my understanding and appreciation of it.

50 It may be confusing to speak of different "I's" but the limits of language leave us little alternative. We need to see this "transcendental I" not as a personality, like the "I" of the natural standpoint, but as a "unit of pure thought," as one of Wilson's correspondents, the psychologist Howard Miller, called it.

51 Wilson, *Beyond the Outsider*, 84.

52 During visits to Tetherdown and the Colin Wilson Collection at the University of Nottingham, I read through some of Wilson's phenomenological journals. They are a remarkable record of and testament to the tenacity of his thought and show that he took his phenomenology very seriously. I am in discussion with other interested parties about the possibility of publishing them.

53 Some readers may question the kind of intention involved in the male response to an attractive female. The point here is intentionality itself, not its target. It is the directedness, the purposiveness of consciousness that is in question here. This is a question Wilson has often had to answer. In many interviews he is asked about the purpose he has in mind. It is not a question of a particular purpose, but of *purposiveness* itself, a directed consciousness rather than a drifting one, a concentrated consciousness, rather than a dissipated one. Whatever one might think about it, it is a fact that sexual attraction has the effect of giving a man's consciousness a more purposive character. It is directed at a goal, rather than idling.

54 J. B. Priestley, *The Magicians* (London: William Heinemann, 1954), 196–7.

55 Colin Wilson, *Super Consciousness* (London: Watkins Books, 2009), 27–41.

56 Wilson, *Beyond the Outsider*, 71–2. Yeats's poem raises the question of what exactly it is that we find beautiful in nature. I am not saying it isn't beautiful, only asking what it is in nature that strikes us as beautiful. We are awestruck by mountains, but they are really only great heaps of soil and stone. Clouds are steam, yet we find them beautiful too. As Yeats knew, we cannot touch the beauty in a mountain or a cloud, but it is nonetheless there. Wilson is suggesting that we respond to the beauty in nature in the same way that we respond to the reality of a sexy picture.

57 Again, Wilson isn't saying that sexual fetishism and mysticism are the same, merely that the mental operations in both are identical. This is the same as saying that a pornographic novel and *War and Peace* both use words to achieve their effect. The same operations are at work with children who endow inanimate objects with a magical life, except in their case, the filtering mechanisms that hamper adults are yet to be in place. Their doors of perception are wide open; it is precisely *because they are* that the force behind life installs the blinders as they get older.

58 Wilson, *Beyond the Outsider*, 164. Wilson condensed his synthesis of phenomenology and creative evolution in an essay, "Husserl and Evolution," collected in *Existentially Speaking*, 71–82.

CHAPTER SEVEN: AMERICA AND THE ROBOT

1 Wilson, "Appendix One: The Mescaline Experience," in *Beyond the Outsider*, 187–206. The book contains two other appendices: "The Rope Trick," on Bill Hopkins's novel *The Divine and the Decay*; and "Culture in the Soviet Union."

2 Wilson was not a fan of drugs—as he states, because they inhibit the will—although he acknowledged that psychedelics could be used in controlled conditions as an aid in exploring consciousness. In *Adrift in Soho* Wilson's hero, Harry Preston, smokes cannabis but is not taken with it. Wilson's intoxicant of choice was alcohol, specifi-

cally wine, about which he wrote a delightful imbiber's tract, *A Book of Booze* (London: Victor Gollancz, 1974).

3 Wilson, *Beyond the Outsider*, 190.

4 Ibid. This is a theme I develop in *The Caretakers of the Cosmos*.

5 Ibid., 193.

6 See Lachman, *The Quest for Hermes Trismegistus*, 46.

7 What Wilson meant by this was that throughout his life Huxley had always had trouble with his vision. Combined with this was his tendency toward abstract thought and intellectualization. Like T. E. Lawrence, Huxley usually saw the world "filtered through by thought," and very rarely experienced it directly. The mescaline quieted Huxley's thinking and allowed him to perceive the world directly. Although an intellectual himself, Wilson was less prone to abstract thinking—hence his predilection for existentialism—and so did not have quite the same distance between himself and the world that Huxley did. That aspect of the mescaline experience did not affect him as strongly.

8 See Lachman, *The Quest for Hermes Trismegistus*, 38–42.

9 Colin Wilson, *Introduction to the New Existentialism* (Boston, MA: Houghton Mifflin Company, 1967), 102.

10 Wilson, *Beyond the Outsider*, 13.

11 Colin Wilson, "Phenomenological Journals," January 15, 1965. A 6th form is a kind of preparatory college for sixteen- to nineteen-year-olds.

12 Ibid.

13 Ibid.

14 Along with the Outsider Cycle and *Ritual in the Dark*, during these years Wilson also published *Adrift in Soho*, *Encyclopaedia of Murder* (1961), *Man Without a Shadow*, *The World of Violence* (1963), *Brandy of the Damned* (a book about music), *Necessary Doubt*, *Rasputin and the Fall of the Romanovs* (1964), and *Eagle and Earwig* (1965).

15 Wilson, *Voyage to a Beginning*, 294.

16 Ibid., 295.

17 Wilson, "Phenomenological Journals," March 23, 1965.

18 Wilson, *Dreaming to Some Purpose*, 237.

19 Martin Gardner, *The New Age* (Buffalo, NY: Prometheus Books, 1988), 180–1.

20 Colin Wilson, *The Quest for Wilhelm Reich* (New York: Anchor Press, 1981), 1–3.

21 Marcel Proust, *Remembrance of Things Past*, Volume One, *Swann's Way*, translated by C. K. Scott Moncrieff and Terence Kilmartin (London: Chatto & Windus, 1982), 48.

22 Wilson, *The Occult*, 10.

23 For the history of this, see my *Turn Off Your Mind* (New York: Disinformation, 2003), 72–9.

24 Judith Campbell Exner, *Judith Exner: My Story* (New York: Grove Press, 1977). Exner also claimed to have had affairs with high-ranking Mafioso leaders.

25 On October 7, 1955, Rexroth served as master of ceremonies at a poetry reading at the Six Gallery featuring Allen Ginsberg, Philip Lamantia, Michael McClure, Gary Snyder, and Philip Whalen, thus inaugurating the Beat movement. He later testified in Ginsberg's defense during an obscenity trial regarding his poem "Howl." Rexroth was eventually critical of the Beats.

26 Wilson, *Dreaming to Some Purpose*, 251–2.

27 Colin Wilson, *Order of Assassins* (St. Albans, UK: Panther Books, 1975), 176.

28 Ibid., 178.

29 *International Times* 10 (October 5–20, 1967).

30 Colin Wilson, *The Mind Parasites* (New York: Monkfish Book Publishing, 2005), 190–2.

31 On exactly how it did, see my *Turn Off Your Mind*.

32 Wilson, *Order of Assassins*, 173–206.

33 *Ritual in the Dark* features two beatnik poets whom Gerard Sorme meets but is soon bored by. Wilson himself had kind words about the poet Peter Orlovsky's collection *Clean Asshole Poems & Smiling Vegetable Songs* (San Francisco: City Lights, 1978). Allen Ginsberg, Orlovsky's lover, expressed surprise at Wilson's appreciation and asked, "How did he get that open mind?" See Allen Ginsberg, "A Literary Incident," in Stanley, *Colin Wilson*, 60.

34 "There has just been a book published by some research team on the effect of total loneliness and silence on human beings—on how they break up." Wilson, "Phenomenological Journals," March 16, 1965. In *Dreaming to Some Purpose* Wilson mentions *Inside the Black Room* (New York: C. N. Potter, 1963), by Jack Vincent. Memory failed him here; the author is Jack Vernon. John Lilly, author of *Center of the Cyclone* (1972), was conducting experiments in sensory deprivation at the same time, and it was the subject of a film, *The Mind Benders* (1962) starring Dirk Bogarde and Mary Ure.

35 Wilson, "Phenomenological Journals," March 24, 1965.

36 Wilson, *Existential Criticism*.

37 Wilson, *Below the Iceberg*, 15–64.

38 Wilson likes to tell the story of when, after giving an impassioned lecture about freedom, Sartre was approached by some inspired students who asked him what they should *do* with their freedom. His answer, "Do what you like," deflated them. Sartre, too, had no idea what to do with his freedom and he experienced it as a burden. His attempt to give his freedom some direction by adopting radical politics was not successful. His major work on uniting existentialism and Marxism, *Critique of Dialectical Reason*, is evidence of this. In his last days he embraced Maoism and urged students toward revolution.

39 Albert Camus, *The Myth of Sisyphus* (London: Penguin Books, 2000), 19.

40 P. D. Ouspensky made the same point in his classic work *Tertium Organum* (New York: Alfred A. Knopf, 1981). "It seems to us that we see something and understand something. But in actual fact we have but a very dim sense of all that is happening around us, just as a snail has a dim sense of the sunlight, the rain, the darkness" (128). To say that the snail's perception of the sunlight, the rain, the darkness is, "relatively speaking," the equivalent of the gardener's standing over him is simply muddled thinking.

41 Wilson, *Introduction to the New Existentialism*, 115.

42 Ibid., 124–5.

43 Ibid., 129.

44 Ibid.

45 He expresses the same opinion in *The Craft of the Novel*. Nevertheless it remains an excellent guidebook for the aspiring writer.

46 Wilson, *Dreaming to Some Purpose*, 258.

47 As Wilson later pointed out in his book on Gurdjieff, *The War Against Sleep* (Wellingborough, UK: Aquarian Press, 1980), this was exactly the philosophy behind Gurdjieff's practice of "super-efforts," and why he made life so difficult for the people around him; his "induced crises" *forced* them to make more effort than usual. A similar idea is behind what William James called the "bullying treatment," a therapeutic practice he shared with C. G. Jung. Neurasthenic patients, who shy from any effort, are "bullied" into making them, which frees them from their paralysis.

48 Wilson, *Dreaming to Some Purpose*, 268.

49 It was originally published by City Lights Books as *Poetry and Zen*; Wilson later expanded this.

50 James Bugental, ed., *Challenges of Humanistic Psychology* (New York: McGraw Hill, 1967).

51 Colin Wilson, "Existential Psychology: A Novelist's Approach," in *The Bicameral Critic*, ed. Howard Dossor (Salem, MA: Salem House, 1985), 38–54.

52 See my essay "Poetry and Mysticism," in *Around the Outsider* (Winchester, UK: O Books, 2011), 116–31.

53 As I mention in "Poetry and Mysticism," Wilson shared this opinion with the writer Arthur Koestler, who spelled out his reservations about "the East" in his book *The Lotus and the Robot* (London: Macmillan, 1960). Wilson knew Koestler's work and admired it—even if Koestler had written disparagingly of *The Outsider*, calling it the "bubble of the year" in his roundup for 1956—and had a copy of Koestler's work in his library. It is unclear if it influenced his ideas about his own robot.

54 This belief was shared by Owen Barfield, who wrote about it in his early work *Poetic Diction* (London: Faber and Gwyer, 1928).

55 This was something P. D. Ouspensky understood. In *Tertium Organum* he remarks on the "incredibly vivid sensation of the difference between factory chimneys and prison walls, a sensation that was like a blow or an electric shock," which is rather like the "Zen effect."

56 Wilson, *Voyage to a Beginning*, 328.

57 Ibid., 330.

CHAPTER EIGHT: MYSTERIES OF THE OCCULT

1 Wilson, *Voyage to a Beginning*, 334.

2 Wilson, *Dreaming to Some Purpose*, 275.

3 Ibid., 1

4 Ibid., 324–5.

5 Ibid., 333.

6 Ibid., 330.

7 Ibid., 331.

8 Ibid., 335.

9 Wilson, *The Craft of the Novel*, 15.

10 For more on *The Morning of the Magicians*, see my *Turn Off Your Mind*, 13–9.

11 Wilson, *The Occult*, 63.

12 Ibid., 64.

13 This scenario informs the narrative of my book *The Secret Teachers of the Western World*.

14 I write about different versions of Graves's "simple method" in my books *The Quest for Hermes Trismegistus* and *The Secret Teachers of the Western World*.

15 See *The Quest for Hermes Trismegistus*, 38–42.

16 One example Wilson often provides is that of the writer R. H. Ward, who recounted his experiences on nitrous oxide in a book that deserves to be better known, *A Drug-Taker's Notes* (London: Victor Gollancz, 1957). Ward writes that after a few inhalations he entered "a state of consciousness already far more complete than the fullest degree of ordinary waking consciousness" (26). Wilson also often quotes Arthur Koestler's account in *The Invisible Writing* (London: Macmillan, 1969, 429) of a mystical experience he had while awaiting his possible execution as a prisoner of the fascists during the Spanish Civil War. To pass the time Koestler scratched out Eu-

clid's proof that there is no largest prime number on the wall of his cell. Koestler had reached a truth about infinity by finite means, and the significance of this hit him forcefully. The sense that this was "perfect" raised him out of the moment and he felt the "fragrance of eternity." Then he was aware of a nagging thought, somewhere in the back of his mind. He realized it was the fact that he might be executed at any moment. His reaction to this was "Is that all? Have you nothing more serious to worry about?"

17 Wilson, *Dreaming to Some Purpose*, 283.

18 Ibid.

19 Ibid., 4–5.

20 See Adrian Lang, *R. D. Laing: A Life* (London: HarperCollins, 1997).

21 Both *The Philosopher's Stone* and *The God of the Labyrinth* involve the kinds of "time slips" that Wilson would write about in *The Occult* and elsewhere. Both are also linked to the writer Jorge Luis Borges. Wilson dedicated *The Philosopher's Stone* to Borges—when he sent the blind writer a copy, he received a warm note of thanks from Borges's mother—and the "Sect of the Phoenix" Wilson writes about in *The God of the Labyrinth* was based on Borges's story "The Cult of the Phoenix."

22 Wilson, *The Occult*, 32.

23 Ibid., 33.

24 Ibid., 33.

25 In *Science Set Free* (New York: Deepak Chopra Books, 2012), Rupert Sheldrake tells the story of a debate about the paranormal between him and Richard Dawkins in which Dawkins declared that he "didn't want to discuss evidence" (255–7).

26 Wilson, *The Occult*, 43.

27 Ibid., 21.

28 David Foster, *The Intelligent Universe* (New York: G. P. Putnam's Sons, 1975). When Wilson referred to Foster's ideas, his book was not yet published. Wilson in fact had already delivered the manuscript of *The Occult* but after receiving a letter from Foster, who had read *Voyage to a Beginning*, he recalled the manuscript and added his reflections on Foster's ideas. He later wrote a preface to Foster's book, which helped get it published.

29 Arthur Koestler, *The Ghost in the Machine* (New York: Macmillan, 1967), 15–9.

30 There was, for example, the case of the *Ammonophilas* wasp, who feeds its young by stinging a caterpillar to paralyze it. If it stings too deeply, it will miss the nerve and kill the caterpillar. If it doesn't sting deeply enough, the caterpillar will struggle and crush the wasp's grubs as they are feeding on it. The French entomologist Jean-Henri Fabre pointed out that the wasp must have learned how to do this *the first time*, not, as strict Darwinists would say, by trial and error and just by chance. Without an accurate sting, there would have been no new generation to inherit the trick. Somehow, the wasp *knew* what it had to do. Another example is the flatid leaf bug, which groups with others to resemble a flower and so avoid predators. But the flatid leaf bug "flower" resembles no flower in nature. This is not the case of an individual insect avoiding its prey through a chance camouflage, but of a whole colony of insects coming together to disguise themselves as a flower that not one insect has seen. Another example is the *Microstomum* flatworm, which defends itself by eating a *Hydra* polyp. The *Hydra* has stinging capsules called nematocysts. These are passed through the *Microstomum's* stomach, then brought by certain cells to the worm's skin. There they act as "guns," which fire the sting when a predator tries to eat them. When the worm has enough capsules, it will never eat another *Hydra*, even if starving. The eminent biologist Sir Alister Hardy suggested that some kind of "group mind" must be in-

volved, a hypothesis unthinkable from the strict Darwinian perspective. (*The Occult*, 126–7.)

31 Wilson, *The Occult*, 37. The passage is on p. 4 of Ouspensky's book.

32 Ibid., 38.

33 Ibid., 40.

34 Some years after reading *The Occult* I followed up one of Wilson's leads and read the remarkable series of books by J. W. Dunne dealing with the phenomenon of precognitive dreams. Briefly put, Dunne, an aeronautics engineer, discovered that he often dreamt of the future, so he suggested that interested readers keep a dream journal, and that by doing so, they would discover that they dreamed the future as well. I took Dunne at his word and discovered that he was correct. I did dream about the future too; many years later I wrote an article about this for *Quest* magazine (winter 1997, pp. 18–23). This experience led to a long interest in the related subjects of time, dreams, synchronicity, and consciousness, about which I plan to write one day.

35 In Allsop, *The Angry Decade*, 154.

36 For Calder-Marshall's encounter with Crowley, see Lachman, *Aleister Crowley*, 273, 290.

37 Wilson, preface to Foster, *The Intelligent Universe*, 19.

38 I have found the same thing happening when writing my own books. I mentioned some synchronicities in *Jung the Mystic*, 241–2, n. 31, 41. One recently occurred while working on this book. I finished my day's work, which involved writing about precognition. When I turned on the television a short while later I watched an episode of the 1960s British spy series *The Avengers*, a program that Wilson himself enjoyed. The plot of the episode involved premonitions.

39 Wilson, *The Occult*, 47.

40 Colin Wilson, *Ken Russell: A Director in Search of a Hero* (London: Intergroup, 1974). There is also a film of Russell being interviewed by Wilson, *Ken Russell, with Colin Wilson* (1973).

41 Wilson, *Dreaming to Some Purpose*, 293.

42 Wilson got the name Saltfleet from a character in David Lindsay's flawed masterpiece, *Devil's Tor*.

43 Wilson, *New Pathways in Psychology*, 34.

44 A. R. Orage, *Consciousness: Animal, Human and Superman* (New York: Samuel Weiser, 1974), 68.

45 Wilson, *New Pathways in Psychology*, 206.

46 Ibid., 22–3.

47 Ibid., 206.

48 Wilson, *Order of Assassins*, 13.

49 Ibid., 50.

50 Ibid., 51.

51 Ibid., 106.

52 Ibid., 111.

53 Ibid., 248.

54 Wilson, *Dreaming to Some Purpose*, 296.

55 Ibid., 296–7.

56 Wilson, *Mysteries*, 23–4.

57 These included a series of illustrated coffee table books on the occult that Wilson wrote for Aldus Books: *Mysterious Powers* (1975), *Enigmas and Mysteries* (1976), and *Mysteries of the Mind* (1978), cowritten with Stuart Holroyd. There was also *The Unexplained* (Lake Oswego, OR: Lost Pleiade Press, 1975) and *Dark Dimensions* (New York: Everett House, 1977).

58　Colin Wilson, *Strange Powers* (New York: Random House, 1973), 73.

59　Wilson did write a short coffee table book about Uri Geller, in which he takes a close look at the popular psychic's powers and concludes that they are real. See *The Geller Phenomenon* (London: Aldus Books, 1976).

60　Wilson enjoyed films and television, as any visitor to his home soon discovered. "I usually write all day; then, at six o'clock, I'm ready to pour a glass of wine and spend a long evening listening to music or reading, or even watching TV if there is some culturally rewarding programme such as *Maigret* or *The Avengers*. I like to 'switch off' and become quietly receptive, and I tend to resent it if I have guests who want to discuss questions of philosophy or psychology; it may be relaxing for them, but for me, it is talking shop." (Wilson, *Strange Powers*, 52.) He also remarks, "My own house, while not exactly chaotic, is never exactly tidy; the floor is usually covered with books, toys and children's records, and if you move the armchair you are likely to knock over a wine bottle that has been there since the night before." (32–3.)

61　Wilson, *Mysteries*, 24.

62　Ibid.

63　Ibid., 25.

64　Ibid., 27.

65　Ibid., 29.

66　Ibid., 45.

67　Alan Hull Walton, *Books and Bookmen*, March 1979, reprinted in Stanley, *Colin Wilson*, 130–6.

68　Kit Pedler, *New Scientist*, September 28, 1978.

69　See, for example, Wilson's review of Koestler's *Bricks to Babel*, a summing up of his career, in *Existentially Speaking* (60–71).

CHAPTER NINE: OUR OTHER SELF

1　Wilson, *Mysteries*, 45.

2　Wilson, *Dreaming to Some Purpose*, 306

3　Wilson, *The Philosopher's Stone*, 110.

4　A good place to begin might be Tom Graves and Janet Hoult, eds., *The Essential T. C. Lethbridge* (London: Routledge & Kegan Paul, 1980), a compilation of Lethbridge's writings, to which Wilson contributed a foreword.

5　This element of the book was in fact one reason why I carried my copy of *Mysteries* with me on my "mini-search for the miraculous," which led to my pilgrimage to Tetherdown in 1983. Part of that search was spent visiting well-known megalithic sites such as Avebury and Stonehenge, but also seeking out lesser known ones—with the aid of ordnance survey maps—and attempting to feel, if possible, any of the kind of force Michell and others suggested could be found there.

6　Wilson, *Strange Powers*, 24. For Wilson's account of his attempts at psychokinesis, the ability to move objects by thought, see 31–2.

7　Wilson, foreword to Graves and Hoult, *The Essential T. C. Lethbridge*, xiii.

8　Colin Wilson, *Poltergeist!* (London: New English Library, 1981), 343.

9　Wilson, *Mysteries*, v.

10　Along with being a paranormal networker, Einhorn—known as "the Unicorn" (his name means "unicorn" in German)—took part in instigating the first Earth Day celebration in 1970, although other participants question his involvement. Sadly he is also known for a darker claim to fame. After more than twenty years on the run in Europe, in 2002 Einhorn was extradited to the United States and sentenced to life imprisonment for the murder of his ex-girlfriend Holly Maddux in 1977; at the time of writing he is still serving his sentence. From all accounts, Einhorn had something of the Right Man in him. I tell the story in the updated and expanded UK edition of *The Dedalus Book of the 1960s: Turn Off Your Mind* (Sawtry, UK: Dedalus Books, 2009), 512–25. I also write about how I carried on a brief correspondence with Einhorn, which came about through our mutual acquaintance, Colin Wilson.

11 Julian Jaynes, *The Origin of Consciousness in the Breakdown of the Bicameral Mind* (Boston, MA: Houghton Mifflin, 1976), 75.

12 Each eye in fact has a left and right field, controlled by the opposite side of the brain, but for convenience's sake I will speak of left and right eye.

13 See David Wolman, "The Split Brain: A Tale of Two Halves," *Nature*, March 14, 2012.

14 Wilson did think that the robot was rooted in the cerebellum, and, following the Huna tradition, that our "lower self," associated with emotion and intuition, is in a knot of nerves in the solar plexus. The left brain houses the ego, while our "higher self" resides in the right. This system—and that of the Hunas—has much in common with the tripartite view of the human psyche presented in Roberto Assagioli's school of psychosynthesis, which Wilson discusses in *New Pathways in Psychology* (209–12).

15 Wilson, *Mysteries*, 523.

16 See Stan Gooch, *The Double Helix of the Mind* (London: Wildwood House, 1980).

17 Wilson, *Frankenstein's Castle*, 13.

18 Wilson relates that in doing the book, he ran into some resistance from Reich's estate. Wilson makes critical remarks about Reich throughout the book, but an unbiased reader is in no doubt that he appreciates Reich's genius and goes out of his way to argue for the importance of his ideas. When Wilson asked the Reich estate for permission to quote extensively from Reich's work, it was refused. Mary Boyd Higgins, Reich's executor at the time, thought the work a "travesty." Wilson wryly remarks that this is exactly the attitude Reich, who believed that "all critics of his work were motivated by malice and dishonesty," would have responded (Wilson, *The Quest for Wilhelm Reich*, v–vi).

19 Ibid., 14.

20 I have had a similar experience when working on different books. For example, while working on my *Madame Blavatsky: The Mother of Modern Spirituality* (New York: Tarcher/Penguin, 2012), I often felt, as I wrote the chapters on her world travels and alleged years in Tibet, that I had spent the day in that part of the world. A long time devoted to focused concentration on a "distant reality" produced the somewhat disorienting feeling that it was somehow "more real" than the reality immediately around me—in this case the four walls of my study.

21 L. H. Myers, *The Near and the Far* (London: Secker & Warburg, 1984), 16. *The Near and the Far* is the first part in the trilogy *The Root and the Flower*; the other novels are included in this edition.

22 Quote in Wilson, *The Occult*, 58.

23 Wilson, *Frankenstein's Castle*, 16.

24 This was recognized in the late eighteenth century by the German Romantic poet Friedrich Schiller in his *Letters on the Aesthetic Education of Man* (1794). Other poets, artists, and philosophers intuited the relationship between our two minds. For a look at some of these, see *The Secret Teachers of the Western World*.

25 Wilson, *Frankenstein's Castle*, 25.

26 Quoted in Wilson, *The War Against Sleep*, 14.

27 See Kit Pedler, "Nikola Tesla," in *Dark Dimensions*, ed. Colin Wilson (New York: Everest House, 1977), 77–9.

28 Wilson, *Frankenstein's Castle*, 76.

29 Ibid., 105.

30 Colin Wilson, "The Laurel & Hardy Theory of Consciousness" (Mill Valley, CA: Robert Briggs Association, 1979), 5.

31 Ibid., 7.

32 See Lachman, *Aleister Crowley*, 118–20, and *Turn Off Your Mind*, 127–30.

33 Colin Wilson and Donald Seaman, *Encyclopaedia of Modern Murder* (London: Arthur Barker, 1983), 17. Wilson likens his own perspective to that of Camus. In *The Rebel* (1951), a work that made him Public Enemy No. 1 with Sartre and the other leftist thinkers, Camus argues that all "philosophies of rebellion" lead eventually to "tyranny and the destruction of freedom." Wilson agreed with Camus that freedom cannot exist "without responsibility and discipline" and he urged that educational institutions would work to discredit "the muddled philosophy of freedom that is undermining our society."

34 Wilson, *Frankenstein's Castle*, 107–8.

35 Quoted in Wilson, "Postscript to *The Outsider*," in *The Outsider*, 301. In recent years much of what Wilson suggested about the relationship between the cerebral hemispheres has received support from a fascinating book, *The Master and His Emissary*, by Iain McGilchrist. While reading McGilchrist I was struck by how often the points he made seemed to echo what Wilson had written. To give one example, speaking of the same story of Wordsworth, De Quincey, and the mail coach from Keswick, McGilchrist writes, "De Quincey tells a story of Wordsworth . . . walking out at night to meet the mail coach from Keswick . . . Lying full stretch on the road . . . his eye happened to chance on a bright star." This "struck him suddenly 'with a pathos and sense of the infinite, that would not have arrested me under other circumstances'. The vision comes because of an effort made and then relaxed." Iain McGilchrist, *The Master and His Emissary* (London: Yale University Press, 2009), 377.

36 Wilson developed an exercise to illustrate this point, what he called "the pen trick." Take a pencil or pen and hold it in front of your eyes a few feet away. Briefly focus your attention exclusively on the pen, ignoring everything else. Then relax and let yourself become aware of the room. Then narrow your attention to the pen again. After you do this about a dozen times, you should start to feel a kind of mental glow, rather like how your muscles feel during a workout. Continue this until you start to feel a bit of pain. At this point Wilson says it is important to keep going; the pain is a sign that we are pushing our "muscles of intention" past their usual limits. If you keep this up for a while, Wilson says a feeling of relief will come over you and you will slip into a mild peak experience.

   Different people have tried this with differing results. I have been able to induce a mild peak in this way, but it usually has a delayed effect. This once happened when I attended a seminar Wilson was holding at the California Institute of Integral Studies, and he had us lie on the floor and practice the pen trick while also doing deep breathing. The sign that it is working, in me at least, has been a sudden bubble of laughter—rather like the giddiness I feel sometimes as I fall asleep and have sudden Faculty X–like memories of places I've visited; I have not been thinking about these, but they suddenly pop up, out of nowhere. I also experienced it once while undergoing an MRI scan. If you are familiar with this procedure, it requires you to lie still in a confined space, rather like a sarcophagus. The concentration necessary to stay still for an extended time had the same effect as focusing and relaxing my attention. In fact, the technicians running the imager had to ask me to stop giggling.

37 Wilson, *The War Against Sleep*, 48.

38 Ibid., 14.

39 Readers can find an account of the efficacy of these, at least in my own experience, in Gary Lachman, *In Search of P. D. Ouspensky*, 2nd ed. (Wheaton, IL: Quest Books, 2006), 291.

40 Wilson, *Dreaming to Some Purpose*, 53.

41 Wilson, *The War Against Sleep*, 81.

42 Quoted in ibid., 81.

43 Ibid., 81–2.

44 William Blake, *The Marriage of Heaven and Hell*.

CHAPTER TEN: INNER WORLDS AND CRIMINAL HISTORIES

1 Wilson, *Frankenstein's Castle*, 95.

2 Ibid., 96.

3 Wilson, "The Laurel & Hardy Theory of Consciousness," 1.

4 Wilson, *Super Consciousness*, 125.

5 Ibid., 126.

6 Wilson "The Laurel & Hardy Theory of Consciousness," 1.

7 Wilson, *Super Consciousness*, 180–1.

8 I experienced an interesting variant on this phenomenon some years ago. I had had a knee operation and was getting around on crutches. One morning I decided to hobble to St. Pancras churchyard, an ancient site, which was nearby and which I often visited, in order to get some air. Because of the crutches, what would have normally been a five-minute walk now took nearly a half hour. One of the drawbacks to using crutches is that your robot wants to walk at your regular pace. But if you do, it hurts. So you have to consciously keep yourself from slipping into your normal speed. This is tiring, as is having to throw the crutches out in front of you at each step. Hobbling back to my flat, I noticed that the sidewalk seemed somehow different. It was shining. I realized that I was seeing the sun's reflection on the chips of mica within it and I found myself looking at it as if I had discovered something. I also found myself looking with deep interest at the cracks in it and at the small plants growing in the spaces between the paving stones. At one point I stopped to rest, and leaned my hand against a wooden support enclosing a recently planted young tree. As I rested I looked at the tree and found myself gazing at it with wonder. I then looked at the sunlight passing through a leaf. It was as if I had never seen this before. The closest I could come to it would be to say it was as if I was seeing it as I had when a child.

What happened, it seems, is that the need for me to *slow down* and countermand my robot's usual forward drive forced me to focus my attention. Because of the crutches my head was looking down and as a result I found myself looking at the sidewalk intently. I was seeing a *complexity* in it I would normally not notice—which is another way of saying that it suddenly looked *interesting*. Likewise the tree and the leaf. My handicap had the unexpected result of making me more aware of things. This led to the insight that *interest* is a function of *attention*.

9 Sir Patrick Moore, foreword to Edgar Allan Poe, *Eureka* (London: Hesperus Press, 2012), vii–ix.

10 In *Art & Physics* (New York: Quill Books, 1991), Leonard Shlain tells the same stories and adds that Swift may also have anticipated black holes. He quotes from Swift's short poem "On Time": "All devouring, all-destroying / Never finding full repast / Till I eat the world at last" (357). The thesis of Shlain's book is that art anticipates the discoveries of science—physics, in particular. He bases his idea on the

differences between the twin cerebral hemispheres. His later book *The Alphabet Versus the Goddess* also concerns the differences between our two brains. I write about Shlain's ideas in *A Secret History of Consciousness* and *The Secret Teachers of the Western World*.

11 Colin Wilson, *Starseekers* (London: Hodder & Stoughton, 1980), 20.

12 Leonard Shlain argues this point in *The Alphabet Versus the Goddess*.

13 http://www.bbc.co.uk/news/science-environment-24026153.

14 Steven Weinberg, *The First Three Minutes* (New York: Basic Books, 1993), 154.

15 Wilson, *Starseekers*, 260–1.

16 Ibid., 259.

17 Colin Wilson and Una Woodruff, *Witches* (London: A&W Publishers, 1981).

18 Colin Wilson, *Access to Inner Worlds* (London: Rider and Co., 1983), 37.

19 I discuss "active imagination" at length in *Jung the Mystic* (New York: Tarcher/Penguin, 2010), 115–22.

20 Wilson, *Access to Inner Worlds*, 51.

21 See note 36 from chapter 9.

22 Wilson, *Access to Inner Worlds*, 11.

23 Ibid., 12.

24 Ibid., 15.

25. I write about Moskvitin's work in *A Secret History of Consciousness*. Moskvitin was a musician and composer as well as a philosopher. I sent him a copy of the book on publication and corresponded with him intermittently until his death in 2005.

26 Wilson, *Access to Inner Worlds*, 71.

27 In *Demian* Herman Hesse writes about precisely this phenomenon. Speaking of how "a certain strength and joy, an intensification of my self-awareness" came from "prolonged staring into fire," Hesse's protagonist Emil Sinclair remarks about the "state of mind in which we are unable to decide whether the images on our retina are the result of impressions coming from without or from within." Through this exercise we can, Hesse writes, discover "to what extent we are creative, to what extent our soul partakes of the constant creation of the world. . . . If the outside world were to be destroyed, a single one of us would be capable of rebuilding it: mountain and stream, leaf, root and flower, yes, every natural form is latent within us" (*Demian* [New York: Harper and Row, 1965], 107–8). Hesse seems to have known of what Moskvitin and Husserl speak. This should not be surprising; as a poet he had an intuitive understanding of the creative character of all perception. His belief that, should the world be destroyed, a single consciousness would be sufficient to re-create it is a version of the Hermetic doctrine of man as a microcosm, or "little universe." Needless to say this is a complete rejection of the modern view, based on the psychology of John Locke, that "there is nothing in the mind that was not first in the senses."

28 Wilson, *Access to Inner Worlds*, 76.

29 Paul Ricoeur, *Husserl: An Analysis of his Phenomenology*, quoted in Wilson, *Super Consciousness*, 171.

30 Quoted in Wilson, *Access to Inner Worlds*, 72.

31 Aldous Huxley, *The Doors of Perception and Heaven and Hell* (London: Grafton Books, 1987), 69–70.

32 Wilson, *Access to Inner Worlds*, 55.

33 In *The Caretakers of the Cosmos* (138–9), I suggest that western society as a whole has entered the self-esteem level of Maslow's hierarchy. My evidence for this is the widespread popularity of social media through which we compete with others for attention and recognition. I also suggest that this may mean that there is a generation of

self-actualizers that constitute what Bergson called a "creative minority," quietly working away at evolving. Members of this creative minority do not attract attention to themselves because they have passed beyond the self-esteem needs and in any case are too busy self-actualizing to care if anyone likes them or not.

34 Colin Wilson, *A Criminal History of Mankind* (New York: G.P. Putnam's Sons, 1984), 12.

35 Ibid., 15–6.

36 In the early 1960s, Ian Brady and Myra Hindley, his accomplice, who died in 2002, committed a series of sex murders, mostly of children, and buried some of their victims on Saddleworth Moor, near Manchester, UK, hence the name "Moors murders." Brady believed his actions were a legitimate protest against a corrupt society. Exactly how many murders were committed is unknown. Wilson began a correspondence with Brady in 1991, and was impressed by his intelligence. In court Brady had surprised the judge with his eloquence and had defended his actions through voicing a "philosophy of freedom" based on reading the Marquis de Sade and an admiration for Hitler. Brady was a dominant individual who embraced a philosophy of sadism and fascism and believed that the strong have the right to dominate the weak. He believed—as many modern philosophers and artists have—that everything is permitted and that morality is only a means by which the status quo maintains its power. Brady wrote a book, *The Gates of Janus* (2001), about his beliefs; Wilson wrote an introduction to it and found it a publisher. Wilson broke off his correspondence when it became clear that Brady would never see his crimes objectively, that is, he continued to defend them vociferously in his letters. Wilson defended the book's publication because it is "the only work in world literature in which a criminal Right Man argues his case that society is really to blame for his crimes." He has no illusions about Brady, though, who is "paranoid, obsessive, and wrong-headed." (Wilson, *Dreaming to Some Purpose*, 323–4.)

37 Wilson, *A Criminal History of Mankind*, 11.

38 Other writers also added to the list of "gratuitous acts." In his *Second Surrealist Manifesto* (1930), André Breton writes, "The simplest Surrealist act consists of dashing down into the street, pistol in hand, and firing blindly, as fast as you can pull the trigger, into the crowd." *Manifestos of Surrealism* (Ann Arbor: University of Michigan Press, 1974), 125. It seems that many terrorist groups today employ similar surrealist tactics. Such gratuitous acts also became part of radical politics in America in the 1960s. See Lachman, *Turn Off Your Mind*, 358–60.

39 Ibid., 12.

40 Ibid., 670.

41 Ibid.

42 P. D. Ouspensky, *A New Model of the Universe* (New York: Alfred A. Knopf, 1969), 305. "One history passes by in full view and, strictly speaking, is the *history of crime*, for if there were no crimes there would be no history." This could serve as the motto for Wilson's book.

43 Wilson, A *Criminal History of Mankind*, 6.

44 Ibid.

45 Ibid., 49.

46 Jaynes, *The Origin of Consciousness*, 214.

47 Leonard Shlain, *The Alphabet Versus the Goddess* (New York: Penguin Compass, 1998), 69.

48 This is a point also made by George Steiner in *Language and Silence* (New York: Atheneum, 1982), 55–67.

49 Arthur Koestler, *Janus: A Summing Up* (London: Pan Books, 1983), 18.
50 Wilson, *A Criminal History of Mankind*, 142.
51 Ibid.
52 Ibid., 178.
53 Ibid., 179.
54 Ibid., 178.
55 Ibid., 149.
56 Ibid., 56.
57 Ibid.
58 Ibid., 59.
59 Ibid.

CHAPTER ELEVEN: PSYCHICS, SPIRITS, AND UPSIDE-DOWNNESS

1 *Time Out*, March 29, 1984: 18–19.
2 Laurie Taylor, "The Dark Side," *New Society*, March 29, 1984, 488–9.
3 During my first visit to Tetherdown I spent some time with Wilson's mother while Wilson, Joy, and their sons headed to the beach. I stayed behind because Wilson had given me the manuscript of his book on Jung, not yet published, to read. His mother said she was very proud of the books, but admitted that she had no idea what they were about, as she had never read them.
4 Colin Wilson, *The Psychic Detectives* (New York: Berkley Books, 1984), 224. The exception in question involved a quadruple murder in Edmonton, Canada, in 1928. The psychologist Maximilien Langsner, who had studied with Freud, was deeply interested in telepathy and other psychic phenomena, and had recently solved a jewel robbery case in Vancouver simply by reading the mind of the suspect. Now he was able to tell the Edmonton police that the person responsible for the murders was the same one who had alerted them. The murderer had developed a hatred of his domineering mother, and in a fit of rage, had shot her in the back of the head. Realizing others on their farm would suspect him, he shot them too. Langsner got this information by reading the murderer's mind. He was also able to uncover the rifle used. Confronted with this evidence, the murderer confessed.
5 Ibid., 157.
6 Ibid., xx.
7 Lyall Watson, *Lifetide* (London: Coronet Books, 1980), 19–22.
8 Ibid., xxi.
9 Ibid. Wilson was not the only parapsychologist with a bone to pick with Watson. In *The Double Helix of the Mind* (235–41), Stan Gooch makes some similar points against Watson and what he feels, for him, to be his less astringent approach to investigating paranormal claims.
10 Colin Wilson and Christopher Evans, *The Occult: An Encyclopaedia of the Supernatural* (London: Orbis Books, 1975) and *Index to Occult Sciences: A New Library of the Supernatural* (London: Aldus Books, 1975).
11 See *The Caretakers of the Cosmos* (190–2), for a comparison between Wheeler's ideas about a "participatory universe" and more occult or metaphysical ones, specifically the work of Owen Barfield.
12 http://www.astrologer.com/bio/gauquelin.htm.
13 Wilson, *The Psychic Detectives*, xxiv.
14 Stan Gooch agrees. "I do not mind what the truth turns out to be. . . . And I am always ready to abandon whatever I currently believe is the truth if I find something that looks or works better." (*The Double Helix of the Mind*, 240.)

15 Quoted in Wilson, *The Psychic Detectives*, 11–2. Buchanan's ideas were very similar to those of T. C. Lethbridge, whose work Wilson writes about in *Mysteries*. In short, Lethbridge believed in the "recording" theory of ghosts. He believed that strong emotions could be imprinted on the surroundings in which they occurred. The strongest emotions are generally those of fear or pain, and Lethbridge suggested that what we may experience as a ghost is a kind of videotape of some unfortunate event, the emotions of the person experiencing it having been impressed on the place where it took place. Similar experiences of an unpleasant feeling, and not a visible ghost, he called a "ghoul." Lethbridge writes of feeling an unaccountable irrational fear on one occasion while walking along some cliffs. The feeling covered a specific area and Lethbridge could literally walk in and out of it. These recordings were associated, Lethbridge believed, with certain kinds of "fields," and were strongly related to water.

16 William Denton, *The Soul of Things* (Wellingborough, UK: Aquarian Press, 1988), with an introduction by Colin Wilson.

17 Wilson, *The Psychic Detectives*, 121.

18 Ibid., 122.

19 Ibid., 187.

20 Ibid., 231.

21 Ibid., 192.

22 Ibid., 198.

23 Ibid., 112.

24 Ibid., 224.

25 Ibid., 251.

26 Ibid., 225.

27 See Lachman, *Rudolf Steiner: An Introduction to His Life and Work*, 166–9.

28 See Lachman, *Madame Blavatsky: The Mother of Modern Spirituality*, 148–51.

29 Wilson, *The Psychic Detectives*, 118.

30 For an account of Steiner and hypnagogia, see *A Secret History of Consciousness* (Great Barrington, MA: Lindisfarne, 2003), 85–94.

31 Wilson, *The Psychic Detectives*, 34.

32 Ibid., 247.

33 Wilson, *The War Against Sleep*, 9.

34 Crabtree also wrote one of the best books on hypnotism, *From Mesmer to Freud: Magnetic Sleep and the Roots of Psychological Healing* (New Haven, CT: Yale University Press, 1993).

35 Colin Wilson, *Afterlife* (New York: Doubleday, 1987), 244.

36 Ibid., 256.

37 Ibid., 254.

38 Wilson, *The Bicameral Critic*, 98.

39 Colin Wilson, *The Essential Colin Wilson* (London: Grafton Books, 1985), 326–36.

40 Colin Wilson, *Rudolf Steiner* (Wellingborough, UK: Aquarian Press, 1985), 9–11.

41 For an account of Webb, see my *Revolutionaries of the Soul*, 183–92.

42 Wilson, *Dreaming to Some Purpose*, 334.

43 Colin Wilson and Donald Seaman, *Encyclopaedia of Modern Murder* (London: Pan Books, 1989), 1, 4.

44 Colin Wilson and Donald Seaman, *Scandal!* (London: Weidenfeld and Nicolson, 1986), 1.

45 Wilson, *Dreaming to Some Purpose*, 335.

46 Ibid., 340.

47 I've mentioned Sidney Campion's book. Others include John Weigel's study *Colin Wilson* (Boston, MA: Twayne Publishers, 1975); Clifford P. Bendau's *Colin Wilson: The Outsider and Beyond* (San Bernardino, CA: Borgo Press, 1979); Nicolas Tredell's *The Novels of Colin Wilson* (London: Vision Press, 1982), the revised and expanded edition of which is mentioned earlier; and K. Gunnar Bergstrom's *An Odyssey to Freedom: Four Themes in Colin Wilson's Novels* (Uppsala, SE: Uppsala University Press, 1983). Colin Stanley's Paupers' Press publishes several shorter studies of particular aspects of Wilson's work, to which I have contributed two titles: *Two Essays on Colin Wilson* (Nottingham, UK: Paupers' Press, 1994) and, with John Shand, *Colin Wilson as Philosopher* and *Faculty X, Consciousness, and the Transcendence of Time* (Nottingham, UK: Paupers' Press, 1996).

48 In "Dear Mrs. Thatcher," his contribution to *Dear (Next) Prime Minister: Open Letters to Margaret Thatcher and Neil Kinnock,* ed. Neil Astley (Newcastle-upon-Tyne, UK: Bloodaxe Books, 1990), Wilson spells out his disenchantment with the "Iron Lady," and calls for her to resign.

49 Wilson, *Beyond the Occult*, 17.

50 Wilson, *Below the Iceberg*, 126.

51 Wilson, *Beyond the Occult*, 21.

52 Ibid., 22.

53 Ibid.

54 Ibid., 34.

55 Colin Wilson, *The Mammoth Book of the Supernatural*, ed. Damon Wilson (New York: Carol & Graf, 1991), 27.

56 Wilson, *Beyond the Occult*, 39.

57 Ibid., 40–2.

58 Ibid., 43.

59 Ibid., 44.

60 Henri Bergson, *Mind-Energy* (London: Macmillan, 1920), 56–77.

61 For more on Bergson and the link between his intuition and the right brain see *The Caretakers of the Cosmos* (2011), 84–5.

62 Wilson, *Beyond the Occult*, 33.

63 Ibid., 99.

64 Ibid., 148.

65 Ibid., 150.

66 Ibid. Synchronistically enough, I experienced a synchronicity myself while writing this chapter. When I mentioned Daskalos, the "magus of Strovolos," earlier, I needed to check the exact spelling of Strovolus. I grabbed my copy of *Beyond the Occult* and opened it at random. The first words I saw were "the magus of Strovolos." The angel of the library strikes again.

CHAPTER TWELVE: MISFITS AND ATLANTEANS

1 Wilson, *Below the Iceberg*, 137.

2 Ibid., 139.

3 Ibid.

4 Ouspensky once said that in order to really know something one must teach it, meaning that the renewed attention given a subject and the effort of explaining to others focuses our own understanding of it. From my own experience I can say this is true. I thought I knew all about Wilson's work, yet in the process of writing this book, new insights into his ideas and their connections to others came to me regu-

larly. Again it is a question of not taking things for granted. Focused attention has the power of revivifying what has become stale and dull.

5 Wilson, *Beyond the Occult*, 332.

6 Ibid.

7 This was an insight he shared with Gurdjieff, who told Ouspensky that our "higher centers" already exist and are waiting to be used, *when* we know how to use them. A similar idea, Wilson saw, was part of the Huna tradition too.

8 Wilson, *Beyond the Occult*, 343.

9 Ibid., 349.

10 Ibid., 41–2.

11 Ouspensky, *A New Model of the Universe*, 303.

12 Readers of Ouspensky's early works such as *Tertium Organum* and *Strange Life of Ivan Osokin*, written before his encounter with Gurdjieff, can recognize a more poetic character than the stern taskmaster of "the work" that emerged after his meeting with that remarkable man. See Lachman, *In Search of P. D. Ouspensky*, for more on Ouspensky's early work and the change he underwent during his time with Gurdjieff.

13 Wilson, *Beyond the Occult*, 349.

14 Ibid., 350.

15 Ibid., 359.

16 Wilson, *Below the Iceberg*, 142.

17 Wilson, *Dreaming to Some Purpose*, 341.

18 Friends were not the only ones who suspected this. In *Against Our Will: Men, Women and Rape* (New York: Bantam, 1990), 326–7, Susan Brownmiller writes of Wilson's "attraction to male slayers of women," calling his *A Casebook of Murder* a "sprightly compendium of sex slayings," in which he displays "no queasiness." Wilson's failure to display queasiness, Brownmiller suggests, places him in close proximity to the subjects of his investigations. The fact that murder interests Wilson because it is "the most extreme form of the denial of human potential," as he says in the introduction to A *Casebook of Murder*, seems to have escaped Brownmiller's notice.

19 Wilson, *The Misfits*, 19–20.

20 Ibid., 20.

21 Ibid., 21.

22 Ibid., 22.

23 Ibid., 24.

24 Ibid., 26.

25 Ibid.

26 Ibid., 42.

27 Ibid., 39. Wilson disagreed that the male sexual drive was to *become* the female, as Charlotte Bach argued. It was rather to *possess* her, which ultimately is an expression of will. He also disagreed that the behavior of the male stickleback and zebra finch showed that role reversal is a common feature throughout nature. He suggested that in these cases, the male may be trying to *remind* the female of what she should be doing, while defusing his own frustration in what psychologists call "displacement activity." In effect, the male here is using his *imagination* to "pretend" to be the other in order to solve a problem.

28 Ibid., 44.

29 A similar paradox confronts the perpetrator of a "perfect crime." He feels he has achieved something of note and his self-esteem revels in it. But he cannot share his glory with the world, because of the obvious consequences. So he must celebrate in

silence, which annuls the motive for committing the crime, that is, to show the world he is "somebody."

30 Ibid., 262.

31 Ibid., 247.

32 Ibid., 75–7.

33 Wilson, *The Craft of the Novel*, 42.

34 Wilson, *The Misfits*, 78–9.

35 Ibid., 46.

36 Ibid., 47.

37 Ibid., 48.

38 Ibid.

39 Ibid., 54.

40 Ibid., 58.

41 Ibid., 87–8. Wilson points out that there seems to be a biological basis for the male interest in the forbidden. Sex itself for the male is an act of penetration, to some degree, what we might call "breaking and entering." It pierces the barrier of alien flesh and invades it. But once pierced, a particular barrier no longer is forbidden. Wilson points out that animal breeders know that a male will mate with a female only a few times before losing interest. A new female will revive it, but if a female with which the male has copulated is introduced again, the male will ignore her. Wilson speaks of what is known as the "Coolidge effect," named after the American president. President and Mrs. Coolidge were inspecting a government farm and taken on separate tours. Mrs. Coolidge asked her guide how often the rooster copulates a day. He replied, "Dozens of times." Mrs Coolidge said, "Please tell that to the President." When the guide saw the President he passed on the message. The President asked, "Does the rooster choose the same hen each time?" The guide said, "No, a different one each time." President Coolidge said, "Tell that to Mrs. Coolidge." Wilson jokes that this is the basis of the "she is not my wife" advice that a therapist gave a husband suffering from impotence.

42 Another problem with the forbidden is that in order for it to provide the required "kick," the very law de Sade wanted to abolish *must* be maintained; otherwise the meaning of the forbidden would dissolve. When "nothing is true and everything is permitted," as de Sade would have liked it, nothing would be forbidden and hence de Sade would lose all the fun of breaking the rules. It also requires one to remain *immature*—as Charlotte Bach advised—because only children enjoy doing what they shouldn't.

43 Wilson suggests that Rupert Sheldrake's idea of "morphic resonance" may have played a part in spreading the interest in superheated sex. The intensity of the experience enjoyed by the Romantics was picked up by the "morphogenetic fields" that Sheldrake proposes as the agency of evolutionary transmission. This would suggest that even without actual contact with the "imagination explosion" through reading, its effects would spread throughout society. This can explain why rural areas, unaffected by the urban stress usually offered as a reason for the rise of sexual deviancy, saw a rise of sex crime, just as much as cities did (Wilson, *The Misfits*, 256–8).

44 Ibid., 160.

45 Ibid., 161.

46 Ibid., 167.

47 Men's attitudes toward the fact that women defecate vary. In his poem "The Lady's Dressing Room," Jonathan Swift bemoans the fact, but a century and a half after Swift's death, some appetites for superheated sex positively celebrate it. http://www.poetryfoundation.org/poem/180934.

48 Ibid., 168.

49 Ibid., 246.

50 Joyce had a penchant for soiled panties and flatulence; Ellis took a mystical delight in watching women urinate. Paul Tillich, the existential theologian Wilson saw lecture at Georgetown University decades earlier, was obsessed with pornography. T. E. Lawrence enjoyed being beaten; the composer Percy Grainger was obsessed with giving and receiving pain. With all, in some way their creativity and perversity were linked. The reader can find other eccentricities throughout the book.

51 Wilson, *The Misfits*, 254.

52 Ibid., 260.

53 Harry Ritchie, *Success Stories* (London: Faber and Faber, 1988).

54 "Outside Loon," *Private Eye*, February 19, 1988.

55 It remains unpublished in English, although a Russian version, from which Wilson saw no income, did appear.

56 In *Meetings with Remarkable Men*, Gurdjieff speaks of acquiring a map of "pre-sand Egypt."

57 *The Necronomicon*, ed. George Hay (Jersey, UK: Neville Spearman, 1978); *The R'Lyeh Text*, ed. Robert Turner (London: Skoob Books, 1995). As far as I can tell the film was never made.

58 Wilson, introduction to *The R'Lyeh Text*, 22.

59 Colin Wilson, *From Atlantis to the Sphinx* (London: Virgin Books, 1996), 87.

60 Readers may know that some of Hapgood's ideas were used in Roland Emmerich's 2009 disaster film *2012*.

61 Wilson, *From Atlantis to the Sphinx*, 3.

62 "Egypt Serves Up New Twist to Mystery of the Sphinx" *Los Angeles Times*, October 26, 1991.

63 Wilson, *From Atlantis to the Sphinx*, 7.

64 This is a view shared by other thinkers as well; I look at some ideas about it in *A Secret History of Consciousness*.

65 R. A. Schwaller de Lubicz, *The Temples of Karnak* (Rochester, VT: Inner Traditions, 1999), 15.

66 See Lachman, *The Secret Teachers of the Western World*, 39.

67 Ibid., 37–40. See also *The Caretakers of the Cosmos*, 83–8, in which I link all three to Whitehead's "meaning perception."

68 Wilson, *From Atlantis to the Sphinx*, 9.

69 Ibid., 10.

70 Ibid.

71 Ibid., 243.

72 Ibid., 268.

73 Ibid., 271.

74 Ibid., 272

75 Ibid., 277.

76 Ibid., 281.

CHAPTER THIRTEEN: ALIENS AND ANCIENT SITES

1 W. B. Yeats, "The Second Coming," Poem of the Week, http://www.potw.org/archive/potw351.html.

2 The program is available on YouTube, but unfortunately it is in Japanese. I have been unable to find an English-language version. https://www.youtube.com/watch?v=n2Mpkn5nUnY.

3 Colin Stanley, *The Ultimate Colin Wilson Bibliography* (Nottingham, UK: Paupers' Press, 2015), 553.

4 Wilson, *Dreaming to Some Purpose*, 365.

5 I visited Tetherdown in September 1995, following the Rosicrucian Enlightenment conference hosted by the New York Open Center and *Gnosis* magazine in Český Krumlov, in the Czech Republic. While there I interviewed Wilson for *Quest* magazine and had the rare delight of accompanying him in his old Jaguar to the Tesco—a UK supermarket chain—in Truro, where I helped him pick out groceries. What started as a brief visit turned into a two-week stay. I was also pleased to see that he got his fish and chips from a place called Atlantis. (Gary Lachman, "Romanticism, Optimism, and Consciousness: A Conversation with Colin Wilson," *Quest,* Summer 1996. A shorter version of the interview, "The Sage of Tetherdown: A Visit with Colin Wilson," also appeared in *Gnosis* [Winter 1996].)

6 Gary Lachman, "Stone Records of the Age of Leo," *Gnosis*, Fall 1996. Also reviewed is Hancock and Bauval's *The Message of the Sphinx*.

7 It aired in the United States on the Discovery Channel. An English version with Portuguese subtitles is available on YouTube. https://www.youtube.com/watch?v=X ayY04P7JKM.

8 Wilson, *From Atlantis to the Sphinx*, 104.

9 The syllable *atl* is itself seen as evidence of a very earlier connection between the Old and New worlds. It is of Mayan and Nahuatl origins, and means "water." Atlahuac was the patron god of Tenochtitlán, which the Aztecs built on a lake. Plato's lost world was Atlantis, lost in the Atlantic Ocean (Colin Wilson, *The Atlantis Blueprint* [London: Little, Brown, 2000], 147).

10 Wilson suggested that whatever power was used to move the blocks, it may have been known to Edward Leedskalnin, an eccentric Latvian-American who, between 1923 and 1951, built Coral Castle, a strange sculpture garden in Florida made of megalithic blocks of coral stone weighing up to thirty tons each. No one knows how Leedskalnin moved the blocks and he was never witnessed working on his "castle." When asked how he did it, he said he knew "the secret of the pyramids." http://coralcastle.com/.

11 Wilson, *From Atlantis to the Sphinx*, 36.

12 Ibid., 37.

13 David H. Kelly and Eugene F. Milone, *Exploring Ancient Skies: A Survey of Ancient and Cultural Astronomy* (New York: Springer Books, 2005), 460.

14 John E. Mack, *A Prince of Our Disorder: The Life of T. E. Lawrence* (Boston, MA: Little, Brown, 1976). Mack won a Pulitzer Prize for the book.

15 Colin Wilson, *Alien Dawn* (London: Virgin, 1998), 4.

16 In 1994, following publication of *Abduction*, Daniel C. Tosteston, dean of Harvard Medical School, initiated a confidential review of Mack's handling of the "alien abductees" he had interviewed. The gist of the complaint was that it was "irresponsible" for Mack to take his patients' abduction stories seriously, which he did. Although the review carried on for more than a year, in the end Mack's credentials as a serious scientist were upheld. See http://news.bbc.co.uk/1/hi/magazine/4071124.stm.

17 His books included *Missing Time: A Documented Study of UFO Abductions* (New York: Ballantine Books, 1988) and *Intruders: The Incredible Visitations at Copley Woods* (New York: Random House, 1987).

18 http://news.bbc.co.uk/1/hi/magazine/4071124.stm.

19 http://www.aetherius.org/.

20 Ronald Story, *The Encyclopaedia of UFOs* (London: New English Library, 1980), 155–7.

21 Colin Wilson, *Alien Dawn* (London: Virgin Books, 1998), 9.

22 Ibid., 14.

23 Ibid., 15.

24 Wilson's old friend Stuart Holroyd would later recap the tale in his equally mind-numbing *Prelude to a Landing on Planet Earth* (London: W. H. Allen, 1977).

25 Wilson, *Mysteries*, 545.

26 Wilson, *Alien Dawn*, 45.

27 Ibid., 73–4.

28 Ibid., 73.

29 Ibid., 304–5. http://gutenberg.net.au/ebooks07/0701231h.html.

30 Wilson, *Alien Dawn*, 294.

31 Wilson, *The Mind Parasites*, 192.

32 Ibid.

33 Wilson, *Alien Dawn*, 295.

34 Ibid.

35 Ibid., 305–6.

36 Ibid., 306.

37 Wilson worked on another novel, *Lulu*, based on the femme fatale from Frank Wedekind's play *Erdgeist* for years but never finished it. I read some of the manuscript of it during a visit to Tetherdown in spring 2015. It is unclear why Wilson was never able to finish it.

38 Colin Wilson, *The Books in My Life* (Charlottesville, VA: Hampton Roads Publishing, 1998), 11. The book began as a series of essays Wilson wrote for a Japanese magazine *Litteraire*; parts of it were also published in Paul Newman's *Abraxas* magazine.

39 Ibid., 8–9.

40 http://www.theguardian.com/world/2014/jun/09/worlds-oldest-man-dies-new-york-111.

41 Wilson, *Dreaming to Some Purpose*, 379–80.

42 Ibid., 380.

43 For a strange take on this journey and the whole of the ancient civilization milieu see Lynn Picknett and Clive Prince, *The Stargate Conspiracy* (London: Little, Brown, 1999).

44 Colin Wilson, *Atlantis and the Kingdom of the Neanderthals* (Rochester, VT: Bear & Company, 2006), 17.

45 Ibid., 27.

46 Ibid., 25.

47 See Paul Devereux, *Stone Age Soundtracks: The Acoustic Archaeology of Ancient Sites* (London: Vega Publishing, 2002).

48 Wilson, *Atlantis and the Kingdom of the Neanderthals*, 27.

49 Ibid., 31.

50 Ibid.

51 Rand Flem-Ath and Colin Wilson, *The Atlantis Blueprint* (London: Little, Brown, 2000), 29.

52 Today this date has been pushed much farther back. The most recent findings seem increasingly in line with the kinds of dates suggested in Wilson's and other authors' works on ancient civilizations. See https://www.newscientist.com/article/2080549-oldest-ever-human-genome-sequence-may-rewrite-human-history/.

53 As mentioned, many of Gooch's ideas about Neanderthal were before their time and he suffered ridicule because of them. Today many of the them have been vindicated.

54 In the late 1960s, through one of his students, Hapgood became involved with the American psychic Elwood Babbitt, eventually coauthoring three books with him. *Voice of Spirit: Through the Psychic Experience of Elwood Babbit* (New York: Delacorte Press, 1975) is a scientific study of mediumship. *The God Within: A Testament of Vishnu* (Flagstaff, AZ: Light Technology Publishing, 1982) and *Talks with Christ and His Teachers* (Fine Line Books, 1984) are essentially transcriptions from "trance lectures" given by spiritual teachers through the medium of Babbitt. That Hapgood made the fascinating but highly dubious books by James Churchward about the "lost continent of Mu" a research assignment for one of his students suggests that he had a refreshingly open mind.

55 https://www.forbiddenhistory.info/?q=node/70.

56 The Golden Section: take a line A–C, and divide it at B, so that A–C is longer than A–B in the same way that A–B is longer than B–C. Related to the Golden Section is a sequence of numbers known as the Fibonacci series. In this each number is the sum of the preceding two numbers: 0,1,1,2,3,5,8,13,21,34,55, and so on. These mathematical constants can be found in the arrangement of leaves around a stem, pinecones, the petals of a flower, even the human body. Schwaller de Lubicz believed the ancient Egyptians were aware of phi and used it in their understanding of the universe.

57 For a full account of the Nineveh number, see Maurice Chatelain, *Our Cosmic Ancestors* (Flagstaff, AZ: Light Technology Publishing, 1988).

58 One argument Wilson makes against the ancient astronaut idea is that one bit of knowledge they would certainly have passed on was that the precession of the equinoxes, about which everyone from Plato to the hippies of the 1960s made much, did not reveal some mystical plan of the universe, but was produced by a wobble in the earth's rotation. No wobble, no precession. The idea that the constellations do a stately backward round above our heads, shifting from one "age" to another—Aries, Pisces, Aquarius—is, from this perspective, an illusion, caused by an imperfection in the earth's spin.

59 Wilson, *Dreaming to Some Purpose*, 376.

60 216,000 / 360 = 600.

61 Ibid., 378.

62 Wilson, *The Atlantis Blueprint*, 252.

CHAPTER FOURTEEN: ON THE WAY TO SUPER CONSCIOUSNESS

1 Wilson, *Dreaming to Some Purpose*, 378.

2 I read Wilson's article and did, by joining the hundreds of people atop Primrose Hill in North London, an old Druid site and purported to be at the crossing of several important ley lines.

3 Colin Wilson, *Daily Mail*, November 9, 1994; *Daily Mail*, March 28, 1998.

4 Colin Wilson, "Solstice at the Stones," *Daily Mail*, June 22, 2000.

5 http://news.bbc.co.uk/1/hi/england/bradford/4451508.stm.

6 Wilson, *Encyclopaedia of Murder*, 37.

7 Colin Wilson, "Hanging Ian Huntley Would Have Been More Humane," *Daily Mail*, March 23, 2010.

8 Barbara Godlee, "The Maddest Messiahs," *Times Literary Supplement*, May 5, 2000.

9 I can add to the editorial mistakes. In the analytical table of contents, chapter eight, "Strange Powers" mentions "Gurdjieff and the war against sleep. Ouspensky and his

London group. His disillusionment with the system." These are not discussed in the chapter, or anywhere else in the book. Even the Outsider nods.

10 Wilson, *Below the Iceberg*, 63.

11 Ibid., 89.

12 Ibid., 102.

13 Ibid., 106.

14 Ibid., 111.

15 Colin Wilson, *The Devil's Party* (London: Virgin Publishing, 2000), 82.

16 Ibid., 133.

17 https://www.poets.org/poetsorg/poem/stolen-child.

18 http://www.bartleby.com/146/4.html.

19 Colin Wilson, *Rogue Messiahs* (Charlottesville, VA: Hampton Roads Publishing, 2000), 142–3.

20 Ibid., 288.

21 Ibid., 280.

22 Ibid., 289.

23 Colin Wilson, *The Outsider* 2nd ed. (London: Phoenix Books, 2001).

24 Ibid., 318.

25 Ibid, 305.

26 Ibid., 312.

27 Ibid., 318.

28 Wilson, *The Age of Defeat*, 11. If he did not feel this when looking back on *The Outsider*, it is most likely because he had already written a postscript and introduction to various editions and had come back to the work over the years.

29 http://www.allmusic.com/album/anatomy-of-a-poet-mw0000235494.

30 http://sydneybanks.org/.

31 Wilson, *The Age of Defeat*, 33–4.

32 Readers may not know that the *Fortean Times* is named after the great anomalist Charles Fort (1874–1932).

33 I should mention that two good friends and fellow *Fortean Times* writers, Mark Pilkington and Mike Jay, were also featured speakers. I gave a separate talk myself, "somewhat worse for an evening with Colin Wilson and several bottles of wine" on my book *Turn Off Your Mind* the next day. Jack Phoenix, "Fortean Times UnConvention 2002 Report," http://www.ufoupdateslist.com/2002/may/m11-001.shtml.

34 Ibid.

35 Part 1: https://www.youtube.com/watch?v=8WWeE1GnZjA; Part 2: https://www.youtube.com/watch?v=Fgf79P4mEHk. The text of the interview is available at http://www.intuition.org/txt/wilson.htm.

36 Another English writer of ideas I interviewed, Owen Barfield, said practically the same thing. http://www.intuition.org/txt/wilson.htm.

37 André Gide, *Le traité du Narcisse*, in *The Oxford Book of Aphorisms*, ed. John Gross (New York: Oxford University Press, 1983), 1.

38 Terry Welbourn, "The Man Who Saw the Future: Colin Wilson and T. C. Lethbridge, a Personal Appreciation," in *Around the Outsider*, ed. Colin Stanley, 291.

39 Ibid., 292.

40 Ibid., 291.

41 A short clip of the event is available on YouTube: https://www.youtube.com/watch?v=TwvVqIix2Ww. I should point out that Cope was not the only rocker who enjoyed Wilson's work. *In New York Rocker: My Life in the Blank Generation* (New York: Thunder's Mouth Press, 2006), 226–7, I tell the story of being asked to leave

David Bowie's midtown Manhattan loft because of a disagreement with him about Wilson. *The Outsider* was among Bowie's top one hundred books (http://www.tele graph.co.uk/books/what-to-read/david-bowie-the-man-who-loved-books/). When the filmmaker Nicolas Roeg mentioned to Wilson that Bowie was a fan of his work, he replied that he was sorry he couldn't return the compliment, but he had no interest in rock music and so had never heard Bowie. Another major figure was Donovan, in the mid- to late 1960s, as big a name as the Beatles, Bob Dylan, and the Rolling Stones. In his autobiography, Donovan says that it was a reading of *The Outsider* that set him on his bohemian trail. See my review: http://www.theguardian.com/books/2005/oct/08/featuresreviews.guardianreview10. As mentioned, I first came across Wilson when playing in Blondie.

42 http://www.spiked-online.com/review_of_books/article/3515#.VvQh3eKLTIU.

43 Ibid.

44 The Colin Wilson World website has published the e-mail exchange between Wilson and Carpenter. It makes for infuriating reading. http://www.colinwilsonworld.net/#!colin—humphrey/c1jnl.

45 Wilson told me that when his American publisher, Crown, read the book, they asked if he could put more sex in it. Wilson said, "I'd put in anything they liked. Sex with an elephant perhaps? So the US edition is somewhat longer."

46 He is the author of *The Secret History of the World* (New York: Overlook Press, 2010) and other works. His nom de plume in the United States is Jonathan Black.

47 Colin Wilson, "Bertrand Russell," *Abraxas*, November 1, 1991.

48 I should point out that another literary magazine Wilson was associated with for a long time was the now defunct *Books and Bookmen*, whose editor paid little but allowed Wilson to write about whatever he wanted to, a largesse also granted him by *Literary Review*.

49 Colin Wilson, "Against Gardening," in *Colin Wilson Festschrift* (St. Austell, UK: Paupers' Press, 2003), 26–9.

50 Ibid., 26.

51 Gary Lachman, "Inside the Outsider," *Fortean Times*, March 2004.

52 Ibid.

53 Ibid.

54 http://www.theguardian.com/books/2004/may/30/biography.features1.

55 http://www.nytimes.com/2005/08/17/books/philosopher-of-optimism-endures-negative-deluge.html.

56 http://www.spectator.co.uk/2004/07/stranded-by-the-tide-of-fashion/.

57 http://www.independent.co.uk/arts-entertainment/books/reviews/dreaming-to-some-purpose-by-colin-wilson-731298.html.

58 Back cover of *Dreaming to Some Purpose,* paperback edition (London: Arrow Books, 2005).

59 http://www.savoy.abel.co.uk/HTML/odyssey.html.

60 Noel Rooney, "Necrolog: Stan Gooch," *Fortean Times,* March 2011.

61 Brad Spurgeon, *Colin Wilson: Philosopher of Optimism* (London: Michael Butterworth, 2006), xxvii.

62 Ibid., 27.

63 Ibid.

64 Ibid., 28.

65 Ibid., 46.

66 Ibid., 68.

67 Ibid., 37.

68 Ibid., 46.

69 Ibid., 60, 69.

70 Ibid., 70.

71 Ibid., 50, 61.

72 Ibid., 77.

73 Ibid., 53.

74 Writing about the terrible floods that struck England in 2000, in the context of Nostradamus's prediction for some global catastrophe in 2001, Wilson assured his readers that they did not presage the end of the world. They may, though, be a sign of the "difficult time before some great change." At nearly seventy, he felt he may not be around to see it, but his natural optimism "inclines me to hope so." ("Did This Year's Floods Prove Nostradamus Right?" *Daily Mail*, December 30, 2000.)

75 Wilson, *Atlantis and the Kingdom of the Neanderthals*, 261–8.

76 Ibid., 250.

77 Ibid., 251.

78 Ibid., 270–2.

79 Ibid., 270–81.

80 http://www.bbc.co.uk/news/science-environment-35595661.

81 Wilson, *The Angry Years*, xv.

82 Ibid., 160.

83 Ibid., 154.

84 Ibid., 56.

85 Ibid., 181.

86 Ibid., xv.

87 Ibid., xvi.

88 Ibid., 140.

89 Oddly enough, Doris Lessing died less than a month before Wilson did, on November 17, 2013. She was ninety-four.

90 Gary Lachman, "It's Time to Look Back in Anger," *Independent on Sunday*, April 29, 2007.

91 http://www.artcornwall.org/features/Colin_Wilson_Paul_Newman2.htm.

92 Ibid.

93 Colin Wilson, *Super Consciousness: The Quest for the Peak Experience* (London: Watkins Books, 2009), 6.

94 Ibid.

95 http://www.watkinsbooks.com/shop-history.

96 In 2015 I was asked to teach an online course about Wilson's ideas; the main text for my students was *Super Consciousness*. "Phenomenology as a Mystical Discipline," California Institute of Integral Studies, Summer 2015, http://www.ciis.edu/academics/course-descriptions/phenomenology-as-a-mystical-discipline.

97 Wilson, *Super Consciousness*, 12.

98 Ibid., 15.

99 Ibid., 204.

100 Ibid.

101 Wilson, *Beyond the Occult*, 347.

102 Wilson, *Super Consciousness*, 205.

103 Ibid.

104 Wilson, *Beyond the Occult*, 348.

105 Ibid.

106 Ibid., 349.

107 Wilson, *Super Consciousness*, 87.
108 Ibid., 25.
109 Spurgeon, *Colin Wilson*, 28.
110 Wilson, *Super Consciousness*, 208.
111 Ibid., 208.

CODA: WITHOUT THE OUTSIDER

1 Andrew Philip Smith, "An Interview with Colin Wilson," *Gnostic*, Autumn, 2009.
2 Ibid.
3 Ibid.
4 Ibid.
5 Ibid.
6 Ibid.
7 Ibid.
8 Ibid.
9 Ibid.
10 Ibid.
11 Ibid.
12 Ibid.
13 Ibid.
14 Ibid.
15 Colin Wilson, *Existential Criticism*, 152.
16 Ibid., 1.
17 Ibid., 42.
18 http://www.adriftinsoho.com/.
19 https://vimeo.com/91219063.
20 https://www.youtube.com/watch?v=Jqa-2nV4Vzo.
21 https://www.youtube.com/watch?v=PZyeKAplD4I.
22 http://www.nottingham.ac.uk/ManuscriptsandSpecialCollections/News/2009/ColinWilsonCollection.aspx.
23 Colin Stanley, ed., *Around the Outsider* (Winchester, UK: O Books, 2011).
24 Colin Wilson, "A 100,000 Year Old Civilization?" *Fortean Times*, March 2011.
25 Ibid.
26 http://themurderofmeredithkercher.com/Main_Page.
27 Copies of *Abraxas Unbound*, a collection of articles compiled from the pages of *Abraxas*, are still available from Lulu: http://www.lulu.com/shop/paul-newman/abraxas-unbound-omega/paperback/product-4946735.html.
28 Gary Lachman, "Necrolog: Colin Wilson," *Fortean Times*, January 2014.
29 http://www.independent.co.uk/arts-entertainment/books/features/colin-wilson-eternal-outsider-8994131.html.
30 Wilson, *Voyage to a Beginning*, 336.
31 George Bernard Shaw, preface to *Back to Methuselah*, in *The Complete Prefaces of Bernard Shaw* (London: Paul Hamlyn, 1965), 546. In the preface Shaw writes, "I exploit the eternal interest of the philosopher's stone which enables men to live forever," a hint, perhaps, of the source of Wilson's title.

INDEX

ABOUT THE AUTHOR

GARY LACHMAN is the author of many books on consciousness, culture, and the western esoteric tradition, including *The Secret Teachers of the Western World*; *Rudolf Steiner: An Introduction to His Life and Work*; *In Search of P. D. Ouspensky*; *A Secret History of Consciousness*; *Politics and the Occult*; and *The Quest for Hermes Trismegistus*. He writes for several journals in the United States and the UK and lectures on his work in the United States, the UK, and Europe. His books have been translated into more than a dozen languages and he has appeared in several radio and television documentaries. He is assistant professor in Transformational Studies at the California Institute of Integral Studies. A founding member of the rock group Blondie, he was inducted into the Rock and Roll Hall of Fame in 2006. He can be reached at www.garylachman.co.uk.